ON THE CONTRARY

History is written backward but lived forward.
Those who know the end of the story can never know
what it was like at the time.

CV WEDGWOOD

ON THE CONTRARY

Tony Leon

To his,
Best wishes,
Tony Leon

JONATHAN BALL PUBLISHERS
JOHANNESBURG & CAPE TOWN

This edition first published in hard cover and trade paperback in 2008 by
JONATHAN BALL PUBLISHERS (PTY) LTD
PO Box 33977
Jeppestown 2043

Hard cover ISBN 978-1-86842-305-7
Trade paperback ISBN 978-1-86842-259-3

Editing by Owen Hendry for Wordsmiths SA, Johannesburg
Index by Frances Perryer, Johannesburg
Cover design by Flame Design, Cape Town
Design and reproduction of text by Triple M Design, Johannesburg

Set in 11/13pt Bembo Std
Printed and bound by CTP Book Printers, Cape

Contents

To the men and women of the Democratic Alliance of South Africa;
they willingly and loyally stood alongside me and sustained me in all
the battles and campaigns described in this book.
They kept faith with our cause. They have never been, in the glorious
words of Theodore Roosevelt, 'in the ranks of those cold and timid
souls who have known neither victory nor defeat.'

This book is dedicated, with my deepest gratitude,
to their endeavours for a better South Africa.

Of all the campaigns I fought, the most important was
winning the heart of my wife, Michal.
She has transformed my life. And this book is dedicated,
with my boundless respect and profound love,
to her as well.

On Golden Notebooks

Writing a book is an adventure. To begin with it is a toy and an amusement;
then it becomes a mistress, and then a master, and then a tyrant.
The last phase is that just as you are about to be reconciled to your
servitude, you kill the monster, and fling him out to the public.
WINSTON CHURCHILL

In October 2007 it was announced from Stockholm that Doris Lessing
had won the Nobel Prize for Literature. Other than the fact that we both
grew up in southern Africa (she in Rhodesia) and shared a detestation for
the tyrant's heel then choking Zimbabwe, we have little in common. I
hardly make any claim to her literary fluency, and do not share her political *Zeitgeist*.

We also emerged from different ages and from vastly disparate circumstances. However, while I was at university I enjoyed reading her grim
frontier tale of coming-of-age and a loveless marriage in *The Grass is
Singing*. But it was, according to the *New York Times*, her critical master-
piece, *The Golden Notebook*, that was emblematic of her œuvre. In the book
Anna, the heroine, divided her experiences into four notebooks, black, red,
yellow and blue: each dealing with different aspects of her life.

According to Michiko Kakutani, the literary critic, Lessing suggested
that out of these disparate pieces 'come something new and transformative, a fifth, golden notebook, where things have come together, the divisions have broken down, and there is a promise of unity.'[1]

On the Contrary, a title which came to me as I pondered why it was that
I had spent all my political life in opposition, is, as it were, my own golden
notebook: a pulling together of my personal threads, background experiences, political impulses, and my rather definite views on South Africa and
the wider world it shares, after my 22 years in public life. As readers will
glean should they press on beyond this introduction, I have tried to sketch

a voyage from my Durban boyhood through my moulding in the institutions of an English boarding school in KwaZulu-Natal and the South African military, into my shock therapy of radical politics at the University of Witwatersrand.

The narrative then concentrates on a far more political theme: from the deepest pit of hand-to-hand political warfare in Johannesburg and inside my own party, to the ascent of loftier planes as South Africa scaled the heights of negotiation politics. Much of it is about my assumption, as paradoxically both a battle-scarred and somewhat unready 37-year-old, to take up the reins of my party's leadership.

For over half my life, I lived under the system of apartheid, entrenched and institutionalised in every stage and every facet of everyday life in South Africa. I witnessed some of its cruelties and absurdities from a privileged place in the country's then prevailing ethnic hierarchy.

Yet, as both this book and any reading of an objective history of South Africa will attest, there was always a group of white South Africans who opposed the system of racial supremacy and the tyranny of its oppression, and held fast for a more just and humane political and economic order. Of the many blessings my parents bestowed on me, inculcating this different view of the prevailing racial order at the time of my birth was, in many ways, the most significant.

Every white person had a choice in how to respond to apartheid. Most supported it – but a minority did not. It could be said that every black person, by definition, was the object of a pattern of discrimination as pervasive as it was unfair. But equally, not every black person, or group, responded in like fashion. Some took up arms, some were imprisoned and brutalised, some were executed, and some went into exile.

But some others actively collaborated with, and profited from, the apartheid order. It was a brutal, yet complex, system and the responses to it, in all communities, were by no means uniform.

Indeed, while it is unarguable that the ANC government that today governs South Africa was the primary liberator or resistance movement pitted against the National Party in its fastness, it was by no means the only one. And, at various stages of the struggle, it appeared to be more surprised by, rather than master of, the revolutionary events which swept across South Africa and which I either witnessed or participated in. Given the dull patina of political correctness which for many years of my later political career had settled heavily upon South Africa, it might surprise some to learn that key events in the calendar which are celebrated today as milestones of liberation came from quarters either largely forgotten or conveniently omitted from official memory.

For example, the 1960 Sharpeville massacre was a police response to a Pan-Africanist Congress protest against the pass laws. The 16 June 1976 Soweto riots were a student uprising triggered by the Black Consciousness-inspired Soweto Students' Council. Its leader, Tsietsi Mashinini, died a lonely exile in Guinea – completely outside the circle of ANC insiders; and today languishes as a forgotten, barely mentioned, footnote in the current history of our times.

Then again, while the ANC was a decisive voice abroad in attempting to ratchet up the pressure against – and increase the isolation of – apartheid Pretoria, it was arguably the machinations of a New York banker that did more to bring down South Africa's financial house of cards than any number of speeches at the United Nations. In 1985, for example, the appositely named Willard C Butcher, head of Chase Manhattan Bank, pulled the plug on South Africa's dangerously exposed loan position. It was probably this action more than the more modest military accomplishments of Umkhonto we Sizwe that pushed the National Party to the brink of the abyss.

And again, staring into that deep and dangerous pit a few years later it was a '*murg-en-been*' Afrikaner Nationalist leader, FW de Klerk, who turned his back on it and marched his forces and his people in a different and unprecedented direction. His extraordinary act of political apostasy, no less than the moral compass of Nelson Mandela, guided South Africa's often dangerous transition, whose outcome at the time was never as assured as it now appears to have been.

Their courage and flexibility cannot be overestimated.

I mention these facts, and elaborate on others in this book, not to negate the role of black suffering and oppression, nor to minimise the centrality of the majority's chosen leadership, the African National Congress. However, it is important to mention that neither our history nor our future can be crudely reduced into a single narrative comprising permanent heroes and implacable villains. South Africa's history and future were, and are, far more subtle and contradictory than that.

Almost immediately on my election to the leadership of the party in 1994, and for the 13 interesting, and often hair-raising, years that followed, I found myself embroiled in many battles. One was against those who were determined either to denigrate the liberal contribution to change in South Africa as either resistant to it in the past, or complicit with frustrating its attainment in the future. At one level this was simply anti-intellectual, ahistoric, jejune political posturing – an attempt to cut out debate or to question the credentials of an opponent by using, in Robert Conquest's useful phrase, 'thought-blockers'. At another level, it was of a piece with the determination of the cadres of the 'national democratic revolution' (as the ANC – oddly, I have always thought, for a modern party participating in a constitutional democracy – chose to style its movement) to divide South Africa, and its people and polity, into a Manichean universe where you were either 'for us' or 'against the will of the people'. This book is, in part, an attempt, entirely from my perspective and ringside seat, to fill in the missing blanks of so much of our current history.

There are, however, some who claim to tend the uncertain flame which flickers around the liberal camp of South African politics who would doubt my credentials for this task, and have certainly questioned my fealty to its first principles. In their cases the fire against me could not be characterised as 'friendly'. But while often irritated by my critics, I have never been too concerned with labels in politics. I share the judgment of my friend and colleague Robin Carlisle that 'liberalism in South Africa would have died of malnutrition' had the Democratic Party and later the Alliance not pursued the course I helped steer it by. But I hope that I also have (as Helen Suzman affirmed in the foreword to my previous book *Hope and Fear* in 1998) 'stood foursquare in the liberal tradition'. That tradition includes the advancement of constitutionalism, the rule of law, social justice, free markets, and the rights and obligations of personal freedom. It is by no means a closed list, but I reckon these to be its essentials.

'Liberalism' is a much contested term, both in South Africa and abroad. It has application to a wide range of political positions, from the libertarianism of *laissez faire* economics to the democratic egalitarianism of the welfare state. One of the continuous battles in South Africa, during apartheid and afterwards, has been the encroachment of state into the life and activities of the citizen, and vice versa.

Thomas Nagel, professor at New York University, concluded: '[All] liberal theories have this in common: they hold that the sovereign power of the state over the individual is bounded by a requirement that individuals remain inviolable in certain respects, and that they must be treated equally.'[2] This fight of ideas is by no means over, and while the state might have changed hands, the hegemonic impulses of government have not. But as readers will gather, I always felt that leadership, and the liberal cause it was elected to serve, was required to be adaptive to the often stony conditions of the South African soil. The reader is invited to judge how successful or futile this adaptation has been. But events dictated that if we had stood still on the tiny patch of political earth bequeathed to me in 1994 it could well have disappeared from under our feet entirely.

So although I have at various stages of my career been either close to or distant from some of the more famous proponents of the liberal ortho-doxy in South Africa, for example, Colin Eglin, Zach de Beer and Helen Suzman, let me pay unreserved tribute to their pioneering efforts.

When, in 2003, Jonathan Ball suggested that I consider writing my politi-cal biography we both agreed that it should be as honest and forthright and lively as possible. My mandate was not to provide a complete, or even partial, history of the five decades of my journey as a South African. In any event the difficulty and frustrations which were attendant upon writing this book convinced me that simply a polite or politically correct – I am probably congenitally not predisposed to either condition – recitation of facts, speeches and anecdotes was hardly worth the effort.

I have also included in this work criticisms levelled against me – from the politically trenchant to the personally vicious. Perhaps I can be, there-fore, forgiven for mentioning the generous encomium recently written to me by one of my student assistants (or 'liaisons' as they are perhaps mis-leadingly named) at Harvard University. Kenzie Bok wrote: 'You are an example I will not soon forget – of a leader who takes his ideas seriously, but not himself.' I sincerely hope her remark finds reflection on these pag-es: South Africa has been involved in – and remains challenged by – some life-and-death issues. But I have never believed that their contemplation or resolution requires its politicians to lose their humour or have an over-inflated sense of their personal importance.

I have attempted to describe, hopefully with not too heavy a touch, the key events of my own life and provide an insider's view of what happened, when it did, and for what reason. There will be, no doubt, many alterna-tive or flatly contradictory views of the more controversial personalities and areas covered by this work. In a pluralistic society and in a functioning and contested democracy, disputations should be welcomed, not shunned. I believe that one of South Africa's chief weaknesses since the onset of for-mal democracy in 1994, and one of the contributory causes of the mistakes in governance which have occurred since then, has been an increasing and intolerant tendency by the country's majority leadership: its self-belief that it is in sole possession of the truth.

As a signed-up member of the Isaiah Berlin fan club I can only com-mend his words written in a letter over twenty-five years ago: 'It is a terrible and dangerous arrogance to believe that you alone are right, and have a magical eye which sees the truth, and that others cannot be right if they disagree.'

In this task I have relied on memory, research notes, contemporaneous diary entries, and the various works and articles cited. On many occasions I made a note after an important meeting or event. Also, as a politician who enjoys not only talking (most do) but also writing (which in my view not enough politicians do), I have been aided by the many op-eds and journal and newspaper articles which I penned. Since 2003 I have written a weekly political column on the Internet. This has also been an invaluable tool in my research. My researchers and I have attempted to authenticate every media cutting with a date and reference. This has not proved possible in every case, although each comment cited was noted at the time of its utterance.

I have been hugely assisted in writing this book by the prodigious research efforts of several people: *primus inter pares* is Joel B Pollak, my speech-writer and confidant for a critical four-year period of my leadership. I owe him a special debt, specifically for his considerable assistance in drafting elements of some key chapters. They were all of a piece with the many speeches and articles that he wrote for me: rigorous, articulate and opinionated. In 2006 Joel left my office to pursue his studies at the Harvard Law School. His successor, Dr Guy Willoughby, has also provided me with thoughtful insights and well-honed prose. Gareth van Onselen, another friend and colleague, head of the DA Research and Media Department, gave me specific inputs and suggestions for the final chapter, 'Future Imperfect'. His capacity for research is matched only by his unflinching commitment to our political project, which he has done so much to sustain.

My publishers engaged senior DA researcher Julia Frielinghaus to undertake further research and fact-checking. She tackled this task with her customary brio and thoroughness. The noted political journalist Jan-Jan Joubert, aided by his encyclopaedic political memory and general knowledge, painstakingly read this manuscript and corrected many of its errors. Those that remain are, irritatingly, my own.

The book itself was written over a three-year period. Fits of zealous application were interrupted by long periods away from it owing to political and leadership pressures, or by the perils occasioned by either demoralisation with the project or the work-avoiding demons to which I am subject, and which Michal did her best to keep at bay. Through it all, however, I was sustained by the bonhomie, the belief in its merits and the positive energy radiated by my publisher, Jonathan Ball. We share a similar worldview, and I found his support and encouragement quite infectious.

Less voluble, but equally committed to this project and its perceived merits, was my dedicated editor, the journalist and writer Peter Wilhelm. He laboured mightily and uncomplainingly to knock my prose into shape and systematise the chapters and the ideas which comprise this book. He too is a fellow-believer in the kind of South Africa which we set out to achieve but which we have not yet fully sighted.

At a later stage in the writing process, Jeremy Boraine was appointed publishing director at Jonathan Ball. I was a happy recipient of both his efficiency and his charm. My boundless thanks as well to Owen Hendry for final editing, and Francine Blum for production.

A lifelong friend, Shirley Eskapa, herself a noted writer, provided encouragement and invaluable advice throughout this project.

While I wrote this book in the midst of a media revolution, characterised by MySpace pages, Facebook online friends, YouTube videos and the like, it was actually written in what my technophile stepson Etai would perhaps scornfully describe as 'an old, if not antique, bubble'. Like a pre-Gutenberg monk I wrote most of the text long-hand. It then fell, as ever, to my full-time secretary and part-time soul mate, Sandy Slack, to transcribe them onto disc and often redo the same chapter half-a-dozen times until it was ready for editing. It would be a stretch to say she did it all uncomplainingly. But she undertook the task with the exemplary dedication, deep affection, singular loyalty and occasional irritations which have been the mutual basis of our working and personal relationship for nearly a decade-and-a-half.

My staunch colleagues and dear friends, Ryan Coetzee, James Selfe, Douglas Gibson and Mike Ellis, were kind enough to read portions of the draft text and furnish their comment and suggestions, some of which I have included. Two other friends and colleagues, Sandra and Andries Botha, lent me their magnificent Plettenberg Bay beach house immediately after I stood down as party leader in May 2007. Its impressive and tranquil surrounds inspired me to write a chapter-and-a-half in just one week.

Appropriately much of this book was drafted in Cape Town and in Johannesburg and on airplanes and in hotel rooms on and off the various campaign trails I have journeyed along. Perhaps, however, it was my greatest fortune to receive a fellowship at the Institute of Politics, Kennedy School of Government, at Harvard University for a four-month period from September to December 2007. If it is possible to have a formative experience at the age of 50, then this was it.

At Harvard, I interacted with super-bright and positive, yet respectful, students. I was exposed to the extraordinary intellectual giants who comprise much of the faculty. I met with a range of visiting political leaders and policy-makers at the top of their game. It was both exhilarating and refreshing. When I arrived one of the IOP staff described the Institute in which I enjoyed my fellowship as the political equivalent of the Betty Ford Clinic for recovering politicians. 'You come here to detox,' he said. Given the mephitic nature of some of the political waters in which I have swum, my experience at Harvard was indeed restorative. What impressed me most about the Institute of Politics was its Kennedyesque belief that its fellows and students should seek to share a view that 'politics matters': that it is a noble profession worthy not merely of the best minds of our time but of individuals possessing exceptional character and a tremendous commitment to the common good.

This indeed sets the bar very high; but in South Africa, no less than in America and the rest of the world, we should aim no lower. In addition to the goodwill of Congressman Jim Leach, the acting IOP director, and the fellows' co-ordinator, Eric Andersen, I was hugely inspired and sustained by the other fellows. They were drawn from the upper ranks of American politics, public policy-making and journalism. We soon became kindred spirits and good friends. My warm appreciation goes to Dr Meghan O'Sullivan, Mayor Bill Purcell, Noelia Rodriguez, Maralee Schwartz and Congressman E Clay Shaw Jr.

It was, in fact, Meghan, who arrived to join us directly from her time in the White House as Special Assistant to President George W Bush on Afghanistan and Iraq, who expressed in her crisp and articulate way the environment in which often hugely consequential decisions are made: 'The essence of being a policy-maker is making decisions with real consequences with imperfect information and with too little time.' While the decisions made in the White House were of greater reach than any to emerge from the parliamentary office of South Africa's opposition leadership, this volume is my own personal testimony to the accuracy of those words.

My time at Harvard also afforded me the chance to learn first-hand from some of the frontline experts on the South African economy. Its Center for International Development has been retained by South Africa's National Treasury to advise it on our growth rate. Interacting with professors Ricardo Hausmann, Robert Lawrence and Matthew Andrews, and reading the papers prepared by the international panel, helped refine my own thinking on the complex topic of South Africa's political economy and its growth diagnostics. Professors Niall Ferguson and Samantha Power also provided me with remarkable, and fresh, historical insights.

It was during my Harvard sojourn that the witty and candid memoirs of one of its most distinguished alumni, the historian and Kennedy confidant, Arthur M Schlesinger Jr, were published posthumously.[3] Gossip is the universal staple of politicians and academics alike, and Schlesinger did not disappoint on this score. I read his prose suitably enthralled. However, deep in his diaries I stumbled upon an uncomfortable definition which he termed 'Prichard's Law', which he described as: 'Absence of power corrupts, and total absence of power corrupts absolutely.' This was a light-bulb moment. In a far less elegant but personally directed jibe, a semi-local detractor of lesser eminence had once accused me of 'having run nothing more important than my mouth'. Were my years in politics proof of the salience of Prichard's Law? I certainly hope not.

Some, a distinct minority I suspect, of politicians – locally and overseas – are perfectly content to spend their political lives in opposition. Indeed, it is often easier to critique administration, without the burden of implementation or the frustrations imposed by government. While I never entered public life to achieve executive office, I certainly would have relished the opportunity of converting principles and policies into laws and governance. I would, also, doubtless, have enjoyed some of the appurtenances of power. But I have observed, often with a queasy dismay, how the baubles and status of office have so easily and quickly corroded – and overwhelmed – even the most independent and seemingly incorruptible of men and women. Yesterday's struggle icons and human rights activists in South Africa have often become, in office, today's insensitive and unaccountable mandarins and overlords – abusing means and confusing them with ends.

But while the challenges (and temptations) of direct power have eluded me (or in the case of Nelson Mandela's offer of a seat in his cabinet, have been declined), the opposition benches proved not to be a permanent relegation to the sidelines of influence. I entered parliament at the precise moment of South Africa's interregnum, which Gramsci defined as the political twilight between the dying of the old epoch and the uneasy birth of the new. During this exciting, unpredictable and often dangerous phase of upheaval a unique moment presented itself for those in the political minority, even bit players, to help shape (and, in my case, even draft) certain outcomes – constitutionally and legislatively. I certainly seized some of those opportunities.

One of the most contested issues during South Africa's political transition, as I record in the pages which follow, was the political weight and influence to be accorded to the political minority (which in South Africa's race-based politics and electoral outcomes is largely, although not exclusively, the sum of its ethnic minorities). In more settled and mature democracies, such as the United States, the institutional and constitutional design ensures a powerful, sometimes even paralysing, role for the minority party. Just witness the current difficulty afflicting the Democratic majority in the US Congress in driving through its legislative agenda in the teeth of a determined and unified Republican minority.

For reasons of history and suspicion, South Africa's Constitution provided little institutional power for the future opposition. Such other constraints on untrammelled majoritarianism imposed by the post-1994 order were fairly easily breached by the new government. It was not simply a question of their zeal, but also a consequence of 'the morality of struggle' which was invoked by the ANC at every turn in justification of every act and decree – the good, alongside the constitutionally dubious or even the legislatively dangerous. 'I am in power, therefore I can' was often the unspoken subtext of great swathes of half-baked, ideologically driven ministerial and legislative enactments.

In the teeth of such an approach, the opposition which I led could more often note and protest, rather than amend, block or influence. But while 'bearing witness' is more appropriate to a clergyman than to a politician, it was often necessary for the opposition to act as 'the canary in the coalmine': adverting to the dangers which lurked above or below. And while these warnings often went unheeded at the time, some proved prescient and were later taken up by others either when it was safer to do so or when self-interest kicked in. Our early warnings on Zimbabwe, my initial furious spat with Thabo Mbeki on AIDS, our constant campaigning against crime, and warnings on the excesses of the cronyism and nascent corruption embedded within the paraphernalia of the apparatus of transformation, did indeed later become, if not the conventional, then at least the critical wisdom outside the opposition benches.

But that lay in the future. At the time these criticisms were first ventilated, a strange silence or quiescence had settled on the country. It was neither a case of superior morality nor any gifts of special insight which compelled me to speak and act on these issues. It was simply a combination of belief and determination to use the space which the constitutional order had opened up. I also reckoned that if not used and ventilated then such space would close down soon enough.

I sometimes felt most uncomfortable and even inwardly nervous (although I affected never to show it) when I pushed up hard against the presidency of Thabo Mbeki. I knew it was necessary to expose and oppose the excesses – and sometimes even the abuses – of power which happened on his watch. The disdain of his approach and the reinvigoration of race-politics which accompanied it made me ever more determined. But the reverential awe with which Mbeki was received in parliament, and the opprobrium screamed at critics such as me, was to prove utterly misleading. I always thought that such excessive deference, such as the ANC MPs displayed, was dangerous in any democracy, especially one as young and fragile as South Africa's. I had little idea (and doubtless so did the president) that like a character from Wagner's *Ring des Nibelungen*, the ANC rank-and-file would 'rise from their long slumber' and decapitate their own leader.

But that is precisely what happened in December 2007, when Mbeki was ejected from his party leadership by his by-now-growing ranks of inside critics. They would repeat, in far more extreme language than my own, many of the same warnings that I had first uttered and which they dismissed as *lèse majesté*. Such is the wheel of politics, turned it would appear, as Niall Ferguson once observed, by the god of irony.

But while I believed that creating, often in the teeth of the fiercest resistance, the space for opposition, and establishing the legitimacy of its critique, was a necessary and important task, I also knew that in South Africa such virtue was insufficient. That is why much of my leadership was spent in building a stronger opposition force and ensuring that wherever possible we created enclaves where we could win power locally, even if it eluded us nationally. I still nurse some psychic wounds from the rather harrowing, in fact shotgun, marriage which I willed upon the Democratic Party with the New National Party. The events around this saga are also ventilated in this book. But the formation of the Democratic Alliance was based on the fact that the fractured opposition needed more unity and power in order to extend its reach.

That task is by no means complete, and our political control today of Cape Town, and most Western Cape municipalities, is hardly overwhelming proof that South Africa enjoys normal multi-party politics. But it is a necessary and important start of a much longer journey, which must be completed by my political successors. Hopefully when South African politics normalises, becomes less racial, and the national government changes hands (presumably after the majority party splits), we will have completed the second phase of our democratic voyage.

There was an additional bonus to my stay in Cambridge, Massachusetts.

I had the opportunity to be an interested bystander in the democratic spectacle of the US presidential election. Although only to be finally concluded in November 2008, by the time of my arrival, in September 2007, the campaign had already been under way for most of the year. As a contrast to the semi-opaque nature of the ANC presidential race which was under way at the same time in South Africa, I thought the open and inquiring nature of the American process (despite the obscene amounts of money thrown at it and its exhausting length) had much to commend it.

However, my home thoughts and analogies from abroad were extended even further when my long-time South African friend Cliff Garrun was visiting me in October. We both decided one unseasonably balmy fall evening to join some ten thousand others in the urban parkland of Boston Common. Our attendance there was to hear Barack Obama, presidential candidate for the Democratic nomination. I thought I had maxed out on political speeches and was generally long past being impressed by fellow politicians, however elevated their status or office. Yet Obama managed to sprinkle magic dust in the eyes of his audience that night, including, I later realised, in my own. I wondered whether this was because his election, however likely or improbable, gave an African-American the first serious chance of occupying the White House and heading a country whose racial history and current antagonisms are perhaps as severe as, or even exceeded, those of South Africa.

Then I thought, perhaps it was a demonstration of America's political maturity that three of its presidential candidates at the time (Senator Hillary Clinton, a woman; Governor Mitt Romney, a Mormon; and Obama), each represented a group outside the mainstream moulds from which American presidents are traditionally cast. But on closer reflection, I realised both the real power of the Obama candidacy and the depth of his personal conviction: in his speech that night he never once referred to his colour, his suffering or his people's struggle for equality. As the thoughtful commentator on public affairs, Andrew Sullivan, commented: 'Race is what makes Obama a transformative candidate: not because of his emphasis on it but because of his real unwillingness to pick sides in a divide that reaches back centuries and appears at times unbridgeable.'[4]

'Why,' I thought to myself, 'couldn't South Africa have this kind of transformation?' It seemed far more inclusive and inspirational than the hollowed-out version of this neologism currently practised in my own country: a sort of ethnic-holding race politics, with generous lashings of an exclusionary nationalism. This had informed so much of our past. And it seems to have continued, after a brief pause, since 1994. When South

Africans made their own great leap forward to an inclusive democracy I had, quite wrongly as it now transpires, assumed that we had also buried racial nationalism in history's graveyard of discarded ideologies and faulty practices.

Why we have not done so – and why we need to recapture that brief, shining moment of non-racial hope and democratic possibility that flickered so brightly on that glorious autumn day in May 1994 when Nelson Mandela was inaugurated as president – forms the bulk and substance of this book.

The flip side of my personal journey along South Africa's political highways, and inside its darker labyrinths, has often been accompanied by an intense background noise. It has been almost as incessant as the cry of the hadeda bird on a Highveld afternoon after a summer rainfall. Its essence boils down to a formula of words asked either out of genuine concern or with an angry resentment: 'Can a white person lead a political movement in Africa?' (Or should racial minorities be involved at all in the public life of their country?)

Robert Mugabe in neighbouring Zimbabwe began to destroy his country in 2000 after he unexpectedly lost a referendum. Peter Godwin (whose occasional advice to me on writing this memoir has been invaluable) captured that moment of seething resentment perfectly. In his memoir of Africa, *When A Crocodile Eats the Sun*, he writes:

'[Mugabe] was boiling with the public humiliation. How could he, who had liberated his people, now be rejected? How could they be so ungrateful? It couldn't be his own people who had done this (even though 99% of the electorate was black). It must have been other people, white people leading them astray. He would show us ... we had broken the unspoken ethnic contract. We had tried to act like citizens, instead of expatriates, here on sufferance.'

I am a third-generation South African; I was also its third, and, thus far, longest-serving, leader of the parliamentary opposition since the advent of democracy. I am also white. But I never entered into 'an ethnic contract' nor have I ever considered myself bound by its terms, real or implied. As I attempt to demonstrate in the pages that follow, the basic bargain underpinning South Africa's constitutional order is both the claim and the promise of equal citizenship in all realms of life. But the difficulties in fulfilling this commitment, on all sides, and how far we have strayed from our Constitution's founding premise, has been a central theme of my political life, and my primary motivation in often going against the grain of consensus at times when it was difficult to do so.

I believe that the abyss into which Zimbabwe was plunged by Mugabe is not the inevitable destination for South Africa. But it is not an impossible one either. Kenya is an even more recent – and cautionary – African tale of how the illusion of stability and democracy can be ripped asunder quite easily, when elections are stolen and simmering ethnic tensions are inflamed. The xenophobic killings and attacks in South Africa's townships and squatter camps which shocked South Africa and the world in May 2008 are a potent and baleful reminder that the 'rainbow nation' is in fact composed of highly flammable and combustible ingredients. South Africa's future depends on our actions and reactions in resisting, democratically as citizens, not as supplicants, the totalitarian temptation in whatever guise it appears and whenever it needs to be interdicted.

CAPE TOWN
May 2008

PART ONE

PATH TO LEADERSHIP

CHAPTER I

In My Beginnings

The past is a foreign country; they do things differently there.
LP HARTLEY

We all come into the world with baggage which, in the end,
we have no hope of reclaiming.
ROBERT HUGHES

I

Wednesday 8 May 1996 promised and delivered a far from routine sitting of the parliament of the Republic of South Africa. A hubbub of excitement and expectation resonated in the chamber since we were about to ratify the new national constitution. In my brown leather front-bench seat – somewhat to the side of the 'football-style' legislative chamber with its origins in the discredited Tricameral parliament of PW Botha – I waited to see the vestiges of the old order eradicated.

It was a day that dawned almost thirty months after the inauguration of the Interim Constitution, which had ushered in the most truly epoch-changing transition to our new democratic order. Immense haggling and bargaining underlay this historic compact – not least because the atmosphere was replete with drama and trauma as the Inkatha Freedom Party of Mangosuthu G Buthelezi had refused to participate in the proceedings of the Constitutional Assembly; the far-right Afrikaans party, the Freedom Front, had indicated an abstention; and the fringe African Christian Democratic Party, with two members, dissented and voted against.

The Democratic Party which I led consisted then of only seven MPs and three senators. All ten had been up deep into the night reaching for agreement on whether to support the final passage of the constitution, or not. One of my colleagues, Kobus Jordaan, had become deeply emotional during our final discussions after a rather brutal put-down by our chief constitutional negotiator, the redoubtable but gruff Colin Eglin.

The weariness gave way to the normal adrenalin surge. I was ready and waiting to make my speech when called on to do so by the chairman of the Constitutional Assembly, Cyril Ramaphosa – previously the ANC secretary-general and soon to become one of South Africa's leading businessmen.

The entire tone of the debate was set by the deputy president, Thabo Mbeki, who struck an extraordinary note of dramatic reconciliation and rare eloquence, when he stated: 'I am an African.' In a remarkably articulate speech evoking the flora, fauna and tumultuous humanity of our nation and continent, he orchestrated the debate.

Mildly panicked, I realised that my introduction would have to change so that I, too, could acknowledge the refrain 'I am an African' – taken up by the leader of the National Party, FW de Klerk, and others who spoke before me.

When I rose on behalf of the Democratic Party to support the passage of the constitution – despite our reservations on some provisions – I entered into the spirit of the moment: 'I too make claim to being an African, not just by birth, but by choice … Others have spoken of their origins and journeys into the new South Africa. Three generations ago, my great-grandparents fled the oppression of a distant country on another continent. They came to a country where rights were granted to the few, but denied to the many. I am humbled and privileged today to be part of a process rectifying that historic wrong – and extending those rights, from the few to the many.'[1]

Who were these great-grandparents of mine? What were the family origins that had catapulted me, a representative of the current generation, to a ringside seat in the parliament of one of the world's newest democracies, previously its pre-eminent festering trouble-spot and certainly one of the morality plays of the 20th century?

The story requires a little disentangling.

Almost every South African Jewish family's provenance can be traced back to the Pale of Settlement created in 1791 by Catherine the Great.[2] It lasted until the First World War and confined the Jews of eastern Europe to 25 provinces including the Ukraine, Lithuania, Belarus, Crimea, and part of Poland. Most Jews were specifically expelled from Moscow and St Petersburg and forced into the Pale. Later they were also evicted from rural areas within the Pale and forced to live in ghettos, known as 'shtetls'.

Despite abject poverty, Jews in the Pale developed an extensive social welfare system that was so effective that rabbis were compelled to decree a halt to conversions of non-Jews in order to keep out free-riders.

The late 1800s saw a wave of pogroms against Jews in the Pale. This persecution coincided with rapid industrialisation in the Americas and western Europe, and the discovery of gold and diamonds in South Africa. Jews began emigrating in droves. Between 1881 and 1917, more than two million left Russia: about two million went to the United States; twenty thousand immigrated to Great Britain; a hundred thousand went to Canada; forty thousand to South Africa; and thirty thousand resettled in Europe. Thousands also left for Palestine. Of South Africa's Jewish immigrants in this period, roughly 80% were from Lithuania and 20% from Poland.

Most of my forebears can trace their origins to the Pale.

Shmuel Zvi Herman was born in Kovno in Lithuania. He married Chaia Rabinowitz whose name was anglicised to Clara Robinson. Of their nine children, one Samuel Herman (Sam), my maternal grandfather, was born in Bradford in England to where the family had moved and from where he, in turn, emigrated to South Africa with his father – fleeing the poverty of their origins. Little is known of their life in Lithuania or England; there is a generalised account of poverty and struggle.

Sam Herman arrived in Cape Town in 1912 – a city dominant in the life of my family, and where I ultimately made my home. He was industrious and intelligent and, unlike succeeding generations, devoutly religious. Shortly after the First World War, the Hermans moved to Johannesburg and Sam, with his brother-in-law Louis Traub, established the firm of wholesale wool merchants, Herman & Traub.

The family lived in Saratoga Avenue in Doornfontein, Johannesburg – a suburb which at the time attracted many Jewish immigrants.

In 1923, with a prospering business under his belt, Sam married my maternal grandmother, Rachel (Ray) Kowarsky, whose family immigrated to South Africa from Vilnius in Lithuania – the ancestral home of many Jewish South Africans. They did particularly well in the early 20th century with a fresh produce business and a bag and bone company (which literally collected bags and bones by horse cart), called Sand, Kowarsky & Co.

Ray grew up in a splendid old house in Empire Road, Parktown, Johannesburg – today part of the Pieter Roos Park bordering Hillbrow and the Parktown Ridge. The house remained in the family for many years, since it was bequeathed by Ray's father, Noah, to her sister, my great aunt Rose. My brother Peter and I spent many happy holidays in Johannesburg in its splendid garden, with an orchard on one side and a swimming pool on the other.

Sam and Ray were a fortunate couple, Ray a highly attractive woman, and Sam a devout man who prospered in business and made good provision for his future family.

In 1929 my mother, Sheila Jean, was born in Johnson Street, Berea. In 1935 the business had flourished and they were able to move to Observatory, a more upmarket suburb, where Sheila and her older brother Neil delighted in their new status symbol, a tennis court. It seemed a happy trajectory.

Three years later, tragedy. My grandparents sailed for England. Sam took ill and was diagnosed with then-fatal pleurisy of the lung. In the background was Munich and the 'peace in our time' crisis. Because of the onset of winter and uncertainty about the European situation, Sam was urged to leave England, but developed septicaemia on the passage home. This was before sulphur drugs were in general use, and he died shortly after returning in February 1939, at the young age of 47.

More than any other event, this was to blight Sheila's life; to create in her a sense of impermanence and insecurity that played out with far-reaching consequences for her family, including her children.

Sheila, in the immortal words of Queen Mary, was 'a pretty kettle of fish'. Devastated by Sam's death – she was nine – she strengthened the bond with Neil, four years her senior. She went to boarding school at Kingsmead, one of the top private schools of its time, and once related that she got her first party dress at 17, when she was allowed to dance with a boy.

My father, Ramon, advocate and judge, had forebears who found their way to South Africa by a not dissimilar route. But his mother, Tamara Drusinsky, was, all agreed, an exotic beauty and hailed from the Russian Crimea. She was the daughter of Dr David Drusinsky and his wife Bluma. Drusinsky was born in the Crimea in about 1850, and unusually for a Russian Jew was allowed to qualify as both a doctor and a dentist at the Moscow Medical School. Despite the apparent concessions his family received, he too left Russia as part of the massive migration to South Africa in 1896, bringing Tamara. His two adult children Abraska and Panya remained behind, and nothing is known today about them or their fate.

Tamara's 'Russianness' gave me a conversational gambit when I met Vladimir Putin on his state visit to South Africa in September 2006. My ANC colleagues, especially parliament's Speaker, Baleka Mbete, regaled President Putin with stories from their Moscow days and invoked the wonders of Soviet support for 'the struggle'. Then when the Speaker called on me to address some remarks to Putin, I thought to mention that I was certainly the only South African in the room with him who had a Russian grandmother.

In his intense, polite fashion Putin deadpanned in response that the Crimea was now part of the Ukraine, but he was 'very pleased' that Tamara had given South Africa such an 'important legacy' – myself. My ANC colleagues were taken aback.

Actually Tamara, or 'Granny T' as we called her, was born when the ship docked in Constantinople in the Ottoman Empire (now Istanbul in Turkey), and arrived in South Africa as a babe-in-arms. Dr Drusinsky apparently had to obtain permission from the president of the Transvaal Republic, Paul Kruger, to practise as a dentist, which he did in Barbican Buildings in downtown Johannesburg until his death in 1921.

In 1999 a vast fuss was generated in the media and among my political opponents when the majority of Afrikaans-speaking South Africans voted for the party which I led. However, this 'toenadering' hales back to Dr Drusinsky's time in South Africa – since, apart from his dentistry, Kruger thoughtfully appointed him as one of his official translators from Russian into English and vice versa.

Ramon's paternal line was also tinged with the exotic. While his grandfather, Barnett Leon, was born in England in 1845, the Leons were originally Polish and had lived in Spain for several hundred years. The mists of time have descended over whatever connection might ever have existed between the family name and the eponymously named corner of the Spanish kingdom.

As it happened, Barnett seems to have been the least successful – financially – of all my ancestors. He arrived in Cape Town from England in 1869 at the age of 23 or 24, and must have had a little money since he started a jewellery business in Cape Town. From this source he gave his cousin, George Albu, some trinkets to help him on his way to Kimberley, fame and fortune.

Albu, who was knighted in 1912 for his services to mining, was with his brother Leopold the founder of the General Mining and Finance Corporation – later merged with the Union Corporation to become Gencor. According to Mendel Kaplan,[3] George was particularly far-sighted, 'one of the first to experiment with the deep levels of the Witwatersrand'. The first blasting experiment on a South African gold mine was conducted on a property controlled by the Albu brothers.

The less fortunate Barnett's wife was Amelia Freeman, one of 12 children, born in Penarth near Cardiff in South Wales in 1864. She arrived in South Africa with her parents, Joseph and Emma Freeman, who brought all their children, bar one, to Cape Town in 1880. Six years later, Amelia and Barnett were married in the Mother City, exactly 104 years before my wife Michal and I tied the knot there. Shortly after the betrothal they took the coach for Kimberley in the hope of emulating the more famous cousin, George. But after failing to find either fame or fortune in Kimberley – and certainly no diamonds – they arrived in Johannesburg in 1889.

It was there that Jack Leon – my paternal grandfather – was born on 16 January 1892 in End Street, Doornfontein, an inner-city suburb of a Johannesburg founded only six years before his birth. A Rand pioneer, his advent coincided with the years of Paul Kruger's presidency. At the outbreak of the South African War in 1899 he was able to observe Barnett – who unlike Amelia did not sit out the war in England – 'help the Boers' at the same time that his business career took a direction opposite to that of George Albu.

First he owned a bar, the Trocadera, and later a spectacularly unsuccessful bookshop. Barnett was also responsible for introducing into the family line the concept of divorce – practically unheard of in the early 20th century: he divorced Amelia. My own parents divorced in 1965, and six months later my father's only sister, Valerie, was divorced. My mother Sheila was to marry three times; my father Ramon twice; and I married a divorcée. Only my unmarried brother seems to have escaped the curse.

In this long fault line of broken marriages we find the extraordinary circumstances of Jack and Tamara's union. They had met before the First World War and became engaged. When Jack announced his intention of fighting the Germans in East Africa, Tamara retorted: 'If you go to the war, Jack, I will break the engagement and marry someone else.' I must have inherited my obduracy and obstinacy from both, since my grandfather duly went up north and my grandmother, as promised, broke her engagement and married another, Herman Cohen, with whom she had a daughter, Valerie.

But when Jack survived the war, his imprisonment and a near-fatal bout of the Spanish flu – a pandemic that swept South Africa after 1918 – he and Tamara reunited; she duly divorced the unfortunate Mr Cohen, and married Jack in 1922.

In 1925 my father, Ramon Nigel Leon, was born in Page Street in Yeoville, Johannesburg. His first home was alongside the municipal ward of Bellevue, which I was to represent as city councillor more than fifty years later.

Jack was in many ways an inspiration. So much is spoken in South Africa about previously disadvantaged individuals – known by the acronym 'PDIs'. But when I think about my grandfather's life and career, he truly deserved the title. He was forced to leave school at 14 because of the poverty of his profligate father and his impoverished mother. Nevertheless, he went to night school and learned shorthand and typing. This secured him a job with another famous Randlord, Sir Thomas Cullinan, after whom one of the most famous diamonds in the world was named.

In this manner he landed up as company secretary to Cullinan Diamond Mine – outside Pretoria – and he used to regale us with stories about its founder, who once asked him to order a library from England. When Grandpa enquired which books he would like, Sir Thomas replied: 'Never mind the titles, Jack, order them by the yard.'

In 1930 Jack briefly prospered with his own business, the Glencairn Lime Company. However, like his father before him, his success was temporary and illusory; he gambled it all on the stock exchange – and lost.

His brother Billy, however, started a hugely successful motor dealership, Leon Motors, a company listed on the JSE in 1935, and it held the agency for the major cars of the time: Packard, Pontiac and Vauxhall.

Billy set Jack up in the motor business in Durban, to which my grandparents departed in 1934. Grandpa prospered again for a while and then blew it all again 20 years later when he retired and decided to invest his small fortune in a chicken farm on the Natal South Coast which went belly-up.

Jack suffered from the defects of his qualities. His trusting nature made him vulnerable to others with lesser scruples. His easygoing, carefree attitude made him careless about saving money – another trait I have inherited.

When Tamara and Jack came to Durban they became very friendly with an 'old Durban family', Rupert and Claire Ellis-Brown. Jack shared a poker table with Rupert, his brother Tick and four others, all gentiles. On one celebrated occasion my grandfather was the only winner. He rose at the end of the game: 'Thank you, gentlemen,' he said: 'This must be a case of Jewish luck beating Christian Science.'

Grandpa Jack was a fine and amusing man who spent many evenings entertaining my brother and me with tales of the war and stories of old Johannesburg and his extremely chequered career in business. He had a common, endearing touch; a wry sense of humour; and a most gentle philosophy of life. He was well-loved, and lived to a great age. On his 90th birthday in 1982 my father organised a big celebration in Durban. My brother Peter proposed the toast for the grandchildren: 'Grandpa's life is proof that learning does not lie in learning, and riches do not lie in riches.'

Jack lived on for another two years.

I find the American habit of using and promoting one's family to illustrate a political principle or illuminate an issue mawkish or vulgar or
both. However, by the time of the Democratic Alliance's 2004 congress I
was sick and tired of the caricature of myself as a child of privilege. The
volume was invariably ratcheted up to distract public attention from the
obscene amounts of money being acquired by ANC fat-cats through deals
based on political cronyism or the worst sort of rent-seeking. So, at our
party congress and after the 2004 elections, I had this to say:

'My grandfather [had little] because of the poverty of his family. He
had to leave school at 14 and make his way in the world as best he could.
[Yet] because of the opportunities he opened for the next generation, and
which society helped him to provide, his son became a Supreme Court
judge. And his grandson stands before you right now ... In those days,
there were only opportunities for some. Today there must be opportunities for all. And this opportunity which my family has had, these blessings
I have received – this is what the DA seeks for the whole of South Africa,
for all the people. Every South African counts. No one should be left
behind ...'

By all accounts my father's childhood in Durban was uneventful and
happy – his parents combining the virtues or defects of strictness and love
in more or less equal measure. He attended Durban High School, then the
premier government day school of its kind in the city. He went straight
from university in Pietermaritzburg, where he prospered, to the Bar in
Johannesburg where he was admitted as an advocate on 20 April 1948, just
before the National Party won power in the fateful general election.

The Nationalists' shock election had profound consequences for my
father's incipient career at the Bar. The first National Party minister of
Justice, CR (Blackie) Swart, began to appoint members of the Bar to the
Bench, not on merit, but for political reasons. Like the ANC government
after it, the new government almost immediately began to use its power
of patronage.

My father recounts another problem: most of the leading senior counsel
or silks at the Johannesburg Bar were Jewish, but now Jewish appointees
to the Bench were apparently few and far between – the first such by the
National Party was made only in 1955. The result was to create a tremendous bottleneck at the Bar: the silks did not become judges, and senior
juniors could not take silk, and the junior juniors could not inherit the
work of the senior juniors.

Life at the bottom of this food chain was difficult for my father. Nonetheless, he commenced practice on the tenth floor of His Majesty's

Buildings next door to Joe Slovo, who was to achieve notoriety and fame over the next five decades.

My father was to achieve great distinction, some controversy and a considerable reputation as both a lawyer and a judge. Oddly, he did not believe that he ever had what might be called a natural aptitude for the law; as he put it: 'I lack a particularly subtle mind.' What he did have in those days was the ability to see the real point in a case – and a flair for advocacy.

In many ways, his career mirrored the political developments and social mores of the land. Thus it happened that my father was on the Western Circuit of the old Transvaal of 1951 and acting as a prosecutor against a white man charged with raping a black woman. The minister of Justice had forgotten to direct that the trial be held by a judge and assessors – and the accused wisely elected to be tried by an all-white jury. The result was inevitable, but it was assisted by some fine advocacy by Charl Theron, a great jury advocate. He had the ability to make small discrepancies assume monumental proportions, and his closing address was superb. My father says that he sat up until 4 am with the assistance of the court stenographer, Bernard Pitt, preparing his address to the jury in Afrikaans. An unavailing labour: the accused was acquitted.

There was a corroboratory lesson in racial legal manoeuvres in a similar case some years earlier, when a white accused appeared before Mr Justice Greenberg charged with raping a black woman. After deliberating briefly the jury returned and the judge asked the foreman to state the verdict. 'Guilty but insane,' replied the foreman. 'What?' said the judge; 'all nine of you?'

A year before that, in 1950, my father had a brief to defend a white man from England and his co-accused, an allegedly Coloured woman, charged with contravening the Immorality Act. It was common cause that the couple were living together as man and wife, but the question was whether the Crown could prove that the female accused was not white but Coloured. The detective sergeant who arrested the woman said that she seemed to be Coloured in appearance and lived in an area mainly inhabited by Coloured people and that her brother also appeared to be Coloured.

My father's cross-examination was selective and extremely brief. Having asked the accused to pull up the sleeve of her dress he proceeded thus:

'Sergeant, you will see that her skin is lily white. Do you agree?'

'Yes.'

'Is not the skin on her face just the same?'

'Yes.'

'Why did you arrest the accused?'

'Because she has high cheek bones.'

'Is there anything unusual about that?'

'No.'

'Do you, yourself, not have high cheek bones?'

'Yes.'

My father sat down. The accused were acquitted but a storm erupted. In a leading article entitled 'The woman who had high cheek bones', the editor of the *Star* wrote:

'Once again, a woman has been dragged into the courts and accused under the Immorality Act because a policeman thought she was Coloured ... [S]o long as the race laws remain on the statute books, they must be obeyed, but how can the law be truly interpreted when it is not precise? ... If parliament cannot decide on something better, MPs of every political shade should insist that decent investigations are made without embarrassment to the suspected individual, before a woman who may merely have been having sun-ray treatment is subjected to the indignity of an arrest.'[4]

Absurd as this case and this cross-examination appear from the moral heights which South Africa has now reached, we can see the hurt and humiliation of those at the receiving end of the mad hatter's ideology of apartheid.

On New Year's Eve, 1953, after my father had been in practice for about five years, he became engaged to my mother, Sheila, after apparently only six dates. They were married three months later on his 29th birthday, on 31 March 1954.

My mother had apparently enjoyed a very full social life and a number of romantic liaisons. Her mother, Ray, who subsequently escaped widowhood by marrying a mining engineer, Jack Grusd, exercised a great deal of control over her wilful daughter. Ray's idea of perfection was that both her children, Sheila and Neil, should 'marry well' – i.e. into the Jewish haute bourgeoisie – and 'preferably a professional man', she instructed my mother.

Sheila, who was a curious and intriguing amalgam of contradictory impulses, simultaneously sought to defy and to obey Ray. So she conducted a secret liaison with a leading young physician in Port Elizabeth who met all my grandmother's requirements, except – horror of horrors – he was a gentile! Whether on the rebound or not, my mother's meeting with my father, arranged by a mutual acquaintance at the Bar, was exactly to my grandmother's taste and delight.

Sheila was then 24 years old and had emerged from the University of the Witwatersrand with a BA and already spent some time abroad, where she was wined and dined by admirers from Oslo to London. When she met my father she had begun a career in public relations and was deeply involved in promoting the recently launched South African National Tuberculosis Association in Sandton.

She was undoubtedly the greatest single influence on my life, part flapper, part intellectual and part bohemian. One of her close friends, Roseline Shapiro, described her much later as 'a non-conventional conformist' or as 'a conforming non-conventionalist'. Whatever … I inherited many of her flaws but also some of her attributes, two of which were a social conscience and elements of her piercing wit and humour.

Barbara Bush, matriarch of the eponymous American political dynasty, has been described as 'prickly, tart-tongued, and an injustice collector' – and in many ways that described Sheila at her brilliant best and irascible worst. Her wonderful gift of friendship was matched only by her penchant for petty squabbles and fallouts with seemingly good friends. Many years later I accused her of keeping a 'grievance bank', into which, I noted, there were far more deposits than withdrawals.

Shortly after my parents returned from their honeymoon my father discovered that his practice was not moving as fast as he thought it ought to. Chance intervened. He was involved in two cases in Durban and was persuaded to start a practice there; the opportunities were so much greater. Reluctantly, my mother agreed to leave her family and friends and they decamped to Durban on 1 September 1955. My brother, Peter, had been born earlier that year in Johannesburg. I arrived on 15 December 1956 at the St Augustine's Hospital in Durban, and was named Anthony James Leon. Almost from birth, and certainly from my earliest recall, I was called Tony, except by Grandpa Jack who always called me Toto. My teachers used my formal first name.

The sultry climate of Durban was the warm, if humid, background to my early life, my formative years and my first political stirrings.

The historian Paul Johnson is fascinated by the dates when people are born and die, and the events that surround them. He says: '[K]nowing your own historical context gives you a perspective on events, not always reassuring.'[5]

In the year of my birth, the National Party under the leadership of JG Strijdom, the so-called 'Lion of the North' – even in the context of his times regarded as an extremist hardliner – held sway. Already in power for eight years, the Nationalists had commenced assembling the legislative foundations of apartheid, having been elected on the promise that only the total separation of the races would prevent a move towards equality and the overwhelming of white South Africa by blacks.

While other discriminatory societies at that time – such as the United States – maintained the legislative and political fig-leaf that 'separate means equal', South Africa's unique system was untarnished by such hypocrisy. For example, the minister of Native Affairs, Hendrik Verwoerd, introducing the Bantu Education Act (1953), decreed that blacks should be sealed off from the relative advantages of state education, and created a separate, grossly inferior, system for blacks. African pupils would be 'trained in accordance with their opportunities in life', which he considered 'did not reach above the level of certain forms of labour.'[6]

In the month of my birth – December 1956 – the Soviet army brutally suppressed the Hungarian uprising. At home, the year marked the end of a titanic and futile battle to invalidate the government's attempts to remove the 'Coloured' (as distinct from African) voters in the Cape Province from a common roll. This singular instance of multiracial exceptionalism dated back to an historic compromise at the time of the formation of the Union of South Africa itself in 1910. Since 1951 the National Party had been attempting to circumvent the constitution or alter its entrenched provisions, but it lacked the requisite two-thirds majority.

Furthermore, the United Party opposition in parliament showed uncharacteristic grit and determination. They ultimately persuaded the highest court in the land to throw out the National Party's attempt at constitutional gerrymandering.

However, the court indicated that its powers were extremely limited. It could, in terms of the Union constitution, only determine whether the procedure employed by the legislature was legally competent. So after half-a-decade of struggle, the Nationalists succeeded in their quest by the simple expedient of packing the Senate with nominated members and achieving – albeit artificially – a two-thirds majority.

From 1949 onwards, the first apartheid parliament commenced the systematic codification and ratification of discriminatory patterns and practices which had been evolving since white settlement first came to South Africa some three hundred years before. In the NP's world order, apartheid began at birth with racial stratification under the Population Registration Act (1950) and continued through every stage of life's journey. Even at its end the separation was maintained in (legally decreed) segregated cemeteries.

2

Probably as an intended insult, one of my predecessors as leader of the opposition once described my political and parliamentary style as 'pure Westminster'. This was a dig at a certain perceived 'unAfricanness' which became the form of background noise of what passed for political discourse in the late 1990s. However, Frederik van Zyl Slabbert, my accuser, was closer to the truth than he realised since my first home was at 22 Westminster Drive in the middle-class enclave of Durban North.

However, my earliest memories relate to our next home – a formidable three-storey pile atop a hill, 240 South Ridge Road, Durban, where the panoramic sweep south took in Manor Gardens and the University of Natal campus at Howard College; while eastwards, or straight ahead from my bedroom, were the twinkling lights of Durban harbour at night – and the shimmering waves of the Indian Ocean by day.

Durban – Africa's biggest port and the country's third-biggest city – was noteworthy for its population mix. The province was a demographic fruit salad of Zulu, Indian and white. Zululand was almost a different country, although the Tugela River – its western boundary – was only about eighty kilometres from our home. We vaguely heard stories of King Shaka and his Zulu impis, whose forces had shaken the British army before ultimately being crushed in the Battle of Ulundi on 4 July 1879. The province of Natal – of which Durban was the most important city – had its name bestowed by explorer Vasco da Gama who allegedly first saw the coastline on Christmas Day, 1497.

But what distinguished Natal and Durban from the rest of the country was neither its Portuguese precursors nor its humid climate and sunspeckled beaches. It was the only part of the Union (as South Africa then was) where English-speakers formed a majority of the white population. In the Transvaal and Orange Free State, Afrikaans was the *lingua franca* and the dominant influence in the political life of their white citizenry; in Natal, Englishness, and to an extent the Indian population, set it apart.

While English and Afrikaans whites collaborated to maintain their hegemony over blacks, they divided – sharply – on the 'Imperial Connection', attachment to the English motherland. Further, a basic detestation of their Afrikaans-speaking fellow citizens was a feature of 'English' Natal life and politics until the late 1960s.

Notably, much myth and guff surrounds the alleged warmth (or at least understanding) between black and Afrikaans South Africans today, allegedly because of their shared attachment to and roots in the soil. A strict contrast is drawn with the alleged *uitlander* mentality of English South Africans. Like all racial generalisations and stereotyping, there is a pebble of truth in this – but a boulder of mythologising.

As recently as 2005 I was told by a departing foreign diplomat that a preference for the Boer-Black axis – and a concomitant disparagement of the English – is very much a prejudice shared by President Thabo Mbeki. As the emissary, known to be close to Mbeki, put it: 'He can't stand the English, but has a sneaking regard for the Afrikaner.' It was not a sentiment that many reciprocated; many whites today regard Mbeki as having an anti-white perspective – without linguistic distinctions.

While the province of my birth did not differ from the rest of the country on the fundamentals of race and politics, its close colonial ties to Britain did set it somewhat apart from the other provinces, from Union (1910) to the establishment of a Republic in 1961. In a study of the *British Civic Culture of Natal South Africa, 1902-1961*, PS Thompson makes the pertinent point that a constant in Natal history was that the Union of South Africa was greeted with a singular lack of enthusiasm, as was the succeeding Republic. This was more than a question of establishing – and bitterly preserving – white minority rule 'in a land full of blacks'; in Natal the process was reinforced by the predominance of 'the British' at the time of Union – then making up perhaps 74% of the white population of the province.

Of course, we had the skins of privilege, and my father's burgeoning legal practice – supplemented by Granny Ray's material generosity. We had all the accoutrements of an advantaged elite: weekends at the Oyster Box hotel in nearby Umhlanga Rocks, holidays in the mountains of the Drakensberg and in Johannesburg; a legion of servants and nannies; and the effortless assumption that a private-school education could ensure that 'the blessings' (as our parents called us) would be insulated against the travails of Christian National Education then being imposed by the Nats on the public schools – promising us the best kind of life as scions of the elect.

Nevertheless, the political climate into which I was born was not simply set by the National Party's grim and benighted legislative railroad. There was, too, African resistance. My first conscious awareness of politics was when my brother and I stood on the veranda of our house on the crest of South Ridge Road and excitedly watched South African Defence Force Saracens, or armoured cars, on their way to subdue the densely populated African township of Cato Manor, which practically bordered the leafy and salubrious area in which we lived. To a four-year-old and his brother, this was all a game, like war or a sophisticated version of the cops-and-robbers

we played at nursery school. In fact it was the deadly face and force of
the government imposing the first state of emergency since the advent of
National Party rule. It was 1960.

Cato Manor loomed large in my family's life that year. My father, at the
extremely young age of 33, had 'taken silk', attaining the rank of 'Queen's
Counsel' or Senior Advocate. He was one of the youngest QCs in the
country, and was briefed to lead the team of lawyers to defend the 'natives' who had rioted when the police entered the township to confiscate
and impound illegal liquor. This routine raid had lit the simmering fires
of resentment smouldering in the vast, teeming township – and nine policemen were killed in the encounter. Twenty-eight 'non-Europeans' were
charged with the murders of 'four Europeans and five natives'.[7]

My father recalls that the proceedings 'lasted for 87 court days; at that
time it was the longest murder trial in South African history. The trial was
a trial in more ways than one for me: it became a tribulation, it nearly
caused me to have a nervous breakdown and came close to ruining my
practice.'

A major issue was why a trivial liquor raid had given rise to such a
brutal and merciless attack upon the police. It became clear to Ramon
that 'a large part of the population of Cato Manor bore feelings of hostility towards the uniformed branch of the South African Police in January
when the attack took place.'

'I contended that in the year 1960 the philosophy of an eye for an eye and
a tooth for a tooth was to be rejected. The law had been implemented in such
a way that the inhabitants of Cato Manor had been harassed by the police to
the point where a most trivial incident had sparked off an explosion ...

'The cause was exceedingly unpopular, the prosecution very hostile,
and the court did not display any particular sympathy towards the defence.
The prosecution gave no quarter and we had to fight every inch of the
way.'

There was an inspection *in loco*: 'Within minutes of our arrival a crowd
of several hundred black people gathered. They watched intently as we
moved around the area guarded by policemen armed with Sten guns. By
the time we left some hours later the crowd had swelled to more than a
thousand strong. And there were others watching from in front of their
huts on the surrounding hillsides.'

At the time, 'Cato Manor was a slum consisting for the most part of
closely packed corrugated-iron shacks. It was an unhygienic, overcrowded
shack town.'

After about three exhausting months, the Crown case finally closed.

My father relates: 'We had hoped that about half would be acquitted and that we might be able to avoid the death sentence for some of the others. In the event 18 were convicted and ten acquitted ... [E]xtenuating circumstances were found in the case of eight of those convicted, with the consequence that ten were sentenced to death. Our argument on general extenuating circumstances was rejected; still, the evidence which had been led had not been in vain, for in the case of three of the accused extenuating circumstances were found, partly because of the alcohol consumed and partly because "the instincts of the chase" had got the better of the accused.'

The trial ended on 15 December 1960, my fourth birthday. When asked later about how I grew up under apartheid, my mother stated: 'In our home he was exposed to liberal values.' Indeed I was, and that year had a particular resonance for my parents.

3

In 1960 both my parents became more closely bound to the political realities of the land. While my father wrestled in court with the unpleasant consequences of the police action, my mother was immersed through the Women's Section of the Institute of Race Relations (which she helped establish in Durban) in a musical named *Mkumbane*. Its significance in Durban in 1960 was what the *Natal Mercury* described as its 'all-native' cast of 130.

Staged shortly before the grim onset of the state of emergency, the play was also noteworthy for the collaboration between its lyricist, Alan Paton, and its composer, Todd Matshikiza. Matshikiza went on to fame, if not fortune, with *King Kong*. Paton, of course, is known worldwide as the author of *Cry, the Beloved Country*.

Mkumbane is the isiZulu name for Cato Manor, and translates as 'the village in the gulley'. The Institute (in particular, my mother) threw its energies into making a success of the production, which depicted township life in a manner little known to white Durban. Its run at Durban City Hall was a sellout: Sheila handled marketing and publicity.

Paton was president of the Liberal Party (to the left of the Progressives, and in consequence even more electorally unpopular); he became a frequent visitor to our house. And after the production's great success, the Natal chairman of the Institute, Archbishop Denis Hurley, presented my mother with an album of photographs and press cuttings. In an inspiring inscription, he wrote:

'To Sheila Leon – This album commemorating *Mkumbane* is presented to you by the Natal Region of the Institute of Race Relations as a small token of our deep appreciation of your very valuable contribution to the success of this memorable production. We hope that in the years to come it will recall that at a time when there was little laughter and joy in our country, *Mkumbane* was to all of us a symbol of what can be achieved by men and women who forget the petty things that divide in the pursuit of a noble goal that unites.'

Hurley was at the time the youngest archbishop in the Roman Catholic world, and bore prophetic and prescient witness. After my mother's death in December 2001, I felt that the album – with its precious and unique memories – more rightly belonged to the Matshikiza family than to my own. Accordingly, I sent it to Todd's son, John, an actor and writer living in Johannesburg.

What was *Mkumbane* about? I was too preoccupied with playing marbles and rounders at school, and staying out of trouble. And indeed I did increasingly find myself in trouble – though for being unpunctual, untidy or speaking out of turn.

What I specifically recall was an injunction from Sheila never under any circumstances to refer to blacks as 'natives' or to Indians as 'coolies', but to call them Africans and Indians. We were instructed to stand when *any* adult entered the room.

Another form of early 'conscientisation' was when she piled Peter and me into her blue Morris Minor, and drove us around Umlazi (black) and Merebank (Indian), to grasp the true context in which we lived. My mother's great fear, at that stage, was that her children would simply accept 'Granny's Ray's bourgeois or middle-class (Jewish) values' as the norm. There was a much wider and harsher world outside the relatively protected and privileged suburbs, and Sheila Leon was determined that her children should experience it, or at least be aware of its existence.

Although most of Sheila's enthusiasms and projects were temporary, she strongly imbued us with an early and permanent sense of the gathering apartheid injustice.

In Christopher Hitchens's masterful study of George Orwell[8] he observes that, living and writing as Orwell did, he 'discredited the excuse of "historical context" and the shady alibi that there was, in the circumstances, nothing else people could have done.' Forty years on, it is easy to say that my parents and their circle could have 'done more' or that their opposition to apartheid was feeble. But it was an inescapable fact that white

Durban, and South Africa, were deeply conservative and inherently racist. My parents' behaviour needs to be seen against that backdrop.

In 1981, when I was a student of the Witwatersrand law faculty, one of my father's close friends and eminent judicial colleagues, John Didcott, was invited to address our annual law dinner. He was a pre-eminent and crusading liberal jurist with a brilliant mind, if an occasional intolerant manner. Appropriately for the time, he dissected the dilemma of participating in an unjust system, rather than working for its revolutionary overthrow. He was characteristically frank:

'The idea that by working within a system one "lends respectability" to it, and thus strengthens it, is fast becoming a cliché. It is a peculiarly modern one, what is more. Human society would have made little progress had that view prevailed throughout history … If one is too fastidious to soil one's cuffs [one cannot change] society … To change that, one must remain part of it, involved in it, even at the risk of being called a collaborator.'[9]

After democracy came in 1994, John went on to further fame as a Constitutional Court judge.

Perhaps the most formative political event of my very early years was my parents' decision to involve themselves in the formation of the Progressive Party in 1959. Shortly after the Cato Manor trial they committed themselves to the establishment of South Africa's newest political force.

'The Progs' (as they were soon christened) were a liberal breakaway from the ossifying official opposition United Party. The breakaway issue – the reneging by the UP on its previous commitments in terms of the so-called 1936 Hertzog 'settlement' which provided more land for African reserves – was merely the last straw for the more enlightened wing's determination to rupture the reactionary NP-UP duopoly.

Led by the Cape UP leader, Jannie Steytler – a Queenstown doctor, whose father had been an Anglo-Boer War hero – the Progressive ranks attracted just under a dozen of the UP's more enlightened MPs; and, crucially, the major backing and financial support of mining tycoon and former MP, Harry Oppenheimer. Of its founding members, three – Helen Suzman, Colin Eglin and Zach de Beer – were to play immense roles in the struggle for principled opposition in South Africa over the next 30 years. Each – plus Oppenheimer – was also to have an enormous and varied role in my own (as-yet unglimpsed) political career. In short order, my father was elected the party's Natal coastal region chairman and a member of its governing National Executive. In reality this meant he became second-in-command to its first provincial leader, former Durban mayor, Leo Boyd.

My mother, a copywriter at the Durban office of the international advertising agency, J Walter Thompson (JWT), took charge of the local publicity machine.

The Progs' first political test came when Verwoerd decided to hold a referendum on the issue of an independent republic. In many senses this was a legal formality, since the country had enjoyed sovereignty under the Statute of Westminster for the preceding 40 years. However, symbolically, the poll was seen as the fulfilment of Afrikaner Nationalism – the *volk* unshackled by any overwhelming attachment to the British Crown. Since Natal had just such an attachment (as did the English throughout the country), the province returned a huge 75% 'No' vote. But some 52% of white South Africans supported the Republic – and it was duly declared on 31 May 1961.[10]

Such details were unknown to me at the time. In my final year of nursery school, I was handed a small orange, white and blue South African flag and a gold (or gold-coloured) medal, and told by a teacher to 'put it in your satchel, because the Natives will be upset.' The referendum was also the final form of co-operation between the UP and the Progs. Thereafter it would be a fight to the political death for the relative crumbs of the opposition vote. The contest would be most bitter in Natal.

Later in 1961, Verwoerd tapped into the prevailing republicanism and called an early election. I vaguely recall the excitement as leading figures of the Progs, such as Steytler and De Beer, came to stay. 'You know,' Steytler said to my father, 'the day will come when the Nationalists will adopt the politics of our party.' 'Nonsense,' argued Ramon. 'I am quite right,' Steytler said, 'because I know my people.'

Steytler was both prophetic and about thirty years premature. South Africa would yet have to endure three decades of repression and struggle, vast amounts of violence and the fundamental degradation of civil liberties and human rights.

From today's vantage the Progressive philosophy seems mild beer. The party's key principles were defined at its inaugural congress in November 1959. They were:

- the maintenance and extension of the values of Western civilisation; the protection of fundamental human rights and the safeguarding of the dignity and worth of the human person irrespective of race, colour or creed; and
- the recognition that in the Union of South Africa there is one nation

21

which embraces various groups differing in race, religion, language and traditions; that each such group is entitled to the protection of those things and of its right of participation in the government of the nation.

However, the National Party and its press thought otherwise. AK Heard[11] summarises their response:

'*Die Transvaler* [the official organ of the NP in the Transvaal] particularly decried the "one nation" concept ... "If words mean anything," it wrote, "[they mean] that this party seeks to create a new unity out of many faces. Boer, Briton, Jew, Bantu, Indian and Coloured will all form 'one nation' together ... This is the most open and fatal point of view ever adopted by a political party in our country."

'A few days later, the same paper attacked the party as revolutionary: "The white man does not intend to surrender his future voluntarily; and if in the final analysis it has to be defended, he will defend it with blood."'

It never happened. Indeed, by the time of the Progs' formation, FW de Klerk was an enthusiastic young Nationalist member who – no doubt – vigorously agreed with the newspaper's thundering denunciation of the 'revolutionary' Progressives (his father was, after all, a director of the newspaper group that published *Die Transvaler*). It would be him and a much-reduced National Party that would 'surrender the future', as the newspaper ranted.

Still, at the time of its debut, the Progressive Party crashed to defeat in its first election in 1961. It retained Houghton, which became, nearly thirty years later, the constituency that elected me to parliament at the tail-end of apartheid.

4

My early years were probably similar to those of tens of thousands of other white middle-class children born in the baby-boomer years of the consumer age. We enjoyed the 'unasked for, but unearned, apartheid dividend', to borrow the accurate phrase of journalist Rowan Philp.[12] I attended a local nursery school, where in July 1960, when I was three-and-a-half years old, the principal noted: 'Tony has a very happy nature.' However, I could be frustrating because my results in 'cutting out' and 'painting' were not as good as Peter's.

My brother and I are temperamentally – and in many other ways – very different. Yet we were, and remain, very close. The nursery school noted that by the time Peter had to leave for primary school, I 'became weepy and upset'. I have probably toughened up in the intervening 45 years, but an early characteristic I have never entirely shed was what was presciently described as a 'not-too-long attention span' and the fact that 'he becomes bored quickly'.

My primary schooling commenced at Chelmsford, on the edge of Musgrave Road, the artery which snaked across the Durban Berea. I was mostly miserable – bored in class since I could already read by the time I started lessons – and somewhat terrified by our severe and forbidding head-mistress, a certain Miss Sissons. For unexplained reasons (owing nothing to feminism) all our teachers, all women, taught under their maiden names.

My first report, dated 29 June 1962, described me as follows: 'Tony is very keen and made very good progress. His mental work is better than his written work.' The phrases 'very untidy' and 'not always attentive' would become the mantra of all my succeeding school reports. By my second year my arithmetic was 'rather slow and unsure'; while my English was 'excellent'. This divide, in my brain or elsewhere, would reach its zenith and nadir in my matriculation ten years hence.

When Peter went on to Clifton Preparatory School for Boys I was disconsolate. So I started agitating to go there as well; I reckon my unhap-piness at being at school was initially in contrast to my huge enjoyment of being at home. In South Ridge Road we had a big garden, where I played war with my first friend, Tom Sulley. We imagined being soldiers in some faraway combat zone that we read about in our Marvel comics, on which I spent my pocket money. Sheila abhorred 'bad literature' – my photo comics, Enid Blyton, and 'Classics Illustrated' with their marvellous, bowdlerised and easily understood versions of every book and author from Jules Verne to Mark Twain.

I had the radio – Springbok Radio with its 'serials' in particular. But in the sixties there was no TV, no video games, no Sunday shopping, no mov-ies, no Sunday sport (except, curiously, for soccer); just a dour Calvinism imposed on a quiescent population by a nervous government in thrall to the serried ranks of the NGK church hierarchy. There was official terror of any concession to popular culture: godless secularism from a corrupted West was to be kept at bay. Fundamentalist Nationalists were determined that shameless decadence was to be suppressed and avoided; mild girlie magazines were banned and seized at all airports; and the cabinet's en-forcer-in-chief – the goatee-bearded ultra-nationalist, Albert Hertzog – decreed TV to be the 'devil's box'. Political repression was meshed with joylessness.

In 1965 there were major changes. Happily, I moved to Clifton Preparatory, a private school, fairly relaxed, with small classes. Many of my friends were moulded by (in Durban standards) old money, and lived in enormous houses which made our comfortable family pile seem modest in comparison. For example, the Levy family, whose son Steven was an early friend, owned Budget Rent-a-Car; another classmate, Kevin Dawson, was the grandson of the founder of the John Orr's department store; while another, Doug Saunders, was the son of Natal's pre-eminent sugar baron, Chris.

For all the advantages it bestowed on those who passed through its gates, Clifton was not always an inoculator against personal failure and even extreme forms of sociopathic conduct. One of the 'naughty boys' in my class transmogrified in his post-school years into a member of an infamous gang of armed robbers who terrorised banks in suburban Johannesburg in the late 1970s. He was subsequently captured and convicted and was sentenced to, and served, a hefty jail sentence.

My school reports remained ambivalent. Thus, in standard five: 'Anthony has continued to show much ability in English and in History and Geography, where his very good general knowledge can be used most effectively. Mathematics and Afrikaans need a more concentrated effort, and written and illustrated work, although enthusiastically tackled, is sometimes spoiled with careless presentation.' The headmaster was more severe: 'Intellectual endeavour is a strict discipline and it is obviously important for him to control, though not suppress, his laudable enthusiasms.'

In British public school culture, prowess at sport is highly esteemed. I tried. However, my very flat feet and indifferent eye-ball co-ordination meant that cricket and rugby had me exerting maximum effort and minimum talent.

An enduring memory comes from my final year at Clifton in 1970. The entire school was marched several kilometres to the Kingsmead cricket field to watch the first test between South Africa and Australia. Clifton's most famous old boy, Barry Richards, was debuting as opening batsman for the Springboks and almost scored a century before lunch. Alas, Richards's international cricketing career came to an abrupt and tragic end that very year. A decision by Prime Minister John Vorster to ban an MCC side from touring in 1968 – because South African-born Coloured Basil D'Oliviera was a member – precipitated our isolation from world cricket within three years. The ban was over time extended by our international competitors to most other sports.

Our headmaster, Tim Sutcliffe, was an extraordinary figure. Today we would call him a polymath – equally conversant in Maths, English and Latin.

Aside from his day job he was a great actor on Springbok Radio. He and his wife starred in all the soap operas; today one also calls them celebrities.

Sutcliffe was a remarkable person, capable of acts of great kindness and instant cruelty. He once slapped me across the face several times for being rude to him; and would march us into his office in order to flog us for often very trivial reasons. Corporal punishment was freely and ferociously administered, and my punishment was generally for 'answering back' or 'being cheeky'. I had a real fear and loathing of the cane; yet, oddly, my abiding recollection is of a fairly blissful environment. Even as odd, perhaps, was that my stay at Clifton commenced with a shatteringly sad and unexpected event which accompanied me like a constant, dark shadow.

In late 1965 my parents decided to divorce. My mother had met a Charlton Heston semi-lookalike, Dick Prior, a Durban yachtsman who was advertising manager for the *Daily News*. My mother would eventually deeply regret her impulsiveness; but for my father – a proud and essentially sensitive man – there was to be no turning back.

The practical – as opposed to emotional – consequences meant a weekly oscillation from my mother's new home in Westville to my father's new bachelor quarters in an apartment in Musgrave Road, where we spent every weekend. My mother's second marriage was even less successful than her first, and while I got on very well with Dick Prior, who introduced my brother and me to the pleasures of fishing and yachting, he was a better stepfather than husband: Sheila divorced him after six fairly unhappy years.[13]

The other big event, the consequences of which would be felt many years later in my political career, was my father's decision to accept an appointment as a judge in the Natal provincial division of the Supreme Court. Judicial appointments were, in those days, relatively rare: there were, for example, only 12 judges in Natal; fewer than seventy-five judges in all divisions across the entire country.

Today there has been an explosion in judicial numbers and a corresponding decline in the status of the office.

It was also the custom that if a senior advocate declined an appointment by the Minister of Justice, he was unlikely to be offered it again. As my father tells it, two factors weighed against acceptance: his liberal predilections would make the implementation of apartheid law difficult; and second, although my mother bitterly complained of the alimony from my father, the divorce agreement obliged Ramon to pay for the education of his children at private schools. His earnings as a QC were considerable; his salary as a judge would be fairly modest.

On the political issue, he believed it would be possible on occasion – as he demonstrated – to push the judicial envelope against the semi-authoritarian state. Here he had the example of some stellar liberal jurists who preceded him: Oliver Schreiner, Solly Miller, Albert Centlivres, Leopold Greenberg, Denis Fannin and Sandy Milne, for example. And my father would, shortly, be joined on the Bench of Natal by one of his closest friends, the ultra-liberal John Didcott.

As for income, my father decided that the honour and status of the position outweighed financial disadvantages. Thus on 1 January 1967 he was sworn in as the youngest (at 41) and most junior member of the Natal Supreme Court.

I began to develop a keen and precocious interest in politics. My mother took us to political meetings and functions organised by the local Progressive Party. Soon I was hooked, and the narcotic of political activism and involvement has remained a life-long habit.

At a Prog fête in 1969, at the age of 12, I met a gangly teenager with an intense and arresting manner – the chairman of the Young Progressives. His name was Bobby Godsell and he would subsequently become known as one of the country's most significant mining chiefs (becoming in time CEO of AngloGoldAshanti). But at the time his army of young activists knocked on doors, put up posters, and did the drudge work of electioneering. Bobby signed me up and within months I was immersed in the 1970 general election campaign in the Durban constituency of Musgrave.

My family's old friend Jannie Steytler was our candidate. His opponent, the incumbent UP MP, George Hourquebie, was colourless and undistinguished. In my childlike way, I assumed the righteousness of our cause would prevail. The United Party campaign was captured by their extraordinary slogan poster: 'Want TV? Vote UP.' But when the votes were counted on 22 April, Steytler was smashed. The Progressive Party kept Houghton, while the UP was returned as official opposition with 47 seats. Elsewhere the National Party garnered 117 MPs.

This, then, gave me a foretaste of many electoral false dawns. Yet if hard logic rather than youthful exuberance had been the measure, I would not have been disappointed. After all, a few years before, when Ian Smith declared UDI in Rhodesia,[14] Durban cars were emblazoned with stickers declaring 'Forward Rhodesia', 'Good old Smithy', and the like. Britain's prime minister, Harold Wilson, became a hate figure, and we seemed isolated in resolute opposition to 'Smithy's' antics.

Then came a series of jolts. At the end of my primary school years at

Clifton, my mother, still feebly stoking the dying embers of her marriage to Dick Prior, agreed to his request to improve his job prospects by moving to Johannesburg.

I was bitterly unhappy. My friends in Durban were moving on to various boarding schools in the Natal hinterland. We would have to leave our idyllic house in Haraldene Road, Glenwood. There would be no more afternoons on the beach. And I would miss weekends with my father – seeing him only during school holidays.

Perhaps most of all I was bitterly upset at parting with my beloved Boxer dog 'Kimmy', a faithful companion for six years who could not be accommodated in our new Johannesburg apartment.

And I intuited a deep malaise in Sheila's marriage. I later learned that Dick was serially unfaithful – but in our family, when the grown-up spoke or commanded, that was the end of it. No negotiation, no turning back from an adult-decreed decision.

So then: Johannesburg. We lived in a flat opposite the Houghton golf course where, unhappily, a previous tenant had committed suicide in the main bathroom. Even this sombre augury was picayune compared with the intense culture shock waiting for me on my first day of high school at King David. My brother had already commenced his senior schooling at a Jewish school, Carmel, in Durban. It was therefore felt he would acclimatise better at a similar establishment in Johannesburg; and as the younger brother I was expected to tag along.

King David High, in Linksfield, emphasised Judaism. The variety to which I had been hitherto exposed was secular and culinary. I had learned my bar-mitzvah portion by heart off a tape recorder (then, as now, unable to speak a word of Hebrew); and while we attended, largely unwillingly, the Durban Synagogue on high and holy days, my closest acquaintance with the religion of my birth had been my enjoyment of such festive dishes as chopped herring, liver and 'tzimmes' (a concoction of prunes and brisket) served with loving relish by Granny Ray.

My Clifton schooling was notionally Christian, with morning renditions at assembly of the Lord's Prayer, recited on succeeding days in English, Afrikaans and Latin. I took no part in the youth activities provided by the Durban Jewish Club, except for weekly tennis, and all my friends, with the exception of Steven Levy, were Christians. I knew Jews to be 'different' – but I experienced no anti-Semitism from my schoolmates, only curiosity about Judaism, about which I knew little.

When in 1967 (I was in standard three) Israel's very existence was threatened, we all gathered around the radio for the news bulletins, and I surged with childish pride when the dashing Moshe Dayan emerged as an international hero. Sheila ensured that I learned about the Holocaust. In *Five Chimneys* by Olga Lengyel I read of the 'nightmare horror of Auschwitz and Birkenau where day and night, five flaming smoke-stacks belched out the odour of burning flesh.' I still have the battered paperback.

Had I but known, I would have realised that Durban's Jewish Club itself was a monument of sorts to the ingrained and institutionalised anti-Semitism of my home town. It was established by benefactors of the Jewish community because Jews were not, generally, admitted for membership of the Durban or the Country Club. Such restrictions have long since gone, but the Jewish Club still stands near the beachfront.

5

King David in 1971 was bewildering, like arriving in a foreign country. I had little in common with the boys in my class, who had an easy confidence and in-group attitude. Daily prayers, which we were obliged to attend, struck me as bizarre and ritualistic. We had to 'lay tefillin' which meant strapping two boxes of biblical verses to your arm and head – regarded by Orthodox Jews as an essential element of the morning prayer service. I was also obliged to attend Hebrew classes; and the headmaster was an irascible man, Norman Sandler, who early on decided I was one of several candidates who required 'sorting out'. That meant more lashings.

I was not comfortable in an exclusively Jewish school. I identified, later in life, with the famous British politician Lord Keith Joseph who on being asked, 'What sort of Jew are you?' responded: 'Minimally practising, but maximally acknowledging.'

Towards the end of my brief stay at the school, I was most uneasy when we assembled to listen to visiting Israeli intelligence chief General Chaim Herzog (later president of Israel). The flowery introduction of the chairman of the school board embarrassed me. With great solemnity he pronounced: 'We regard the twenty acres of the King David schools complex as being God's twenty acres of holy chosen ground.' No doubt if I had stuck it out, my schooling there would have ended happily: among my closest university friends were Diane Levy, Laurence Kaplan and Brian Schneider; and all had been at Jewish day schools.

During a school vacation that I spent with my father in Durban, Steven Levy spoke with wonder and excitement of his first months at the Natal boarding school, Kearsney. Particularly impressive was his account of the length of the school holidays. (He omitted to tell me this was compensated for by attending school every Saturday morning.) So I began canvassing both my parents for a transfer; they agreed.

Kearsney, affiliated to the Methodist Church, is situated on rambling grounds at Botha's Hill – close to the scenic Valley of a Thousand Hills. It is almost equidistant between Durban and the provincial capital of Pietermaritzburg, and is on the route of the Comrades Marathon, South Africa's most famous road race.

The school was founded in 1921 as Kearsney House, near Stanger on the Natal north coast, by Sir James Liege Hulett – Natal's original sugar baron and founder of the eponymous sugar corporation Huletts. The name 'Kearsney' is apparently derived from an old village and medieval manor near Dover in Kent. This is a clue to its educational ethos: deeply, almost reverentially, influenced by the English public school tradition. In many ways a sort of Victorian or Edwardian spirit still held sway.

Even primogeniture had its place: the headmaster during my Kearsney years, James Hulett Hopkins (known universally as 'Jimmy' or 'Hoppy'), was the great-grandson of the founder. He was a decent and humane man, although extraordinarily conservative.

'Character' was all, and sport and its traditions were seen as the best way of moulding it. Many years before I arrived at the school, one of my father's colleagues, Justice Frank Broome, reflected on a similar institution of his youth:

'Boys were told to play the game; unethical conduct was described as "not cricket"; selfishness was rebuked as not playing for the side; sexual immorality was condemned as undermining physical fitness. And the system worked well, except that the deification of physical prowess tended to embitter the intellectual and unathletic and make of them the communists and racists or cranks of the future.'[15]

If the Duke of Wellington really did say that 'the Battle of Waterloo was won on the playing fields of Eton', it's noteworthy it was not in the classroom, or the library, but on the sports field that character was supposedly forged.

With this ethos went the usual attributes of the public school. Elements of what Broome described at Hilton in the 1930s were still evident in 1970s Kearsney. Thus bullying was common, and corporal punishment institutionalised.

There was a macabre weekly ritual known as the 'hit parade'. If you committed an infraction (such as leaving your socks out of the laundry locker or, my usual offence, 'talking after lights-out') your name was recorded by a prefect and on Thursday night after prep you ended up with your fellow offenders outside the door of the junior common room. Inside, the head prefect (who generally seemed twice your size) made you bend your head under a desk while he took a run at your exposed backside and belted it with what was euphemistically called a 'flogging slipper' – a thick piece of floppy leather with a hard handle.

The pain was mind-numbingly searing and the humiliation extreme. The big test was whether you could emerge with your dignity intact, walking, not running; shaken perhaps, but never crying. I sometimes failed that test.

Other elements of 'school tradition' now seem to me arcane in the extreme. We had to learn by heart the names of the members of the school's 1st cricket XI or 1st rugby XV, depending on the season. Juniors (those in the first three forms) had to keep both blazer buttons fastened and could not put their hands in their pockets. As for 'fagging', once every few weeks a junior was assigned to a house prefect as a sort of domestic servant. For seven days you rose before the school bell, which rang grimly at 6 am, winter and summer, got dressed, woke up the prefect, made his bed and tidied his room; and then, after breakfast, carried his books to class.

Yet Kearsney did practise a form of egalitarianism: we were not allowed civilian clothes on the basis that boys from modest homes (scholarship boys or those granted the fee discounts offered to sons of Methodist ministers) might be 'shown up'.

However, this exclusionary rule extended to a ban on radios and other home comforts. In fact, despite some boys from fabulously wealthy backgrounds, the pre-eminence or financial standing of your parents made little impact on your place in the school food chain. Another privation was extremely limited 'home leave'. We were kept in school for all term weekends, except for one long weekend and two 'free Sundays'. Parents were allowed to visit on Saturday afternoons. I still remember my father (and occasionally my mother) arriving at the school in his grey Rover, with a much welcome spit-roasted chicken, which my friends and I would devour hungrily – a weekly respite from the grim boarding school fare which consisted of such delights as curried eggs, a grey-looking mince concoction, or powdered scrambled eggs.

Status was largely sports-driven, though Kearsney made space for other attributes. Dramatic productions, trips to view rock art in the Drakensberg, and photography were encouraged. I tried public speaking. The school had a mock parliament, divided into government and opposition; and in my matric year (1974) I became 'Leader of the Opposition'.

Not only did my natural talent in debating assist my later career, it compensated for my singular lack of prowess on the sports field. Boys were roughly divided into the 'main okes' and those generally disparaged as 'naffs'. My performance at the podium – and in winning all the public speaking cups and contests in the school – helped me move into the coveted membership of the first group. At school, as in life, it helped to have some or other distinguishing attribute; yet friends were crucial.

As for the masters, some were genuinely inspirational. Our English teacher, Clyde Broster, was one. In the third form, one of our setworks was *Cry, the Beloved Country*, and he used the fabled work as a template for an intense political discussion on the current racial order and its devastating consequences. At the time Paton lived at Botha's Hill, just outside the college grounds. He spoke once to our matric class, and while, in Conor Cruise O'Brien's memorable phrase, he somewhat resembled 'an angry baboon', his talk was one of grace and passion.

We ridiculed Clyde Broster (behind his back) for his peculiar hairstyle – and nicknamed him 'Ziggy Stardust' after one of David Bowie's incarnations. Yet his articulate and empathetic method of instruction still stands today like a rock in my memory. And then there was our physical science teacher, MA Thiselton, known universally, and with awe, as 'Mat'. He dealt out fearsome beatings; yet, paradoxically and perhaps unusually in such a conservative school setting, Mat was an unashamed political liberal. One day when our standard seven class had performed with its usual lack of distinction, Mat flung the exercise books on the floor and shouted: 'You are over-privileged and undeserving. Look at the opportunities you have. There are black children in this country who would give their left testicles to enjoy the sort of education you have and which you so dismally squander.'

The class gasped, not so much at the racial point he was making – unusual though it was at the time – but at his explicit reference to the sexual organ, much discussed by schoolboys, but never by the masters.

I was deeply unhappy and thoroughly miserable in my first year to eighteen months. We lived in barrack-like dormitories, subject to bizarre rituals and endless bullying; some seriously sadistic seniors did much to aggravate my sense of homesickness and alienation. Nearly thirty-five years later, I still associate Sundays with maudlin gloominess. The college was particularly grey and sombre in winter when the mists of Botha's Hill would envelop the school. On the rare Sundays we were allowed home, a few hours of intense pleasure in Durban would rapidly give way to mounting depression as I readied myself to go back to school. However, since I, rather than my parents, had elected to become a boarder, I was determined to stick it out and hoped for an improvement in the overall bleakness.

The change came in the fourth form, my penultimate year. Suddenly, or so it seemed, I had a whole group of 'main oke' friends; and one must suppose that boarding school was useful preparation for the pitiless rigours awaiting me, especially on the sometimes hard benches of opposition politics. But I can't help but think that adding a necessary hard carapace onto my sensitivities and vulnerabilities as a child also led to the disappearance of something quite vital and important.

I also became friendly with the rebels, who had a penchant for breaking the rules, bunking out of school grounds, or misusing officially sanctioned outings into the Valley of a Thousand Hills for the purposes of smoking or even drinking. Disastrously, given its deleterious impact on my health later, I became a keen charter member of the 'smokers' club'. Smoking was illicit – so, in my contrarian way, I greatly enjoyed, at 16, indulging and, unlike Bill Clinton, inhaling.

As always, we and those we know often walk in the dark.

One of my 'naughtiest' friends at school was Chris Stemmler, whose father was a well-known Durban society doctor. Chris enjoyed living life on the edge. Shortly after we matriculated, he joined the South African Police as an alternative to compulsory military training; one night a suspect, with whom he was alone in a patrol car, shot him with his own service revolver. He was the first person I knew who would die in such a violent manner. Unfortunately, he was not the last.

My other friends included Peter Crossley, Rob Nathan, Peter Forsyth, Steve du Toit, Gappy Smythe; my old Clifton connections, Steven Levy and Mark Witney; and a host of others. Some of those friendships remain intact to this day. Outside school I socialised with a diverse cast of characters – Debbie Goldberg, Mandy Levy, Jeremy Schmahmann and Gavin Varejes – these too have proved to be enduring relationships.

We would spend hours at school, often whispering deep into the night, discussing our personal futures and the country's direction. Those of us with a liberal, non-racial perspective were in the distinct minority. The majority were fairly reactionary – they could not imagine a country in which black people governed; their minds were full of the darkest foreboding about 'savage' revenge being meted out to the whites – and some actually viewed blacks as being congenitally incapable of governing. I am sure that today they have accommodated themselves to the new order – a remarkable fact about South Africa, a transition not all multiethnic countries have managed.

6

In 1972, in my second year, my father's judicial office led to me acquiring the nickname 'Judge'. This had little to do with my friends being impressed with high office or parental titles, since they profoundly and splendidly were not. It had much more to do with the one commodity pubescent boys in a monastic environment obsess about and have only derivative knowledge of – sex.

The most popular legal publication to which many boys subscribed was a peculiarly indigenous creation called *Scope* magazine; it contained scantily clad centrefolds, the wrath of the censorship regime placated by the minimum apparel over the forbidden bits of the female anatomy. The school was opposed to such prurient filth; one speech day the head lamented 'the collapse of moral standards'. The Kearsney tradition of neatness and good manners 'had to be protected against such inroads.'[16]

In truth, of course, the boys were desperate to be part of the 'permissive society': hence the massive enjoyment of *Scope*, *Playboy*-lite, of which our supply was permanently threatened when, in May 1972, the Publications Control Board banned an edition of the magazine. Far worse was the censor board's decision to 'ban all future editions' of the periodical. The matter came before my father as an urgent application. Bannings could then be appealed to the judiciary.

It emerged that one of the main grounds for the banning was the large photograph of 'a non-white shirtless young man embracing a white girl openly in what appears to be a street in Greenwich Village, New York, where, as was stated in the accompanying caption, it was "with it" among young folks to spoon across the colour line.'[17]

I had never heard the word 'spoon' (nuzzle and kiss) in such a context. At any rate, the magazine had conjoined the two great no-no's of 1970s South Africa – sex and race – in one revealing photograph. Hence the lifelong ban. The reasons for the prohibition that the court squeezed out of the Publications Board appear today risible; but they provide insight into the mind, such as it was, of official South Africa at the time.

In essence, the Board's thinking was along these lines:

'[Youth], both white and non-white, is prone, if not eager, to follow trends of licence and promiscuity current in other places, and they may very well be encouraged herein by such an open example of what is described as being "with it" to disregard the provisions of the Immorality Act ...

'The photo of the white girl and the Negro is objectionable in that it portrays intimacy between black and white persons … It is harmful to public morals in that the photos [deal] in an improper manner with scant or inadequate dress and physical poses. It is calculated to stimulate sexual desire in the male youth by means of these suggestive poses … These provocative photos are considered to be indecent or obscene and likely to deprave or corrupt minds of young people.'

The Board was certainly correct about *Scope* using pictures to stimulate sexual desire in males generally – but it was arguable whether *Scope* itself caused the phenomenon. My father, himself pretty strait-laced, though not naïve, had to pick through this zealous officialese to decide how 'a substantial number of likely readers' would react. He said: '[It] is not irrelevant to observe that attitudes have changed towards the human body and the method of dress employed to cover it to a lesser or greater extent.'

He was equally dismissive of the Board's view on the corrupting effect of the offending picture: 'I regard the views of the Board on this point as being far-fetched in the extreme. It is, I consider, important to bear in mind that the photograph depicts an event in New York, and not one in Johannesburg … The photograph is merely a pictorial representation of a fact of life in another country … How this can be said to be an encouragement to the youth of this country to commit criminal offences [is quite] beyond my comprehension.'

He similarly dismissed the Board's argument concerning photographs of 'partially exposed breasts' and 'some exposure of the human body'. He threw out its argument and set aside the Board's declaration of *Scope* as an undesirable publication. So Dad struck a blow for free expression and inadvertently boosted my standing among my much-relieved peers, whose supply of *Scope* would now continue!

More serious consequences of this judgment would soon be felt. The Nationalists paid lip-service to an independent judiciary; but did not enjoy being thwarted by it, especially not by the more enlightened English-speaking Bench in Natal. Within 18 months an amending statute was rammed through parliament, the Publication and Entertainments Bill. It simply removed the right of appeal from decisions of the Publications Control Board to the Supreme Court.

When Abba hit the hit parade for the first time – with 'Waterloo' – in 1974, I entered my final year at school. In public life it was another year of a proclaimed change in government policy – relying essentially on the windy rhetoric of the NP tub-thumper, Pik Botha, then in full flight as ambassador to the United Nations. In one of his dramatic but ultimately empty speeches to the Security Council he said, 'South Africa will do everything in its power to move away from discrimination based on race or colour.' He would 'not die for an apartheid sign in the lift.'

Aside from such bombast, there had been some minor easing of 'petty apartheid', but this was virtually on the absolute fringe. Thus, during the school holidays in Johannesburg, my mother took us to the Koffiehuis restaurant at the new five-star Carlton hotel in Johannesburg – designated an 'international hotel' which allowed multiracial dining. That, and the desegregation of certain parks and libraries, represented the horizon of change.

We also had a certain hopeful expectancy when Prime Minister Vorster ventured onto the bridge at the Victoria Falls and met the Zambian leader, Kenneth Kaunda, to convene talks in a railway carriage between the warring parties in Rhodesia. The sight of the dour epitome of apartheid co-hosting a gathering of his prime ally Ian Smith with the dread terrorists (as they were routinely depicted) led by Joshua Nkomo created expectations that were not fulfilled for another six bloody years there, and only 16 years later in South Africa.

The one event that did profoundly change the entire political landscape was the coup in Portugal. Within months this signalled the end of the oldest colonial empire on the continent and, as the *Kearsney Chronicle* noted, 'moved the border of black Africa 1 000 miles southward from the Ruvuma to the Pongola.'

Our matric year was accordingly profoundly unsettled, since we could now look at our call-up papers for military service the following year. The incipient civil war in Angola, in the wake of the abrupt Portuguese flight, would escalate and ensnare many young conscripts within the next two years.

Of more immediacy was the 1974 election, which completely dominated my Easter holidays. I immersed myself as a 17-year-old activist in the Houghton seat (where we lived) of the party's mega (and perhaps only) star, Helen Suzman. Helen's re-election was assured; but so was the NP's certainty of winning its 7th consecutive election by a large margin. For us, the critical factor was whether the United Party would begin to reflect in its returns the desiccation that had enveloped its internal structures.

The antagonists were a reformist young Turk faction led by the newly installed Transvaal leader, Harry Schwarz, and the conservative mainstream rump led by the party chief, Sir de Villiers Graaff. Without proper justification, Graaff and his coterie were probably seen by the Young Progressives as a sort of prime evil – Vorster and the Nats being beyond the pale. But because of the intensity of the intra-opposition fight, and after 13 long and unyielding years in the political desert, some hope and stirrings of a Prog breakthrough out of Houghton could be entertained.

I enjoyed the juvenile dirty tricks in which we indulged: pulling down UP posters and going to call-boxes to ring all the opposition office telephone numbers and then leaving the phones off the hook. Beyond our electioneering and silly pranks, there was genuine outrage at how the UP had finally sold the pass on civil liberties.

The American constitutionalist, Benjamin Franklin, had famously observed 200 years before that 'those who would give up essential liberty, to purchase a little temporary safety, deserve neither liberty nor safety.' Well, the UP had so temporised, and in our view deserved the political bullet.

Rage was precipitated by the UP's participation in one of government's political star-chambers: the Parliamentary Internal Security Commission (instantly dubbed by the opposition press as 'Piscom', or the 'Schlebusch Commission' after its NP chairman). Its findings led to the banning of eight student leaders of the leftist National Union of South African Students (Nusas), whom the Commission branded as 'traitors, guilty of providing support for terrorist groups'. Without due process or any shred of justiciable evidence, the leadership was effectively house-arrested and the organisation severely restricted.

With some of my fellow Young Progs I attended the rallies of our opponents – real eye-openers. The NP gathering at the Johannesburg City Hall introduced me to a white South Africa of which I had read and heard, but never actually seen. Thousands of Afrikaans-speaking whites assembled; the massive stage organ ground out various patriotic anthems; and our small coterie of fresh-faced northern suburbanites felt utterly intimidated and totally alien.

The hall lights were dimmed and the crowd broke into paroxysms of joy and rapture when Vorster entered and addressed his enthralled supporters. I remember nothing of what he said; but it was spoken slowly, loudly, effectively and menacingly. In Natal Afrikaans was poorly understood and certainly undertaught; we left wondering if we shared the same value system, and country, as the faithful.

Then there was a UP meeting in Greenside addressed by their star reformist provincial leader, Schwarz. I went determined to despise him, but came away secretly impressed. A powerful orator, Schwarz did what clever lawyers always do: he played up his strongest arguments, ignored the gaping holes in his own flank, and bore in on the enemy's weakness. Strangely enough – because it struck such a chord – I still remember him mocking the Progressive Party for its moral hypocrisy. I did make a mental note that he was never to be underestimated.

To my intense dismay I had to return to boarding school ten days before the election on 24 April. The kindly Pembroke House matron, Mrs Higham, knowing – as did the whole school, apparently – of my intense interest in the outcome, lent me her transistor radio. While my schoolmates slept, I stayed up the whole night cheering silently as one UP bastion after another fell to a resurgent Progressive team, led by Colin Eglin. In objective terms, the UP only lost six seats to the Progressives (who added a seventh soon after in a by-election). But in the more important political world of perceptions, the UP slide soon became an avalanche.

Within a year Schwarz led a reformist breakaway into a merger with the Progressives. By 1977 the Progressive Reform Party (as the merged entity became) ousted the UP as the official opposition. In fact, shortly before that election, the UP disbanded into a renamed New Republic Party. Many years later, when the once-mighty NP faced electoral immolation at the hands of the party which I then led, it too tried to rebrand itself by adding the prefix 'new' to its name – proving that cosmetic changes and marginal tinkering cannot arrest political sclerosis.

I received a warm letter of thanks for my efforts from Helen Suzman, who added, no doubt as a throwaway line to as ardent a fan as me, 'It's good to be back in parliament with Progressive colleagues … perhaps one day you will join us there.'

I was soon distracted (with no particular difficulty) by the suggestion of one of my schoolmasters that I enter the prestigious inter-schools debating competition, the Jan Hofmeyr Speech Contest. I needed no persuasion. I chose from a list, as my setpiece speech, 'Jan Hofmeyr – Moralist and Statesman'. As I delved into his extraordinary achievements and politics, I had difficulty in imagining that such a prodigious genius had been at the centre of political life in South Africa just over a generation ago.

Born into an eminent Cape Afrikaans family, Hofmeyr was indeed a boy wonder: he matriculated at 12; had a Bachelor of Arts in the sciences at 16 (he attended the University of Cape Town in short pants); obtained the degree of Master of Arts at 17; and a degree from Balliol was conferred on him at the tender age of 21. Just three years later he became principal of Wits University (then the Johannesburg School of Mines); and in 1924 at 29 he was appointed by Jan Smuts as the Administrator of the Transvaal.[18]

During the Second World War, as Smuts's deputy prime minister, he was responsible for seven cabinet portfolios. He apparently memorised his speeches, holding the pages behind his back and turning them over as he – from memory – completed a page. However, he apparently had no private life to speak of and was ruled by his possessive mother. As his biographer Alan Paton noted:

'Two personal relationships to a large extent ruled his life. His attitude to Smuts was ambivalent: sometimes he came close to veneration and sometimes close to hostility. Hofmeyr was like a great hill under a great mountain. He was 24 years younger than Smuts yet he died two years earlier. He had in fact spent his life as Smuts's lieutenant, and in Smuts's shadow.'

Paton asks the question which, years after Hofmeyr's death at the young age of 53, remains unknowable: 'If Hofmeyr had outlived Smuts, would he have become prime minister? He had two great handicaps. One was his liberalism, which frightened and antagonised white South Africa. The other was his phenomenal childhood and boyhood, and the possessiveness of his mother. This was the second personal relationship that to such an extent ruled his life.'

At its height, the United Party was – as Paton remarks – led by 'two of the most gifted Afrikaners of their time. Geniuses in fact.'[19]

I loved the contest; the debates, the extempore speeches (which each contestant had to deliver in addition to the set pieces) and, most of all, landing up in the finals as the first Kearsney boy to so qualify.

I didn't win, and ended up – bitterly disappointed – in second place.

As the school magazine records it: 'Kearsney's entrant, Anthony Leon, was faced with the ordeal of having to speak before his own school fellows and staff, which appeared to make him more nervous than usual. He spoke on perhaps the most difficult topic, a history of the life of Jan Hofmeyr, and acquitted himself admirably. Unfortunately he attempted a little too much in his impromptu speech, speaking on "being selective about comic strips".'

As a compensation the school jointly awarded me the trophy for 'cultural leadership' (together with my friend Peter Crossley) and school colours. It was 'not done' to express too much disappointment; but I was angry at not winning and still, in that sullen teenage way, resented that I had not become a school prefect at the beginning of the year. As the famous American college football coach Henry 'Red' Sanders (later plagiarised by Richard Nixon) put it: 'Winning isn't everything, it's the only thing.'

Strange, therefore, that my passion for winning did not embrace – indeed, by-passed – my studies for the matriculation examination which determined entry into university and was the real point of 12 years of schooling. Most of my school subjects bored me, and I had an almost fatalistic nonchalance about how to overcome my scholastic nemesis of mathematics.

I was further distracted by my father's decision, the same year, to remarry. His new wife Jacqueline was a cultural shock to us all: she was a beautiful French Mauritian. And she had definite ideas about where and how teen-age boys fitted into the pecking order. I found her sudden presence in my father's – and our family's – life strange and initially alienating. Like some of the ingredients in one of her more exotic culinary concoctions we were not, initially, an easy mix. However, my father was totally smitten, and after a fairly solitary decade was delighted to be married again.

Over time – and notwithstanding a few fiery clashes – I grew excep-tionally fond of Jacqueline, who was not simply supportive of my father through various vicissitudes, but from inception actively encouraged my political career. She died suddenly in November 1996 (my father believes needlessly) and remains warmly remembered and much cherished.

I acquired not only a stepmother, but a burgeoning social life. During holidays we would walk to the beach, spend the day in the sun, buy a hamburger and coke at the Cuban Hat on the North Beach for 30 cents, and catch the bus home for 12 cents. It was cheap to enjoy life. We would party at one another's homes to meet girls. We listened, endlessly, to the 'Cold Fact' album of the smart cynical singer Rodriguez, and the more romantic ballads of the pop groups Bread and The Strawbs, then in their ascendancy. Durban even had a disco – 'Dorian's' – at the swanky beach-front Edward hotel.

Nonetheless, through my precocious political involvement and obses-sive reading of the daily Durban newspaper the *Mercury* I gained some knowledge of events unfolding outside the cloistered confines of Kearsney and our enjoyable, but no doubt banal, social life. I learned that Ahmed Timol, a Muslim teacher, had, in my first year in high school, fallen to his death in suspicious circumstances, from the tenth floor of John Vorster Square, the Johannesburg headquarters of the South African Police. His was the 17th – but by no means the last – death in detention (inevitable, given the battery of security legislation promulgated to suppress black resistance after the bloody repression of the Sharpeville demonstration of 1961).

Perhaps more immediately, since it was spawned in Natal, I read with close interest of the 1973 strikes in the local textile industries, triggered by the near-starvation wages of the workers. This event had profound and lasting consequences for the revival of the trade union movement which was to play such a decisive (or as Marxists put it, a 'vanguard') role in the struggle ahead. Vorster made the extraordinary admission that the black strikers were 'human beings with souls'.

None of these events being sketched – and rewritten – on the increasingly bloodied and turbulent palimpsest of South Africa were to be gleaned from the history syllabus then being drummed into us at school. The rather anodyne *History for Standard Nine and Ten* by AN Boyce contained within its pages reams about 'the causes of the Great Trek' and 'the arrival of the 1820 English Settlers and its consequences', but precious little of the real and genuinely burning issues which were stalking the country and which would engulf it shortly after we left school.

All these extracurricular readings and activities had a disastrous effect on my preparations for the looming matric exams. I did exceedingly poorly, failing both mathematics and biology. I was blown away when the results arrived at Sheila's apartment in Johannesburg. She was upset; I was disheartened; my father was furious.

I was immediately recalled to Ramon's house in Durban and told that my feckless and undisciplined attitude was the cause of my woes and would have to be redressed in supplementary examinations three months hence. I deeply resented my father's attitude then – but have remained grateful to him ever since for snapping me out of my hitherto casual approach to life and learning. I also received a letter of support from our family's close friend, Shirley Eskapa – by then a well-known novelist living in London. She wrote, 'Let adversity be your spur.' I took that to heart.

Under my father's watchful eye, I enrolled in the local cram college, Damelin, and was forbidden social contacts between Monday and Saturday afternoon. I set about correcting my self-inflicted failure. The foolhardy and misplaced confidence which accompanied me into the original exams gave way to an anxious but determined discipline. In the event, I raised my marks overall by 20% and achieved the university entrance certificate which had previously eluded me.

The net effect of this unpleasant diversion was negligible: once I had been called up to the army for 18 months' national service in July, I could only start university in 1977.

Although I spent fewer than four years at boarding school, there is more than a kernel (perhaps, indeed, a boulder) of truth in the adage that while I 'left Kearsney behind, it never really left me.' Almost a generation later, in August 2003, I was invited back to the school at Botha's Hill to address the 75th Anniversary Dinner of its Old Boys' Club. Of course the school had physically and attitudinally changed out of all recognition. It was modern and comfortable, and reflected the opulent circumstances of most of its young 'customers'. The Dickensian dining hall and the bleak, institutional dormitories of my youth had disappeared. The culture of physical punishment – now taboo – had given way to an authority more based on reason and persuasion. It had also – most notably and praiseworthily – shed its uniracial character and was now genuinely non-racial in its student body.

But to me – not Kearsney's greatest scholar and certainly no sports star – what school had helped inculcate was a set of values. In part, I said this: 'In South Africa, we have overturned an odious system that made race the basis of elite membership. Today, when we look around at the few that have become rich and the many that remain poor, we see that a new upper class is forming on the basis of wealth alone. But if South Africa is to excel, we must embrace a social vision that rewards excellence, hard work, and virtue ...

'We need to set standards and expect them to be met. Kearsney is living proof that some ways of doing things might change over time, but that others cannot. Our most important change here is the increasingly non-racial character of the school. But when it comes to learning, and integrity, and character, Kearsney has always stood for the notion that there is a right way and a wrong way. We cannot dismiss this fundamental truth, or brush it aside for reasons of political correctness or even propaganda.'

7

After my examination detour I returned to Johannesburg, to fill in the four months before my military call-up. Sheila had by then trained as a producer and researcher for the SABC, then about to launch South Africa's much-delayed, much-anticipated television service. Her home, which I was to share for the next five years or so, was a meeting point of sorts for many of the guinea pigs – members of Johannesburg's and Cape Town's artistic and intellectual communities – around whom she structured her programmes before the official launch of the service in 1976. Many of them became firm friends of hers, particularly the satirist Adam Leslie; the theatre impresario Pieter Toerien; the radio broadcaster Wouter de Wet; and the academic David Welsh.

My mother's customary cultural ambivalence and intellectual doublethink reached its zenith during her TV years, which lasted until heart disease took its toll in 1987 and she retired prematurely. On the one hand she loathed the NP government, and her particular *bête noire* were the grey-shoed bureaucrats and Broederbonders who swelled the ranks of SABC directors. She disparaged them with piercing put-downs, much to the amusement of her 'chums'. On the other hand, she loved the entrée to a more stimulating and professional world that her new-found TV cachet granted her.

I used the gap between school and the army to work as a junior organiser in the Southern Transvaal head office of the Progressives. I was put in charge of the organisation – such as it was – of the party's fledgling structures in Hillbrow and Von Brandis (the CBD area). In truth, I was also used as an all-purpose gofer; and my unswerving youthful belief that the Progressive philosophy was right meant that no task was too menial, no job beyond my enthusiasm.

The office was headed by Peter Soal with humour and guile; he later became an MP. I found myself on occasion handing out refreshments to journalists being briefed by the party boss Colin Eglin on his return from a foray into Africa; or counting the bottles after a function at the opulent estate of Gordon Waddell, the immensely wealthy MP for Johannesburg North. The party was also in the midst of awkward negotiations with the Schwarz faction of the UP. Schwarz's disagreements with Graaff and the UP establishment had led to his expulsion, and he and a group of like-minded 'reformists' (including Douglas Gibson) had founded the Reform Party. Clearly, they and the Progressives needed an accommodation, although there was much bad blood and personal enmity between the personalities in both formations.

Down in the bowels of the party, as it were, I discovered that the Progressive Party – for all its virtues and political coherence – had an unattractive side. It consisted of several personalities who exuded an exclusionary snobbishness and moral superiority which grated and alienated those outside their magic circle.

In some ways, the party operated as a political extension of an Anglo-Jewish social club, with much of its activist membership drawn from a narrow social base in the leafy northern suburbs of Johannesburg and the southern suburbs of Cape Town.

While it had certainly (to its electoral cost) held the ring – morally at least – against the Nationalist juggernaut, it too had temporised and compromised core convictions to stay in business. Notably, by the time of my employment, 14 years after its foundation, neither Helen Suzman nor the party had embraced the cause of universal franchise. It had also decided to carry on operations (in 1969) when the government decreed that no political party could have mixed-race membership. To comply with the

42

provisions of the Prohibition of Political Interference Act, the Progressives purged their membership rolls of all African, Indian and Coloured supporters. The Liberal Party stuck to its principles and exited the political arena.

This is why I am still angered, after all these years, by those who wish to score a point against the DA, or me personally, by incorrectly suggesting that the Progressive Party was an outpost of ideological and political purity. The organisation made significant compromises and concessions to the political climate in which it operated. It trimmed its sails; and the same was true of its successors.

In a speech in Houghton in 2006, I drew attention to the fact that the opposition project had been consistently faced with 'fateful choices'. In 1983, for example, the PFP (as the Progs became) campaigned against the introduction of the Tricameral parliament, which excluded black participation, yet went on to serve in it. My conclusion: '[The] history of the Progressive Party that we rightly celebrate is not that of a pristine political priesthood, but of a political party that had to make pragmatic ideological compromises in order to stay competitive and relevant.'

My practical involvement in the looming merger with the reformists was slight, but comic. Peter Soal said the party leadership needed to be better informed about the thinking inside the Schwarz camp – so he obtained a Reform Party membership card for me, and I enrolled so that I could attend one of its regional council meetings in northern Johannesburg. I was duly despatched with a tape recorder, on which I taped the proceedings, and gave them to Soal at party headquarters for dissemination.

In the end, the Progressive and Reform parties merged in July 1975 in Johannesburg under the name of The South African Progressive Reform Party (PRP). Eglin became leader of the merged entity, and Schwarz chairman of its National Executive. It thus held 11 seats in the 171-member House of Assembly. In September 1977, the PRP ranks were augmented by a further breakaway from the UP. Veteran politician Japie Basson led that group which duly merged with the PRP to become the Progressive Federal Party (PFP). It became the official opposition in the general election three months later, with 17 seats.

All too soon I found myself at Milner Park station, then opposite Wits University, nervously awaiting embarkation with hundreds of other conscripts. Our destination was the military establishment of Potchefstroom in the western Transvaal. My call-up for basic training was to the 14th Field Artillery Regiment there.

Boarding school had been a picnic.

The rigours and privations visited on the unsuspecting 'troopies', as the new intake was branded, were severe. Military service for white males, over eighteen, was *de rigueur*. The End Conscription Campaign which advocated non-compliance with the call-up was launched only a decade later. So the only escape was to defer service – then possible in terms of the law – until completing university studies. My father, peremptory on such matters, indicated that this was not an option: he predicted, accurately, that if we deferred our service on leaving school, we would face a military stint of far longer duration in a far more hostile environment. So we went.

'Potch' was a dusty field in the Afrikaans heartland – the place where the first shots were fired in 1880 in the first Anglo-Boer War. It was also the place where the *Vierkleur*, emblem of the South African Republic, was first designed and hoisted.

None of this was of the slightest interest to me. Surviving basic training in the bitingly cold, alien environment topped my personal agenda. The camp, such as it was, was new and had no permanent structures. We were accommodated in dozens of khaki tents dotted around the bone-dry parade grounds. There were no ablution facilities to speak of; a mobile shower unit was provided every second day; and we waited nearly a week for our regulation brown uniform and marching boots.

From early morning to night we were harried by undereducated and over-sadistic NCOs – corporals and sergeant-majors – whose terms of greetings and endearment always commenced with the Afrikaans word *fok* (fuck), as in *fok jou, fok julle, kry fokken rigting*, and other niceties.

I knew no one at the camp. Fortunately my first Saturday coincided with the running of the annual July Handicap in Durban. During my years at Kearsney, and inspired by Grandpa Jack's lifelong encyclopaedic knowledge of horse racing, I had become something of a self-taught expert on equine matters (I could recite in consecutive order all the winners of 'the July' from the year of my birth onwards).

On July Day, 1975, I encountered a group of fellow rookies (newly conscripted 'grunts') clustered around a transistor radio. They were sons of bookmakers or had worked in and around racing and bookmaking enterprises; and they became my first army friends. Having spent my entire life mixing with children from my own English-speaking middle-class milieu, the army proved a great and jolting leveller. We might as well have been from different planets. Interestingly, the July was won that day, on an objection, by Principal Boy, owned by Harry and Bridget Oppenheimer.

One of our first tasks was to familiarise ourselves with the 25-pounder cannon, a Second World War special. Seven or eight of us had to lug this monster up and down the hills – and the '25 pounds' referred to the weight of the projectile, not the gun, which (to us) weighed about the same as a VW Beetle.

The best feature of the camp was its exit, and the highway to Johannesburg and Pretoria. For once I was hugely advantaged by my flat feet, which had impeded my schoolboy sports career but now saved me from hideous exercises. These feet turned up in my medical examination, which included such standard humiliations as having my testicles squeezed with the demand that I '*hoes*' (cough). The doctor declared: '*Daardie plat voete van jou is niks werd nie*' ('Those flat feet will take you nowhere'). He promptly marked my card as 'G4' – medically unfit for training. Joy.

Eventually (I recall it took about two weeks of processing), I was batched with dozens of other physically challenged servicemen (and no small number of malingerers who had successfully hoodwinked the authorities) and boarded a train for Pretoria. Here our basic training occurred in the less-severe confines of Diensvakskool in Voortrekkerhoogte.[20]

My brother had completed his own military service in 1974 working at the Defence Force magazine *Paratus*, and was now studying at the University of Cape Town. He requested his former commanding officer to get me a posting there; and certainly a job at *Paratus* looked like the nirvana of all military alternatives. I embellished my very modest role as the Kearsney editor of a private schools' newspaper, and applied for a slot at the periodical. After three months of drilling, endless inspections and the other mind-crushing banalities of basic training, I was indeed posted there.

The magazine operated out of a building in downtown Pretoria, where we were dumped each morning from a Bedford truck from the Wonderboom military camp where most of the troopies assigned to work in Pretoria were housed.

Wonderboom was pretty awful. It also accommodated the military police with their complement of some seriously dodgy, if not deranged, individuals. A night or two after arriving at the camp, one of the MPs, apparently high on drugs or alcohol – or both – attempted to commit suicide by slitting his wrists in a toilet. He was unsuccessful: but the camp commander's response was to remove all the doors of the toilets, with de-lightful consequences for all of us henceforth answering nature's call.

Paratus itself was interesting – and revealing. It was one of the few units where certain skills could be acquired that might later be of some use. According to my later political detractors, it was at *Paratus* that I became a propaganda supremo in service against the 'total onslaught' of apartheid's enemies. (More of that in a moment.) The reality was that I learned to type; after a writer's copy was complete, it was sent to one of the permanent force editors for checking and editing and then, laboriously, despatched by driver to the printers.

Again, though designated a 'reporter', I spent much of my time in the darkroom, learning photography but mainly assisting with the printing of endless photographs. These were used as a form of *baksheesh* (or 'baksies' as we bastardised the term) to extract favours from one or another military panjandrum.

For example, on one occasion, when sent to cover a military dance, I spotted a man of great significance to those of us marooned every evening in Wonderboom. He was an administrative officer at the defence headquarters personnel unit, near the *Paratus* office. This unit was the ultimate in sleeping accommodation because of its proximity to the magazine and its ease of access to the Pretoria-Johannesburg highway. I arranged an array of shots of the officer and his wife, then presented myself in his office a few days later. I said I had a gift for him and handed over a dozen glossy photos (8" x 10") of the officer and his lady. I mentioned that a billet at DHQ personnel would greatly aid my ability to do my job. A transfer followed.

So photographs became a form of currency, and human vanity – or venality – was never to be underestimated, even in matters so trivial.

I also made some good friends – of whom Roger Wolfsohn, today a New York psychiatrist, remains one of my closest – and learned various revealing facts about the Defence Force. *Paratus* was a bivouac for some fairly ropey journalists horizontally inserted, as it were, from various newspapers into the ranks of officers. Our commanding officer was a South African Navy captain, Kosie Nieuwoudt, who, when I later temporarily joined the ranks of the navy frigate, SAS *President Kruger*, was disparaged by another navy man as 'a fat-arsed, desk-bound four-ringer'. The others were all total strategy types, no doubt cogs in the propaganda effort of which *Paratus* was a fairly minor outpost.

All military establishments operate, in varying degrees, on 'the need to know' basis. National servicemen, at the bottom of the chain of command, were deemed receivers of orders, not originators of ideas or strategies. Of course, we fervently dreamed up assignments, such as an article on the naval printing works in Simon's Town, which got us a trip to the Mother City. But in the main our assignments consisted of covering medal parades, mess reunions, and *Damesfederasie*-type functions.

From an extreme distance I got sight of the top brass of the military establishment. I could never have imagined that one of them, Lieutenant-General Bob Rogers, then Chief of the Air Force, would take his place alongside me – or perhaps in deference to his vast seniority, the other way around – as a fellow new arrival backbench MP in the DP caucus of the 1989 parliament. Bob (whom I would have stiffly saluted at the time) became a friend and a good political ally. When, in 1993, I was visiting Israel, I was introduced to the country's president Ezer Weizmann. Learning I was from South Africa, he asked if I knew Bob Rogers. I told him we were now colleagues. Weizmann, one of Israel's top fighter pilots and previously head of its legendary air force, lit up and said in his earthy way: 'Bob Rogers is one of the best pilots I ever met. We flew Mustangs together in Korea, and he was damn fine.' Praise indeed.[21]

Rogers, of course, was something of an anomaly – one of the very few in the top defence nomenklatura who was English and not aligned to the Nat establishment. Far more typical was the chief of the army, Lieutenant-General Magnus Malan, who went on to become, in my time in the army, Chief of the Defence Force. In due course, he followed his father to parliament and soon became, thanks to his closeness to PW Botha, Minister of Defence. In this capacity I first met him properly when I became an MP. By the early 1990s he was surrounded by controversy because of the actions of covert military units – such as the CCB and the notorious Vlakplaas – in extra-judicial killings and dirty war activities aimed at ANC operatives.

Botha, too, was actually a distant, unsmiling presence. Many hours were spent in the darkroom where, to improve the standing of our CO, we had to develop dozens of photographs of Botha's family. I never met him – although bizarrely he telephoned me, for the first time, in 2006 to point out the disastrous impact that flooding had had on the Kaaimans Pass on the N2 highway, near his retirement home in Wilderness in the southern Cape. We had two lengthy conversations about the imminent danger to local infrastructure, but never discussed politics. In that year the DA controlled most of the municipalities in the southern Cape, including Botha's old constituency of George.

I have elaborated on these personalities and my objective location as a minor cog in the Defence Force of the time because fully 25 years after my 18-month stint of national service, my scribblings at *Paratus* would be disseminated – or more accurately, sliced and diced and ruthlessly decontextualised – by ANC bigwigs to portray me as, variously, 'on the payroll of the SADF',[22] 'one of apartheid's chief apologists',[23] and '[heaping] hymns of praise on the apartheid war machine'.[24]

The reality behind these laughable, if lurid, pronouncements was this:

- Every national serviceman was paid approximately R35 a month (which increased by about R10 when after 12 months I was promoted to 'one stripe' as a lance-corporal, the highest rank I was to attain); and
- long after I had forgotten what I churned out at the time, the Minister in the Presidency, Essop Pahad, and his cronies exhumed them from wherever the dusty *Paratus* archives repose to try and establish some basis, however marginal and elliptical, for their extreme assertions.

The source of these investigative revelations was the head of the periodical's section during my time of service, one Brigadier Kobus Bosman. Bosman had been an apparatchik at the SABC, where he knew my mother. She once described, with some hilarity, how he visited her apartment where, due to his immense bulk, he leaned forward in one of her delicate antique chairs – and broke it! In any event, he was a marginal figure in my military career. Whether he approved or disapproved of my output as a 19-year-old conscript, he held his counsel at the time.

However, on leaving the military, he too entered politics, first as a National Party MP of no great distinction in the 1980s and 1990s, and then as a member of the provincial legislature in Gauteng from 1994. There he encountered my brother Peter. Bosman, never noted much for diligence or leadership, deeply resented the fact that despite his seniority in terms of service and the NP's position as the second-largest party in the legislature, he had been passed over for the chairmanship of the Safety and Security Committee in favour of Peter, who led the small five-man team of the DP in the legislature. Then, within four years, the NP in Gauteng, as elsewhere, was reeling on the ropes against our resurgent party. He began to make increasingly sour attacks on the DP in debates. In November 1998, he unveiled a 'revelation':

'I wonder if the honourable member is aware of the fact that while I was in the Defence Force, I had a very talented young man who did his national service indirectly under my command. He was very talented, Sir, because he was a journalist with *Paratus*, one of the better journalists, and he was one of the best propaganda writers for the Defence Force at the time. As a matter of fact, Mr Speaker, he was very effective … [That] man, Sir, was Mr Tony Leon.'[25]

This proved to be unexpected manna for the ANC – which was, of course, Bosman's intent. In particular, it was an oleaginous West Indian lawyer-cum-writer, Ronald S Roberts, a close cohort of Pahad's, who then apparently scoured the back issues of *Paratus* in search of ammunition. Roberts arrived in South Africa in 1994, long after the battle against apartheid ended. Undeterred by being 'missing in action' he proceeded to establish a decidedly mixed – if not overwhelmingly negative – reputation as a polemicist and author of various bilious diatribes.

His general *modus operandi* was to ingratiate himself with the ascendant political-intellectual elite, collaborate with them – usually in the form of co-authorships – and then use their renown to boost himself. However, in a somewhat small world, he harboured another less endearing and (in my view) entirely characteristic habit: he quickly fell out with his associates. Soon after producing various tracts, he ceased to be on speaking terms with Albie Sachs, Kader Asmal and his wife Louise, and, famously and very publicly, with Nadine Gordimer, the über-ANC liberation novelist who withdrew her authorisation to Roberts to write her biography, which he had already done by overstepping the boundaries she had set.

However, his co-operation with Pahad and Mbeki, of whom Roberts penned a hagiographic tract on his 'intellectual tradition', whatever that might imply, appeared to be made of sterner stuff. Accordingly, he wrote various poison-pen tracts after trawling through the *Paratus* archives.[26] In turn, Pahad would then 'quote' Roberts (with whom he had no doubt conspired) in the National Assembly as proof of my role in the 'total strategy against the total onslaught'.

Among the extraordinary array of ANC politicians I have met, from the good and the great to the mediocre and the awful, Pahad, with his menace and penchant for viciously personalising every issue, occupies a league of his own. Indeed, it is piquant to be lectured by Pahad on the evils of propaganda. He is more Stalinist than most of his comrades and churned out a string of defences in the *African Communist* for the most rights–delinquent and repressive behaviour his Soviet masters meted out to their eastern European satellites – including, in 1968, the rape of Czechoslovakia.

He was, into the bargain, one of the worst speakers in parliament, barely lifting his eyes from his text to acknowledge or interact with the audience. He brings to mind – on a puny scale – Clement Attlee's description of the old monster, Stalin, himself: 'He reminded me of the Renaissance despots – no principles, any methods, but no flowery language – always yes or no, though you could only count on him if it was no.'[27]

The authentication of such assertions as 'dignifying the apartheid military machine' or 'portraying apartheid as God's gift to the white population' – in the measured words of the ANC's Smuts Ngonyama[28] – was risible and would have failed a basic ethics test. Nonetheless the evidentiary basis of the statements was irrelevant to the 'big lie' technique.

Having rummaged through what must have been dozens of eminently forgettable and marginal pieces, my enemies produced as 'exhibit A' a piece that I penned on the Transkei 'independence' celebrations in October 1976. My and my photographer's assignment had been to cover the SADF's participation and logistical support for the bantustan's formal accession to 'independence' from South Africa. It took our train about two days to reach Umtata, where we were billeted in a tent. We were then obliged to get up, after about four hours' sleep, to scurry around snuffing up material to suggest some fizz and élan in what would otherwise have been one of history's great non-events. The overwhelming bulk of the Transkeian population was resolutely opposed to being denationalised as part of the logic of the bantustan policy.

About the worst that Roberts-Pahad could produce from my no doubt execrable article was the headline proclaiming 'a magnificent freedom day'. Toe-curling indeed! But hardly demonstrative of some sinister, later buried, agenda on my part to hide the apartheid state's evil and nefarious intent.

Some three years after Pahad's exposé (which no doubt had the president's approval), his master, Thabo Mbeki, in 2003 presided over the state funeral ordered up for Kaizer Matanzima, who led the Transkei to 'independence' and was easily the most notorious black comprador in the service of apartheid. Yet, to secure his Eastern Cape base, Mbeki heaped praise on Matanzima and practically co-opted him from his place in the Pantheon of apartheid collaborators into a hitherto unlikely role as one of the progenitors of the black struggle against the system that spawned him.

And then, to add to my mirth, Stella Sigcau – whose father was inaugurated as 'State President of the Transkei' – took office in 1994 as an ANC cabinet minister. She too had been in the special VIP section of the Umtata independence celebration on which I reported in 1976. At the time the 'Pondoland Princess' was a minister in Matanzima's cabinet.[29] Leading the parade that day was a star graduate of 1 Transkei Battalion, Bantu Holomisa – shortly to become the officer commanding the Transkei Defence Force and lead a putsch against Stella Sigcau after she succeeded George Matanzima (brother of Kaizer) as prime minister.

However, politics in 2000 dictated that I, lowly scribe of the obscure *Paratus*, would be roughed up to suit the demonology of the ANC in government.

1976 was my final year in the army. Before my mustering out, in addition to our humdrum reportage and photography, *Paratus* was inspanned into covering the border war between South Africa and Swapo insurgents in then-South West Africa. Of course, the country was actually (although largely secretly) involved in a full-scale incursion into Angola where, apparently at the behest of Secretary of State Henry Kissinger and the US administration of President Gerald Ford, the SADF was fighting alongside the Unita and FNLA forces against the Cuban-aided forces of the MPLA.

Our first inkling of this major but unreported war came one Friday. All Pretoria-based units abruptly had their weekend leave cancelled. Instead of retreating from the boredom of army life to the discos of Johannesburg, we were loaded into Bedford trucks and deposited at the sprawling Voortrekkerhoogte compound of '3 Supply and Transport Unit'. There we were told, on 'hush-hush' terms (there were hundreds of servicemen involved), that we were not to report to 'anyone at all' about our exercise.

So it was that our particular shroud of secrecy included mountains of tinned food. We formed a human conveyor belt and spent the evening and next day painstakingly removing all the labels from the cans and replacing each with a blob of paint: I recall red for processed meat, green for tinned vegetables, and blue for fruit salad. No official explanation was offered; however, word passed down the line that the victuals were destined for our troops already deep inside Angola, and it was necessary to disguise their origins.

Of course, most of the troops in Angola would be white and mostly Afrikaans-speaking. Disguising the source of their food was absurd.

Apart from painting tins of food my other 'contribution' to the war in Angola was more of a piece with *Paratus* work: flying up to the South West Africa/Angola border in lumbering and extremely noisy C-130s to such places as Ondangwa and Otjiwarango in northern Namibia, and reporting on the SADF's humanitarian side. This comprised doctors, nurses and other personnel assisting the refugee columns flowing in to escape the ravages of the civil war. The fact that the SADF was actively aiding – and fuelling – the civil war was, of course, unmentioned. One uncharacteristic sight for those times and my naïve eyes was a column of dispirited-looking, poorly clothed white Angolans clutching suitcases. Many years later, Harry Schwarz told the story of his own encounter with such a group. Schwarz spoke to a man with a suitcase-full of worthless Angolan currency, who

told him: 'If you had come to me two years ago and told me to give up
10% of what you have in order to keep 90% of what you own I would
have told you to get lost. But I have now lost everything! My home, my
business, my cars, my dignity; so if you said to me today, you have to give
up 90% of what you have in order to keep 10% of what you own, I would
grab the offer with both hands.'

I have little doubt that the refugees I encountered would have made the
same concession – which usually comes too late. South Africa was later to
prove a remarkable exception to this general, if gloomy, rule on the politics
of compromise. While Roberts and Pahad have tried to paint my period
in the military as the 'loyal service of atrocity', the true *reductio ad absurdum*
of their garbage came from an ANC hack in the National Council of
Provinces (NCOP), parliament's other chamber – a certain TS Setona MP.
In an extraordinary outburst – faithfully and duly noted in *Hansard* – he
had this to say in 2005:

'It reminds [sic] of 1976 when some of the members who are now audacious to stand in front of this house and talk about a lack of libraries and
resources in schools, tend to forget that they are led by a person who in
1976 when the students were revolting against this brain damaging colonial education system, was in a helicopter up there, monitoring, shooting
and maiming our people ... Hon [Shelley] Loe [a Democratic Alliance
NCOP MP] does not even know the history of her party and the history
of her leaders. [Interjections] Tony Leon was a soldier and he was one of
the soldiers, a lance-corporal in a helicopter above the streets of Soweto,
firing tear gas and bullets at the armless students. Thank you, very much.
[Applause]'[30]

Clearly Setona was deeply damaged by the education system he decried. In fact, on 16 June 1976 I was thousands of miles away from South
Africa, on a South African Navy frigate approaching the eastern seaboard
of America. This extraordinary odyssey was an unasked-for bonus of my
military service, and led to me enjoying the doubtful distinction of becoming, apparently, the first South African army national serviceman to
travel overseas with the South African Navy in peacetime.

With very little warning the US government decided – apparently at
the very last moment and doubtless in the confident expectation of rejection – to invite isolated South Africa to send a warship to participate
in celebrating the US Bicentennial on 4 July 1976. The SADF obviously
leaped at this opportunity to sail out of the political deep-freeze into
which apartheid had consigned it, and one of the three serving anti-sub-
marine frigates, the SAS *President Kruger*, was quickly prepared for the

16 925-nautical-mile round trip. The *Paratus* officer class was, naturally, falling over itself to join the ship. However, after much negotiating with naval headquarters in Simon's Town, it was decreed by the men in white that there was no room on board for another officer, and a 'rating' would have to be sent to report and photograph the voyage.[31]

Both the invitation and the wrangling were unknown to me and my fellow troopies when one May morning we gathered to work out the day's assignments (or more likely how to minimise them). There were no navy servicemen in the *Paratus* head office at the time, and I was hastily called to the office of the commanding officer – Captain Kosie Nieuwoudt. Would I be interested in leaving 'the next day' for Simon's Town to join the crew of the *President Kruger* for its voyage to America?

I couldn't believe my luck, at 19, to join the navy for a 65-day epic voyage all the way to America! At the end of standard nine, in 1973, I had cashed in the money I received as gifts for my bar-mitzvah three years before, and gone with my brother to friends and family in Switzerland and London. That was hitherto my only exposure to the joys of overseas travel.

Twenty-two years later, a latter-day conspiracy theorist, James Sanders, produced a tract on the rise and fall of South Africa's secret service. In his volume, *Apartheid's Friends*, he seized on my assignment to locate me as a sort of apparatchik of the sinister and secretive forces abroad in the military at the time. He opined:

'He [Tony Leon] did not report for *Paratus* on this intriguing visit by the South African Navy to the United States but apparently "provided" a colour picture for the "cover" of the magazine. It would seem likely that at such a sensitive time, a few weeks after the Soweto uprising, the personnel on this trip would have been closely vetted by both the MID [Military Intelligence Department] and the dominant Department of Information …'[32]

Practically every 'fact' in the paragraph is an invention. Accordingly, I never bothered to read beyond page two. In fact, the ship cast off a full two weeks before the Soweto uprising and I still have, yellowing with age, the four-page special supplement which *Paratus* printed of our voyage based on my shipboard diary and the photographs which I took. My superiors had deemed I was sufficiently quick-witted to master both halves of the photo-journalist divide; and I was despatched, on the day I was told of the assignment, for some crack lessons on how to frame a picture and how to set the 'f-stop' aperture to achieve the best results with high-speed film in the decidedly old-order Canon camera with which I was entrusted for the trip.

Two days later I reported for duty, in biting wind, at Simon's Town.

While the voyage was long – over two months – and took its 236 crew members to New York via Walvis Bay, Abidjan, Las Palmas, Norfolk VA and Charleston SC, it was far from a pleasure. I quickly learned why no officer could be sent. I was accommodated in 'mess 9', with 30 other communications and radar operator ratings. It was way below the waterline and it was dark except when the lights were switched on. I was presented with a hammock and told to make the best of it. During the day we stowed them, and by night strung them up from hooks. A hard mattress was encased by canvas and that was my abode for over two months.

Far more than the unfamiliarity of the sleeping arrangements, I had to overcome the initial hostility of the seamen to an army presence and the oddity of one brown uniform amid the sea of blue. I described it in the supplement: 'While, after a time, I seemed to interact reasonably well with my fellow travellers, I was the constant butt of practical jokes and irreverent comments for being the only army man aboard ship. To them the idea of a "pedestrian" (navy disparagement for army personnel) afloat was inconceivable.'

I was constantly tired owing to the swaying motion of the ship. I was not a regular cleaning or maintenance hand, but there was general cleaning; and every Saturday, mess decks were immaculately cleaned, scrubbed and shone. Whether I had to shine all 35 lockers, scrub the deck or wash the bulkheads, it was three hours of hard work and reminded me of basic training at Voortrekkerhoogte.

One day while the *President Kruger* was in mid-ocean from a refuelling and refurbishing stop in Las Palmas en route to Norfolk, Virginia, the largest naval base in the US, the telex in the signals room spewed forth pages which told a tale of unimagined rebellion and repression. It was 16 June 1976. We received, naturally, a highly selective, state-sanctioned account of events. But the facts could not be disguised. Shortly before our ship berthed in America, on 25 June 1976, we received the sombre, awful death and casualty figures from the riots, which soon spread from Soweto to engulf most of the other Reef townships and extended as far as the Western Cape.[33] Eventually 70 townships witnessed disturbances and rioting leading to loss of life and property. Soon the initial educational reforms demanded by the students had morphed into a hitherto unheard of militancy for change and liberty.

The response of the government was to increase repression. The minister of Justice, Jimmy Kruger, announced in July that unlimited detention without trial would be used 'against all persons threatening public order'; all public gatherings were banned; and all schools in the riot areas closed down. However, the immediate response of the Black People's Convention turned out to be the most prophetic:

'The National Black People's Convention declares that the severe riots have ushered in a new era of political consciousness.'

Indeed, the tide of violence and repression unleashed on 16 June was far from spent by the time we reached America – or when we returned home. So elemental – and unexpected – was its force that the smug certitudes which had characterised the Vorster administration and the white community it represented were no longer tenable.

However, in the tiny universe of the *President Kruger*, these things and their consequences could barely be imagined. The immediate concern was whether South Africa's floating emissary would be targeted for demonstrations or damage when we entered New York on the eve of Bicentennial day, 4 July 1976. From the naval perspective there were two advantages. The first was the non-existence of any strong anti-apartheid organisations and structures in America. (It was only ten years later that pressure created by black community leaders such as Andrew Young, Randall Robinson and Jesse Jackson led to powerful financial sanctions and disinvestment.)

The America we arrived in was still led by Gerald Ford, and the target of the agitators and demonstrations, such as they were, was the even more repressive (and much more geographically relevant) regime of Augusto Pinochet of Chile. The Chilean sloop, *Esmeralda*, which had been used as a site of torture of dissidents, took the heat. South Africa was barely noticed.

For a 19-year-old serviceman, entering New York as part of a 49-mile-long column of naval vessels – the largest collection of warships to form a single convoy in peacetime – was a thrilling moment. Under the giant span of the Verrazano-Narrows Bridge, an estimated thirty thousand pleasure craft thronged. Overhead flew Zeppelin-style blimps, and on the water fireboats gushed arcs of water eighty feet high, while helicopters dipped overhead. We dropped anchor in the Hudson River, in the shadow of the famous Liberty statue.

The big action was the next day, 4 July, when America celebrated, in typical big style, the 200th anniversary of its independence. The *President Kruger*'s job was to be part of the international naval review, which meant it and some fifty other naval ships formed a floating guard of honour for Vice President Nelson Rockefeller aboard an ultra-modern amphibious ship. It was the next sight that I will never forget: 225 sailing vessels from around the world. This convoy, known collectively as 'Operation Sail 1976', was also a modern first — apparently the greatest armada under canvas since the Battle of Navarino off the coast of Greece in 1827.

My crewmates and I were overwhelmed and excited as we took our first tentative steps in the Big Apple. We were nervous of New York's fierce and scary reputation — but there were some ten thousand other sailors enjoying a 'liberty boat' (which means time off), and New York was one giant party, which we drank, literally and figuratively, to the dregs.

In all, I spent 65 days aboard the *President Kruger* and regard myself as one of the fortunate 236 to have witnessed — and in my case photographed — such a sweepingly epic event. The rest of my national service was, for obvious reasons, a boring anti-climax. When I '*klaared* out', I was presented with a government cheque of R750 for serving an additional six months — which I did to avoid call-up camps in the future.

I then headed off to the radically different environment of the University of the Witwatersrand.

CHAPTER 2

Dancing with Dialectics

The age of gold of the human race is not behind us, it lies ahead of us,
it consists in the perfection of the social order. Our fathers have
not seen it; our children will arrive there one day;
it is for us to mark the path.

HENRI DE SAINT SIMON

I

The University of the Witwatersrand, Johannesburg (Wits), is at the fore-front of academic and scientific endeavour and research in South Africa. It was also, during the Nationalist years, an outpost of continuous opposition to apartheid and its seemingly relentless march to a closed and racially dis-crete society. This stance was completely antithetical to the ethos of liberal inclusivity and openness which Wits proclaimed and attempted – with variable success – to practise.

I was involved with the institution – intimately and more or less con-tinuously – for nearly twenty years: as a student, a campus politician, a lecturer and – in my final incarnation – a member of its executive govern-ing council.

Firstly, though, after the fairly narrow strictures of boarding school and the army, campus life was new and pleasant. There were the distractions of orientation week; campus 'razzles'; and the discovery of 'sex, drugs, and rock 'n roll'. There was neither a huge nor copious amount of these es-sentials, but enough to realise that life on the Braamfontein campus, where Wits is housed, was to be qualitatively different from my previous, essen-tially monastic, experiences.

Since politics was already embedded in my DNA, I contemplated – having previously had no idea of anything vaguely like a career path – enrolling for a Bachelor of Arts degree, majoring in political studies with sub-majors in international relations and industrial sociology. My ardour vis-à-vis the Progressive Party continued – and indeed with some return

of affection, for while I was an ingénue in the ways of Wits I rapidly ascended in the Prog ranks. I was elected as regional youth chairman and
landed a place on the National Executive which, at the time, as its youngest member, seemed a far bigger deal than it probably was.

While I imbibed (or perhaps, with the aid of an occasional joint, more
accurately smoked) my new environment, the biggest change was my academic and intellectual exposure to the ideas of the hard Left. While we
were not literally force-fed Marxist dialectics of arcane historical material-
ism, the diet was heavy on radical starch, with extremely spare dollops of
liberal theory – and a scarcity of any conservative roughage!

Wits in the late 1970s was in thrall to the whole schtick of André Gunder
Frank's 'development of underdevelopment' theses, and other intellectual
camp-followers in left-wing historiography and sociology. The lonely exceptions were the departments of international relations and classics – the
former headed by a mellifluous German historian, Professor Dirk Kunert,
of whom his unkind detractors said: 'His mother got in the way of the
Soviet army when they invaded Berlin.'

The latter department was chaired by the extraordinary and eccentric
Michael Arnheim. He arrived at lectures in a formal gown, announcing
to his class (which overflowed out of the lecture hall, since Latin was still
a requirement for law undergraduates): 'The only reason I wear this garb
is to remind myself – and you lot, in particular – that this is actually a
university.' Arnheim wrote a tract denouncing, amazingly, Vorster's almost
non-existent reforms as paving the way to full-scale majority rule. He was
much ridiculed, but those such as the extreme rightist Herstigte Nasionale
Party (HNP), who had been pounding the same drum for years, were bereft of Arnheim's classical vantage.

But in the main, my academic attentions were forced leftward and I
struggled through the various tomes, such as *Das Kapital, Karl Marx: An
Introductory Reader*, and *Industrial Relations: A Marxist Introduction*. Despite
a most repressive, even paranoid censorship regime, none of these – and a
myriad companion pieces – were banned or censored. Quite possibly, and
perhaps rightly, the benighted censors knew that both their length and
impenetrability weighed against their being widely read.

The Wits social sciences departments contained a number of interesting personalities who interrogated our not-altogether fascinated classes in
various tutorials. Once again the wheel of fate and connectivity was to
turn up in my life: my industrial sociology lecturer, Belinda Bozzoli[1] (at
the time a radical feminist), was the daughter of the outgoing and eminent
vice chancellor, Professor GR Bozzoli.

What neither she, nor I, could even have remotely forecast was that her then two-year-old son, Gareth van Onselen, would some twenty-three years later land up as the diligent and driven head of my office in parliament.

The department of politics was headed by the immensely likeable, but not always understandable, Professor Alf Stadler. The three years of undergraduate politics was spent, essentially, studying Marxist and Hegelian philosophy, with a dash of the revolutionary and enlightenment thinkers – Hobbes to Rousseau – thrown in for good measure. The politics department – no less than the others – was also in the grip of 'developmentalitis'. Perhaps the attraction of Gunder Frank *et al* was their faith that the capitalist world economy was in a state of advanced, if not sclerotic, crisis and would, sooner rather than later, fall and be replaced by a more humane, worker-orientated order.

Although only fleetingly referred to by my lecturers, the real bogey they sought to refute was the orthodox liberal academic mainstream – people like Leo Kuper, Hobart Houghton and Michael O'Dowd. Their essential thesis, usefully summarised in a more contemporary context by fellow liberal academic and left-wing scourge, Hermann Giliomee, was that as economic growth accelerated, apartheid would fade away.[2] Democracy and the sway of markets would ultimately solve ethnic conflict. This was anathema to the Left, for whom capitalism and segregation were two sides of the same coin. In this view, the impoverishment of the African homelands was the essential precondition for the supply of the mass of cheap labour needed to dig and drill the very deeply located ore that was the basis for South Africa's dominant gold mining sector.

Mining was a major field of interest for the Marxist scholars. The university itself, just like the city of Johannesburg, was founded on the industry. It was first established on the Rand in 1904 as 'The School of Mines'. For many faculty members, Wits continued to serve the predominant interests of the mining elite, hence their vehement critique.

A particular flavour of the month, if not the decade, was the work of a Canadian 'Marxist-structuralist', Frederick Johnstone, who interpreted race relations in class terms. His analysis was based largely on his empirical study of the mines between the First World War and the white miners' revolt of 1922. Much less attention was paid to more contemporary, liberal theses suggesting that apartheid was – when we were students – 'being undermined by the resilient capitalist economy's need – in the 1970s and 1980s – for labour, goods and markets which the apartheid system was stultifying.' John Kane-Berman was later to codify these thoughts in his aptly entitled tract *South Africa's Silent Revolution*.³ He posited that the steady growth of the economy – which then exceeded Japan's – had ensured the rise of black workers to 'strategic levels of the labour ladder' regardless of whether they lived in the homelands or in urban areas.

Another favourite polemicist much beloved by the Left was the radical existentialist Frantz Fanon. *The Wretched of the Earth*, although published in 1962, was very much still in vogue at Wits in the 1970s. The historian Paul Johnson has dismissed him as the avatar of 'the theology of violence', which has validity. For Fanon, violence was a necessary form of social and moral regeneration. Although largely drawing on his own study and experience of French colonisation – especially the bloody decolonisation of North Africa – Fanon was highly rated since the Left viewed South Africa as a mutation of colonialism, 'colonialism of a special type', as the jargon had it.

I, however, was much struck by a passage which describes what happens to the state after independence, when the so-called 'native bourgeoisie' takes control. It is eerily prophetic; and it is perhaps ironic that no less a student of Fanon than Thabo Mbeki became a latter-day champion of what he termed the 'patriotic bourgeoisie'. Fanon's bleak description of post-colonialism could, in part, be an accurate depiction of post-Mandela-ism and the unhappy epitaph of the Mbeki presidency:

'The institutions of the state are progressively reduced to those of the president and his circle. The party becomes a mere shell, and actually "an implement of coercion". The leading posts in the bureaucracy are entrusted to men from the leader's tribe, sometimes directly from his own family. Parliament becomes little more than an adjunct of the Presidency where a legislative veneer is fitted over the wishes of the autocracy in return for higher salaries and some licence to ventilate popular sentiments (though not, of course, sentiments critical of the president) ... Elections "circulate the elite", contribute to the mystification of the voters, and thus help to preserve the elite's freedom to go on enriching itself without interference from below.'⁴

Why did Marx and Marxism hold such a grip on so many fine academics? It was apparent, even by 1977, that capitalism was not on the verge of collapse; and no proletarian-led transition to socialism could be sighted. Where indeed Marxism was applied, in the Soviet bloc, in China, and in parts of the Third World, the misery index rose and democratic institutions were trampled under the tyrant's heel. Yet dissent was dismissed on the basis that what we observed in the real world was a 'distortion', or a form of 'state capitalism'. The brilliant English historian, resident at New York

University, Tony Judt, demolished such sophistry in a powerful put-down:

'Marxism as a doctrine cannot be separated from the history of the political movements and systems to which it led. Moreover Marx's other youthful intuition – that the proletariat has a privileged insight into the final purposes of history thanks to its special role as an exploited class whose own liberation will signal the liberation of all humankind – is intimately attached to the ultimate communist outcome, so that Marxism becomes difficult to distinguish from communism ...

'And the daily deployment of Marxist categories for the vulgar purpose of suppressing freedom – which was their primary value to communists in power – detracts over time from the charm of the theorem itself. This clinical application of dialectics to the twisting of minds and the breaking of bodies was usually lost on Western scholars of Marxism, absorbed in the contemplation of past ideals or future prospects and unmoved by inconvenient news from the Soviet Union.'[5]

Although having learned from my matric debacle that exams are not passed without a fair amount of backbreaking preparation, I began to read and explore ideas and authors off the course and away from the curriculum. Jean-Francois Revel and Raymond Aron became two particular favourites. Revel's conclusion that the communist system could never democratise without destroying itself would over the next dozen years prove accurate and confirm Marx as a failed prophet.

I also started dipping into the essays of Isaiah Berlin and through him into the 'open society' writings of Karl Popper. They assisted me in clarifying the romanticised Marxist and neo-Marxist philosophies to which we were exposed. As Popper pointed out, any philosopher attached to a closed and complete system of thought – such as Marxism – helped lay the foundations for totalitarianism by breeding hostility to 'openness', whether in respect of science or of democratic societies themselves.

Then there was Berlin's famous aphorism: 'Liberty is liberty, not equality or fairness or justice or human happiness or a quiet conscience.'[6] Berlin also (as one of his intellectual disciples Mark Lilla recounts) pointed out a central paradox of modern thinking on liberty, that it is often those most attached to freedom as a political value who end up supporting ideas or measures that reduce its sphere or seek to extinguish it.[7]

But of all the works that gripped my imagination at that time, and one that still does, was a volume by the British historian and journalist, Paul Johnson, *The Enemies of Society*.[8] Johnson, who was to achieve international fame with his later work *A History of the Modern World*,[9] had himself undergone an interesting, if circuitous, journey from socialist editor of the

New Statesman to an early cheerleader for Margaret Thatcher. His conclusion that the millenarianism of ideology did little to improve the lot of Fanon's 'wretched of the earth' is worth recalling: 'New tyrannies have replaced old ones, and fresh injustices have been generously heaped on the heads of countless innocents in every quarter of the earth.'

He also seemed to have a much shrewder and more realistic analysis of the illusoriness of devising permanent and equitable solutions to problems which have always sprung from the nature of human beings – not arithmetical units – themselves. For him history proved that a flourishing middle class was the bellwether of economic prosperity, political stability and individual freedom. Importantly, Johnson noted that the health of the middle class is probably the best indicator of the health of society as a whole.

Not only did these views completely contradict the prevailing intellectual winds – at least in the small universe of a university – but his powerful polemic on freedom provided me with a lodestar to navigate the murky waters into which South Africa was sailing, and in which I was to immerse myself for the next 25 years.

2

Much of my time was not spent reading tracts or disputing my lecturer's dialectical interpretation of history. It was spent meeting and befriending a variety of people, largely from the more affluent sections of Johannesburg Jewish society. That they were – or proclaimed to be – keen adherents of socialism and rather mocking of my attachment to the PFP did not impair our socialising. However, one friendship was to provide the basis of a most durable political partnership both on and off the campus. Donald Rallis was the politically canny and intellectually witty son of the Dean of Men's Residence, and we were to spend the six years of my student life creating a liberal presence on the SRC and using the PFP youth movement as a battering ram against – ironically – the more conservative elements of the party.

Donald left the country in 1982 to avoid military conscription, and settled in America where he is today an associate professor of geography in Virginia. Had he stayed, he would have achieved a front-rank position in liberal politics. Alas, like so many others, my friend is a member of the diaspora of talented South Africans around the world.

One of my first ventures as Young Prog chairman was to organise a conference with the rather vacuous (I probably thought 'grand') title: 'South Africa: Where do you stand?' The anti-apartheid speakers – at least those who still had a legal voice – gathered, and this was my first opportunity to meet and hear Desmond Tutu, then secretary-general of the South African Council of Churches. Tutu's address, in his characteristic, charismatic style, was blunt and prophetic. He told our all-white, rather polite Young Prog assembly:

'The miracle is that blacks still talk to whites after all their ghastly treatment. Let the whites use our transport, run the gamut of police roadblocks and see if they agree that this system is evil, unjust and immoral and for those reasons bound to fail. I must issue a warning,' he went on, 'that if the present things continue then as sure as day follows night, we are going to have a blood battle in South Africa.'

However, in what was to become his most familiar trait, he laced his doom-laden (and largely accurate) foreboding with humour: 'I often wonder what the white parliament would talk about, if there were no blacks in South Africa!'

A few months later, the world would witness – again – just how 'evil, unjust and immoral' the system really was, when Black Consciousness leader Steve Biko died in police custody in 1977. The circumstances, even by the grisly standards that had made the security branch infamous, were deeply shocking. Despite at least a dozen injuries in the eight days preceding his death – including extensive brain damage – Biko was manacled in leg-irons, and driven naked for over seven hundred miles – from Port Elizabeth to Pretoria – in the back of a Land Rover. He was dead on arrival.

At a mass meeting at Wits in September I was mesmerised by the main speaker, the East London newspaper editor Donald Woods, who delivered a thundering denunciation of the minister of Police, Jimmy Kruger, whose utterance that Biko's death 'left him cold' would enter the lexicon of political infamy and imbecility. Within months Woods would flee to escape the privations of the banning order Kruger vengefully slapped on him, shortly after the student rally.

Biko's shameful death and the outpouring of local protest against it had significant and lasting consequences. In the immediate aftermath, the apartheid government decided to raise, rather than relax, levels of repression: it declared 18 organisations unlawful, and arrested 70 activists (including most of the reformist members of the Soweto Committee of Ten); banned several people (including Woods); and closed down the largest black newspaper, the *World*. Vestiges of peaceful political activism as then existed were effectively choked off. In consequence, what began in the 16 June 1976 revolt was taken further: the further radicalisation – if not revolutionisation – of black opinion.

Another fact highlighted by Biko's death was the extremely threadbare state of the rule of law: the apartheid apparatchiks had gutted its substance. This was particularly true of the magistracy, which had none of the independence of the jurists in the superior courts. One such, a certain Marthinus Prins, presided over a 15-day inquest into Biko's death, with South Africa's foremost advocate, Sydney Kentridge SC, acting for Biko's family. Kentridge made legal mincemeat of the policemen who interrogated Biko; and in a spellbinding four-hour address he called for the verdict that Biko died as a result of the criminal assault on him by one or more of the eight security policemen who had him in custody. Early the following year, Prins dismissed Kentridge's contention with a three-minute finding that no one could be held criminally responsible for the death.

These events were played out on the grand stage of South Africa's meta-conflict; but there was, too, drama in the much smaller sideshow of white politics in which I had by then something of a bit part. The United Party took the spectacularly ill-starred decision to disband and relinquish its battered brand to create – with a maverick Nat breakaway, Theo Gerdener – the New Republic Party. From my early childhood, the UP had seemed a permanent, if increasingly enfeebled, presence. So this was an early lesson in 'the impermanence of the permanent'. Even mighty structures on the surface of politics and society can disappear in an unexpected swirl of events and circumstances.

The National Party, more than two decades later, also disappeared into the elephants' graveyard of South African politics. What made the UP's move odder than most was that its death was by its own hand. To be fair, its leader, Sir de Villiers Graaff, still holds the dubious distinction of being South Africa's longest-serving – 21 years – leader of the opposition. But he desperately wanted a political realignment; and it simply didn't work. His successor, Radclyffe Cadman, had the equally dubious distinction of leading his 'new' party for just five months before losing his own seat when the NRP sank outside Natal and yielded its official opposition status to the PFP.

Much to the irritation of the UP, the Young Progs (and I) held a demonstration outside their dissolution congress, inviting them to join the PFP.

In my second year I was elected (along with Donald Rallis) to the Wits SRC for the first of three terms of office. Dr Henry Kissinger once famously remarked that the reason why academia is such a vicious rat-race is 'because the stakes are so small'. He had obviously not spent time in the hothouse atmosphere of student government. Herein an envenomed atmosphere prevailed – replete with personality disputes, arcane debates about abstruse theory, and vicious jockeying for position and status. I was no choirboy, and Rallis and I (elected respectively vice president and deputy president on the Exco) delighted in pricking the balloons of those we dubbed 'the sack and sandal brigade' of the Left.

The Wits SRC was intensely politicised. It reflected – in a small way – the academic cleavages on campus and the politics of wider South Africa. Broadly, the council was divided into the Left, which tended to dominate through organisational discipline; the liberals, whom Rallis and I led; and the right-wing conservatives, a distinct minority whose support generally came from engineers, Rhodesian students and the tiny band of NP supporters on campus.

The latter were eventually led by Russel Crystal, whose provocative obnoxiousness and contrariness vastly exceeded my own anti-Left inclinations. The fact that he was Jewish, with a capital 'J', appeared to rub some nasty salt into the wounded feelings of his fellow Semites who found his politics total anathema. Many years later, when I was the newly elected leader of the Democratic Party, Russel's decision to quit the NP and join our party caused me to blanch. Nevertheless, I thought we should publicly welcome his act of political apostasy. ('But you didn't have to welcome him with a brass band,' an angry Helen Suzman phoned to tell me.)

It was ironic, therefore, that Russel then set about helping to destroy, most effectively, the very NP machine to which he had been so attached in his student years.

If Crystal leaned more to the Left in later years, another distinct character on campus who swung radically in the opposite direction was the resident SRC anarchist, Dan Roodt. At the time pro-Nusas (the National Union of South African Students, and intellectual incubator of Left student politics) and anti-establishment, Roodt would clown at student meetings and use witty invective and his formidable reserves of intellect to advocate his brand of nihilism. Only the shifts in South Africa's political tectonic plates would transmogrify Roodt, in ANC South Africa, into a 'taalaktivis' of very right-wing views unfathomable to those who had encountered him across the SRC table.

Left-wing students, in my view, projected a blend of censorious smugness and intellectual pretentiousness. Many lived together in communes in Crown Mines, south of Johannesburg – today the headquarters of the

Oppenheimer-dominated De Beers diamond company, one of the prime villains in the demonology of the student Left. They sometimes seemed to fit the Nat caricature of Johannesburg's northern suburbs, where the residents 'could buy their own apartheid'. But some were formidably clever and personally brave: at least six student politicians whom I knew (at Wits and UCT) were severely harassed by the security police – and in one case, severely tortured. Two were served with banning orders during our time in student government.

Of course there was one overriding factor for a certain unity: apartheid and the increasingly repressive shroud in which the government was wrapping South Africa.

My first tangle with government on student affairs was both telling and trivial. One of my early tasks was to help organise the 1979 'Free People's Concert', an assemblage of rock bands to round off orientation week for the first-years. The university insisted that we obtain the then-required permit for mixed-race gatherings. My job was to apply to the Orwellian Department of Plural Relations (previously Bantu Administration) for such a permit. A mere two days before the scheduled event, the hardline deputy minister Dr AP Treurnicht, 'after careful consideration', refused us. No reasons were given, and no appeal was allowed. We decided to cancel the concert and I explained our decision to the student newspaper: 'All students must be allowed to attend all university activities. The SRC is not prepared to compromise because of an absurd apartheid rule. Education does not end in the classroom. It should encompass all aspects of university life.'[10]

Much of my political time was spent promoting the key issue of academic freedom – not a topic in which the student Left was much interested. Trade union rights and the ubiquitous question of 'development' dominated their thinking. The centrality of the issue on campus arose because of the ironically titled Extension of University Education Act (1959) which excluded blacks from admission to traditionally white universities except with ministerial permission (there were seven hundred to eight hundred at Wits during my time).

On 16 April 1959 Wits had held a general assembly which affirmed a dedication, which even today reads as a clarion call to the liberal ethos: '[It] is our duty to uphold the principle that a University is a place where men and women without regard to race and colour are welcome to join in the acquisition and advancement of knowledge and to continue faithfully to defend this ideal against all who have sought by legislative enactment to curtail the autonomy of the University.'

During my time, the centrepiece of our activities, at which the dedication was reaffirmed, was the Richard Feetham Academic Freedom Lecture. Presumably thanks to what the Australian art critic and polymath historian Robert Hughes called 'the colonial cringe', the tradition was to secure a high-profile overseas speaker to address the gathering. By 1979, South Africa was beginning to feel the effects of the academic boycott, which many academics and politicians abroad were beginning to implement.

Quite aside from the importance of the lecturer, the idea of securing a well-known speaker from abroad appealed to my sense of political theatre. So I embarked on a blunderbuss approach. I sent off ten or so letters to various international liberal politicians, hoping to persuade at least one. When a committee member asked the obvious question – 'But what will you do if more than one accepts?' – I brushed it aside and hoped like hell we would not face such a dilemma. I pinned my hopes on Senator Edward Kennedy, whose slain brother Robert, my early political hero, had galvanised South African campuses in a series of barnstorming speeches in 1966. I knew one or two South Africans acquainted with the Kennedy dynasty, and they encouraged him to come.

In the event he declined, but sent an encouraging note, which at the time I treasured. It read: 'Thank you very much for your kind invitation to come to deliver the annual Academic Freedom Lecture at the University of the Witwatersrand. I deeply appreciated your words of support and encouragement.

'Much as I would like to accept, it will not be possible for me to schedule a visit at this time. I continue to hope that it will be possible for me to visit in the future. I wish you and your colleagues every success in your important struggle for justice. You will continue to have my strong support.'[11]

I was to meet Ted Kennedy and enjoy a cup of coffee with him some twenty-seven years later, when I was appointed a Fellow at the Kennedy School of Government, Harvard University, named after his other slain brother, President John F Kennedy. I reminded him of the invitation, of which of course, in such a long and event-laden life, he had no recollection. He was, however, extremely warm and deeply interested in developments in South Africa. By then he was also a fairly aged and overweight figure – few traces were left of his youthful svelteness and political drive. He had moved from being a presidential hopeful to being dubbed the 'last liberal lion' in the Senate.

Eventually, however, my various entreaties paid off and the then-rising star of the British Labour Party, Dr David Owen, agreed to come. One of the youngest-ever Foreign Secretaries, he and his party had – fortunately for our purposes – just been ousted by Margaret Thatcher's resurgent Conservatives. We were aware that many whites detested him because of his outspoken views on Rhodesia, Namibia and apartheid South Africa; and that such black activists as remained above ground regarded him as too gradualist.

Our invitation incensed the daughter of Richard Feetham, a certain Mrs Hahn of Johannesburg, who wrote furiously denouncing us for inviting the 'terrorist-friendly Dr Owen' to South Africa. She also wrote directly to Owen – and to my amazement and his great credit he sent her a carefully crafted and well-reasoned response. And we did manage to arrange meetings for him with some leading struggle figures, including Desmond Tutu, Mangosuthu Buthelezi, and the famous anti-apartheid cleric, Dr Beyers Naudé, the previous head of the Christian Institute. Since Naudé was banned, this meeting presented difficulties. We settled on a one-on-one meeting in a Braamfontein tea-room. I took Owen – and was naïvely shocked that two obvious security policemen followed Beyers to the meeting and sat in plain view watching the entire encounter.

Owen had acquired – long before his arrival – a reputation for prickly sensitivity and irritability and for being something of a prima donna. He was the first international politician I had ever met, and while somewhat star-struck at the prospect, I found him reserved but largely pleasant and engaged, though given to occasional stiff silences if he grew bored or annoyed. However, his charming and gregarious American wife, Debbie, was a delight. She was an exceptionally successful literary agent (Georgette Heyer, Jeffrey Archer) and seemed genuinely interested in our group – peppering us with questions and amusing us with her quick-fire humour. She certainly leavened the occasional atmospherics generated by her husband.

The lecture itself was a huge success, with over two thousand five hundred students, academics and guests packing the sports union to hear him speak on 12 September 1979, a date chosen because it was the second anniversary of Biko's death. He told the audience that he was indeed a 'gradualist' in applying economic and social pressure on South Africa, and argued that successful transitions in Namibia and Zimbabwe would pave the way for internal negotiations in South Africa. He concluded on a rousing note, which I then thought to be misplaced, but the accuracy of which would be revealed a decade later: 'It has often been claimed that history is on the side of those who advocate violence and revolution. Our task is to defy that trend and help bring peace to South Africa.'[12]

Owen had been regarded as a natural leader and the obvious successor to James Callaghan. His comet-like rise and then disappearance from
frontline politics provides a cautionary tale of how the many gifts he possessed – intellect, courage, charisma – can sometimes be outweighed in
politics by a poor sense of judgment and timing.

3

Shortly before Owen's visit, I was rebuffed in my efforts to attain the
SRC presidency. Donald Rallis and I had put together a liberal ticket for
the elections, and after a lively campaign he finished first and I third in a
crowded field. The top candidate of the Left, Norman Manoim, came in
fourth. I shall describe my feelings after a small diversion into the state of
Progressive politics.

On 3 September 1979, the PFP congress convened to choose its own leadership. I was still a member of the party's National Executive, although not
privy to its inner machinations. Colin Eglin had been pushed aside, largely
because Gordon Waddell (former son-in-law of Harry Oppenheimer, and a
leading MP) and others wanted a fresh approach. They specifically wanted as
leader the much-admired academic-turned-politician Dr Frederik van Zyl
Slabbert; and Slabbert's election was essentially a coronation.

The Waddellites had also decided to remove Harry Schwarz as chairman
of the National Executive and replace him with Slabbert's close confidant,
the former Methodist minister-turned Anglo American executive-turned
politician, Dr Alex Boraine. At that stage I did not particularly like Schwarz;
indeed, we had clashed at several congresses because the youth movement
found his reflexive support for the South African Defence Force repugnant. However, I felt his skill and articulacy lent the party credibility. I also
found the machinations – and overweening arrogance of Slabbert's lieutenants – grating. When the National Executive met to choose its chairman, I cast my ballot for Schwarz. Not for the first time I was on the losing
side, as Boraine romped home.

When the SRC gathered to elect its president, Norman Manoim defeated me by two votes. One of the members who turned against me was
Schwarz's youngest son, Michael, who told me in tones of deep emotion
before the meeting that 'the PFP with your help ousted my father, so don't
expect my support tonight.' My laboured – and truthful – explanation that
I had voted for his father cut no ice.

Losing my bid for the SRC presidency left me feeling – at the ripe age of 23 – utterly defeated and deeply bereft. The consolation prize of being elected SRC vice president seemed small – and flat beer indeed. But then I received a note from one of my international relations lecturers, Peter Vale, which said: 'Just remember – the disappointment of failure is always much greater than the pleasure of success.' This proved a useful star to steer by, both in the small stakes of student politics, and in the somewhat larger arena of national politics where I was to spend most of my adult life.

I will not say appropriately, but at the time, and again reading off the course, I looked into Richard Nixon's memoirs. Perhaps I had a macabre fascination with someone whose prodigious talent and political drive was outweighed by flaws – which became fissures in his presidency – of truly Shakespearean proportions. Anyway, I reckoned – faults and all – Nixon knew how to come back from defeat. What arrested my attention was his citation of a speech by another former American president, Theodore Roosevelt, in an address to the students of the Sorbonne in the early 20th century. It read in part:

'It is not the critic who counts; not the man who points out how the strong man stumbles, or where the doer of deeds could have done them better; the credit belongs to the man who is actually in the arena, whose face is marred by dust and sweat and blood; who strives valiantly; who errs, and comes short again and again because there is not effort without error and shortcoming; but who does actually strive to do the deeds … who spends himself in a worthy cause, who at the best knows in the end the triumphs of high achievement and who at the worst, if he fails, at least fails while daring greatly, so that his place shall never be with those cold and timid souls who know neither victory nor defeat …'

I laboriously copied this out in 1979. I keep it as a reminder and guide.

Despite the competitive – and often vindictive – nature of my political nursery, I forged some significant friendships on the SRC, apart from my co-conspirator Rallis. Gilbert Marcus, today a leading senior legal counsel, was even when much younger a sage presence on the council, and he and his girlfriend (now wife) Jenny and I became close friends. And there was romance – especially since my partner at the time avowedly did not believe in the radical feminism that some of the Nusas clique of women espoused, that 'penetration was inherently degrading to females'.

Another strong memory of the SRC is of Mike Roussos, a melange of Catholicism and socialism, living in extreme penury in a murky commune in Berea. He was unusual for a man of the Left – an engineer, in an overwhelmingly conservative faculty – and had a lively sense of humour.

He was severely maltreated, after graduation, by the security branch, as his involvement in the burgeoning trade union movement intensified.

I truly expected him to see his commitment through – not to emigrate like so many hardliners who prophesied an African future only to decamp when that possibility became real. And indeed, Roussos stayed, emerging after 1994 as a key functionary in the Gauteng provincial administration, after having held key positions in the private sector. I never even contemplated that he might be remotely materialistic – he seemed utterly incorruptible. With amazement I read in 2004 that he was facing corruption charges at Johannesburg's specialised commercial court (the charges have not, to date, been processed). Whatever the validity of those charges, it was clear, simply from the quantum involved and the opulence of lifestyle sketched, that he had shed his university asceticism. So it sometimes goes.

Two of my most enduring friendships originated in the unlikely environment of the All Sports Council, where as an emissary from the SRC I was initially treated with much hostility by the campus sportsmen, who had a profound detestation of student politics. Once they grasped that I was not a Nusas spy sent to undermine their activities, the atmosphere improved considerably. There I met Clifford Garrun and David Greenstein – from the Wits rugby club – who became my closest friends on campus. We studied law together; went 'jolling around'; and remain close to this day. David emigrated to Australia after marrying (as did many friends and contemporaries in the 1980s); but Clifford stayed and prospered in his family insurance business. Our friendship lit a political spark in him, and he went on to become a Johannesburg city councillor in 1988.

The foremost event arising out of the SRC-All Sports Council collaboration was the rugby intervarsity between Wits and RAU (Randse Afrikaanse Universiteit). It was played at the Wanderers stadium since Ellis Park was being refurbished. Suffice to say, there were Anglo-Boer War connotations. However, most Wits students present saw the match as an occasion – or excuse – for unbridled exuberance, helped along by copious quantities of Klipdrift brandy and other student-favoured libations.

Unfortunately, the Wits vice chancellor, Professor DJ du Plessis, seized the opportunity to showcase his university to a number of distinguished guests, who were seated with him, the SRC president and me in the long room. Du Plessis had a fearsome reputation (he was nicknamed 'God' by his fear-struck minions); he had been Professor of Surgery before his appointment to the university's highest office.

A stickler for discipline and good manners, he was – on a good day – actually quite warm and even witty. He was also, given his conservatism, surprisingly liberal on most political matters. Now, as the students began to shed their inhibitions, they also began to shed their clothes. The most rowdy and intoxicated, stark naked except for their blue and yellow Wits scarves and pom-poms, proceeded to bare their backsides to the crowd and wave at the glowering Du Plessis, who left the match in high dudgeon.

The consequence – two days later – was an early-morning summons for the SRC Exco to report to the vice chancellor's office on the 11th floor of Senate House. Du Plessis commenced proceedings with a vintage display of ire by invoking the stinging words of his wife: 'Events at the Wanderers were a very sad evening for Wits.' We were then commanded to respond, which we did in predominantly mealy-mouthed terms. Du Plessis then rounded on his extremely diffident deputy, Professor Ellison Kahn; 'Professor Kahn,' Du Plessis intoned, 'we have not heard your views.' *Sotto voce*, Kahn responded: 'I don't know what you do with animals, except to put them into cages.'

Naturally there were numerous run-ins between the student leadership and Du Plessis's administration. The most notable – perhaps a metaphor for the times and the power structure on the campus – was Du Plessis's decision to ban an edition of the student newspaper which unveiled the fact that several members of the governing university council were members of the ultra-secret Afrikaner Broederbond. *Wits Student* responded by publishing an edition with a photograph of the council on the front page, removing the names and faces of the Broeders. At a mass meeting I moved a motion of no-confidence in the vice chancellor, stating that 'critical awareness is the best defence against creeping authoritarianism.'

Actually, I held Du Plessis in high regard. He was tough-minded, but not inflexible, and there was more to him than a forbidding exterior. He was a reformist and for the first time allowed student observers to attend meetings of the hitherto secret council. I was in the first batch admitted to this inner sanctum of the university's government.

In fact, the covert nature of *government* operations exploded into the biggest political scandal of the time – indeed of the NP administration's entire tenure. The 'Information scandal' was a saga that began to unravel towards the end of my second year. One of my father's friends on the Natal Bench, Judge Anton Mostert – enquiring into exchange control violations – disclosed and published evidence of massive government corruption. Famously, this included secret funding of the pro-government Johannesburg newspaper, the *Citizen*. Mostert had a characteristic blend of courage and obduracy, and ignored a request from the newly installed prime minister PW Botha not to publish his findings. Instead, he walked out of Botha's office, stating that no one, 'not even a prime minister', could prescribe to a judge his duties and functions.

A wave of events was unleashed by the revelations. They soon washed over the Presidency itself, sweeping John Vorster[13] from office. In January 1979, the NP's erstwhile crown prince (whom Botha had defeated the year before in the race for the premiership), Dr Connie Mulder, was forced to resign his seat, having already been dismissed from the cabinet by Botha. Three years later Mulder helped found the largest right-wing breakaway from Botha's Nationalists, the Conservative Party. He died in 1987, but his two bright sons, Pieter and Corné, became the standard-bearers of conservatism in parliament and represented (between them) half the parliamentary presence of the Freedom Front in the post-apartheid National Assembly.

During a long conversation with Corné on a visit to Germany in 1994 – in the improbable locale of the Reeperbahn in Hamburg's red-light district – I discovered just how deep and everlasting his family's resentment was towards the NP for what they perceived to be the party's brutal treatment of their father. In many ways the politics of resentment and revenge, commingled with ideology, fuelled the right-wing forces at large in the 1980s.[14]

Aside from this rare instance of political accountability, other consequences of the saga were more negative and baleful. The government introduced a bill which created an Orwellian office of 'Advocate General' aimed at preventing anyone from publishing material 'relating to the alleged misappropriation of state funds without the prior written permission of the Advocate General', whose enquiries were to be kept secret.

We organised a huge protest at Wits, perhaps the largest since the early seventies. I strongly asserted that 'press restrictions, enshrining cover-up and corruption as the law of the land, are symptomatic of the South African state on the march to fascism.' Probably despite associated civil society protests across the country, the government later removed the most contentious and draconian provisions of the legislation.

The controversy over the bill underscored the Botha government's least attractive feature: a reliance on state-imposed mandarins and structures designed to shield it from scrutiny and place it beyond accountability. On the other hand, Botha had (halting) instincts for reform, and early evidence of this rendered aspects of our final-year industrial sociology course almost instantly obsolete. The much-banned, harassed and outlawed black trade union movement had been plunged into a gloomy universe. Suddenly the Wiehahn Commission report into the issue helped change the landscape.

Its proposals were radical at the time, and included one that black trade unions be legalised and registered; and that an Industrial Court be established to arbitrate labour litigation. Botha accepted the recommendations 'in principle', later enacting their core elements.

It was just as well I attended the lectures concerning this reform, since most of my days on campus were taken up with student politics, and my time off campus on Progressive Federal Party matters and bouts of distinctly non-political partying. However, I passed my finals – not particularly spectacularly – with upper and lower seconds in my majors.

At the end of my undergraduate degree, I persuaded my ever-generous grandmother Ray (then bedridden since, horrifyingly, both her legs had been amputated consequent on severe circulatory disease) to sponsor me on a trip to America. Two friends and I criss-crossed the US in the back of Greyhound buses – a cheap though far from cheerful way to travel. Despite the intense excitement of new and dynamic destinations, I was increasingly uncertain about my future academic and professional route. I decided to enrol for an honours degree in political science and international relations.

Yet just as the academic year was about to begin, I happened to go to a Friday night movie with my friends Jenny and Gilbert Marcus. It was fairly typical Hollywood fare – *And Justice for All*, starring a youthful Al Pacino. The main character was a heroic public defender trying to come to terms with his father's legacy.

The movie was hardly a classic, but it profoundly unsettled me and my tentative academic and career choice. Gilbert was also, as always, enthusiastic about his enjoyment of law. However, the reason I had shied away from studying law was that I didn't want to enter a profession in which my father was locally famous, and in which my brother (on full scholarship at Cambridge) was an academic star. I didn't want the comparisons that could be drawn. My mother, however, urged me to be pragmatic. 'Well, Tone,' as she often called me, 'if you get a law degree, you can at least have more choices afterward.' I switched courses, entered the Wits Law School and enrolled for an LLB.

4

The Law School was then headed by Louise Tager[15] who resembled a fashion mannequin rather than a legal scholar. Some of the best and brightest

Right: RUSSIAN ANCESTORS: my paternal great-grandparents, Dr David Drusinsky and his wife Bluma. They migrated to South Africa from the Crimea via Constantinople in 1896. My grandmother, Tamara, was born en route.

Below: MY DIRECT ORIGINS: on 31 March 1954, my parents Ramon and Sheila were married at the Great Synagogue, Wolmarans Street, Johannesburg.

Above: DURBAN CHILDHOOD:
with my mother Sheila and my
brother Peter when I was four
years old, *circa* 1960.

Above right: Pictured at the
family home, 21 Empire Road,
Parktown, Johannesburg. We
spent many happy holidays
in Johannesburg visiting my
grandmother and her sisters.

Opposite above: 'Untidy' and 'a
short attention span' were some
of the remarks recorded on my
early school reports. Formal
school photograph, age 7.

Right: Pembroke House,
Kearsney College, 1971: my
Natal English boarding school
had a profound effect on
shaping my life and some of
my views. I am in the front row,
appropriately enough at the
knees of the housemaster,
Peter Metcalf.

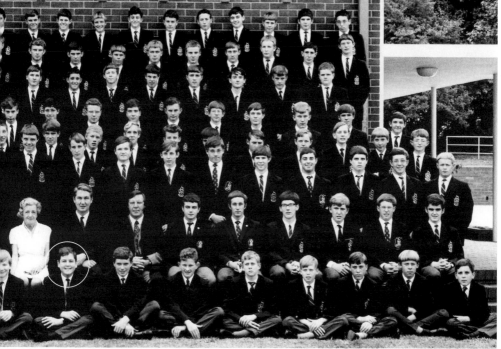

Top: IN THE ARMY: during my 18-month compulsory service; my journalistic post at *Paratus*, the South African Defence Force magazine would be 'the gift that kept on giving' to my later opponents in the ANC. I never rose beyond the rank of lance corporal, in which capacity I met Lieutenant-General Jack Dutton, Chief of Staff of the Defence Force.

Above: The Wits Students' Representative Council (SRC) was dominated by the left, although I did get elected to it in three elections. Despite the smiles there was great enmity among some of the student politicians portrayed in the photograph.

'DANCING WITH DIALECTICS' is what I have entitled the chapter that describes my experiences at the University of the Witwatersrand. This was the mugshot used for a student election campaign in 1980.

Left: INTO POLITICS: my first election was as Johannesburg city councillor for Bellevue, in February 1986. Pitching in to help were my friends Susan Scott, Diane Levy and Lauren Kaplan. (*STAR*)

Below: SCRAPING HOME: I just made it by 39 votes after a titanic struggle in Bellevue. The relief at my victory was shared by my election agent Alan Gadd, on the right, but Harry Schwarz MP, on the left, seemed more pensive. (*STAR*)

Opposite above: ASPIRING LAWYER: my father delivered the graduation address when I was capped with my LLB degree in February 1983. It was a happy and proud moment for us both.

Opposite below: SAYING 'NO' to the 1983 Tricameral Parliament: despite Helen Suzman's enormous stature, her own constituency of Houghton voted 'Yes' for PW Botha's incremental reform measures. On referendum day my mother, Helen Suzman and I made a vain effort to turn the tide. (*STAR*/STEVEN DAVIMES)

Top: LEADER OF THE CAUCUS: in 1988 I was elected leader of the Progressive Federal Party municipal caucus in Johannesburg after its veteran leader deserted. It was a tense time for us all, which is reflected on the faces of my colleagues. From left, Les Dishy, Paul Asherson, Rae Graham and Pat Rogers. (*Star*)

Below: UNEXPECTED VICTORIES: the PFP municipal team did far better in the 1988 local government elections than our many doomsayers and critics predicted. Here I pose with my council candidates, including two of my close friends, Clifford Garrun (just below my hand) and Claire Quail, front right. Judith Briggs, who went on to many years of service on the council, is at front left. (PFP)

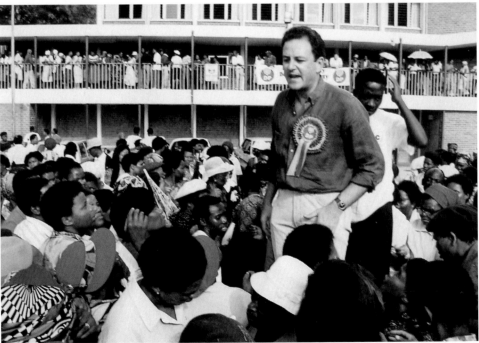

Top: HIGH-WIRE ACT: emerging from a marathon negotiation session in November 1993 with the National Party Justice Minister, Kobie Coetsee. In what was billed as 'the most dramatic turnaround' in the Kempton Park negotiations, I managed to achieve a breakthrough on the critical issue of judicial selection. Extraordinarily, Coetsee used me as the whistleblower on the agreement he had signed with the ANC. (PICTURENET)

Below: SOUTH AFRICA'S FIRST DEMOCRATIC ELECTIONS: the huge audience I targeted at an open-air rally in my Houghton constituency flattered to deceive. Most of the attendees did not vote for the Democratic Party, which was nearly immolated in the poll.

Top: In the 1994 campaign, there was little enthusiasm for an opposition presence in ANC strongholds. I was chased off the campus of the University of the Western Cape after futile appeals from ANC luminaries, such as professors Jakes Gerwel and Kader Asmal, to allow me to speak. 14 April 1994. (*CAPE TIMES*)

Above: ELECTED LEADER: the Democratic Party Federal Council elected me to the leadership of a dramatically shrunken party when I defeated Ken Andrew, on the left. Party chairman Dave Gant shakes my hand, and deputy chairman Chris April joins in. April would later defect to the ANC, but our party forged ahead. 23 May 1994. (*ARGUS/*ROY WRIGLEY)

Top: LEAN AND MEAN: a very small Democratic Party caucus poses for a photograph outside Parliament in March 1996. Despite our low pecking order in terms of strength and size we set out with a single-minded determination to become the largest opposition force in the land, something we achieved three years later.

Above: Within ten years we had more than quintupled our number of MPs, as this photograph of our 2005 parliamentary caucus illustrates.

Top: MADIBA MAGIC: President Nelson Mandela lifted me out of my initial post-1994 electoral blues. Despite his worldwide iconic status, he greatly enjoyed his interaction with his political opponents. Although we sometimes sharply disagreed, we enjoyed a warm relationship which continues to this day. This photograph was taken at a state banquet in 1994.

Above: DO OR DIE: in the 1995 municipal elections I told the party it would have to improve on the dismal performance of the year before or close up shop. In Gauteng, at least, the voters responded and we did considerably better than in the previous year's election. In the photograph I line up to vote at my local polling station in Orange Grove, accompanied by my brother Peter, then the leader of the party in the Gauteng legislature, my mother Sheila, and provincial legislator Jack Bloom (*left*). (*BEELD*)

Top: TENSE TIMES: a difficult moment in the Constitutional Assembly as DP negotiators join other opposition members in seeking to stop the ANC juggernaut. It proved to be an uneven exercise.

Above: MAY 1996: the day before parliament finalised the constitution, MPs gathered for a photograph on the steps of the Senate. The light-heartedness I shared with NP chief negotiator, Roelf Meyer, and Deputy President FW de Klerk belied some serious points of reservation between us, and, indeed, as it later transpired, between them. Meyer would shortly quit the NP to co-found the United Democratic Movement. (*CAPE TIMES*)

Top: COSATU'S FIST: COSATU called a general strike to oppose the lock-out clause in the constitution, which the DP favoured. For my pains I was assaulted outside Parliament by a member of the Trade Union Federation. Douglas Gibson (behind me) looks suitably concerned, while Joe Marks and EK Moorcroft try to guard my back. 1 May 1996. (*DIE BURGER*/BRANDEN AMRON-COETZEE)

Above: 15 DECEMBER 1996: the constitution is squared away and I celebrate my 40th birthday in the company of Labour Minister Tito Mboweni. He would go on to become Governor of the South African Reserve Bank and establish a reputation as a monetary hawk. Notwithstanding our fierce disagreements about labour law, we maintained a friendship while serving together in parliament.

Left: TOUCHED BY STARDUST: an early appearance on Pieter-Dirk Uys/Evita Bezuidenhout's TV show 'Funigalore' bolstered my public profile and allowed me to observe, at close quarters, South Africa's master satirist. Here we pose at my alma mater, the University of the Witwatersrand. (M-Net)

Below: A VISIT TO NEWLANDS: in 1999 Hennie Bester, on my right, the Western Cape leader of the Democratic Party, and I met with Hansie Cronje during a cricket test. Cronje was one of South Africa's most successful cricket captains before his involvement in a betting scandal the following year, which brought a premature and controversial end to his career. He was tragically killed in a plane crash in 2002, aged 32. (*Die Burger*)

Top: GOLDEN TOUCH: South Africa's Olympic champion swimmer Ryk Neethling attended a Democratic Alliance caucus meeting where he was warmly received by suitably star-struck parliamentarians. Here he poses with me and colleagues Roy Jankielsohn MP and Sheila Camerer MP.

Below: POP ICON: I campaign with Steve Hofmeyr, whose mega record sales and popularity in the Afrikaans-speaking community were used in an unsuccessful attempt to retain the name of Pretoria, which the ANC council renamed Tshwane. 20 February 2006. (*BEELD*/FELIX DLANGMANDLA)

jurisprudential highbrows were on the faculty: the remote but scholarly Ellison Kahn; the formidable and intimidating – but actually fun-loving – Paul Boberg, king of torts or delict; and the intellectually stylish criminal law professor Roger Whiting (who also enjoyed his nights on the town with his students). Then there was the tart-tongued, high-octane June Sinclair – expert in the law of persons. Intellectual depth ran even deeper. We had the highly rated public international law supremo John Dugard and my cousin, David Zeffertt, by then South Africa's pre-eminent expert on the intricate law of evidence. The junior ranks also revealed that the next generation could possibly outshine its masters. Edwin Cameron and Carole Lewis – both to become Appellate Division judges in the new order – lectured on the arcane mysteries of Roman law. We were taught constitutional and administrative law by the intellectually towering, young Etienne Mureinik.

Halton Cheadle, who went on in 1994 to draft South Africa's new labour laws, was a recently unbanned trade unionist who taught us the then-greenfields subject of labour law.[16] The book of *Genesis* records that: 'There were giants in the earth in those days.' I'm not sure whether the Wits Law School, circa 1980, housed the exact academic equivalent; suffice to say we were taught by some pretty big and impressive intellectual beasts.

The distance between staff and students, a feature of my undergraduate years, was far less characteristic in the postgraduate milieu of the Law School. We spent inebriated evenings in the bars and restaurants of Braamfontein and Hillbrow, fraternising with the staff and 'pulling all-nighters' under the baton of the Law Students' Council social programme. This was, of course, years before sexual molestation – and the sex pest – became a social and legal taboo. One or two otherwise famous academics who blatantly hit on some of my very pretty female co-students of the 1980s are fortunate indeed that this change in mores happened only in their dotage.

Although the curriculum was approximately three times larger and more complex than the lightweight arts degree I had completed, I thrived in my new environment. I enjoyed many courses and was intrigued – occasionally entranced – by the logic of legal reasoning and the rigour of many court judgments we pored over.

It was not all a question of deduction from first principles and a close reading of texts. One of the keys to exam success was to 'have a good set of notes'. One of my friends, David Sash, who fancied himself as something of a roué, prided himself on never attending lectures, yet solved the problem in the run-up to exams by taking out to dinner 'the plainest girls' in the class; the underlying theory being that their gratitude would allow them to part with their notes – which Sash reckoned would be meticulous given their empty social calendars. My political involvements furnished a similar dilemma; but I was fortunate in that another friend, the scholarly and conscientious Cecil Wulfsohn, was a year ahead of me and passed on his scrupulously written, perfected tomes. These were often better than the textbooks we studied. Not surprisingly, Cecil won every major academic award and is today one of the country's leading commercial attorneys.

Studying constitutional law allowed me to familiarise myself with 'consociational theory', which despite its unpromising and politically unsexy title, was much punted by PFP leader Van Zyl Slabbert and his academic collaborator, Professor David Welsh. It was a means of reconciling the need for majority rule with minority protection. Pioneered by Professor Arend Lijphart[17] of the University of California, 'consociational democracy' is the antithesis of majority rule – democracy as prescribed by the Westminster model. I liked the thesis that the primary meaning of democracy is that (in Sir Arthur Lewis's formulation) 'all who are affected by a decision should have the chance to participate in making that decision, either directly or through chosen representatives.' Its secondary meaning is that 'the will of the majority shall prevail.' But if this means barring the minority from influence or governmental decisions, it violates the primary principle.

Many years later, in my ringside seat in South Africa's first democratic parliament, I saw the ANC repeatedly use its majority and dominance as a legislative steamroller to violate that principle.

The reason why the PFP constitutionalists – and other liberal initiatives such as the Study Project on Christianity in Apartheid Society (Sprocas – 1973) and the Natal-based Buthelezi Commission (1982) – desired a consociational outcome was easy to fathom. The position was best articulated by the sociologist Pierre van den Berghe, who with deadly accuracy about the emergent South African polity had postulated in 1979:

'If your constituency has the good fortune to contain a demographic majority, racism can easily be disguised as democracy. The ideological sleight of hand, of course, is that an ascriptive racially defined majority is a far cry from a majority made up of shifting coalitions of individuals … [Majority] rule in Africa can thus easily become a veneer for racial domination.'[18]

In our deeply divided society the exclusion of the political (and racial) minority is likely to be permanent. Consociational theory – to meet Lewis's primary principle – demands that executive power be shared among all significant social segments.

The advocacy of this system by Slabbert *et al* meant it was not then entertained by the National Party, who dismissed it as over-sophisticated hokum; and it was rubbished by the ANC-in-exile. By the time for real negotiations to commence, a decade hence, the DP (political heirs to the PFP) had jettisoned it. Ironically, only the NP at Codesa advanced the concept of permanent power-sharing and minority vetos. A few vestiges of consociationalism featured in the Interim Constitution of 1993 but were dropped entirely from the 1996 document – a classic example of good ideas being doomed by timing and their provenance. Their opponents saw behind it a ruse to perpetuate minority rule.

While I was immersed in the study of law, I had not yet, by 1980, entirely left student politics. I was still SRC vice president, serving unhappily under Norman Manoim and a Left-dominated executive. I had decided to stand down when our term ended; but a number of younger liberals had been elected to the SRC and they pressured me to stand for the leadership. By then, political antagonism between Left and liberal had reached an intensity unseen for years on the campus. I, somewhat against my better judgment, decided to head up a list and made it clear I was standing for president, and the campus poll should be a referendum between the two sides and their leadership contenders.

A record number of students – 46% – streamed to the polls. In the 26 years since then, that percentage has not been bettered. I won, as they say in racing, 'going away', 300 points ahead of the Left's standard-bearer, Sammy Adelman. However, the weighted nature of the preferential ballot and the diffuse constituency which I represented told against the liberals. Only one other of the six on our list made it, while all six of the Left ticket were elected together with a fruit salad of maverick anarchists, Christian activists and faculty representatives who made up the new SRC.[19]

It was clear that in the ultimate ballot for president my bid, while enjoying strong endorsement from the student body, would be scuppered by the SRC. Donald Rallis and I decided to proceed with my nomination at the inaugural meeting of the Exco, and in the inevitable event of its defeat to resign from the body. So it came to pass, with the newly elected president (Adelman) declaring in his victory speech: 'I'm not sorry to see Messrs Leon and Rallis go. Whatever my relationship with Tony, he is a very clever politician … So Tony is capable, Tony is experienced, but Tony has chosen for his own reasons to resign. Tony felt that Tony Leon was more important than the SRC.'

I responded in *Wits Student*, which ran the story under the headline:

'Tony tumbles and Donald ducks'. As I elaborated, 'We had a very strange election. The [radical Left] ticket were all elected and the [liberal] ticket was not, yet I topped the poll by 300 points. While I believe there is no substitute for victory, I am happy in this particular defeat [for the presidency] because it is much better to be defeated for a cause that will ultimately triumph, than to triumph in a cause which will be ultimately defeated …'

The editor of *Wits Student* felt obliged to add a footnote: 'Mr Leon's accomplishment in the art of rhetoric is an undisputed fact. It is precisely the absence of this kind of indulgence which facilitated the smooth functioning of the last SRC meeting.'

The somewhat acidic editorial was penned by Sheldon Cohen, who despite our political differences at the time was generally a person of estimable cheerfulness and civility. In late January 2008 he was shot dead, aged just 47, by an armed robber, while waiting for his son to finish soccer practice at the Balfour Park sports ground in Highlands North, Johannesburg. Sheldon's stupefying murder further traumatised a community already reeling from a crime wave which seemingly was without end.

However, there was another strange and sad footnote to the saga, this one related to Adelman. After I resigned from the SRC, he pushed the council ever further leftward and increasingly entangled himself in direct confrontation with the state. He was banned and fled the country, initially aided and sheltered by Hollywood star and activist Jane Fonda and her husband, Tom Hayden, whom Adelman had invited to South Africa. Sammy landed up at Sussex University where he completed his PhD.

In 1990, shortly after I was elected to parliament, a vaguely familiar voice came across the telephone. It was Adelman. FW de Klerk had just announced his dramatic changes, and Sammy was anxious to return to see his ageing and sick parents. Since he had left illegally, he needed official sanction to return. I was happy to oblige. A few weeks later Sammy duly – and legally – arrived back. Old enmities evaporated, and we had an animated discussion about his adventures and prospects. He had involved himself in the activities of the ANC in London, an experience rather like being in snakebite territory.

I did not see him again. Despite his courage and disregard for his own safety he is, today, a non-person in the ANC's hall of heroes, neither mentioned nor remembered.

At my final Nusas congress in 1980, I decided to go out on a splenetic note: 'You claim to be in favour of democracy, you claim that the university is, itself, unflinchingly authoritarian and unsusceptible to grassroots opinion and critical inputs. Yet your own adverse and paranoid reaction to criticism, to dissension within the ranks, your branding of your opponents as BOSS agents and police activists, is McCarthyism of the worst sort.' I felt better for saying this, but the following wind among the Left was all in the other direction. The *Star* newspaper characterised my speech thus: 'Voice of dissent raised at Nusas congress'.[20] Indeed, the congress passed a resolution against the 'insidious notion of private property', while another condemned all forms of advertising.

After that I became president of the Law Students' Council in my final year, after having happily spent time editing and publishing the law students' newspaper, aptly entitled *De Minimis*.[21]

A few months later, during the run-up to the 1981 general election, in which both Donald and I were once more active in the PFP campaign, we invited a series of speakers from participating parties to address the students. The first two events were well attended, with the PFP's Slabbert enjoying strong support and the New Republic Party's enormously rotund leader Vause Raw getting a barracking – but being allowed to express his views. We struggled to obtain a suitable speaker for the NP until Russel Crystal told us he could 'secure' Dr Piet Koornhof, the well-known and much parodied minister of the (yet-again-renamed) Department of Co-operation and Development.[22]

Donald and I organised meetings with an entire swathe of South African opinion-formers, including Helen Joseph, Ntatho Motlana, Ndabaningi Sithole of Zimbabwe, and Helen Suzman. None generated as much heat as Koornhof. In essence, there was no meeting, or at least not one where Koornhof was heard to utter more than a few audible words. He was literally screamed and shouted down.

The *Rand Daily Mail*'s political correspondent was the young Helen Zille, who years later was to take over leadership of the DA when I resigned. Her report is worth recording: 'Pandemonium reigned for almost an hour at the University of the Witwatersrand yesterday as the guest speaker, Dr Piet Koornhof, battled to shout a few disjointed sentences of his speech above jeers, shouting, singing and cheering. The noise came from about 300 of the 1 200 students who packed the Great Hall for the lunchtime meeting ... As Dr Koornhof walked onto the stage he was greeted with chanting of "Amandla", "Sieg Heil", "Free Mandela", "Get out" and "Remember Sharpeville" ...

'Dr Koornhof attempted to start his address in a jovial mood, battling against the roar to "thank" the students for a "warm and hospitable welcome". He was soon drowned out with shouts of "Get out, fascist", "Bull★★★★" and "Where's your pass?" Dr Koornhof responded: "At least it's exciting at Wits."'

By the end, a visibly furious Koornhof was being pelted with paper balls, mostly crumpled posters. Twice, several hundred students stood to sing *Nkosi Sikelel' iAfrika*, the anthem of the banned ANC. Koornhof challenged the students to sing the official national anthem, *Die Stem*. Some did. Koornhof joined in. The majority of students who had squeezed their way in sat in silence, overwhelmed by the rival groups.

Zille wrote: 'At one point Dr Koornhof attempted to silence the students, and the audible words over the microphone were: "You are a disgrace to your University and South Africa ... I am a Minister of State." He was soon drowned out by shouts of "Mandela can't speak, Mandela can't speak."

'On three occasions the chairman, Mr Tony Leon, attempted to take the microphone and call for a vote on whether students wanted the meeting to continue. Dr Koornhof did not hand over the microphone, saying repeatedly he was determined to stand there for the full hour ... After the meeting scuffles between opposing sides broke out in the aisles of the hall.'

While writing this book I contacted Donald Rallis in Virginia, USA, to ask for his recollection of events that March – 25 summers ago. He sent this response:

'With the benefit of decades of hindsight, I don't see the issue now as being as clear-cut as I did then. I now understand the views of the other side better than I did, and I respect their sincerity. But I still think that we were right. We believed in making use of what freedoms of speech there were in South Africa; we were confident enough in our ideas to believe that giving a platform on campus to Koornhof, and juxtaposing it with an appearance by Van Zyl Slabbert, would help our cause, not Koornhof's. The Left believed that allowing Koornhof to speak legitimised the cause he represented. I suspect that they never did believe in freedom of speech, limited or otherwise.'

I agree with Donald's analysis, and would add that what happened started a clear and regrettable process which saw the exclusion of more and more voices from the campus, which surrendered to what Ronald Dworkin has described as 'the heckler's veto'.

It came as no surprise to me that a few years later, the redoubtable anti-apartheid critic and scholar, Dr Conor Cruise O'Brien, was hounded off both the Wits and Cape Town campuses; while by the time of the 1987 election, Helen Suzman was denied a platform at Wits. The silencing of O'Brien and Suzman enjoyed the official imprimatur of the university authorities themselves: clearly the academic leadership had decided to honour the adage, 'If you can't beat 'em, join 'em.' So much for academic freedom and tolerance for dissenting views.

By 1982 – my final year – I was exiting student politics. But the political climate of the country was inescapable. The young trade unionist Dr Neil Aggett was found dead in his cell in John Vorster Square. He and other unionists had been detained in solitary confinement for three months. Again, the verdict after a 64-day inquest was, incredibly, that 'no one was responsible for his death', the 46th of its kind in South Africa's grim history.

Another apartheid-inspired death had even wider ramifications. In August, ANC activist and academic and the much-feared Joe Slovo's wife, Ruth First, was assassinated by letter bomb, posted to her in Maputo. At the TRC, many years later, Craig Williamson – a high-level security policeman – confessed to the murder. Williamson and two cohorts had served on the Wits SRC many years before my own time. Later they were unmasked as security police spies; but by then Williamson had successfully penetrated, and achieved high office in, various international student-affiliated bodies closely linked to the ANC-in-exile. A consequence of the existence of a spy ring was that when I reached the SRC, we were obliged at the commencement of our term of office to take an oath that we were not, nor would become, spies or informers.

One of my best friends on campus was Ruth First's nephew, Jonathan First, and we remain close to this day; his politics was far from his aunt's and nearer to my own. In the sad aftermath of her murder, Jonathan wrote to his grandmother (Ruth First's mother) Tilly, who had been a communist activist. He condoled with his grandmother and indicated his admiration for Ruth's bravery, and his disagreement with her politics. Jonathan showed me Tilly's response, which was maximally political, and minimally warm. I remember one memorable and brutal line to her grandson: 'What do you mean you disagree with Ruth's politics? What are your politics, do you have any?'

Not exactly your typical, doting Jewish grandmother, I thought.

I intensely enjoyed my final year at Wits. Amid the studying, I enjoyed the partying and the socialising even more. But when I sat my finals I was well prepared, and I graduated with a sprinkling of firsts and an average upper second. I was particularly thrilled to be awarded, jointly, the Claude Franks Memorial prize for the best results in jurisprudence and conflict of law, and the Society of Advocates' prize for winning the final year moot court contest. I was 25 and ready to take on the wider world.

5

There appeared little connection between the theory of law and its practice at the offices of Edward Nathan & Friedland Incorporated, whose 23rd-floor threshold in downtown Johannesburg I crossed for the first time in March 1983. I was freshly suited as an 'articled clerk' – in today's euphemism, a 'candidate attorney'. This post was the lowest form of life in law. Edward Nathan was (and remains) one of South Africa's top commercial law firms, and placement there was highly prized. I was considered fortunate in being accepted and doubly so because I was to be articled to Michael Katz, the dominant legal brain and presence in the firm, whose outsized ability and personality tended to define the concern, even though he was not at that stage the senior partner.

Victor Mansell – white-haired, pencil-thin, and 'every inch a gentleman' as he was ubiquitously described – was the senior partner and possessor of much of the firm's institutional memory. This went back to the early days of Johannesburg's manufacturing industry and nascent commercial development, in which Mansell and several of the older partners had been intricately and intimately involved.[23]

However, Katz was the driving force, chief rainmaker, and effectively headed the team of 20 partners and thirty or so professional staff who arrived early every morning (often including Saturdays) and frequently left late at night. It was an intimidating environment for a neophyte professional. The brainpower, collective knowledge and mental acuity of most of the partners brought me crashing down from the 'I-know-it-all-I-am-the-master-of-the-universe' attitude to which good university results and leadership positions in student posts had – in my own mind – elevated me.

Although Katz was my notional boss and I was personally contracted to him under my articles of clerkship, I saw very little of him. He worked extraordinary hours, had the sleep needs of a Margaret Thatcher (about four hours a night), and hugely enjoyed his proximity – and access – to power, economic and political.

As a legal tadpole, I mainly worked with junior partners and professional assistants. This entailed a myriad of seemingly bewildering and taxing tasks – from computing stamp duty on leases, to accompanying nervous divorcées to court.

My first professional brush with Katz came soon after I arrived. 'Tony, it's good to have you here,' he boomed. 'With respect,' (Michael's every second sentence commenced with this formalism) 'you'll need a day or two to acquaint yourself with the place, but have a look at this file in the meantime and see what you make of it.' He then handed across his desk – stacked on every conceivable surface with burgeoning, enormous documents – an intimidating large buff-coloured file whose contents threatened to explode the over-stretched elastic band pinioning its papers. I still clearly remember its contents: it was an 'off-balance-sheet-ledger finance agreement' devised for a client to take advantage of the fiscus's then-benevolent attitude towards rubber plantations.

The further I read, the more confused – and miserable – I became. Most of the agreement and appendices appeared written in impenetrable code: 'put and call options', 'no par value shares', and 'the fiduciary duties of the vendor' could have been in ancient Greek for all the impression they made on me. I had never actually seen a summons or visited the inside of a courtroom. This wasn't so much being thrown in at the deep end; it was like being washed out into the deepest and most shark-infested waters. When I'd finished feeling sorry for myself I stopped wondering why I'd ever done law, let alone entered articles, and urgently sought help and assistance further up the food chain. The kindness and guidance of those further up, such as Hennie Pretorius, Marius van Wyk and Miranda Barker, saved me from committing some unspeakable – and perhaps very costly – blunders and helped reduce the sense of panic which gripped me whenever the phone rang or my code was flashed. (In pre-cellphone and pager days, Edward Nathan had colour-coded lights in all offices, boardrooms and library which flashed in specific combinations. Each legal staffer had his, or her, own code, and when your lights flashed you dived for the nearest phone.)

Slowly, I became familiar with the intricacies and esoterica of legal practice, and the panic lessened, though it never entirely disappeared. Early on, however, I decided that despite the material prosperity and status that a partnership at Edward Nathan bestowed on its directors, I had no great desire to be among their number, a legal nursemaid to hundreds of clients each of whom thought they were the only one you had to deal with, and many of whom possessed the assumption that they had a lien on a portion of your soul.

Thinking back, this changed with circumstance. As a fairly diligent ward councillor and constituency MP – which is what I became, in short and successive order after leaving Edward Nathan – I never resented helping my constituents at any hour.[24] The difference, objectively, is that an attorney can bill his client directly by the hour; yet a politician cannot. I saw politics as a life-long vocation, while legal articles were a necessary means to an undefined end, which I vaguely saw as professionalising my legal qualifications.

The real truth, I suspect, was that I was conflicted. Part of me was a creature, or captive, of convention, holding the view that learning for its own sake was an indulgence; that the true path to success was to find a profession, qualify, marry, raise a family, play golf, etc. Another, the dominant part of me, saw such a 'career path' as death by instalments. I was, however, on my own basis of completing all missions, determined to stick out my articles and pass the tough professional board exam, so that the title 'Attorney of the Supreme Court' could be added to my CV.

I also found elements of legal practice intriguing. Observing Katz – and other formidable lawyers – interacting with clients on a good day was akin to watching a good actor give a spellbinding performance or master-class.

Attorneys were then denied the right of appearance in the high court, and much of our litigation was strategised – and in the end given voice – by the advocates housed across the road in Innes Chambers. Clerks were obliged to prepare the brief thoroughly for the advocate before sending it across in a pale blue folder and green ribbon. You had to familiarise yourself with the claim, prepare witness statements, if relevant, and draft instructions for the advocate.

This stringent regime was not always applied at certain other firms of attorneys. On one of my visits to Innes Chambers, a young advocate told me of receiving a visit from a black client, accompanied by a huge bundle of unsorted papers, from a well-known 'struggle attorney' (a lawyer in constant receipt of legal work relating to anti-apartheid work, usually paid for by overseas funding). After straightening out the sheaths of paper, the advocate discovered that the poor client's house had been attached and already sold in execution of judgment.

The client's misery was entirely a consequence of the gross negligence of the attorney, who enjoyed a lucrative lifestyle funded largely by the anti-apartheid movement! I asked the advocate how he dealt with the situation. He said: 'Well, I shouldn't strictly have said it, but I felt so sorry for the man, who had lost his worldly possessions, that I told him I could do nothing further for him; but that he should leave his current attorney, and engage another one to sue the present one for damages.'

The negligent attorney went on to enjoy a very prominent political career under the aegis of the ANC.

I learned at the feet of the lawmasters. Some of the greatest legal talents ever seen in South Africa were alive and still in practice at the Bar – some at the tail end of their careers: Rex Welsh QC, Sydney Kentridge SC, Arthur Suzman QC, Isie Maisels QC, and Ernie Wentzel SC. All, regrettably – with the singular exception of Kentridge, now knighted and still practising in London in his mid-eighties – are now dead.

What was noteworthy was how quietly spoken Welsh, Suzman and Maisels were, often difficult to hear in open court. While most judges were fairly merciless with inaudible or incoherent counsel, none I ever encountered was anything other than excessively deferential whenever one of the giants appeared in their courtrooms.

Welsh was arguably the most admired and distinguished, and certainly one of the most liberal, of counsel at the Bar. One of his favourite young advocates, then completing his pupilage, Sean Naidoo, had prepared his application for admission to the Bar. I was approached by him to handle the matter, and instructed to brief both Welsh and Edwin Cameron to appear in court. There can be few simpler and more straightforward legal applications. However, I had no prior experience and proceeded to the nerve centre of Edward Nathan, designated 'Wang room', where in quarters closely resembling the set of *2001: A Space Odyssey* a group of typists surrounded by enormous computer consoles flicked a button and, as if by magic, produced a precedent document on every conceivable legal process. This was in the seemingly prehistoric, pre-personal computer and pre-Microsoft pioneering days of what seems now primitive technology. But in 1984 the Wang centre was at the cutting edge of the 'white heat of the technological revolution'.

I eventually despatched the document for signature to Welsh. The next day a chilling message awaited me: 'Contact Mr Welsh urgently.' When I saw him, 'Where is it decreed,' he rasped, 'that the applicant's race is a requirement for admission? You describe Naidoo as "an Indian male".' He went on: 'Edwin Cameron has searched the statutes and cannot find any racial status as a requirement on the admission papers. Where did you find it? Perhaps you have other sources?'

So many legal processes, especially those involving sales of a business or property, required the deponent to state his race, that the safest legal assumption then was to furnish it. But the Admission of Advocates Act did not require it – and I had just learned several important, if not embarrassing, lessons. (Quite what Welsh would make of today's mandatory racial form-filling, *de rigueur* under an ANC government in pursuit of 'transformation', can only be conjured in the imagination.)

Although Edward Nathan was – and remains – pre-eminently a commercial law practice, its directors were not blind to the encroachment of apartheid on civil liberties and fundamental freedoms. To 'do its bit' – or assuage their consciences – the firm signed up its articled clerks on the Black Sash roster for duty in the 'Commissioner's Court' in Albert Street in downtown Johannesburg. This dismal place – housed in an appropriately decaying building – was where 'pass offenders' were tried, a legal charade. It has been estimated that between 1916 and 1984[25] an incredible 17 745 000 black South Africans were arrested and/or prosecuted under a battery of pass laws and influx control regulations. They were designed to staunch the flow of blacks to the urban areas – and maintain tight control over those legally in the cities and 'white' suburbs.

The 'Commissioner' was the 'Commissioner for Plural Relations', and the Black Sash, one of South Africa's most prominent and effective anti-apartheid NGOs – inaugurated by concerned white women to oppose the removal of Coloureds from the voters' roll in the 1950s – monitored the proceedings. They had observed that the average pass offender was 'processed' by the apartheid machine in less than three minutes. Generally, the hapless transgressor was not legally represented. Even the most benevolent employer could seldom afford the time to provide an excuse or explanation for his employee's 'violation'; and many were unemployed, their 'illegal' presence in the city grim testimony to the collapse of the so-called rural 'reserve economy'.

However, the presence of ranks of young lawyers, suitably gowned and armed with the particulars of the law and some form of defence, delayed proceedings and slowed down the grinding bureaucracy. We often succeeded in obtaining a temporary reprieve or getting the matter thrown out.

Duty in Albert Street exposed apartheid's wrecking-ball effect on human lives, and frequently left lawyers far more aware of the conditions that millions of their fellow South Africans endured, usually out of sight of most white South Africans.[26]

The first year of my legal apprenticeship (1983) coincided with events that profoundly affected the political direction of South Africa. The narrow reformist gauge on which PW Botha was driving South Africa gathered a head of steam with the announcement of the creation of a Tricameral parliament. In this, the minority Coloureds and Indians would achieve a parliamentary presence, largely subordinate to and in separate chambers from the white representatives. Inevitably, the internal and external leadership of the struggle intensified their opposition to this perceived tinkering which left unaddressed the question of black inclusion.

The most visible – and violent – indication of the ANC's rejection-ism was the detonation of a car bomb outside the headquarters of the South African Air Force in downtown Pretoria. It exploded as personnel were exiting the building, and 19 were killed and more than two hundred injured. If the ANC could strike at the heart of the apartheid military machine, where, observers asked, might the campaign end – and at what cost?

The Tricameral plan moved ahead largely because of the buy-in which Botha's constitutional architect, Chris Heunis, obtained from the fairly representative Coloured Labour Party. But it also led to the creation of the largest internally based opposition movement, the United Democratic Front (UDF). The new mass-based organisation was effectively the domestic stalking horse for the struggle leadership, largely confined to prison or exile.

The UDF was launched in August 1983 in Mitchells Plain, Cape Town. Dignified by local luminaries including Desmond Tutu and Allan Boesak, it was astute enough not to personalise its leadership in either one man or one organisation. Representing – or claiming to – 320 community groups, trade unions, and women's and student organisations, it present-ed the apartheid state with a multi-headed Hydra, which (correctly) its organisers reckoned made it far more difficult to isolate, ban or detain. Its size and diversity would effectively hamper the state's repressive zeal to close it down.

The increasing polarisation and militarisation of South Africa – now entering a mature and decisive phase – showed up, painfully but clear-ly, the limits of the PFP's reformist stance. While the same was true for Buthelezi's Inkatha movement, he had a force on the ground – and covert state support for Inkatha's increased militancy – while the PFP mere-ly had a parliamentary presence. And while the Progs fully opposed the Tricameral option, they were committed to sitting in the white House of the newly enlarged parliament. This Left-Right pincer movement had a somewhat radicalising effect on the PFP; and when its Federal Congress convened the following year in November 1984, it resolved to open the party's membership to all races, despite the statutory prohibition, and also voted to oppose military conscription.

Botha's National Party decreed a white referendum on the new system to be held on 2 November 1983. Except for managing the operation at Helen Suzman's Houghton Primary School polling station on referendum day itself, I played little part in the campaign – the workload at Edward Nathan precluding any wider involvement.

However, it became apparent that the PFP, estranged from the more direct activism of the UDF, was in serious danger of alienating itself from its own core constituency. This was personally and directly demonstrated to me when I was travelling with Michael Katz to a Reserve Bank meeting in Pretoria. While urbane and socially progressive, Katz also enjoyed his proximity and access to political power, nurturing a particularly close relationship with the Finance minister, Barend du Plessis. He and many other members of the profession, even the most sophisticated, were clearly buying the government line that the Tricameral parliament was 'a step in the right direction'. In the car, I expressed my vehement opposition to the plan, and was not altogether surprised by Michael's response that he intended to vote 'Yes' in the referendum.

The PFP's awkward position was compounded by the unsurprising decision of the rightist Conservative Party also to support a 'No' vote, which meant that Van Zyl Slabbert was asking his supporters to vote along the same lines as Andries Treurnicht. PFP voters deserted the party in droves on referendum day and voted 'Yes'.

The government gained further support from the business community, including certain titans of commerce and industry notionally opposed to the policies of the National Party. With a few notable – perhaps heroic – exceptions, such as Anglo's Harry Oppenheimer and Gavin Relly and Premier's Tony Bloom, a vast swathe of business leadership was delighted that the NP was courting them and they reciprocated the ardour. They sponsored a large advertisement in the *Sunday Times*, urging readers to affirm the Tricameral proposals. Their endorsement concluded with a warning that time would prove to be as fatuous as it was wrong: 'A no vote must have harmful political and economic consequences both nationally and internationally.'[27]

At Houghton Primary, I saw hundreds of normally doughty Helen Suzman-supporting residents avert their gaze as they headed into the polling station to make their mark against us. The results – 65,95% for the Tricameral reforms and 33,53% against in a 76% poll – caused massive and immense gloom in our ranks. An increasingly confrontational and violent phase of politics ensued. (In truth, if spread across the total population of the country, the majority of whom were denied a voice in the referendum, no more than 5% or 6% of the total voting-age population approved the new constitution.)

I was always amused by sometime NP-supporting corporate citizens who seamlessly crossed the aisle to embrace the ANC in the run-up to the 1994 election; and once cynically observed that: 'Business has never met a government it didn't like, either National or African national.' English business interests, long regarded as 'oppositional' by the NP, were now invited to 'sit by the fire' and many leaped at the chance.

The fact that some leading members of the Jewish business community in the 1980s also increasingly and visibly identified with Botha's initiatives – including Sol Kerzner, Sidney Frankel and Louis Shill – caused some unease among more enlightened members of the community with longer memories who were convinced that the NP's reforms would end disastrously. And, here again, the spectre of the '*Hofjuden*' or 'Court Jews' had a lengthy, if not exactly a distinguished, provenance in Jewish European history, from where many South African families originated. Amos Elon, in his riveting history of the Jews in pre-war Germany,[28] highlights the phenomenon with reference to Bismarck's 19th-century banker, Gerson Bleichröder: 'Bleichröder served power, never trying to change it. He was the last of the great German Court Jews ... said to be the richest man in Berlin, he could have been a character in a Balzac novel. Bismarck systematically exploited his hunger for honours and decorations and his craving for social prominence.'[29]

Bleichröder, who became the first Prussian Jew permitted to add the coveted 'von' to his name, had a fair number of kindred spirits in the ranks of South Africa's latter-day business community.

On 13 July 1984 the last all-white parliament terminated, and on 5 September prime minister PW Botha was unanimously elected to the post of Executive President by an electoral college which, conveniently (and again to the disadvantage of minority dissenting parties, such as the PFP), consisted only of the majority parties of all three houses. At a 'thank you' party – or wake – for her Houghton workers after the referendum meltdown, Helen Suzman confidently asserted that the entire Tricameral edifice would 'collapse due to its complexity and unworkability'. In fact, it did not, and endured until the first democratic elections a decade hence.

Although the UDF worked zealously, often using questionable and intimidatory tactics, the elections for both Coloured and Indian Houses went ahead. The Front succeeded in ensuring exceptionally low polls in both communities, which did not prevent the new MPs taking their seats, but placed a major question mark over their legitimacy.

The Coloured Labour Party was the only one of the new Tricameral entrants that could boast reasonable community depth and support. Initially established to oppose the NP's ghettoisation of Coloureds, it became, after 1984, an essential prop in the new design. Allan Hendrickse, its leader, himself a previous victim of detention without trial, accepted a post in

PW Botha's cabinet. Chris Heunis later told me that he doubted whether tricameralism could have endured had the Labour Party boycotted it. He also recalled that Franklin Sonn, later to emerge as an ANC luminary and as South Africa's first post-apartheid ambassador to Washington, played a crucial role in persuading the hitherto anti-apartheid Labourites to 'enter the system to change it from within'.

When I contacted Franklin Sonn to authenticate Heunis's claim, he advised that he had indeed been consulted by the Labour Party on their fateful decision. On his version, he advised the Labour Party that since it was already participating in the Coloured Persons' Representative Council, any decision to join the Tricameral parliament was 'academic'. He did, however, give the Labour Party credit for maintaining an 'opposition' stance which, in the end, 'made the Tricameral government unworkable.' He denied, however, that his role had been 'crucial'.

The most lucid defence I heard on the merits of the system was given at a dinner party I attended when I was an MP, just as the system was on the verge of being scrapped consequent to the Codesa negotiations. One of my fellow guests was Japie Basson, by then retired from active politics, having spent the best part of forty years as an MP, and as a member of no fewer than five political parties. He began his political life as an NP MP from South West Africa; and migrated through various opposition parties, holding high office in the PFP before being expelled by Van Zyl Slabbert in 1980 for arguing against party policy. He served in the President's Council (forerunner of the Tricameral parliament, with advisory, not legislative powers) and so landed up back in the NP.

He was a person of easy charm and affability, and a gifted raconteur, perhaps precisely because of his multiple political peregrinations. He told me that he doubted whether the NP would have been ready to enter full-throttle negotiations with the black majority had its rank-and-file parliamentarians not been sensitised, through the Tricameral window, to leaders of other race groups on a roughly equivalent basis. An interesting perspective.

During the birth pangs of the Tricameral parliament, and my second year of articles, we received the news that my father, then in his 18th year on the Bench, had been elected to the prestigious ceremonial post of Chancellor of the University of Natal, his *alma mater*. In the sweltering March humidity, the family gathered at the glittering ceremony on the Howard College campus, down the road from the South Ridge Road home of my earliest – and happiest – childhood memories.

In the citation which preceded his installation, the university orator

Professor Colin Gardner, later to become an ANC official in Pieter-maritzburg and a fierce critic of mine, described my father as 'a most distinguished son of this university, who has proved to be an outstandingly learned, humane and just judge.' We were all immensely proud – none more so than Grandpa Jack, by then frail but still extremely alert, though deaf and 92. His immense pride in his son's achievements stemmed from the contrast of his own modest and somewhat impoverished childhood.

That evening was the last time I ever saw him. He died, peacefully, six weeks later.

By the end of the year I had completed my articles of legal clerkship and passed the dreaded attorney's admission board examination, notwith-standing its legendary failure rate, said to hover around fifty per cent. Yet my appetite for legal practice had not improved; in fact, I hungered to do something else, preferably political. I was by now considerably out of the PFP loop, and my earlier intense ardour for the organisation had cooled somewhat.

Micawber-like, I thought 'something would turn up', and decided in the interim to stay on at Edward Nathan as a professional associate. I was assigned to work for Philip Pencharz, one of the firm's heavyweights in a practice crowded with legal big-hitters. Pencharz was to have a major influence on my life and learning.

He was forbidding; had silver hair, a beaked nose, and an imposing man-ner – enough to quiet or even sometimes empty a room. Legend had it that when his secretary once twittered, 'Have a nice day, Mr Pencharz,' he responded: 'I have other ideas.' Yet he usually bullied up, not down, so his contempt and temper were reserved for clients or legal opponents try-ing to take advantage of another's culpability, stupidity or inferior status. An excellent commercial lawyer, he remained a glorious old-fashioned generalist. Through his doors paraded an entire spectrum, from terrified divorcées to top business hot-shots.

The most important lesson I learned from him was never to go for half-measures or sloppy short-cuts. Once, pressed by competing claims on my time, I decided to wing it in a somewhat incompetent opinion. He called me in, looked disparagingly at the document, and said: 'Tell me, Tony, would you go into the supermarket and help yourself to a can of food and leave without paying?' Nonplussed, I responded: 'Of course not … that would be theft.' 'Precisely,' he rejoined, 'but why then do you steal my time?'

I never produced another shoddy legal draft for him. Although I spent a lot of my time feeling like a flea on the back of a cat – to transpose

Matthew Parris's felicitous description of working for Margaret Thatcher – I grew to like Pencharz immensely, although I never entirely lost my awe for him. He was also generous with his time, despite his earlier put-down; and this was all predicated on the fact that he liked me and was as kind to those he favoured as he was dismissive towards those he did not. He was an immensely tough, but not unreasonable, negotiator, and sitting alongside him in numerous conversations and encounters taught me some significant lessons and skills for the time when the entire country's future was to be negotiated eight or so years later.

At his behest I returned to Edward Nathan as a special associate when I became an MP in 1990, which position I retained for four years until I became the party leader.

Philip died, close to 90, in March 2003. I was immensely honoured, but deeply saddened, when his widow Anita asked me to speak at the prayers after his funeral. I said, in part: 'Our gallant friend Philip, whose life we celebrate and whose death we mourn today, was like the "giant Cedar tree in Lebanon" spoken of in the *Book of Ezekiel*, "who towered higher than the other trees" in the legal field. For Philip loved law and its practice. He admired its reach and its strength. He always challenged its form, but respected its limits. He observed precedent, but always pushed the envelope of innovation. He practised both brilliantly and combatively for an extraordinary and unbroken 60-year period.'

During my initial 'Pencharz period' I thought all my stars were coming into alignment: I felt more fulfilled at work; I was dating a very vivacious and pretty girl, Carla; and with some financial assistance from my mother, I occupied a nice apartment in Houghton. My then happy but young life nearly ended.

6

On Saturday morning, 31 March 1985 – my father's 60th birthday – I was in Braamfontein at the Varsity Sports equipment shop buying tennis balls for a match I was to play with Carla and a friend on a campus court. After my purchase, I crossed the road and felt a deep – and unusual – pain in my chest, almost as if a pile of bricks had been dropped on it. I immediately sat down at a bus stop in Jorissen Street; and by now the crushing sensation had been replaced by flu-like symptoms – a weariness, and a tightness around my throat akin to swollen glands. I had generally been untroubled by ill-health but this felt like nothing I had ever experienced before.

I managed to walk back to the tennis court where Carla and her friend were waiting. I said I did not feel well enough to play, and when – with my normal hypochondriacal flourish – I vividly described my symptoms, she insisted I see my doctor immediately. I drove myself to the consulting rooms; my GP was distracted by his own poor health, but insisted that I submit to an ECG at a physician.

Strangely enough, a full hour after the initial attack, I felt pretty much recovered and irritated by having to drive through the Saturday morning traffic to the physician's rooms in Jeppe Street. Dr Isaac Cohen ran a series of electro-cardiogram tests. He said the results were 'disturbing, but probably not serious'; I needed to spend 'twenty-four hours under observation in hospital', but that once blood tests had been administered and analysed I would probably be discharged to return home. I headed home to pack a bag, amazed that this minor discomfort could portend such consequences.

As I was getting my pyjamas and toothbrush packed, the phone rang. It was Dr Cohen. He sounded agitated. 'Look, Tony,' he said, 'I've looked at your ECG again. It is definitely very wrong. I think you are suffering a heart attack, but we need to confirm this with the blood tests. You must get to the Kenridge hospital and under no circumstances are you to drive there yourself.' I was staggered and suddenly felt immediately weakened, more by the news than by the coronary episode I had apparently suffered.

I was duly whisked to the Kenridge nursing home by my stepfather Paul, and a wheelchair and nurse awaited me as I was speedily admitted to the coronary care unit where oxygen was immediately administered and a ghastly pill – apparently consisting of TNT, or some such derivative – was placed under my tongue. I thought if the heart attack didn't kill me, the throbbing headache generated by this artery-dilating medicine would.

The next day, after a battery of tests, the gloomy prognosis was confirmed: I had suffered from a 'myocardial infarction' – the destruction of a portion of the heart muscle as a result of the occlusion of a coronary artery, to give its precise medical meaning. I was 28 years old, a fact not unnoticed by the nurses attending me and the other unfortunates in the ward. 'But you're far too young,' one or another clucked solicitously. I felt something of a freak as friends, or mere acquaintances, rushed to my side, no doubt to wish me well, but also, no doubt, to see this phenomenon of one certainly so young and seemingly healthy felled by such a dramatic medical event.

While my mother busied herself chasing away the visitors and bringing me copious amounts of home-made chicken soup ('Jewish penicillin'), I fell into a deep, dark depression. I was resentful and occasionally tearful: how would the rest of my life turn out, or indeed – with this intimation of mortality – how much of life did I have left?

I resolved to give up smoking and to de-stress my life at work. It wasn't so much the work pace that concerned me; it was the essential lack of enjoyment. I had read the cliché (apparently traced back to Confucius) that 'if you choose a job that you enjoy, then you will never have to work a day in your life' – but had yet to experience that reality, if indeed it existed. However, the origins of my heart condition lay neither in the work environment nor in my bad habits, aggravating though they were. The maternal line from which I descended had an extreme disposition to circulatory and cardiac illness.

The year after my infarct, my mother had a major coronary requiring urgent bypass graft surgery. She continued to battle heart disease until her death, at 73, in December 2001. While I recovered fairly quickly from my own situation in 1985, by 1998 I was – on exercise – experiencing severe discomfort from angina. Accordingly I was booked in (after a book-signing tour and a frantic series of rallies) for quadruple coronary bypass surgery, performed at the Milpark hospital on 3 December that year.

It was quite an ordeal, but I walked out of hospital six days after surgery, and six weeks after that led the Democratic Party into the hectic 1999 'Fight Back' general election campaign. My extreme nervousness the night before my open-heart surgery was relieved by an unexpected visit from Nelson Mandela (who was in the hospital visiting someone else, when he heard I had been admitted). A few weeks before he had attacked the DP, and other opposition parties, as 'Mickey Mouse organisations'; I in the same Disneyesque currency had accused him of running a 'Goofy government'. After a knock on my hospital door, I heard the world-famous voice call out: 'Hullo, Mickey Mouse, this is Goofy, can I come in?' It was Mandela. And in he came, radiating his renowned charm. It was a good augury for the operation.

As for the heart disease, I have learned to live with it and the uncertainty it brings, by trying some modest adjustments in lifestyle, doing exercise, having check-ups – but for the rest of the time, essentially forgetting about it. Between my first heart attack in 1985 and my surgery in 1998, I had attempted, with many unforgivable relapses, to give up smoking. The day before surgery I finally stopped smoking, but for the occasional cigar.

While I was recuperating at home from my initial infarct, Louise Tager, dean of the Wits Law faculty when I was a student, came to see me. She was still on the academic staff and said the faculty was keen to recruit lecturers with a professional as well as an academic qualification – and urged me to apply. I did not see myself as an academic, but reckoned that a year or two teaching law might help route my future somewhere beyond law. I had simply a desire to move on – and out – from legal practice. After interviews I was offered a post as lecturer in law at Wits, commencing at the beginning of 1986.

The mid-1980s was a period of extreme violence. ANC guerrilla operations intensified with all manner of targets being hit, usually with limpet mines, from (literally) Wimpy Bars to recreational saloons – the infamous Magoo's Bar on the Durban beachfront being a spectacular example – to attacks on the offices of Anglo American and Anglo-Vaal in Johannesburg; various government, provincial and municipal offices; the homes of Tricameral politicians (including Amichand Rajbansi); various policemen's residences; and the Sasol III and V petroleum plants. The SADF shot up and killed all manner of ANC members and their families, numbering some twelve people, in cross-border raids into Gaborone in neighbouring Botswana.

One ANC operative, who bombed civilians, came to have his name linked closely to my own. He was Andrew Zondo. On Christmas Eve, 1985, he placed a bomb in a flowerpot just outside the Amanzimtoti shopping centre on the Natal South Coast. From some distance away, using a remote device, he detonated the bomb which killed five and injured 40, black and white, all civilians.

A few months later, after his capture, he was charged with multiple counts of murder, and appeared before a judge and two assessors at the Scottburgh circuit court. The judge in question was my father and, in the absence of finding extenuating circumstances, Zondo was sentenced to death. The conviction and death sentence were confirmed by the Appellate Division among whose number sat Judge Mick Corbett, who would preside as Chief Justice of South Africa under both presidents De Klerk and Mandela.

Zondo became a *cause célèbre*, not simply because the ANC saw him as a martyr, but also because it assisted their demonisation of me (as in the case of my military service) as 'the son of an apartheid operative who ordered the execution of comrade Andrew Zondo' – to use one of their more recent depictions of the event.[30]

Shortly before the 1999 election campaign, one of the ANC's more heavyweight members, then-Health minister Nkosazana Zuma, had this to say in a debate in parliament on the Truth Commission on 25 February 1999: 'The depth of our humanity,' she said with her customary immodesty, 'is illustrated by the fact that the judge who had the discretion to hang, or not to hang, a young revolutionary like Andrew Zondo is still a judge, and his progeny enjoys the direct fruit of the very freedom that Andrew died for.'[31]

Zuma was wrong on all counts – my father having long since retired and, in his view, the sentence was mandatory, not discretionary. But Zuma never allowed facts to interfere with her prejudices.

I often wondered whether there was merit in the ANC's attack on my father's judgment, which certainly contrasted with a long line of liberal decisions. But while my father was opposed to the death penalty, he viewed judicial office as a constraint and felt that if the law prescribed the maximum penalty, then he was duty-bound to impose it. While preparing this volume I asked him for his insights into the Zondo case. The essence of his reply is as follows.

Zondo, who was represented by Denis Kuny SC, did not give evidence at the trial itself, but only on the question of extenuating circumstances. The evidence against him was given mainly by an accomplice who was an excellent witness. He testified that the murders had been carefully planned and that after the event Zondo complained bitterly that only five people had been killed. There was also evidence (not challenged) that he had acted contrary to the policy of the ANC not to target innocent civilians.

Zondo said his motive was political and he had tried to warn the public (on this, he was disbelieved). My father's judgment on extenuating circumstances went like this:

'We live in a divided and deeply troubled society: a society divided by differences and deeply troubled by its failure to resolve them. The monopoly of power and its fruits rest in the hands of the white minority while the black majority are less affluent, voteless, and many live in conditions of squalor and degradation. It is against this background that this case must be judged. It had been held, quite rightly in my view, [that] youth, either alone or in conjunction with other circumstances, may be an extenuating circumstance. [The] youth of the accused must be a factor operating in his favour. Moreover the accused did not commit this offence from base motives such as greed, or lust, or envy but because he wished to help his people. That must also count in his favour.

'On the other hand, there are matters which count against him, namely:

'There has been unchallenged evidence that he acted against the clear policy of the ANC not to attack innocent civilians.

'Not only did the accused express no remorse but he complained bitterly that only five people had been killed.

'Finally, there is the nature of the crime itself. This is not a case where a government building or institution had been attacked which would have been serious enough. What makes this crime so appalling is that it was committed against the civilian population as a whole. Young and old, black and white, innocent and guilty. Anyone shopping at the centre on Xmas Eve was at risk of being killed.

'The law requires that the onus of proving that extenuating circumstances are present rests upon the accused, not upon the state. We are unable to find that that onus has been discharged. [Extenuating] circumstances have not been proved to be present.'

The Zondo decision continued as a subject of debate for over twenty years; but another decision of my father's in 1985 had far-reaching consequences – particularly for the thousands of detainees arrested and held incommunicado under the state of emergency proclaimed that year. This was the case of 'Hurley and Another v Minister of Law and Order'.[32] John Hlophe – later to achieve a degree of notoriety as the controversial Judge President of the Cape High Court – was at the time a doctoral student at Cambridge and was moved to write of my father's judgment as displaying 'a relatively liberal attitude … (which) should be warmly welcomed.'

The case arose out of an application brought by Archbishop Denis Hurley for the release of the director of the Durban Christian organisation, Diakonia, Paddy Kearney. The other applicant was Kearney's wife, the noted legal journalist Carmel Rickard. Kearney was detained under the notorious Section 29 of the Internal Security Act (1982). My father ordered his release. It was a landmark, precedent-breaking decision which turned its back on a host of previous judgments which held that for the arresting officer's 'reason to believe' it was sufficient for the functionary only to honestly think that he had 'reason to believe' that the detainee had committed an offence.

The judgment was acclaimed by jurisprudential scholars throughout South Africa and was a decisive blow in favour of the liberty of the individual. Professor Laurence J Boulle of the University of Natal wrote: 'Leon J's judgment establishes a landmark in South African jurisprudence, in the development of administrative law, and in the judicial protection of civil rights. For the first time, a detention order issued in terms of Section 29 … has been invalidated and the detainee's release secured. The decision deals with issues of a deep and universal constitutionality: limited government, separation of powers, justiciability of executive action, and the liberty of the individual.'

If the state intended to use the law as 'an instrument for control and domination', it would have to 'reckon with the judiciary'. Boulle's optimism arising from the judgment was, however, tempered firmly by the objective conditions in which the courts operated and mass detentions occurred: 'Despite "Hurley" many hundreds remain in detention without due process and the system is likely to endure on a large scale in South Africa as long as the constitutional agenda is not properly addressed.'

Needless to say, the ANC in parliament and elsewhere never referred to the Hurley judgment or any other liberal rulings given by my father.

In July 1987, after a bout of ill-health, my father took early retirement at 62. He was also intensely disillusioned by having in 1987 been passed over by the National Party administration for the judge-presidency which his seniority entitled him to expect. He was also, he told me, intensely bored after 22 years of trying cases. His colleagues and the media lauded his life in the law. In a full-page interview in the Durban *Sunday Tribune*[33] he was slightly less cautious in his public pronouncements than usual, but still circumspect when he noted: 'What has happened over the years is that the rule of law has been eroded and the powers of the Supreme Court in that way have been reduced. And the traditional role of the Supreme Court, of standing as a bulwark between the executive and the liberty of the subject, has been reduced and we have become to a large extent, triers of cases.

'I am in favour of a bill of rights. I think it would give us a better chance but until the Law Commission has completed its findings it would be unfair to comment.'

The *Sunday Times*[34] commented: 'Mr Justice Ramon Leon, 62, left more than his chambers on Monday – he also left an impression in South Africa's legal profession which will be felt for a long time to come.' He told us – his family – that on the rare occasions when he imposed the death sentence he would be 'physically ill'. In retirement he became an outspoken opponent of the death sentence.

Undoubtedly the lynchpin event of 1985 – which lit so many of the explosive forces that engulfed South Africa for the next half-decade – was PW Botha's 'Rubicon' speech. The Rubicon is remembered as the name of a small river marking the boundary between ancient Rome and Gaul, which Caesar crossed – in 49 BC – and thereby irretrievably committed his army to war. In modern South Africa it became a synonym for a missed opportunity: the widening gulf between the outer limits of Botha's modest reforms and the minimum expectations of his opponents. The speech was delivered at the National Party congress in Durban on 15 August against the background of increasing violence which Botha's piecemeal reforms had unleashed, and the repressive imposition by the state of a partial state of emergency in 36 key magisterial districts.[35]

Botha and his media managers might have done better to have pondered the truth of Edmund Burke's 'On Conciliation with America'. He wrote in 1775: 'A nation is not governed which is perpetually to be conquered.'

The egregious Pik Botha had traversed the world to proclaim that the speech would herald a new golden age of negotiation and genuine power-sharing, including black participation in government, and even the un-conditional release of Mandela. This build-up flattered only to deceive. No new initiatives were announced. Instead, Botha warned the world 'not to push us too far' – stating he would not succumb to hostile inter-national pressure and agitation, which he considered would only encour-age militants.[36]

He soon descended into a pit of rhetoric which only his immediate audience of the NP diehard faithful could approve. In a searing indict-ment of Botha and his government, *Power, Pride and Prejudice*, the academic Henry Kenney wrote: 'The plain truth was that Botha blew it. No South African leader had ever had so large an audience, for his address to the Natal congress of his party had become a global media event. In front of millions of television viewers Botha chose to deliver the kind of defiant xenophobic speech guaranteed to stir the locals, and equally guaranteed to make foreigners wonder what was happening in South Africa if boors like these were in charge.'[37]

The worldwide disabusal resulted in a serious run on South Africa's hitherto strong currency. Chase Manhattan Bank executed a decision to stop rolling over loans to South African borrowers; they were followed by other financial institutions, leading to a flight of capital from the country and the worst financial crisis experienced in decades.[38]

Nearly twenty years after Botha conspicuously failed to cross his own Rubicon, I was given a fascinating insight into some of the background behind the speech, by his chief constitutional negotiator, Chris Heunis.

Heunis, unlike certain other superannuated politicians, had spent his years since retiring from frontline politics quietly practising law in Somerset West (where he died in 2007). He kept a low public profile, ex-cept when Marthinus van Schalkwyk bowed out of the DA to align with the ANC, when as he put it to me, 'as a matter of principle', he publicly endorsed me at a DA fundraising breakfast in late 2001.

Three years after that, in 2004, one of my parliamentary colleagues, Sarel Haasbroek, as detailed elsewhere, arranged a convivial lunch for Heunis and me in the Cape winelands. Heunis explained that he had written the first draft of the famous speech; but that on the document being circulated to key cabinet colleagues, 'Pik Botha deliberately leaked it to the English press.' A few days before the speech was to be delivered in Durban, Heunis was summoned by Botha to his residence at Groote Schuur. En route there he saw a *Cape Argus* placard proclaiming an 'exclusive' on the speech.

A visibly furious Botha met him at the door, and told him he would certainly not deliver the 'Prog speech' widely trailed in the *Argus*. Heunis said it was unclear whether it was its contents or Pik Botha's leaking of the speech that had infuriated PW Botha more. 'I, however, told him,' Heunis recounted, 'that there was no other speech I could write and that he should do the next draft himself.' This was the only time he, essentially, 'walked out on the president'. Heunis's ideas for bringing blacks directly into the cabinet and other ground-breaking suggestions did not survive into the final draft.[39]

On Rubicon night itself, I was in Clifford Garrun's flat, with a group of friends, watching Botha's dismal performance. It filled me with dread and foreboding. Quite aside from the punitive damage to be unleashed on South Africa by the wider world, it profoundly unsettled my small universe, especially after the coronary episode. I saw little prospect of peaceful change and gave serious thought, for the first time, to emigration.

I went so far as to write to a relative – 'Cookie' Leon, a distinguished Second World War RAF fighting ace – who had tired of the conservatism of his farming neighbours in Tzaneen and in the early 1970s had gone with his entire family to Australia. He readily agreed to serve as a 'sponsor' had I pressed ahead with my initial inkling to 'pack for Perth', which the Nats sneeringly dubbed as the acronym of the PFP.

Fortunately, I never proceeded further. But thousands of white South Africans of similar age and qualifications, depressed by Botha's recalcitrance and shocked by deepening levels of anarchic violence, did leave – taking their skills and expertise.

When I was a backbench MP, in 1992, on a study trip with the parliamentary justice group to Europe, I spent a pleasant evening at a Paris restaurant; and the talk turned to emigration. My Conservative Party colleague, Chris de Jager, MP for Bethal, and later a member of the TRC, said: 'Ag, Tony, it's easy for you to leave South Africa. You can be a Jew anywhere in the world. I can, however, only be an Afrikaner in South Africa.'

I was deeply struck, even moved, by Chris's declaration. However, from the vantage point of 15 years later, Chris was mistaken. Hundreds of thousands of Afrikaners (whites and Coloureds) have emigrated, and today Auckland, Sydney, Perth, Toronto and vast swathes of the south-western suburbs of London are filled with Afrikaans-speaking emigrants, complete – in many instances – with their own churches and schools.[40]

Probably an even greater number of the estimated one million whites who have left since 1994 are English-speaking. Before 1994 they saw the threat as onerous military conscription. Since then, on the anecdotal evidence available, the emigrants have done so from a matrix of motivations, with crime and affirmative action topping the list. Some – I suspect a minority – were unable to reconcile themselves to the reality of majority rule.

Tellingly, in my lengthy telephone conversation with PW Botha, detailed elsewhere, just weeks before his death he told me that, 'strange though it was for him', his eldest son Pieter had settled permanently in England.

Botha died peacefully at home some twenty-one years after the Rubicon speech. He was ninety. I was amazed to read a rambling but essentially fulsome tribute to him penned by Thabo Mbeki in his weekly letter in *ANC Today*.[41] While Mbeki had the intellectual honesty to include many of the vicious attacks the ANC had launched on '*die groot krokodil*', he ended musing curiously on Oliver Tambo and PW and the 'tragedy' that they had never met. He wrote:

'At the beginning of 1989 PW Botha suffered from a slight stroke that ultimately led to his retirement from active politics, having opened the door to the liquidation of the inhuman system of apartheid to whose construction and defence he had dedicated his life. He left the challenging task of the completion of the work he had started to his successor, FW de Klerk.'

Later in 1989, too, Tambo suffered from a massive stroke that took him out of active politics, creating the possibility that his close friend and comrade, Nelson Mandela, would, finally, officially assume leadership of the African National Congress.

So the fates decreed that Tambo, born in 1917, a year later than Botha, should leave the world of the living in 1993, a year before the realisation of his dream of liberation. Botha followed 13 years later. Of them we can say, echoing the Palestinian leader, Yasser Arafat, when he spoke of the Israeli, Yitzhak Rabin, that they were partners in the creation of the 'peace of the brave that is our blessing, but, again, tragically, seems, still, to be beyond the reach of the sister peoples of Palestine and Israel.'

Quite why Mbeki thought a meeting between the two nationalist leaders – white and black – would have proved productive is entirely unclear. The day after the Rubicon address, Tambo (perhaps aided by Mbeki's pen, since the latter was his speech-writer) denounced Botha in extreme, even violent terms: he was the leader of 'a clique of diehard racists, hidebound reactionaries and bloodthirsty braggarts … Posturing like a pathetic dictator in the mould of his predecessor and mentor [Hitler], whose fascist rule was brought to an end 40 years ago, PW Botha stood last night pretending he can withstand and defeat all the forces at home and abroad that are engaged in struggle.'[42]

Whether the thin-skinned and quick-tempered Botha would easily have ignored these damning epithets is seriously open to question. However, it is entirely in character for the ANC to praise in death those they unreservedly damned while alive. As Pieter-Dirk Uys the arch-satirist observed: 'Hypocrisy is the vaseline which lubricates our politics!'

7

I returned to Wits as a member of the academic staff in the law faculty in mid-January 1986. But I unexpectedly became a candidate for the Johannesburg city council. Thus my three-year career as a lecturer coincided with my first – intense – foray into representative politics.[43] This did not prevent me, however, from assuming a hefty lecturing load. While I juggled my academic with my civic duties, I prided myself on never missing a lecture – no matter the turbulence outside the campus in which I was engaged. I decided, given my increasing political profile in the Johannesburg press, never to discuss party politics in the lecture theatre. I didn't want students to feel disadvantaged if their political preferences – and prejudices – did not coincide with my own.

I was nervous at first as a lecturer. However, I took John Dugard's advice on confronting a class of three hundred: 'Attack is the best form of defence.' I picked on various hapless students to answer questions on the readings they had seldom done in advance (exactly as I had not done in my student days) before they could expose the gaping holes in my own knowledge base; or the fact that I was, generally, only a lecture or two ahead of them.

As for marking, there can be few less enchanting tasks than reading up to three hundred versions of the same answer, recycled. Dugard told me the best way to mark an exam script was to think of yourself as the candidate and ask how you'd feel if the marker rushed through, not bothering to read the answer properly. That proved to be a corrective.

The other item of advice from another old hand was that 'the standard sets itself.' I tended to imagine (quite falsely) that the students would attain a certain level of excellence – and marked down my first batch of scripts. Yet if I stuck to my guns most of the class would fail. Accordingly, after reading a few more of their offerings, I went back and adjusted upward the first, more severely marked papers. In this way, the good were lifted up by the bad, and the majority passed on the basis that whatever the lecturer's objective standards might be, you couldn't fail most of the class.

Another consequence of my brief academic career was the opportunity to reacquaint myself with constitutional issues, teaching a course on the subject. Against a background of an ever-widening state of emergency, mass arrests and detentions, and the campaign of ungovernability un-leashed by the exiled ANC and the UDF, abstruse concepts such as a bill of rights and participatory democracy seemed abstract indeed. The climate in South Africa was, to put it mildly, inclement. But there were incipient moves in such worthy organisations as Lawyers for Human Rights, on whose local executive I sat, to create some kind of following wind for a new constitutional order.

The course also gave me – and the students – an opportunity to glimpse the ANC's constitutional thinking at the time. Although texts of the banned movement were totally proscribed for general reading, for academic pur-poses various texts were allowed to be kept 'on reserve' in the Law Library. In the mid-1980s, beyond the level of rhetoric, the Congress was generally unrevealing about a future rights-based jurisdiction. Their most notable legal scholar, Albie Sachs, specifically warned (in an article I prescribed for my students) of the 'danger' of a bill of rights which could (in his phrase) become a form of 'Judocracy' frustrating the popular will.

Sachs's writings at the time were in strong contrast to his activism after 1994 as a Constitutional Court judge – deciding, among other things, to scrap the death penalty and to legitimate gay marriage (or civil unions); whatever the intrinsic merits of both, they went hard against the popular will of the significant majority of all South Africans.

Dugard established, with foreign funding, the Centre for Applied Legal Studies, where some of the best and brightest local luminaries (particularly Edwin Cameron, Gilbert Marcus and Halton Cheadle) held court and pioneered impressive research – tracking and quantifying extensive data on the state's encroachment on remaining liberties.

My professional career at Wits was to be little more than a staging post for a full-time political career. When I was elected to parliament in September 1989 I was – in terms of legislation – obliged to resign, which I did. I retained links with the Law School, however, at Mureinik's suggestion, as a 'distinguished visiting lecturer' for some years.

Far more importantly, however, my Wits law links enabled me to draw on a powerhouse of intellectual talent: first when I was appointed DP justice spokesman in 1992, and shortly thereafter when I persuaded party leader Zach de Beer that the party needed to produce a draft bill of rights for South Africa. Because of my faculty ties and personal friendships I must have been the best-advised opposition politician of the time. Many Sundays in my Orange Grove home were spent with Mureinik, Cameron, Dennis Davis and Marcus, aided by my brother Peter and colleague Douglas Gibson.

Although Cameron and Davis were then decidedly more ANC than DP they were happy to lend their intellectual idealism and pragmatic legal grasp to ensure that I went back to parliament – and later to the constitutional negotiations in Kempton Park – armed and equipped with an impressive agenda and proposals.

My links with Wits were to continue with my election by the Convocation in 1991 to the University Council, the institution's governing body. This was an honour – and indeed several denizens of Johannesburg and South African commerce and industry, and a number of illustrious public figures from judges to politicians, to senior struggle activists, served on it. I felt suitably exalted. However, the sensation was short-lived: the council was soon engulfed and almost consumed by the messy and at times violent process of transformation gripping the country and the universities. The howling demand for root-and-branch change sweeping South Africa meant that Wits, for the next decade or so, became a sort of local lightning conductor for many of the forces contending for national power.

Around the same time as my election, I was invited to the University of Natal in Pietermaritzburg to deliver the Edgar Brookes Academic Freedom Lecture. Borrowing from a heartfelt plea which appeared in a journal by the elegant Cape Town poet and academic Stephen Watson, I described the temper of the times:

'Any university, by definition, is a fragile plant: its defences are easy to breach, because by its very nature it is, or should be, an open institution, susceptible to outsiders. Its barriers, if they exist at all, exist in the realm of academic standards, ideas, argument and discourse, not of physical barricades or heavy-duty metal. The ivory tower, properly so-called, belongs, if anywhere at all, in the intellectual architecture of a university campus. But at Wits and other campuses, the totality of its qualities – openness, moderation and reasonableness – in the temper of the tempestuous 1990s have become the sum of its defects.'

The situation in fact became far worse. Violence erupted on the campus with increased frequency, and I recall attending one council meeting in conditions of actual siege. We were instructed to park our cars, as usual, in the Senate House garage. There we were met by beefy members of the university security department who escorted us to the meeting via a rear elevator to avoid protesting students who threatened to take us hostage.

Not everyone on campus was afforded such protection. In about 1995, one of the university's senior registrars, Bruce Dickson – an estimably polite and diffident man who was in charge of the administrative side of our meetings – was, indeed, taken hostage by the chief shop steward of the militant union, Nehawu, to which many of the university's non-academic staff belonged. More bizarre and brazen was the lack of consequential action. After Dickson was released, his captor, Dan Motaung, was arrested and charged with kidnapping. He was found guilty and given a suspended sentence.

Motaung was also dismissed, quite correctly, from the university. But then – in an attempt to mediate the ongoing trench warfare between the ever-accommodating university authorities and the increasingly militant Nehawu – he (with several others who had been involved in the hostage-taking) was re-employed. Since no manager of any department or division of Wits would have this egregious man on their staff (no doubt fearing, in a dispute, that they too might be taken captive) Motaung was paid a salary for no work. Incredibly – and as an apt *pièce de résistance* of this entire unfortunate epoch – he was appointed by the union as a representative on the selection committee appointed to choose the university's next vice chancellor and principal!

Backsliding and moral equivocation became the standard response of the university administration; those they confronted believed any grievance justified any tactic.

The background to the loss of control on the campus was obscure and complex. In some instances, as in France in 1968, the universities were seen as a site of struggle to be conquered as the logical outcome of the ANC-inspired campaign of 'liberation before education', and the general milieu of ungovernability which walked in awkward lock-step with negotiations with government in the 1990s.

There was also a contestation for power between the radical fringe of black students and union militants emboldened by favourable changes in the political weather, and an increasingly nervous and insecure university leadership unsure of how to deal with the rousing demands for transformation, oft-repeated but seldom defined. Often, individual demands for restitution, no matter how absurd or extreme, were conflated with campus-wide demands for radical change. One such incident affected the tail-end of my father's chancellorship of Natal University in April 1992.

A student at the Durban campus, the spectacularly ill-named Knowledge Mdlalose, was excluded from the law faculty on academic grounds.[44] He had failed numerous exams, but under a very generous provision inserted into the admissions criteria was allowed a further stay of execution. However, the authorities discovered that Mdlalose had abused the provisions of the bridging facilities (to assist educationally disadvantaged students) by applying to different departments with different entry criteria. When they found that some departments had already excluded him, and his academic record justified his final removal, Mdlalose sparked a riot because 'he felt he was being victimised by a certain law lecturer and wished to have his paper marked by an outside academic.'

This extraordinary concession was granted by the principal and vice chancellor, Professor James Leatt, who, in a further attempt to placate angry demonstrators disrupting his campus, agreed to appoint a special Senate Review Committee. It was led by Leatt and comprised three members of staff and two outsiders – one a high-profile ANC activist – to 'form an opinion on Knowledge Mdlalose's future.'

As a wag later commented: 'A little Knowledge is a very dangerous thing.'

My jaw dropped at the appeasement tactics of the university, and I recalled the irrepressible Paul Boberg – my distinguished colleague from the law faculty – who used to dismiss complaining and failing students with the withering put-down: 'You failed the exam because you got too few marks.' Boberg's spirit was not to be found on the timorous Natal campuses.

What made the Knowledge saga more immediate and personal, however, was that the unrest sparked by his proposed exclusion coincided with the university's week-long graduation ceremony – at which, as he had done for the past eight years, my father would officiate and cap the graduands (it was his last week in office). At the medical graduation, earlier in the week, all hell broke loose when a hundred students gathered outside the main entrance to the hall waving banners, chanting slogans and toyi-toying. They hurled insults at the hitherto happy and proud students awaiting graduation, denouncing them as 'sell-outs'. For the first time in the six years since my father had imposed the death sentence on Andrew Zondo, placards appeared stating: 'Leon is a murderer.'

The crowd, according to media reports, were whipped into a frenzy at the prospect of Ramon Leon presiding; whatever the merits or demerits of the Zondo sentence, the activists served early notice that from their vantage the Zondo case would be 'the gift that kept on giving' (as my *Paratus* scribblings were to prove in the hands of Ronald Suresh Roberts and Essop Pahad). As it happened, my father was ill that night and his absence, together with other concessions hastily doled out to the protesters by the hapless and beleaguered Leatt, allowed the ceremony to more or less proceed.

The saga was far from over. The Saturday graduation ceremony had been earmarked as a grand occasion on which the university would confer an honorary doctorate on Nelson Mandela, then president of the ANC, but not yet first citizen of the country. That would be my father's last act as Chancellor.

In the days preceding the ceremony, three people came under immense pressure. The first was Leatt who suggested to my father that he might consider it 'in everyone's interests' not to officiate at the ceremony. Indeed, my father's life 'might be in danger', to which my father apparently coldly responded: 'Well, let them kill me.' My father also − no doubt very frostily − advised that he had every intention of being present and that the university should prepare itself, not least in the matter of its security measures.

Mandela was perhaps the most pressured of all. His normal decorous politeness and sense of *obligé* inclined him to receive the honour from my father; but this ran against the currents unleashed by his own activists who were determined that their icon should not receive his doctorate from one they termed the 'hanging judge'. My father's determination to attend had nothing to do with any bloody-mindedness on his part, but with delivering (as I encouraged him to do) a hard-hitting message about the values which the protesting students, and quiescent administrators, were trampling underfoot.

In the event, Mandela withdrew, citing 'reasons of state'. This, the great Isie Maisels, a friend of Mandela and my father, told me later, was a most 'curious choice of phrase, since Mr Mandela, as of present, does not yet preside over this or any other state.'

The graduation ceremony duly went ahead in the absence of both Mandela and the protesters. My father delivered a farewell message in what the *Sunday Tribune* described as 'a dignified and moving speech'.[45]

For his part, Leatt claimed that in 'this difficult week' Mr Justice Leon had 'kept his cool and his calm'. He had shown he would not be intimidated. Further, Leatt said my father had made 'brave contributions while he was a lawyer, an advocate and a long-serving judge. He made judgments which changed the way the law was understood and interpreted in this country' and had sought to 'keep a semblance of the rule of law and justice' during times of detentions and disappearances of people.

Leatt went so far as to state that the university was 'never willing to yield to pressure', to ask Justice Leon to step down from officiating at any graduation ceremonies.

This remark was of course not accurate. Leatt's public sentiments may have been laudable – but the tidal wave unleashed by various campus forces in the early 1990s was far from spent. Indeed – with singular irony – Mandela himself, when he duly headed the ship of state a few years later, was to feel its eddies. The campuses continued to swirl with militant, often criminal students and workers who looted and vandalised property and kidnapped officials for some years after the ANC's accession to power.

Mandela entered the lists in 1995 (as I reminded parliament) with a strong warning of his own: 'White university rectors are scared of dealing with a disruptive minority of black students. I have literally begged them to prevent the slaughter of our own people. I have closed the chapter. I have begged them. Now they must beg me.'[46]

The University of Natal soon tired of Leatt's ineffectual leadership and he was, in time, replaced as principal.

8

The struggle for transformation at Wits reached its apogee in the long and increasingly vicious and vexatious fight to choose a new vice chancellor and principal. The casualties were not just a number of eminently qualified candidates for the office, and the collateral damage inflicted on the institution itself, but also one of my closest friends, Etienne Mureinik, who in an act of suicidal depression killed himself in July 1996.

I cannot obviously say, nor suggest, that Etienne's death was a consequence of the so-called 'Makgoba affair' which was at the heart of the envenomed feud over the future direction and leadership of Wits. But I can say with direct knowledge that Etienne's toughness of purpose and principle and rigour of intellect hid a sensitivity seldom considered by his opponents – only on occasion revealed to his friends. He was deeply and traumatically affected by the whole messy but defining saga.

It can also be said that the events unleashed by both Professor William Makgoba and his detractors became a full revelation of much of the political drama that would be played out on South Africa's body politic for the next decade or so. In the case of Malegapuru William Makgoba, as Tolstoy described the tree: 'The leaves enchanted far more than the roots.'

By the end of 1993, coinciding with the passing of white rule, Wits's mostly male and all-white top floor realised the necessity for an urgent high-level makeover. The incumbent vice chancellor, Professor Bob Charlton, had, like his estimable predecessor but one, Du Plessis, been drawn from the medical school. Charlton was a decent man of unimpeachable integrity and acute intellect; yet I always felt he lacked Du Plessis's toughness of conviction. In fairness, much of his tenure was beset, if not besieged, by the intemperate protests and demands that rocked Wits by the week.

Charlton's increasing ennui was also a consequence of his — somewhat reluctant — acquiescence to the urgings of council to extend his period in office until 1997. The hunt for a successor, preferably a black, commenced in earnest. When the senior appointments committee went in search of a replacement combining academic excellence and the right colour, it suffered rebuffs and rejection. It could barely believe its good fortune when it interviewed Makgoba in London in 1993. South African-born and educated, he was an outstanding medical graduate who had ploughed his academic furrow abroad with distinction and aplomb. The somewhat jaundiced, but essentially accurate, observations of the journalist Edyth Bulbring sum up the enchanting expectations Makgoba created:

'He was the darling of South Africa's London embassy cocktail parties, he had worked in Britain's finest universities and institutions, he was undisputedly South Africa's leading immunologist, and he had no political baggage ... He also looked right and said the right things. His demeanour at his interview by the senior appointments committee, academics recall, was modest, accommodating and self-effacing.'[47]

The committee, including South Africa's pre-eminent social historian, Professor Charles van Onselen — who was to play a leading role in Makgoba's decline and fall — unhesitatingly recommended him for the post of deputy vice chancellor in charge of academic matters, and in October 1994 he was in place.

To be fair to Makgoba (not one of his own attributes), the assumption by many, not least in the ANC hierarchy, that he would shortly ascend into Charlton's seat was far from certain. Another deputy vice chancellor, June Sinclair, had her eyes on that particular prize, and had some significant backers.

I admired her no-nonsense, tough-minded *modus operandi*. I had been one of her students and she had been my notional boss when I lectured at the Law School. During my tenure there, it is true, she never once asked how I was coping, and her confrontational style never permitted her to exhibit an over-supply of the milk of human compassion. However, Sinclair, sooner than most – and with unerring clarity – realised the need to preserve Wits as an institution of intellectual and technical excellence, and was not timid about disagreeing with those whose desperation for consensus and the quiet life led them to display a singular lack of backbone.

She and her close colleagues, Mureinik and Van Onselen – while in the best sense of the word elitist – had worked long and hard to make Wits responsive to the needs of disadvantaged communities. This they did not by grand gestures or eloquent speeches (although Sinclair exhibited a vivid turn of phrase) but – in the words of one of them – 'by the drudgery of raising funds for bursaries and black staff development fellowships, developing mentoring relationships with black schools, building new residences, devising new courses, and doing more teaching.'

By the time of Makgoba's arrival I had been elected to the executive of the council and thus sat in the *binnekring* or inner council of the university leadership. Because of my efforts as its new leader to keep the DP afloat, and my intense involvement in the final constitutional negotiations in parliament, I was not a permanent presence in the executive's deliberations. However, I got an early, uneasy, feeling that the Dr Jekyll lionised in London could have become, at Wits, something of a Mr Hyde. In 1995 I read an extraordinary interview[48] in which Makgoba stated: 'Power at Wits is concentrated in the hands of a small, highly inbred elite. It is a mockery of democracy – a junta.'

I thought it extraordinary that a senior member of the university could publicly denounce, in such extreme terms, his colleagues and the institution he had just joined. When I and other council members raised our concern, Charlton and the council chairman, Steve Anderson, attempted to defuse the situation with a mild wrist-slap for Makgoba. However, a senior administrator showed me a bizarre letter Makgoba had penned privately to Charlton in December 1994, barely two months after arriving at Wits:

'A group of right-wing liberals have run and influenced the future direction of this institution without opposition for too long.' He labelled the group a 'cabal' whose key members were identified as Sinclair, Van Onselen and Mureinik, among others.[49]

During our occasional interaction, I had found Makgoba charming, soft-spoken and personable. But his use of extreme and denunciatory epithets and his lack of basic collegiality suggested to me – and increasingly to others – something seriously amiss.

Within the year, the Makgoba saga became a full-blown exercise in the politics of racial solidarity, with the professor proclaimed as the victim of a racist witchhunt. Yet when a council Senate committee was appointed to choose a professor for the law faculty, he eschewed any emphasis on pigment and demanded the application and promotion of rigorous intellectuality. I sat with him on this particular selection panel. One of the applicants was Shadrack Gutto, attached to the university's Centre for Applied Legal Studies. He made great play of his racial credentials, but his writings and theorising cut little ice with Makgoba, and even less with Ishmail Mahomed, South Africa's first black Chief Justice, who also sat on the committee. We unanimously declined to appoint Gutto.

Gutto eventually found a berth at Unisa as the chair of the curiously named 'Department of Renaissance Studies', presumably the African, not Italian, variant.

Meanwhile, Makgoba turned his sniping against the Wits leadership into a full-scale assault in the media. He displayed an almost reckless propensity to hurl abuse through the press – or the written word – rather than in direct and personal confrontation. He told one interviewer, for example, that his detractors in the higher echelons of the university were 'a typical group of racists who don't want change.' He added that Wits was a 'place beset with racism'.[50]

Anyone who had any dealings or relationship with Van Onselen, Sinclair or Mureinik could attest to their staunch fealty to the principles and practice of a transcending non-racism at a time when few had glimpsed a future outside the apartheid paradigm. Still, as Mureinik was to observe in an aside which he later elaborated on in an article: 'It's all about stigma-labelling.'

Makgoba's denunciation of his opponents (real or imagined) as 'right-wing liberals' was the forerunner of what would become the ANC's stock response to my own party's opposition – and a generalised race smear against any critic. The impugning of the ethnic credentials of a whistle-blower was an easy response, which conveniently avoided the merits of the issue. Mureinik saw and exposed this, earlier than most: 'It is now obvious,' he wrote, 'that a white person who dares to question a black person's credentials will automatically be called a "racist", a label which makes one a moral criminal, and consigns one to the non-world of those who can safely be ignored.'[51]

Burnt by Makgoba, Mureinik propounded a great truth: the emerging new order aped its predecessor to delegitimise the critique and the critics; liberals would be stigmatised with renewed tenacity. 'Under Verwoerd and Vorster, "liberal" was the stigma label of choice,' Mureinik concluded. It meant 'so far Left as to be almost communist'. 'Liberal' had again become a stigma-label. But now it meant, 'so far Right as to be almost racist. It is a new psycho-trick, calculated to taint the democrats on one's Right with the authoritarianism of those much further to the Right.'[52]

I have used this analysis ever since as the most lucid explanation for much of the background noise – the politically kitsch muzak – of South African politics.

Makgoba's opponents struck back after investigating his *curriculum vitae* (in which they found discrepancies and exaggerations); and having compiled an exhaustive 100-page dossier of his increasingly bilious utterances against the university.

In due course the 'cabal' was joined by eight deans of faculty and comprised 13 very senior academics. The documentation was sent to Charlton as vice chancellor, and the chairman of the council, Anderson. The accompanying letter stated that misstatements in the CV 'raised serious concerns' and that Makgoba's utterances since his appointment cast 'very serious doubt about his fitness to continue in office'. The letter concluded with a request for a formal enquiry, and that Makgoba be 'given the right to defend himself'.

Charlton suggested to Makgoba that an attempt be made to resolve the matter in informal proceedings. This was rebuffed by Ismail Ayob, Makgoba's attorney, who years later achieved infamy in a vicious falling out with his most famous client, Nelson Mandela. Ayob challenged Van Onselen's ethics and integrity: Van Onselen had spearheaded the research into Makgoba's credentials and had used 'underhand methods' to ferret out the incriminating information.

Makgoba's defenders grew in number in proportion to both the severity of the attack on him and the high standing of the attackers. Before the council could decide how to proceed, Makgoba and Ayob brought in the minister of Education, Sibusiso Bhengu, to enquire: 'Whether the utilisation of such scarce resources at the university for [the] purpose, which appears to be a vendetta against one specific individual, enjoys approval or can be justified.'

Various members of the black commentariat also piled in; well-known race warrior and journalist Thami Mazwai denounced the Makgoba dossier as 'a spontaneous white conspiracy against the black intelligentsia'.[53]

Kaizer Nyatsumba in the *Star*[54] spoke of an 'apparent persecution', while the *Sowetan* opined that those responsible for the attack on Makgoba were 'conspirators'.[55]

Clearly, the battle lines would be drawn on a far larger terrain than the cloistered confines of our council chamber; and the matter would be fought on racial grounds.

Since Makgoba had insisted on a formal procedure, the council deemed it most appropriate, and objective, to appoint a tribunal of pre-eminent international academics of 'unquestioned integrity and reputation' from outside South Africa to dispose of, and hopefully defuse, the matter. However, by then the minister of Education had intervened with some extraordinary assertions and claims. I knew Bhengu slightly – he gave parliament an impression of indecision and caution, and was almost openly dismissed by some cabinet colleagues as a serial bumbler. A letter he sent to Charlton indicated that if he was not entirely a captive of the Makgoba group, he was operating in an uncharacteristically decisive and definitely partial manner.[56]

In his letter he spoke of his and government's concern about a 'low-intensity but persistent crisis at the university since 1993'. This was an over-blown description – richly ironic coming from Bhengu who had previously failed to assist the university when asked to persuade the militant elements trashing the campus to desist. He went on to list all manner of requirements for the university to adhere to vis-à-vis Makgoba, calling on the tribunal to look into 'the manner in which the allegations against Professor Makgoba have been investigated'.

Bhengu's intervention was a blatant supplanting of the university's institutional autonomy, and would have been resisted fiercely under apartheid. It did little to placate the militants – now led by, among others, the egregious Gutto – who gathered together in a 'Wits Transformation Front'. No doubt still smarting from Gutto's professorship rebuff, the Front called for the dismissal of the proposed tribunal and direct intervention by the government to resolve the issue.

In an unusually bold but, in my view, entirely appropriate response, the council declined the minister's and the Front's advice. Then matters were ratcheted to an almost unendurable level when Makgoba – via his attorney – released selective titbits gleaned from the contents of the confidential files of his detractors, dubbed 'The Gang of 13'. Makgoba had used his position as a deputy vice chancellor to purloin the information. Unlike a CV, these documents were not in the public domain.

On the basis of the files, Makgoba and Ayob claimed 'evidence of impropriety within the university'. The claim was that this was the real motive of Makgoba's detractors since, as Ayob put it, 'Makgoba's investigations have come to the knowledge of those who have something to hide.'[57]

Makgoba's claims ranged from the merely spurious to the outright ludicrous. Most of them were based on the routine allowances paid to some of the 13 as an entitlement of their office and duties. They were designed to legitimately reduce tax liability, but Makgoba's attorney claimed them as proof of 'widespread tax evasion'.[58] Those singled out claimed the charges to be defamatory (which they undoubtedly were) and called on the council to appoint an enquiry into each allegation. We duly commissioned leading senior counsel plus a tax accountant to investigate. In February 1996 the commission reported, finding none of Makgoba's charges to be justified. There was no misconduct.

However, long before this – simultaneously with faxing the letter to Charlton in late November – Ayob released its contents to the media.[59] At this point, Charlton's long-suffering patience snapped and he promptly suspended Makgoba, sending him a letter advising him that his behaviour amounted to an 'abuse of position'.

Bhengu again entered the lists in early December, demanding that Makgoba's suspension be 'carefully reviewed'. Even the sainted President Mandela, himself a Wits graduate (arguably its most famous son), cautioned that 'government cannot allow Wits University to implode upon itself.'[60]

With Makgoba issuing dire threats that he would 'tame' the 'thirteen monkeys', there was an attempt at informal mediation. It was facilitated by Cecil Wulfsohn and Dennis Davis, but without any involvement on my part (though both were personal friends); they arranged a ceasefire. Makgoba agreed to step down as deputy vice chancellor and accept an academic role, while both sides withdrew their charges and claims.

It was a peace without winners. Mureinik killed himself within the year; the brilliant Van Onselen left Wits and joined the University of Pretoria; Sinclair was denied the vice-chancellorship when it fell vacant a year later after Sasco (the radical students' organisation) launched a vicious assault on her candidacy. The succession process ended up entirely botched when the person chosen as vice chancellor, an overseas import, met the lowest common denominator of the warring factions – but proved to be disastrous once in office. She, too, was fairly swiftly removed.

Makgoba moved on to eventually take control of the University of Kwa-Zulu-Natal. But his leadership there has been characterised by intellectual suppression and internal censorship. As they say: 'Character will out.'

An unintended by-product of the Makgoba crisis was of some direct personal and political relevance. When I arrived on the University Council, in 1991, Helen Suzman was among our number, elected like me by past students of the Convocation. However, this was just two years after my Houghton nomination,[61] and she gave me the cold-war treatment, and ignored my presence and my proffered greetings. Then, as the Makgoba saga unfolded and as we found ourselves increasingly on the same side, she began to thaw. By 1996, she had defrosted to the extent that she engaged in direct conversation. She announced in the press that she approved of my leadership of the party, although she found my manner somewhat 'brash'.[62]

Over the next ten years or so, my relationship with her seesawed. Her absence from parliament by no means indicated her withdrawal from politics. She felt it incumbent to keep up a public commentary on all manner of happenings, from road closures in Johannesburg to the fact that her contribution to South African politics had been airbrushed out of the apartheid museum in Johannesburg's Gold Reef City. I spent a fair amount of private time visiting her and hearing her often acerbic views on the party and the performance of the government. Suzman on occasion publicly backed the Democratic Party; but she equally openly dissented when the Democratic Alliance was formed in 2000.

The relationship was not an easy one to manage and, I suspect, her ambivalence towards me was never resolved.

Makgoba's damage to Wits was profound – but the institution, ten years on, appears to have recovered its balance under new leadership.[63] Makgoba's future is less certain. A few months before his death, Etienne predicted that the strategy and strength of what he termed 'naked, uncritical race solidarity' had proven far greater than most expected. As he wrote towards the end of the dispute (and of his life): 'It [undermines] the hope of a society in which white leaders can call a black leader to account under criteria binding equally on all ... [it] destroys any hope of equal accountability.'[64]

Events in parliament and public life in the decade that followed proved his grim prediction accurate.

CHAPTER 3

Into Politics

*I experienced the high voltage of publicity. It was like picking up a
dangerous wire fatal to ordinary folk. It was like the rattlesnakes handled
by hillbillies in a state of religious exaltation.*

SAUL BELLOW

I

In early January 1986 I was unpacking my books in the ground-floor office allocated to me as their newest addition by the Wits Law School. The
telephone rang. It was Ian Davidson, my former colleague in the PFP
Youth Movement, now a city councillor in Johannesburg. He told me that
Aleck Jaffe, the long-standing councillor for the Bellevue/Judith's Paarl
ward, had died; the PFP was in need of a candidate, preferably 'a young
Jewish professional' to suit the demographics; and, 'Was I interested?'

I took about three seconds to assent. Naturally I was miffed that my
grandiose sense of self had been overlooked by Davidson and his cohorts
as of less significance than my age and religion! He suggested we meet the
next day at a local Melville eatery, down the road from Wits, aptly named
'The Gobble and Gossip'.

Davidson was accompanied by two of his council colleagues, Don
Walton and Paul Asherson. They formed the core of what the party regional chairman – and my later nemesis – Irene Menell condescending-
ly called the 'ginger group'. This was not a reference to Davidson's then
strawberry-blonde hair, but the party's senior establishment perception
that it alone could breathe fire into the PFP's city council presence; a view
reinforced by the hubris of a somnambulant and conservative leadership
drawn largely from United Party elders who had broken rank and merged
with the Progressive Party to form, first, the Progressive Reform, and, later,
the Progressive Federal Party.

I quickly discerned that the active backing of the 'ginger group' was no
guarantee of success in the forthcoming party nomination contest. The

INTO POLITICS

MP for Yeoville, Harry Schwarz, whose bailiwick included Bellevue, was no fan of the progressive wing of the party. He regarded his constituency as a form of extension of his difficult personality.

I had always been fascinated by Schwarz – both as a personality and as a politician. His positions varied: from a hawkish perspective on security, to a social-democratic one on the economy – all of which put him at variance with the party's liberal orthodoxies. He continually clashed with the leadership, despite being one of the party's most senior members and its best parliamentary and platform performer. As I have recalled, his ousting as executive chairman had directly knocked my own chances of election as SRC president at Wits. But Schwarz resented being made to feel an outsider.

Of course, I too had clashed with him at various party congresses as head of the regional youth wing. I once accused him – with all the self-righteous histrionics that an undergraduate can bring to politics – of being 'an agent of neo-colonialism'. After that Schwarz cut me dead.

Asherson, however, had a plan of action. It is difficult to capture Paul in a phrase or even in a book. He had been four years ahead of me at school. While neither a promising student nor sportsman, his was an immensely attractive personality, among the small number of Kearsney boys who took an active interest in politics, and of an even smaller number who defended the Progressive Party. We had lost touch after he abandoned his legal articles in Durban and set off for Johannesburg, where he had made and lost at least two fortunes by the time we were reunited in Melville. He had also transmogrified from the lean schoolboy of memory to his current Falstaffian figure, replete with silk suit and unfiltered French cigarettes which he chain-smoked throughout the meal.

The key architect of my first nomination strategy, Paul would become one of the chief backers of my municipal ambitions – and later my party leadership. His heart and energy were as huge as his appetite for food and life itself (interestingly, he didn't drink). He knew his way about; he cut corners to close deals and 'get things done'. Some of his deal-making might not survive close ethical scrutiny, but to him worthwhile ends justified sometimes dubious means. My affection for him was unbounded, and his loyalty to me total and unwavering.

In May 1999, just after he had accompanied me on an election swing around the Boland in a helicopter, which he personally hired, we returned to Johannesburg – and the next day, with no warning, he died suddenly at the age of 46. I was literally stunned. The next week – when the party famously won the Official Opposition prize from Paul's dread enemy, the

Nats – I saluted him. But all this lay in a future undreamed of on that Johannesburg summer afternoon, when I wondered whether I would even reach the first rung of the ladder he would help build.

Apart from my historic enmity with Schwarz, I faced three others for the nomination. I was a long shot, despite support from Davidson and Asherson. Four years before, while a final-year law student, I lost a party nomination for a city council seat in Braamfontein precisely because my opponent was the preferred choice of the party's council leadership. Back then, the PFP was riven between its component parts. The Progressive Party founders denigrated the newcomers; while the relatively late-breaking Schwarz 'reformists', who stayed with the UP until 1975, resented the superciliousness of the old Progs. While by no means an uncritical subscriber to the establishment, I was seen as a 'Prog'.

Nomination day was 16 January – propitious, since it was my late Grandpa Jack's birthday. My legal mentor, Philip Pencharz, had always cautioned me to take a 'belt and braces' approach in preparing a brief. I tackled the nomination in similar fashion, scouring Ward 30 – the Bellevue/Judith's Paarl/Bertrams area – essentially for the first time. It was one of Johannesburg's poorer white enclaves; and although the southern edge of the ward, in terms of the Group Areas Act, was strictly reserved for whites, it was (as some put it) starting to 'grey'. Increasingly, Coloured, Indian and a few African tenants were being accommodated by rent-racketeering landlords. They had to live in miserable, high-rent conditions – but were surreptitiously moving in anyway.

There was open hostility by some of the (largely poor) white residents to this encroachment. Having spent my years in Johannesburg in an apartment opposite the Houghton golf course this was an eye-opener. What surprised me even more than the broken pavements and uncut grass was how the PFP had won a comfortable three-hundred-plus majority in the seat just four years before. Whatever else my putative new political home offered, it was a refutation of sorts that the Progressives could only win and hold seats in the 'leafy suburbs' of northern Johannesburg and southern Cape Town.[1]

On Asherson's advice I canvassed all the members of the Electoral College. I received a mixed, largely non-committal response. Given our history, I hesitated about phoning Schwarz, but placed a call. I stammered away something or other about standing in the seat, and offered to visit him before the nomination contest. Curtly, but not rudely, he said this would be unnecessary, adding, I thought ominously, 'since I know who you are.'

On nomination night I waited nervously in the reception area of the party's head office; I would be the last nominee to be interviewed. Abruptly, Asherson burst in. His pretext was to answer a call of nature, but he quickly gave me a rundown of the questions fired at my opponents. The clincher (which not one had answered appropriately) was a question from Schwarz as to what issues were uppermost in the voters' minds ('crime' and 'the cost of living' was the answer he sought). He added that at one stage, Schwarz had waved his finger at Irene Menell: 'Tony belongs with you in Houghton, not with us in Yeoville.' Oddly prophetic!

Suitably armed with the unfair advantage Asherson had given me, I dealt with the questions in an appropriate and even, apparently, disarming manner.

I won an outright majority on the first ballot. To his great credit, Schwarz shook my hand and announced: 'The past is the past. You're our candidate now and I will back you.' I would need every bit of that assistance.

The NP nominated Sam Bloomberg, a 60-year-old Jewish businessman. He had eschewed the religious precept that acts of kindness and charity are best done quietly or anonymously, and had hacked out a significant public profile for himself as the head of 'Suicides Anonymous'. This was a voluntary group which provided counselling to those on the personal edge. But the name was a misnomer, at least as far as Bloomberg's very public role in the organisation was concerned. He was also a reservist police colonel, which the crime-pressed residents would no doubt find reassuring – the ace in the NP's hole was that the PFP and its neophyte über-liberal candidate were 'soft on security'.

The oleaginous Bloomberg's first election salvo – a pamphlet – proclaimed: 'The radical PFP is a danger. Ward 30 won't make the same mistake again and support a party that wants to experiment with its untried integration policies on the residents of Johannesburg.' He advised voters to stand against what he piquantly termed 'the PFP's suicidal option of one-man-one-vote'.

Schwarz's chief lieutenant, Alan Gadd – the local provincial councillor who was appointed my election agent – told me to avoid getting into a 'pissing contest' with Bloomberg. I should stick to local topics and personally contact as many of the ward's five thousand voters as I could. So my campaign – largely staffed by personal friends – took off, and I hit the streets, morning, noon and night.

Many of the voters had moved away, and others were chronically 'out' no matter when we rang their doorbells. My intense and uninvited presence on the doorsteps of a myriad of flats in Bellevue and the dilapidated houses of Judith's Paarl did wonders for my personal and political education. I had considered myself a liberal *tout court*. Politics was to be seen in essentially binary terms: white oppression and affluence on the one hand, and black suffering and poverty on the other. I also viewed the police as an extension of the state's repressive apparatus, unfazed by methods that included torture and even extra-judicial killing. My exposure to some of the mean streets began to shift my understanding and infuse it with a reality which my rather sheltered upbringing had largely obscured.

Apartheid provided all whites with an economic leg-up allowing an escape from absolute poverty. But they were by no means rich or well-off. Aside from an ephemeral bohemian presence of young white lefties who were either not registered to vote or who would never deign to do so in an 'apartheid poll',[2] the residents were mainly elderly, scraping by on the extremely derisory monthly state pension provided by a parsimonious government. They were exploited by rapacious landlords; and by marauding gangs of criminals who found, in their vulnerability, easy pickings.

Schwarz – an immensely successful and rich lawyer-businessman – understood better than most in the party the need to distinguish between the call for legitimate law and order, and oppression. He had campaigned relentlessly for a police station in Yeoville, with a characteristic single-mindedness that eventually shamed the government to construct it. He could convey the fears and insecurities of his constituents.

It was Alan Paton who understood and articulated the crucial difference between order and tyranny: 'Order without liberty is tyranny, but liberty without order is chaos.'

I made this mantra my own. On the streets of Bellevue, despite its claims, pretensions and doses of brutality, the NP government had not provided much order against criminals, while removing the vestiges of liberty from its citizens.

Given the immense issues and national questions I would later be privileged to participate in and pontificate about, my first political salvo, back in 1986, was modest and decidedly parochial. My manifesto promised to get bobbies back on the street, and in keeping with the parish-pump strictures of my election agent, I offered the anodyne – but necessary – promise of a 'quiet, safe neighbourhood'.

My mother was an active presence in the campaign. However, she was so appalled by what she perceived to be the grime and filth encasing the 'dungeon flat' – as she described our campaign office – that she spent most of the time in the kitchen, cleaning, and scouring the crockery and cutlery from contamination.

As the campaign entered its last three-week stretch, I felt hopeful. Our canvass results looked good, and whatever public advantages my better-known opponent clearly enjoyed, I compensated by visiting far more voters than him. So it went until Friday 7 February 1986 when the awful and unexpectedly shattering news came through of the self-inflicted (some would say self-indulgent) political hara-kiri that was Frederik van Zyl Slabbert's decision to resign from parliament, where he led the official opposition, and from the PFP leadership, where he enjoyed wide support.

That morning, the then Transvaal leader of the party (later to become one of my closest political allies and friends), Douglas Gibson, phoned me as the candidate in the field, and sounded uncharacteristically grim: 'Look, Tony, there's going to be an announcement in parliament later today which could have a very negative impact on your campaign. What you need to do, however, is just to keep going!' I was mystified and alarmed when he said he couldn't give me details, but told me to listen to the radio that afternoon.

I went about my electioneering chores. That day they centred on addressing the genteel women of the Gerald Fitzpatrick Home for the Aged. They received me very warmly, and I recall reading (and writing it down) a plaque entitled 'From the Old to the Young':

> Remember, friend, as you pass by,
> As you are now, so once was I.
> As I am now, so you must be,
> Prepare yourself to follow me.

This made an immense impression on this 29-year-old candidate, and I have frequently invoked those words in countless old-age homes and retirement villages which I have visited since in 21 years of public and political life.[3]

When I left I heard the extraordinary news on the car radio. Slabbert stated: 'The Tricameral parliament is a hopelessly flawed and failed constitutional experiment.'[4] As it happened, I agreed – the whole party did – but was appalled. I had what I was later to call 'a Myrtle moment' – as the eponymous character in JK Rowling's *Harry Potter* series used to wail from the lavatory at Hogwarts School: 'What about me?'

What, indeed, about me? The voters I then went to visit this afternoon, in the immediate aftermath of the Slabbert bombshell (I still remember, more than two decades later, their names: Philip Herring and his wife Jessie) asked, not unreasonably, why they should support a party in which its leader had so little confidence? Shell-shocked, I relocated the discussion around local issues, and by the time I left they promised firm support on the day. However, I now saw my campaign unravelling under the impact of Slabbert's fiery immolation.

Several years later, Slabbert's successor but one in the leadership, Zach de Beer, described his predecessor to me as 'someone who always quit on the eve of success'. Whatever Slabbert's exit achieved for him and the country – and I suspect its impact over time was far less than he imagined – it devastated his party and stalled my campaign.[5]

Schwarz phoned me that night from Cape Town and warned that we now faced the real prospect of an electoral meltdown. We decided on a public rally in the area to intensify our profile and allow him to reassure the voters that he, at least, was standing firm.

The Nat organisers of my opponent's campaign could not believe the political manna which Slabbert's exit rained down upon them. They immediately announced that their leading vote-getter and crowd-puller, Pik Botha, would also address a rally in the constituency. This was by no means the end of my travails in the beleaguered campaign.

Flak from the opposition-inclined media was unfriendly, unforgiving, but probably just – in the way 'first drafts of history' often are. In the case of the *Sunday Times*, the best read of the lot, it proved sadly accurate: under the headline 'PFP, Alone in a Hot Kitchen' the editor wrote: 'The judgment on Dr van Zyl Slabbert's dramatic exit from parliamentary politics must, sadly, be harsh. He leaves behind him a bewildered party that may well be rent asunder – thus enabling the Conservatives to acquire the enhanced status of Official Opposition.

'Most of all Dr Slabbert will be remembered as a captain who at the height of the most serious storm his country has known laid his own secret plans and simply helicoptered off the ship, leaving officers and crew in the lurch.'[6]

As we regrouped and tried to refine our tactics to meet our new, leaderless situation (it took the PFP a week or so to put Eglin back in the saddle), my opponent Bloomberg thought, as did I, that he had hit the winning run. With just two weeks to polling day, he plucked a would-be suicide from the rooftop of a downtown Johannesburg building. The event did not pass unnoticed or unheralded. The next day's *Citizen* devoted a four-colour picture spread to this feat,[7] while the *Star*'s front page breathlessly informed its readers that 'Mr Bloomberg had spent two hours perched on the narrow ledge of the roof without a safety harness while he spoke to the would-be suicide.'[8]

Then, in what the NP and their faithful retainers at SABC-TV no doubt imagined to be the *coup de grâce*, Bloomberg was featured for eight minutes in a prime-time broadcast on suicide, on the actuality programme *Network*.

If my goose wasn't already cooked, it was certainly being heated up. But then, as braggarts often do, Bloomberg overreached himself. He told a newspaper he would be making election posters of his rooftop heroics and hanging them outside the polling station on election day. This was a solitary ray of light in a very gloomy week. Someone in my campaign team contacted the *Sunday Star* with the details of the unfortunate girl's family; we had been investigating whether the event was real or staged: it was, sadly, the former. Thus the newspaper headline on the front page, three days before polling, proclaimed: 'Family Fury over Suicide Sam'.[9] Her mother was quoted as saying, 'I will personally rip every poster down', while the girl's boyfriend accused Bloomberg of misusing her misfortune in a 'disgusting manner'.

On that same Sunday I had prevailed upon the *Sunday Times*'s editor, Tertius Myburgh, a friend of my mother from their days in Durban, to give me a slot on the op-ed pages to respond to Slabbert's resignation and explain why the party was still worth supporting. The piece now seems fairly trite and tame. But in the hope that some of the good voters of Bellevue would see it, the *Times* gave me a photo and a headline on a prime page – even if the headline, 'Dear Van, Here's Why I'm Staying', was fairly cringe-worthy.[10]

In between my amateur journalism and participating in Schwarz's public meeting (which drew half the audience that Pik Botha achieved for Bloomberg) I ran myself ragged around the ward. Schwarz's wife, Annette, with a team of party veterans, redoubled efforts to trace missing voters across the province, and cajole them to get to the polls.

On election eve, the NP dropped a pamphlet across the ward, proclaiming in a blood-red headline: 'If you vote for the PFP you are voting for the party which is prepared to form an anti-government alliance with the ANC.' The pamphlet listed all manner of 'ANC atrocities' (real: the Pretoria bombing the year before; and imagined or disputed: the campaign of murdering so-called apartheid collaborators). This noxious missive concluded triumphantly, with the flourish of a rhetorical question: 'Are you going to vote for the PFP which is prepared to treat with the ANC, or would you rather vote for Sam Bloomberg, a colonel in the police reserve who protects you and guards your home while you sleep at night?'[11]

I was so outraged and incensed with this smear that I failed to see the hilarity of its lurid and exaggerated prose. Bloomberg, who lived miles from the ward, had not been noticed spending his evenings patrolling his constituents' homes.

Our final salvo was lower in pitch and octave. It was an endorsement by Schwarz, which I thought somewhat tepid and low key: 'Tony Leon is a bright young man, both energetic and principled, and with a realistic approach to life. I commend him to you.'

2

On 26 February 1986, election day dawned, and at 6 am my friend Caron Sandler, who had laboured mightily in the campaign, drove me to the polling station in Bellevue's Hunter Street. The auguries seemed propitious – especially for one as superstitious as me – when Radio Highveld broadcast one of my all-time favourite songs ('Always on my mind' by Elvis Presley) as we strode in.

In those days, with one voting station per ward, election day was intense, direct, and in this case, brutally acrimonious. The Nats scented an historic win in a PFP seat, and we were certainly on the extreme defensive. Every voter was jostled by opposing volunteers, who sought to direct constituents to one or other party registration tent – an absolutely meaningless ritual since a voter could theoretically get his or her number from the NP tent and then proceed to the privacy of the polling station and vote PFP, or vice versa.[12]

Bloomberg and I stood opposite each other, no more than a yard apart, right outside the voters' entrance. I disliked Bloomberg. His oily and instant flattery of each voter struck me as especially false, and I was enraged at his false pamphlets and dubious publicity stunts. In over fourteen hours we exchanged scarcely a word, civil or otherwise. In pictures from that day, I appear young and tentative, while Bloomberg's face radiated confident expectation. But I actually knew the names of many of the residents streaming up the stairs to vote – in stark contrast to Bloomberg who ran a poor second in the greet-by-name contest and relied on his public profile to lift him to victory.

Schwarz and various other local party luminaries also greeted the voters, and both the Nats and PFP deployed dozens of cars and drivers to scour the ward for lost or absconded voters. The sole event on which Bloomberg and I agreed was to take an hour's break from our vigil – in mid-afternoon, before the anticipated 5 pm rush.

I felt wary and expectant in our electoral HQ, witnessing the frantic efforts of our teams of telephonists, led by my redoubtable mother, urging electors to get their vote in. I conferred with Schwarz and Gadd, both extremely concerned with the numbers our statistician had crunched out. Too many voters had been marked by our canvassers as 'doubtful', 'won't say', or 'against'; and simply not enough 'fors' (i.e. PFP supporters) had yet polled. Was it a landslide defeat? Annette Schwarz, determinedly positive (in contrast to Harry's Spenglerian gloom about impending defeat), urged me on: 'It's OK, Tony, it will be OK, you're going to win.'

Back outside, a tall bespectacled man approached me, with an obviously confident air. Paul Asherson once described Francois Oberholzer, chairman of the Management Committee of Johannesburg Council, as resembling a 'Volkswagen Beetle with the doors open' – a barbed reference to his slicked-back hair and prominent ears. However, 'Obie', as he was universally known, exuded power and confidence at all times.

'Well, young man,' he greeted me, 'you've done your best, but I don't think today is your day.' Oberholzer, a holdover from the United Party whose 'Independent Group' ran Johannesburg in coalition with the Nats, despised the Schwarz breakaways who had helped form the PFP. A week before the election, in a full-page ad in the local newspaper, he denounced me as 'a radical Prog leftist (young Turk) who will bedevil your future with untried and untested political games.'

Eventually, after what seemed like 14 days rather than hours, the doors of the polling station closed and Schwarz, Gadd and I entered the room where the council officials stood behind a very long trestle table, ready to open the ballot boxes and separate the papers into piles of 50; check the seals on the back; and then separate them into parcels of 50 for either Bloomberg or Leon. I was so anxious that an irritated Schwarz asked if I couldn't take a pill or something to 'calm down'. Bloomberg and his cronies exuded huge confidence, increasing my sense of foreboding.

Once the seals had been checked, the count began. Gadd, a veteran of many campaigns, said we mustn't worry about our pile of votes but needed to scrutinise our opponent's to ensure none of our lot, mistakenly or otherwise, were assigned to our opponent. The count was unendurably slow, mainly because Schwarz and the returning officer got into a ferocious dispute about a number of ballots that were not clearly marked but which, according to Harry, belonged to us.

The count appeared to be an almost even split between Bloomberg and Leon. But Gadd carefully counted the number of 50-vote bundles awarded to me. He calculated that of the just under two thousand votes recorded I had 18 bundles, giving me the edge. Then an official placed the bundles in two stockpiles; I had only 17, and Bloomberg had gained one more. I felt crushed and almost broken. To have laboured so hard, against incredible odds, and now to lose by so little!

However, neither the officials nor the Nats had reckoned on my counting agents. 'Objection!' Gadd shouted. 'There's a bundle of Leon votes in the Bloomberg pile.' I sent up every prayer I had ever known or heard, and telegraphed to the Almighty to show some compassion. I also hoped that Gadd, an accountant by training, was as good a counter as I imagined him to be. Thank God he was.

The returning officer inspected each bundle – and like a magical croupier who stops the wheel and the ball bounces from the number you haven't backed to the zero you've staked your whole house on, he lifted a pile of 50 Leon votes from the Bloomberg pile and placed them on my own. I didn't bother to look at Bloomberg and his cohorts – I punched the air, embraced Gadd and Schwarz, and impatiently waited for the doors to be opened so that my victory could be trumpeted to the now several-hundred-strong crowd, waiting anxiously outside.

It was my first election, and I had seemed to climb a personal political Everest. In reality it was no more than a foothill. But I now knew I was on my way as a politician – and at 29, the most junior councillor in the city of Johannesburg.

CITY OF JOHANNESBURG: WARD 30 BY-ELECTION

26 February 1986		1982 General Municipal Election	
AJ Leon (PFP)	903	A Jaffe (PFP)	760
SG Bloomberg (NP)	864	I Levine (Ind)	389
Spoilt Papers	9		
Majority	39	Majority	371
% Poll	31	% Poll	28

3

My fatigue was swept away. I was delirious with my extremely narrow victory, a dizzying high quite unlike any other I'd experienced. After the speeches and congratulations, we partied into the night, and for some un-remembered reason I finally slept not at home but on a couch at the home of my now fellow-councillor and soon-to-be close friend and ally, Cecil Bass, and his wife Glynnis.[13]

Winning against the odds – in the dramatic aftermath of Slabbert's exit and Bloomberg's suicide rescue – garnered disproportionate publicity. Even the ultra-cautious, somewhat politically supine *Star* newspaper (whose editor had a few years previously advised his readers to abstain in the crucial Tricameral referendum) was moved to editorialise, with customary equivocation: 'No call to read too much into yesterday's municipal by-election. Still, two points are worth musing on. The first is that "big gun" Pik Botha couldn't swing it for the National Party candidate who had the initial benefit of being widely known as a sympathetic suicide counsellor. And the second is that the turmoil in PFP ranks didn't stop municipal voters from returning a lesser-known PFP candidate. It was a desperately close call but ... it makes you think, doesn't it?'[14]

The party hierarchy in Cape Town was also relieved. Eglin phoned me minutes after the result was known, and a few days later I received a very warm letter from the party national chairman and MP for Cape Town Gardens, Ken Andrew, who thanked me for 'what you have done to keep the party's flag flying high'. We did not know then that eight years later we would face each other for the party's national leadership.

A colleague, Janet Semple, recently presented me with a contemporaneous copy of the *Weekly Mail*, as it was known, as a memento. It published my victory picture, hands in the air, under the caption: 'The just-made-it sort of victory cheer'. Above that was a front-page interview with Slabbert proclaiming: 'I've lost all hope: peace is no longer an option for South Africa.'[15]

I would spend the next few years in the less-than-peaceful political environment deserted by my lost leader, until in 1990, in the Tricameral parliament Slabbert asserted 'could not rid South Africa of apartheid', the change he despaired of came to pass.

My arrival in the council coincided with the 100th anniversary of Johannesburg's establishment as a city. All manner of banquets and self-congratulatory flummery ensued; but no one of any significance in the world deigned to be present. Johannesburg's apartheid city status – its position as the premier metropolis of a country under internal siege and shunned as an international pariah – highlighted our beleaguered position.

My councillorship ran from 1986 until late 1989, a period of violence and political stagnation, as described by Paul Bell, writing in the journal *Leadership*: 'South Africa was a nation on a verge – but of what no one could be sure. The country was haemorrhaging capital and skills, investors had fled, the economy staggered under debt repayments, government was overspending, and people were dying in increasing numbers in daily political violence despite a draconian state of emergency. After four-and-a-half years of upheaval, the military option of PW Botha's government, in defence of a constitution barely 5% of the people had voted for, was a political cul-de-sac.'[16]

Many of my 50 fellow-councillors averted their gaze from the political dead-end South Africa had now reached. It was as if the structures and symbols that had served the white ratepayers' interests required little adjustment or even fewer concessions to the grim and urgent realities requiring redress and manifest change. In some ways this myopia was structural: councillors wore absurd and obligatory black gowns lined with velvet, and the mayor presided over our monthly sessions in a dazzling purple cloak with a large gold chain. Yet they enjoyed little real power. They also received – in comparison with the much larger awards paid to metro councillors today – very modest remuneration. My 'salary' (in reality an allowance) was R750 a month for most of my time there. You certainly could not do the job on a full-time basis, though ratepayers naturally expected full-time attention.

Most of the real power was vested in the hands of the all-powerful Management Committee (today the mayoral committee). Enormous store and prestige was placed in the ascent to the mayoral chair. In reality, the mayor was a figurehead, elected to a non-renewable two-year term, determined on the 'Buggins's turn' philosophy that the most senior councillor would get the chain. (In civic politics at the time the mayoralty rotated between the PFP and NP.) However, each party caucus would resemble snake-bite territory when two or more councillors had equivalent periods of service. Ultimately, the chairman of the Management Committee held the reins of executive authority.

Here again – as while waiting for the Ward 30 result – I came face-to-face with J Francois ('Obie') Oberholzer. He had been Management Committee chair for over a decade, and would hang on until 1988. This political longevity rested on his position as a local city boss unrivalled anywhere in the country in terms of political command and mastery of municipal matters. He was reminiscent of Mayor Daley of Chicago.

Actually, to purloin a description of De Gaulle during the Second World War, Oberholzer played 'a very strong hand from a particularly weak seat'. He was neither Nat nor Prog; but what in the old era was called a '*bloedsap*' (a dyed-in-the-wool United Party man). Extremely conservative, he had joined neither of the larger parties when the UP disintegrated in 1977. Instead he created a vestigial presence of his former party on the council in the guise of an 'Independent Ratepayers' Alliance' (which enjoyed the clumsy and politically dubious acronym 'IRA'). With half-a-dozen colleagues he formed a governing pact with the much larger NP bloc on the council – a stratagem fuelled by his bitter enmity towards his former UP colleagues in council who had made common cause with the Progs. His political skill and cunning ensured that he retained the top job.

Today Oberholzer could also be designated a 'previously disadvantaged individual'; not racially, but in terms of his extremely humble origins. Before his political life he had been a rigger on the mines. He had no formal education to speak of, but his intelligence, charm and vast experience had propelled him to the front rank. I never once saw him stumped for an answer, and he could recall from memory exactly why, months before, for example, the Management Committee had located a building on the north-west rather than on the south-east of a council site. High office did not corrupt him or remove him from his origins. Despite presiding over (by the standards of the 1980s) a huge budget of R1,8-billion – larger than the combined revenues of two provinces – he lived modestly in a flat in Rosettenville (until his death in 2004) and drove a nondescript Toyota.

He also revelled in a form of populist philistinism, which accorded with the sentiments of his own voters. For example, he stormed out of the Market Theatre's opening production of *Marat/Sade* (denouncing it as 'pornographic') and mocked the city's Art Gallery (whose purse strings he controlled) for purchasing, at monstrous cost, one of Picasso's cubist works. Yet the highway network around Johannesburg and the modernisation of much of the municipal infrastructure bore his mark.

I once asked Oberholzer how he coped. The answer, he said, lay in playing a round of golf once a week, and having a nightly glass of whisky before retiring (I adopted the latter habit, but not the former). But while I quickly understood why Obie was the political master of all he surveyed, I realised that his considerable attributes did not include a largeness of political vision. But then, in the cavernous and user-unfriendly Civic Centre atop Braamfontein Hill, I also wondered whether my party in the council had the imagination and leadership to confront the clamour for long-denied change.

I was to spend my next 21 years in various political caucuses, municipal and parliamentary. In the Johannesburg council, our paterfamilias was the avuncular Sam Moss, a former mayor and one-time thespian who spoke in a rounded baritone. While a moderate pragmatist, he had little idea of how we as a group should respond to Oberholzer's political intransigence. He was generally conflict-averse and somewhat mesmerised by the reputation and reality of Obie's talents. Furthermore, in the event, there was a clear line of division between the old guard and the younger 'ginger group'. We thought our leadership stodgy and timorous; and were referred to, inside and outside the caucus, as 'the young Turks'.[17]

Our party caucus – or many of its members – were intensely conscious of status issues, such as where one sat and what one's position was in the mayoral stakes. In some ways, it was as Ian McEwan described a conclave of eminent poets: 'A jealous watchful world in which reputations are edgily tended.'[18]

It was a combustible mixture. Its shifting centre would not hold, and within two years of my arrival some of our 24 members would cross the floor or quit the council. For myself, while fascinated by the intrigues of the caucus, I set about establishing my presence in my ward and driving a more hard-nosed strategy in council. I joined the housing and utilities committee (which Paul Asherson dubbed 'the browsing and futilities committee') in the hope that I could secure a measure of relief for some of my hard-pressed constituents.

Politics is not always about the grand fate of nations.

Within weeks of my arrival in council, an unfortunate young resident in my ward, Patti Smit, was electrocuted to death while using her washing machine. The reason was, firstly, faulty wiring in her decrepit block of flats. However, had the building possessed earth leakage relay protection (standard and compulsory in more modern buildings) she would have received a severe, but not fatal, shock. I was appalled to discover that no owner of a building erected before 1978 – the majority of flats in Bellevue – was obliged to install such protection. The city electrical department immediately cut off power to the building (and a neighbouring one) and gave the landlords 30 days to rewire according to minimum safety standards.

This was where the Catch-22 consequence of the government's rent-control legislation kicked in. Intended as a protection against tenant exploitation, the ability of landlords to increase rents was regulated and circumscribed. When confronted by both the council and me on behalf of his angry and in-the-dark tenants, the landlord refused to make the necessary improvements, claiming that the cost of the rewiring, coupled with 'un-market-related and government-determined' rentals, made the proposition unaffordable.

Some form of compromise was reached. I was instinctively on the side of the tenants – not just because, cynically, they had the votes and the landlords did not; but because simple justice favoured them. However,

I also saw the unintended consequence of government legislation that foisted on the landlord elements of the state's social obligations towards its citizens. How to secure equity?

My solution was roughly as follows. I had discovered that council had a policy which provided soft loans to house owners to improve the wiring in their homes. This benefit ought to be extended to landlords since they, not tenants, contracted with the city for the supply of electricity. Again, we should make it mandatory for earth leakage relay systems to be provided in all inhabited buildings regardless of the year of construction.

My proposals received a reasonably good response; but my self-congratulatory moment soon passed. When the officials reported back (a month later) I witnessed first-hand the frustration which a British cabinet minister once described as the 'tyranny of bureaucracy'. My original proposal was deemed 'unenforceable' and 'beyond council's competence'. A watered-down resolution extended the soft loans scheme to homeowners other than house-dwellers. It was my first, and necessary, lesson in what TS Eliot might have called the 'shadow-land' of politics between the idea and the reality.

Chastened, but essentially undeterred, I set about my ward with a long list of urgent and needed improvements – ranging from broken kerbstones to unenforced noise regulations – which made my presence felt in the minds of my voters. In late November 2006, after I announced my decision to stand down as party leader, I was asked by a journalist to name what permanent monument to my work would remain. I replied, irreverently but not altogether untruthfully: 'Probably the traffic light I persuaded the city council to erect in 1986 on the corner of Rockey and Bezuidenhout streets!'

4

Oberholzer once – with disarming frankness – told the council that 'we have only ever made our planning decisions for whites.' The context was that, years before, the government had removed the control and financing of Johannesburg's black townships from the city council and located them in the hands of discredited and largely bankrupt black local authorities. The Coloured and Indian localities were governed by so-called management committees without independent revenue bases and little support or credibility. By 1986 the government's constitutional engineers – led by Chris Heunis – realised the inherent instability of the situation. Their answer, by the time of my arrival in council, was a truly Heath-Robinson construct aimed at securing at least some funding for the townships while maintaining white rule. This was given effect in the Regional Services Councils (RSCs). The first, known as the 'Central Witwatersrand RSC' (which included Johannesburg), was due to come on stream in July; and I decided to use my first major council budget speech in June to deconstruct this behemoth.

The RSC concept envisaged a sort of supra-municipality. Some existing councils would cede a few core functions and place them and the revenues they generated in the hands of a non-elected RSC – to benefit from mass economies of scale and use the proceeds to uplift the most impoverished (i.e. black) areas. Much-needed infrastructure would be built. However, while the enabling Act described the Byzantine basis for representation on an RSC, it became clear that white municipalities would wield the whip. Stripped to its essence, I calculated that Johannesburg would receive 48% of the votes on the RSC, while Soweto would get a mere 12% despite the fact that (in population terms) Soweto should have been allocated some 40% of the seats.

A fundamental problem – the central flaw of all government constitutional thinking and planning – was to rely on the beleaguered black township councils to provide the representatives from Soweto and other areas.

I decided to visit the Soweto council. Even what I had read and understood of the illegitimacy and unpopularity of black local authorities did not prepare me for what I witnessed. Accompanied by a number of Black Sash activists, including Molly Sklaar, we presented ourselves at the Soweto Civic Centre. The building was barricaded by barbed wire. Municipal policemen, armed with shotguns, stood sentinel around its perimeter. Inside we were introduced to a number of councillors, one of whom harangued us on 'the evils of Desmond Tutu', and others who denounced their participation in the system. I asked another about his greatest challenge, and he replied – candidly – that the Soweto councillors were unable for reasons of personal safety to actually live in Soweto (contrary to the requirement that they be residents of their municipalities).

In my council speech I described the RSCs as perpetuating a 'massive confidence trick'. They had been 'born in infamy' and would 'entrench apartheid instead of eliminating it'. It was possible to applaud at least one genuinely good feature of the model – transfer payments from richer to poorer municipalities – and the first annual budget of the Central Witwatersrand RSC was estimated to be R66-million. This, at first blush, was an impressive figure. But it would not survive close scrutiny.

The current budget deficit of the Soweto council – with no reserves to speak of, and subject to one of the most sustained and almost entirely successful community boycotts of rates and service accounts – totalled around R54,5-million. The proposed RSC budget would be almost wholly absorbed by this fiscal black hole. Further, nearly 80% of the homes in the area had no electricity – which the RSC had neither the means nor the will to address.

In Johannesburg, I was given 30 minutes as a junior councillor to launch my attack. The governing coalition benches were strangely quiet, while the PFP ranks' 'hear-hears' were vociferous.

I was immediately denounced in the most patronising terms by the NP leader, Danie van Zyl, with whom I was to clash frequently over the next few years: 'Mr Leon will mature in a few months. At the moment he is trying to make an impression.'

Actually, my speech did make an impression: on Oberholzer. He devoted most of his reply to my address; and afterwards he sought me out and asked for a copy of my speech. Of course, he did not concede to my analysis. His entire political worldview was animated by a defence of the status quo. We lived in separate political universes. But I had gained his ear, and even, apparently, his respect and affection.

The Regional Services Councils came on stream as scheduled, and lasted vestigially well into the new democratic order. They represented one half of the national government's agenda for local authorities, while, predictably, repression was the other. I stumbled across this truth and the city council's involvement in the tentacles of PW Botha's national security structure more or less by accident.

Johannesburg's traffic department was headed by a bizarre character named John Pearce. He was of enormous girth and easy, if menacing, charm, looming both literally and figuratively at every meeting. The rumour was that he enjoyed an exceptionally close relationship with Pik Botha, the Foreign minister.

Pearce's seeming nonchalance, his swagger and lack of deference to his political masters (in contrast to most other senior mandarins) was long established before I entered council. After one meeting, however, when I criticised his department, he approached me with a 'challenge'. Was I prepared to see the traffic department 'as it really was' – by attending one of their 'briefing and mustering' sessions at their headquarters at the Johannesburg Fort (once a notorious prison, and today the site of the Constitutional Court). I immediately accepted for a few days hence, but was utterly nonplussed when he told me that such get-togethers commenced at 4.45 am and he looked forward to welcoming me at this ungodly hour.

Somehow or other I managed to arrive more or less on time on the appointed day. I was the only city councillor present. The hardware and refreshments were astonishing. Pearce, in a suit, was surrounded by smartly uniformed traffic officers and men in brown camouflage uniforms. There was an array of armaments on display, including an armoured car! Pearce told me this was one of several used to 'guard Johannesburg's eastern flank, in Alexandra Township'. Clearly the department did not confine itself to issuing parking tickets, though none of its security activities had ever been disclosed or discussed in council.

My second surprise was the insistence of my host that I add a large dollop of brandy to the scalding hot coffee I was attempting to drink – along with consuming huge steaks, boerewors and the whole panoply of a typical South African braai, despite the early hour. Since I preferred my liquor after 6 pm rather than before 6 am I politely declined. Pearce, however, persisted and I relented. I don't recall how my morning lectures at Wits were affected, or improved; but Pearce and his colleagues downed several snifters of brandy before the get-together ended.

Clearly, the purpose of my presence was to get me 'on-side' and integrate me into the '*esprit de corps*' of the department's upper echelons. I was not converted. Clearly the elected councillors knew little of the true functioning of key departments. The traffic department, for example, was a form of private army and adjunct of the state then engaged in quelling 'unrest' in the townships.

I received confirmation when one of Pearce's key lieutenants – who had serious differences with his boss's cavalier style and his misuse of office – approached me. He informed me that the information given by the Management Committee to councillors about Pearce's department was 'a joke'. The reality was that they worked 'hand in glove', outside the public and council gaze, as an integral component of the Joint Management Centres (JMCs) of the national security system established by PW Botha.

The JMCs, in particular, were the nerve-centre of the government's councils and networks designed to meet the 'total onslaught' of its numerous external and internal enemies, real and imagined. There were apparently some four hundred JMCs – bureaucrats, technocrats, soldiers, policemen, and Johannesburg's traffic cops; all described by the Defence minister, Magnus Malan, as an 'early warning system to defuse revolutionary unrest'.

It had emerged in parliament that the secretive JMCs' remit included the 'local implementation of policies agreed at national level, including the deployment of the Defence Force, into troublesome "hot spots".' Helen Suzman had warned vividly that the relocation of security affairs outside of parliamentary control 'amounted to a creeping *coup d'état* by consent.' It later emerged[19] that such intervention often involved decisions on the use of powers of detention, restriction, banning, spying and harassment by organs of state, the police force and, indeed, the municipal authorities. Of such matters the Johannesburg city council was, at least in public, unaware.

James Selfe, who at the time was a PFP parliamentary researcher, and who had written a master's thesis on the state security apparatus, pointed out that the entire system, from the cabinet committee at the top to municipalities, operated on 'a need not to know' basis. The top brass issued general directives and deliberately left matters to operatives on the ground to implement and enforce policy 'by any means necessary'. Thus the Truth and Reconciliation Commission found a direct and bloody line of accountability between boss politicians and the foot-soldiers – who saw themselves as broadly mandated to co-opt local politicians or order extra-judicial assassinations by the killing machine of Vlakplaas under the control of the notorious Eugene de Kock.

All this would emerge in all its ghastly detail long after I'd left the council. But at the time, informed by no more than personal hunch and inspired tip-off, I determined to probe the linkage between our council and the JMCs. What I did know was that the JMCs operated outside the normal strictures and were virtually a law unto themselves.

In October 1986 I submitted some sixteen written questions to the Management Committee in an attempt to establish the precise links between the council, Pearce, and the local outposts of the state's security machine – and what council did for it. Oberholzer stonewalled; he claimed it was an 'offence' under the Protection of Information Act (1982) to reveal 'any or all' such details. All I could do was fulminate against Oberholzer for 'hiding under the skirts' of the Act.

Over the next year, Oberholzer ducked and dived for the cover of 'security' when I sought to raise and probe our links with the JMCs. My final recourse was to place a motion on the order paper – for full and open debate – obliging the council to prohibit its officials from participating in the machinery of the National Security Council and its JMCs. Should any of them be obliged by the Administrator of the Province to participate, I added, they would be compelled to report back on the nature and extent of their involvement. Of course, the motion would be voted down; but

I thought public airing of the issue would serve notice to the implicated apparatchiks that they were doing so with some degree of public notice. Eventually in October 1987 the mayor, doubtless on Oberholzer's (and Pearce's) instructions, blocked debate, refusing to consider the motion.

I decided to threaten court action. My great luck was that the eminent Sydney Kentridge SC supported my quest, and penned a written opinion advising that the mayor's decision was *ultra vires*, or outside his power. I backed up this powerful view with an accompanying legal letter advising that if he did not restore the motion to the order paper then I would seek relief in court. The mayor (or Oberholzer) relented, and the motion was eventually aired in council in January 1989, fifteen months after I had raised the issue.

The debate was something of an anti-climax. Aside from pointing out the dangers of municipal officials involving themselves 'without accountability and answerability … [in] a sinister covert government operation' I had little flesh to place on the bare bones of the structures I had outlined. My informant had told me that Pearce and his sidekick Brigadier Jan Visser were apparently involved, as part of their work for state security, in spying on various political organisations; but he could provide no further substantiation. I contemplated throwing this allegation into the debate, but lawyerly caution kicked in: councillors, unlike parliamentarians, did not have unfettered privilege and I envisaged that my moment of glory could see me on the wrong end of a ruinous defamation action. So I left matters. The NP amended my motion to read that 'Joint Management Centres were an excellent system as an alternative to Marxism'. This political gibberish was adopted as the substantive motion after the debate.

Before I left the council in late 1989 for parliament, Pearce was promoted into a new and expanded position as the head of the Orwellian 'Directorate of Public Safety'. In the debate on my doomed motion, a Nat councillor had proclaimed that 'when it comes to security there are no limits.' Just how accurate his chilling declaration was to prove emerged barely a year later in March 1990. The *Star* broke a story providing details of the very spy ring about which I had been tipped off a year before. It was profoundly disturbing.

A member of the ring gave the newspaper graphic details of how Pearce had been the spymaster. The threat of 'terrorism' and 'strikes' was used to mount surveillance and obtain information on trade unions and all manner of liberal and Left political organisations, from the End Conscription Campaign to Lawyers for Human Rights.

Fortuitously the story broke when parliament was debating the local government budget. Both Harry Schwarz and I used our speaking turns to press the minister to appoint a judicial commission of enquiry into the entire saga, which had begun to sound like a Keystone Cops script. One of the targets of the spies was National Union of Mineworkers secretary-general Cyril Ramaphosa – of whom the agents found that '[He] did not have close links with the ANC.' This spectacular lapse of intelligence and attention was exposed within months, when Ramaphosa was elected secretary-general of the ANC!

All this came in the early stages of FW de Klerk's *glasnost*. Since our request for a probe would reflect badly on PW Botha's national security management system (which De Klerk, on taking office the year before, had downgraded) it could do no harm to the new Nat leader. Accordingly, minister Amie Venter, a close De Klerk confidant, instructed the Administrator of the Transvaal to appoint a probe. The following month, retired judge Victor G Hiemstra presided over hearings in the Civic Centre.

I predicted a 'Pandora's Box' of revelations – and indeed the commission's first witness gave sensational evidence. He testified that he had arranged for the illegal surveillance of some forty-eight anti-government political organisations and NGOs. He also said that he had (perhaps predictably) prepared a file on me at the very time I was probing Pearce's department, 'Personal Profile No. 1'. It contained such weighty secrets as my car registration number and some of the places I visited. The witness, Johannes Beetge, revealed that every report prepared by a spy or handler was copied and forwarded to a senior official of the South African Defence Force's Johannesburg HQ at Wits Command.[20]

The evidence of the town clerk, the lugubrious Broederbonder Manie Venter, excited the most interest aside from Pearce's performance. Venter claimed he thought the spy network was involved in securing 'national key points and council property'. He was 'unaware' of any political motive or that Pearce had recruited some of his spooks from the Department of Military Intelligence. Furthermore, according to Venter, a four-man 'security committee' vetted all security matters before they were sent (presumably censored) to the Management Committee. This in turn would perhaps dribble out a few droplets of info to the elected councillors. Pearce, Brigadier Visser, Venter, and Oberholzer's successor as chairman, Danie van Zyl, comprised the committee.[21]

Pearce's evidence was risible and revealing. Pressed and harried by counsel for the End Conscription Campaign (ECC) on why council resources were tied up in monitoring the ECC's activities at Wits, Pearce claimed he was concerned about 'last-minute bussing of students' to the polls in the

October 1988 municipal elections – to disrupt them!

I wrote a commissioned article on the probe, entitled 'Stunned by the Gall of City Hall':'On the one hand we can dismiss the activities of the city council spying department as comic opera. On the other hand they suggest a level of illegitimate activity and an abuse of authority which crosses the threshold so that government itself becomes the law-breaker.'[22]

Between the revelations about the surveillance operation and Hiemstra's findings, power switched in Johannesburg and my successor as DP leader in council, Ian Davidson, became chairman of the Management Committee, with the NP as junior partners in a new coalition. Neither Venter nor Pearce would be welcome in a DP-led city; and Hiemstra's report was the perfect basis for the hasty exit of both. Hiemstra found that the list of people spied upon 'consists entirely of people with leanings against the National [Party] government, and the same can be said of the organisations.'[23]

On the conduct of Pearce, the Commission was damning and unequivocal:'One of the cornerstones of democracy is accountability, and it is on the issue of accountability that John Pearce stands accused.'[24]

5

I visited the Mshenguville squatter camp in Soweto. It was a rough and ready metaphor of all the ills that the Group Areas Act and urban planning legislation had wrought. Initially it was – of all things – a golf course laid out by apartheid's planners as a sort of aesthetic Band-Aid on squalor and overcrowding. Huts and shacks lined a filthy stream which by winter 1988 had completely overwhelmed the fairways and putting greens.

At first glance it seemed yet another repository for the millions of unhoused in South Africa – a bleak monument to human misery. On closer inspection, however, when some of the residents invited me into their dwellings, a different and more hopeful picture emerged. Even the most basic shelter demonstrated inside an almost heroic attempt at creating a home environment based on cleanliness and pride.

Largely spurred on by Josie Adler, a wonderfully public-minded activist to whom I was introduced early in my council career, I began to look into the proliferation of urban squatting – the space occupied by hundreds of thousands of black workseekers who, particularly in the 1980s, defied the apartheid planning laws and arrived in the greater Johannesburg area. At Josie's urging I began to publicise some of the worst cases of suffering.

(One was a destitute group of families who had set up home in a '*spruit*' in Oberholzer's political back yard, Kibler Park.) Often these interventions led to some relief – accommodation in a municipal hostel, or the provision of tents or other assistance.

I realised early, however, that this kind of fire-engine role, however necessary, begged a far larger question and obscured a mightier issue: how informed and ready were Johannesburg's planners for the full-scale arrival of thousands of workseekers who were streaming into the white citadels such as Johannesburg and its outskirts?

The heartstrings of the Management Committee were not easily moved; so I determined on a Gradgrindian 'facts, facts, facts' exercise. The obvious question, which I tabled in January 1988, was: 'How many squatters are currently present in the Johannesburg municipal area?' I knew the officials cocooned the Management Committee in a fool's paradise of undercounting and bureaucratic obfuscation to hide the true extent of the problem. However, even I was staggered when the council agenda revealed the answer to be '96 squatters only'. I personally knew, by name or by sight, double that number.

If the Management Committee figure was correct, I pointed out, something must have happened to the bulk of the 850 000 squatters whom parliament had recently been advised were in the Transvaal. 'It's hardly rocket science,' I said, to understand that the majority of this battalion would be living in and around Johannesburg, by far the largest urban settlement in the province. Of course this kind of denialism simply meant that at a crucial point the political masters of the municipality looked the other way.

While the homeless remained unaccommodated, by the end of 1987 it was estimated that 40% of Hillbrow – adjacent to my municipal ward – had become 'grey' with Coloureds, Indians and Africans moving in illegally but steadily. The PFP set up a group areas committee in Johannesburg to formulate an appropriate response, which I chaired.

Government persisted in ignoring the facts. It announced that neither of the two pillars of residential segregation – the Group Areas Act, and Reservation of Separate Amenities Act – would be purged from the statutes, or amended. The state president did, however, foresee a situation where in 'certain select areas' so-called 'free settlement areas' could be legalised. We rejected this. Marginal legalisation of a few mixed suburbs would be disastrous, creating inordinate pressures in a very restricted space – walling off the rest of Johannesburg as a segregated, though unsustainable, white enclave. As I expressed it at the time: 'Group areas need to go. Market forces need to operate. Selective opening is a recipe for disaster.'

This would be the defining issue in the late 1988 municipal elections.

Not unusually, the PFP was in a demoralised position to confront this electoral hurdle. Its poor performance in the 1987 general election, and the after-effects of the Slabbert desertion – the events were undoubtedly linked – hardly inspired confidence in the ranks or in the electorate. Much to my surprise, Eglin called me in July 1987 to head a national commission to weigh the party's future in local government. Should it participate, and, if so, in what form, in 1988? As one of the PFP's most junior representatives, I was immensely flattered. However, Douglas Gibson brought me down to earth with the reminder that 'when leaders are in doubt, they appoint a committee!'

But my preferment did cause considerable local anger in our senior ranks. Moss, usually affable and accommodating, had a serious case of the sulks, and responded with cold indifference when I sought his views. I did not realise quite how far his nose was out of joint, but we would soon witness his revenge for what he regarded as yet another slight. (The year before he had been elbowed out of a nomination contest against the sitting MP for Parktown, Dr Marius Barnard, brother of the more famous Chris.)

My committee (comprising councillors from across the country) took soundings and, in short order, published a 127-page report. Perhaps weight might have been seen by us as a substitute for depth. At any rate, we proposed that the party participate in the election (a blindingly self-evident recommendation); but did allow for regional opt-outs and variations. However, a proposal that any PFP member seeking election, even under an independent flag, be obliged to join a national 'Association of Progressive Councillors' (and subscribe to a National Municipal Charter based on PFP ideology) was warmly received by the party's Federal Council. My local base had, partly courtesy of Eglin, been given a national lift: newspapers took to referring to the Leon Commission.

I was then in the initial puppy-love phase of what would, over 20 years in public life, become a distinctly on-off affair with the media (see Chapter 12). At the end of 1987 the *Star* picked me as one of its 'Stars of the Community' for my work among the homeless. I was socially courted by the irascible and personally awkward Ken Owen. In the 1980s he was a fan. He was also a proponent of the muscular liberalism I favoured. He would not violate principle, as did the Black Sash, whose ardour for the liberation movements blinded them to deeply illiberal tactics employed by the ANC and PAC, from necklacing to murdering informers. He was deeply suspicious of the ANC in exile, and had little truck with the sanctions brigade at home led by Desmond Tutu.

In fact, Owen also despaired of the PFP's political future and dismissed Slabbert as an 'ethnic carpetbagger'. I suspected that the main reason for my becoming a regular fixture at the dining table of the Owens' sprawling Atholl home in northern Johannesburg was the fact that I was his wife's constitutional law lecturer at Wits. Not that Kate Owen needed any favours from me. We used to euphemistically describe students of a senior vintage as 'mature students'; but she was exceptionally bright and diligent, as her grades reflected. However, this cosy access I enjoyed with a major editor would change. Elsewhere I will record the embittered and envenomed vitriol Owen was to spew against me from 1992 onwards. Our mutual – strictly intellectual – infatuation was to be fairly short-lived.

Sam Moss exploded his own leadership bomb when in March 1988 he and Harold Rudolph (the last-serving PFP mayor of Johannesburg) announced that they were quitting the party and would run as independents in the forthcoming local elections. A cynical friend phoned to ask: 'What sort of outfit do you belong to? First your national leader deserts his post in the middle of battle, and now your local one. Losing one is a calamity, but now two – surely a disaster?' And certainly Moss and Rudolph had kicked their caucus colleagues hard in the political solar plexus and below. Now we were not only divided, but leaderless. Moss claimed that 'party politics had been of no benefit to city government' – a strange claim, I thought, from one who had led a political party in council for the preceding 11 years. But, as always, the political was merely a cover for the personal – the thousand slights, rebuffs and disappointments which constitute the warp and woof of political life.

Owen, as always the intellectual bovver boy, decided to put the boot into Moss and Rudolph. He also decided to articulate why I would be the best successor: 'Cromwell's harsh judgment of the Long Parliament fits the former mayors of Johannesburg, Sam Moss and Harold Rudolph: they have sat there for too long for any good that they have done ... The future lies in the hands of a younger generation. The most prominent claimant [for the leadership] is Tony Leon. As a law lecturer he has kept abreast, as the old guard have hardly done, of the constitutional changes and their impact on local government. In the council he has been aggressive, probing and effective. His youth and energy are as much an asset as Moss's age and lethargy are a liability. The only question is whether PFP councillors are prepared to unite behind tomorrow's men or whether they will hide behind yesterday's.'[25]

When Paul Asherson, Ian Davidson, Cecil Bass and I gathered in my

Illovo flat following the Moss–Rudolph exit, I announced that I would stand for the leadership. The great advantage of being 31 years old is that the certainties of youth have not yet given way to the self-doubt and reflective questioning of middle age. My friends, more or less, agreed to support my bid, and I set about canvassing my council colleagues.

My proposed candidacy received fairly wide support. Although I was irredeemably stamped as a 'young Turk' insurrectionist, I had ties with some of the old guard in our ranks, particularly the father–son members Max and David Neppe; Monty Sklaar, a former mayor; and the old Prog warhorse, and scion of an old Cape family, Christopher Newton Thompson. Claire Quail, whom I sat next to in council, was my strongest backer. However, a strong minority felt my swift ascent should not go unchallenged. They coalesced around the candidacy of one of the venerable aldermen and one of the remaining past mayors in our ranks, Issy Schlapobersky, a UP veteran who had long eyed Moss's post as his rightful due.

Issy and I were on perfectly civil terms. The contest, whatever its outcome, would not result in lasting enmity; but the caucus I was hoping to head comprised very fragile material. The once-significant PFP presence in council was now more of a rump: its tantalisingly close proximity to power had, through desertions and emigration, been reduced to 19, and the *Star* predicted we would win, in the looming poll, no more than twelve seats.[26]

A sombre atmosphere, appropriate to our reduced circumstances, prevailed when the PFP caucus gathered in the Civic Centre on Monday 28 March 1988 to choose its new leader. Schlapobersky and I were the only candidates nominated. I suppose the entire process took about three minutes, but it seemed like thirty. I won, 12–7. I was seized with a sense not of manifest destiny, but of hope that I could turn our situation around.

My ascent to the municipal leadership coincided with changes elsewhere in the battered PFP. Eglin was giving way to De Beer. I believed that part of the PFP's poor performance against both Left and Right was part of a deeper intellectual failure to define itself properly. We had become part of the mush in the middle. Writing for *Frontline*, I suggested that the PFP's preoccupation with ridding South Africa of apartheid had blinded it to the need to defend its own ideas from the encroachment of the liberation forces, whose own agenda and practices were deeply inimical to sound liberal values.

I said: 'The PFP is burdened with a stereotype … Although labels are the parsley on the plate of politics, we need to be muscular liberals. This is because liberalism is too often confused with a negative passivity, strong on critique, soft in defence of society, and anarchic by disposition ... In reality and on close examination the liberal credo is at considerable variance with the radical chic analysis that "the people" and "the oppressed" should (in all circumstances) prevail ...'

While this was aimed at the Left, which I recognised as the coming force in South African politics, my immediate and full-time opponents in the council were, in fact, on the Right. Oberholzer had announced his resignation to coincide with the forthcoming municipal election. His place as Management Committee chairman would in due course be taken by the NP leader in the council, Danie van Zyl.

In any scenario, political or otherwise, it would be difficult to imagine two more opposite characters than Danie van Zyl and me. He was, even in the PW Botha era, an arch-reactionary. A former boxing promoter and owner of a building construction company, he approached politics as a blood-sport, unrelenting in his political pugilism. A caricature of the time was that Nat bureaucrats wore grey shoes. Van Zyl did wear them – to match his shiny grey suits. A countervailing caricature was that I was a 'Yuppie'.

To me Van Zyl represented all that was wrong and backward about the management and politics of Johannesburg. Unlike the case of Obie, I was unconstrained by affection or respect when it came to taking the attack to him.

In my first speech as the new leader, I attacked the Management Committee for its 'champagne and caviar taste' for first-class overseas junkets 'while pleading poverty when it came to Johannesburg's urgent needs'. Bobby Godsell (who with his wife, Gillian, would be immensely helpful in providing intellectual rigour to my leadership) arranged for some of the sharpest financial minds at Anglo American to review the city's finances and help me fashion an intelligent and economically literate response. When I immersed myself in the small print, I noticed – for example – that R50 000 was allocated for 'flowers for the mayoral parlour'. I picked on such items, reckoning, accurately, that they would attract headlines as proof of wide-ranging 'wasteful expenditure'.

Local politics feed on vanity, a destructive fault. This affected the PFP's standing in council. One councillor lost a nomination contest and promptly quit the party to stand as an independent. Then the incumbent deputy mayor, David Neppe, requested an urgent meeting. I had known and been friendly with the Neppe family since I first became active in the PFP in Johannesburg. I had even saved David's father Max's floundering political career when, some five years earlier, I had rallied the Hillbrow PFP, which I then led, to support his candidacy for a by-election after Max had lost his own seat earlier in the year.

At the time, the immensely grateful David told me I would have 'the eternal gratitude' of the family. Well, an eternity in politics is strictly time-limited. Another lesson is that – in politics – 'no good deed goes unpunished'. When David arrived in my office he was flustered and embarrassed. He said: '[With] tears in my eyes I have to resign from the party.' I was completely winded. Of all people, I had assumed the Neppes were stalwart behind both the party and me. Not, apparently, with the mayoralty at risk.

David babbled nonsense about the mayor needing 'to stand above politics' (a novel proposition). Only after he hastily exited my office did I learn the sub-text: the Nats had told him they would only support him for the mayoralty if he stood against the PFP as an independent. Neppe actually prevailed in the election – though his dubious acquisition of the mayoral chain was short-lived. After six months, he was chopped and the Nats installed one of their own.

6

Spurred by these travails, I applied the excellent maxim of French general Ferdinand Foch, during the first battle of the Marne in 1914: 'My centre is giving way, my right wing falling back. Situation excellent. I am going over to the attack.'[27]

In various public meetings and articles I said Johannesburg was 'at the crossroads'. Under its current management it was doomed to remain shunned and isolated as a racist backwater (twinned with the city of Santiago, then under the dictatorial grip of Augusto Pinochet); or, I suggested, in the parlance popularised by Clem Sunter: 'We can adopt the high road, and make ours a modern, harmonious and multiracial city.'

Behind this boilerplate cliché we had drawn up a raft of policies ranging from municipal policing, and acceptable non-racial community standards, to proposals to return power transparently back to the council, and away from both the Management Committee mandarins and their political masters. I purloined a catchphrase from Jesse Jackson, and our slogan – 'Vote your hopes, not your fears' – sprouted from posters across the suburbs in the PFP red-white-and-blue livery.

We were seriously short of quality candidates. Not for the last time in

144

my political life, I reached into my own social set – or at least twisted a few arms to persuade them to stand under our colours. Many declined, but three agreed: Clifford Garrun, Lester Fuchs and Carl Stein. They were subsequently elected. Eventually we nominated about thirty-seven in wards across the city, and hoped on a good day to win about half.

Meanwhile, my just-held ward of Bellevue-Judith's Paarl had been de-limited out of existence. Schwarz was keen that I remain in Yeoville, but Suzman said: 'You must be mad! Take a safe seat in Houghton.' It proved a fateful remark. A new seat had been created there – joining the stolidly respectable Highlands North area with the leafier, high-income suburbs of Oaklands and Orchards. I decided to stand in what was named Ward 17; and while as leader I was unopposed for the party nomination, I found myself in a three-way fight against a Nat and an independent.

With some anxiety, I contemplated just how many, or few, colleagues would be joining me. The NP confidently projected a thirty-seat sweep, and the PFP, with a host of defectors standing against us in our normally safest seats, looked imperilled.

In Cape Town, the party national congress in August formally installed De Beer as leader, giving me an opportunity to grandstand about our efforts to revive the party in Johannesburg. This attracted media attention. David Breier wrote in the *Saturday Star*: 'The moribund PFP is beginning to display faint signs of life as the brash young breed of Johannesburgers known as the "young Turks" inject new energy into the party.

'These "practical Progs" believe they are more in tune with what the ordinary voter feels than the Progs have been for a long time … [In Cape Town] there were the obligatory standing ovations for Colin Eglin who was retiring as leader and for Dr Zach de Beer who took over the leadership, but it was the speech by "superturk" Mr Tony Leon, leader in Johannesburg city council, which set the congress alight.'[28]

In another interview,[29] which journalist Patrick Laurence headlined as 'PFP's Leon turns out to be a tiger', I said liberals had to strip themselves of their soft, effete image. While the PFP was 'justly famous' for attacking institutional forms of oppression, we also needed to start attacking crime in the streets, hence our call for municipal policing.

The municipal election campaign coincided with the 40th anniversary of Nat rule. Rallies were held throughout the country. In Houghton we inverted the celebratory mood of our opponents and held our own com-memoration – a public meeting to denounce the misery that misrule had wrought. Suzman, as always, was the star turn at the Houghton Primary School. My role was as the warm-up speaker. After paying appropriate obeisance to Helen's significant and historic role, I aimed my pitch at my own peer group:

'Many of us in this hall, the under-forties, are indeed the children of apartheid. [It] matters little whether we are the so-called benefactors or victims of the most enduring system of racial injustice in the modern world, of one of the most pervasive forms of racial engineering ever undertaken by a government which calls itself "civilised".'

Suzman was in vintage form, mocking the Nats and performing a hammed-up imitation of the dour minister of Law and Order, Louis le Grange, and his accented English. The audience was convulsed with laughter. The next day I got a different take on the meeting, from an unlikely source. At Wits I was collared by Edwin Cameron, a colleague and friend, who had been at the meeting and who was way to the Left of Suzman and me. He observed that the party would never attract Afrikaans support if it mocked the way Afrikaners spoke English. (Edwin is, in fact, half-Afrikaans.) Since then I have never attempted to win an easy laugh by imitating anyone's accent.

Another decision was to turn down an arrangement which allowed councillors to buy back their pensions to a maximum of fifteen years, at little cost (R1 from the councillor matched by R7 from the ratepayer). I felt I should attach personal cost to my endless proselytising about the 'snouts in the trough' trope of municipal and national politics.

My steady girlfriend of the time, Beverley Gurwicz, loyally and tenaciously trudged the streets of my new political ward canvassing voters alongside me. She also had the inspiration of printing a carrot cake recipe, emblazoned on the back of my manifesto, surmising that this practical ruse might entice voters not to instantly consign my promises to the rubbish bin. And the celebrity-worshipping *Sunday Times* dubbed me 'a delicious hunk' and ran a profile claiming: 'Tony Leon looks as though he's stepped out of the pages of the male equivalent of *Vogue* magazine.'[30] It did wonders for my ego.

As our campaign began to power along at a reasonable tempo, our rallies were enthusiastically and well attended, and there were signs of a revival – and precisely then, the Nat bruiser Van Zyl struck. He proclaimed that he would lobby government to declare that any ward which voted PFP be immediately opened to all races, under the proposed Free Settlement Act, while all NP wards would remain segregated. The inference was obvious: whites voting PFP would be visiting on themselves massive overcrowding and worse.

He received a withering response from our campaign manager, Peter

Soal:'I have news for Mr van Zyl. One day the whole of South Africa will be open to all races, including the suburb he ran away from [there had been a CP threat in Newlands, Johannesburg] to the one in which he is now standing in Linden.'[31]

Beeld, normally staunch in its support for the NP, turned its guns on Van Zyl's '*swart gevaar*' tactic. It was outraged that Van Zyl could caricature the free settlements proposal as something to be 'visited on your worst political enemies' rather than as a reform.[32]

I pointed out that the PFP stood for the total scrapping of group areas, not the creation of social pressure-cookers.

De Beer's leadership proved a boost. Crucially, he ensured that our campaign was properly funded. During this period I was first introduced to – and dined with – Harry Oppenheimer and his formidable, but intensely warm, wife Bridget. This relationship was to become significant and enduring. Oppenheimer kindly agreed to address a fundraising dinner for our campaign (as did his son, Nicky); his pulling power ensured a sell-out evening, generating further funds for our election efforts.

I had little time to reflect on, or perfect, the art of leadership. I simply led on instinct and applied as much energy to the job as possible. The day before polling, Bobby Godsell sent me an inspiring fax: 'I want you to know that whatever tomorrow's result, you have already achieved a very important thing for the PFP, for liberalism and for South Africa. I am sure that the party can now survive and I know that it is in no small measure consequent on your leadership of the campaign you have created here in Johannesburg.'

It was apparent on election day, 26 October 1988, even before the doors opened at my polling station at the Laërskool Dirkie Uys in Orchards, that my new ward was to be a far safer political base than my old one had been. From about 6.30 am a queue of voters stood in line at our registration table, while my opponents' reception areas were literally deserted. Zach de Beer arrived shortly after 7 am, and we then went to visit the polling stations in the key marginal wards which the PFP had to win in order to stay in business. The signs everywhere looked hopeful.

I entered my own count that night buoyed up with expectation. My own result was declared early. The signs had not been misleading. I received 72% of the vote.

CITY OF JOHANNESBURG: WARD 17: 26 OCTOBER 1988:
OFFICAL RESULT

AJ Leon (PFP)	2 144
M Rosen (NP)	545
M Carel (IND)	269
Spoilt papers	0
Majority	1 599
% Poll	57

At the party's Houghton headquarters we gathered to hear the results. We picked up three wards we never expected to win – including to our ecstatic amazement the scalp of the NP deputy leader, who lost his safe seat in Melville to our young student candidate, Deon van Greunen. We also beat Sam Moss in his own back yard in Killarney, thanks to Carl Stein's efforts. Cecil Bass, whom I'd persuaded to run again in a different seat, snatched back the ward in Lyndhurst which had been thrown away five years before. We just lost Hillbrow to the Nats; and Jack Bloom, who would later make a name for himself in provincial politics under DP colours, agonisingly forfeited Cyrildene by 20 votes to the son of my previous nemesis, Sam Bloomberg ('Son of Sam' seemed a particularly apt name for this deeply unattractive character).

Around 5 am Zach laconically concluded: 'Not a bad day at the office. Not bad at all.'

The PFP won 18 seats; the NP 26; the Conservative Party, four; and the independents held three of 51 seats. This gave the NP a perilous overall majority of just one seat in the reconfigured council. *Business Day* editorialised: 'The PFP staggering to its feet after disasters and setbacks that began with the abdication of its most charismatic leader has reason for modest satisfaction. In Johannesburg, especially, a strategy of long-term reconstruction pursued by Tony Leon has paid off handsomely ... Leon takes into the council a team of people of a quality and seriousness not seen in many a year.'[33]

Favourable media publicity focused on how in five months I had led the PFP turnaround. Nationally, the party also received a huge boost from Johannesburg: not only the largest municipality, but the only one where the PFP had contested the local elections with party candidates, not aligned independents, fighting on a broad front.

We had laid the foundation for a DP takeover of the city council within two years of the election, when an internally riven NP caucus effectively toppled its own leadership.

Among the many thank-you notes I penned after the results were known was one to Zach de Beer, whose leadership and fundraising acumen I was certain had boosted our result. His own reply concluded: 'I do very much hope that we can do a few more things like this campaign in the future together. I am sure that you have a great future in politics, and if I can do a bit to get it on the road, I shall be delighted.'

Zach's promissory note came in handy a few months later, when I contemplated a move from local to national politics. My decision would rock the foundations of the very political establishment then toasting my success in Johannesburg.

CHAPTER 4

The Battle for Houghton

Nor law, nor duty bade me fight,
Nor public men, nor cheering crowds:
A lonely impulse of delight
Drove to this tumult in the clouds.

WB YEATS

I

At an absurdly young age I decided to become a member of parliament. Perversely – to family and friends – I admired politicians; if not the generally conservative, crimped and curmudgeonly South African variant of my childhood, then certainly overseas role models. In standard four, when I was at home sick for a day, the news came through that Senator Robert Kennedy had been assassinated in Los Angeles. It was as though a close relative had been slain. All my early role models were of the liberal-Left.

Three years later, on New Year's Eve 1971, I went to the cinema with my mother to see the Costa Gavras movie *Z*. I was transfixed; I identified with the Yves Montand role, the Greek left-wing politician Gregoris Lambrakis. Once again an assassination was involved – and an insurgent politician.

I soon localised my political ardour and fixated on a future in South African politics. If there was one political figure who typified the best of political virtues – and star power – it was Helen Suzman, in whose constituency I was serving as a city councillor by 1989. The two critical events which catapulted me from the front rank of Johannesburg politics to the back benches of the South African parliament – and on – were the formation of the Democratic Party, and Suzman's decision to retire after 36 years as an MP.

Houghton occupied a special place in South Africa's political history. It was Suzman's domain for nearly four decades, and represented a small, enlightened, well-to-do corner of the white population. One negative impression was well described by the acerbic Ken Owen in *Business Day* in October 1989: 'Houghton in a sense is a metaphor for many old prejudices: middle-class distrust of rand-barons, hostility to capitalism, Afrikaner dislike of the toffee-nosed English upper classes and a deep, deep resentment of Helen Suzman's 30-year display of actual, not pretended, moral superiority.'[1] In the somewhat bare cupboard of white liberal politics, Houghton was the most glittering prize on display.

Helen was effectively the only star of the Progs; she was its sole representative in parliament for 13 of her years in the national legislature; and I got to know her well through my precocious involvement in the constituency and party. The assumption – somewhat arrogant in the view of many – was that when she retired the succession would pass to her long-time provincial councillor and constituency chairwoman, Irene Menell.

Irene was a cousin of Helen's and the wife of Clive Menell, scion of the Anglo-Vaal mining empire. The Menells led what passed in Johannesburg as a social and political salon for the right-minded and powerfully connected; their graciously appointed Parktown home, Le Tholonet, was directly opposite the Oppenheimers' grand sprawl, Brenthurst.

Irene was highly intelligent, and possessed a manner that hovered between the dismissive and the diffident. She and Clive, doubtless unfairly, were regarded by some of the constituency activists as relentless social mountaineers: but the flip side was that they used their great wealth and standing to pursue causes by no means typical of white society, from interracial dialogue to adult literacy. With the tact of a young bull who had run out of china shops, my eventual decision to challenge the apostolic succession would have wide-ranging consequences for me – and for my relationship with Helen and Irene.

I anticipate: 1989 was, in Roy Jenkins's felicitous phrase, a 'junction year' for the country, the DP and me. None of us emerged in the same direction in which we began. Above all, the 11-year rule of PW Botha began to unravel when he was felled by a stroke. The personal consequences were calamitous; he attempted to retain the presidency while relinquishing the party leadership. Ironically, nearly two decades later, Thabo Mbeki, Botha's successor but two as president, would attempt the opposite exercise – retaining the party presidency while yielding the country's leadership. The result was equally dismal. Education minister and Transvaal leader, FW de Klerk, hitherto the champion of those who had not followed Dr AP Treurnicht into the Conservative Party, narrowly beat the Finance minister Barend du Plessis, perceived as representing a more enlightened nationalism.

Botha's plans to split the leadership between himself and De Klerk proved unworkable, and the *Groot Krokodil* was forced out. In a bitter, denunciatory speech on television, he quit the presidency in August. His acrimonious departure occurred when the national state of emergency had been renewed for a fourth successive year; his sprawling national security management system (which Suzman had accurately summarised as 'a creeping *coup d'état* by consent') had seen nearly fifty thousand anti-apartheid activists detained – and some tortured – without trial. Botha represented the bleak face of white oppression.

A militarist by instinct, not by training, he ceded vast political power to the South African Defence Force. Yet in the month before his resignation, he became the first head of state to receive then-jailed icon Nelson Mandela in his office for tea and talks. Mandela later reminisced to me that he preferred dealing with Botha to De Klerk, since 'you at least knew where you stood'. (The comment came in 1995, at the height of the tensions in the Government of National Unity, in which De Klerk served uneasily and apparently unhappily – so perhaps it can be somewhat discounted.)

Botha had partly dismantled elements of grand apartheid. The recognition of trade union rights for blacks and the permanence of blacks in urban areas (a recognition of reality) required a hitherto uncountenanced degree of apostasy. Botha also removed some of the most egregious elements of petty apartheid, including the Prohibition of Mixed Marriages Act. But he was, in his bullying and charmless manner, a 'reformer without results'. While prepared to create a right-wing opposition force, he faltered at the essential step: the acceptance of black South Africans within the central political system.

Any hope that Botha might lift South Africa out of the quagmire was effectively dashed on 15 August 1985 when he declined to deliver a much-promised 'Rubicon Speech' at the NP Natal congress (see 'Dancing with Dialectics', Chapter 2).

At the same time that the NP was undergoing its leadership crisis – which within a year would lead to the unbanning of the ANC – the Democratic Party went about being formed. The 1987 general election was a crushing disappointment to the Progressive Federal Party. After the shock resignation of Van Zyl Slabbert, Colin Eglin had been persuaded to resume the leadership from which he had been forcibly ejected some eight years before. He was obliged to discard the sage advice of the Greek philosopher Heraclitus: 'You can't step twice in the same river. Everything flows, nothing stays.' The PFP lost a dozen seats to the NP, and the Conservative Party became the official opposition.

Trudging along the streets in support of the PFP that year, I personally heard the disillusionment of our core supporters. They wanted 'something new', 'something different'. And in Helderberg, near Stellenbosch in the Cape, former Nat constitutionalist and ambassador to London Denis Worrall had taken on Chris Heunis in his own stronghold. Worrall had dramatically resigned his post and formed a fledgling 'Independent Party' as a reaction against the Nats' unwillingness to embrace reform, and in particular the Buthelezi-inspired KwaZulu-Natal Indaba. This forum had negotiated a constitutional model which would have seen Natal accord full political and civil rights to blacks, with protection for minorities. The product was less important than the process: in a country starved of negotiation politics it shone like a brief shooting star.

Worrall's decision was seen as a brave repudiation of a political life of ease and repose. In reality, he had been sidelined after incurring the wrath of Botha and Heunis. Nevertheless, he added much-needed glamour and freshness to the opposition terrain.

Closer to my own bailiwick, Wynand Malan, a *verligte* NP MP from Randburg, left his party at the time of the Worrall insurgency and formed a new movement with four PFP defectors. Malan retained his seat, and Worrall ran Heunis exceedingly close – losing Helderberg by an agonisingly narrow 39 votes.

In the grisly aftermath of 1987, the PFP groped for the way forward. Robin Carlisle, who lost Wynberg, was a likeable if natural-born intriguer; he began a low-key revolt against Eglin's leadership. A year later, Eglin signalled his readiness to give way to his long-time friend and political ally, Zach de Beer. De Beer had unfailing civility, great personal charm and warmth; he was possessed of a first-rate intellect and *noblesse oblige* acquired over 25 years in the Anglo American empire. However, his removal in 1961 from the political front line extinguished much of the fire in his belly. Assuming the leadership of a battered political party at the age of nearly sixty – Churchill's example notwithstanding – was probably not the most rejuvenating step the PFP could muster.

But there were no other takers or prospects; and Zach was quite forcefully persuaded that duty required he answer the call. His reluctance arose, in part, out of his deep fear of offending Eglin. The matter was settled by Harry Oppenheimer – appropriate in view of his role as the party's chief financial backer and his close relationship to both men.

In August 1988 De Beer was unanimously elected leader of the PFP in his home town, Cape Town. In his acceptance speech he stated his intention of unifying the fragmented white opposition. Not without irony, he invoked the words of the first NP prime minister, Dr DF Malan: '*Bring bymekaar daardie mense wat van innerlike oortuiging bymekaar hoort.*' ('Bring together those who out of inner conviction ought to belong together.')

Simultaneously, there were calls in the opposition media and business community for a more rational alignment of the anti-apartheid parliamentary opposition. Even those not at all associated with the unrewarding grind of politics – such as the rugby supremo Louis Luyt; FW de Klerk's older brother, the journalist Wimpie; and maverick Stellenbosch academic Sampie Terreblanche – signalled support for a new movement. This set off a series of negotiations between De Beer, Malan and Worrall.

Neither Malan nor Worrall was particularly liberal, but there was no disagreement on the broad principles that a new opposition force should follow. It was apparent that any disagreement between the three was minor compared to the major chasm which yawned between the government and the extra-parliamentary forces on its Left.

Indecisions and delays in forming the new party related, as these matters often do, to position and pre-eminence. There was also a large body of opinion in the PFP (whose heirs evinced the same sentiments and obduracy when I merged the DP and NP into the DA, 11 years later) that since they had toiled longest and hardest, they, and not political arrivistes, should be represented in greater numbers in the new leadership.

Although by then quite prominent in the PFP, I fortunately took no part in the negotiations that led to the formation of the DP. This unhappy task was left to the party's four provincial leaders. The results: a new party name and logo, and a troika leadership of Malan, De Beer and Worrall with equal representation for each element on the party's National Board. I had no doubt the Democratic Party (DP) was an absolute necessity – and the 'something new' our voters yearned for. However, I shared the old Progs' dismay at how we had discounted our strength in the negotiations (the PFP membership, voter base and financial resources vastly outweighed the combined strength of the other movements) and settled on unfavourable terms.

Suzman shared none of my enthusiasm for the new project and all my misgivings about the negotiations. She described the party formation acidly and amusingly as 'the biggest hijack since Entebbe – and there aren't any Jews around to rescue it.'

There was at least one. And I (with De Beer's active support) decided to move a resolution at the PFP closure congress in Johannesburg, in April 1989, that the new party junk the troika leadership with dispatch and elect a single leader. The 500 delegates enthusiastically supported it – many

because it was the only meaningful way they could register their disapproval of the so-called 'hijacking'. I deployed an inelegant metaphor: that
the party 'needed to soar like a bird, and no bird can fly with three heads.'
This resolution found no favour with the DP congress at year end.

Eglin, the outgoing chairman of the PFP, said aptly of the party's decision to dissolve into the DP the next day: 'Our task here is to bring down
the curtain on a worthy era but to do so in a way that we are more effective than we have been in the past.'[2]

The PFP had to choose four representatives to the newly constituted
National Board. Harry Schwarz and I – perceived by the delegates to be
the most hardline PFPs – were elected over the heads of all the provincial
leaders; and together with MPs Eglin and Tian van der Merwe formed the
party's complement at the top table.

In the Linder Auditorium of the Johannesburg College of Education, I
sought refuge in the classics, quoting Victor Hugo's aphorism that 'nothing
is as powerful as an idea whose time has come.' The speeches of the three
joint leaders were, appropriately, studies in contrast. Zach was worthy but a
little flat; while Malan was almost semi-mystical, invoking 'paradigm shifts'
and 'flex flows' which I thought verged on mumbo-jumbo. Worrall, however, set the congress alight with a barnstorming extempore (it seemed)
performance, perhaps somewhat light in content. The excellence of his
bilingual delivery electrified the crowd.

Internal machinations within the National Board pointed early to fundamental differences between its components. The first fuse was lit when
Malan demurred at the prospect of the DP fielding candidates for the
Indian and Coloured chambers of the Tricameral parliament, in addition
to the white constituencies we would be contesting in the general election on 6 September.

Malan saw himself as the party's avatar of extra-parliamentary activity
– and its essential link to the mass-based democratic movement. He was
terrified of giving offence to that sector, and there was a rough logic to his
calculus: the white representatives in parliament were supported by their
community, while the Coloureds and Indians were generally not. Many
of us, however, thought the logic of selective participation specious, and
deeply disrespectful to PFP members in the Indian chamber, particularly
the MPs Pat Poovalingam and Mamoo Rajab.

Poovalingam – an old-style liberal from Durban, who had been a confidant of Alan Paton's – denounced Malan as a 'racist'. And then an enormous row erupted between Schwarz (who took offence easily) and Pierre

Cronjé (who had defected from the PFP to Malan's group and now found himself back with his adversaries) who detested each other. The notional issue was whether another ex-PFP renegade, Jan van Eck, then sitting in parliament as an Independent, should be admitted into the party and allowed to contest the election under its colours.

In the end, participation in the election in all chambers was agreed upon, more or less in exchange for Van Eck's readmission.

2

Such petty manoeuvres were symptomatic of the uneasy basis of the recently consecrated marriage. It had certainly not been conceived in sin, but was the product of necessity, far more than love.

I had misgivings about Malan and his crew and some of the Worrallites – although not Denis and his chief lieutenant, David Gant, whom I grew to like. But this did not quench my belief in the party itself. A week after its formation, I went to East London to address a gathering; my enthusiasm was manifest when I said, no doubt with as much hyperbole as sincerity: 'The founding of the DP is the most exciting thing to have happened in South African politics for thirty years. During that time every merger, reduction or splitting of the parties of the opposition in parliament, has been hitherto a basic rearrangement of the furniture of the old United Party. This time it's different, we have brought together the opposition elements and added to them a "fourth force" of enlightened modern Afrikaans-speaking opinion.'

I urged the party – and the audience – to stand up to both the 'false patriotism of the NP and the AK-47s of the ANC'.

Frantically involved as I was in assisting the new party to get going – and heading the Johannesburg city council caucus – I nonetheless contemplated the forthcoming election. I had decided to act on my long-nurtured (I was then 32) ambition of going to parliament. My fervent hope was that – although abandoned by people like Slabbert – a parliamentary process of peaceful change was still possible. Although I shared my party's disbelief that De Klerk would deliver on his reformist noises, I believed the leadership shake-up in the governing party could yield change.

I also had been thoroughly demoralised by so many of my close and good friends' decision to emigrate. I would stay – and wanted to be involved in a forum that would allow me to help shape the future of the country I loved. A delusion? Not to me.

On a more prosaic level, my intense involvement in politics had reduced me to singularly part-time habits in my full-time job as a law lecturer at Wits. Further, I did not see my future in academia, or in legal practice. The American football coach Yogi Berra once advised: 'If you come to a fork in the road, take it.' I couldn't. I chose to put forward what I perceived as my claim to stand in Houghton.

At around this time, a seemingly flattering article appeared in the *Star* newspaper with the somewhat sinister heading: 'Leon could be too ambitious'.[3] Whatever it had to say of my perceived merits, there was a clear message which I did not doubt came from party elders close to the Irene Menell camp: 'Charismatic Tony Leon's meteoric rise continued at the weekend when he outstripped several PFP heavyweights to be elected one of the PFP's four members on the DP's new executive. His rapid rise in municipal ranks from ordinary councillor to leader of opposition pales in comparison with his progress in party politics. The 31-year-old "yuppie" attorney and lecturer undoubtedly has his eyes set on a parliamentary seat.

'But ironically, his extraordinary flair for politics could count against him. For some of his party seniors believe he should for the time being stick to his present job of changing the country's biggest city into what he called "a shining city on the hill".'

My ambition to succeed Suzman had been boosted by a number of approaches I received from key constituency activists and leadership figures. Many stalwart 'true blue Progs' supported my candidacy; and it soon became apparent that Menell had made – no doubt unintentionally – many adversaries. Many of my most ardent backers, I concluded, were more passionate about blocking a dynastic stitch-up, and also in 'stopping Irene', than they were in promoting my career.

One of my offstage backers, the eccentric billionaire Graham Beck, fell into this category. Over drinks (with him it was always several, the whiskies huge) during the preceding Christmas holidays at his St James mansion near Cape Town, he vented his spleen: 'If you have enough fucking guts to take her on and beat her, I'll back you!'

Graham was astonishing. He had turned his father's modest fortune into a massive empire of mines, wine farms, racing studs in Kentucky and the Cape, and one of the largest yacht-building businesses in Europe. Exceedingly generous and crassly earthy, he had an enormous capacity for both warmth and harshness. Crucially, in my modest financial situation (in all DP 'safe seats' the candidate had to pay the costs of the election), he was a man of his word. When I did beat Menell for the nomination he stumped up the sum of R100 000 to pay the entire costs of a very well-resourced campaign. (In today's money, that is about – in purchasing power terms – the equivalent of more than a million rands.)

Another whose enthusiasm for my candidacy was genuine, and was also beset by doubts about Suzman's hand-picked successor, was the legendary former newspaper editor Joel Mervis. Mervis, who resembled a sad bloodhound, had great intellect and a trenchant humour; massive charm (if he liked you), haughty disdain if he did not. He and my mother were close; but Joel was closer to Helen, with whom he played bridge and whose political career he massively assisted when he wrote an editorial – in the difficult 1966 election – supporting her hold on Houghton despite the *Sunday Times*'s strong support for the UP. When Mervis retired after his astonishingly successful editorship, he went on to a second career, for ten years, as a PFP provincial councillor.

When I sought his views on my candidacy, he was strongly in support; he would 'stand all night in a draughty hall' to make sure I won. I knew I had a real chance.

Far more important than Beck's financial muscle and Mervis's political sway was the support of the key constituency activists. In this I was well-placed: my position as Johannesburg city councillor gave an almost automatic political lien on the allegiances of the city councillors. Two of them, Claire Quail and Cecil Bass, were close personal friends. In the event, all five of the local authority councillors declared for me. Friendship was decisive when it came to the constituency vice-chair, Brian Doctor (Menell was chairman). Brian, his wife Estelle and I were – and remain – extremely close. After returning from abroad in 1980 he entered a glittering career at the Johannesburg Bar, before returning to London where he is now a distinguished Queen's Counsel. We first met in the unlikely surrounds of Edwin Cameron's wedding.

The crucial key to my nomination lay with a group of doughty campaigners, mostly women – Robin Harvey, Jill Wentzel, Jennifer Soicher, Dorothy Eskapa and Corinne Evans – who had maintained Houghton as impregnably Progressive against all-comers. They were led by Robin, for years head of party headquarters in Johannesburg – a no-nonsense, tough-minded, plain-speaking liberal – and Claire Quail. They were determined that I should be Helen's successor.

I mention these local details and personalities since shortly after the nomination was concluded, my defeated opponent – and those close to her – put it into circulation that I had been successful thanks only to energetic 'rigging', and the active importation of 'outside elements'. However, the significant weight of the long-time members did not want Irene Menell as the successor to Helen Suzman.

Helen's own role vacillated. Initially, she stated that both Irene and I were worthy, and while she would give the nod to Menell, she would not involve herself in the actual process. I hesitated to speak to her frankly and discuss my intentions explicitly. But she resolved my indecision by inviting me for drinks at her baronial home in Hyde Park. She could not have been friendlier, even encouraging, maintaining her support for Irene, but saying: 'I'm sure you'll do very well and you would be a very good MP.' Perhaps her assumption was that I would lose, and she might as well sound encouraging.

I indicated that having the year before – at her suggestion – moved from my marginal Bellevue/Yeoville ward to Highlands North in the constituency of Houghton, I had no desire to become a 'suitcase politician', moving constituencies each time a new nomination was sought. I was relieved by Helen's reasonable tone and relative spirit of even-handedness.

All this was to change over the next few weeks. Helen's initial benevolence turned to outright partisanship for Menell; and when I eventually won, to extreme and embittered hostility which lasted for upward of six years. Many years later, while abroad with a veteran colleague – who was extremely close to Helen – I got an inkling of an explanation. He suggested that Helen had realised, as my campaign gained critical mass, that by not retiring two years earlier in 1987, she had made it difficult for her loyal lieutenant Irene to succeed her: of all Helen's manifold virtues, blaming herself for an avoidable error was not high on the list.

Ken Owen – himself very close to Suzman – editorialised on the issue: under the heading 'Fiefdom at Stake', the abrasive editor wrote: 'Had Helen Suzman quit before the 1987 election, there is practically no doubt that Irene Menell would have taken her place, and she is now claiming delivery on that long-standing, if implicit, promise. Suzman's decision to remain in parliament, however, put Menell into limbo, and she vanished from the public eye.'[4]

Parliamentary nominations in the DP at the time were determined by an electoral college, 50% of whose members (15 of the total 30) were chosen by the local constituency, the remaining from the regional candidates' committee. So winning delegates in the constituency was the decisive key to locking up the nomination. Although the PFP in Houghton had simply morphed into the DP, each constituency was obliged to convene a new general meeting to select office-bearers, including members of the electoral college. Houghton's AGM was scheduled for 24 May.

Between deciding to stand and the date of the Houghton meeting, I studied the DP's new rules and discovered there was no minimum time limit between joining the party and voting in an internal election. One could sign up new members and they would more or less immediately be permitted to participate in internal party processes. This was an excellent and rules-bound manner to bolster my local momentum.

My team energetically recruited hundreds of new members for the constituency. Nor were there any residential requirements for membership: a DP member could choose which constituency he wished to join, even if resident in another. Because of this oddity, Helen Suzman, Max Borkum and Irene Menell and other grandees of the constituency could be members since they all lived outside the boundaries. I felt, however, that my potential members should have some linkage; so I consulted my socialite friend Philippa Sklaar, who probably knew more people than anyone else in the northern suburbs of Johannesburg. She was also, crucially, married to one of Houghton's councillors, Carl Stein, an attorney, whom I had persuaded to stand and win a seat for us the year before.

Carl and Philippa – and her formidable mother, the former Johannesburg mayoress, Molly Sklaar – had run a Rolls Royce campaign with hundreds of helpers. I asked Philippa to sign up all those involved in that effort. She complied with gusto, even throwing a huge social function for signatures. The upshot was pivotal – on deadline day I handed in 350 new members for the constituency.

Irene had not bothered with the recruiting open to her. Word was that she expected to win easily. She signed up 15 new members, including her husband Clive who curiously had never been a member of the party (or its predecessor).

Meanwhile the media had a field day. On the Sunday before the showdown, a large spread appeared in the *Sunday Star*. In very purple prose under the lurid headline 'High noon in Houghton', David Breier wrote: 'The Houghton Mafia are dusting off their violin cases as they prepare to shoot it out for a successor to the Godmother who has held sway over her family for 36 years. When Mrs Helen Suzman announced this week that she was retiring from politics as MP for Houghton, the Democratic Party nomination struggle burst into the open after a long period of silent lobbying. The contenders are Mrs Irene Menell (56), representing the old Houghton dynasty, and the brash young Mr Tony Leon (32) ...

'Mrs Suzman herself is not entering the fray but has expressed a clear preference for Mrs Menell, who is said to be backed by former Transvaal Prog chairman, Mr Max Borkum. Other old Progs are said to back Mr

Leon. Former MPC and editor, Joel Mervis, gives the nod to Mr Leon. Mr Mervis said he believes Mr Leon has the aggression and leadership needed in parliament.' Breier further delineated various class and social trivia which could have a bearing on the nomination.[5]

The day the article appeared, my brother and I had lunch with my father and step-mother, Jacqueline, who were visiting Johannesburg from Durban. While the whole family was enthusiastically behind my bid, 'the judge' was nonplussed by the media depiction of his son as an 'outsider from nowhere' pushing against the gilded and fortified gates of the Houghton establishment. I suspected he was somewhat miffed that his position as a Supreme Court jurist and university chancellor had been overlooked in the stereotyping of the two rival candidates.

The evening of the Houghton showdown arrived some three nights later. I had attempted unsuccessfully to persuade Irene to relocate the meeting to a local school hall; but she insisted that since the AGM was always held at her home, this was to be treated the same. A tent was pitched on the lawns of Le Tholonet to take the overflow. My existing and new supporters were present, with young helpers in the garden guiding people in with torches, handing out pencils to fill out ballot forms, and a printed list of the names on my slate for the electoral college. Irene's list included Suzman, despite her previous avowal to remain aloof from the nitty-gritty. I thought it odd – if not demeaning – that the outgoing MP, praised across the world for her achievements, should seek to end her association with the constituency in this manner. Second, with hundreds of my supporters primed to vote for my elector's slate, which did not include Suzman (since she had indicated she would not be involved), there was every chance that, having entered the ring so late, she could end up not being elected. It was too late to do anything about it.

Somewhat bizarrely, Irene's husband Clive sat in the middle of the lounge – surrounded by dozens of people – serenely reading the *New York Review of Books* wearing impressively monogrammed maroon carpet slippers!

Irene and I exchanged a few glacial pleasantries until she saw the ranks in the outside tent swelling with people she had never seen before. We eventually got down to the balloting for the 15 members of the electoral college. I obtained a full house of all 15. Menell did not get a single delegate, and Suzman, as I feared, was excluded. This particular stain on her escutcheon, plus her inability to influence the succession, led to a cold fury on her part which cast a shadow over my subsequent entrance to parliament. There were several years of snubs, barbs and an essential pettiness.

In the immediate aftermath of the results, Irene rounded on Claire Quail, an essential pillar in my victory, and, as Claire put it, 'The mask dropped and she shouted at me: it's all your fault, it's all your fault.'

My supporters and I had meanwhile decamped to my brother's nearby flat where we celebrated. When the Houghton delegates met their regional counterparts a few weeks later, I won the final contest 22–8. *Business Day* led with a front-page headline: 'Leon landslide in Houghton'. Their comment: 'Irene Menell, Helen Suzman's chosen successor for the Houghton nomination, was soundly trounced by the DP's rising star, Tony Leon, in a DP constituency election last night. About three hundred members attended the first DP Houghton constituency AGM during which its representatives on the party's electoral college were elected. Leon's entire slate of fifteen nominees were all returned, leaving Menell without a single representative. Even Suzman was not elected.'[6]

Accompanying the article was a photograph of me kissing Irene. The next day, in the tea room of the Wits Law School, my academic colleagues were warm and congratulatory. Roger Whiting waved the *Business Day* picture around and intoned with mock solemnity: 'Beware the kiss of the spiderman, for it brings death.'

Graciousness in defeat was not to be the hallmark of the establishment. In the *Star*[7] Suzman complained that 'Mr Leon's lobbying effort to achieve nomination made Tammany Hall look like a teddy bear's picnic.' She repeated that remark in the 1994 update of her memoirs. I have never responded in public, although grossly unfair, inflated and unjustified were the facts as I perceived them.

Nor was there any shortage of public pundits who expressed themselves on my attainment. The acerbic Johnny Johnson, editor of the right-wing *Citizen* (which had always disparaged the Progressives and now the DP, but who admired Suzman personally), gave vent to his considerable displeasure:[8]

'Mr Leon, whose abrasive personality and tough politicking caused several Prog stalwarts to leave the party, is still at it. He will get the Houghton nomination, since he is an ambitious young man and not for nothing has he been named the Rambo of politics. But in climbing to the top, he has pushed aside members of the Prog old guard who have devoted their lives to the liberal cause. He may think he is the cat's whiskers, but parliament has a way of cutting politicians like him down to size.'

While I regretted the fallout with Suzman, I thought the remarks and allegations were proof of entirely what was wrong with the long-held assumption that a seat in parliament was in the gift of the departing member.

This had been exemplified when one of my team, David Unterhalter, today a leading SC and law professor, went to solicit the support of former MPC and councillor Dr Selma Browde. She was firmly with Menell: 'Irene has paid her dues … it's her turn after all those years.' David's riposte – that 'handing over the seat of Houghton should not be like a gold watch for 25 years of service' – was deadly accurate, but did not close the deal. I also felt an effete preciousness in the constituency leadership (as in the upper echelons of the recently disbanded PFP). South Africa was about to enter a new age, and I was sure that the old, noble verities which had sustained the PP needed refurbishing and reinvigoration.

However, my old opponent on the Johannesburg city council, JF Oberholzer (who had stepped down the year before as chairman of the Management Committee), paid me an unusual tribute. He had, as I have recorded, with great effectiveness and extreme conservatism governed Johannesburg for 15 years. We seldom, if ever, agreed on an issue, but always got on well despite our differences. Doorstopped by a newspaper reporter[9] on my future, he responded: 'I have watched Tony Leon very closely … he will go very far. He is extraordinarily gifted and versatile. He is a possible leader of his party.'

Under the energetic leadership of my campaign manager, Barbara Friedman, we set about turning our constituency insurgency into a fully fledged campaign for the general election on 6 September. The skirmishing around the nomination was to leave me with a reputation for rapacious ruthlessness in pursuit of an objective, unmindful of the political corpses I left in my wake. To others, it was a breath of new life for an old cause. I didn't see either view as wholly accurate, but the mould had been set.

3

Although 1989 propelled me into national and parliamentary politics, I was still immersed in my civic leadership role. Since the 1988 municipal elections, much attention had been focused on the former urban NP East Rand strongholds of Brakpan and Boksburg, which had fallen to the rightist Conservative Party. The newly installed mayors banned blacks from all public open spaces – a reversion to 'petty apartheid' which most municipalities had abandoned. In an article I penned,[10] I pointed out that the excesses of the CP were only a few degrees worse than the Johannesburg set-up run by the NP, whose political head was the so-called enlightened Foreign minister, Pik Botha. I said: 'Suppose Johannesburg installed a

Conservative Party council. It would find that the 29 pools controlled by the Parks and Recreation Department were strictly segregated, except for the occasional swimming gala. Turning to its 21 recreation centres ... With a single exception, these amenities exclude blacks as a matter of specific policy.

Johannesburg had planned its facilities for whites only – it had ostentatiously refused to take into account the real, inextricably integrated population of the city. But what to do? In a caucus discussion Councillor Carl Stein noted that the Reservation of Separate Amenities Act required a specific reservation or bar on the entry of blacks to, for example, a swimming pool. He instructed the articled clerks at his law firm to unearth a specific proclamation which racially reserved municipal pools. They couldn't.

We decided to test the proposition. So, on a wintry June highveld morning, 20 DP councillors arrived at the entrance to the Hillbrow indoor swimming facility, operated by the Johannesburg Council. There was a huge media contingent present, but our entry was blocked by a group of far right-wing militants of Eugene Terre'Blanche's Afrikaner Weerstandsbeweging (AWB) sporting the red and white AWB flag with its swastika motif, chanting 'AWB! AWB!' Some local Nat officials linked hands with them, shouting 'We don't want blacks swimming in our pool.'

At this moment, the South African Police arrived. But – to my surprise and pleasure – instead of stopping us, they pushed the right-wingers out of the way. We entered, changed, and swam. Unfortunately one of our group had difficulties (apparently he couldn't swim) and a press photographer leaped into the water to rescue him. But the point had been proved. The NP leadership was extremely embarrassed at being shown as little different from their mortal opponents in the CP.

The following day my nemesis, the *Citizen*, echoed the Nat view:[11] 'The swim by a group of DP councillors, blacks and Indians was a farce that nearly turned into a tragedy with a press photographer having to save an Indian from drowning ... Mr Leon succeeded in attracting a host of foreign press men so that they far outnumbered the swimmers ... We do not think that city councillors should disport themselves in such a fashion ... Leon, of course, has introduced confrontational politics into the city council and likes to attract attention to himself and his causes in a most aggressive way. [But] opening municipal facilities is a thorny issue that should be dealt with in a calm way.'

The *Star*'s Carol Lazar wrote: '[A] group of Johannesburgers having a friendly swim – something that in any other country in the world would be the norm. But in South Africa, on this particular morning, a friendly neighbourhood swim was a little piece of history in the making.'[12]

Within weeks of our swim, the city council abandoned the endorsement of segregation in all its pools and recreation centres.

Another 'little piece of history' was being crafted by the shrewd and energetic head of the anti-evictions watchdog group, 'Actstop', Cas Coovadia. Cas today heads South Africa's Banking Council. Back then he was fighting apartheid in the heart of the Johannesburg CBD. Although the Group Areas Act was on the statute books, it was increasingly being honoured in the breach. Owing to an endemic housing shortage – and the location of so-called 'new white' housing huge distances away from the commercial heartland – thousands of black, Coloured and Indian families had moved at first stealthily and then more openly into vacant apartments in the Johannesburg business district and in the inner city suburbs of Hillbrow, Berea, Doornfontein, Braamfontein and Bertrams.

The new residents lived in precarious and generally appalling circumstances. An inventive and far-reaching judgment by Justice Richard Goldstone stymied the Group Areas Act's full application, holding that authorities applying its provisions needed to promote alternative accommodation in the designated area. In this combustible cauldron, the landlords, many little better than rapacious racketeers, preyed on the illegal occupants' vulnerability by maximising rentals and minimising services. Most of the flats were run-down tenements, overcrowded, with unsanitary conditions; they were literal death-traps.

Actstop accordingly launched a campaign headlined 'the Gandhi Gambit'. In the spirit of the Mahatma's passive resistance, they intended to demonstrate the plight and precariousness of the inner city dwellers. I accepted an invitation, with some fifty other whites, to participate in 'an inner city encounter'. Accordingly, I spent two nights in a cramped apartment in Export House, Bree Street. I had never lived in the CBD, and nothing I had read or heard prepared me for the two tiny bedrooms in the very grim block (previously an office building) with its broken lift and fused bulbs. I declined my host's kind offer of their bedroom, and spent the evenings in their lounge on a sleeping bag.

Today, nearly twenty years later, while the Group Areas Act is a dim and unpleasant memory of our apartheid past, the housing crisis is worse than it was then. However, on a recent visit which I paid to the same Johannesburg business district, I was delighted to see that while many grim tenements remained, many other buildings had been rejuvenated and refurbished and were being sold to first-time home owners – mostly the increasing ranks of young black professionals – or 'buppies' as they became known in advertising argot – who saw the situation as an opportunity to gain a foothold on the property ladder.

Shortly after the Houghton saga, the leader of the NP in the Johannesburg city council, Danie van Zyl, died prematurely – he was in his early fifties – of leukaemia. His death created a vacancy in his ward in the relatively wealthy, predominantly Afrikaans north-eastern suburb of Linden. This was the DP's first electoral test. After a hard-fought campaign, we managed to wrest the seat – in the middle of Pik Botha's Westdene constituency – by the relatively wide margin of 340 votes. I was ecstatic and told the media that we had been told this was the NP's new leader FW de Klerk's 'first test'. 'In that case,' I harrumphed, 'he has failed it miserably.'

The newspapers proclaimed such wonders as: 'DP shows it can win Nat voters' and 'Fourth force on the march'.[13]

Linden proved to be, if not a false, then a premature dawn. In the general election three months later, the NP held off the DP in most of their traditional seats: DP gains were made largely by recapturing traditional opposition seats which in the PFP meltdown of 1987 had moved to the Nats.

The second consequence of Van Zyl's demise was a rearrangement of the Nat leadership at city council level. Our irrepressible chief whip, Paul Asherson, decided to take advantage of the becalmed Nat ranks. While Van Zyl's long-time deputy Jan Burger was a shoo-in to become chairman of the Management Committee, there was much unhappiness in their party ranks about the proposed deputy, Marietta Marx. Asherson appealed to the vanity of a former Nat mayor and Johannesburg councillor, Ernie Fabel, and persuaded him to stand. Since there were only four votes separating the Nats from us, Fabel and another voted with the PFP and he was elected. This caused chaos and concern in the normally disciplined NP ranks. Their caucus looked as if a daisy-cutter bomb had decimated them when the result came in. I announced: 'This is the first time in living history that the NP has split in council. It indicates massive dissension in their ranks.'

I was immensely satisfied. The bedraggled and disunited PFP council group which I had inherited just a year before was now vigorous and united. The previously sturdy Nat fortress appeared now to be made of little more than papier-mâché. We were on the march. It was also time for me to exit the municipal scene.

In due course, after the September election, Ian Davidson – who had recruited me into the council and over whom I'd jumped to become leader – won the leadership once I had vacated it. Within months, further internal Nat wrangling – with Asherson enlisting dissidents on the inside – forced them to sue for peace with the DP. It was then Davidson who assumed the chair of the Management Committee in a DP–NP coalition. He was to remain at the helm through the turbulent transition until 1994.

In May, while I was immersed in the affairs of Houghton, a university colleague and significant anti-apartheid activist, David Webster, was assassinated outside his home in Johannesburg's eastern suburbs. I attended his memorial service in downtown Johannesburg cathedral, and was struck at how openly and brazenly the government's extra-parliamentary opponents wore ANC insignia and Communist Party emblems. At the time, notionally at least, such a show of defiance led, on conviction, to an automatic and lengthy jail term. Clearly the apartheid state was losing control.

After winning the nomination, I embarked on a campaigning tour around the country. I was dubbed – looking back now, at least, in cringing and toe-curling terms – as the 'DP's rising yuppie star'. Indeed the *Sunday Times* even ran a feature article in which I and the other leading 'thirty-something' candidates were paraded under the ghastly headline: 'Yippee for the yuppies'. Typecasting in politics can be difficult to shrug off if more serious purposes are at stake. But I was hardly publicity shy, and enjoyed the new challenge and the prospect of entering parliament.[14]

De Klerk, as the new Nat leader, had promised voters that the NP would seek a new constitution for South Africa. Based on his own well-documented and articulated conservatism and the NP's dismal track record on reform, I sneered: 'Instead of frankly engaging with the ANC, and other banned organisations, and acknowledging the failure of government constitutional engineering, they will tinker around the margins of the system without dismantling its structure.'[15]

Events and De Klerk himself would within months turn my prophecy to ashes. To be fair, though, the facts were on my side. My colleague, the politically gifted and immensely likeable Tian van der Merwe – who was to die tragically in a motor car smash just two years later – pointed to the De Klerk track record. Tian said De Klerk's 'new liberal image' was at odds with the 'conservative reality he has established over many years'. He specifically drew attention to De Klerk's call – shortly before the 1987 election – for 'every white resident to report to the police any person of colour who transgressed the Group Areas Act'. In a TV debate with Conservative leader, Dr AP Treurnicht, in March 1988, De Klerk had committed the NP to maintaining separate beaches for whites. As recently as nine months before, when leader of the (white) House of Assembly, De

Klerk had suspended the Rules of Parliament to push through bills tightening up apartheid education policy.[16]

De Klerk and his camp would, with some justification no doubt, cite with approval the observation of Lord Salisbury, thrice prime minister of Britain in the 19th century, that the 'commonest error in politics is sticking to the carcass of dead policies' to explain his political epiphany. Perhaps, in the words of one of Salisbury's later successors, Harold Macmillan, it was a case of 'events, dear boy, events'.

Nomination day in Houghton arrived in August. No one was prouder than my mother, who paid the electoral deposit of several thousand rands and gave me – in her flamboyant style – a red envelope containing a red card to underline what she considered a 'red-letter day'. I still have the note, one of the few which survives her death. It reads:

'Tony darling – A red-letter day indeed! It is with much joy and pride that I am paying in this deposit for your parliamentary nomination. This day will be surely the start of your incredible political career in the really big stakes ... Thank you for having been a source of joy (and occasional irritation!). Fondest love, Ma.'

My opponent was Dr Shlomo Peer, a former insurance tycoon, Israeli-born, and a close friend of FW de Klerk. It was noteworthy that every one of my three NP opponents (Peer and the two municipal candidates I opposed in 1986 and 1988) were Jewish. This gives the lie to later attempts by elements of South Africa's Jewish leadership to try and depict the Jewish community as uniformly pro-struggle and anti-apartheid. The truth – as ever – was far more complex.

Aside from the Houghton stalwarts who had helped me win, our election headquarters in Norwood were abuzz with dozens of young students – many of whom I had lectured. We set out visiting on foot and telephoning each of the 18 000 voters in the seat. Since a deep, if not arctic, chill emanated from Suzman and Menell who both indicated that they would play no role in my campaign, I turned to some old Progs for help.

First off, I asked Zach de Beer as both DP co-leader and a figure of immense authority to write a letter of formal introduction to my constituents. Even by his generous standards, it verged on the excessive; but I was delighted to have it. It read, in part:

'In Helen Suzman, the voters of Houghton have had a great member of parliament for the past 36 years. In Tony Leon they are being offered another very remarkable person ... [He] is the most exciting young politician to have emerged in recent years.

I also decided to invite Colin Eglin to my first public meeting. His closeness to Suzman, I felt, would rebut some of the subterranean murmurings that I was, if not quite an impostor, then a usurper. I had grown to like Colin for his intellect and perseverance. Unlike him, I could never imagine myself ousted as leader, yet forging on for another 12 years.

At the meeting, I outlined two propositions which I felt were of the essence:

- Negotiations: the DP had a 'let's-talk' philosophy, which meant we would sit down and talk with our opponents wherever possible; 'real negotiations' with the real black leadership could not be delayed or postponed.
- The economy: the NP had distorted the concept of public service by making service to the state a means of enrichment. For ordinary South Africans bond rates had risen 50% in a year; petrol by 40%; and the price of food by 1 000% over the past 17 years.

In addition, recent research revealed the full extent and true cost of the 'homelands' and the Tricameral parliament with its racial divisions and duplications of 'own affairs' for whites, Coloureds and Indians; and so-called 'general affairs' which usually meant legislating for the absent black majority. All this made South Africa one of the most over-governed and over-burdened countries in the world. Should I be elected to parliament, I would be a member of one of 13 parliaments and national legislatures in the country (three in the Tricameral parliament; four in the so-called independent TBVC states; and six in the self-governing, non-independent black homelands); and be one of 1 270 MPs gracing one or other of these chambers! To maintain these edifices and the army of satraps they spawned cost about 15c out of every one rand of government spending.

I invited Dr Peer to debate me at the meeting. My opponent declined my invitation (he spoke poor English) but held a rally at Houghton Primary School, where De Klerk also spoke. We did debate the issues in a weekly paper which afforded the opportunity. I took advantage of my space to stretch the somewhat sketchy DP constitutional policy into something akin to my own position – achieved largely as a consequence of having lectured in constitutional law for the past few years.[17] I wrote that the NP was not centrist 'but represents the muddle in the middle'.

It was in the gift of government to abolish or repeal the Reservation of Separate Amenities Act and the Group Areas Act – but they chose not to. I also noted that three of the schools in my constituency were grossly under their quota of pupils, but government policy would not admit blacks desperate for decent education. The NP's rhetoric was substitution for reform which sought to 'Max Factorise' apartheid without committing itself to any specific or practical proposal: 'Having brought South Africa to the brink of political collapse and financial ruin, we are now told that the architects of this sad state of affairs are the very people who are going to rectify it.'

The DP was planning for a post-apartheid era with an orderly transition to a secure, prosperous and non-racial South Africa. To achieve this we needed:

- a constitution that would free South Africa by limiting the state;
- recognition that every citizen is entitled to vote and participate in society without reference to race;
- negotiation of an inclusive system of democratic bargaining to achieve an acceptable dispensation;
- protection of fundamental freedoms and human rights in a bill of rights;
- proportional representation as an alternative to domination and the spectre of a one-party state;
- an independent judiciary with testing power of legislation – so that fundamental freedoms were not subject to the whims of parliament;
- the protection of democracy through the maintenance of law and order and security;
- the proscribing of violence as a means of political change; and
- the genuine devolution of power and dispersal of authority through a federal, rather than a unitary, state.

My conclusion: 'Only a party that explicitly rejects racism, tricameralism and the ethnic partition of government has the ability to achieve this peaceful transition.'

Looking back, after nearly two decades, it is fortifying to note that those elements are today commonplace, and were enshrined – in theory at least – in the constitutional settlement that followed some four years after the election. The NP's so-called 'five-year action plan' (September 1989) was easy to dismiss as the sort of tribute vice occasionally pays to virtue. But its prescriptions quite closely resembled the ANC-revised constitutional guidelines, published the year before. The Nat document stated: 'South Africa is one undivided state with one citizenship for all. Every South African has the right to participate in political decision-making on all levels of government which affect his interests, subject to the principle of no domination.'

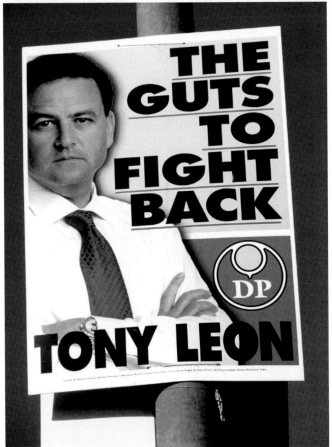

Above: FIGHTING BACK: a sign of the revival of our political fortunes was on display at a fundraising dinner on the eve of the 1999 general election, which was attended by every living leader or patron of the party and its forebears. Here I pose with Colin Eglin, Helen Suzman, Dr Frederik van Zyl Slabbert, Harry Oppenheimer, Dr Zach de Beer and Harry Schwarz. (*Sunday Times*)

Left: The slogan that stirred the electorate and future controversy. (*PictureNet*)

Although our campaign was targeted at minorities, I spent a great deal of time in the 1999 election campaigning among the majority. Here, on a rainy day, I take our campaign to Soweto.
(ASSOCIATED PRESS)

Top: Zapiro was predictably unimpressed: he had a very specific view on how the DP could appeal to black voters. (ZAPIRO)

Above: CELEBRATING IN PHOENIX, KWAZULU-NATAL, IN 1999: the Democratic Party made a significant breakthrough in the Indian community, sweeping the boards in Chatsworth and Phoenix, the largest concentration of Indians outside the sub-continent of India itself. Unfortunately this was not followed through in subsequent elections. 2 August 1999. (*DAILY NEWS*/PETER DUFFY)

Top: FORMATION OF THE DEMOCRATIC ALLIANCE, JULY 2000: the Democratic Alliance was formed by merging the Democratic Party and the New National Party. The first meeting of the party's national management committee was held in Parliament shortly thereafter. In the front are our party chairman, Joe Seremane, me, deputy leader Marthinus van Schalkwyk, and mayoral candidate for Cape Town Peter Marais. (*ARGUS*)

Above: TAKING THE SHOW ON THE ROAD: the leadership trio takes our campaign 'for all the people' across the country. 15 October 2000. (*RAPPORT*)

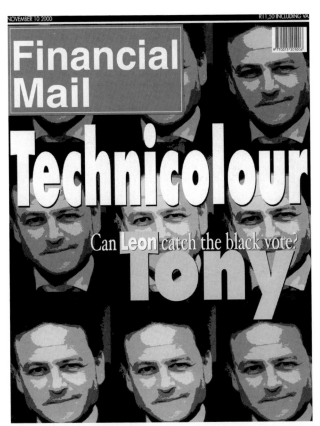

Left: The *Financial Mail* anticipated our good showing in the 2000 municipal elections by plastering a multi-coloured version of my face on its front cover. 10 November 2000. (*FINANCIAL MAIL*)

Below: Our eve-of-poll rally in December 2000 at the Standard Bank Arena in Johannesburg attracted the largest crowd ever assembled at a Democratic Alliance event.

The most important event for me at the end of 2000, the most crowded of years, was personal: Michal and I were married at the Mount Nelson hotel, Cape Town, where we were photographed with the family: my father Ray, mother Sheila, and young Etai Even-Zahav in the front; and my brother Peter behind me.
10 December 2000.
(*Die Burger*/Esa Alexander)

December 2000: opening of the South African Jewish Museum: Nelson Mandela greets Michal, with Chief Rabbi Cyril Harris in the background. (*Argus*)

Above: THE CHAMPAGNE SOON WENT FLAT: in December 2000 the Democratic Alliance's top structure *(from left,* premier Gerald Morkel, deputy leader Marthinus van Schalkwyk, mayor-elect Peter Marais, and I) cheer our victory in Cape Town and across the Western Cape. Within months every personality in this picture would be at war; either with one another or with the party itself. 8 December 2000. (*Argus*/Leon Muller)

Above: HIGH NOON: in October 2001 I arrive at a meeting of the National Management Committee to terminate Peter Marais's office as mayor. He awaits his fate grim-faced. (*Sunday Times*)

Above: 2001 proved to be an *annus horribilis*, as this Zapiro cartoon indicates.

Left: Funding crisis and floor-crossing: the media had a field day with German fraudster Jurgen Harksen's claims of dirty money, which blackened the hitherto corruption-clean image of the Democratic Alliance. The floor-crossing saga also bolstered the new ANC-NNP coalition. 30 May 2002.

Top: A HARD DAY AT THE OFFICE: my pensive demeanour in parliament at the height of the floor-crossing and funding sagas led a newspaper to observe that I 'seemed to be carrying a weight on my shoulders ... he does not look happy.' Indeed, I had no reason to be. 25 October 2001. (*CAPE TIMES*/LEON LESTRADE)

Above: A BETTER DAY IN PARLIAMENT: the Democratic Alliance front bench pictured before the 2004 election: Joe Seremane sits up front, with chief whip Douglas Gibson and senior MP, Ken Andrew, just behind. (*SUNDAY TIMES*)

Top: Visiting DA members in Crossroads, Cape Town, who had been subjected to a vicious and continuing assault by ANC supporters on the ground. One of our members was shot and died in an inter-party fracas, which occasioned our visit. 26 April 2002. (*Die Burger*/Joanne Cavanagh)

Above: Rallying the party in Alexandra township. (PictureNet)

LENDING A HAND: at the height of my cold war with his successor, Thabo Mbeki, I sought the counsel of Mbeki's illustrious predecessor, Nelson Mandela. In September 2002, when we met at his Houghton home, Mandela advised me to seek the intervention of Jacob Zuma. (IMAGES24)

Top: HONOURING HELEN SUZMAN: Michal, James Selfe MP, Dene Smuts MP and I attend the inauguration of the Helen Suzman exhibition by the South African Jewish Board of Deputies in Cape Town in 2005. (PRIVATE COLLECTION/SHAWN BENJAMIN)

Above: TAKING A GAMBLE: the Durban July race day in 2003 was spent in the company of then deputy president Jacob Zuma (*on the left*). Michal, Zuma and I were hosted by the ebullient Bill Lambert (*centre*).

MARQUEE DAY IN PARLIAMENT: the annual opening of Parliament and State of the Nation address. Michal always injected both colour and glamour into the proceedings. 3 February 2006. (PictureNet)

I spent a great deal of time and political effort in and around South Africa's townships. Although the results were modest electorally, I believed that first-hand, on-the-ground observations were absolutely essential. (PICTURENET)

TANGLING WITH THE LADY:
my parliamentary and personal
tussles with Winnie Madikizela-
Mandela occupied considerable
time and effort, but I felt that
the 'mother of the nation'
mask needed to be ripped off.
(PICTURENET)

Crime and corruption are the
evil twins poisoning the roots
of the new South Africa. Here
I join a midnight patrol on
the mean streets of Hillbrow,
Johannesburg.
(SUNDAY INDEPENDENT/TJ LEMON)

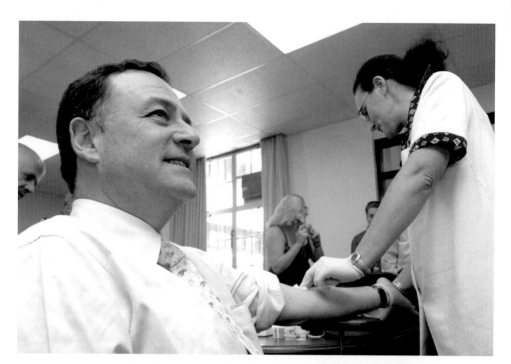

Top: SOUTH AFRICA'S LONG AIDS BATTLE: a wall of silence and official obfuscation and denialism characterised Thabo Mbeki's policy on AIDS. In November 2004 I underwent an HIV test, having been advised that testing was an essential key to an effective AIDS-fighting strategy. (*SUNDAY TIMES*)

Above: Holding up front page of a Zimbabwean newspaper in a 2001 parliamentary debate which focused on Mbeki's temporising with the tyranny of Robert Mugabe. Six years later little had changed. 13 February 2002. (*CAPE TIMES*)

The ANC had said: 'South Africa shall be an independent, unitary, democratic and non-racial state. Sovereignty shall belong to the people as a whole and shall be exercised through one central legislature, executive, judiciary and administration.'

4

Some three weeks before polling day, PW Botha resigned as president. Enoch Powell once famously observed that 'all political lives, unless they are cut off in midstream at a happy juncture, end in failure ...' Botha's finalé was no exception. He complained on TV about a cabinet mutiny, and press speculation was rife that FW de Klerk had moved in – understandably – for the political kill since Botha's desire to separate the presidency from the party leadership was clearly unsustainable.

Another feature of the election was growing unease – and incipient disunity – within the DP about how to deal with the extra-parliamentary Left. The party was implacably opposed to the NP's apartheid system and *faux* constitutional reforms. That by the end of the eighties was the easy part. But did the party believe its heart and soul lay in a broad alliance with the Left; or going it alone; or even in some association with the moderate right, such as Buthelezi's IFP? These were the existential issues which would confront the party in the next parliament, and nearly tear it asunder.

I had no doubt that simply because the MDM and UDF opposed apartheid did not make them our natural allies. Their call for an election boycott by whites infuriated many in our party. At an election meeting in Camps Bay, Cape Town, I took them on. Their boycott call was 'an extraordinary self-indulgence which would only strengthen the NP and CP.' 'If the white Left wants change,' I gratuitously advised, 'it should participate in the parliamentary process, even at the risk of being called collaborators in certain radical-chic circles.'

What I wanted to do was put down a public marker, a sign of what I perceived to be the battle to come in the DP parliamentary caucus, which I soon hoped to join.

My campaign proceeded apace. Canvassing results were excellent, and the tide, at least in opposition areas, appeared firmly in the direction of change. The Botha era had fuelled the emigration of young whites, turned the black townships into battlefields, and caused economic hardships.

For the end-of-poll rally that we held in part of my municipal ward (Orchards), which was also in the constituency, I recruited my old political boss, Harry Schwarz. He was unopposed in neighbouring Yeoville and had great pull with the Jewish community – which my Israeli-born opponent was wooing. I also, silently, knew that it would drive Irene Menell mad. There was simply no way Schwarz – a long-standing foe of Suzman – would have been invited to the constituency under the old order I had supplanted.

Schwarz delivered the goods. However, he seemed less than thrilled by my preceding remarks. I had again put my own individualistic view on the theme of the nearly three hundred people facing the death penalty. My speech was widely publicised, drawing a furious response from NP MP Hernus Kriel (appointed to the cabinet after the election).

My contention was that most of the condemned had not had fair trials. They were defended generally by *pro deo* counsel, usually the junior legal ranks. This was aggravated in the rural 'circuit courts' where often the advocate had little more than an hour with the accused pre-trial, and usually had to conduct proceedings without an instructing attorney. This was 'an unequal contest with the full resources of the state'.

I called for a moratorium on the death sentence and a stay of execution. Government, especially its reform-minded Justice minister, Kobie Coetsee, should revoke the compulsory imposition of the death sentence and provide an automatic right of appeal. And government should enhance legal aid for all such cases.

For reasons entirely unrelated to my pleading, a few months later De Klerk gave concrete legislative expression to a package of reforms drafted for capital cases. He also invoked the moratorium for which I had called. I concluded my speech that night with a quote from one of my favourite Kahlil Gibran passages. It seemed apt for one as young as me, about to take over the most venerable 'opposition fiefdom' in the land:

> Your children are not your children ...
> You may give them your love but not your thoughts
> For they have their own thoughts;
> You may house their bodies but not their souls,
> For their souls dwell in the house of tomorrow
> Which you cannot visit, not even in your dreams ...

As usual on election day, I was up at dawn pumped up with an excess of adrenalin and what the brilliant novelist Ian McEwan has phrased as 'the irreducible urge to win, as biological as thirst'. Brian Doctor collected me, and we spent the day and early evening visiting the five constituency polling stations. Each party had its reception tents, tables, posters and banners: ours looked fantastic – decked out in the blue and yellow livery of the DP and mountains of posters, courtesy of Graham Beck's largesse. The queues were relatively long, and voting was brisk until the 9 pm closure. While I knew instinctively I couldn't lose Houghton for the DP, after my first narrow scrape in Bellevue vote-counting always made me apprehensive. I need not have worried.

I significantly increased our votes and nearly doubled the previous (PFP) majority of two years before:

HOUGHTON CONSTITUENCY

1989 Result		1987 Result	
AJ Leon (DP)	10 003	H Suzman (PFP)	8 635
S Peer (NP)	3 702	GUAN Pagan (NP)	4 784
DP majority	6 301	PFP majority	3 851
Percentage poll	67	Percentage poll	65

A long and liquid party was held in a tent in nearby Parktown – where all the DP victorious winners and unlucky losers gathered. In the event, the DP gained 12 seats to finish with a total of 33 (recouping ground lost by the PFP in the last election); but the rightist CP won 17 NP seats to entrench itself – with 39 MPs – as the official opposition. Despite its losses the NP had a comfortable overall majority of 21 seats.

After months of nervous energy, epic battles and ceaseless activity, I was exhausted – and depressed. I realised the latter was the symptom that always comes when a major deadline has been reached and a long-held personal goal achieved – 'like the dog who finally catches the bus'. And where was it all going?

However, my sense of uncertainty was soon assuaged by what I would soon discover to be the politician's narcotic – the fix of overseas travel, from which I was far from immune. Immediately after the election I had been invited, by their respective ambassadors, to visit Britain and Germany.

When in London I met Ken Livingstone who, as the leader of the Greater London Council (GLC), had run such a virulent oppositional campaign against the then all-powerful prime minister, Margaret Thatcher, that she had abolished it. Livingstone had then migrated, as I had, from local politics to the national stage, and by the time of my visit was becalmed on the back benches as a Labour MP for the London suburb of Brent. He had been variously described as leader of the 'loony left' and by the *Sun* tabloid as 'the most dangerous man in Britain'.

Much to my amazement he agreed to meet with me. We met at a wine bar on the South Bank across the Thames River, together with my foreign office minder. Livingstone was extraordinary: part comedian, part conspiracy theorist, part regular guy. I was not surprised when fifteen or so years later, millions of Londoners, many of whom detested his political prejudices, voted for him as the first directly elected mayor, essentially because of his 'cheeky chappie' attitude. In May 2008 he was defeated by Boris Johnson, of whom more in Chapter 20.

Our conversation commenced with a question from him along the lines of, 'Tell me, Tony, do the police in South Africa murder political suspects and detainees?' I answered him in the qualified affirmative, and gave him a condensed – I hoped, accurate – version of some of the more egregious examples of torture and deaths (or 'suicides' as they were sometimes inaccurately dubbed) at the notorious John Vorster Square in Johannesburg. 'That's what I understood,' he answered. But what he next said took my breath away and nearly caused (so she later confessed) my foreign office minder to drop her glass. 'Of course,' opined Ken, 'that's exactly what the British forces do in Northern Ireland.'

Having, in his view, established a form of moral symmetry – and a parallel which enjoyed extremely little credence outside the command structures of the Irish Republican Army – we got on famously. I was interested in his view on current politics, especially since Margaret Thatcher was looking increasingly vulnerable. Indeed within a year she would be toppled from office in a party coup, a sort of internal tidal wave, whose eddies are still being felt by today's Conservatives. Much to my amazement, Ken spent little time dealing with his nemesis Thatcher, and most of the evening in a very amusing – but deeply vicious – denunciation of his own leader, Neil Kinnock. It was easy to understand how a divided Labour Party would wait nearly a decade more before its return to power, notwithstanding the vicissitudes that would continue to beset the Tory government.

My visit to Germany was fascinating and personally significant. Most Jewish households, including my own, were deeply scarred by the Nazi epoch, and if not anti-German, then they had deep feelings of ambivalence towards all matters in the Rhineland. My mother had, in 1980, to the chagrin of some members of Jewish society in Durban and Johannesburg, taken as her third husband a German gentile, Paul Schulz. The fact that he had fought as a conscript for the German army in the 1940s outraged some friends and family, and led one elderly member of my mother's circle to raise her arm and murmur 'Heil Hitler' on hearing the news of her impending nuptials.

But it was not simply the past and the reconciliation of the ambivalent pulls of its own dark history which now compelled interest. It was the prospect of visiting, in depth, the Federal Republic of Germany at a time of transcending change in eastern Europe that filled me with great anticipation. I was not disappointed. By the time I reached divided Berlin in October 1989, the sense of impending change was palpable. I had little idea that within days of my departure the Berlin Wall would be breached and the map of Europe would be changed irrevocably; and the Cold War could be won, finally and decisively, by the West.

My visit also allowed me to establish my first ties with Germany's Free Democratic Party (FDP), an allied organisation of the DP's through Liberal International, and with the German liberal think tank, the Friedrich Naumann Stiftung. Both organisations would, after I assumed the party leadership several years hence, be our key – and closest – international allies. It was through them that I became close to one of Germany's truly significant liberal post-war statesmen, Otto Graf Lambsdorff (or 'the Count' as he was affectionately known). A one-time party leader, he espoused the sort of muscular, no-nonsense liberalism which I thought was crisply clarifying as opposed to much of the sentimental hand-wringing which often passed for modern liberalism.

Meanwhile, back at home De Klerk claimed a mandate for reform (though only by combining the NP and DP totals); but this did not quell civil unrest. The installation of yet another Tricameral parliament seemed to arouse the flames of insurrection anew. Yet shortly after his installation as president two weeks after the election, De Klerk started sending real and substantive signals that he was a qualitatively different leader from his predecessors. First he released seven senior ANC leaders, including Walter Sisulu and Govan Mbeki. Next, the police essentially did not interfere when a giant rally was held by the (still banned) ANC to welcome back the seven to South Africa.

Next, De Klerk disbanded the deeply distrusted and rightly maligned National Security Management System (NSMS). By year-end he halved the compulsory two-year military conscription for whites. These important reforms gave no inkling of the big bang he was to detonate when he formally opened the second session of the ninth parliament early in the new year.

While awaiting this momentous session, in late 1989 the DP went about holding its first national congress after the election. The dominant issue was whether the party should continue with its three-man leadership – or dump the troika for a single leader. The gathering – in Durban's Royal hotel – precipitated huge recriminations, since in the build-up most of the old PFP elements (in which I had a very public role) wanted De Beer as leader, while Malan and Worrall's troops preferred the status quo.

By a margin of 330 to 213 the congress rejected the idea of a single leader. One old Prog was heard, by the press, to mutter: 'The Nats already have the government, now they've got the opposition too. Unless you're Afrikaans and not an old Prog you don't have a chance any more.'

My contribution to the proceedings was entirely negative and deeply unhelpful to the cause I was seeking to promote. I can't remember now whether it was a reckless bloody-mindedness or simply a tin ear for the political background noise that impelled me to goad the congress with a speech and performance which – to put it at its mildest – was spectacularly ill-judged. The *Star*'s political correspondent Peter Fabricius records the proceedings:[18]

'The mood of the congress hit young Mr Tony Leon – the Prog whizz-kid from Houghton – like a freak arctic wave. He was one of the first speakers in the debate, and in his usual spunky style went straight into the attack.

'"I find it an extraordinary suggestion that anyone should consider continuing with the status quo," he said. And the congress jeered. Undeterred, Mr Leon retorted: "I've been attacked by Nats before" – and that really set them off. Later Mr Leon thought he'd let them know who they were dealing with, and said he had ten thousand voters in Houghton behind him. That was the clincher. Whether Mr Leon completely misread the congress or intended to provoke it, was not clear. But with that remark he lost it completely. The rich Anglo-Jewish Johannesburg northern suburbs were as far from the nerve centre of this congress as possible. The focus of this congress was somewhere in the platteland.'

The reporter was either too kind, or too unobservant, to record that I was then slow-hand-clapped off the stage altogether.

Five years later, to the month, at the same venue, I was elected unopposed and with acclamation, as the single leader of the Democratic Party.

CHAPTER 5

Present at the Creation

Being a Member of Parliament feeds your vanity and starves your self-respect.
MATTHEW PARRIS

*All fixed, fast-frozen relations, with their train of ancient and
venerable prejudices and opinions, are swept away, all new-formed ones
become antiquated before they can ossify. All that is solid melts into air,
all that is holy is profaned.*
KARL MARX

I

I arrived in parliament in the spring of 1989, flush from my big victory in Houghton, which gave me high, and as it transpired misplaced, expectations. I was at the summit of my young political ambition, achieved at 32. I expected my service as opposition leader in Johannesburg and membership of the party's National Board to propel me to at least a senior position in the party's parliamentary corps. The governing realities of my new environment savaged my expectations.

Parliament at the fag-end of Tricameralism resembled nothing so much as a curious combination of boarding school and an Old Boys' club (there were then few women members). An exaggerated sense of deference by the staff and officials, to those onto whose names the electorate had affixed the magical letters 'MP', prevailed. While there were three racially discrete chambers – white, Coloured, Indian – the essential power was wielded, fairly effectively, by the white house and, more pertinently, by the Presidency. Under the complex constitutional arrangements of the time, it was the dominant institution.

However, while race remained the determining factor of political power, the binding glue of the entire institution was rigid application of the rule of seniority. This meant that what for many of my colleagues were life-and-death matters, such as where one sat in the chamber, and which office you were allocated, were determined – with an obsessive, almost comical sense of solemnity – by how long you had been an MP or, in the cases of equal service, how old you were.

Being the second-youngest MP in the DP caucus meant I that got one of the worst seats in the back row of the House of Assembly, and was allocated a windowless cell on the fourth floor of the parliamentary new wing where our party MPs were housed. While such a derogation delighted officious DP whips who determined these matters – and whose opinion was that I was too 'uppity' and high-profile – I was far more interested in the portfolio I would be allocated. From this I could expand the causes which had propelled me into parliament.

To my disappointment, the 'Buggins's turn' principle was again at play. Portfolio appointments were rigidly and zealously driven by 'who came first'. The fact that some of the party front-benchers were – as the British put-down has it – 'bed-blockers', or exhausted volcanoes, counted far less than their years of service.

Thus I found myself a junior member of the party's justice and local government groups – the former headed by David Dalling, a perfect product of the now-extinct United Party machine who had steadily tacked (in his case under the influence of his new young wife) from the right to the left of the opposition spectrum. He had a reputation for bullying his secretaries and being rude to waiters; but by the time I arrived he was bored with the routine minutiae of legislation, of which the Justice Committee was to produce a great deal in the next few months. (To be fair he gave me many opportunities to participate and speak in parliament.)

If I found my own party environment somewhat stifling, it was nothing compared to the '*Führerprinzip*' prevailing in the National Party, and which infected the senior office-bearers of parliament drawn exclusively from its ranks.

It was the custom for new MPs to introduce themselves to the Speaker, parliament's most senior office-bearer. So, shortly after my arrival, I made an appointment to take tea with this institutional heavyweight. Louis le Grange had achieved local and international notoriety as PW Botha's minister of Law and Order. In his dour Potchefstroom way, he personified the hard-headed, and even cold-hearted, application of the apartheid regime's rule-by-emergency-decree, detention without trial, police brutality and multiple bannings. His bowler-hatting to the symbolically significant – but politically powerless – position of Speaker was a straw in the wind of regime change to come.

Le Grange was tall and imposing, and resembled a latter-day Clark Gable.

Over tea, he proceeded to lecture me on the wisdom of retaining one's own counsel: he told me that in his first five years in parliament he had spoken in his caucus only twice and made but one or two parliamentary speeches. Then he was appointed a deputy minister! I realised that in my first two weeks in the DP caucus I had exceeded his total for five years!

There were few topics on which I did not have an opinion. Nor could I imagine how, if you did not vigorously and volubly participate in parliament, the world would have any idea of your thoughts and worth. Indeed, I assumed the major purpose of being there was to do precisely that. The NP code worked differently.

It quickly became apparent that Louis (which I never called him: the formalism 'Mr Speaker' was to be used at all times) and I inhabited different universes. 'It is important,' he intoned, 'that you keep your family close at all times. They should accompany you to parliament during the session if possible, and you must not allow your political commitments to lead to the neglect of your family.' I interrupted to explain I was unmarried. He looked at me with a degree of incomprehension, and doubtless wrote me off as either louche or a deviant, inhabiting a cosmopolitan world so far removed from his in the western Transvaal mieliebelt as to be unfathomable.

The parliamentary caucus – which convened every Thursday morning when the House was in session – was a scorpion's nest of conflicting ambition and unresolved tension.

The caucus was an uneasy amalgam of old-school liberals, wannabee activists, and younger *arrivistes*. While by age and inclination I fell into the latter group, youth itself was no determinant of ideology. My friend from the city council, Lester Fuchs, now the new MP for Hillbrow, and I were firmly in a group that wanted the party to redefine the liberal agenda for the next phase of our politics; while some of my other new and more youthful colleagues, particularly Wessel Nel from Mooi River, Geoff Engel, whom I'd helped secure a winning nomination in Bezuidenhout, and Rob Haswell, a geography lecturer from Pietermaritzburg, were of a more radical bent.

We made common cause mocking the stuffy pretensions of our new home and some of its arcane and meaningless rituals. These included the fact that in the parliamentary dining room it was unheard of to break bread with colleagues from another party; you dined (and occasionally wined) only, and at all times, with your own political kith and kin. Lists were drawn and redrawn by the whips to indicate who was where on the front, or in my case the back, benches, and other meaningless rituals were obsessively followed.

While parliament had briefly assembled in late 1989, it was only formally opened by the newly enthroned state president, FW de Klerk, on 2 February 1990. His speech that day, the first of its kind I had ever witnessed as an MP, was of thermonuclear intensity. Its effects are still being dealt with today, nearly a generation later. While De Klerk had used the months preceding this event to indicate a significant change of gear from the PW Botha regime, there was no great expectation that he would fundamentally overturn the 350-year-old South African order – not least its incarnation over the past half-century.

De Klerk was an unlikely iconoclast. He was a conservative 'Dopper' (the more orthodox believers of the Afrikaans protestant tradition) and his effortless rise to the top had not salted many clues that he would be the agent of the most profound change ever witnessed in parliament since the decision to enter World War Two on the Allied side.

Indeed, De Klerk, by any measure of background, instinct and culture, was a conservative agent in a regime which by the time he assumed its leadership was looking distinctly tattered. Many years later, when reading Tony Judt's great work on post-war Europe,[1] I realised that De Klerk's conversion to democratic negotiation and consequent personal and political self-abnegation was not without recent precedent. When sweeping democratic change engulfed southern Europe in the 1970s (particularly in Portugal and Greece, just as in the Soviet Union a few years later under Gorbachev), the leadership figures there – Constantine Karamanlis, Antonio de Spinola and Adolfo Suarez – were all characteristic products of the system their reforms helped dismantle.

De Klerk, superficially, seemed both self-confident and grounded; he bore no chest full of medals; carried no homburg hat; nor did he strut with the overbearing sense of self-importance I had long associated with the leadership of the ruling party. Yet when he stood behind the podium of parliament and in increasingly assertive cadences buried the apartheid way of doing business forever, he seemed immensely elevated and strong.

The speech lasted for not much longer than forty minutes, and with the flourish of a theatrical showman, or seasoned trial lawyer, he saved the most dramatic and far-reaching announcements for the end: a moratorium on the imposition of the death penalty, the acceptance of a negotiated new constitutional order with all leaders and, as a consequence of this, the unconditional release of Nelson Mandela in the very near future – as well as the lifting of all legal and other prohibitions on the ANC, PAC, SACP, COSATU, UDF and allied organisations.

Actually, for all its stupendous impact and the political courage it took to conceive and implement it, the opening line of De Klerk's address contained a half-truth or a white lie, when he proclaimed: 'The general election of 6 September 1989 placed our country irrevocably on the road to drastic change.'

In reality, De Klerk's mandate was far more ambiguous than that: he never came close to intimating during the election campaign the agenda which he unveiled for the first time on 2 February. Indeed, the anti-DP propaganda launched at us by De Klerk's political machine had as its centrepiece a poster depicting an ANC puppet-master manipulating the strings of the DP troika above the legend 'Three Blind Mice'. I didn't mind the creative fiction, although my joy was tempered by my realisation that our entire election manifesto had just been taken (or stolen) by our chief opponent. As the former PFP leader Frederik van Zyl Slabbert later observed: 'There is ample and comprehensive evidence that De Klerk's speech on 2 February ... was a sell-out of everything the NP had held near and dear since 1948.'[2]

Intense speculation continues to this day as to the cause of his about-turn. De Klerk claimed a 'spiritual conversion' (*geestelike oorspronging*), while the choice he made was massively assisted by the autocratic culture of National Party decision-making. I was staggered to learn, as in a mentally shell-shocked state I exited the chamber, that my NP colleagues were en route to a caucus meeting where their '*hoofleier*' would brief them on his speech after he had already delivered it!

While the Nats were caucusing, a couple of the neophyte DP MPs were invited to join one of our own leaders, Wynand Malan, for lunch in the agreeable surrounds of the La Perla restaurant on Sea Point's beach-front. We speculated on the implications of the morning's events. Malan, who had previously been a National Party parliamentary colleague of De Klerk's for nearly a decade, seemed the right man to ask. So I said, over the bread rolls: 'But how, Wynand, will De Klerk take his people with him?' To which Malan responded: 'I know my people, they will respond to strong leadership and vision.'

A year or so after the event I reviewed a biography which FW's brother, Wimpie, had penned on his more famous sibling.[3] I read that FW de Klerk's conversion, according to this account, was not Damascene but reflected his calibrated rationality: a combination of strategic conservatism and a 'Calvinistic sense of vision' which apparently and open-mindedly made him able to do 'magical things' with and on behalf of the Afrikaner.

Whatever his motives and their background, he was frank enough to stare impending doom in the face and attempt to turn the ship of state around in mid-course.

There was little doubt that De Klerk's performance caught all his opponents on the hop. The ANC in exile was scantly prepared for its now imminent return; the official opposition Conservative Party fulminated about betrayal – which left the Democratic Party precisely where? We were somewhat like the Liberal Party in England, circa 1920, as the historian George Dangerfield suggested. The liberals had won everything they wanted, had exhausted themselves in the process, and had run out of a *raison d'être*. What purpose had they left? As this existential question began to exercise my colleagues, the fragile unity of our caucus soon unravelled.

Some two years later (with five of our MPs joining the ANC), Ken Owen, who constantly disapproved of the party and its leadership, wrote scathingly that the DP had 'provided a haven for closet revolutionaries, Stellenbosch socialists, draft dodgers, homeless federalists from the United Party, Afrikaans carpetbaggers, and sundry flotsam from the apartheid era.'[4] While exaggerated, it was a reasonable working description of a caucus, and a movement, whose essential glue was the fight against apartheid. And now that this system was to die – or be negotiated away by its own progenitors – our party was to come seriously unstuck. Thus the DP, founded only a few months before, would become the site of leadership crises, splits and walkouts as the party battled its way in a new terrain – which it had devoutly fought for.

2

The initial, overwhelming response to De Klerk's speech was hugely positive. His local and international status was immeasurably enhanced, although as the negotiations which were to stretch out over the next four years were to reveal, his new-found celebrity – which often seemed to drive his decision-making – would become a mixed blessing.

De Klerk was something new. Shortly after his famous speech, waiting for parliament to start, some colleagues and I were astonished when the state president strolled in, pumped our hands, wished us well, and had an animated discussion with us on the rigours of his TV encounter with the American supremo Ted Koppel, broadcast the night before. We were immensely flattered by his approach. So apparently were the members of his own caucus, still slightly shell-shocked from their membership of the caucus under PW Botha, who apparently barely greeted them, while their new boss invited them round to the presidential residence for a braai.

Both as a citizen and as an MP, I was caught up in the swirl of events consequent to De Klerk's big bang. I therefore found myself on the Grand Parade on Sunday 11 February, along with thousands of others, awaiting Nelson Mandela's expected 3 pm appearance on the balcony of the City Hall. This was my first direct experience of an ANC event, and it was not auspicious.

The crowds in front pushed backwards and those behind pushed forward. The middle ranks, where I was standing (perhaps an appropriate metaphor for the political ground my party occupied) were being squeezed out. When the delay mounted and the crowd's irritation grew to unrest and some rioting broke out on the fringes, I decided to retreat home. To my amazement, when I presented myself some four hours later at an ambassador's residence for a cocktail function, I discovered that the world's most famous political prisoner had not yet arrived to speak. In the event it was not a great or reassuring message, since the script (apparently) was written by a committee and promised lashings of nationalisation of industry and the other delights plucked from the then decidedly threadbare cupboard of international socialism.

But, I was to soon realise, in Mandela's case (like Marshall McLuhan's description of media), 'The medium is the message.' He was to prove the most powerful and important messenger and medium on South Africa's stage from that day onward.

The previous Tuesday, I had been allocated six minutes in the appropriation debate to disport myself of my maiden speech to the chamber. Furthermore, I had been allocated the graveyard slot of 6 pm (shortly before the House rose) for my debut. I doubted that too many in parliament would pay it much attention, although Tertius Myburgh had agreed, on reading it, to place it prominently in that week's *Sunday Times*.

The topic (which according to quaint, and antiquated, custom was required to be non-controversial) I could best address was the need for South Africa to be governed by a bill of rights. Hitherto the courts had been largely unwilling and unsuccessful in resisting apartheid's encroachments on individual and civil liberties; and this was not simply the consequence of deference to the executive by the judges. It was consequential on the doctrine of the supremacy of parliament – giving it the right to legislate without a higher body of law interfering in its decision-making. I reckoned De Klerk's speech contained an acceptance, in principle and for the first time, of a bill of rights. So I began:

'Despite the positive developments of the past fortnight, we still live in a divided and troubled society. Divided by differences and troubled by our abilities to reconcile them. It is therefore of the utmost importance that we seize the initiative given by government's acceptance of a bill of rights. A bill properly enacted and justiciable by an independent court could be a bridge over the troubled waters raging in our land – a bridge over the conflicting ambitions for absolute power. Such a bill will be a neutral ar-biter in whose favour each side – the majority and the minority – could safely relinquish the claim to absolute power since the bill of rights would embody a set of even-handed rights.'

I had, as noted, been an intensely fascinated observer of the historic col-lapse of communism in Europe in the latter half of 1989. There were dots to be joined between those epic events – especially *perestroika* and *glasnost* in the Soviet Union, then rapidly unbundling – and De Klerk's recent announcements. I therefore ended by quoting from the inaugural speech of Vaclav Havel as the first president of a free Czechoslovakia in over fifty years, delivered weeks before my own, more modest, debut:

'I dream of a republic, independent, free and democratic; of a republic economically prosperous and yet socially just. In short, of a humane re-public which serves the individual and which therefore holds the hope that the individual will serve it in turn.'[5]

3

The parliamentary Justice Committee went about converting the prom-ises of the speech into legislative action. The reform of the death penalty was the first item of business. Given the fact that my last speech during the 1989 election called for its abolition, because of the inherent lack of protection for, especially, indigent (essentially) black accused persons, I immersed myself in the details of the draft bill and the measures it now provided to strengthen the rights of defendants.

In those days committees met behind closed doors, inaccessible to the media. This, of course, was bad news in terms of openness and account-ability, but did mean there was far less grandstanding when it came to debating the clauses and purpose of the legislation. In the event, we pro-duced legislation which should have massively decreased the prospects of an innocent – or legally underrepresented – accused person facing the gallows. The bill radically curtailed the crimes for which the ultimate sentence applied; South Africa in 1990 was not that much more advanced than Victorian England in terms of the harshness of its jurisdiction.

The bill we crafted, much to the intense pleasure of my father who on his retirement from the Bench had become an ardent abolitionist, also restored judicial discretion: hitherto judges who could not find extenuating circumstances were statutorily obliged to impose death by hanging. I know how much anguish this had caused judges of my father's sensibilities – and I was pleased to have been a minor legislative cog in the improvement of the position.

I unearthed the startling fact that half of the 4 278 executions which occurred in South Africa between 1911 and 1988 had taken place in the last 20 years, exactly coinciding with the surge of violence against the apartheid state. Clearly judicial executions were a potent and blatant weapon of oppression yielded by the state against its opponents. In 1987, of the 164 persons executed 97% were black. While over one hundred black men had been executed for raping white women, not a single white had ever been hanged in South Africa's entire history for raping a white female.

The bill, important as it was at the time, was effectively moot. De Klerk's moratorium was extended until South Africa's new democratic order was born in 1994; whereafter, in short order, the new Constitutional Court outlawed capital punishment.

I was, in due course, to change my standpoint on the death penalty.

Before the anticipated talks between the recently unbanned ANC and the South African government could commence, and indeed before such struggle luminaries as Joe Slovo, Thabo Mbeki and Mac Maharaj and the entire ANC leadership in exile could return to South Africa, parliament had to undo reams of legislation which made it a criminal offence, among other things, simply to be a member of a banned organisation. For these and related offences, including convictions on acts of political violence, most of the ANC top cadre would, according to law, face either jail or immediate arrest on setting foot back in South Africa.

The government and our Justice Committee decided that the best method was to draft a broadly phrased indemnity bill which would allow the president, by regulation, to grant temporary indemnity to people convicted of crimes of political violence and related matters – and to do so retrospectively. While this was far from ideal jurisprudentially and open to potential political manipulation, government promised that in due course it would, by regulation also, set up an indemnity or amnesty committee of eminent jurists to deal with future cases.

The parliamentary debate that took place in May 1990 was overwrought. The charged atmosphere of venomous vituperation was largely occasioned by the official opposition Conservative Party, appalled and disbelieving that the South African government was about to negotiate – and it reckoned, sell the pass – to 'criminal terrorists' to use one of their more decorous epithets hurled into the debate.

I decided to try and turn the tables, and reminded the Conservatives, who regarded themselves as the living political heirs to the Boer War combatants, that they had in fact ignored their own history. Having just reread Thomas Pakenham's epic history of the Boer War, I calculated that the most egregious insult which could be levelled at a Conservative Party MP was to accuse him of behaving like Lord Milner. Milner, the British high commissioner in South Africa, was of course not simply anti-Afrikaans, but had played a big role in establishing the concentration camps where Boer women and children were interned. He remained, even at this time, one of the most hated figures for Afrikaans traditionalists.

I stated: 'The pig-headedness of the Conservative Party's opposition to this bill resembles nothing so much as Lord Milner's act of aborting the Middelburg peace talks between Lord Kitchener [the officer commanding the British troops] and Louis Botha [the great Boer War commandant]. Kitchener wanted a free hand to grant amnesty to the Boers of the Republic and also to the colonial rebels in the Cape Colony and Natal who had taken up arms on the side of the *volk* against the British flag.

'Milner's refusal delayed the end of the Boer War by over 15 months. Thus immeasurably more lives were lost, more concentration camps built, and more earth was scorched. Yet when peace eventually came there was a general amnesty and an indemnity from prosecution for acts previously committed.'[6]

The bill had a noisy but overwhelmingly easy passage through parliament. But the entire question of granting indemnities or amnesties for political crimes was to prove one of the most vexed and contentious issues of the entire negotiation process. Central to this controversy was who determined whether an offence was 'political', and how. South African jails at that time contained hundreds of prisoners, many of whom were on death row. Their offences were far from 'technical': often involving gruesome murders, including the infamous 'necklace' technique with which alleged informers were despatched to a savage end by being constrained by a rubber tyre and then doused with petrol and burnt to death, often to the delight of the frenzied toyi-toying crowds.

In any event there were some four hundred affected prisoners in jail at the time – often serving long sentences after convictions for such common law crimes as murder, arson and assault; but each of whom had one or another political motive. The first full-scale government-ANC meeting, the so-called 'Groote Schuur talks', were scheduled for March but postponed to May because of the Sebokeng massacre which saw 11 ANC-aligned demonstrators allegedly killed by IFP members – the ANC simply demanded the unconditional release of all 'political' prisoners.

Another former Wits colleague, the international law expert John Dugard, had given me sight of his paper on the 'Noorgard principles', devised by the Norwegian academic Karl Noorgard, and used recently to great effect in Namibia to determine whether common-law prisoners who were also Swapo members were genuine political prisoners who should be released to create a climate of normalcy pending democratic change. I used Dugard's gloss on the subject to construct a speech which suggested that in the absence of few other international precedents, the Noorgard-Namibian example was the best on offer. Among its other precepts it required that a prisoner seeking an amnesty or conditional release would need to show that his crime was 'proportional' to the political objective being sought; and importantly did not involve the gratuitous or indiscriminate killing of civilians. In my speech I specifically singled out Robert McBride, the ANC operative whose bombing of Magoo's Bar on Durban's beachfront in 1986 had killed three women and injured 69. According to Dugard, McBride would not qualify under the Noorgard test.

The Justice minister, Kobie Coetsee, approached me after the debate for a copy of my text. He said he wished to 'study it'. In the event, and whether or not linked to my speech is unknown, after the Groote Schuur talks and consequent to the regulations under the Indemnity Act, the government appointed an indemnity committee specifically to weigh and evaluate the claims for release of each 'political' prisoner. And the person Coetsee chose to head the committee was my father, then retired from the Natal Bench. Thus not for the first time in my life, the circle was joined again between the two of us.

The activities of the year 1990 could be termed 'the negotiations about negotiations'. The full scale Convention for a Democratic South Africa (Codesa) would only convene late the following year, in December 1991. Meanwhile the ANC and NP engaged in a 'getting to know you' exercise, no doubt to improve their comparative advantages. It was quite clear, from all the manoeuvring and delays, that neither side was seized exactly with a keen sense of urgency to thrash out a common understanding and basis for settling the big constitutional issues.

But during this interval, there was also increasing and dramatically dire, almost daily, evidence that violence in the black areas was to be a grim and constant companion on South Africa's journey down an uncertain road to an unknown destination.

It subsequently emerged that the National Party government and the ANC had been involved in low-key but exploratory talks in England even before De Klerk's accession to power.[7] But there was little in De Klerk's, or his cabinet's, background to suggest that their bottom line entailed more than the relinquishing of some power to maintain its essentials. As recently as two years before his presidency, De Klerk was asked by an interviewer whether he believed in one man, one vote. His answer was emphatically and unambiguously negative:

'I reject it if it is within the framework of "one man one vote" in a unitary state or in a typical federal state. [I believe in] one man, one vote for your own [racially defined and determined] institution ... Self-determination of each group is insured within its own group power base and its own structures.'[8]

De Klerk had undoubtedly calculated that he was entering the negotiations with a strong hand, forcing the ANC, stripped of its Soviet paymasters' resources and its unique occupation of the moral high ground abroad and at home, to occupy a weak seat with what he, De Klerk, no doubt calculated was a pretty poor set of cards.

While the initial meeting between government and the ANC at the government presidential compound, Groote Schuur, in May 1990 apparently evinced and yielded 'good body language and unexpected optimism', in the words of one eyewitness, this appearance flattered to deceive.[9] The extremist outriders on both sides had little stomach for what they saw as an elitist conspiracy which appeared (in the words of Slabbert *et al*) to keep 'their respective constituencies in the dark about how they were bargaining away fundamental policy positions that they had promised were completely non-negotiable.'[10]

This saw in quick succession the resignation of PW Botha from the NP and, at the other end of the spectrum, the unearthing of an apparently unauthorised ANC plot ('Operation Vula') aimed at overthrowing the state. When ANC senior operative Mac Maharaj was arrested and 40 others detained it was clear that the ANC either was suffering from an incoherence of tactics and an infirmity of strategy, or else was playing both ends (negotiation and armed struggle) off against the decidedly makeshift and fragile middle which was now emerging in South Africa.

By the middle of the year, the process begun on such a high note in February was now stuck in what mariners call the 'horse latitudes' where ships sailing around the equator find themselves either becalmed or thrown off course by baffling, unpredictable winds. Violence accelerated in the urban townships, especially around Johannesburg. To overcome this impasse, especially the suspicion aroused by the Vula plot, Mandela, apparently on Slovo's advice, suspended the armed struggle, which was codified in the Pretoria Minute co-signed with De Klerk, in August 1990. Slovo later confided to Patti Waldmeir, one of the best and most accurate chroniclers of the history of those times, that '90% of ANC supporters thought the decision was a sell-out.'[11]

Meanwhile, the Democratic Party, apart from helping the parliamentary legislative process, essentially took the role of interested bystander. Part of this was due to the objective (or as Marx would have it, the 'motive') forces of history unlocked by the ANC/NP power play. But it was also in keeping with the essentially passive personality of our most senior leader, Zach de Beer. He and much of the caucus were mesmerised by the sheer force of Colin Eglin's personality and analysis. Eglin, who became the party's chief negotiator when full-scale talks finally started, was of a mind (and he seldom changed it, once made up) that the party's role was essentially that of 'a facilitator of convergence'. At one level the DP was hardly a minatory presence in the body politic, and perhaps this was the best approach in the circumstances. But, at another level, I thought the strategy to be self-immolating, and told a student conference in Midrand in July:

'The DP has to decide its future as a matter of urgency, and any deferment of our positioning could simply see the party's eclipse by larger forces on the political horizon. The DP, in a sense, is caught between the hammer of NP power and the anvil of African Nationalism. [But] I have little doubt that if we position ourselves as a "radical centre" party – radical in resolve and centrist in positioning – we can play a major role into the future. A party pugnacious in its defence of commonsense solutions and implacable in opposition to tyranny, collectivisation and mob rule will have an assured and growing role in South Africa.'[12]

While the headlines which followed my speech were no doubt intensely irritating to De Beer and others, he was too polite to say anything about my gratuitous advice. In any event, he was no doubt preoccupied by the sudden and essentially unexplained departure of his co-leader Wynand Malan, whose public comment that De Klerk's speech had achieved what he came to parliament for seemed to underline our irrelevance.

Our inconsequentiality at this time seemed to release and fan the simmering tensions. I well remember earlier in that year when we were discussing the killings in Sebokeng – apparently perpetrated by IFP-supporting hostel dwellers from the nearby Sebokeng hostel, with much of the blame being attached to them and the police and/or some 'third force' element – one of the ANC sleepers then resident in the DP, Jan van Eck, stood up to denounce Inkatha in withering terms. My colleague and friend, Robin Carlisle, turned on him and said: 'You know Jan, if a five-year-old child was wearing an IFP T-shirt and she was hacked to death by an ANC mob, you would have no qualms in blaming the child for being provocative.'

I had no doubt that the party should be wary about the NP, but we had little in common with the ANC. At a report-back meeting, in August in Norwood, I told my constituents: 'The ANC should stop relying on a victim psychosis and start doing something creative. Its reliance on "popular frontism" in place of clear politics is a store of trouble into the future.'

I was unaware of the immense behind-the-scenes role Joe Slovo was playing to steer his party into more appropriate and moderate positioning for the forthcoming negotiations. However, I had ploughed through his 100-page polemic, 'Has Socialism Failed?', and was fairly nauseated by its ex post facto rationalisations. He suggested that Stalin, Mao, Pol Pot and Ceausescu were not the personification of, or representative of, the entire communist experiment which had seen tens of millions murdered in the course of its implementation, but simply extreme mutants of an otherwise laudable economic and political system. I described him, at the meeting, as 'an economic illiterate promoting a minimal programme of meaningless populism'.[13]

In truth, while my remarks were ostensibly aimed at the ANC, my real targets were their fellow-travellers within our caucus. They responded predictably, vehemently and immediately: Jan van Eck claimed my speech was aimed at sabotaging a forthcoming DP and ANC meeting, and demanded I 'retract [my] negative remarks.' Van Eck, at least, more or less had struggle credentials of his own, which was more than could be said for the NP-crossover in our midst, Jannie Momberg. But he too had apparently decided to hitch his somewhat over-burdened (by past association) wagon to the ANC star. He made an extraordinary statement in which he claimed it was important that I and others 'understand the difference between the ANC's rhetoric and the reality of its deeds.'[14]

Peter Gastrow, another left-leaning colleague, who despite pressure from his wife did not join the others two years later in crossing the floor to the ANC, decided to personalise the issue by attacking me for 'coming from Houghton and living in splendid isolation from what is happening on the ground elsewhere.'[15] It was left to Zach de Beer to pick up the pieces. In his droll way, Zach said: 'Tony Leon is a young man with a strong mind and a rich vocabulary, but all his criticisms of the ANC seem to contain substance.'[16]

I defended myself in an interview by re-stating my inner beliefs: that I saw both the ANC and the NP as 'instrumentalists' – they both saw democracy as an instrument for retaining, or attaining, power – not as a political philosophy to be defended and propagated in its own right, for its own virtues.

As the DP lurched and listed we headed into our annual congress where De Beer was to be opposed as leader by a colleague, Tian van der Merwe – the troika leadership having, thankfully, on Malan's exit, become redundant. Worrall's star was in sharp decline and he didn't even bother to make a fight of it (his descent was sealed the following year when, despite being the party's parliamentary spokesman on constitutional matters, he was passed over in favour of Eglin as the negotiations commenced at Codesa).

Bobby and Gillian Godsell and I were intimately involved in De Beer's campaign for the leadership, and in fact together drafted his speech for the congress. I had immense personal affection for De Beer, and despite being very friendly with Van der Merwe, I was uncertain where he stood in terms of the party's future alignment. But Tian, at least, and despite his chronic disorganisation, projected a youthful dynamism.

In truth, and friendships aside, I had deep misgivings about Zach's 'chairman of the board' style leadership, no doubt a hangover from his Anglo days. I also constantly expected the 'old Zach' of party mythology to appear: the one-time boy wonder who apparently, according to old Prog hands, had blazed a trail of intellectual brilliance and charisma across the South African political scene in the 1950s and 1960s. But by 1990, at the age of 62, the fires which had apparently burned once so bright within him had been all but extinguished. Instead, he seemed redolent of a past age offering very little promise for the future. It was not known generally, as well, that he was ill: on medication for high blood pressure, and declining.

I hesitated when it came to marking my ballot. But in the end, my sense of loyalty to him overcame my foreboding for the future: I voted for Zach. He beat Tian, but by no huge margin, and the next few years would – sadly – confirm the doubts about De Beer's leadership mettle and projection. Tragically, Tian was to die in a motor car collision six months later.

4

In the run-up to the congress, the violent wave of criminality sweeping the country directly confronted me. For the second time in five years in my relatively young life (my heart attack in 1985 being the first such unhappy intrusion) I was given an intimation of mortality. By 1989 there was a robbery every ten minutes or so of every day – 150 000 in that year alone. By 2005 the situation, notwithstanding over a decade of democratic governance, had barely improved. My evening of reckoning came after a concert which I had attended at the city hall with Edwin Cameron. We decided to have dinner at a small Italian restaurant in neighbouring Braamfontein.

This, as I wrote it down at the time,[17] then happened:

'Edwin interrupted our chat, saying *sotto voce*, "There's a robbery happening here." I spun round in my seat and came face-to-face with a menacing man pointing a revolver. He was accompanied by five others who commanded us to "get on the floor". About fifteen fellow diners and I promptly obliged. I thought no brave thoughts and simply wanted to survive … One of my fellow diners jibed, "My coffee's getting cold!" The response was immediate: "Sleep – or we'll shoot you!" I shuddered. Moments later the looting of valuables began. I was kicked on the soles of my shoes. My watch and the leather jacket on my back were demanded and quickly given. The robber then demanded my shoes. But the attempt to take them off while lying on the floor took too long for his satisfaction – and he moved on to the next victim.

'After what seemed hours – but was in reality perhaps no more than fifteen minutes – we were forced to move into a back office in the restaurant. We expected the worst, and the expressions on my fellow guests' faces must have mirrored my own fears. Some women sobbed. The restaurant owner, who had been manning the till, had been smashed over the head. Then it was over: R25 000 taken in cash, and they left.'

When the state loses the capacity to protect its citizens against violence, it loses the primary reason for its existence and we descend into the state of nature under which, according to Thomas Hobbes – in 1657 – the life of man becomes 'solitary, poor, nasty, brutish and short'.

Many residents of the Transvaal townships were far less fortunate. Within weeks of the Pretoria Minute being signed, some five hundred people lay dead as a consequence of vicious fighting, on the trains and in the streets, between Zulu hostel dwellers and township residents. The dragon of a frenzied and thuggish murderousness had been unleashed – but by whom exactly? Was it:

• the security forces, mandated or unmandated, determined to destabilise the ANC and secure an advantage for the forces of the status quo by a hideous and cynical manipulation of ethnic and political tensions?

- some variant of this, a so-called 'third force' determined to fan the flames of terror and stop the process of 'giving away South Africa'?
- Buthelezi's revenge at his de facto exclusion from the alliance being forged between Mandela and De Klerk?

Or was it a combination of them all?

Whether in an effort to uncover the truth or to buy time by deflecting the focus away from his government, De Klerk appointed Richard Goldstone, an astute Transvaal judge with impeccable liberal credentials and a talent for publicity, to head a commission into the violence. His initial task to investigate the earlier Sebokeng massacre was later widened to uncover the causes and location of the incipient anarchy sweeping the land. Goldstone probed, and by 1992 he had 'found some evidence of a third force' – more, in truth, a ragbag of dirty tricks unleashed against the ANC.[18]

Just six weeks before the general election in 1994 he dropped his biggest payload: he released a report alleging that top South African Police officers had supplied illegal weapons and ammunition to Inkatha Freedom Party operatives, and alleged that the 'architects of the oppressive system are still in place.' Extraordinarily for a jurist of Goldstone's eminence, however, he fingered the second-in-command of the Police, Lieutenant-General Basie Smit, and other top brass by way of a press interview, not by putting any of the allegations to any of the officers implicated or by charging them in court.

Shortly before the election, Basie Smit's daughter – a Pretoria lawyer – requested an interview with me in our campaign office in Norwood, Johannesburg. My amazement increased when she arrived the next day with her now infamous father. He told me he remembered me as 'straightforward and honest', and simply wished to state that despite the seriousness of Goldstone's revelations, he, Smit, had never been asked by Goldstone, or the Commission, about their veracity or his culpability. When I asked him what he wished me to do with this information, he responded: 'I want you to do nothing with it. I simply want you to know.'

That lay in the future.

In the intervening period parliament and the public debated endlessly the existence of the 'third force' and, more crucially, whether it was still extant and whose interests it served. What was being done to stop it before the violence killed not only innocent township dwellers, but the very fragile negotiation process itself?

The state attempted to interact and cauterise the killing fields in the townships around Johannesburg first by declaring a state of emergency in late August 1990, and then by launching 'Operation Iron Fist'. A few weeks after its inception I went with two DP parliamentary colleagues to see for ourselves conditions in the violence-wracked East Rand township of Thokoza, the very centre of the blood-filled storm.

We travelled in a police Casspir into the area, where only hours before rival armies had attacked each other leaving the site devastated. It looked as though aerial bombing and heavy artillery had devastated the pathetically flimsy shack structures: fires still smouldered, shelters of corrugated iron had been reduced to waste, and women and children picked their way through the debris. One source of the conflict, the adjoining Zulu migrant workers' hostel, had no roof (it had been razed in the ongoing violence).

A street barricade set up to prevent vehicles entering and leaving forced us to circumvent it, and we promptly hit a ditch which shattered the steering column. The next Casspir sent to transport us fared little better. One of its tyres – despite approximating the circumference of an elephant's thigh – punctured promptly on thick nails which had been used to booby-trap the Thokoza main road.

Law enforcement was sporadic and ineffective, with the police welcomed in some quarters and widely feared in others. The Katlehong station commander told us he had never in his lifetime seen so many AK-47s: 'The supply seems endless.' The neighbouring white local authority threatened to switch off the electricity that night, making what passed for law and order a total impossibility. Fortunately our negotiations averted that disaster, temporarily at least. But our meetings with local community leaders showed more of a desire to cast blame than to resolve violence.

In truth, I thought 'Operation Iron Fist', or at least the manifestation of it which I witnessed that day in the East Rand, could more appropriately have been dubbed 'damp squib'. But whether the homicidal frenzy could be blamed on De Klerk (as the ANC would have it) or was what the government descriptively, but unhelpfully, termed 'black on black' violence seemed often beside the point. The finger-pointing continued.

While De Klerk seemed to remain in what Patti Waldmeir aptly described as a state of 'negligent ignorance',[19] his choices were in fact severely circumscribed. On the one hand the ANC – and indeed the bulk of South Africans committed to a democratic future – needed him to stay in office to see through the momentous changes he had inaugurated. But to do so he could hardly fire his top echelon of security generals and tip their support – and armoury – to the far right, which under the bellicose Eugene Terre'Blanche and the quieter, but far more significant, ex-SADF chief, General Constand Viljoen, was mobilising and spoiling for a fight.

The following year's parliamentary session – violence notwithstanding – saw De Klerk and his Nationalists in buoyant mood: he clearly believed he had the upper hand. His reforms continued to impress the world, and he clearly enjoyed the spotlight. More importantly, his major opponents, the ANC, were battling through the undergrowth of new terrain. Its uneasy components – returned exiles, released Robben Island prisoners, and the grassroots resistance organisations spawned by the UDF and the trade unions – continued to manifest 'struggles within the struggle'.

5

I enjoyed my work as an MP. While Zach de Beer, who represented the constituency of Parktown, next to my own in Houghton, once remarked, 'The voters of Parktown do not bother me, and I certainly don't bother them', I revelled in the nitty-gritty of constituency work. I was not unaffected by *Die Burger*'s description of me as 'the DP's most promising newcomer'.[20] Nevertheless, my own no doubt inflated sense of political self-worth was not shared by all my colleagues. I noticed a distinct hostility from some, particularly those who were not opposed to my view on the much-contested political direction for our party, but who seemed personally resentful of my activities and profile.

Peter Soal, with whom I had enjoyed a friendship before I came to parliament, seemed in the forefront of this brigade. I found his attitude and increasing antipathy somewhat strange and disconcerting (it continues to this day). When I put my frustration to Zach – who was friendly with both of us – he told me to pay no heed. 'Soal is a good soldier,' said the leader, 'but he suffers from many petty jealousies ...'

Difficult as I often found the hostility in my own ranks, it only emboldened me and made me determined to work harder and prove perhaps more to myself, even more than to my detractors, that I was in politics to play a purposeful, perhaps eventually a leading, role. I was impassioned about our cause and credo having relevance and salience in the new South Africa.

In May 1991 I was invited by the student body of the University of Natal in Pietermaritzburg to deliver the Edgar Brookes Memorial Academic and Human Freedom Lecture. I used the occasion to try and delineate and differentiate modern liberalism from the other far more powerful political forces in play in the country. I expressed myself in forthright, and I hoped clear, terms:

'Liberalism is the only reliable barrier between apartheid and communism. Both those systems depend on the enslavement of the individual conscience to the creed of the collective. Liberal values are not weak, watered-down bourgeois values of other greater, more compelling truths. They are values which must apply here and now and after the creation of a new South Africa.'

I warned the students about the 'fallacy of genesis', the philosophical, and bogus, construct that invalidates good ideas because of their origins, and the reverse: 'Do not be mesmerised by a fraudulent course of action simply because it is authored by an heroic organisation, and do not doubt your own principles if they are accepted by previously oppressive parties. To do so would be to inhabit the slum of moral relativism.'

I felt my own party was in some danger of temporising its principles. In truth much of my thinking had been influenced by the then recently axed prime minister of Britain, Margaret Thatcher, whose moral certitude and political clarity had revolutionised her country away from the drift and purposelessness which had characterised its post-war decline.

She had once famously handbagged consensus-politics, with one of her withering disparagements: 'To me consensus seems to be: the process of abandoning all beliefs, principles, values and policies in search of something in which no one believes, but to which no one objects: the process of avoiding the very issues that have to be solved ... what great cause would have been fought and won under the banner "I stand for consensus"?'[21]

As it happened, shortly after the lecture Mrs Thatcher, licking her wounds and in search of an admiring audience elsewhere, was in Cape Town. Flown in by Anton Rupert's private jet, she comported herself more as a potent regent than as the vanquished force she in reality had become. De Klerk fussed over her, De Beer was summoned to an early morning encounter, and I was invited by the British ambassador, Robin Renwick, to a garden party at his Bishopscourt residence in honour of the lady. She was escorted around the grounds by a young embassy official bearing a large umbrella, no doubt to protect her peaches-and-cream complexion from the unseasonably harsh Cape sun rays.

As she did her rounds, we met. I somewhat breathlessly introduced myself, and jabbered on about how interesting she must have found her meeting earlier that day with the iron man of South Africa's right, the Conservative (far removed from her own) Party leader, Andries Treurnicht. 'Yes,' she responded, 'one must negotiate with all parties.'

I was both irritated with myself for asking her such a banal question and incredulous that Margaret Thatcher, of all people, could utter such a platitude when the body of her life's work had actually vividly demonstrated the very contrary proposition. Our brief encounter was, however, saved from complete inconsequence by my colleague Dene Smuts who was standing next to me. Perhaps because of her journalistic background (before entering parliament, Dene had been an acclaimed editor of *Fair Lady*) or owing to her honest forthrightness, Dene asked the question everyone wanted to, but nobody dared put to her: 'Gee, Mrs Thatcher, it must have been tough to have been dropped [from the leadership] in the way that you were?'

It was as though Mrs Thatcher had been waiting to be asked: she launched what I recall to be an animated form of venom against those who felled her. She pointed to the figure of Pik Botha who was standing about one-and-a-half metres away from us, and said, 'Foreign ministers are usually the least trustworthy of the lot', clearly more a reference to Geoffrey Howe, her nemesis in the Conservative Party, than to his local opposite number.

De Klerk's belief that he could surrender power without losing it was manifested in the government's constitutional proposals published in early 1991. The document, '*Deelnemende Demokrasie in 'n Regstaat*' ('participatory democracy in a constitutional state'), was, at best, a flight of fantasy that still clung to the delusion that the NP's past dominance was an accurate guide to its future prospects. De Klerk's model proposed a rotating presidency consisting of the leaders of the three to five largest parties elected from the lower House of Parliament, presiding over an all-party cabinet; and envisaged a super-sized senate with disproportionate representation for minorities. The Nats also proposed very high thresholds for enacting key parliamentary bills and for amending the constitution. Mandela archly – and perhaps accurately – dismissed this scheme as a 'loser takes all' system.[22]

Although events over the next two years would mock this plan, at the time of its publication De Klerk believed that he, not the ANC, was the driver of events; and that he could determine, if not dictate, terms for the final resolutions.

I took particular note of the government's charter of fundamental rights, published at that time, and the equivalent proposals of the ANC. Both reflected an essentially illiberal approach to protecting individual rights against all claimants, including an over-intrusive government.

I wrote in the *Sunday Times*: 'Both have dressed up their political manifestos as bills of rights. The government sees the role of the future judiciary as the sultans of the status quo. Their bill of rights protects the old empire in all its vastness – from ownership to pensions. In the ANC's version, the judges will be busybody social engineers intruding into every nook and cranny of social and economic life consistent with its vision of a welfare state buttressed by massive doses of affirmative action …

'Where liberals require a bill of rights as a shield to protect individuals in a zone of privacy and in the protection of rights which are bestowed innately not as a favour from the government, the left (read ANC) views a charter of rights as a battering ram to enforce a range of issues essentially beyond adjudication: moral claims more than legal rights.'

While I thought the ANC's version to be predictable, what alarmed me about De Klerk's proposals was their government-centric nature. The NP clearly believed it would be in power for some time to come, and had fashioned its key assumptions in a manner that was more protective of the state's interests than of the individual citizen.

One of the members of De Klerk's cabinet at the time, who today serves as the Democratic Alliance caucus chairman, Dr Kraai van Niekerk, confirmed to me when I was writing this account that the predominant cabinet view – vouchsafed by De Klerk – was that there would be a very lengthy 'transition period' before the majority party would be empowered to assume all the reins of government – and even on that date its power would be circumscribed by the restraints contained in the NP model.

The state of the ANC at the time was cause enough for the NP's misplaced optimism. Its organisation was chaotic, its membership recruitment anaemic, and it was, aside from struggle slogans, essentially bereft of coherent policies.

As Waldmeir recounts: '[B]y the time the ANC met for its first conference, in July 1991, meeting inside South Africa for the first time in more than three decades, the situation for them was desperate.'

The desperation was not simply a consequence of its internal dynamics. It was also a manifestation of a degree of powerlessness by the then-powerless. The serpent of violence continued to wrap its deadly coil around black South Africans. The Swannieville massacre in May that year saw a group of over eight hundred Inkatha supporters invade a West Rand squatter community and leave 29 residents dead (an uncorroborated report in the *Sowetan* claimed that the attackers were escorted back to their hostel by armoured vehicles). The ANC's response, as hitherto, was to use the widespread violence as a brake on its negotiations with government.

De Klerk dictated the pace of change. Parliament continued to repeal the legislative edifice of apartheid – from scrapping the Reservation of Separate Amenities Act and the Group Areas Act, to repealing the central lynchpin of codified segregation, the Population Registration Act. My party and I were merely bit-players on a stage on which the reformist president starred.

However, the ANC conference was to prove seminal. In electing Cyril Ramaphosa, a hardened trade unionist who had stared down the mighty mining conglomerates over the bargaining table, as its new secretary-general, it signalled that it was single-minded in its determination to impose a hitherto-lacking sense of order and discipline in its movement. Ramaphosa – aided by Mandela's ascent to the party presidency to replace the ailing Oliver Tambo – also executed a strategic shift of seismic proportions. No longer would it allow violence to stop the pace of change – but the ANC would now use it as a pivot to force concessions from government.[23]

6

At almost exactly this time a political bombshell detonated which would severely dent De Klerk's image and credibility. The *Weekly Mail* provided details of how covert funds had been channelled from the state, via the South African Police, to Inkatha to underwrite the costs of its trade union arm. In addition, the South African government had provided some one hundred million rands in secret funds for the opposition to Swapo in the run-up to the Namibian independence election some two years before. This exposé not only knocked De Klerk off his moral perch, it forced him to demote two of his key securocrat ministers (Magnus Malan and Adriaan Vlok) and allowed the ANC to demand, successfully, a postponement of the looming Codesa talks. It was clear that time was now to operate in the ANC's, not De Klerk's, favour.

At the time of the 'Inkathagate' revelations, I was in Washington DC. Owing to the untimely death of Tertius Myburgh (who as editor of the *Sunday Times* had done much to bolster my ascent into parliament, and whom De Klerk had appointed as ambassador-designate to the United States), the government had taken the extremely unusual step of appointing Harry Schwarz, from the opposition front bench, to the front ranks of international diplomacy as South African ambassador to the United States. It was interesting that Schwarz, who would be very critical of my own later moves with the National Party, eagerly accepted this plum diplomatic bauble from the hand of the party and government he apparently so despised.

Schwarz's primary mission, at that stage, was to encourage members of Congress to revise and rescind the comprehensive Anti-Apartheid Act which the Democratic Congress had forced on a reluctant President Ronald Reagan. Now that De Klerk's reform process was proceeding at full pace, and Reagan's successor, President George HW Bush, was keen to see the legislation scrapped, Schwarz believed that two of his former colleagues – Lester Fuchs and I – would be of assistance to him.

We cleared the trip with De Beer, who assented without demur. I'm not sure what affect or influence we had on the Congress, probably very little. The Republican members we visited with were already on-side, some Democrats were open-minded, but most were waiting for a signal from Nelson Mandela, not at that stage forthcoming.

Of more significance, however, was the sage advice I received at a meeting which Schwarz arranged for us with the distinguished Dr Chester Crocker, who had served as Reagan's assistant secretary of state for Africa. On his watch the Angolan morass had been cleared and the endless procrastinations which marked the passage of Namibia to independence had been finalised. Crocker asked me for an update on the negotiations in South Africa. I painted what I believed to be an accurate but gloomy picture: a stalled process, spiralling violence, mutual distrust, if not actual detestation, between the main players – and now the spectre of Inkathagate was likely to haunt both the start and even the outcome of the talks when they finally occurred.

'I respectfully disagree with you,' Crocker quietly interrupted my ramblings. 'How come?' I enquired. 'Well, you see,' he responded, 'in my experience, process overcomes problem. If you get the process of negotiations right, then I suspect even seemingly insurmountable obstacles will be resolved.' In fact the prescription would prove, over the next tumultuous two-and-a-half years, to be eerily prophetic.

However, my presence in Washington – at the time of Inkathagate – also provided my caucus nemesis, Jan van Eck, with a club with which to beat me. Van Eck (himself no stranger to parliamentary-sponsored trips of all descriptions) happily tore into Lester and me in the most extravagant terms: he claimed our visit 'drags them [Leon and Fuchs] into the Inkatha funding scandal to the extent that they are allowing themselves to be used by government to promote its hidden agenda.'

Quite what secret plot we were meant to be complicit with was never elaborated upon; but I returned to South Africa more convinced than ever that the ill-fitting mask of DP unity would soon be ripped off. But before that event occurred, early the following year, on the eve of our party's congress in November, we managed to lose one of our safest municipal seats in Johannesburg in Killarney and Houghton where Zach de Beer and I served as the parliamentary representatives.

Asked by a newspaper to comment I put it down to 'the ANC tendencies in the party'.[24] This, predictably, enraged one of them, David Dalling, and we tore into each other at the party's national council meeting on the eve of the congress. Both the pro- and anti-ANC factions in the caucus and party disgracefully (and I was complicit in the disgrace) leaked selective titbits to promote their agendas and discredit their opponents in the media. This led Zach to tell the congress that MPs should leave the party 'if they can't curb their tongues'. But aside from offering such admonishments, he had little to offer the party by way of a road map into the future.

The response from informed analysts was, in my view, deadly accurate: 'Who needs bridge builders when the two parties have already crossed the chasm?' enquired Shaun Johnson and Peter Fabricius in the *Star*.[25]

In response to my head-butting with Dalling, his friend Allister Sparks, the former editor of the *Rand Daily Mail*, entered the lists with a sneering, smear-by-association attack on me, published with great prominence in Johannesburg. While I thought Sparks a fluent writer and able chronicler of events, I found (and still do) his analysis to be shaky and his predictive abilities even worse. There was also in his high-minded, smug censoriousness – which always verged on pomposity – everything that was alienating (to the majority outside its embrace) to those outside the left-liberal-WASP enclave which Sparks inhabited, both mentally and physically.

He described Dalling and his cohorts in the party as 'the progressives', while I (and others who shared my distaste with the ANC '*toenadering*') were stigmatised as 'conservatives' and 'the reincarnation of the [Vause] Raws and [Douglas] Mitchells of 1959'.[26] This was, of course, a reference to the UP old guard who drove Helen Suzman and the progressives out of the party. I thought the comparisons to be one-part hilarious and one-part odious.

Whatever else politics in South Africa had become in the 1990s, it bore little resonance to bygone intra-opposition quarrels. Anyway, I accused Sparks of envisaging the role of white liberals as 'lying prostrate' before South Africa's dominant black political organisation.[27] But while this sniping on the sidelines of South African politics very much preoccupied me, the big elephants on the political savannah, the NP and ANC, finally got it together along with the minnows to convene the politically unprecedented and dramatic 'Codesa' talks in December of that year.

Although I had been immensely active in drawing up a raft of position papers and discussion documents for the party, Zach as usual chose the DP delegation to the Codesa talks on grounds of seniority. When he offered me a back row seat as an 'observer' I – in retrospect – childishly and churlishly refused, thus ignoring CP Snow's wise injunction that 'the first law of politics is to be present.' My hissy fit ensured that I watched one of the great political dramas of our time – the fierce fight between Mandela and De Klerk – at home alone and on TV!

Many years later, when I was on the receiving end of the manoeuvrings and manipulations of the NP leadership, I developed considerable sympathy with Mandela's outrage at how he believed De Klerk had tricked him into allowing the state president the final word at the Codesa opening. The substance of De Klerk's attack, however, did contain a boulder, not just a grain of truth: 18 months after signing the Pretoria Minute, the ANC still had intact both a guerrilla army and arms caches, which De Klerk demanded be disbanded and decommissioned. But Mandela, with a seldom-seen (in public at least) display of fiery temper, literally spat back. De Klerk, he said in response, was head of an 'illegitimate, discredited minority regime with very little idea of what democracy means'.[28] I chortled in agreement, and indeed the NP's performance at the negotiations henceforth would underline the accuracy of Mandela's utterance.

The only substantive achievement of the so-called Codesa convergence was the agreement on a declaration of principles, which I thought sound but unobjectionable. They were later used as a pretext by an increasingly alienated IFP to walk out of the talks – believing that the word 'undivided' in the adjectival description of the principle of a democratic South Africa precluded the federal option.

However, less dramatically but in process terms more importantly, it was agreed, on a key concession by De Klerk, that Codesa would write the Interim Constitution, but that an elected Constitutional Assembly would draft the final document. Ex post facto pundits and chroniclers of those times – from Slabbert to Waldmeir – believe that the president was again displaying signs of political hubris and personal vanity. He believed he could achieve permanent power-sharing in the first document and use it and other institutional brakes and balances to continue wielding power into the foreseeable future.

How seriously such 'delusions of grandeur' weighed on his judgment is unknown – but the practical upshot was that Codesa devolved into five working groups, each to hammer out key agreements needed to shape the new constitution. Thus when De Beer offered me a post as one of the 'advisers' to the DP negotiators, Colin Eglin and Denis Worrall, on Working Group 2, I did not retreat into a sulk again, but leaped at the chance.

Of all the five working groups, No. 2 was the most significant. Its purport was no less ambitious than to determine how South Africa was to be governed. It had to bargain on such fundamentals as the constraints to be placed on majoritarianism, the role of power-sharing, and the threshold majorities needed for all legislation – especially the constitution itself, including the bill of rights. Between January and May 1992 we met in lengthy sessions in one of the cavernous rooms in the jerry-built and grandiose and inaptly named 'World Trade Centre'. It was in Kempton Park, only minutes away from the airport. Apparently its owner was a close friend of Pik Botha's, which might have explained government's eagerness (it was footing the bill for the venue).

So, along with other colleagues, I shuttled each week between parliament in Cape Town and the new and now much more politically relevant site of political struggle. But in truth, while I had been given a ringside seat along with the other DP adviser, David Welsh, the professor of politics from the University of Cape Town, we were in his words 'advisers to someone who doesn't take any'. Indeed, on Eglin's table directly in front of us were a small, but growing, pile of notes and *aides mémoires* which Welsh and I had prepared for Eglin, either ignored or glanced at without comment or response.

The basis for agreement at Codesa was the purposefully vague requirement of 'sufficient' consensus. And while some nineteen political organisations were gathered around the rectangularly constructed tables, to achieve such a desirable outcome, Cyril Ramaphosa, the ANC's chief negotiator, told the ever-reliable Waldmeir in pithy and brutal terms how to deconstruct the phrase. Officially it meant the agreement by all those who needed to agree, but in reality 'it means that if we, the NP and the ANC agree, everyone else can get stuffed.'[29]

Ramaphosa's opposite number on the government side was the intellectual heavyweight minister of Constitutional Affairs, Dr Gerrit Viljoen, but whether the atmospherics at Codesa or some extraneous factors led to his indisposition, he apparently suffered some form of nervous collapse, and before anything of significance could be agreed Viljoen resigned from government and exited Codesa, never to return.

This was by no means the biggest calamity which befell the NP at the time. An electoral earthquake in the western Transvaal appeared to cause the ground to fall from under De Klerk's feet. It happened in the constituency of Potchefstroom – where De Klerk had attended university, and where he was currently enthroned as chancellor – and was occasioned by the death of my erstwhile lecturer on parliamentary silence and family values, the Speaker of parliament, Louis le Grange.

The by-election in February 1992 was a triumph for the Conservative Party, enjoying a resurgence in its fortunes due to the sense of increasing isolation and bewilderment felt by hitherto-staunch Nationalists at the tenor and pace of the reforms (or 'sell-out' as CP posters proclaimed) initiated by De Klerk.[30] If that result was replicated throughout the country, De Klerk would lose his majority in parliament.

The day after the Potchefstroom debacle, De Klerk entered parliament looking, I thought, preternaturally calm and amazingly confident for one on whom the electoral ceiling had apparently fallen; and when he was called to the podium for a special announcement, the reason for his sang-froid was revealed. De Klerk, in one stroke, unleashed a weapon which would prove to be an instrument of ultimate destruction to his opponents on the right. He declared, to an unusually hushed House, that a referendum among white voters would be held on 17 March to give the NP a mandate to continue with negotiations leading to a democratic constitution – or, indeed, to revoke it.

As the referendum results rolled in some weeks later, De Klerk's two-thirds affirmative vote proved him to be, at the very least, a masterful, even brave, tactician. He certainly, in electoral terms, routed his rightist opponents; but for all his undoubted tactical strengths, the events which followed on his referendum triumph suggested that his strategic grasp was much less certain. As Jonathan Freedland wrote in another context, 'He could see the next hill, but he could not grasp the entire mountain range.'[31]

For the duration of the referendum campaign, the DP found itself alongside the NP in urging a 'yes' vote from its constituents (as indeed, with qualifications, did the ANC) for De Klerk, or, as we put it, for negotiations. My constituency of Houghton was galvanised for the campaign as never before. Even my most apolitical of associates and friends pitched in to help, realising just how dire the consequences for the country and their futures would be if the white community turned tail on the incipient negotiations process.

I need not have worried: the constituents of Houghton and most DP areas voted affirmatively by a majority of over 95%. In fact De Klerk's referendum was carried by hefty majorities in every voting district, bar the ultra-right holdout of the far northern Transvaal (today Limpopo province). It was – and remains – the only voting day of my life when I have been on the same, winning, side as the national majority![32]

The referendum was, I believe, the high-water mark of the De Klerk presidency. He appeared to be master of all he surveyed and he apparently enjoyed the elevated view provided by the result. Later events suggested he believed that his renewed mandate was not confined to the white electorate. He clearly thought that he could both out-negotiate the ANC and thereafter run them very close in the all-race election to follow.

7

I played a far more active role in the semi-implosion of the DP. Both the left and right of the party, an inexact but useful shorthand description, despaired of the party making much progress in its current unaligned form. Both Dalling and I, working separately, prepared memoranda for the party caucus, each of which contained a gloomy – but as events would later determine, accurate – prognosis of the party's ailments and prospects. I said that current traditional support for the party had 'shrunk alarmingly' and that we were displaying 'no growth' in the black community. I suggested that the DP consider what I termed a 'reverse take-over' of the NP which I believed was struggling with issues of legitimacy, and we could – DP and NP – create the basis of a new party provided it had a commitment to 'fundamental liberal democracy'.

Since, next to Mandela, De Klerk was the most popular national leader, I suggested we place him at the helm of the new alignment, the very creation of which would give the NP a reason to disband. Dalling's paper, which shared my analysis of our future prospects, needless to say came to the opposite conclusion, and suggested an alignment or association with the ANC. Two strong minorities in the caucus shared one or the other perspective, but the leadership – De Beer, Eglin and Ken Andrew – favoured continued ploughing on. As the *Sunday Times* the next weekend reported it: 'The caucus meeting ended inconclusively, leaving the Democrats more divided than ever before.'[33]

Although I was, over the next few months, approached by several NP leaders to throw in my lot with them, I never seriously considered joining that party as it was then constituted. But I was deeply concerned that the DP was on the scree-slope to electoral oblivion, and some other vehicle would be needed to take the party's principles forward.

However, my ANC-leaning colleagues were, unbeknown to the rest of us, involved in deep discussions with their soon-to-be political masters. During the parliament Easter recess, five of them resigned from the DP and were welcomed into the ANC fold by a beaming Nelson Mandela.[34] The ever-scornful Ken Owen had an overdose of bile in his *Sunday Times* column that weekend. But since the 'gang of five' (as we soon dubbed them) were at the receiving end of his acerbity I rather enjoyed his rantings. He was especially scornful of Dalling:

'The most intriguing comment of the week was the assertion by David Dalling, the MP for Sandton who lives in Stellenbosch, that his switch of allegiance, if that is the right word, entailed no change of principles. The implications are perplexing: are the principles of the ANC to be deemed identical to those of the DP? Or did Dalling not as a member of the DP subscribe to its principles? Or has he taken his principles intact from the UP to the RP, to the PFP, to the DP and the ANC with nary an ethical wobble along the way?'[35]

Our much beleaguered caucus could now at least cohere, more or less, around some sense of common purpose; and at the very minimum, the poison which hung in the air of our weekly parliamentary get-togethers was largely removed, together with the air of recrimination and ceaseless media leaks. Secondly, and with typical generosity given the bleak prospectus I had only recently penned about the dark prospects under his leadership, Zach appointed me party spokesman on justice in Dalling's stead. This gave me a frontline position both in parliament and in the constitutional negotiations.

Back at Working Group 2 of Codesa we were racing towards a self-imposed May deadline. The full plenary of the body was due to meet in the middle of that month to confirm the outline of an agreement. But in the absence of Viljoen, De Klerk had not appointed a cabinet member to replace him on Working Group 2 (Viljoen's successor, Roelf Meyer, was involved in another working group). Instead it was left to Viljoen's deputy minister, Dr Tertius Delport, to carry the fight against an immensely strong ANC team consisting of Cyril Ramaphosa and Joe Slovo and, on occasions, Valli Moosa.

Delport – who in Waldmeir's account was 'despised by the ANC' – was not equal to the task.[36] This was not in my view an assessment of his talent or lack of it, but was painfully demonstrated by the fact that he had no real authority: our group meetings constantly had to adjourn as Delport left the room to get instructions, or approval, by telephone from De Klerk! The crisp, make-or-break issue, at that stage, was the crucial question of the percentages required for passage of the final constitution to be drafted by the new parliament (sitting as a Constitutional Assembly).

All parties agreed that the constitution – and especially provisions relating to a bill of rights – would require more than a bare majority. The NP finally tabled a proposal requiring a two-thirds majority on all clauses, and a super-majority of 75% for sections relating to the bill of rights, provincial powers and so-called 'minority rights'; clearly believing (post-referendum and in view of the parity of parties at Codesa, then more or less split between them and the ANC) that they could block an ANC government in the future. They also proposed an upper house senate – with over-inflated minority representation – which would need, on a two-thirds vote, to assent to the final constitutional packages. On the morning of the day when the plenary was scheduled to meet, our working group was still haggling around those provisions.

Clearly, the minority power, on this proposal, would have a blocking power which was precisely the kernel of the NP proposal. Ramaphosa, uncomfortable with the Nat offer, but wanting to appear accommodating on minority rights, especially in the eyes of the smaller parties dotted around the table, then proceeded to gazump Delport. He upped the NP suggestion to 70% for all clauses and agreed to 75% on the bill of rights – but then added a caveat, lethal to the entire construct behind the NP grand design: if the Constitutional Assembly could not agree to a new constitution within six months, then a referendum among all voters would be held to ratify the constitution.[37]

The Nats, clearly seeing a huge and obvious downside in this proposal, demurred, and Codesa was essentially now deadlocked. 'Hindsight,' Joe Slovo later observed, 'is the most perfect and irritating of all sciences.' Well, of course, 18 months later the NP government settled on considerably worse terms (66⅔% on all clauses of the constitution, and a referendum after two years if there was no agreement). Both the ANC and NP obviously thought that the passage of time would increase their strength – but it was to prove a disastrous miscalculation for the NP.

Codesa proceeded thereafter in fits and starts. De Klerk again changed his negotiators. The hardline Delport made way for the recently elevated Roelf Meyer, a man of easy charm and good manners, who was far more to the ANC's liking and seemed to embrace the spirit of majoritarian democracy more than his predecessors. While he was no doubt appointed to help grease the stuck wheels of the rapidly rusting Codesa machinery, he was hardly a match for the wiles and shrewdness of Ramaphosa and company. But before any substantive progress could be chalked up, the Boipatong massacre occasioned the total breakdown of negotiation, with Mandela announcing that this was now well and truly 'the last straw'. The

ANC walked out and convulsed the country with a series of strikes, mass marches and protests which seemed to prove the revolutionaries right: the country was indeed ungovernable, and the men (and women) of moderation had been usurped by those baring the mailed fist, the panga and the necklace.

But as with most grand and dramatic power plays, events on the surface hid an underlying reality, of which I only became fully aware some thirteen years later when I attended a gathering to which Meyer – by then long retired from frontline politics – gave a fascinating account of those times.

He said he had recently been appointed by De Klerk as the chief negotiator on the government's side, and he was watching the TV news as Mandela with Ramaphosa at his side announced that they were 'finished' with the South African government and with talks with them. Meyer told us that he had no idea what to do as he did not see any way to overcome the ANC's new intransigence.

Halfway through the news broadcast his phone rang and, to his amazement, it was Cyril Ramaphosa on the other side. He said: 'When can we talk?' So, here was the man who had just authored the announcement of the breaking-off of negotiations phoning his chief opponent to find out when they could chat.

Meyer told us that while Boipatong was the proximate cause of the break-up, the real cause had been the direct, or indirect, way in which the South African government had been demanding either continued white control or co-governance. Meyer said that he was steeped in the ideology and practices of the National Party and, indeed, had been born in Kareedouw in the Eastern Cape, one of the most conservative bastions in South Africa; he had been weaned on the same thinking. He said before they regrouped with the ANC 'channel' (the informal negotiations between the ANC and the government while they were officially suspended) a government official (whom Tertius Delport later told me was Fanie van der Merwe) had said that the only way the talks could be successfully resumed would be for the National Party to undergo a 'paradigm shift'. By this he meant it would have to relinquish its essential claims: rotating presidencies, minority vetoes, extreme federalism and the like – and would have to settle for a bill of rights based on individual rights. Meyer said that when this thinking started to percolate through the talks, a real change started to happen.

Boipatong itself, even by the standards of the blood-dimmed tide which had engulfed South Africa for the two-and-a-half years before its occur-

rence in June 1992, stands out in memory. Nearly fifty residents of the
Vaal Triangle township were killed in a murderous rampage by local Zulu
hostel dwellers. It not only gave an increasingly militant ANC a reason to
leave the talks ('I can no longer explain to our people why we continue to
talk to a regime that is murdering our people,' said Mandela) but allowed
the ANC to internationalise its cause again and discredit De Klerk's world
standing.[38]

The United Nations Security Council called a special emergency session
to allow every Codesa party to address it on South Africa's apparent and
precipitous lurch from negotiation to confrontation. As it happened, both
Ken Andrew, the DP national chairman, and I were in New York for another
purpose, to attend Bill Clinton's coronation as the US Democratic Party
presidential candidate at its convention at Madison Square Garden. Andrew
and I were told by De Beer to put the party's case to the council. So we
busied ourselves writing a statement for Ken to read out – of which no one
took the slightest notice – since all eyes were on Mandela and Pik Botha.

What to make of the presence of Yusuf Surtee, for some reason wandering
around the floor of the Security Council that day in New York, looking
as if he owned the place? When I had felt deeply extravagant or self-
indulgent I had purchased clothes on occasion from his vastly over-priced
clothing emporium in Hyde Park, Johannesburg. But Surtee (who clothed
Mandela at, I understood, far more discounted prices than I paid) was a
shadowy, although friendly, all-purpose, fix-it man for the ANC (or so
he held himself out to be). But he certainly, whatever the accuracy of his
claims and his true role in the organisation, was very well connected. He
suggested to me, as some minor homeland potentate from Codesa addressing the Security Council, that we repair to the delegates' lounge so that I
could 'get to know Thabo'.

Given Mbeki's later rise to domination of South African politics, at that
stage he was a very marginal figure at the constitutional negotiations where
his arch-rivals, Ramaphosa and Slovo, held court. Indeed, I had never had a
conversation with this eminent ANC dauphin. In the agreeable surrounds of
the lounge, overlooking New York's East River, Mbeki, Surtee and I drank
and conversed. I recall nothing of the conversation; it was not of the sort that
I noted afterwards, but I distinctly remember being impressed by Mbeki's
ready charm and obvious comfort in those surrounds. It was a promising,
but illusory, start to a relationship which would, over time as we both ascended to the top of our respective political piles, sharply deteriorate.

Also during that visit to New York I again met up with Schwarz, accompanying Pik Botha around New York. Schwarz had offered Ken Andrew – much to the annoyance of some of the South African government officials – full access to the legion of staffers scurrying around Botha's baronial suite at the Helmsley Palace hotel in Manhattan. This at least enabled us to get our presentation to the UN typed and copied. During our visit Schwarz told me he was so unimpressed with the way De Klerk kept chopping and changing his constitutional negotiators, and with the quality of the output, that he telephoned the president and asked him, 'Why don't you simply go to the Johannesburg [advocates] Bar and hire for yourself the four or five best senior counsel there? They are likely to get a better result for you.' De Klerk did not heed the ambassador's advice.

While the ANC continued – away from the abandoned World Trade Centre – to flex its muscles in the streets, I busied myself in parliament with the raft of legislation emanating from Kobie Coetsee's Justice ministry. In fact, it was in some ways the most productive and rewarding period of what is now my very long career as a legislator. The National Party government had committed itself to a '*rechtstaat*' (constitutional state) and this was evidenced in the draft legislation of the time.

This was particularly true of a range of bills from internal security to telephone tapping and drug trafficking, which contained provisions providing for limited detention without trial. I was able to introduce, and get the ministry to accept, dozens of amendments which vastly strengthened the rights and protection of detainees. Even on the floor of parliament I succeeded in convincing Coetsee to accept certain modifications before the final passage of legislation. (I had had similar success the year before with the minister of Finance, Barend du Plessis, who was persuaded to abandon a proposal to impose value added tax on municipal rates, which I convinced him was a 'tax on a tax'.)

When parliament adjourned for the year, and before the disbanded negotiations were recommenced, I busied myself in my constituency. As I was preparing myself for the annual public ritual of the Houghton report-back meeting, a constituency committee member suggested, more I suspect as a gimmick than anything else, that I invite the person who was unarguably now Houghton's most famous resident, Nelson Mandela, to attend. He had recently moved into the area, in a house which he later told me was purchased for him by France's president François Mitterrand. Well, I thought, that's a nice idea, and I hand-wrote an invitation and delivered it, together with a chocolate cake, to his residence in 13th Avenue, Houghton, a day or two before the meeting. I hardly expected him to avail himself of the invitation, which indeed he did not.

However, the night following the meeting, when I returned home, a by-now world-familiar voice had left a long message on my telephone answering machine. Mandela explained how touched he was by the cake and how pleased he was to have such an energetic representative in parliament. He also added, quite unnecessarily I thought, that he was indeed sorry he could not have attended the meeting, but looked forward to inviting me 'and one or two other DP chaps' to his house for dinner.

As good as his word, a few days later his secretary made arrangements for Ken Andrew, Zach de Beer and me to join him for a meal. On the appointed evening we presented ourselves, where after a minimum of security clearance we were ushered into a cosy, but by no means sumptuous, ground floor living room, to await the arrival of the great man.

I had never before met Mandela face-to-face, nor indeed conversed with him, although his ceaseless appearances on TV made him seem somehow very familiar. When he entered the room, casually attired in slacks and T-shirt (we were all suited up for the occasion), his famous warmth and conviviality took over and made me feel immediately at ease. I had just returned that day from a lengthy conference in Durban – the so-called British-South Africa meeting, where the good and the great of the UK met with the full range of South African political actors to discourse about the 'way ahead' and related anodyne matters in the climate of suspended constitutional negotiations.

As one of the rapporteurs of the meeting I had been quoted, in a single paragraph buried deep within the story, in that afternoon's edition of the *Star*. To my utter amazement, after warmly greeting us, Mandela proceeded to explain that while he understood my perspective, he wanted to explain the ANC's viewpoint. I was smitten! Thus began a relationship which continued and strengthened over the next 15 years.

Mandela, who was unaccompanied at our get-together, then offered us drinks. Since it was about 7 pm, Zach and I (rather than Ken, who was slightly more abstemious) were intensely relieved; but on eagerly accepting his offer, we were somewhat nonplussed when Mandela proceeded to pour us each a glass of port. Out of politeness – since I can't stand the drink – I quaffed mine.

Before the meal we asked Mandela about the evolution within the ANC which was starting to manifest itself on key economic issues. Mandela's response was typical of his candour and directness: 'Well, you know, earlier this year I was a guest at the World Economic Forum in Switzerland, and some of the biggest and most influential businessmen in the world were there. And they were very happy to meet me, but practically every one of them bashed me over the head because of our policy on nationalisation [of industries]. So when I got back to South Africa, I got hold of our economics team in the ANC, and said to them, "Boys, we are going to have to change our policy in order to be taken seriously in the world." And they agreed ...'

I had no idea whether Mandela's encounter in the Swiss Alps was the proximate cause of the ANC's move away from the socialist model; but I loved the story and the humorous and self-deprecating way Mandela told it. I also thought that even if much of the World Economic Forum's annual extravaganzas at Davos consisted of pretentious photo opportunities and high-minded junketeering, it had on this singularly and important issue to my country and its future wellbeing become a sort of modern day secular Damascus.

8

It seemed by September that 1992 would be chalked up as one of the most dramatic and politically turbulent years in South Africa's history – the Codesa break-up, the referendum, the defections and Boipatong. But even more dramatic events were to unfold in its final quarter. As far as the party was concerned, Zach thought the worst was over and believed, as he put it, 'The resurgent DP forms the centre of South Africa's political spectrum, promoting liberal democracy, left of the NP and right of the ANC.' A predictably unimpressed Ken Owen waspishly poured scorn on this high-mindedness:

'Unhappily the DP has lost confidence in itself, and has adopted the role of facilitator, willing to sacrifice its own interests to carry the brief-cases of greater men. The attempts to broaden its base have been left, too often, to the inventive but restless mind of Tony Leon.'[39]

In this instance, however, the 'inventive but restless mind' happened to agree four-square with the acerbic editor. But by then, and henceforth, I was to occupy pole position in Owen's considerable gallery of demons. I was told by an interlocutor later that he believed (wrongly, as it happened) that I had referred to him as a 'wholly owned subsidiary of his [immensely wealthy] wife'. He used whatever public space remained available to him in the following years to avenge this imagined and misreported slight.

On 7 September 1992 I found myself taking a mid-day refreshment on the manicured lawns of the presidential guest house in Waterkloof, Pretoria. I was there to represent my party's viewpoint and interests at a get-together De Klerk had convened of 'interested parties' to discuss the question of federalism and its location in the new, but not yet sighted, constitution. Midway through the afternoon's proceedings, De Klerk announced that he needed to excuse himself because of an 'extreme urgency' – words to that effect.

The one hundred or so attendees with me were somewhat puzzled, but we quickly learned that South Africa's 'annus horribilis' was continuing. Another massacre had occurred, this time in far-off Bhisho, capital of the notionally independent homeland of Ciskei. However, when the smoke had cleared, and the 28 dead bodies had been removed and the injured hospitalised, it soon became apparent, vehement protestations to the contrary, that the ANC, or rather one of its senior men, Ronnie Kasrils, was primarily responsible for this latest bloodbath. Kasrils was an amalgam of charm and menace, with an almost *Boy's Own* penchant for military adventurism and derring-do. However, from all reports, on this occasion he had displayed wilful and reckless disregard for the lives of his followers.[40] When the Goldstone Commission investigated the massacre it called on the ANC leadership to 'publicly censure' Kasrils and other ANC leaders for 'knowingly or negligently exposing marchers to the danger of death or injury.'[41]

If Boipatong caused the talks to break down, then Bhisho (formerly known as Bisho) shocked the parties into the realisation that their urgent resumption could not be postponed.

The much-hyped 'Record of Understanding' concluded in September between Mandela and De Klerk was a prelude to the resumption of full-scale negotiations. But it extracted a fearsome price when De Klerk infuriated an already marginalised Buthelezi and set in train a chain of events and agreements which would see the NP eventually surrender most of its thus far 'non-negotiable bottom lines'. Ever one to scent weakness in his opponents and trumpet the capitulation, Slovo triumphalised: 'They [the NP] caved in on everything.'

The Record of Understanding revealed De Klerk as a much-reduced negotiator. He seemed to have given the ANC everything they wanted and demanded: the fencing-off of IFP-supporting hostels; the ban on Zulu traditional weapons; and most painfully for the president, the release of further political prisoners who had been refused indemnities by the committee chaired by my father, including the opprobrious Robert McBride.

De Klerk ultimately gave way on this demand. As one observer famously put it, 'The National Party had blinked.' One of my NP parliamentary colleagues at the time put it to me that since the only visible concession

De Klerk had wrung from the ANC was an agreement to restart negotiations, this in and of itself was a Pyrrhic achievement – since 'there's nothing left to negotiate, my party's given it all away.'

In fact there were crucial issues still in play, and the ANC would towards the end of that extraordinary year make some vital concessions – especially on power-sharing arrangements – which would drive the process towards its ultimate, and more or less successful, conclusion.

The prisoner release – one consequence of the Record of Understanding – had an electrifying sequel in parliament in which I was centrally involved. In order to give a shroud of ex post facto legality to the 'dirty deal' which De Klerk had struck with Mandela on the release, a special session of parliament was summoned in October. Its essential purpose was to ram through a further indemnity bill that gave statutory respectability to the Pretoria Minute. This had not only seen McBride's release, but had also thrown into the exchange another infamous killer, from the other end of the political spectrum: Barend 'Wit Wolf' Strydom, who on a November day in 1988 had walked into Strijdom Square in Pretoria and gunned eight Africans to death (and wounded 16 others), claiming some inner voice made him do it. At the time of his release on parole by De Klerk he was on death row in Pretoria. His application for indemnity had, like McBride's, been turned down for the obvious – indeed grotesque – lack of proportionality between the supposed political objective being pursued and the result.

De Klerk's motivations were not simply legalistic (in truth, as state president with the power of pardon he didn't really need the legislation); he was also alarmed by an increasingly nervous security establishment agitating for a general amnesty before the regime-change occurred. When the bill was published I described it as a 'back door amnesty' and worse: its sweeping provisions provided for a committee (meeting behind closed doors) to provide amnesty for any person who committed 'a politically motivated crime'. It did away with all the other cautionary tests, and its worst provision, in my view, was the clause that provided for the publication of the names of persons released without linking them to the crimes and acts on which they had sought indemnity.

While our Justice Committee was convened in urgent session to consider this appalling legislation, De Klerk made a speech to the Transvaal Law Society in which he made the fatuous claim that he 'knew of no state employee who had committed any crime that might require an indemnity in terms of the bill.'[42] I immediately drew attention to the case of Major-General Lothar Neethling then being exposed for a series of state-sponsored criminal activities. I also asked aloud precisely who employed Eugene de Kock – who had told the whole world that he was part of the Vlakplaas killing machine sponsored by a South African Defence Force offshoot.

When I spoke in parliament on the issue, I flayed both the government and the bill, declaring it to be 'a charter for crooks, criminals and assassins'. I said the legislation massively widened the net of bombers, state-sponsored killers and others who would now qualify to walk away from their deeds – 'unnamed, undisclosed and unpunished'.

I sat down knowing that I had delivered my best speech in parliament; 15 years later I am still of that view. Indeed I received a pile of congratulatory notes from all sections of the House, including an unprecedented missive from Dr Andries Treurnicht, the leader of the official opposition, stating, appropriately in both official languages, 'Excellent – *ek dink u was baie doeltreffend*' (I think you were very effective). Zach de Beer, courteous and fulsome as always, told me that 'with your speech this morning, you have joined the ranks of the truly fine parliamentary orators.'[43]

But, of course, my rhetoric did not change votes, since the NP had an inbuilt majority in two of the three Houses of Parliament, having recently, through floor-crossing, taken over control of the Coloured House of Representatives from a fast-imploding Labour Party. But, in a fit of uncharacteristic conscience and defiance, the Indian House of Delegates gave De Klerk the finger. Despite the intense negative energy and publicity unleashed by the debate and the humiliation of not securing its passage, since all three Houses were required to assent, De Klerk sent the bill to the President's Council which, under the rules, had the power to break the deadlock. It nodded the legislation through.

In fact this 'victory' proved to be something of a chimera for the NP: the provisions of the bill were undone by the constitution a year later, which made provision for the future Truth and Reconciliation Commission based on the precise formula of 'knowledge and acknowledgment' that I had argued for that day in parliament.

My father, appalled by the way in which his indemnity committee had been gerrymandered by the new provisions of the bill, promptly resigned from his position. And when, a month later, Amnesty International produced a hard-hitting report on the abuses – including summary executions, torture and lengthy detentions in the ANC camps in Angola, Tanzania, Zambia and Uganda – De Klerk and the National Party were unable to derive much political purchase. Their bill, now the law of the land, would enable those responsible, whose number included such luminaries as Jacob

Zuma and future Defence minister, Joe Modise, to escape scot-free.

With the restart of multilateral negotiations proper early the following year, I found myself back at Kempton Park in a small room trying to thrash out the outline and content of South Africa's new bill of rights. Because we met out of the public gaze, we started to make some progress on the thorniest issues, such as property rights and the limitations clause of the bill itself. By this stage each of us, the NP, ANC and DP, had produced our own draft bills of rights. We each accepted that at least some of the rights we were proposing for inclusion could not be absolute, and that they had to be capable of being limited (e.g. if the right to free speech is unlimited, legal remedies for defamation or prohibitions on child pornography would become invalid). Thus the overall effectiveness of the bill of rights is largely dependent on the wording of the limitation clause. What was striking when we examined the three drafts was that the NP's proposed limitation clause was looser than any of its rivals. The effect was to make the NP's bill the least effective in constraining abuse of government power. Even more perverse was that the ANC – the government-in-waiting – was proposing tighter restrictions on government power than the NP. I concluded that after nearly five decades in government, the Nationalists were basically incapable of acquiring an opposition outlook.

Fortunately, the NP negotiator on our committee, the deputy Justice minister Sheila Camerer, proved amenable to the DP-ANC proposals on the limitation issue, and most of our formulation made itself into the final version accepted by the multi-party process. (When the talks resumed, the Codesa acronym was dropped, but the parties never got around, or couldn't agree, to a new name. Thus rather like a supermarket no-name brand, we described the constitutional conference as 'The Multi-party Negotiations Process'.)

After our committee couldn't agree on a formulation on property rights (being split between those who wanted the right entrenched firmly and those who wished a much more fluid formulation to make expropriation easier), I paid a visit, in some despair, to my friend Professor Carole Lewis, the resident academic expert on the subject at Wits University. She suggested that I go back to the committee with a set of general principles on property rights, obtain agreement on them, and then draft the clauses, instead of the upfront haggling around terms and words in which we were then engaged.

Lewis's suggestion (and she drew up the principles herself) worked, and the logjam started to break. The ANC negotiator Penuell Maduna, who in his subsequent incarnation as a cabinet minister earned a deserved reputation for hotheadedness and overweening arrogance, could not – in those distant days – have been more amenable to reason and compromise. He certainly helped our committee make real and rapid progress. In fact, the first two clauses of the property rights provision in the bill of rights came almost word-for-word from Lewis's early formulation. The expropriation clause consisted of a laundry list of factors, balancing or cancelling each other out, which the court would have to weigh in determining the quantum of compensation – a reasonable compromise.

I realised (particularly after strenuous urgings from Etienne Mureinik, at all times as my adviser) that none of the rights in the bill would be worth much if we accepted the Technical Committee's proposal – that the entire bill be interpreted in a manner consistent with a democracy 'governed by the principle of equality'. Without qualification this could simply flatten out individual claims based on liberty and lead to many kinds of totalitarian temptations well into the future. I had a number of sharp altercations, in public, with the Technical Committee chair, the intellectually towering but clearly ANC-sympathetic Arthur Chaskalson. Eventually he conceded the issue, and we managed to conjoin 'liberty' with 'equality' in the relevant clauses.

The Easter recess loomed. I had been invited on another overseas junket – and left Johannesburg on the calm of Good Friday and stopped off the next day to see friends in London, before going off to Norway. That afternoon, in the interval of a play I was watching at the National Theatre, I phoned an ex-South African friend who was not much seized with political matters. However, her opening sentence chilled me. 'Tony,' she said, 'there's been some terrible assassination this morning in Johannesburg. I think the victim was the head of your Communist Party, Chris something-or-other ...' Of course, it was Chris Hani, a pillar of the ANC-SACP leadership; a figure of immense popularity and significance – and he had been shot dead outside his home in Dawn Park in Boksburg.

9

The South Africa we returned to a few days later was a vastly changed place – again moving frighteningly close to the abyss of violent and anarchic confrontation. The forces of anger and recrimination unleashed by the Hani murder were only barely held in check by the masterly moderation of Nelson Mandela, who appeared to have, effectively, taken over the country, or who certainly gave it its voice, while De Klerk remained on the sidelines at his holiday home in Hermanus on the Cape coast.

De Klerk was soon to pay a high price for this de facto transfer of authority when the next session of the negotiations got under way. In truth, the Hani assassination was a tipping point, and now, beyond doubt or argument, power tipped in the direction of the ANC. Before the talks resumed, there was a session of parliament when, during the debate on De Klerk's Presidential Budget Vote, I opined that in view of the mass protests, marches and killings around the Hani funeral service 'like an ancient mosaic long covered by sand and now exposed to the howling gales of change, the South African legal order is now disintegrating ... meanwhile South Africans walk around in a state of stunned uncertainty.'[44]

Beyond the incipient anarchy consequent on Hani's assassination lay the continually shifting bottom lines of the South African government on constitutional issues. This was thrown into sharp relief when, later at the negotiations, Joe Slovo demanded that before any issues of significance could be concluded or debated, there had to be agreement on an election date. After some wrangling and protestation, the NP negotiators, with the DP's concurrence, yielded. I sharply disagreed with our support for the ANC on this issue, but the party leadership clearly decided that a deal was more important than anything else.

A disaffected unnamed Afrikaner described his view to Waldmeir with accuracy and poignancy: 'It's like handing over the title deeds to your farm without first knowing the price.' According to her account Mandela forced this fundamental concession on De Klerk by playing on his vanity for overseas acknowledgment. Both of them were due to accept jointly the prestigious Liberty Medal in Philadelphia on the fourth of July. Mandela, without whom there would have been no ceremony, said that unless De Klerk agreed to the election date, he would not attend.[45] In fashioning the Légion d'honneur, Napoleon once observed, 'Men are led by toys.'

As it happened, around the time of this fundamental breakthrough (or capitulation) I attended a small dinner at the French ambassador's residence in Pretoria in honour of the former prime minister of France, Michel Rocard. Among the guests was Roelf Meyer, the government's key negotiator. I put it to Roelf that having conceded the election date of 27 April 1994 nine months in advance, they had yielded all the advantages to their opponents who simply had to wait it out, while the South African government would now have to negotiate against an immovable deadline without having reached an agreement on key issues. Meyer was frank: he said that once the government had lost control of the security situation, it wasn't really in a position to control much else.

Whatever the real reason or motive for this most fundamental of all concessions, the NP government had handed the initiative to its opponents before having settled the most contentious issues; and now had to go along with their proposals.[46]

Since the country was to go to the polls relatively soon, I spent as much time as possible when not required at the negotiations trying to assist our organisation with its preparations for this make-or-break event. 'More break than make' was my gloomy conclusion. Despite having attracted over two thousand local domestic workers to a rally I organised in my constituency in January 1993, I was under no illusion that the party was going to make little headway in the majority voting market. To the extent that our message resonated at all with black South Africans, a meeting we attempted to hold at the vast squatter settlement at Orange Farm, and which was violently broken up even before I could speak, indicated that the message would not be heard at all in many parts of the community. This was rammed home by the Sanco (the South African National Civics Organisation) secretary-general who announced that 'white parties must stay out of the townships'.[47]

From an ANC perspective, this was hardly necessary. Outside Natal, their majority and dominance of the black side of the divide was unchallenged, and essentially unchallengeable. On the other side of the divide, however, all the polling and much anecdotal evidence seemed to suggest that white voters were flocking, across party lines (including, I gloomily noted, my own), to seek De Klerk's protection. Meanwhile, for what it was worth, I moved up the short but greasy pole of DP politics, and was in September elected unchallenged to head the party in the PWV/Gauteng province, electorally the most significant. This would likely secure me a seat in the next parliament – but how many, or more likely how few, fellow DP MPs would I be among?

My upward mobility in the party was not high enough as far as my friend and colleague Lester Fuchs was concerned. In late September he took himself off to Zach de Beer's Saxonwold home and told him point-blank to resign and make way for me as the leader if the party was to have any hope of even moderate success in the election the next year. Zach declined the invitation; but yet another 'caucus meeting to clear the air' was held, at which Zach said he intended to stay at the helm, but would go anywhere or do anything the party required of him. At this, the irrepressible Robin Carlisle leaped up and said, 'Well, Zach, you must lead and we will follow. But if you simply carry on as before you will lead us over a cliff!'

I had, in any event, firmly decided against standing for the leadership against Zach at the party congress in November, and said so publicly. The *Financial Mail*, as usual, no doubt well-fed by titbits of information from all sides, reported with accuracy: 'It is clear that some of the support for Zach de Beer is based partly on a dislike of [Tony] Leon. Leon's backers, on the other hand, believe he is the only one capable of giving the DP the sort of profile it needs to draw significant support.'[48]

By year-end 1992, after some energetic and skilful arm-twisting by the ubiquitous Joe Slovo, the ANC had accepted the concept of 'sunset clauses' for insertion in the new constitution. This would legally sanction mandatory coalitions in both the national and regional (provincial) cabinets. They also agreed to protect the pensions of senior civil servants, and expressed themselves amenable to some form of amnesty, with full disclosure. The ANC's new realpolitik marked a decisive shift on its part, and helped move matters to the decisive phase of the negotiations in the August-November 1993 period. The ANC conceded considerable protections for minorities at local government level, and gave (strictly limited) independent powers for the newly created provinces.

Power was slipping markedly from De Klerk's grasp, although there remained real problems. After a fortnight of negotiations in November 1993, there was still no consensus on the holdover issue of percentages required to pass the final constitution, and, from De Klerk's perspective, the even more vexed question of the percentages needed in cabinet for decision-making – though the ANC conceded that for the first five years, at least, South Africa would be governed by a multi-party cabinet.

Then there was the role of De Klerk himself. The NP had long held out for a deputy-presidency going to the leader of the largest minority party. If he had given way on other issues, De Klerk was not giving up on power itself; but the Nats were, on this issue, again outsmarted by the ANC. They gave De Klerk a deputy-presidency, but coupled it with one of their own: there would be two deputies, one for the winning party, and one for the also-ran party. It did not require prodigious amounts of insight to reasonably estimate the pecking order of the proposed presidential troika.

Meanwhile, I was embroiled in an even more contentious – and perhaps more vital – matter of contention which would arguably impact even more fundamentally on South Africa's future and its democratic wellbeing. The issue related to the appointment of South Africa's judges. Since agreement had been reached that the constitution, rather than parliament, would be the overlord of South Africa's new democracy, those entrusted with its interpretation would be the most important sovereigns in the new order.

On Thursday 11 November 1993, before the last week of negotiations, I found myself at my law office at Edward Nathan, where I managed to fit in some lawyering as a special associate, in addition to my constituency, parliamentary and constitutional duties. There I received a fateful telephone call: it was the private secretary of the minister of Justice, Kobie Coetsee, who rang and asked me to hold the line for the minister.

In my capacity as DP justice spokesman, I had got to know Coetsee reasonably well. However, no one (not even his wife, I sometimes suspected) really knew him at all. He seldom revealed his true thinking on matters, and managed to literally smile and wink his way out of many tight corners. However, he was certainly a reformist Justice minister and had the trust of De Klerk. He had been PW Botha's first line of contact with the imprisoned Nelson Mandela, and his close proximity to Mandela and his then wife, Winnie, had also (in my view) led to her under-prosecution for very serious crimes.

Coetsee and other senior cabinet ministers had just emerged from a *bosberaad* (literally, a gathering or meeting in the bush) with their opposite numbers in the ANC in order to resolve outstanding issues.

When Coetsee came on the line he was, even by his own standards, more cryptic then usual:

'Are you near a fax machine?' he asked.

'Yes,' I replied.

'Well, I'm going to fax you a document and you might wish to sound the alarm on it,' he said mysteriously.

'What's it about?' I countered.

'Just read it and see,' he responded, and terminated the call.

A few minutes later the fax arrived. It was an outline agreement in the name of Coetsee and his ANC equivalent on justice matters, Dullah Omar, the contents of which took away my breath. In it was a joint South African government-ANC proposal for the appointment of judges to the new and all-important Constitutional Court, whose jurisdiction and reach encompassed adjudication on the final constitution itself, and the no-small matter of determining the constitutionality, or invalidity, of all acts of parliament and lesser bodies to be established under the new order.

The kernel of the document was that all ten of the Constitutional Court judges would effectively be appointed by the president and the cabinet, with four positions reserved for serving (old order) judges; while the Chief Justice would be appointed by the president. In other words, the lynchpin of the new legal order would be open to blatant political manipulation, at the level of selection at least, and would simply ape the discredited appointment mechanism of the past. However, this court would be entrusted with far greater and more sweeping powers than any other in South Africa's history.

In terms of the ANC–NP agreement (which I was to learn later, with some stupefaction, had been authored by Coetsee himself) the cabinet, with a likely and hefty ANC majority, and the president, undoubtedly Nelson Mandela, would handpick their own judges! Dumbfounded as I was by the agreement Coetsee had authored and agreed to, I was even more perplexed as to why he was now the whistle-blower on his own compact.

I later learned that certain of Coetsee's cabinet colleagues whom he had not consulted before inking his signature to the agreement were appalled at what he had done. He was clearly looking for an escape hatch, and while he would oscillate in all directions over the next few days, blowing both hot and cold on the document, he had apparently decided that I constituted the best getaway vehicle if he needed to resile from his commitments.

I needed no persuasion that this document consecrated a pretty rotten and cynical deal. My problem was not an unwillingness to blow the whistle on the accord, but how to do so with any prospect of success in the extremely reduced time available. It was proposed to table the document for discussion the very next day, and to reach finality on the matter by Monday – with the entire constitution agreed by Wednesday of the following week.

Shortly before 7 am the following morning, I gathered my DA legal 'brains trust' around my dining room table in my Orange Grove home. Douglas Gibson, who was my co-negotiator for the DP in the justice section of Kempton Park, was there, as was my brother Peter, and my young, even by my comparative youthfulness at that time, parliamentary colleague and fellow-lawyer, Hennie Bester. But most crucial of all was the presence that morning, and over the following days, of Etienne Mureinik, my former colleague from Wits.

Quite aside from his brilliance, Etienne had a brave tenaciousness which would stand us in good stead, as he mobilised key constituencies, stared down the ANC in various corridors of the World Trade Centre, and, most importantly for me, provided the intellectual and legal ammunition I would need in the fight ahead. Events would soon cascade the row over judicial appointments into what one newspaper commentator described as 'perhaps the most dramatic turnaround in the entire negotiations process'.[49]

But before the turnaround we needed to launch the fight back. My dining room table group, fed prodigious quantities of hot coffee by my kindly housekeeper Elsie Ramathoka, produced a statement which we immediately released and which Douglas and I then sped off with to Kempton Park, where the public battle was about to begin. The crisp point of our appropriately alarmist statement lay in our warning that 'whether the Government of National Unity [the multi-party cabinet] is controlled by one party or two, or more, it is profoundly wrong that membership of so immensely powerful a judicial body as the Constitutional Court should vest entirely in the hands of the government. However high-mindedly the new cabinet approaches the question, politicians always have a responsibility to deliver the best deal possible to their supporters. They might well believe it their duty to appoint politically sympathetic people to the body which will yield supreme power under the new constitution.'

We also pointed out the supreme irony in the NP-ANC bilateral deal: it accepted the DP proposal for an independent Judicial Service Commission to recommend ordinary judges for appointment, but 'declined to apply the same principle [for appointments] to Constitutional Court judges who will wield so much more power, and upon whose integrity and independence the fate of the new South Africa depends.'[50]

At the negotiations plenary I read out the full statement and proposed a series of amendments – the effect of which was to invest a Judicial Service Commission (consisting of members of government, the judiciary and the independent legal profession) the power to recommend judicial appointees to the cabinet.

My full-throttle denunciation of the NP-ANC deal did not go down well with some of the government-in-waiting's luminaries. Mac Maharaj, for example, accused me of using the 'banner of democracy to [try] and whip up fears among those who distrust the capacity of this process to bring about democracy.' A very accurate distillation, as it happened, of my own fears!

Outside the meeting room, Etienne Mureinik collared the ANC's Albie Sachs who, ironically, was soon to don the robes of a Constitutional Court judge, and demanded that as a legal scholar he should denounce the proposal as well. Etienne later told me that Sachs brushed him off with the rejoinder that whatever the merits of our opposition, 'he could never align himself with "the grandstanding of Tony Leon".'

Matters were adjourned until Monday when Coetsee and Omar would be offered an opportunity to respond. As I left the talks that afternoon, in a grim mood, I was approached by a wire-service journalist who asked how the DP would respond should the ANC-NP deal be bulldozed through. I responded without too much thought: 'If this thing is adopted we will walk out of negotiations and have nothing further to do with this constitution.' The next morning's *Citizen* proclaimed: 'DP walkout threat'.[51]

This infuriated certain of my colleagues, particularly Eglin, who as chief negotiator was unaware of my comment until an equally infuriated Dene Smuts reported it to him. However, while their displeasure was undoubtedly justified, I became increasingly aware of something else at play. The party was, like the NP-ANC nomenclature, so fixated on signing a deal that a flawed inclusive new order was preferable to the discredited and exclusionary old one; even the negation of a key principle would not cancel our assent.

This was confirmed to Douglas and me when we confronted Zach at Kempton Park and told him that if the party agreed to the constitution with the fatal provision retained, we would both resign our party spokesmanships. We would be minded to vote against the constitution itself when it came to ratification by parliament in December. Zach indicated that he would support the constitution, and would advise the party to do the same.

By this stage there was a deep mood of unhappiness that permeated the DP's basement office at Kempton Park. Others on our negotiation team, particularly Andries and Sandra Botha from the Free State and Wessel Nel from Natal, piled the pressure on both De Beer and Eglin, and indicated they would not support the clauses on the judiciary as they then stood. Meanwhile, over the weekend between council meetings, De Beer worked the phones and expressed directly to Mandela and De Klerk his fundamental opposition to the proposal and requested its urgent reconsideration.

Zach's calls had one direct effect that weekend. I was at home on the Sunday evening preparing for an early-morning TV debate with Coetsee on the proposals, preparatory to the negotiations on the issue continuing, when the phone rang. This time it was Coetsee himself, extremely peeved: 'Well, I see you don't trust me … you got your leader to call the president despite our "understanding".' Since there had been no communication between Coetsee and myself bar his cryptic call on the Thursday, I was completely nonplussed and told him so.

The TV debate was something of a non-event. Coetsee mounted, I thought, a defence of the bilateral agreement which I found both lame and, not unsurprisingly, strange. He said that the advantage of cabinet picking the judges was that it 'would avoid public hearings or investigations that would impair the dignity of judges.' More promising, I thought, was his claim that the 'deal was in its initial stages' (in fact it had been signed and sealed: hence his tip-off to me). This at least, I thought, opened the window a little.

After the TV joust, Coetsee arranged for one of his staff to drive my car to Kempton Park, so that he could brief me on his 'game plan' for the day's debate. Once again, he was characteristically vague and indirect, but indicated he would ensure the whole proposal was sent back to the Technical Committee. When the debate recommenced it was clear from the ANC side that they were infuriated that their generally supportive press had turned against them.

Coetsee's performance was of a piece with his general behaviour. His interventions that day, in the piercing observation of journalist Edyth Bulbring who observed proceedings, 'vacillated between being defensive to apologetic, to hostile, to unco-operative.'[52] The ANC decided to turn its guns on me, with Slovo blazing away and announcing that he was 'startled to hear the DP was a prisoner of the past' – based on his premise that the current judiciary was 'a pillar of oppression'.[53] Omar reacted with loud fury in response to a list I read of some sixteen university law faculty heads, which Etienne had procured, and their statement opposing the NP-ANC proposal. After noting (inaccurately) that they were 'all white', he proceeded with an *ad hominem* attack castigating me for my 'hysterical outbursts' which, he speculated to the meeting, probably 'arise from the fact that for the first time in our history we are going to have a black president.'[54]

Despite the pillorying, Coetsee at least obtained a deferment of the final decision 'for further consultations'. But the clock was now really ticking. The entire constitutional package needed to be wrapped up in the next 48 hours, and while, like the proverbial Russian, I was largely fixated on the belly-button of the issue and assumed it was 'the world', I was, together with the rest of the country, cognisant of the fact that agreement had not been reached on other vital subjects. There was the method of decision-making – and veto rights – in the future Government of National Unity, and another crunch matter: whether or not South Africans would have one or two (for separate provincial legislatures) ballot papers to mark, clearly of huge importance to national parties with strong regional bases, such as the NP in the Western Cape and the IFP in Natal.

Die Burger, normally the staunchest NP press ally, thundered against Coetsee and claimed in a shattering editorial that his proposal amounted to 'the castration of the constitution'. This, and the undoubted internal pressure mounting against him in his own ranks, led finally to Coetsee dropping his legendary equivocation. We were now, finally, on the same side. Edyth Bulbring, despite her close friendship with Coetsee, later in her weekend account of events somewhat cruelly dismissed him as 'a small man on his way out of the big league armed with a proposal that was all too clever for his own good.'[55]

The next two days passed in a blur: I basically camped out at the World Trade Centre, as Coetsee, Omar and I (assisted by Douglas Gibson) now attempted to reach a settlement on the issue. While there was a willingness to entertain some compromise, Omar was adamant that the president should not be 'fettered' in his judicial appointments – precisely the bottom line of our minimum demand. Coetsee had to exit our makeshift meeting room (which was in the suite of offices reserved for the South African government) to conduct the debate in the conference plenary, on the yet-incomplete provisions in the constitution relating to the national defence force.

It is, in retrospect, quite extraordinary how the outgoing government thought it could secure its best interests when two such crucial components – defence and justice – relating to the outline of the new state were entrusted to one man. But our discussions on the fringes of the negotiations were all of a piece with the proceedings elsewhere – and happening at all hours – which gave an accurate impression of chaos as the deadline for agreement came.

In fact, by the Wednesday evening the deadline had already been missed. The showcase plenary at which the constitution was due to be ratified by all parties was already five hours behind schedule. But as the clock went into the red zone, Omar (once Coetsee could finally attend our meetings) started to yield. He left our meeting clutching bits of paper containing our reformulation which he needed to clear with Mandela and Ramaphosa, muttering 'this is our bottom line'. I kept urging him to 'have another go'.

Shortly before the dinner adjournment that night, Cyril Ramaphosa entered our meeting room clearly desperate for a deal and for the much-delayed show to commence. I said if the ANC could accede to our demand that the JSC needed to nominate the judges and the president could only choose them from a closed list prepared by the Judicial Service Commission, and not substitute his own names for those on the list, then, indeed, we could agree. Ramaphosa assented.

As we adjourned to take a hurried meal, there was another drama on the go, which revealed Ramaphosa at the height of his negotiation powers, and somewhat cruelly showed the DP in the most naïve and unforgiving light. This power play was contemporaneously described by Bulbring:

'That night just before supper a deal was struck (between Omar, Coetsee and Leon). But while this was going on, the negotiating council was debating whether to allow voters a second ballot paper to choose their regional representatives. The DP and other smaller parties favoured a two-vote system: the ANC and the government, which had settled on one ballot as part of a trade-off on another deal, stood together. They needed the DP to break the deadlock to get sufficient consensus. As Mr Leon left his trilateral talks, having settled – but for one issue – the new procedures for the appointment of judges, Dr de Beer was collared by ANC secretary-general Ramaphosa with an offer to De Beer: the ANC will give you your demand on the Constitutional Court judges if you give in to a single ballot on elections.

'[De Beer was not to know that] the ANC was ready to concede to Mr Leon's demands on the Constitutional Court, and in their desperation to finalise a settlement, were wavering on the single ballot issue. He assented.

'The DP leader has been truly gazumped. No wonder Mr [Colin] Eglin had said he felt "unclean" when he rose to tell the council his party had reverted to horse-trading on a matter of principle.'

But De Beer was not the only one to blink that night. De Klerk gave way to the ANC demand that cabinet decisions in the GNU would be based on effective majority decision-making, receiving in scant compensation the insertion in the constitution of a vague and essentially nebulous formation that 'the cabinet shall function in a manner which gives consideration to the consensus-seeking spirit underlying the concept of a Government of National Unity as well as the need for effective government.'

De Klerk's spokesman, Dave Steward, tried to put a brave face on it, claiming 'a deep and underlying sense of the symbiotic relationship between the ANC and NP rather than legalised percentages will sustain and cement power-sharing.' Cyril Ramaphosa, later that night, crowed with far greater accuracy about 'the complete government collapse'.[56]

At around midnight the much-delayed and deeply contested draft constitution was put to the full plenary of the negotiations process. It was passed with acclaim.

10

In the aftermath of that extraordinary evening – the culmination of six days of the most dramatic, high-wire and exposed process I had ever been a major player in – I felt a sense of relief and accomplishment. My 'fifteen minutes of fame' was generally appreciated. The *Sunday Times* was, however, cynical in its assessment, describing me as 'young and pugilistic ... who spotted a popular fight that was bound to put himself and the sagging DP on the front pages.' Britain's ambassador to South Africa was kinder. Sir Anthony Reeve posted me a note saying: 'Dear Tony, many congratulations on a famous victory! It shows what can be achieved with the right mixture of eloquence and determination. I am full of admiration.'

Thursday 18 November was to provide De Klerk and Meyer with a major hangover. Senior members of De Klerk's cabinet were in open revolt against the terms of the constitutional agreement. At a 7 am cabinet meeting, my future colleague Tertius Delport (then De Klerk's minister of Local and Provincial Government) shook with rage. Many years later he recounted to me the dramatic moments of his confrontation:

'When Roelf Meyer and Fanie van der Merwe briefed the cabinet to sell the deal (which in fact had already been concluded the night before), they claimed "We [the South African government] have got everything we wanted." I was enraged, and I pulled out a booklet which I had prepared in advance, which contained all the NP's constitutional proposals and bottom lines, and showed them how most of them had been lost and conceded in the negotiations.'

In an effort to bring Delport (and five or six other cabinet colleagues) on board, De Klerk suggested a private discussion with Delport. But there things got even worse, with – according to Waldmeir's account – Delport grabbing De Klerk's lapels and demanding to know, 'What have you done? You have given South Africa away.'

This (early morning) shoot-out was, of course, unknown to me at the time, and De Klerk managed to preserve his cabinet's unity. But when parliament met the following week to debate the new constitutional agreement, De Klerk was enraged when I suggested that the constitutional talks had finally put the lid on the NP's coffin. I declared – no doubt he thought presumptuously and prematurely – that 'the NP's historic mission is over. Undoing what they did [under apartheid] is the end of their historic mission. They can never be the torch-bearers of liberty, human freedom and the rule of law.'[57]

I was mostly not involved in the crises that followed, and spent my time and energies trying to organise my provincial party for the looming polls. But I was more than an interested bystander, often thinking that this interregnum between the fading old order and the new republic could become a semi-permanent and paralysing condition. Inkatha and the ragbag of white right-wingers, together with Bophuthatswana's Lucas Mangope, banded together in a so-called Freedom Alliance. The sight of Mangosuthu Buthelezi standing shoulder-to-shoulder with Eugene Terre'Blanche of the AWB and Dr Ferdi Hartzenberg, Treurnicht's successor as leader of the Conservative Party, was not a pretty one. Nor was it intended to be: the constitutional-rejectionists were signalling the fight to come.[58]

Of more significance than the alternating clownish and brutal Terre'Blanche was the presence of General Constand Viljoen in the line-up. His stated aim was a '*volkstaat*' (an ingathering of like-minded Afrikaners with protected rights in the realms of language, culture and religion). But early claims by the ANC, in which Mbeki was the leading role player, that some sort of deal, scant on detail and bereft of any proposed physical manifestation on the '*volkstaat*', had been achieved was shattered with the formation of the Freedom Alliance.[59]

Matters came to a head finally in March 1994 – a month of living dangerously in South Africa. In an attempt to woo Inkatha into the polls which as yet they were determined to boycott, Mandela ('going down on his knees', as he phrased it)[60] met with his arch-rival Buthelezi and offered to refer disputes around the constitution (essentially relating to the role and place of the king of the Zulus in the new dispensation) to 'international mediation' in exchange for Inkatha registering for the election, which an apparently flattered Buthelezi agreed to do, but only on a provisional basis. As an additional sweetener the NP-ANC negotiators threw in a double ballot, the denial of which remained one of the more disgraceful diminutions of democracy, in which the DP had been complicit, agreed in the helter-skelter of the last night at Kempton Park the previous November.

But of course those were mere fig-leaves of concessions. The IFP wanted far more autonomy for the provinces, or at least the one it was likely to control – in Natal – while the ANC was not going back on the huge concessions the negotiations had achieved for it in terms of a unitary South Africa.

In Bophuthatswana, Lucas Mangope decided to test the limits of the independent sovereignty Pretoria had always claimed, facts notwithstanding, was legally and constitutionally his right. He announced there would be no election in independent Bophuthatswana. The rioting and unrest which this brinkmanship caused could hardly be met with help from De Klerk – so Mangope called for help from his Freedom Alliance ally, Constand Viljoen. Viljoen mounted a force, from which he carefully excluded, at Mangope's insistence, AWB elements. But with his tin-ear firmly on the ground, the AWB's Eugene Terre'Blanche marched in anyway. Chaos and a revolt from Mangope's army ensued. Viljoen ordered his men to leave – and after some '*skiet en donner*' the AWB contingent followed suit. But three of their number were intercepted by black members of the Bophuthatswana police forces and executed, at point blank range, while fleeing Mmabatho.

That scene, captured on TV and screened that night on SABC, is perhaps more than any other from the tumult of those times, to borrow Günter Grass's phrase, 'carved into the onion skin of my memory'. But its effect and demonstration of the white right's reversal of fortune had, far more significantly, a profound effect on Viljoen. That very night, as it happened, the deadline for the registration of political parties, Viljoen and a swathe of Conservative Party renegade MPs registered a new party – the Freedom Front – and signalled his participation in the election and his final break with delusional separatist options based on violence.

With the right split, the military establishment sent an even more important and weighty cue. The chief of the Defence Force, General George Meiring, sent in the troops to restore order and bring the Bophuthatswana homeland back under South African control. The three dead AWB members sent an electrifying signal of the price of rebellion.

But Buthelezi was still holding out – and just how determined he was to resist was graphically demonstrated to me on 28 March 1994, when I was driving my car down Jeppe Street, Johannesburg, in, as it transpired, a vain attempt to reach my law offices further down the street. I was confronted by thousands of IFP-Zulu demonstrators, and they were not exactly in peaceful mood. Swinging clubs, sticks, pangas and 'knopkieries', and with red bandanas across their heads, they were a frightening sight.

When they began to rock my car, and started banging on its roof and denting it, I became very frightened as well. Just as I was contemplating my career, and life, ending at the wrong end of an assegai, two traffic officers materialised, I thought miraculously from nowhere, but doubtless a more prosaic explanation exists, and they eased my car through the chanting crowds. I hot-footed the accelerator and careered the car down a side street and retreated to our offices (which shortly afterwards were fired at, and the massive glass entrance windows shattered by stones). But I and other unfortunate motorists caught in the melee were simply collateral victims of the mob's fury. The real target was the ANC and their nearby regional office in the venerable old Lancet Hall building, and the national headquarters of the movement, across the road at Shell House.

The shoot-out from that building became the subject of my first major parliamentary joust with the ANC two months later: but on that day, or at the end of it, when the thousands of IFP supporters disbanded, eight had been shot dead from fire by ANC operatives inside Shell House, and dozens of others were fatally wounded in the downtown area, most of them IFP marchers.

The wells of any ANC-IFP co-operation now seemed to be truly poisoned. The toxicity was apparent when the international mediators arrived a few weeks later and left almost without even unpacking: both sides could not even agree to the terms of reference for their dispute, and Buthelezi refused to signal whether he was prepared to countenance participating in the election, an improbable event, it seemed, given the poll's proximity then just two weeks away. At this point, a Kenyan, Washington Okumu, entered history. His long-standing friendship with the Zulu prince and their 'walk in the woods' moment (which apparently only happened at all because Buthelezi's plane developed engine trouble) led, a week before the election, to the missing piece finally completing South Africa's most complex jigsaw: the IFP was, finally, contesting the poll – all the significant democratic stars were now, more or less, in the same alignment.

Had Buthelezi been bluffing all along – and was his decision to participate at the last minute simply a tactical masterstroke ensuring his pre-eminence as the leading actors were starting to fade? Or did he genuinely agonise and, finally, in Waldmeir's words, 'calculate his options and choose the least costly one'? Having got to know Buthelezi reasonably well in the 13 years after he exercised his fateful – and I am certain, correct – choice, I do not presume to know the answer. But I do believe that with Buthelezi's weighing of options, the one he chose was in all likelihood taken with very strong reservations.

Foremost, the IFP failed, to any significant degree, to achieve federalism. They allowed the central government to override the provinces on the basis of widely drawn and vaguely crafted interventions.

The Nats' negotiating and constitutional eggs were all in the basket of 'power sharing'. Since by the 1990s they had become a pork-barrel party, this perspective made sense to them. They began with the wish to entrench special majorities for cabinet decision-making, giving minority parties veto power. Once this position could not be held, they essentially forfeited the gain made with the entrenchment of power-sharing, by allowing the majority to decide in a very unequal cabinet.

The problem was compounded by inept negotiations further complicated by early agreement on an election date: a reality that meant a fixed date for the end of NP rule. The dozens of smaller parties increasingly aligned themselves to the next ruling party – the ANC. That took away support from the NP and its positions; and their negotiators were demoralised.

The NP must then have reckoned that they would be a very powerful force in the next government and well into the future – a complete self-hoax. The electorate, of course, would decide otherwise, by which time self-deception was pervasive.

Of course, all this is now history. But times produced a flourishing – even, for some, profitable – cottage industry around the all-South African 'negotiations miracle' of how clashing parties submerged their power-lusts and ancient enmities in a marvel of constitutional conciliation. The brutal truth – that most of the negotiating traffic was largely one-way – was elided for such purposes. Given the new nation's need for foundational mythology, I suppose it did little harm – perhaps even some good.

But when – with I thought a degree of vainglorious over-reach – Thabo Mbeki and his presidential team decided this model was also built for export, even into the cauldron of the Middle East, I became more sceptical. I was not alone. In 2004 I attended a dinner in Cape Town for a group of politicians from the Israeli Likud Party, then in power. One of the delegation, an impressive although hardline young cabinet minister who had been, in his Russian youth, a Soviet prisoner of conscience, had as part of his itinerary met Roelf Meyer and Pik Botha.[61] This duo apparently were – and are – ever available to meet visiting political tourists and explain 'how to negotiate with your enemies' and to learn first-hand from the 'South African experiment'.

I asked the Israeli minister what he had concluded from this particular encounter. 'Well,' he replied wryly, 'we now know who to contact if we want to give up power. But that's not actually on our agenda.'

PART TWO

LEADER OF THE PARTY

CHAPTER 6

New South Africa, New Leader

There is a stark and dramatic contrast between the past in which
South Africans were trapped, and the future. The past was pervaded by
inequality, authoritarianism and repression. The aspiration of the future
is based on ... a legal culture of accountability and transparency.

CHIEF JUSTICE ISMAIL MAHOMED

In one of his typically nonconformist essays, Bertrand Russell once
dissected the fallacy of regarding oppressed peoples as morally superior.
The fact that they are tyrannised, the British philosopher observed, does not
mean that they will perform wonders of nobility and high-mindedness
once given their freedom.

TIME MAGAZINE

I

South Africans entered 1994 with a sense of wonderment and nervous expectation. The election on 27 April was its date with a future over which
much blood and backroom haggling had been expended. Its new constitutional order, agreed the previous November, appeared no more than
rickety and makeshift, until the forces of extreme right-wing rejection-
ism and Zulu nationalism were either suppressed or squared away.[1] Many
white households nervously stockpiled tins of food and bottled water,
anticipating a countrywide shutdown in the aftermath of an ANC victory;
however, the very prospect of Nelson Mandela assuming the presidency
was a cause of unbounded joy and hope for millions of his constituents.

In an article for the *South Africa Foundation Review* I sought to pitch our
contribution: 'The job of the liberal democrat is to keep the government –
any government – honest and accountable and transparent ... [Rounds] of
negotiations at Kempton Park have taught us that, despite their new policy
garbs, the ANC is not at home with freedom and the NP never will be. In
a bizarre sense, these two parties are like Siamese twins separated at birth.

They followed very different routes to power, but their genetic composition is essentially authoritarian.'[2]

My attempt to dissect and explain the DNA of the two major contenders for power cut little ice, not even within my own circle. A friend of mine, David Pitman, thought an elementary lesson from music, rather than biology, best explained our dilemma. Quoting Scott Joplin on the piano he wittily and witheringly dismissed my efforts: 'You can play on the white keys or the black keys, but not on the cracks in between.'

Mandated by the party hierarchy, Ken Andrew and I were dispatched to Johannesburg's hottest advertising agency, The Jupiter Drawing Room, to devise a campaign. But whatever the company's claims on our behalf ('If the Left gets in there will be nothing right, if the Right gets in there will be nothing left') the jury that really mattered was the voters.

Meanwhile, there was the no-small matter of who would claim the apparently few seats available for the DP in the new parliament. Although the party exuded a sense of optimism about its prospects, privately there was a growing realisation that we would do well to achieve 5% (the minimum percentage required to participate in the Government of National Unity). There was, too, the issue of whether, if we qualified, we would participate in the GNU or pursue an opposition role.

Constituencies were abolished, and half the 400 seats in the new parliament were allocated to the nine provinces and half drawn from each party's national list. As party leader in the PWV, I was automatically allocated the top position on our list for the National Assembly. To test the waters of my standing in the party as a whole, I also made myself available for selection on our national slate, chosen by a special meeting of the Federal Council in Cape Town in late February. Since the party leader, Zach de Beer, was communicating a deeply ambivalent message about his long-term availability for the top post (the *Sunday Times* called it 'the retirement syndrome'), this contest was seen as a reliable indicator of the eventual succession.

I was elected first on the preferential ballot – placing me just behind De Beer (who as national leader had the reserved top slot) on the national list. I was hugely encouraged and awestruck. De Beer was not well, and signalled that he was not a long-term leader. I was 37 years old. Was I on the verge of achieving the party leadership?

I had many opponents within the party ('enemies' would be an apt description of some), yet the result indicated strong national support. But would I be offered the chance to put my plans into action, and if so, when? The date came far sooner than any of us expected when the election revealed how little of the DP remained to be led.

When my home province held its own list election, certain dynamics came into play. As the provincial boss I held considerable sway over the voting delegates who were to choose, in ranked order, the party candidates for the National Assembly and the provincial parliament. A dispute developed between my best friend in parliament, Lester Fuchs, who had loyally backed me in my multifarious disputes and ambushes in the caucus infighting of the previous four years, and Douglas Gibson, who arrived in parliament in a by-election in 1991. While Gibson was 15 years older than me – and had previously served as provincial leader – De Beer appointed him as my deputy in the Justice portfolio. He was to prove indispensable.

Gibson told me, plainly, that I had to indicate whether he or Fuchs should get the second slot on the provincial list to the National Assembly. I was torn between my personal loyalty to Fuchs and my political judgment that Gibson was the better parliamentarian. This indicated how few seats we actually – and accurately – believed the party would ultimately win. I gave the nod to Douglas, and since Fuchs's fourth place on the list knocked him out of parliament, he has barely spoken to me again.

I was bitterly upset that politics, and my objective choice, had destroyed a friendship. However, my fallout with Lester, and Douglas's subsequent indispensability, reinforced the wisdom of this painful early choice: to do your political duty may require the neglect, even negation, of personal preferences. Later, as leader, I tried never to practise the maxim 'reward your friends, punish your enemies'. In many cases, I did the reverse.

Gibson and I were to establish an infrangible bond that helped steer the party's revival over the next 13 years.

But this spat was not the only dynamic to play out in the nominations. My brother Peter decided, without much prior warning to me, to make himself available for the provincial parliament. I had spent my entire childhood in his shadow. My early years and his scholastic brilliance threw into sharp relief my own more modest efforts on the academic front. And Peter had played an essential supporting role, even serving as Houghton constituency chairman, in my scramble to the top. Now he reckoned it was his turn to shine as well. He was elected to the provincial parliament; but events over the next five years created a tension between the roles of younger brother and party leader: an inversion of the familial relationship in which he had always been the senior, and would now, objectively, be the junior.

Ironically, Lester Fuchs introduced the most alluring, but combustible, element into my personal and political life on the day the PWV list was compiled. He thought it a good idea that we add some glamour and

237

pizzazz to our ticket, so he persuaded a former Miss South Africa to add her name to the candidate's slate – in an unelectable position, but on the understanding that she would help promote the party cause.

Michelle Bruce was undoubtedly the most beautiful woman I had ever seen in the flesh. We locked eyes when the local party campaign was launched at the Carlton hotel in February, and despite her no-hoper place as a candidate, she entered into the campaign with a gusto and determination few other, better-placed, politicians displayed. I suppose my over-bustling and excessively busy public and political life mirrored an emptier personal one. I had known no shortage of liaisons and flings, but my attempts at personal, long-term relationships usually ended not so much in acrimony, but disappointment for both. On one level, I yearned 'to settle down'; on another I enjoyed flitting from date to date, encounter to encounter, unprepared to make the sacrifices of true commitment.

Into this vacuum came Michelle, with her feline grace and charm. I soon discovered that this was an overlay for an intense, appealing vulnerability and insecurity. The campaign drew us close; and some combination of personal chemistry and need drew us even closer – and more dangerously so. She was married, although in the process of separation. No doubt my wanton recklessness enraged her husband.

On the eve of the election, I was with Michelle at my Orange Grove home when her husband Ian demanded entry and confronted us with a string of epithets and threats. My political anxiety was now conjoined to something intensely personal. At that moment of maximum vulnerability I confided in a most impressive and astute VIP security officer, whom the state had thoughtfully assigned to me for the campaign. While Rory Steyn went on to great heights as head of President Mandela's security detachment, his presence then was to keep me safe from political wild men. Steyn sat Ian down for a cup of coffee on election day – and his formidable powers of personal and physical persuasion lessened the immediate hostility.

In the aftermath of the election, I brazenly decided to take Michelle to the historic inauguration of Nelson Mandela as president at the Union Buildings on 12 May. Despite the presence of luminaries such as Prince Philip, Benazir Bhutto, Hillary Clinton, Fidel Castro and Yasser Arafat, Michelle and I drew a disproportionate amount of paparazzi attention. A huge colour photograph of us appeared in the *Sunday Times* that weekend under the banner: 'Just the Occasion Brings DP Couple Together'.[3] The text declaimed: 'Senior DP member Tony Leon caused a stir at this week's presidential inauguration when he arrived with another man's wife on his arm. Eyebrows rose when Mr Leon, tipped as the DP's new leader, was spotted holding hands and cuddling with former Miss South Africa Michelle Bruce, who is married to lawyer Ian Stern ... But Mr Leon and Mrs Stern have denied they are having an affair.'

Quite what I was thinking I cannot fathom. Perhaps the intense campaign had exhausted and impaired my judgment. Certainly, my intensity of feeling overwhelmed more sober considerations. We 'outed' ourselves at the most visible public event yet seen in South Africa. The narrow, technical verbal contortions that Bill Clinton later made infamous matched my statement of denial to the *Sunday Times*. It was only after Michelle left her husband later that year that our relationship flowered. We lived together for a short while; but it had ended by March 1995. There was little acrimony, just some lingering regret; but an essential incompatibility had emerged.

My love affair with Michelle was, in one sense, a positive and even happy outcome of a campaign that was pitiless and disappointing for the troops of the DP and its leadership. Perhaps the party's lacklustre showing was preordained. Outside Natal, black South Africans almost unanimously backed their liberators, the ANC, and Nelson Mandela. For once the ANC campaign slogan – 'Mandela for President – The People's Choice' – did not lie. Against him stood De Klerk, who in truth had done much to bring about the historical reality of the new South Africa. It cost his party its hold on power. Against two such waves of history, the DP was swamped.

Our situation appeared bleak, a fact well captured by leading journalist Brian Pottinger in his headline: 'Watchdog Yapping at the Heels of Giants'. His text was based on one of the many election rallies I addressed in a futile attempt to explain the apparent joys of proportional representation:[4]

'Tony Leon, pugnacious crown prince of the DP, uses a full pitcher of water and two empty glasses to demonstrate to his audience the power of their vote. He pours water from the pitcher marked ANC into one labelled "DP" and one labelled "NP". Lo, the majority party loses exactly the sum gained by the combined opposition vote.

'"This," Mr Leon tells his audience, "is the advantage of proportional representation. Every vote cast for an opposition party diminishes the overall majority of the ANC. Your vote for the DP does count."

'There are about 250 000 hardcore DP supporters out there. Battered by defections, fissions and leadership struggles, they still cling to the hope that somehow, somewhere their "vision" – a liberal democratic society – will prevail. But it has proved hard to convince them that the DP is the right vehicle – with or without Mr Leon's conjuring.'

Despite the gloomy prophecy, I became the party's surrogate campaigner-in-chief across the country. It was all strictly do-it-yourself. I recall waking up in Estcourt in northern KwaZulu-Natal; an exhausting round of campaign meetings; and then driving myself back to Johannesburg for an evening rally in Saxonwold with Zach de Beer and the Anglo dauphin, Nicky Oppenheimer. Ours was an unforgivably amateur campaign: no advance work for rallies, and unscripted appearances in townships. The harsh light of television soon showed up the idiocy of this approach. Peter Soal made arrangements for the SABC to cover Zach in an address to a 'guaranteed capacity crowd' of black supporters in the far reaches of the northern Transvaal. But busloads were intercepted or hijacked by the ANC, and the net result was the 8 o'clock TV news showing a forlorn De Beer surveying an empty field, an exquisitely painful moment.

Television also highlighted a key element of the election: a full-scale one-on-one debate between Mandela and De Klerk. Although objectively I assessed De Klerk as outperforming his opponent, when Mandela – with apparently impromptu brilliance – reached over and took De Klerk's hand, our game was up. Mandela, the moral giant, was signalling to South Africa and the world the essence of the choice – ANC or NP – and gave his paternal 'approval' to his most significant opponent.

De Beer had a poor campaign. The party rank-and-file fumed at public utterances about his possible retirement, signalling impermanence and uncertainty at the top. However, my efforts did not go unnoticed by an increasingly aggressive De Klerk. In Port Elizabeth he paid me a backhanded compliment: 'The DP is strong on billboards and weak on policy. Take Tony Leon away from the DP and you are left with nothing,' he intoned.[5]

We were met by utter indifference or extreme hostility. Paul Asherson, our PWV campaign manager, hired a municipal bus with an open top deck, painted in the party's colours, with loudspeakers, to drive around as a moving billboard and public address platform. We went to the East Rand to tour the area's townships and shopping centres. Blaring music and sound bites attracted barely an onlooker. This apathy was complemented by the frisson of intense anger my appearance sometimes commanded at ANC strongholds elsewhere in the country.

Nothing in the campaign exceeded what happened when I appeared at the University of the Western Cape near Cape Town airport. It was the final lap of the campaign, and I certainly didn't lack a crowd that lunchtime in mid-April. The auditorium was packed to the rafters, unfortunately for me by ANC supporters. I usually thrived in front of a hostile or barracking audience. But this crowd was unlike any other I ever encountered. I was allowed to speak for a few minutes, but given the palpable tension, decided to abandon my prepared talk and defend the new constitutional order, including its provision for free speech. 'The most important thing,' I declared, 'is that the hard-won freedom of South Africans throughout the country is not submerged by those who will not give others an opportunity to put their point of view. That is the principal issue here and everywhere.'

A political reporter wrote that 'shortly after [those remarks] … a deafening cacophony of shouts, chants and whistles burst from the crowd, most waving ANC flags, and continued for over ten minutes.'[6] The rector, Jakes Gerwel, and ANC resident academic Professor Kader Asmal (both soon to be catapulted into high office) appealed for calm. The crowd would have none of it. An entire phalanx rose and advanced on me. On the advice of the university security detail we headed out. Instead of dousing the passions, my exit inflamed and emboldened them. As we made towards our car, the students smashed through glass doors and charged us, hurling bottles, cans and stones, and screaming abuse. I was bundled into the vehicle and we sped away.

I was deeply antagonised by the gross vein of intolerance displayed by the ANC supporters − which was to dog other forays of mine, and of De Klerk (on ANC turf, no opponents were welcome). The media reflected my disquiet, except for a young reporter at the *Mail&Guardian*, one Mondli Waka Makhanya. According to him, the ruckus was all part of an elaborate stratagem which I had set up to boost the sagging profile of the party. As he put it: '[What] was most surprising about the shouting down and eventual stoning of Leon and his entourage was the ease with which the students fell into the DP's trap. By going to a hostile campus and getting thrown out, Leon achieved maximum media exposure for the DP.'[7]

Actually getting silenced and stoned was not part of any plan. But Makhanya was, a few years later, to ascend to lofty editorial heights as chief of the mighty *Sunday Times*.

2

On 27 April I arrived in the crisp autumnal morning sun at Houghton Primary School where a huge − and for the first time multiracial − crowd was queuing to cast its vote. Employers and employees, businessmen and blue-collar workers, the rich and poor, black and white, every extreme together with the mainstream and the marginal, stood together, and patiently waited to do their duty. They entered the polling station as unequal citizens and emerged (with an indelible mark on the thumbnail to prove it) as political equals, since each ballot, like their future citizenship, was of equal worth.

Conditions in Houghton were, as expected, orderly. Scenes at some polling stations elsewhere were rather more chaotic. Among the gremlins: wrong ballot papers; absent stickers for the last-minute entrant, Inkatha; reports of pirate voting stations in KwaZulu-Natal; and widespread intimations of ballot stuffing. The scheduled two-day election stretched out to three, and our worst fears of an out-of-control process seemed confirmed when the ballot boxes were eventually transferred for counting to the cavernous halls of Nasrec, an exhibition arena south of Johannesburg.

The station was responsible for all of Johannesburg, its suburbs, and the whole of Soweto. Instead of an orderly transport of secured and sealed papers by Independent Electoral Commission (IEC) officials, DP members and I saw ANC officials, and even taxi drivers, delivering boxes of ballots (some with broken seals) to Nasrec. Journalists breathlessly noted the presence in South Africa of some seventy thousand election monitors, including 5 000 from overseas, who were deployed at polling stations throughout the country. They certainly did not accompany many of the boxes we witnessed arriving in the hall.

I had expressed surprise – and reservation – when Dr Selma Browde, a well-known former PFP politician who had decamped to the ANC, was appointed by the IEC as the chief returning officer for greater Johannesburg. Selma was an old friend of my father's and a person of warmth and vitality. Yet she was hardly independent, and I never reckoned that her considerable intellect was matched by administrative zeal. And so it proved – though not because of Dr Browde.

Bedlam might be too modest a description for a counting process which slowly degenerated into chaos and recrimination: first between the parties and then between an unlikely NP-DP-ANC alliance against increasingly hesitant and nervous IEC officials. The nub of the problem (repeated throughout the country) was that many local election agents simply never certified that the ballots in their boxes numerically matched those issued at the designated polling station. This meant that without a legally mandated reconciliation process there was no way of telling how many ballots had been genuinely cast and how many had been filled in after the polls had closed. This potential – or actual – fraud had been aggravated by the absence of a voters' register. Anyone in possession of a valid document could vote anywhere in the country. IEC chairman Justice Johann Kriegler was now controlled by a process he was meant to control.

The NP was exceptionally concerned as the count dragged on for the best part of a week (instead of the 24 hours set by the IEC for the declaration of a result). They reckoned that with every disputed ballot box being counted their real score was reducing by the hour. Peter Leon (legally mandated by the local DP to monitor the situation) contacted Roelf Meyer and, separately, the NP and DP approached an increasingly exasperated and tired Kriegler at his headquarters in downtown Johannesburg. It was explained to him (though he knew) that in terms of the law the entire election could be invalidated by order of court, since unverified ballots were being counted.

Kriegler told Peter that we could approach any court we wished, but that if we did so, 'then be it on your own head.' He subsequently told the warring parties that while in law there was a requirement for ballot reconciliation, the matter was far larger than that: we are involved, the judge informed us, in a process of national reconciliation!

In the end we left matters as they stood.

Witnessing the count at Nasrec, I realised that the DP was going to perform even more dismally than my own gloomy predictions. On the eve of the poll James Selfe had predicted 'a million or so votes for the party'. When the count was finally concluded (or, as informed sources suggested, squared away by agreement between the ANC, NP and IFP) his assessment was out by two-thirds. We got barely over 350 000 votes nationally, a dismal 1,7% of the total – meaning just seven seats in the new Assembly. The NP achieved a disappointing 20,8%, after confidently predicting over one-third.

Twenty-two million South Africans voted for 19 parties, of which seven secured representation in parliament. The DP was in fifth place, ahead of only the Pan-Africanist Congress (PAC) and the African Christian Democratic Party (ACDP). The NP at least had some consolation prizes: its national disappointment was augmented by an outright win in the Western Cape, and they achieved a deputy-presidency for De Klerk. The IFP's late surge gave it control of KwaZulu-Natal, and a respectable 10% national total.

National power, the most glittering bauble on offer, went to the ANC with a hefty 62,7%.

There were no consolation prizes for the DP, although my own fortunes were about to change. As Douglas Gibson and I waited for the results at Gallagher Estate in Johannesburg on 5 May 1994, I was called urgently to the balcony studio of Radio 702. In anticipation of being questioned about our poor showing I composed some lines about 'soldiering onward … a small band of MPs, big on convictions and principles'. That question was never put. Instead I was asked for my reaction to the press release just received from Zach de Beer announcing his immediate resignation as leader of the party, and, in his good-soldier fashion, shouldering the blame for our evisceration.

While I personally felt sorry for Zach – a decent and humane man – he had done the right thing. I also realised that I had a clear shot at what was admittedly a devalued coin: the leadership of the party. But before any formal announcement, I needed to confer with Gibson, my brother Peter, Cecil Bass and Paul Asherson – the core of my emerging leadership campaign group. I commented to an enquiring hack from the *Sunday Times* that 'I was going to re-read Nixon – he knew how to come back after a defeat.' The amused reporter wrote, 'For the moment, at least, Mr Leon has retained his sense of humour.'[8]

Two Sundays later, after the epoch-changing inauguration of Mandela and our swearing-in as MPs in the new parliament, a forlorn group of DP national councillors gathered in an appropriately grey Cape winter morning at Ellerton Primary School in Sea Point to elect a new leader. The hall we were using was fitted out with small chairs and diminutive tables, no doubt appropriate for its young scholars – and I thought entirely apt for our diminished status in the body politic.

Ken Andrew, the national chairman, had also decided to contest the leadership. Our respective campaigns had been low-key, almost entirely without rancour. Gibson and I had worked the phones the week before and received an extremely mixed response from the sixty or so voting delegates. I was 'too arrogant'; or 'lacked the common touch'; or was 'too brash'; or 'too young'. But my supporters were fervent. However, one of my foremost critics in the party, Kobus Jordaan, who had managed to claw back his way into parliament, mounted a campaign, essentially for himself, stating that we needed a 'caretaker leader' pending the recruitment of a suitable black person of eminence.

Jordaan's comments in the meeting were scarcely an improvement on the obituary notices that peppered the press predicting the party's imminent demise. For example, the *Sunday Times* satirical columnist, Hogarth, joked: 'The Democratic Party is due to elect an acting leader in Cape Town [today], but Hogarth wonders if it is worth the bother. The party might do better to follow its federal instincts and devolve leadership to each of the nine provinces.'[9]

The *Argus*, the day before, had written an even bleaker epitaph. After our 'abysmal showing in the general election, the Democratic Party has cause to ponder its future. What may be said, at best, is that the party has survived. But only just. What sort of future it has – if it has one at all – is another matter.'[10]

I thought the 'death notices' premature and Jordaan's approach non-sensical. When I motivated my candidature, I told the delegates to forget an outside rescuer, and that 'our fault (and fate) lies not in our stars but in ourselves.' I promised a 'radical change of doing business in the party – which, while it will not make us popular with our enemies and even our fair-weather friends ... will provide you with a party which, over time, will again take its place in the front rank of our politics.'

My speech and a yearning for something and someone very different from the past seemed to do the work. I was elected acting leader with a 49-16 margin.[11] My immediate and patent joy was soon tempered by an almost Spenglerian gloom. How was I to navigate the wreck I had just been elected to steer? I was reminded of the ancient Chinese curse: 'Be careful what you wish for.'

I quickly began an assessment of where the party stood. As I anticipated, the view was hardly propitious, but there was a glimmer of hope.

Of the parliamentary seats, 94% were occupied by the three parties in the GNU. Of the scattered remnants outside the GNU, the Freedom Front, PAC and ACDP were, respectively, too narrowly focused, too internally riven, or too small to mount an opposition charge. This actually created a window of opportunity for the DP. I was determined to throw it wide. I had a small team, but nine of them were experienced parliamentarians[12] and the tenth – William Mnisi – had the apparent advantage of being the only black member of our then all-white enclave. Between us, I reckoned we could make a fight of it. There would soon be plenty of ammunition which government fed us by way of issues and scandals that would sustain us in establishing a strong parliamentary presence (see Chapter 10).

The *Financial Mail*, about the only journal that saw any light for us at the end of an apparently endless tunnel, got it right: 'There is little doubt that [Tony Leon] will introduce a far more abrasive approach and it may bring him into conflict with old-guard members ... Mr Leon has never been one to keep quiet and he will certainly not do so now.'[13]

However, Allister Sparks, as usual, captured the prevailing media and majoritarian sentiment when he described 'the decline and threatened demise of the DP' as one of the 'more intriguing phenomena of South African politics'.[14]

I was determined, over time, to put the doomsday scenarists to rights. In responding to Sparks who described me as 'bright but brittle … with an infusion of Thatcherite ideas'[15] I pointed out that South Africa actually required aspects of Thatcherism to restore the dismal and empty economic larder which the profligate NP government had bequeathed its successor. But I drew as much from the social democrat Roy Jenkins: 'We need the innovative stimulus of the free market without its indifference to unemployment. We also need the acceptance of a broad division between the public and the private sectors. The latter must be encouraged to create as much wealth as possible, but the wealth created must be used to give a return for enterprise and to spread the benefits in a way that helps remove from our land the scourge of poverty … [This] requires the state to steer the ship but not to row the boat at the same time. We need to create a nation of independent citizens, not dependent supplicants; people who are free to govern themselves and choose their own destinies.'[16]

The party would evolve over the next 13 years, but I never saw the need to depart from this analysis. I still believe it prescribed and applied the correct – and sometimes complementary and conflicting – roles between the citizen, the state, and the private and public realms of the economy and society.

There was one immediate problem. At the time the DP controlled Johannesburg, and its political chief, my old colleague Ian Davidson, had ordered, on a cold wintry night, the destruction of shacks erected illegally onto a parcel of land which the council had allocated for new housing. It was a complex case, and the facts – including the massively inconvenient one that Davidson had the backing of Mandela's Housing minister, Joe Slovo – did not deter our critics. I was not surprised at Ken Owen's denunciation – 'A party that demolishes homes just isn't liberal' – but Helen Suzman's invective about 'an apartheid-style demolition' suggested our party was not merely small, but irrevocably divided.[17]

3

The early days of leadership were not uniformly bleak. Parliament was far livelier and – racially and otherwise – more colourful than its unlamented predecessor, although the enthusiasm and informality of the new intake was not to last. However, we had also become, with Mandela as the major draw, a compulsory stopover for world leaders.

The first big beast from the international arena to address parliament was the ageing and sickly[18] French president François Mitterrand. When he glided into parliament on a July morning in 1994, resembling some living combination of the Sphinx and the Mona Lisa, I was struck by his semi-regal bearing – allowing one to forget that he was a socialist, at one stage red in tooth and claw. But as he waxed on about the links of solidarity between the French Republic and the 'noble struggle' against apartheid I could not help but conclude that he was also something of an old hypocrite. The nation had been informed, breathlessly, on the morning TV news that Mitterrand's Boeing 747 had been escorted into Cape Town by South African Air Force F1 Mirages purchased (for hard currency) by the former oppressive regime from a very willing French government.

That evening Mandela hosted a state banquet at the Mount Nelson hotel. What intrigued and mystified us was the president's rapid departure from the scene barely after the first course. We were not to know that a big-bang announcement would follow the next day (5 July) – although my interaction with Finance minister Derek Keys that night held a clue.

I admired Keys. De Klerk brought him into his cabinet in December 1991. He was urbane, sophisticated, and very smart; and having left the commanding heights of industry and mining, he had little need of political office to augment his ego or income. Notionally a Nationalist, he wore his party label lightly and greeted me at the banquet with his signature line of banter: 'I am having trouble with my DP wife!' (His wife, Silma, had, in fact, helped draw up our provincial arts policy for the 1994 elections.) Then, fairly abruptly, he turned serious. 'The time has come,' he said (disconcertingly in the third person), 'for Derek Keys to leave government.' I was shocked and disappointed. But Keys's resignation was already a *fait accompli*, and Mandela's hasty exit was to enlist banker Chris Liebenberg as his successor.

Given Mandela's thorough way of reconciling sectors of society, this step required not only Liebenberg's assent but that of business moguls such as Harry Oppenheimer, Donald Gordon and several others, each of whom – that very night – were called by the president. However, assuming that Keys's comment was simply projecting ahead, I demurred. The highly sensible fiscal and monetary policies initially emanating from government would be adversely affected by his departure, I believed.

He assured me the contrary was the case: 'I only came in again to see FW through the transition, which has been concluded with the budget I have presented.' (It was ushered through parliament a few weeks before.) I urged him to hang on. 'No,' he insisted, 'it's unnecessary because the new government has committed to my policies. Anyway, if I had your youth and energy it might be a different story.'

His resignation was made public a day later. Mandela's announcement and Keys's budget signalled that the new government had chosen the path of the so-called 'Washington consensus'. To the Left globally, and to South African socialists – particularly in the ranks of the ANC – this was anathema. This particular package of free enterprise measures – dubbed the 'golden straitjacket' by globalist Thomas Friedman – required a diet of fiscal discipline, eased exchange rates, privatisation and government collaboration with the private sector to drive export-orientated growth.

Aspects of the 'consensus' would be accelerated by Keys's and Liebenberg's successor, Trevor Manuel, who was appointed in 1996. After a shaky start, Manuel calmed the markets and proved in South Africa in the 1990s what Nixon had established with his groundbreaking visit to China 25 years before: those who are best at promoting a policy – especially one that runs contrary to the natural grain of your supporters – are those who start from the other end of the ideological spectrum. Manuel's home-grown struggle activism and socialist inclinations allowed him to steer economic policy in a manner owing more to Milton Friedman (or Derek Keys) than to Karl Marx.[19]

Our handful of MPs had to straddle a half-dozen or so portfolios each, in addition to constituency and party-building tasks. I was obliged to spend much time outside the House – primarily passing the tin cup around to an ever-shrinking donor base and traversing the length of the country to cheer our understandably dispirited, even shattered, local structures. I shadowed the Presidency, and could afford only one other portfolio. Gibson and I were the only trained lawyers in the team[20] – and he had his hands more than full as chief whip, spokesman on justice, safety and security, correctional services, and much else. More by default and desperation, I was obliged to appoint myself as spokesman on labour. This enabled me to witness the entire gamut of South Africa's creaking and anachronistic industrial relations regime undergo a radical redesign.

It also gave me a close-up view of the men and women of COSATU, whom the union federation had seconded to parliament via the ANC lists. Few had any appetite for the 'Washington consensus' formula initially introduced by Keys and cemented later by Manuel. This led to certain inherent inconsistencies in ANC rule.

First, the enactment of four cornerstone acts[21] – and the final 1996 constitution[22] – tilted the legislative balance in favour of organised labour. This gave the Left a chance to claw back from the free market, via the back door, the hostages which Mandela's government released through the front. Indeed, for all the acres of space and paeans of praise which the media and business pundocracy had poured on Manuel's head, few bothered to note that the new labour regime foisted on South Africa contradicted the stated intention of the Growth, Employment and Redistribution (GEAR) structural adjustment programme, which promised 6% growth by 2000 – and a million new jobs – largely premised on a more flexible labour market.

The essentially negative activities of the Portfolio Committee on Labour – by the end of the first term of the democratic parliament in 1999 – meant that South Africa's growth rate was just over half the promised figure. And instead of the anticipated boost in employment, we managed to shed half-a-million jobs.[23]

This enactment of political schizophrenia engaged my energy and attention for long periods. I underwent a crash course in labour law, from bargaining councils to closed shops. To be fair to my committee colleagues, all labour legislation – before its arrival in parliament – had to pass through a corporatist wet dream called Nedlac (an acronym for 'The National Economic Development and Labour Council').[24] So much for oversight. The council was intended as an all-purpose clearing-house where business, labour, the state, and a vestigial group of 'organisations of community development interests' would hammer out a consensus on all relevant legislation.

I was sceptical about the arrangement. Far from considering all viewpoints, this legislative cabal would soon ensure that only the voices of big business and the large trade union federations would be heard. It was clear to me that if some dent was to be made in the massive unemployment situation – an inherited one – then less, not more, regulation of the market was essential. But in Tito Mboweni, Mandela had appointed a Labour minister with a strong appetite for power (particularly his own) and a huge investment in Nedlac. He was seen by government as having the drive and energy to deliver, via legislative fiat, on the massive IOUs which the ANC had to redeem to its then most faithful and significant ally, the trade union confederation, COSATU.

I don't think Mboweni and I ever agreed on any major element of labour law piloted through Nedlac after 1994 to be dutifully enacted by parliament. However, he was very bright and immensely likeable. He was also (compared to most of the cabinet) cast in the Mandela mould; he had genuine self-confidence, enjoying intellectual engagement, even combat, and never played the race card. Of all the ANC ministers of the time, I got on best with him. His presence at my 40th birthday in 1996 and at my wedding four years later proved, I suppose, that Venus and Mars can indeed cross each other's orbits.

However, I very much doubted that his proposed brave new world of industrial relations – conflated in the 300-page, 214-clause Labour Relations Bill, which hit our desks in 1995 – would ever be realised. On the contrary, the legislation was likely to overturn the conversion of Manuel and Alec Erwin to fiscal fundamentalism.

While Mboweni was the law's most ardent and articulate promoter, it had in fact been crafted by my former Wits colleague, the implacably pro-union labour lawyer Halton Cheadle. The legislation was the most sweeping redesign of labour relations since the enactment of industrial councils in 1924. I agreed with stripping away the repugnant racial discrimination characteristic of the previous labour dispensation; but felt it hugely ironic that the new bill was the product of an inferior process to that which attended its predecessor.

During my industrial sociology studies, Eddie Webster, my Marxist professor, regaled us with accounts of how the old parliament took evidence from white stakeholders across the country for almost the entire 1923 session, while the bill was only finalised at the end of the 1924 session! In the new, transparent and democratic order we were given precisely eight working days to consider the detail and implications of its 1995 successor. When I protested, the stock response was that 'it had been considered already by Nedlac'. The views of the unemployed, and small and micro-businesses[25] – the engines for job creation according to the Department of Trade and Industry – had not been considered.

At the heart of the new order was a centralised system of bargaining councils which was accorded vast and interventionist powers to regulate disputes and impose collective agreements (minimum wages and the like). When I proposed that non-parties to collective agreements (those small and micro-enterprises) be exempt from the bill's provisions, the committee rejected the idea. Indeed, the bill went in the other direction: it empowered the Labour minister to extend collective agreements to non-parties, even in sectors where organised trade unions represented as few as thirty per cent of the workers.

The legislation also entrenched the very provisions which New Labour leader Tony Blair had vowed would never again return to Britain: the closed shop and secondary strikes – measures which had crushed job-creation prospects elsewhere in the world.

Why did organised business prove so pusillanimous in submitting to the fierce restrictions of the revised labour regime? My colleague, Kobus Jordaan, was so incensed with the back-sliding of the private sector that when we attended a dinner arranged for us at the sumptuous Sea Point apartment of the Chamber of Mines, he bluntly said to our host, and president of the Chamber, Attie du Plessis: 'Why do you people go around the place saying "*jammer dat ek leef*"?' ('Sorry that I'm alive.') My belief was that business was so grateful that its worst nightmares – a confiscatory regime of nationalisation, penalty taxes and the like – had not been realised that it decided 'to go along to get along'. In truth, big business could absorb the costs of compliance: the few witnesses from the emerging and 'survivalist' enterprises who managed to actually address our committee made it clear that they could not. They were utterly ignored.

The bill, unadorned by any amendments of significance, arrived in parliament for debate on 12 September 1995. I made an impassioned, but futile, call for the members to remember that only 7% of the economically active workforce was likely to be absorbed into the economy. The legislation gave a politician (the minister of Labour) sweeping powers 'to act as a super-conductor of all labour and economic policy, instead of allowing the real and unvarnished facts on the ground, and at factory-floor level, to determine economic outcomes.' My argument was met with jeers, and the COSATU boss, Mbhazima (Sam) Shilowa, sat stony-faced in the gallery. He smiled broadly when I said: 'Mr Shilowa told television viewers this morning that the big winner in the passage of this bill will be COSATU. In that I believe he is quite right.'[26] He knew it too – and so did the ANC.

4

For much of the early years (1994-1997) of my leadership I felt as though I had been given a poisoned chalice. At times it tasted like (as *The Economist* later put it) 'something rustled up by Lucrezia Borgia on one of her more vengeful days.'[27]

My plans for the party were clear: cleanse it of ideological ambiguities; create an effective opposition presence in all legislatures where we had members; and rebuild on the ground. But, initially, there was no meeting of minds. During an early joint caucus meeting in June 1994 in Cape Town, the old warhorse Colin Eglin weighed in that 'the party had lost its soul, and should show a more caring side.' Roger Burrows, the KwaZulu-Natal leader, felt the fundamental problem was a division between 'liberal and social democrats'. To compound the infirmity of approach, the Western Cape leader, Hennie Bester, had already publicly informed one newspaper that 'the jury was still out as to whether the party had any role at all.'

I was determined to rid the party of the incubus of perceived irrelevance and recreate a spirit of can-do optimism and professionalism. A start could be made with our parliamentary team. Although representative of the diverse strains of opinion in the party, they were at least dedicated to getting the job done. Two, Douglas Gibson and James Selfe, would soon respectively be chairman of the party executive and chief of the organisation; and they were prepared to shoulder major organisational responsibility for hacking our way out of our electoral near-wipe-out.

We used our somewhat slender financial resources to start professionalising our parliamentary operations. First we poached ace Institute of Race Relations researcher Julia Frielinghaus,[28] and then appointed a young returning diplomat, Robert Desmarais, as chief of our parliamentary operations.[29] Practically every evening after the session, Douglas, Robert and I would retreat to my fifth-floor attic office in the Marks Building in the parliamentary precinct, pour large tumblers of whisky, and plot, deep into the night, how to advance our cause and make it relevant and visible.

Visibility was hugely augmented by our energetic representatives in parliament, a fact acknowledged by the then broadly sympathetic press. John Maclennan, an old press gallery hand, enthused in the *Sunday Tribune* (August 1994):

'The DP returned to parliament with a tiny presence after being trampled by the giants in the election. But it is calling the shots as it has not done for years. [It] enjoys a parliamentary profile out of all proportion to its size. This is because it is not encumbered by the joint responsibility of the unity government. In addition to the freedom this offers, the party also has the will, more than any other, to call a spade a bloody shovel.

'The DP might be small, but this makes for a lean and effective team. The caucus is a more cohesive, united and spirited group than it was when it had 35 MPs.'[30]

Our presence and performance could take us only so far. Money is the mother's milk of politics – and ours was running out, other than the loyalty of our existing donors. Harry Oppenheimer was by far the most significant and hitherto generous. Yet despite his link to the liberal cause, his close association with the party had also been cemented by warm personal ties to Suzman, De Beer and Eglin. I had previously met him once or twice, but as the new leader I presented myself at the Main Street headquarters of Anglo American, and sat nervously waiting for my first audience with Oppenheimer since the election.

Zach de Beer had warned: 'HFO – although exquisitely polite – bores easily. Try to tell him something he doesn't know. He will enjoy political anecdotes and a bit of gossip, in addition to your plans for the party.' Forewarned, I provided Oppenheimer with such titbits as I could muster. He was diminutive, and at 86 looked frail. However, he was empathetic and affirming, gently probing our future prospects. At the end he gave me a warm handshake, and pledged continuing personal and corporate support.

I was to remain in contact and enjoy Oppenheimer's support, counsel and even friendship (augmented by the warmth and hospitality of his wife Bridget and daughter Mary) for the remaining six years of his life.[31] Indeed, after I had taken the decision to merge the DP with the NP to create the Democratic Alliance (see Chapter 16), I thought it prudent and appropriate to get his blessing in 2000.[32]

On 23 October 1994, the DP rank-and-file gathered in Durban's Royal hotel at its first post-election congress. Five years after I had been jeered off the stage at the hotel, I was now confirmed as sole leader. I told the delegates: 'For perhaps far too long now, the DP has been a sort of political fruit salad – with a range of different groupings and ideologies mixed together. Now, in post-apartheid South Africa we are required to become something different.'

I also drew the congress's attention to the need for a major political realignment, feeling confident enough to assert: '[The] current political groupings are artificial. The ANC comprises a group spanning liberal democrats to unrehabilitated Stalinists, while the NP is a group of confused and dispirited politicians ... [The] healthiest development for South Africa would be a fundamental realignment based on a shared agenda [and] common vision ...'

I also had to address the concern that our slender numbers in parliament cemented our irrelevance. I quoted the anthropologist Margaret Mead: 'Never doubt that a small group of concerned people can change the world. Indeed it is the only thing that ever has.' The delegates cheered mightily.

The Daily News also seemed in agreement, editorialising – under the headline 'New Lease on Life' – that 'Tony Leon brings much-needed qualities to the leadership of the DP ... [Chief] among the thirty-something MP's attributes are vigour, fresh ideas, a combative political style and good public projection.'[33]

In time the very qualities that the newspaper identified in me would fairly rapidly be perceived by the press as defects. But that was after the party's base began to expand rapidly, and the newspapers – particularly their editors – underwent 'transformation' in an attempt to make them more congenial to the new political order.

I indicated at the time to James Selfe that by our next congress we had to unpack a more modern version of the liberal agenda rather than claim victories against apartheid – akin to asking people to 'vote for a better yesterday'. He was firmly in agreement, and we set about commissioning policies and proposals, which we were to describe as the 'Agenda for a Better Country' – whose acronym, ABC, I thought a good marketing contrast to the ANC's RDP.

The entire package, unveiled at our August 1995 Muizenberg congress, was premised on the need for at least 6% annual GDP growth (the precise target set by government some eight years later). In the words of our economics spokesman, Ken Andrew: 'If poverty is to be alleviated then there is no substitute for economic growth.' Andrew had also repeatedly drawn the government's attention to the failure of state initiatives to date. Having performed an economic U-turn away from dirigiste interventionism to the discipline of the market, they treated this as a smorgasbord from which to pick a few tasty morsels (such as fiscal discipline) while ignoring indigestible ones – such as privatisation and labour market flexibility. I advised the delegates – in a splendidly mixed metaphor: 'You've got to swallow it all and go the whole hog.'

My constant reading in and around economic and political issues had introduced me to the American philosopher Gertrude Himmelfarb, who called for a 'remoralisation of society'.[34] She did not mean the creation of a supernanny state telling people what they could read or what they could do with their pregnancies.[35] Rather, I interpreted her to mean – for our purposes – that the country had to undergo a refurbishment of its economic and political institutions.

For capitalism and democracy to work, they had to co-exist with certain cultural habits. While law, contract and economic rationalism are necessary conditions for economic growth, they are not sufficient to achieve the sort of success evidenced by the so-called South-East Asian 'tiger economies'. We needed to learn their moral lessons as well: respect for education, a work ethic, a willing embrace of property rights, and a reliable code of reciprocal obligations between the community and the individual.

As my speech to the congress on the ABC emphasised, the most gaping hole in South Africa was the spiralling crime wave and government's feeble efforts to interdict it. I pointed not merely to the mind-numbing statistics which, at that stage, were more of a blight on the previous government than the new one, but to the mixed messages about fixing it: 'In the past decade – between 1984 and 1994 – 140 000 South Africans have been murdered. That is more than the total number of Japanese killed at Hiroshima, and three times more than the total number of Americans killed in over a decade in Vietnam ... Yet at the heart of our government we see a lack of resolve: 15 000 prisoners are given early release, and police numbers are allowed to shrink. What we need are more armed and effective policemen and more prisons, and a more effective criminal justice system.'

Our new policy detailed how to achieve these aims. But the headline which greeted us after the congress in the next *Sunday Times* suggested, for the first time, that I had jolted the party sharply to the Right. Ray Hartley's piece was headlined: 'The Man Who Talks Like Margaret Thatcher'. It was an attack dressed up with a few back-handed compliments: 'Inside the hall the DP's Tony Leon ... delivered the opening speech to his party's congress and, yes, it was replete with the aggressive, free-market and privatisation messages pioneered by the Iron Lady.'[36]

Hartley then went on to describe me (notwithstanding my attention to Mandela's many successes) as 'spurning the rainbow nation policies'. However, he did report that despite his disapproval of my message, as the messenger 'he got the delegates to their feet chanting, "Tony, Tony, Tony". For the first time since the DP was humiliated in last year's election, they swayed their arms, waved party flags, and cheered their leader ... Mr Leon sounded more like the head of a thriving opposition, rather than the last hope of a party representing less than two per cent of the electorate.'

I was irritated by Hartley's hatchet job – but pleased that the party was conveying a new-found optimism. However, Hartley was dead right that unless we shook off the 'less than two per cent' tag, any other claims or pretensions would amount to self-deluding piffle. Municipal elections loomed as the best and obvious place to prove our detractors wrong; but the struggle was to be arduous, yielding decidedly mixed results.

Notwithstanding plaudits in the press on the back of our exposés of corruption and rigour on crime, there appeared to be a remarkable continuum in the ecology of the electorate as the 1995 and 1996 municipal elections neared. There seemed to be a general acceptance – by many within the organisation – that the DP could continue to coast as a sort of moral witness and political watchdog without expanding its base. To some, indeed, 'small is beautiful'. I felt it time to move out of our comfort zone.

So we kicked off our campaign in February 1995 in Orlando, Soweto. I received a rousing, spontaneous reception from the nurses at the Chris Hani Baragwanath Hospital, and told the accompanying media that it was now 'do or die for the DP'.[37] I warned that should the party not 'significantly improve' on its abysmal 1994 vote in the forthcoming poll, we might as well pack it in as a political party. The fluttering in the party's dovecotes was palpable.

The day after, one of our parliamentary researchers, given to occasional hysterical outbursts, declaimed aloud: 'Leaders come and leaders go, but we, the grassroots, will decide the future of the party!' As it happened she left shortly afterwards while I continued as leader for more than a decade – this time (this was my genuine message) we were running to win.

Most of our efforts were concentrated in Johannesburg, our previous heartland, where in 1994 the NP had cut great swathes into our northern and eastern redoubts. This year we had to win it all back; and in addition, we fielded a full slate of ward candidates in Soweto and Alexandra and the East Rand township areas. For the first time the party had something of a local black presence on the ground.

The Soweto effort was headed by a crossover from the ACDP, Dan Maluleke. With his good looks, imposing bearing and imperious manner he appeared to personify the black leadership the party so desperately craved. Yet when he opened his mouth he had little of substance to say to the press or his fellow candidates. Once, while lunching with writers from the *Star*, Maluleke was asked what he considered the greatest problem confronting Soweto. 'The absence of trees,' he responded. He spent an inordinate amount of energy ensuring that no one else in Soweto – other than himself – rose to prominence or attained visibility. In his gatekeeper's view, 'Dan was the man.'

None of this, least of all his personal dismal showing in the November poll, stopped his upward trajectory in the party. Within four years he was a member of parliament; three years later he was elected a federal vice-chairman of the party; and three years after that, in 2005, he crossed the floor to the ANC. In his first speaking opportunity as a turncoat, he denounced the party which had lifted him to prominence.

However, our real battle for survival and reinvention in 1995 lay in proving we could reverse our fortunes in the old Prog citadels lost the year before to the Nationalists. Since De Klerk was still popular and had a profile as deputy president, we tactically turned our guns not on him but on the ANC. But Mandela transcended both race and party; he even boasted with complete honesty of having gone door-to-door in Houghton recruiting over 150 members for the ANC in a morning. When he recounted his triumph to me, I responded, with no great confidence: 'Well, of course, they love you, but not necessarily your party.' When he repeated the story to Helen Suzman she was more direct and, indeed, accurate: 'Just see what they do on election day, it will be a different story.' She had won Houghton in nine successive general elections.

We decided the ANC's area of maximum vulnerability was the spiralling crime wave. At the beginning of 1995 in his opening address to parliament Mandela made what I termed a 'brave speech'. It contained a specific commitment to 'take the war to the criminals and no longer allow a situation in which we are all sitting ducks for those in society who are bent on engaging in criminal activities.'[38] Yet since then the country found itself reeling under a crime wave of egregious proportions.

I saw two essential reasons for this failure. There was an inability – stretching across all realms of governance – to match concrete deed to fine rhetoric. Worse, government actions tripped each other up. Six weeks after Mandela's fierce attitude had been communicated in 1994, the minister of Finance cut the Police budget by 4%. A few weeks later the minister of Correctional Services – warmly applauded by the minister of Justice – released (without regard to the seriousness of the offence) all juveniles from prison to scantily secured places of safety, from which most subsequently escaped.

At precisely this time figures revealed that a staggering 110 000 vehicles had been hijacked or stolen in a year, up by 30%.

Government initiated a series of high-profile steps and actions, many of which, I said, 'bear all the hallmarks of desperate improvisation and U-turns, rather than acts of deliberate and decisive planning.' The Police cutback announced in the April budget was re-routed back in October via the RDP fund – just some two weeks before the municipal polls. Likewise, eight months after the release of the juveniles, the minister of Justice introduced legislation to halt their indiscriminate release. The nub of the problem was revealed by figures we prised out of government: 40% of the posts in the criminal justice system were vacant, and only some eight hundred South African National Defence Force personnel were on hand to assist the police in crime-fighting.[39]

Our efforts on the crime front signalled a revival in our political fortunes, as the *Sunday Times* observed ten days before the election. The headline read: 'Tony Leon Surfs South Africa's Spiralling Crime Wave'. And political editor Mike Robertson observed the shifts in the traditional opposition electorate: 'The ANC has hastily put up posters across Johannesburg saying "tough on crime: tough on the causes of crime". Not a bad slogan – except that it happens to belong to British Labour Party leader, Tony Blair, who coined the phrase and is so associated with it he might as well have copyright. What is most peculiar about this intellectual theft on the part of the ANC is that it has been prompted by the performance of a man who should, politically speaking, be dead and buried now.

'Tony Leon's Democratic Party did so badly in last year's election that even in Houghton it polled fewer votes than the NP. But since taking over as leader of the Democrats, Mr Leon has managed to give the party a focus, and the DP has not only managed to recapture many of its traditional supporters but ... to win approval, if not yet backing, from important people and institutions normally associated with the NP.'

After noting how Izak de Villiers, editor of the mass-circulating Afrikaans Sunday newspaper *Rapport*, was quoting my utterances with approval, Robertson delved into the crime issue and how it was affecting suburban preferences: 'While the white middle classes are the biggest beneficiaries of ANC economics, they are scared and angry because of crime. When Nelson Mandela and Gauteng Safety and Security MEC, Jessie Duarte, addressed an ANC rally at Temple Emanuel (in Parktown) she was booed. This by people who later adoringly lapped up every word the president uttered. Mr Leon has tapped into this anger.'[40]

We did improve our position in Gauteng, winning over eight per cent of the total vote – up 53% from the year before. The party did particularly well in Johannesburg, obtaining 19 council seats in the eastern municipal substructure (compared to the ANC's 32 and the Nationalists' six). In Houghton, despite Mandela's personal campaigning, the DP's candidate Mike Moriarty won by a hefty margin. Our Soweto and Alex candidates performed uniformly poorly, except in one seat, in Alexandra, where we tallied a respectable 500 votes. However, because of the staggering of polls across the country, we now had to focus on the next battleground, Cape Town metro, scheduled to poll in late May 1996, followed a few weeks later by the local election in KwaZulu-Natal.

Cape Town provided a bleaker outcome. FW de Klerk's decision to pull his party out of the GNU in May 1996 (just days before the Cape Town election) galvanised his party. In Mitchells Plain, the heartland of the majority Coloured voters, whatever appeal the DP held in the suburbs, its reach on the Cape Flats was exceedingly small – loyalties there were firmly on the side of the Nationalists. As we desperately scrambled to maintain our foothold, the NP, buoyed by the prospect of delivering a double blow against the DP and ANC, redoubled their efforts. Even in traditional DP territory, such as the southern suburbs, our canvassing revealed a potential meltdown.

When election day arrived on 29 May, I accompanied local MP Dene

Smuts to the polling station at the Fernwood Parliamentary Club. As she acidly observed, many of the residents lining up to vote had avoided our gaze by staring fixedly at their shoes: 'They know they should be voting for us, but they will not be doing so today.' And so it proved – for although the ANC's fashionable candidate Revel Fox finished a very distant third in the ward, our local councillor Ian Iversen barely held off his NP challenge. The estimable Belinda Walker (who would in time, after the next election, prove a great asset to our municipal administration) was buried by an NP avalanche in the next-door city bowl area. And so it went across the Peninsula.[41]

If King Claudius was right that 'sorrow comes not in single spies but in battalions', I suspected that the knock-back we had received in Cape Town would be compounded by a dismal showing in KwaZulu-Natal, due to vote on 26 June. Apart from the despondency in our battered ranks, we were also running low on money – having exhausted our resources in Gauteng and Cape Town. Our campaign management in KwaZulu-Natal was also desperately short of volunteers to bring out the vote. It seemed pretty hopeless.

I decided to borrow Churchill's maxim of 'in defeat, defiance' and announced a few days later in Grahamstown that the whole party would be mobilised and decamp to Durban to make a stand – not our last, I hoped. No doubt to outside ears I sounded somewhat frenzied, if not irrational, when I declared: 'Durban will be our Stalingrad!' But it did the trick within the party ranks.

We temporarily closed down every party office in the country – including our parliamentary operations – and arrived with assorted MPs, secretaries and researchers to do battle in Durban and Pietermaritzburg. We discovered we were broke. As the dire financial situation was being explained to our members, Jack Bloom, a Gauteng MPL who had come to Durban to take charge of the media campaign, responded quietly: 'I will advance the money.' There and then he produced his cheque book and stumped up an amount of R30 000! I have never forgotten this.

We fought hard. Fortunately, De Klerk's star did not shine as brightly on the east coast as it did on the west – except for the Indian community, which was still then in thrall to the Nats. We also tried to translate our successes – and scalps obtained – in parliament into a local narrative, with our stump pamphlet proclaiming: 'Whether it is COSATU, Winnie Mandela, Allan Boesak, *Sarafina 2* or Shell House, Tony Leon and the DP are not afraid to speak out where others are silent.'

By our modest (and the media's non-existent) expectations, the results were resoundingly favourable. We won 16 wards in Durban, six in Pietermaritzburg (pushing the IFP there into third place), and improved our provincial tally by over fifty per cent from the previous year to a modest, but life-saving, 3,35% of the total. We could now face the future with a certain confidence that was far more than rhetorical.

5

There would be big shifts in South Africa's political headwinds, sooner than anticipated. By 1999 the terms of trade, on the opposition side, were mostly in favour of my party, willed by our efforts in part, but also by a fundamental change in the political weather to which I had pinned the DP's future. However, the politics and temperature of the first democratic parliament can largely, and I believe correctly, be measured by the conduct and personalities of the four men (there were no women in this line-up) who led the three major parties: President Nelson Mandela and his heir presumptive, First Deputy President Thabo Mbeki; Second Deputy President FW de Klerk (he loathed his place in the pecking order); and Mangosuthu Buthelezi, who sat, often extremely uncomfortably, in the GNU by virtue of his presidency of the Inkatha Freedom Party.

Objectively, if there was a fifth leader, it was myself – I led the fifth-largest party. I interacted intensely on occasion with each of the 'big four'; and our encounters spanned the full range: many were warm, some frosty, others extremely fraught. Local issues and political dramas, the banal and the significant, formed the template of our interactions.

It was Mandela who pulled me out of the slough of despondency that initially settled on me after I became party leader. I had sent the president a letter warmly congratulating him on his election and expressing the hope that the DP could be of service in the new South Africa. I added, as an afterthought, that perhaps we could meet at some stage 'to develop a creative dialogue on the road ahead'.

The letter was sincere – though strictly speaking a courtesy to which I expected no response. On the evening of Mandela's first address to parliament, in May 1994, as I was pottering about my mother's Camps Bay holiday flat, a Cape Town base, the telephone rang at 10 pm. I was stunned: it was Madiba, hero of the world, phoning the leader of a minor opposition party for a chat. He talked at some length about his appreciation of my sentiments, asked warmly after certain DP figures, and invited me to join him for breakfast at his Cape Town residence in two days' time.

I presented myself at the white-gabled Cape Dutch mansion which sits atop the rather grand and rolling Groote Schuur estate in Newlands, Cape Town, and which serves as the official residence of the president and numerous cabinet ministers. After a brief wait I was escorted upstairs to a small dining room where an impeccably groomed Mandela welcomed me with his famous smile. Accompanied by only his secretary and an over-anxious air force chef, we sat down to *spanspek*, Jungle Oats, scrambled egg for me, and toast and jam for the president.

Mandela was exceptionally welcoming, full of personal praise for my 'leadership ability', and pronounced himself determined to enjoy a close relationship with the DP. I found it interesting that he singled out Harry Schwarz as 'a champion of the poor' – essentially correct in my estimation, but contrary to the old Prog caricature of the then ambassador to Washington as a 'right-wing hawk'. I, too, spoke warmly about Schwarz, but put in a plug for my vanquished predecessor, Zach, suggesting he would make a fine diplomat, an entreaty subsequently taken up by Mandela who later appointed De Beer ambassador to the Netherlands.

What I found most revealing and refreshing was Mandela's openness and candour. When I spelled out how I saw our role as a 'loyal opposition', he immediately agreed on the need for such a parliamentary watchdog but assured me that on all major issues there tended to be huge areas of disagreement within the ANC itself. Pivots of division vested in a triptych of former Robben Island prisoners, the formerly exiled leadership, and the internal activists. These elements comprised the ANC's own (self-sealed) 'opposition'.

For some reason Mandela introduced the subject and complex personality of Inkatha president Mangosuthu Buthelezi, who seemed in our later talks a semi-permanent presence in the mind of Madiba. He launched into an essentially psychological deconstruction of his opponent from KwaZulu-Natal, telling me that to understand Buthelezi you had to appreciate his past, especially his childhood.

I was tempted to tell Mandela that if he looked into my own background, with my mother's multiple divorces and the like, he might also find the origins of my own personal anxieties and insecurities – but thought better of it! We concluded our discussion over one-and-a-quarter hours later. What shone through for me was how well-grounded he was; as the French say: 'He wore his own skin.' I couldn't help but think that he must have had impressive and deeply nurturing parents as well.

Of course, by embracing me in his circle of confidence he presumably figured on inoculating himself against any prospect of personal attack. Not that the world, or South Africa, would have taken much notice had I been stupid enough to take him on. However, I decided that I would not allow myself to become a sort of pet-poodle placed on the opposition benches. Part of the DP's past mistakes had flowed from a desperate desire to be affirmed by the liberation camp.

To explore our options for co-operation elsewhere, I arranged to meet Buthelezi. We met in his ministerial office in the HF Verwoerd Building (soon to be rechristened as plain '120 Plein Street'). A large portrait of Margaret Thatcher enjoyed pride of place: she had always been an admirer of the 'Zulu chief', and her ardour was reciprocated.

I thought etiquette weighed heavily upon him: yet though formal, he was also warm and expressed deep appreciation for our party's role, and his personal admiration both for my political progenitors (especially Helen Suzman and Ray Swart) and for my father whom he knew quite well from Natal. I suggested we co-operate on constitutional issues, an idea he welcomed in view of the forthcoming tussle in the Constitutional Assembly to finalise the constitution. He also told me he was 'very uncomfortable' in the GNU, and that he had accepted Home Affairs because of 'intense pressure' from the IFP leaders.

Buthelezi's ambivalence – between co-operation with the ANC and intense opposition to it – was to play itself out over the next ten years. A junior partner in government, he was head of the majority party governing KwaZulu-Natal, where the ANC served as a minority component of the provincial government. Deference to his status was at all times to be observed – for a politician of his longevity he was almost exquisitely sensitive to slights, and one of the most litigious figures in public life. But, from our first meeting, we forged a bond of friendship.

As for Thabo Mbeki, my suggestion to Mandela that Zach de Beer be appointed an ambassador led to our meeting to resolve the fact that the proposal was not apparently welcomed by Mandela's cabinet colleague, Zola Skweyiya. Mbeki, as deputy president, was in reality the de facto head of government. (Eglin referred to Mandela as the 'Lord Mayor of Africa' and to Mbeki as the 'country's CEO' – an astute observation.)

In contrast to his later metamorphosis into a chilly, distant eminence, dismissive of critics and often sneeringly sarcastic in his political approach, the Mbeki of 1994 was a much nicer person, far more approachable and accommodating. He was quite frank about 'the extremely slow and frustrating nature of cabinet' and the 'sheer weight of bureaucracy which pulled and directed government, rather than the other way around.'

It was apparently in this process that Zach's nomination was ensnared. Perhaps it was his early and unhappy encounter with Mandarin-style procedures that helped firm Mbeki's later instincts for control and centralisation. He also admitted that one of his greatest frustrations was the absence of time to pursue essential policy development and implementation. In the event, he kept his door wide open to me for the next four or so years; and shortly after our meeting, Zach received his ambassadorial posting.

That door slammed shut after a meeting in late 1998, as I recount in Chapter 14, never to reopen until I stood down in May 2007.

Of the GNU leaders, De Klerk was undoubtedly having the hardest time. His status had been much diminished under the new order, and his emerging key lieutenant, Marthinus van Schalkwyk – yet to play a profoundly destructive role in my later political life – was at the time an amiable colleague. Over a long tea session he told me how difficult matters were for the NP: 'Thank heavens we have discipline, it's about the only thing which keeps the party together.' Privately he admitted what had become utterly apparent publicly – that the NP had become 'the punch-bag of this parliament. We cannot – and will never – be allowed to shake off our legacy, and no self-absolution is possible.'

Later I learned, through brutal first-hand experience, that Van Schalkwyk was equally capable of honest self-reflection and candour, and of manipulative dissembling. However, on this occasion he seemed genuine. His further complaint that De Klerk had been 'let down' by the NP's appointees in the cabinet (Pik Botha, Dawie de Villiers, Roelf Meyer, Kraai van Niekerk and Abe Williams) was later echoed by Mandela, who told me that he had once urged De Klerk 'not to speak on every issue before cabinet'. His deputy president said he did so out of necessity, since his NP colleagues did not back him up.

Instead of fixing his internal problems, De Klerk determined to strike at the DP. In one week in August he attacked the party three times. Strangely, he had earlier chosen to 'wish me well'. That was the first occasion on which we had met since the election, and I noted in my diary that he 'retains his charm and skill, but is a much-reduced figure. His speech in parliament is polished – but what does he have to offer? He can't pull any more rabbits out of the hat. As president he was brilliant with the dramatic announcements, but now he has only the trappings of high office, but little or none of its substance.'

In September 1994 John Major and a huge entourage from Britain arrived in parliament for the first visit by a British prime minister since

Harold Macmillan's groundbreaking 'wind of change' speech in 1960. He was pithy, witty, historical and substantial – elucidating at length on the ties of history, affinity and culture which bound our countries together. When I mentioned my impressions to the minister responsible for international development, the voluble and energetic Linda Chalker, she remarked: 'Well, it should have been good – it went through 17 drafts.' Mandela, ever the considerate host, introduced me to Major. I flatteringly but truthfully told him: 'Your speech was far better than anything we heard from Mitterrand or Mugabe [another visitor].' Mandela and Major grinned.

On this occasion De Klerk buttonholed me: 'It's high time we got together for a chat and tea or coffee or whisky.' A meeting was duly arranged at his office in the Union Buildings for early the next month. I had always had a high regard for De Klerk's intelligence, and at times admired him for his conspicuous displays of courage and steadfastness. That was him at his best. But I also realised that he could be crafty and manipulative – perhaps essential ingredients for high-wire politics.

Our relationship with the NP was uneasy and, at that initial stage, very uneven given that they outnumbered us in parliament by a factor of ten (82 MPs against seven). However, we were making the running as an opposition force as the NP tried (with far less apparent success than Inkatha) to straddle its ambiguous role. I had also come to the conclusion that while there was no immediate quick-fix to my own party's growth problem, a short-term route to political relevance was to go after the low-hanging fruit of disenchanted NP voters: essentially we represented broadly the same constituency.

The constitutional negotiations had yielded high office for De Klerk and a half-dozen holdovers from his faded regime. But for the rank-and-file Nat supporters the new South Africa was neither rosy nor as secure as their political masters had promised. After surveying the results of the Kempton Park process, Van Zyl Slabbert had apparently observed: 'The rich Afrikaners sold out the poor ones.' Such was the background to my first get-together with De Klerk.

He was persuasive and plausible, if not slightly formal. He informed me that the DP, Dene Smuts and I were 'attacking the wrong target. You should concentrate your fire on the ANC. They are the common enemy.' He sought my views on the advisability of forming a joint caucus to approach the final constitutional haggling as a united entity (a 'patriotic front' was his unfortunate term). I felt such an idea would be a disaster, not simply because the ganging-up would drive the ANC into a hardline or rejectionist stance (although it would) but because it would diminish our influence on key issues.

I felt that separate but broadly converging approaches on those issues would be more effective. In fact, there was little NP/DP common purpose in the Constitutional Assembly, though De Klerk was animated on the need for closer co-operation – at least at local level, where he believed the opposition should work together 'to cut the ANC down to size'. I agreed with his general thrust, and we resolved to devolve the matter to our respective regions. There this high-born idea was duly killed by the competing intra-opposition interests of both parties.

However, my conviction that a more unified opposition was necessary and possible had been confirmed by De Klerk. Yet when that unity was eventually attained, six years later, De Klerk had long retired from active politics and his party entered the DA as the junior partner.

6

When the British royal family visited South Africa in March 1995, Mandela grabbed my arm as I was about to enter the formal dinner at the Cape Sun hotel in honour of Queen Elizabeth and Prince Philip, and insisted I join him and senior government ministers in an ante-room for personal introductions. The Queen extended a gloved hand to me, but offered no word as I bowed my head, merely smiling and moving down the line.

However, when Mandela advised Prince Philip that 'Tony Leon is the leader of our Democratic Party', the Duke of Edinburgh decided this was a moment for interrogation and royal repartee. 'So you're democratic?' he enquired. 'Yes.' 'Well, aren't all your parties here now democratic? What sort of democrats are you?' 'We are liberal democrats,' I answered. 'Oh,' he rejoined, 'we've got plenty of liberals in Britain, why don't you just call yourselves liberal?' I advised His Royal Highness that the term 'liberal' was not particularly popular in our part of the world. The Prince then retorted: '[The] problem with the word "democratic" is that all those Soviet republics in eastern Europe used to describe themselves as democratic and they were anything but! Ha! Ha! Ha!' He moved on, having delivered himself of what I judged to be an accurate, and princely, take on the political lexicon.

Almost immediately after this close, if brief, encounter with royalty I departed for Switzerland to join my father and his wife's family (her oldest son had a mountain lodge in Champéry in the Alps) to celebrate my father's 70th birthday. At the small pension where we were overnighting in

Carouge, outside Geneva, I was interrupted by the manager before break-fast, shouting in indecipherable (to my ears) French something along the lines of 'le telephon' and 'le president'.

Mandela's secretary was at the other end. She had tracked me down from Mozambique, where Mandela was visiting, and told me the president needed to speak to me urgently. I had no idea what had caused the latest crisis. His familiar voice told me we needed to resolve swiftly a problem relating to the DP's 'proposal to nominate John Dugard to the soon-to-be-established Human Rights Commission [HRC]'. While 'government had the highest regard for Professor Dugard' they felt it was necessary for Helen Suzman to add her expertise and stature to the new body. He was certain that the DP would want to support her.

I was completely caught off guard. After Dugard's excellently merited nomination to the Constitutional Court had been rejected the previous year, my parliamentary colleagues and I felt most strongly that this man, one of the prime exponents of a human rights discourse in South Africa during the long apartheid night, would be a worthy commissioner. We had accordingly strongly motivated his candidacy. Mandela made it clear that it would be 'disproportionate' (or words to that effect) if the liberal/DP camp had more than one nominee – and he required me to choose. I had not been aware that Helen had sought, or received, nomination, but I immediately realised how politically and personally perilous it would be for me and the party to be seen not to support her.

I was appalled at the prospect of Dugard being dropped again – and mortified that I was being railroaded into exercising a choice, which I made in favour of Suzman. (I did think she too merited inclusion, and her service on the HRC was exemplary, if brief.) I never discerned why gov-ernment was so resolute on not appointing Dugard, hardly a DP partisan such as Suzman. It might have been those racial, gender or quota-filling requirements which soon – on an ever-accelerating basis – became the raison d'être for all public appointments. Or perhaps senior ANC figures bore some personal animus towards the mild-mannered, distinguished professor. The mystery has never been explained, and Dugard was to be a double-casualty of the democratic transition to which he had so resolutely dedicated himself.

Another source of tension between Mandela and me arose in the trou-bled kingdom and province of KwaZulu-Natal. The always ambivalent re-lationship between Madiba and Buthelezi began increasingly to fray some eighteen months after they were conjoined in the GNU. A promissory note thrown by Mandela and De Klerk at Inkatha during the helter-skelter

Top: BLESSING: meeting His Holiness Pope John Paul II in Pretoria, 1995.

Above: THE NATURAL: in March 1998 President Bill Clinton delivered a mesmerising address to parliament, and met thereafter with the opposition leadership. His singular charisma embraced all present: my colleague General Constand Viljoen and me, and the Speaker, Dr Frene Ginwala, on the right.

Top: INTO AFRICA: Colin Eglin and I made several visits to Africa, meeting on this occasion in July 1998 in Kampala with Ugandan president Yoweri Museveni.

Above: My gift of a bottle of South African grappa to the then British Minister for Africa, Peter Hain, *(left)*, did not persuade the European Union to drop its requirement that our local liquor be rebranded. Hain, although later felled in a funding scandal, proved to be a seminal voice on Zimbabwe's dramatic implosion. 4 February 2000. *(DIE BURGER)*

Opposite above: In January 2001 FW and Elita de Klerk invited Michal and me to meet Margaret Thatcher and her husband Denis, and her, later notorious, son Mark, at a gathering on the De Klerks' beautiful farm in Klein Drakenstein near Paarl, Western Cape.

Opposite below: TWO LEADERS OF THE OPPOSITION: I meet my opposite number in Britain and Thatcher's Conservative Party successor but one, William Hague, in London.

Top: ACROSS THE DIVIDE IN THE MIDDLE EAST: Michal and I met Israeli strongman, Prime Minister Ariel Sharon, the year before he was felled by a massive stroke. He advised me that South Africa could play no role in the Middle East process: 'Your government is totally pro-Palestinian.'

Above: In September 2002 I lunched in Ramallah with Sharon's arch adversary, Yasser Arafat, President of the Palestinian Authority. Arafat was extravagant in his hospitality, notwithstanding his embattled conditions, but he accepted no responsibility for the Palestinian predicament.

Opposite above: GALLIC GREETING: French prime minister, Lionel Jospin, came calling in Cape Town some years before the 2004 elections. He asked me the essential question: 'Are you an opposition or an alternative?'

Opposite below: In Dharamsala, northern India, March 2006, meeting with His Holiness the 14th Dalai Lama. He is one of the world's great moral leaders whose struggle for justice and dignified adherence to principle ranked him, in my view, with the 'good and the great' of the 20th century, alongside Mahatma Gandhi and Nelson Mandela.

Top: VISITING THE FORBIDDEN CITY: I led a Democratic Alliance delegation to mainland China where we were wined and dined by senior members of the government, and given their perspective on both Tibet and Taiwan, and on economic matters.

Above: VICE-PRESIDENT OF LIBERAL INTERNATIONAL: in this capacity I traversed the globe attending various gatherings of Liberal International. In October 2003 its first-ever congress was held on African soil in Dakar, Senegal. In the photograph I am second left in the front row. In the centre is the Senegalese president Abdoulaye Wade.

Opposite above: A BRIEF DISCUSSION ON OUR RUSSIANNESS: I accompanied Russia's President Vladimir Putin when he signed the visitor's book in Parliament on a visit in September 2006.

Opposite below: Addressing the Oxford Union in October 2006: apart from its historical surrounds, the debate gave me an opportunity to delve deeper into the critical issue of climate change.

Above: 2004 ELECTION: campaigning with Theuns Botha, Western Cape provincial leader, and energetic local councillor James Vos, in the Democratic Alliance new stronghold in Goodwood, Cape Town.

Left: Michal and I launch the 2004 general election campaign at Vista University in Soweto. The enthusiasm of the crowd proved to be something of an electoral false dawn. 23 February 2004. (*SOWETAN/* PETER MOGAKI)

IFP president Mangosuthu Buthelezi and I launch the 'Coalition for Change' at a rally in Soweto, in 2003. When the results rolled in it proved to be an illusion.

Above: DOORSTOPPED ON THE DEATH PENALTY: during the 2004 election campaign I was bounced with a question on the death penalty outside a jail in Bloemfontein. My answer, that in certain exceptional cases it should be considered as an appropriate sentence, infuriated some but echoed the sentiments of many. Andries Botha on the left, the Free State leader of the DA.

Below: Addressing the media in the aftermath of the 2004 general election when the DA comfortably retained its position – and increased its support – as the largest opposition grouping; but the ANC grew by even more. 16 April 2004. (*BUSINESS DAY*/ARNOLD PRONTO)

Top: I reach across the aisle in Parliament to congratulate Thabo Mbeki warmly on his re-election as president. However, my attempt at *glasnost* proved unsuccessful: the ANC later said, 'Keep your hand to yourself.' 23 April 2004. (PICTURENET)

Above: RE-ELECTED LEADER: the party Federal Congress in Durban in November 2004 re-elected me unanimously as leader of the party. Unbeknown to them or to me at the time, it was to be my last term.

Opposite above: DEMOCRATIC JIVE: celebrating at the 2004 DA Federal Congress in Durban with re-elected chairman, Joe Seremane.

Opposite below: I redouble my efforts to reach out to communities and to experience life where people live, work and learn. Interaction with students at Bosmansdam High School outside Cape Town.

Top: Last electoral hurrah: the 2006 municipal elections yielded a good result for the Democratic Alliance. Our 'stop corruption start delivery' campaign was launched in festive conditions at the Boland Cricket Stadium in Paarl, Western Cape. 23 January 2006. (*DIE BURGER*/LEANNE STANDER)

Above: In 2008, with my strategist and confidant Ryan Coetzee in Parliament. He envisaged the Democratic Alliance mission before anyone else. (DEMOCRATIC ALLIANCE)

Above: PEACE AT LAST: President Thabo Mbeki and I had a warm discussion at a private meeting in Pretoria in May 2007, days before I stood down from party leadership. (*Sunday Times*)

Centre: The family joins in the farewell: a splendid send-off was arranged by the party on the eve of my final congress as party leader, in May 2007. Noa, Michal and Etai were on hand to celebrate. In the background is my chief of staff, Paul Boughey.

Left: As Fred Mouton of *Die Burger* attested in this cartoon, Thabo Mbeki in his farewell remarks promoted me up the canine ladder from a chihuahua to a bull terrier. (*Die Burger*)

Left: PARTING SHOT: my final speech to Parliament as Leader of the Opposition. 14 February 2007. (*Cape Times/*Alan Taylor)

Below: GOODBYE AND HELLO: On 6 May 2007 I stood down as leader of the Democratic Alliance and embraced my successor, Cape Town mayor, Helen Zille. (*Sunday Times*)

AT HARVARD: I was appointed a Fall Fellow at the Institute of Politics, Harvard University in Cambridge, Massachusetts. If it is possible to have a life-changing experience at the age of 50, then this was it.

preceding the 1994 election – promising 'international mediation' on issues such as the degree of federal independence – had not been honoured by the ANC. As a consequence Inkatha boycotted the Constitutional Assembly, and the political temperature – never particularly low – in the garden province of KwaZulu-Natal glared red.

In a May Day speech in 1995 delivered in the populous and poverty-stricken township of Umlazi, south of Durban, Mandela lost it – blaming Inkatha for the upsurge of violence in the province. In bare-knuckled fashion he told his audience that he would 'cut off the funds to the province' – a blatantly unconstitutional threat. These provocative remarks were in response to Buthelezi (termed by Mandela 'a certain leader in KwaZulu-Natal') in a speech at the same venue, when the Inkatha boss announced that 'he would organise people to revolt against the government.' Mandela warned: '[Those] who call on Zulus to resist the authority of Pretoria don't know what they have started. Those responsible for violence will be dealt with.'⁴²

The very next day, 2 May, was a marquee event in parliament, the president's own budget vote. As I grappled with preparing my own speech for that afternoon's debate, I received a call from Mandela. He requested me to forego my speaking turn until he had had an opportunity to brief me personally on the situation in KwaZulu-Natal. I explained to him that if I was to accede I would be knocked out of the debate until the following day, rendering my contribution largely pointless. I also sensed that after a private briefing from the president, my guns would effectively be spiked.

Mandela then suggested we meet after the debate. I agreed, and used the talk to implore him to meet the IFP's demand for mediation, however eccentric and moot it now might appear. As the private dialogue flowed to and fro, the president interrupted me with a personal and unmerited compliment ('You are a brilliant young man') and a warning: 'The matter is essentially political and my patience with Buthelezi is now exhausted.'

The debate was strange. Mandela never once referred to the storm which had erupted over his KwaZulu-Natal speech. Buthelezi's contribution went for the jugular, directly referring to the president's 'threats' and launching a lengthy justification of his own position, quoting himself as saying that South Africa and KwaZulu-Natal must rise and resist the central government 'which has given a clear indication of pressing plans from which great evil arises.'⁴³ Jeers from the ANC benches punctuated his presentation.

For my part, I told parliament I was shocked and saddened by the events in Umlazi – 'a vivid example of the gross vein of political intolerance and violence which is still alive in our country.' Here I had in mind the fact that apparently several hundred IFP supporters had tried to storm Mandela's rally and allegedly shot and injured several people inside the stadium. I said that in my party's 'objective view' international mediation should continue, even on the terms of reference agreed to 13 months before which had themselves now become a source of disputation. I suggested less confrontation.

When I later met Mandela (with Eglin, whom the president suggested accompany me), he appeared perfectly calm, though determined. He elaborated on the violence and intimidation meted out to his supporters throughout KwaZulu-Natal – although nothing seemed to justify the threat of 'turning off the taps' to the province. Then in his reply to the debate the next day he drew a clear line between the precepts of the constitution and the necessity of saving human life: 'I do not believe the constitution to be more important than human lives ... [The] constitution is very important, and it is a matter of serious concern when the president of a country threatens to change the constitution, but I am determined to protect human life. The perception that whites in this country do not care about black lives is there. I may not share it but it is there. The discussions [during this debate in parliament] where reference is not even made to the principal reason for my having taken this tough line to protect human lives, unfortunately goes a long way in confirming this perception.'[44]

The immediate crisis passed. The threats and counter-threats lessened. There was, however, no mediation – but also no cut-off of funds. Thereafter, Mandela's method of dealing with Buthelezi went from cajoling to charm. He repeatedly appointed Buthelezi as Acting President when both he and Mbeki were out of South Africa (a frequent occurrence). If he was not entirely mollified, this ensured Buthelezi's continuance in the GNU.

The squalls, squabbles and heated exchanges between the ANC and me were more the exception than the rule in the 'Prague spring' of the first years of South Africa's transition. However, my constant parliamentary skirmishes with the ANC relating to 'the Shell House massacre' on the eve of the 1994 election were to cast something of a pall over my warm relationship with Mandela (as I detail in Chapter 10).

But looking back now at the events and major political personalities of this brief era, and my own role, I am struck by how relatively at ease the top echelon of the ANC government appeared – at least initially – with the form of robust opposition practised by the DP. Perhaps nothing better demonstrated the general spirit of amity than an early scandal concerning the ANC's favourite cleric and sometime leader in the Western Cape, Allan Boesak. Somewhat portentously, at the commencement of the 1995 session, ANC minister Kader Asmal gave parliament this categorical assurance: 'We must be bound by higher standards of conduct than those which governed our predecessors ... [Those] who use office for money are taking food from children's stomachs.'[45]

Barely two months later, Boesak, who had been nominated as South Africa's ambassador to the UN in Geneva, was named and shamed by the release of a detailed forensic legal report (on behalf of the Nordic donor organisation Danchurch) which stated that he had been involved in major improprieties relating to his Foundation for Peace and Justice (FPJ). Boesak had directed the FPJ during the heyday of the struggle. In meticulous and legalistic detail the report stated that Boesak had misappropriated the fund, contrary to the donor's wishes, to enrich his personal lifestyle and fund the career of his TV-producer wife, Elna. It also appeared that money had been diverted to finance the travel arrangements of various ANC politicians during the 1994 election.[46]

As it happened, the report had been drafted by a university friend of mine, Greg Nott, a person and lawyer of immense probity and decency.

At the same time as the report surfaced, the state's anti-corruption arm, the Office for Serious Economic Offences (OSEO), was also probing Boesak on the same matter, with a view to prosecuting criminal charges against him. Extraordinarily, Deputy President Mbeki leaped into the fray on the basis of an extremely flimsy report prepared by his own legal adviser, Ms Mojanku Gumbi. I had never before heard of Ms Gumbi; she would soon, however, become known to the entire nation as one of Mbeki's most powerful and influential advisers. (She later said we were in law school together, although I have no recollection of her presence.)

Her report purported to exonerate Boesak of all allegations, and conveyed the clear impression that Nott's law firm (Bell, Dewar & Hall) agreed with her contentions. The lawyers shot back that her information was faulty, unsourced, and based on her own highly selective quoting from a response she had received from the firm. For example, Gumbi claimed that in its response to her 'findings' Bell, Dewar & Hall admitted that 'in certain instances their report is wholly incorrect'. In fact, the firm had done no such thing! They had merely summarised Gumbi's own statement and, at length, refuted it. Extraordinarily and unethically, Gumbi had lopped off the refutation. Mbeki, however, en route to Australia, gave Gumbi's botched investigation his imprimatur, declaring Boesak exonerated and claiming, bizarrely, that 'far from misappropriation of funds' (earmarked for the victims of apartheid) he in fact was owed money by the Foundation and was guilty of nothing more 'than inadequate supervision of the fund'.[47]

I was incensed at this farcical and far-fetched ruse, and told the media that Gumbi's report was questionable in terms of its 'appropriateness, timing and motive'.[48] I also accused Gumbi of 'astonishing judgment in making elementary errors when reading a simple document'. Nor was I the only unimpressed party: the OSEO's Jan Swanepoel proclaimed himself 'surprised and taken aback by [Mbeki's] announcement which was made in the middle of the police investigation.'[49] The *Sunday Times* went further: Gumbi's efforts were 'shallow, inconsequential and in some cases patently wrong';[50] while Bell, Dewar & Hall dismissed her efforts as 'incorrect' and 'preposterous'.[51]

In attempting to offset the damage to Boesak, Mbeki damaged himself and the ANC. He was dubbed the 'Velcro man' since 'everything thrown at him sticks' as the *Sunday Times* tartly observed. This was not simply a reference to *l'affaire* Boesak (in due course convicted by the High Court and carted off to jail precisely for the reasons contained in the legal report that Mbeki-Gumbi disputed), but to his mishandling two weeks previously of the dismissal of Winnie Mandela as a deputy minister. She had to be 'refired' later when it transpired that the provisions of the constitution had not been properly applied in the first attempt.

Unfortunately Boesak was not an isolated swallow that summer. The sky blackened as one after another ANC appointee became mired in allegations of corrupt practice. Some were prosecuted; others were never probed properly – or at all. The standard defence had been ventilated by the ANC over Boesak: 'The DP and NP should come to terms with the fact that they had lost last year's election and remained minority parties ... Reverend Boesak was constitutionally entitled to basic norms of justice.'[52] No question here, or ever, about the merits of the accusation, the judgment, or the fitness for office. To be perfectly fair, however, the ANC did not on that occasion – as it was ceaselessly to do henceforth – play the race card, and the brouhaha around Boesak scuppered his ambassadorial posting.

I believed that my justified roasting of Mbeki and Gumbi's 'efforts to whitewash the stain of corruption allegations off Boesak' would poison, or at least contaminate, the warmth which had hitherto apparently characterised my relationship with the deputy president. Yet when we met shortly thereafter at an agreeable cocktail function hosted by the Australian Foreign minister, Gareth Evans, Mbeki slapped me on the back, and when

I introduced him to my friend Steve du Toit who accompanied me to the function (to celebrate a Rugby World Cup match which the Springboks won), Mbeki expressed close interest when Steve said he and I had been at boarding school together. 'Well,' joked the deputy president, 'it's just a pity that your school didn't remove all Tony's rough edges!' Mbeki then promptly invited me to join him on a government-business delegation to Switzerland. A few days later he sent me a follow-up note with the relevant documents, adding wittily: 'Unfortunately for you (and I), Ms Gumbi will not be on the delegation. Regards, Thabo.'

Even more unfortunate, however, was the fact that the myriad demands of parliament, the party and my portfolio committee precluded me from accepting. I have since pondered, without resolution, how and why the apparently engaged and informal Thabo Mbeki became, in a relatively short period, a baleful, broody and withdrawn figure as the cares of office apparently began to weigh more heavily upon him. There is no simple or apparent answer in the case of this most complex and enigmatic of political figures.

7

To an extent, the honeymoon between Mbeki and me appeared to continue. Several months after the Switzerland invitation, I received in my office a highly agitated group representing the senior leadership of the South African Jewish Board of Deputies. They were extremely concerned about reports that the South African government was about to invite or receive a group of the Palestinian terrorist organisation, Hamas, in the country.

At that time, March 1996, Shimon Peres had assumed the leadership of Israel in the wake of the terrible assassination of prime minister Yitzhak Rabin the previous November. Peres and Rabin were the co-architects and prosecutors of the Oslo Peace Process which held out the prospects of 'a new Middle East based on peace and the mutual recognition of Israeli and Palestinian rights'. Hamas, of course, was dedicated (as it still is) to the destruction of the peace process and of Israel itself. Hence my visitors' fear that Mandela and the government would legitimate and enhance the bloody hand of Hamas. It seemed apparent to me that the route of resolution was, again, to speak to Mbeki and outline the Board's concerns and add a few of my own.

The deputy president indicated an immediate appreciation of, and sensitivity towards, the issue. I was also deeply impressed with his apparent knowledge of the thicket of issues which hemmed in the Middle East combatants, and his thoughtful approach to peacemaking in the region. He promised to investigate the Hamas matter; and a few days later (3 March 1996), when we were both in parliament, he sent me the following note:

Dear Tony –

I spoke to the President about Hamas. He will not meet with them. A statement will be issued to this effect. It will be worded in a way which will ensure that we do not lose the main point the President was making – that the campaign of terror should come to an end and that we fully support the peace process – and the peace-makers in the Middle East.

Best wishes, Thabo.

Of course Mbeki's eloquence did not outline the roadmap which government would in fact follow – least of all when Mbeki assumed the presidency three years later. However, in Israel itself the defeat of Peres at the hands of hardline Likud leader Benjamin Netanyahu, two months after Thabo's note, scuppered the entire Oslo Peace Process and vanquished, with help from Yasser Arafat, the peacemakers in the Middle East.

The hard fact is that South Africa's foreign policy under the aegis of both Mandela and Mbeki was to remain contested terrain. It was never clear or consistent. The designated minister, Alfred Nzo, was amiable but ineffective and inert, and policy lurched between high-minded principle and the lowest common denominator of Third World struggle solidarity. While the ANC leadership greatly enjoyed hobnobbing with the G-7 (as it then was), it appeared equally happy rubbing the West the wrong way by parading its allegiance with the countries and regimes that lost the Cold War.

Initially I assumed that the struggle debts included consideration for the party's cash funders. When I visited Taiwan as a guest of its government at the end of 1994, our ambassador there (we still maintained diplomatic links) cheerfully told me that when Mandela visited the pariah island (as mainland China designated it) he directly requested the staggering amount of US$10-million from President Lee Teng Hui. The full amount was granted 'within minutes'. But although Mandela was absolutely candid when pressed on this issue by the media a year later,[53] he claimed 'a donation is not a bribe.' Taiwan's largesse to the ANC – buttressed by a further R14-million donation in 1995 for a Defence Force vocational training scheme – did not prevent South Africa from severing their diplomatic ties in November 1996 in line with the worldwide trend to recognise only one China, namely Beijing.

No one could raise funds for the ANC quite like Mandela. He told me that in his first year out of prison he raised a staggering R66-million for his party from African leaders alone. He was not at all ideological, requesting and receiving funds from such mutual enemies as Angola's José Eduardo dos Santos and Zaire's Mobutu Sese-Seko. The ANC's attachment to the Polisario Liberation Front did not preclude Mandela from seeking and receiving cash from their nemesis, the King of Morocco. He succeeded with every African potentate he called on – bar Egypt's Hosni Mubarak.

Party-political fundraising in South Africa remains a wild and unregulated frontier, without limits or prohibitions. After the ANC assumed power, I received credible reports of how official state visits were used, in part, to recruit these funds. When the DP attempted to probe this point we were met with non-answers, not denials.[54]

What influence such financial grubbing had on foreign policy posturing was difficult to discern. When challenged about his close links with Libyan strongman – at the time a fomenter of world terrorism – Muammar Gaddafi, Mandela simply advised the enquiring reporter 'to take a jump in the pool',[55] as he quaintly expressed it. When I questioned the Libyan link, that country's energetic ambassador to South Africa asked to meet me. We did so in my Johannesburg home and his easy charm was as disarming as his 'gift of friendship to the DP': a bottle of Chivas Regal, surprising, I thought, given its Muslim provenance.

While accommodating myself and the party to aspects of Mandela's embrace of, and invitations to, the world at large, I drew the line at meeting Iranian president Hashemi Rafsanjani in August 1996, and when Fidel Castro received a hero's welcome in parliament in October 1998, the DP benches were empty, following our caucus decision to boycott the event. This drew howls of outrage from the ANC, the media and the occasionally crude but exquisitely politically correct cartoonist Zapiro, who penned a caption under my caricature: 'I have a double standard to maintain.'

The government's posturing overtures to rogue regimes and dictators were one thing – I thought them counter-productive to the national interest, but essentially harmless. However, a full-blown military invasion of a neighbouring state was quite another matter. In September 1998 a morning news show wanted my comment on the fact that the South African National Defence Force, together with its Botswanan counterpart, had 'invaded Lesotho to restore democracy.' I mumbled something anodyne and rushed to the office to find out more about this astonishing occurrence. To compound the situation, both Mandela and Mbeki were abroad and the operation had been authorised by the acting president, none other than Mangosuthu Buthelezi.[56]

Opposition leaders were summoned that day to the Presidency for a briefing. I found Buthelezi, on this occasion, very unconvincing, and expressed my doubts as to whether all other, more peaceful, avenues of resolution had been exhausted before the 'invasion'. Buthelezi took extreme umbrage, informing us that South Africa's 'assistance' was requested by Lesotho and mandated by the Southern African Development Community.

Mandela, who was in January 2003 to join worldwide condemnation of George W Bush's pre-emptive invasion of Iraq, later described the operation in Lesotho as 'an intervention to restore democracy and the rule of law. There is a responsibility to intervene when democracy is under threat.'[57] A party colleague later described his ex post facto justification as 'pure Bush doctrine three years before Bush himself enunciated it.'[58]

The waters were to remain chilly for some time between Buthelezi and me. It is, however, worth reflecting how swiftly, if cack-handedly, South Africa responded to the apparent threat to democratic governance in Lesotho, and how gingerly, quietly and irresolutely the same government acted in the face of Robert Mugabe's self-destruction of the last shreds of democracy in Zimbabwe, which commenced just 18 months later. Was it a case of once burnt, twice shy; or were there two (or more) sets of rules and standards to be applied in the region and across the wider world?

But during the heyday of Mandela's presidency, the approach to international relations was broadly ecumenical, and the foreign leaders, of all ideological stripes, kept pouring into the country. President Bill Clinton, in the midst of the Monica Lewinsky saga, descended on parliament in March 1998.

He held the usually restive National Assembly spellbound with his masterly performance. Unusually for a visiting head of state, Clinton had expressly requested a private meeting with the entire parliamentary opposition leadership. Thus, after his address, we arranged ourselves in a reception line for the president and first lady, Hillary Rodham Clinton.

Standing far behind us was a gaggle of nervous and wide-eyed waitresses ready to serve the tea. When Clinton, accompanied by members of his entourage, entered and started shaking hands with us, he immediately saw the tea ladies – none of whom remotely resembled Monica Lewinsky or Gennifer Flowers. Yet with a special grace and instinctive feel, he reached beyond our line-up to greet them also and shake their hands. When a biographer admiringly referred to Clinton as 'the natural', I thought it a masterly understatement.

My then low position in the opposition pecking order gave me a pro-tocol-mandated seat towards the edge of the table. However, when one of my colleagues proceeded to bend Clinton's ear on various complaints, and the travails he saw afflicting South Africa, Clinton looked suitably interest-ed, and then responded with what I thought to be an astute description of political reality. 'You know what I think,' the president countered, 'I think South Africa today is fantastic: not because you don't have problems and unresolved issues. But the only question in politics to ask is "compared to what?" And compared to its past, South Africa is doing pretty well.'

The rapid re-integration of South Africa into the international or-der also opened a window for Colin Eglin and me to attempt to ensure that our brand of liberalism enjoyed wider reach and resonance in Africa. At a meeting in Malawi we helped launch the Organisation of African Liberal Parties. Our host was the recently elected president of Malawi, Bakili Muluzi. Like another charter member of the African liberal family, Abdoulaye Wade of Senegal, Muluzi's party became steadily more illiberal once in power; but his young Education minister, Sam Mpasu, was both impressive and plain-speaking.

His description of what he termed 'the incomparable paradoxes' of Africa caused me to scribble down his diagnosis which, some twelve years later, still remains sadly relevant. Mpasu said that Africa's paradoxes included:

'A continent which is richly endowed with human and mineral re-sources and yet is the poorest continent in the world; a continent which has tracts of arable land large enough to feed a continent, yet which can-not feed itself; a continent which is blessed with lakes and large rivers and yet suffers from droughts and where her people die of thirst; and, the strangest paradox of all – the poorest continent on earth which has some of the world's wealthiest leaders.'

A few years later, in 2001, Eglin and I were to meet with one of the poster boys of corrupt old Africa, Daniel Arap Moi of Kenya, which in three decades as president he had converted from a country which at in-dependence in 1964 famously enjoyed a GDP equivalent to South Korea's into an impoverished kleptocracy. I was appalled, but not surprised, at how the public squalor of Nairobi, with its crater-sized potholes, pestilential squatter camps and imploring beggars on every corner, contrasted with the sumptuous luxury, and the splendid façade and lavish interiors, of State House where Arap Moi held court.

As we were ushered into a palatial reception room for our meeting with the president, Eglin urged me to be restrained and polite. I could not, however, prevent myself from raising the corruption issue which had become the only distinguishing feature of Moi's regime. Midway during our conversation, during which Arap Moi expressed doubts and scepticism about Mbeki's African Renaissance project then much in vogue, I asked him what he thought of the usefulness of legislative and institutional methods to curb government corruption, choosing for the immediate sake of etiquette an example of the Australian state premier who had been recently jailed for acts of financial impropriety. Moi smiled blankly and countered mystifyingly, 'Corruption lies in the hearts of men and women, and it is there you must deal with it.'

8

The atmospherics of reconciliation created by Mandela were soon replaced by a far more strident racism. It was perhaps appropriate that ANC firebrand Tony Yengeni gave early warning of the shift: in March 1996 he announced that whites had accumulated their wealth by stealing from blacks.[59] This was of a piece with Jacob Zuma's attempt to defend his maladroit then-wife Nkosazana Zuma for her public squandering of monies on the *Sarafina 2* debacle by saying she would not have been attacked if she had been white.[60]

I attempted to position the DP by indicating that we were not to be found in the corner of the new racists. Responding to a vicious attack by a journalist, Jon Qwelane, in the *Star*, I wrote: 'The reason why liberalism and liberal institutions like the DP are the subject of sustained attack is simply that our worldview denies the centrality of race. We see the real issue an emerging democracy has to face up to is an understanding that the quality of a person's life will approximately reflect the quality of efforts you put into it.'

I no doubt compounded the felony of colour-blindness by quoting an African-American scholar, Shelby Steele, of an even more conservative inclination than my own, who described 'race-holding', of which Yengeni and company were prime exemplars, as 'a form of justification of a person's fears, weaknesses and inadequacies. The race-holder complains indiscriminately – he is a victim and he is thus not responsible for his condition, and by claiming a victim's status, the race-holder gives up a sense of personal responsibility to better his condition.'[61]

Qwelane responded by labelling the DP as 'pathetic reactionaries'. He said: '[The] reason [is] that the DP and certain sections of the liberal white community were guilty of some serious charges, to wit, self-serving hypocrisy, false morality and convoluted sophistry.' He added gratuitously that 'liberalism in South Africa, like Christianity, was very poor in its choice of representatives.'[62]

While the second-string race-warriors were beating the tom-toms with increasing vehemence, it was Mbeki who gave his state-sanctioned imprimatur to the approach. Again it was the debate around Mbeki's budget vote as deputy president (this time in June 1997) that provided the occasion. The background was the report of the auditor-general, Henry Kluver, for the 1995-1996 financial year in which he noted that as a consequence of the rapid deskilling of the public service and affirmative action, 'the quality of financial management and administration in many institutions has deteriorated ... caused by a shortage of staff with the necessary experience and skills.'[63] This naturally was political manna from heaven for the opposition, and we focused on the consequences and shortcomings of such an approach. When Mbeki came to the podium he gave early notice of how he would short-circuit any such criticisms. However, since he delivered his speech in his typical dead-pan manner, redolent of a suburban bank manager, the initial impact of his remarks was not quite as devastating as intended. This is what he said:

'During our debates in this House, the issue of affirmative action arises repeatedly. As with other matters on which we all assume there is a national consensus, comments on this issue are normally prefaced with professions of support for the objective of creating a non-racial society and understanding for the need to employ affirmative action as one of the means to pursue this objective. Argument then follows, which effectively seeks to rule out such affirmative action, in the name of non-racialism, buttressed by further arguments about experience and efficiency.

'For example, assertions have been made about the declining financial management standards in government, which is attributed to inefficient blacks, who it is said occupy their positions by virtue of misplaced affirmative action policies. In reality we are not far from the day when the diplomatic language will slip and a point will be made openly, that "the Bantus are not yet ready to govern".'[64]

Deconstructing that speech, it became very clear that, in the words of a close political observer, 'Mbeki was determined to prevent any real or far-ranging discussion on the merits of the question by simply implying that the critics of the process were motivated by racial prejudice.'[65]

In my response I decided to quote Moeletsi Mbeki, the deputy president's brother and an increasingly strident critic of Thabo's policies: '[Shoving] shares into the hands of black businessmen to be used for their own benefit is not what black empowerment is about ... [Nor] do black conglomerates promote great competitiveness within the private sector which is what is required for entrepreneurship to flourish.'

I reminded Mbeki that in his first budget address (in 1994) he had made bold to say that good opposition meant 'the need for openness and candour, the need for good and robust debate, and the need to accept the *bona fides* of government's interlocutors.' Now, a mere two years later, he was clearly turning his back on this commendable approach: '[On] every major occasion when legitimate opposition has been raised, it has generally been met with the spectre of race and race-baiting in response. I have a list here of no less than 17 major issues – ranging from *Sarafina 2*, to universities, to labour, to legal immigrants, to youth commissions, to sport, to finance ... [When] legitimate questions ranging from corruption to the squandering of public resources are aired, the ANC has invariably begun with a reference to the pigmentation of the accuser or some implied racial prejudice utterly irrelevant to the merits of the issue.'[66]

It was becoming clear at this early period that the sort of exceptionalism which South Africa had proclaimed for itself in terms of reconciliation was to be more mythology than reality. Certain commentators were later to comprehend the first term of the ANC government as a 'pause for breath' to stabilise its position in power and to move on to capture the commanding and lesser heights of both the state and the whole of society. There was a flurry of legislative activity to give bricks and mortar to the approach which Mbeki had indicated was neither to be criticised nor slowed. And then there was Mafikeng.

9

By the time the ANC met in Mafikeng in December 1997 for its watershed 50th National Conference, the legislative process for the reracialisation of South Africa was all but in place. However, there apparently existed a consensus of party opinion that white South Africans needed a wake-up call, and that 'Mandela was the man to deliver it.'[67]

SABC–TV thoughtfully arranged for its viewers to watch Mandela's address to the conference live. I began observing proceedings early on the morning of 16 December before wending my way to a wedding. When I returned home from the happy nuptials and a splendid lunch, I was amazed to see Mandela still on the platform delivering his speech. It was a marathon four-hour address, interrupted by a meal break. Mafikeng was not simply to be a changing of the guard between Mandela and Mbeki – the latter elected unopposed as ANC president and therefore the man who would incontestably become the next national president after the general election 18 months hence. It was also to set the seal and draw together all the strands of the race agenda which had by then become the predominant feature of our public and political life.

By the time of its conference the ANC was unquestionably in control of South Africa. The largest opposition grouping, the NP, was in the process of rapid disintegration. Little had come of the much-threatened right-wing revolt or rebellion against the new government's rule; and despite occasional squeals the government enjoyed wide support from previous opposition bastions such as the English-speaking press and the universities.

Mandela's address was in its own fashion unprecedented and revealing. Gone was the gentle, national conciliator and the emblem of South Africa's rainbow aspirations. Apparently Mbeki wrote the speech – or was much involved in its drafting. It was clearly good politics from an internal point of view to infer that the Mbeki age of transformation had the blessing of Mandela, and the president certainly lived up to this requirement. He gave clear notice that the heights which the ANC commanded across politics and much of civil society were insufficient for the party's appetite.

Yet since the ANC held such a predominant position, he nonetheless had to conjure up some ghosts and phantasms to make it clear that the organisation, far from being secure, was in fact under some kind of threat. He turned his attack bare-fistedly on the opposition, claiming somewhat risibly that the 'NP had not abandoned its strategic objective of the total destruction of our organisational movement … and is involved in a desperate attempt to find ways and means to destroy its historic enemy [the ANC].'[68]

Of course, I was not unduly sympathetic to his enemy, which was also my own. But I was staggered when he went on to accuse the DP of 'engaging in a desperate struggle with the NP to convince the white minority that they are the most reliable defenders of white privilege.' Nor did 'the bulk of the mass media' – as Mandela chose to characterise what I actually regarded as a fawning press – escape his wrath. Their crime? Setting themselves up, in Mandela's words, 'as a force opposed to the ANC ... to campaign against real change and the real agents of change as represented by our movement.'

While Mandela's speech caused some concern and grabbed the headlines, it was immediately discounted by many as simply addressing an internal audience, placating some of the wilder ANC elements to accept the endorsement of the macro-economic approach embodied in the GEAR document. This immediately led ANC-inclined sympathisers to play down the rhetoric as being of less importance than the economic substance. But those who assumed that the surrender of socialism meant the abandonment of the party's national revolutionary agenda were mistaken. As James Myburgh pointed out in his careful analysis of Mafikeng, 'the ANC simply sought a racial rather than a socialist transformation of South Africa.'[69]

The resolutions flying out of the conference included a demand for even more rapid affirmative action focused primarily on Africans, and called for the South African National Defence Force and the Police Service to be made even more demographically representative.

The Mafikeng conclave followed on a seminal decision which occurred some six weeks before. At a Tripartite Alliance summit in October the movement outlined a plan to capture the state in its entirety. A key document – 'The State, Property Relations and Social Transformation' – explicitly rejected the idea that the state should be 'a neutral non-partisan entity'. It endorsed the notion that the state was 'an instrument in the hands of the liberation movement'. It also affirmed and embraced the Leninist notion of crushing the old order 'to extend the power of the national liberation movement over all levers of power: the army, the police, the bureaucracy, intelligence structures, the judiciary, parastatals, and agencies such as regulatory bodies, the public broadcaster, the central bank and so on.'[70]

By November 1998 the ANC National Working Committee established a National Deployment Committee, headed by Jacob Zuma, and adopted a strategy for the employment of ANC cadres in all areas of government and society which 'the movement regarded as crucial for the transformation of the project.' Now only the Police remained outside the control of the party in the sense that its head, the commissioner, was not yet a party faithful. This was to change in October 1999 when Jackie Selebi, a former ANC MP and diplomat, was made commissioner with no police background.

The non-racial prospectus of the Freedom Charter that 'South Africa belongs to all who live in it, black and white' was no longer sufficient for the ANC: proportion of population was what really mattered – along with ANC party membership.

I still held the view that Mandela himself, although undoubtedly responsible for events at the conference and for the speech he delivered at it, should be judged for the many things he had got right. Therefore, when it came to the State of the Nation debate in parliament following on Mafikeng on 10 February 1998, I tried to square the circle between Mandela's decency and his stance at Mafikeng. I said: 'His moral stature may not be in doubt but his political judgment may well be. To stamp us [the DP] as part of some dire conspiratorial web hellbent on destabilising the new order in South Africa, beggars the imagination … [The] depiction of opponents of the ANC as racist enemies of transformation determined to sabotage our fragile democratic order is a sinister attempt to stifle dissent and distort debate. This, Mr President, is a journey down a populist blind alley … You do not build democracy upon the delegitimisation of your opponents; you do not cement freedoms by excoriating the media; you do not bind the wounds of our suffering nation with a populist band-aid.'[71]

Parliamentary rhetoric was one thing, but the DP needed to document when the Rainbow Nation succumbed to something darker. We launched one of our most controversial pamphlets as a response to the post-Mafikeng situation, entitling it:[72] 'The Death of the Rainbow Nation: Unmasking the ANC's Programme of Reracialisation'. Our 75-page document, authored by James Myburgh, sought to explain how the ANC had moved in three years from a vision of South Africa as a society – in Mandela's words – 'inspiringly united around the commitment to a common future'[73] to one of racial division.

The policy malaise was located in the misconception that the advancement of blacks and minorities was mutually exclusive, and opportunities finite. Government white papers and affirmative action policies assumed that demographic representivity was synchronous with equality. Yet affirmative action did very little to improve the lot of the poorest. Indeed, race-based affirmative action was the flip side of race discrimination: for everyone being discriminated against, someone else was being affirmed.

The document was highly contested within the party (a parliamentary colleague referred to it as 'the death document'); and in it we drew attention to the fact that racial bean-counting had become so pervasive in government departments that massive numbers of crucial posts were left vacant when only white appointees qualified to apply for them. The same government departments were simply re-engaging as expensive consultants those who left with golden handshakes.

One ANC politician, Firoz Cachalia, called our report 'a crude apology for apartheid'.[74] The DP's attempts to draw attention to the shortcomings of racial transformation 'amounted ... to a demand that nothing be done to fully address the imbalances which existed.' Much could be done, and we could point to various policies involving skills training, opportunity vouchers, and the like; but as I indicated in a response to Cachalia: 'Race makes good politics but it too often leads to bad policies because it provides the policymakers with an excuse to avoid the really difficult problems.'[75]

The transformation agenda under Mbeki gained ascendancy – one reason being that it met an internal ANC need. The Alliance was fairly fractured, particularly over economic policies. Having less and less in common with its partners, the ANC turned to the pursuit of imaginary enemies – such as the DP – and the recalibration of race to restore urgency and purpose in reuniting the governing Alliance. I also reflected at the time of Mandela's 80th birthday party celebrations on 19 July, that while in the following year's elections Mbeki would notionally be opposing a range of parties from Left to Right, in reality he would be running against the immense popularity of Nelson Mandela.

Generally – with the gaping exception of Mafikeng – Mandela transcended the narrow partisan and racial divisions of South Africa; but Mbeki tended to reinforce them. My forebodings would be proven startlingly correct and in more ways than I could ever have imagined.

However, it was not always clear in the 1994-1999 period that I and my party would in fact remain in opposition, and indeed, what form that opposition was to take. This leads me to a significant and related event: the offer of a cabinet post from Mandela in his government, and change and fluctuations in the fortunes of South Africa's opposition parties.

Motorists driving home in Cape Town on 23 January 1997 must have been surprised to see the *Argus* billboards proclaiming: 'Tony Leon for the Cabinet?' Not, however, as surprised as I had been a week before the speculation entered the public realm.

My enjoyment of the prospect of a *tête-à-tête* with Mandela – requested by him through his secretary, Mary – had been offset to an extent by her insistence that I present myself at his Houghton home for breakfast at 6 am. Early rising was an ingrained habit of Mandela (who usually tried to retire at 9 pm), but my body clock worked in the opposite direction.

However, a presidential summons required punctuality, and after making my way through a thicket of security personnel I found the president on his doorstep, needlessly apologetic for the early morning scheduling necessitated by the fact that he was to depart at 7.30 am for an ANC *lekgotla*.

We sat down to a breakfast far more sumptuous – fruit, porridge, eggs, fish and coffee – than my constitution could allow me to enjoy fully at that early hour. Towards the end of the meal Mandela dropped a thunderbolt: 'Would you consider joining me in the cabinet and helping to strengthen governance?' I was blindsided; and could think of no appropriate response, except to thank him and ask for time to consider the implications.

I did have the presence of mind to use an item currently in the news as an indicator of how Mandela and the government were dealing with a controversial issue, and whether any putative DP presence in the cabinet could be remotely compatible with an opposition perspective. South Africa was set to sell R3-billion of tank-firing systems to Syria. The cabinet committee charged with ensuring we did not export ordnance to rights-delinquent regimes or high-conflict areas was chaired by Kader Asmal. Had his attention been elsewhere? The ruthless Baathist regime of President Hafez al Assad, and the potential abyss of Middle East conflict, should have immediately spiked the suggestion.

Mandela became extremely agitated; he told me the matter was far from concluded, but that he was 'infuriated' by America's reported response to the deal. He then launched 'the struggle defence' – he said he and the ANC looked at the world as divided between countries that fought against apartheid ('which was criminal and lacked any respect for human rights') and those which supported it. Hence, Syria was pro-ANC and America pro-apartheid. I countered by pointing out that for at least the last two decades of apartheid, most of the West prohibited arms sales to South Africa – and whatever role Syria played in support of the ANC at the time, I thought it ill-behoved our country to embrace and arm its regime.[76] Our breakfast time ran out.

I set in process a series of discussions with trusted colleagues as to whether, in principle, we should explore the matter further. I was equally determined not to leak any suggestion or hint of the offer to the media, realising that apart from the gross discourtesy to Mandela which this would involve, the feeding-frenzy of speculation would impair a proper and sober evaluation. However, 'a source in the Presidency' (for which Mandela apologised, by phone, on the evening of our early morning meeting) was not as restrained. Within a day or two it was all the stuff of headlines.

My only public comment was diplomatic: 'It would have been churlish not to have taken into account Mandela's hand of friendship,' I told the *Sowetan*.[77] They informed their readers that the 'DP's participation in the GNU seems a foregone conclusion.'

However, Mandela was not our only political suitor. The day before my dawn meeting, the leader of the opposition – which he had become after his exit from the GNU – FW de Klerk called me. The NP was also seeking our hand, and four days hence he would be announcing a 'new initiative' possibly leading to a new party contesting the next election. He was sure, he added, that the DP, IFP and NP held enough 'common values' to enthuse millions of voters who currently supported parties more for reasons of history than of current reality. He requested me 'not to shoot down the idea'. I gave him the assurance he sought.

The Mandela offer was generally welcomed by the party; De Klerk's new initiative was not. I also sought an early meeting with Buthelezi – who seemed, after three years, to have adroitly straddled the conflicting demands of government and opposition. Also into play came the minuscule PAC and its diminutive new leader, former bishop Stanley Mogoba, a person of great warmth and naïveté, to whom Mandela's offer had also been extended. Buthelezi told me (and Douglas Gibson and Roger Burrows) in late January that should the PAC accept Mandela's offer, and we reject it, prospects of racial polarisation would increase, with three essentially black parties in government arraigned against mostly white parties outside. He said the DP joining would be 'a good thing'.

I also met Mogoba, who struck me as sincere and engaging, belying the radical, fire-eating reputation of his party. He was of a mind to accept the offer.

Amid public speculation and private soundings I oscillated: was it a golden chance or a poisoned chalice? In the midst of my uncertainty, I bumped into senior Anglo executive Les Boyd and sought his counsel. 'Following your gut instinct is always the best way to resolve a finely balanced question,' he wisely advised. 'But, Les,' I responded, 'the problem is that my gut keeps changing on this matter.' 'In that case, follow your first one.' Useful: but all I could remember was deep ambivalence.

Harry Oppenheimer and Bobby Godsell believed we should 'give it a go'. However, bumping into Van Zyl Slabbert at a cricket match, he urged me to stay out. Helen Suzman did not wait for me to contact her, and warned me, via the press, that 'it would be a big mistake' and one 'sorely disappointing to hardcore DP supporters'.[78] But Suzman was not the only person going public on the issue. An 'unnamed government source' quoted by the *Mercury* informed its readers (and me) that I would be offered the post of Minister of Public Enterprises.[79] Here, I thought, would be the rock on which my party and government would wreck our incipient relationship. An ardent privatisation zealot sent into a department of statist officials? A poacher turned gamekeeper indeed.

My unease hardened when I reread Mandela's 8 January statement on his party's expanded and expansive view on the role of 'the cadre': these appropriately Leninist figures were to be deployed everywhere: 'In places of residence, in schools, places of worship, in the workplace, on the sports fields, in government, in the legislatures.' They should be neither 'political' nor ANC simply 'after hours'.[80] I envisaged myself as a minister atop a department stuffed full of ANC apparatchiks, answerable and unswervingly loyal to the party of which I was most decidedly not a member.

Still, I was sincere when I told the *Citizen* that 'an offer to join a government has to be taken very seriously. It's not something I would dismiss out of hand, but it's not something I would accept without qualification and very serious thought.'[81]

While my office was negotiating a time to obtain some specificity around his proposal, I received a call from a casualty of De Klerk's previous government, the former Health minister, Dr Rina Venter. Venter, who would soon join the DP, warned me that the biggest mistake De Klerk had made – and doomed his ill-starred role in the GNU – was his inability, at any stage, to pin down Mandela as to the precise ground rules for minority parties in the coalition government. The essence of the issue was to obtain, explicitly, a manner enabling the DP to publicly distance itself from policies agreed to in cabinet from which it fundamentally dissented. If De Klerk, with six colleagues to back him up and whose membership of Mandela's government was mandated by the Constitution, could not achieve such an agreement, how could I succeed where he had failed?

During the annual State of the Nation debate in mid-February I told parliament what I really thought: 'South Africa is governed by an administration with a clashing agenda of competing and contradictory priorities; a ship of state which sails without a moral compass and a government of hindsight, not foresight. The ANC reminds me of priests who have kept their faith but lost their religion … I see a revolutionary movement, which stood for perhaps the greatest universal good in the second half of the 20th century – the eradication of racism and the elimination of apartheid – now practising so many instances of new racism.'[82]

Such admonitions did not seem to trouble the ANC. Indeed, one of its more thoughtful members, Willie Hofmeyr, soon to exit parliament, wrote perceptively: 'A decision by the DP to join the GNU will bring little direct benefit to the ANC, but is primarily based on the interests of the country.'[83]

I finally met once more with Mandela in Pretoria towards the end of February, literally two days before the DP's Federal Council was to meet in Durban. Mandela pointed out that there were often vehement disagreements in cabinet, and members were free to express their viewpoint. 'But what if we wish to go public with our dissent?' I asked the president. His immediate answer sealed the matter for me: 'We must go out and face the world with one voice, just as Mugabe and Nkomo do.'[84]

The DP Federal Council accepted my advice that it would be impossible, on the basis outlined by Mandela, for the party to participate in government and maintain any role as an opposition. I had also gained the impression – although he never said so – that Mandela was relieved when I indicated that I thought the ANC would find it difficult to accept the proposal. It may well have been that significant elements in his own circle jibbed at the idea of one Tony Leon becoming a cabinet minister.

I thanked the president for his 'generosity of spirit and his nation-building efforts of which this move was evidence.' *Die Burger* praised our decision for 'striking a blow for democracy'.[85] However, writing in the *Pretoria News,* the normally cautious commentator and veteran radio journalist Chris Gibbons let rip at us: 'The decision [by the DP] to remain in opposition will see the party permanently sidelined; with support slowly ebbing away until it vanishes into a richly deserved obscurity.'[86]

Fortunately, events were to prove his prediction almost entirely wrong.

10

The first half-decade of democratic governance was inextricably linked to the decline of the once mighty National Party. Having failed to entrench power-sharing in the final Constitution – which the Nats half-heartedly affirmed in parliament on 8 May 1996 – De Klerk immediately withdrew his party from the GNU and became 'Leader of the Opposition'. I was fairly scathing in my assessment of this move, telling the *Star*: 'It's politically expedient, churlish and a complete negation of the NP's insistence that power-sharing was critically important to the stabilisation of South Africa.'

I noted that De Klerk's caucus had been deeply divided in its support for the new Constitution, and his precipitate move out of government was a 'temporary dressing on the wounds that divide [the NP]'. I made bold to predict that the NP had 'failed as a government, and by its own admission had been of no consequence as a junior partner in the GNU, and would do no better as an opposition.'[87]

Behind my rather sharp put-down was a deep anxiety whereby I felt that our hitherto high-profile role as parliament's watchdog could be eclipsed by the arrival of the much larger NP (with more than tenfold the number of MPs we had at the time) with far greater firepower and the not inconsiderable charisma of De Klerk to lead it.

Shortly before De Klerk's move, the *Sunday Tribune*'s John Maclennan published another huge op-ed piece about the DP's role and performance which described, in somewhat extravagant but pleasing terms, the distinctive niche which our small parliamentary presence had achieved at this time.[88] In exultant prose he wrote: 'If there was no DP someone would have to invent it. There is a need for it and that is proved every week in parliament. It seems to have the only clear policies and it has a genuine set of tested principles. This enables it to say what it means and mean what it says. It does so often and with great effect. This is why there is always a chorus of jeers when DP leader Tony Leon gets to his feet. His audience has no other way of deflecting his uncomfortable truths. The DP may have only seven MPs out of 400, but the lean team plays a role far out of proportion to its number.'

I felt confident that over time we would start to win over new ground with the electorate. Indeed, I had underestimated (as no doubt did De Klerk) the dire effect on his party's morale and personnel when he removed its oxygen of ministerial patronage. His key senior lieutenants scattered: Pik Botha (who intensely disliked De Klerk) to a grumpy and far-from-quiet retirement; Dawie de Villiers to a grace-and-favour job in world tourism; Leon Wessels to a perch at the Human Rights Commission; Deputy Speaker Bhadra Ranchod to a foreign ambassadorship. De Klerk's key young Turk Chris Fismer used his high office as a minister in charge of gambling legislation as a revolving door to head up the Gaming Board. And so on.

Of those who remained there was a fierce internecine struggle between Roelf Meyer, whom De Klerk had appointed party secretary-general, and who wished to wrench the party from its ancient anti-ANC moorings, and Marthinus van Schalkwyk – rising up the ladder, positioning himself as the champion of fierce opposition.

However, De Klerk and the NP's future prospects were not undermined so much by internal dissent and the flight of defrocked cabinet ministers as by the public exposure of its misdeeds and misanthropic governance which the Truth and Reconciliation Commission (TRC) highlighted in gruesome – although often unverified and highly contested – detail from its first sitting in April 1996 over the next two years.

Established by the Promotion of National Unity and Reconciliation Act 30 of 1995, the Truth Commission had three key purposes:

- to obtain and ventilate testimony from victims and gather information about human rights violations in South Africa between 1 March 1966 and 5 December 1993;
- to consider applications for amnesty from prosecution for those perpetrators of human rights abuses and atrocities (dealt with by a variety of specialist amnesty committees, each headed by a judge); and
- to provide recommendations to government on a system of reparations for victims.

Allister Sparks wrote approvingly about the TRC's work and accomplishments, noting that it 'became a series of travelling confessionals' that investigated 31 000 cases in three years, presenting President Mandela with an interim report in October 1998 of over a million words. However, while TRC head, Archbishop Desmond Tutu, had a universal respect and commanded national credibility, second probably only to Mandela's, not every section or leader of South Africa's communities was a signed-up fan of him or of the TRC. Almost from the outset, the composition of the Commission (weighted hugely in favour of the ANC), its terms of reference, and its *modus operandi* were hugely contested. In one of several parliamentary debates on its genesis, IFP firebrand MP Albert Mncwango dismissed both Tutu and the TRC in an unforgettable (and, to many, unpardonable) slap-down as 'a sensationalist circus presided over by a weeping clown'.[89]

The TRC – and reactions to it – cast most of the major political players in a poor light.[90] Thabo Mbeki argued that different standards of justice had to be applied to the ANC and the apartheid government: one side had been morally right, the other morally wrong. He was backed up by a bevy of radical intellectuals, such as Robert Suresh Roberts and Mahmoud Mamdani, who wanted the TRC to go further in blaming and punishing whites in general. Mbeki was also supported by the ANC's ideological prejudices – its 'penchant for self-exoneration' in Martin Meredith's words.[91]

The ANC resisted the TRC despite the fact that the hearings and their conclusions were fairly biased in their favour. Survivors of the ANC's detention camps, for example, were often prevented from telling their full stories when TRC commissioners turned off their microphones, saying their time had expired. Those who spoke out about the party's grim secrets were disciplined and ostracised. The list of those directly involved or who knew about the human rights abuses but did nothing to stop them included many past and present senior leaders of the ANC, including current and former cabinet ministers.

The ANC's moral high ground was held by virtue not of its own conduct but of the odious nature of the regime it opposed. Some in the movement's armed wing used violence in a limited way, and were careful to avoid injuring the innocent. Others were merely sadistic thugs who killed for very different reasons other than bringing about democracy. The ANC killed far more black people than white people in the name of overthrowing the white regime. Even as apartheid began to reform, and it became clear that non-violence was again an option, the ANC accelerated its armed struggle. The TRC failed to scrutinise this period properly; it failed to examine the ruthless resort to violence that occurred in the trade union movement, for example.

When the final report came out, the ANC was not satisfied that the TRC had read history in its favour; it wanted references to its sins expunged. Mbeki even tried, via a court challenge, to stop publication of the TRC's interim report. He failed.

In response to Mbeki's challenge, Tutu threatened to resign: 'If parties are able to grant themselves amnesty, what is the point of having a Truth Commission?' he asked.[92] More alarming was the ANC's attempt to use its political leverage to force the TRC to rewrite its final report. Mbeki continued to maintain that the TRC had been 'wrong and misguided' despite Mandela's endorsement of its findings.[93]

What Mbeki could not achieve in court, he attempted to do once he assumed office. In 2002, he pardoned 33 convicts who had been denied amnesty by the TRC for their crimes, including several Pan-Africanist Congress and Azanian People's Liberation Army members.

Whatever unhappiness the leadership of the ANC and IFP displayed towards the TRC, they both ran a very distant second to the harsh gaze of the Commission's focus on De Klerk and the NP. In part, this was due – as De Klerk was later to complain bitterly – to the bias in the TRC and to serious lapses in its procedural conduct and evaluation of evidence. But, overwhelmingly, the weight of information and the nature and conduct of the apartheid government placed the burden of opprobrium on De Klerk's head – as the extant NP leader and as a serving cabinet minister during the apotheosis of apartheid.

The NP's security state was put on public display: from the grotesque and ghoulish detail of its killing machine presided over by the head of the Vlakplaas special defence unit, Dirk Coetzee, to aspects of chemical warfare, right through to the murder of Steve Biko and the Cradock Four. TRC deputy chairman, Alex Boraine, with some feeling, described the revelations as 'a huge sewer spilling out its filth and stench'.[94] It was all broadcast live on radio and TV, daily, and probably did more then anything else to undermine the claims of the NP to a permanent and rejuvenated place in the new South Africa.

Former president PW Botha, on whose watch most of the abuses and violations occurred, simply refused to obey a subpoena calling him to testify. De Klerk, however, appeared three times. Many in his circle and some outside it, such as a prominent Afrikaans-speaking editor, approached me and stated that the TRC was nothing more than a 'witch-hunt', determined to railroad the Afrikaans minority as a whole (and not simply its political leadership) into a position of permanent moral inferiority.

Meredith viewed De Klerk's performance as distinctly unimpressive: '[He] turned out to be a petty politician, concerned only with trying to absolve himself from personal blame ... blaming "rogue elements" for taking "unauthorised action" and "lower ranks" for "misinterpreting" government policy.'

This damning conclusion flowed from De Klerk's second appearance at the TRC on 14 May 1997. He apologised 'once and for all' for apartheid and 'the hurt caused by his policies' but reaffirmed his assertion that murder and torture never formed part of government policy – although he was careful to qualify this by referencing it to his period at the helm from 1989 onward.

The TRC never did exhaustively complete its investigations into the abuses of the apartheid regime, leaving victims feeling unfulfilled and suspicions hanging in the air. Much was still unknown about the operation of the state security apparatus, and those who directed it. In addition, while many former apartheid operatives were denied amnesty, relatively few actually came forward at all. The TRC's final report castigated De Klerk for failing to deal with the 'third force' blamed for much of the political violence of the early 1990s, and accused him of not making a full disclosure.[95]

The 'bad apples' whom De Klerk had denounced and distanced from his party felt deeply aggrieved and abandoned: after all, as an editor of a waveringly NP-supporting newspaper confided in me at the time: '[Those] *vuilgoed* [rubbish] of the security forces were bad, but they allowed the NP leadership to sleep at night. You don't leave your wounded on the field of battle. You pick them up.' It was indeed striking how, in comparison, the ANC leadership tried to protect their own operatives, even the worst of them.[96]

But before the TRC was to complete its first report, in October 1998, De Klerk was felled by a blow from within: his presumptive crown prince and key constitutional negotiator, Roelf Meyer, upped sticks and resigned from the party he had unsuccessfully attempted to reform and reposition. Meyer's move, which he declared with much fanfare on 17 May 1997, came at a useful and happy moment for my party.

Two months before, the DP snatched an unexpected victory from the NP in a municipal by-election – Kempton Park, the East Rand suburb where Meyer had starred in the Codesa negotiations just three-and-a-half years earlier. In the previous (1995) municipal election we obtained barely a third of the vote; now we notched up 76% of the total. What made the victory improbable was the identity of our candidate: Mike Waters, a highly effective and courageous local councillor (who made it onto the council previously as a proportional list councillor) was English-speaking and gay – and now represented a blue-collar, predominantly Afrikaans ward. This swallow presaged a wonderful summer: in short order the DP then won previous NP strongholds from Witbank in Mpumalanga to Margate on the KwaZulu-Natal South Coast – in most cases quintupling our percentage votes, routing the previously impregnable NP.

The tectonic plates were shifting, at last. Ironically – shortly before Meyer opted out of the Nats and established a strangely named political entity called the 'New Movement Process' – he had led a number of NP delegations to meet the DP to explore prospects of closer intra-opposition co-operation.

This placed us in something of a quandary. Nothing irritated our current and newly available constituency more than internecine opposition squabbles. They wanted the parties to co-operate or merge the better to take on the ANC.

Yet the natural and immediate area of growth for our party lay at the expense of the NP. We clearly needed an overarching strategic roadmap; and James Selfe, no mean military strategist, and the party's CEO, arranged a meeting to determine our approach.

We met – in conditions of deep confidentiality – in the agreeable surrounds of Dave Gant's[97] majestic fruit farm 'Lourensford' outside Somerset West on the slopes of the Helderberg. The party's senior leadership was present: Hennie Bester, Ian Davidson, Peter Leon, Colin Eglin, Douglas Gibson, Eddie Trent, Mike Ellis, James Selfe and me.

In his meticulous manner and copperplate handwriting, James recorded the full discussion, just one sentence of which was to inform our approach for the following three years: 'The DP's strategic objective is the destruction of the NP as an institution.' As he wrote down those fateful words, he said as an aside to my brother: '*Carthago delenda est*' ('Carthage must be destroyed'). Indeed, we were to take apart the once-mighty NP edifice, brick by brick, in by-election after by-election, until they appeared to surrender their name, cause and leadership to our not-so-tender mercies in the winter of 2000.

However, Meyer's defection created both opportunity and a challenge for our grand scheme. He was seen by many (including some in our support base) as the coming man in a fluid opposition scene. Within days of his announcement, we met on a Sunday evening, alone, at a rather bleak hotel in Midrand. I thought him a person of some charm and ability, but had hitherto regarded him as something of an empty suit. Still, I admired his courage in turning his back on the party to which he had dedicated his entire political life; and was also impressed that he was prepared to stalk into the financial wilderness, since his resignation from the NP entailed both the loss of a parliamentary seat and forfeiting the cabinet minister-level salary to which his post as NP secretary-general was linked.[98]

Meyer told me that he had been advised by 'many people' to 'simply join the DP'. However, while agreeing with our principles and practices, he was not seeking to simply consolidate the 'traditionally white' opposition, but wanted a wider, more racially inclusive alignment. I thought this approach admirable in theory but problematic in practice, since there were not many political movements or individuals who shared our world-view and were prepared to challenge the ANC. Meyer countered with the name of Bantu Holomisa.[99] Holomisa was on his own trajectory, although his route to our corner of the political landscape was circuitous and unconventional.

Holomisa was, of course, far from being alone in the ANC government as a one-time compradorist prop of the apartheid homeland system. The ANC was an open house for even the most inside-elite members of a now disreputable class of black apparatchiks who had helped grease the apartheid wheels. Ahead of him in this queue was Stella Sigcau.

She had served as minister of Education in Transkei, and then briefly as prime minister before Holomisa forcibly ejected her from office in December 1987. In August 1996 Holomisa went before the Truth Commission and alleged that gaming and casino tycoon Sol Kerzner had bribed the then Transkei prime minister George Matanzima to the tune of R2-million for exclusive gaming rights in his territory. That much was in the public domain. But, explosively, Holomisa now disclosed that Stella Sigcau had also received a cut (in the rather measly amount, I thought, of R50 000) and that Kerzner had 'donated' a further R2m to the ANC for the 1994 election.

Holomisa claimed: 'As a loyal ANC member I want to resist the inference that the price that our organisation had to pay in return for financial assistance was that in the event our organisation became the majority party in government – as it indeed is now – Sol Kerzner would not be prosecuted.'[100] Kerzner never was prosecuted.

This revelation was deeply embarrassing to the ANC. Sigcau was apparently well regarded by the ANC hierarchy, so Holomisa was drummed out of the ANC in September 1996; and by the time of my meeting with Meyer was well on his way to starting yet another opposition movement christened the 'National Consultative Forum'.

Meyer and Holomisa eventually launched a new party, the United Democratic Movement (UDM), in September 1997 with Holomisa as president and Meyer as his deputy. As I gleaned, they were preoccupied with their positioning and far less concerned with either principles or policy: indeed they seemed to inhabit a virtually ideology-free political zone. However, Holomisa's incontestable blackness and sometime ANC credentials impressed some in the media and a scattering of businessmen.

Meyer's immediate effect on the NP was to increase the haemorrhaging from its ranks. These defections, our by-election successes, and the moral artillery of the TRC clearly affected De Klerk. No doubt wishing to be remembered – at home and abroad – for the things he had got right on 2 February 1990, his last great and unexpected surprise came when he quit his post as leader of the opposition and the NP in late August 1997.

I told the media – correctly as it has transpired – that 'he will be much better judged by history than he is now.'[101]

De Klerk played an instrumental role in ensuring that his hand-picked successor, Marthinus van Schalkwyk, succeeded him. Events would reveal that any prospect of this seeming political ingénue shaking off the NP's crisis of credibility was misplaced. Van Schalkwyk was in fact a political knife-artist when it came to the dark arts of party infighting and his own preferment. Of course, as his nickname 'Kortbroek' ('Short pants') revealed, his boyish appearance gave him a resemblance to a bespectacled and puffy-cheeked cross between a boy scout and Billy Bunter; a man with scant presence.

Van Schalkwyk, relying on a relationship stretching back to his arrival in parliament in 1990, immediately put out feelers to me; I listened and responded appropriately, but while we could talk, there would be no deals at this stage. *Carthago delenda est.*

The DP Federal Congress convened in the newly Democratic territory of Kempton Park. The party that *Business Day* had in a 1995 editorial[102] written off as 'a desolate shack' had reconstructed itself into something larger and more durable. I needed to address the issue of opposition co-operation and realignment – and told the delegates we should seek a 'Codesa of the Opposition', which provided a nice headline for the *Sunday Times*;[103] but I believed in a more rational approach to opposition-building against the ANC: 'If it emerges from such a Codesa of the Opposition that we all agree on fundamental principles, then this could lead to a merger of parties. [There] is no other party with whom we share an identical set of principles, but in the absence of a full-scale merger, partnerships and co-operative agreements are quite possible. Our overriding duty to South Africa is to prevent ANC dominance.'

My positioning of the party at the centre of an anti-ANC alignment passed without demur, while my organisational reforms scrapping the party's national list as a basis for electing MPs, and substituting provincial lists for the same purpose, were also nodded through. This diminished the disproportionate preferment Western Cape MPs had enjoyed despite the fact that the party got far more votes from Gauteng; henceforth MPs would be drawn from the provinces where the votes were obtained. However, my desire to allow the party leadership greater and (I thought) much-needed control over the finalisation of the preferential placements on the party's electoral lists was resisted – and this was eventually achieved only in 2004. Nevertheless, the congress firmly placed me as the leader of a clearly revived political animal in a much strengthened position.

The one party which I did think we could co-operate with at some future stage was Buthelezi's IFP. I kept the channels open to him. After our next formal (IFP-DP) meeting the following May, Buthelezi told the media: 'Of all the parties in parliament, we are the closest to the DP on a number of issues.'[104]

II

The Western Cape DP was possibly the most liberal – and anti-NP – bastion in the party. A peculiar twist of fate was that it should now provide what was to prove a template for closer union with the former enemy.

The NP's Hernus Kriel presided there as premier and was casting around for a new partner to shore up his administration. Kriel, who combined the survivalist talents of a political street fighter and a Lyndon Johnson-like cunning for sizing up an opponent's weakness, quickly discerned that the DP provincial leader, Hennie Bester, would be amenable to a post in government. Kriel's instinct was entirely correct. Bester's slight frame encased outsize ambition. Over time I had warmed to Bester since becoming leader. His personal ambition was matched by a considerable intelligence and a sharp intellect. He and I also read the Western Cape tea leaves in the same way: the NP's shrinking national base would erode its position in the province, but it was likely still to emerge after the next election as the largest party, in the context, however, of a hung legislature. The DP could be the kingmaker in this scenario, able to throw its support behind either the NP or ANC, and thus be the lynchpin in a new coalition.

Bester wholeheartedly agreed with our emerging strategy that we should create an opposition-led government, and not simply cede more power to the ANC. He indicated that his early accession into Kriel's cabinet would convert the current breeze into a headwind for such a future reality. In due course, he requested my presence at a meeting with Kriel where the premier told me directly that he wished to appoint Bester to his cabinet, preferably before the year's end.

However, having a few months before rejected Mandela's proffered cabinet post because of the muzzle it would have placed on our opposition voice, I was insistent that we obtain a written agreement which would explicitly not bind the DP to cabinet co-responsibility for decisions with which it disagreed. To my surprise, Kriel readily assented to this requirement. On 11 December 1997, Bester was appointed as the provincial minister of Trade and Industry and Tourism.

Our accession to the Western Cape government actually attracted less hostility and national attention than the more spectacular news which followed shortly from the Eastern Cape: a former stalwart of De Klerk's cabinet, Dr Tertius Delport, had joined the DP.

Delport, post-1994, had served as NP provincial leader in Bhisho and in the provincial government there until 1996; now he was caught up in a process of serious disillusionment with his party. He had been subsequently ousted as provincial chief, and I was surprised when DP provincial boss, Eddie Trent, asked me in December to fly to Port Elizabeth to meet our potential and most controversial new recruit.

Trent was in favour of accepting Delport, and indicated he would raise funds to ensure the party could pay Delport a monthly retainer (for agreed work) as compensation for the loss of income Delport would suffer consequent to his proposed defection. He would be obliged by the anti-defection clause as it then stood to forfeit his seat in the legislature. But Trent's ardour was not to last: he and his strong-willed wife Elizabeth were shortly to fall out with Delport, and I was to spend time trying to mediate and patch their quarrels.

I had spent much of the preceding year trying to make the party more accommodating towards Afrikaans-speakers. Although we had some very high-profile Afrikaners in our senior ranks (Hennie Bester, Dene Smuts and Wessel Nel among their number), they tended to be pre-eminently liberal rather than emblematic of their communities. It was noteworthy that each had been first elected from overwhelmingly English-speaking constituencies; and this was, I discovered, not simply political. The party and its forebears had little attraction for generally conservative Afrikaans-speakers. There was also an effete snobbery and a degree of cultural imperialism in certain senior ranks; I was sensitive to its presence, and happy to make common cause against it: I think I managed, in poor Afrikaans, to communicate my sincerity.

Delport – a Broederbonder and NP heavyweight – was cut from a very different cloth than, for example, Smuts or Nel. It was also his perceived reputation as a conservative, antagonistic to the more liberalising Roelf Meyer, that I knew would raise some red (or true-blue) flags. However, I viewed Delport as a potential signal to an increasingly untethered NP base that it was safe to cross the waters, poisoned as they had been by a history of enmity and mutual suspicion dating back to the Anglo-Boer War of 1899.

I was receiving a blizzard of invitations to address Afrikaans organisations. They were demoralised by the TRC; they felt duped by De Klerk's exit from politics; and, to put it politely, they were underwhelmed by his successor. They needed a new political home.

I was satisfied that Delport had, for whatever reason, crossed his own Rubicon, and we settled the terms and the timing of his arrival in our ranks.

When the announcement was made in the middle of January 1998, it again catapulted the party into the news. Van Schalkwyk, fighting to quell ever-growing doubts about his foundering leadership, struck back by suggesting that the big fish we had landed actually belonged in other waters. He announced on the evening TV news, with the calculated malice which he hid behind his, as ever, po-faced expression: 'We expected Dr Delport to leave the NP, but thought he would join the CP. It is clear that the DP has the ability to attract certain rightist elements.'[105] However, a trickle then a stream of NP politicians and party office-bearers left the NP in all directions, mostly to the DP and Meyer's UDM.[106]

All manner of commentators eager for evidence of my alleged right-wing shift started to unsettle some in my own ranks. Some in the DP judged Delport as simply a bridge too far. They also seemed, sometimes, to accept the caricature painted by our opponents of the party as some form of reactionary redoubt. In Johannesburg in early 1998 I decided to take them on. This is part of what I said as an 'answer to the critics':[107]

'Some of our new recruits come from conservative backgrounds. I regard this as a compliment, not as cause for regret, for it proves exactly in practice the words uttered by JP Landman[108] to our Federal Executive last year – that the only worthwhile value system for South Africans, including minorities, under a new constitutional dispensation is that provided by liberal democrats. I am delighted as well that in government ranks there are whites, Coloureds and Indians in the cabinet. That is what normal politics is about. We are only interested in competence and commitment both in our party and for our country. White men are not second class citizens – they must take their chances with everyone else …

'This party stands for individual merit … [We reject] as a false antithesis that there are only two choices: one starkly "transformation at all costs" and the second equally crudely labeled "privilege", as though there were no middle way in between … It is appalling to think that in post-apartheid South Africa a political view has to be determined on the basis of bogus racial distinctions when … we need to create a coalition around values.'

Delport's arrival was grist to the mill of Ken Owen. He disliked him with a furious hatred which exceeded even his own intense dislike of me. He was soon to launch forth into a post-retirement career as a regular columnist for *Business Day*. In it he spewed forth with monotonous regularity about how I had sold out the party's liberal values, usually citing Delport's arrival as exhibit 'A'. This continued with increased vituperation for a few years, until the column rather than the columnist died. Owen lives on in Cape Town, finding, no doubt, other demons to exorcise. He announced to a journalistic colleague that his purpose had been to 'destroy Tony Leon'.

Nonetheless, our mojo appeared to work wonders with the electorate: in a dramatic week in May 1998, the DP captured three hitherto impregnable NP electoral fortresses, in Bergvliet in Cape Town, Brakpan on the East Rand, and most striking of all, a stunning 89% of the vote in

Rosettenville in the southern suburbs of Johannesburg. The week before, somewhat unwisely, the local NP MP Sheila Camerer had described the latter seat as the 'safest' NP area in South Africa.

Like a fast-fading summer tan, the initial euphoria, felt across the entire country on Mandela's inauguration in 1994, and the unexpected capturing of the Rugby World Cup by South Africa the following year, had peeled off three or four years later.

On the inside pages of the *Sunday Times*, Carol Paton, who unlike many other, lazier members of her journalistic tribe had actually visited the newly won DP areas, penned a report from our new front line. It was entitled: 'The Gatvol Vote With Their Feet'.[109] She described the scene from the polls at Rosettenville as marking a shift in both our electoral pitch and the response from our new electorate:

'The DP slogan this time was different from its usual waspish approach. "Gatvol" said the posters in Rosettenville where the DP scored an astonishing 89% victory over the NP (ten years ago it got 100 votes there) … [Bricklayers], electricians, teachers and shopkeepers were among those who for the first time voted DP. Its slogan tuned in to where they were and summed up their attitude. They were *gatvol* [fed up], and the DP was the party they hoped could do something about it.'[110]

It was not only the profound alienation felt by white voters which moved the electoral wave in our direction. The party had put in place a professional team to capitalise and capture this momentum, creating a group around me whom I could completely trust with the communication, organisation and policy production that are the necessary staples of a modern and effective political movement. These key elements had been largely absent as some of our earlier amateurish, finger-in-the-wind approaches made evident. And by early 1998 I had found in Greg Krumbock – a quietly spoken, immensely intelligent and passionately political accountant in Pietermaritzburg – someone who could take the reins as party chief executive. He applied number-crunching skills to by-elections with a breathtaking single-mindedness and accuracy that enabled us to marshal our resources on the basis of science rather than sentiment.

At around the same time, Robert Desmarais decided to leave his post as head of our parliamentary operations. The position was filled by a bright-eyed, fearsomely intelligent 24-year-old former party youth activist, Ryan Coetzee. Of all the personnel appointments I was to make or green-light in my 13-year leadership, his was the most significant. His intellect was marshalled, often with ruthless single-mindedness, to the benefit of the party. He was utterly unconcerned with the mannered etiquette some felt in approaching the party leader. Sometimes brusque, even rude, he never unsettled me – even when he occasionally stormed out of my office after a disagreement.

As Ryan set about sharpening our parliamentary operations, he became my most valued and among my most trusted counsellors. There was no danger of him ever succumbing to the fawning obsequiousness which sometimes characterises the party chief's inner circle. I admired his courage as much as I respected his clarity of thought.

Russel Crystal, whose controversial arrival into the party from the NP in 1996 I have already described, soon became deputy chief executive. With the flourish of an expert, though ill-tempered, theatre impresario he quickly set about converting the church bazaar, amateur-hour public party meetings of the past into something far more futuristic. He converted our public events into carefully choreographed, made-for-TV (where we now occasionally featured) showcases which belied the fact that we were still only, despite our by-election successes, a 1,7% party.

However, as Ryan, Greg and Russel willed a reality which was not yet objectively there, a Markinor opinion poll of the electorate's likely voting intentions in September 1998 suggested the DP was level-pegging the NP, each with about ten per cent support. With an eye to nudging the 1999 elections in the hopeful direction to which the polls pointed, our core group – which included Douglas Gibson and the ever-dependable James Selfe – set about marketing me as the next Leader of the Opposition.

To some this seemed vainglorious, but the polling seemed favourable and it was deemed appropriate to go public with me as the political equivalent of a sort of rock star-cum-evangelical preacher. When the scion of the more famous OR Tambo, Dali Tambo, held court on Sunday evening TV with a soft, celebrity-focused show ('People of the South') I was the featured guest he persuaded to sing 'My Way' to the nation. Friends and family cringed, but it appeared to work in terms of 'humanising' me.

Then in October 1998 Jonathan Ball, South Africa's leading publisher, produced a volume of my speeches and writings which we launched, accompanied by a nationwide tour, under the title *Hope and Fear: Reflections of a Democrat*. It was carefully edited by Professor David Welsh, who gave it a semblance of thematic structure. Helen Suzman wrote a generously worded introduction, signalling that the issues which had cast such a pall over our relationship were now in the past. She wrote:

'Tony and I have had our differences ... [However] I give him full credit for a splendid performance in parliament and for reinvigorating the party. The essence of liberalism is a staunch commitment to civil rights and to the rule of law, and a total opposition to racial discrimination. Tony Leon stands squarely in this great tradition.'[111]

Suzman's imprimatur was helpful with one section – the traditionalists – in our enlarging constituency. It was also immensely useful to receive the private advice and occasional speech draft from Professor RW ('Bill') Johnson, a high-octane – but controversial – intellectual who returned to South Africa from Magdalen College, Oxford, to take the reins of the Helen Suzman Foundation. The Foundation had been one of the few liberal NGOs to withstand the howling gales of political correctness. In a private communication addressed to me many years later, Johnson described the moral backsliding of those times and the sense of isolation it created for some who resisted it, but also the bonds of solidarity it engendered.[112]

He noted that I (as did he) 'had a visceral dislike of hegemonic and authoritarian behaviour.' This left him in no doubt that, whatever the ANC's historic merits and achievements, in the new dispensation these traits had to be resisted firmly if a democratic space was to be left open and if any of the liberal promise of the Constitution was to take shape. 'The alarming thing was how few people were really willing to stand up with a straight back against the pressures of fashion, patronage and political correctness, all of which pushed strongly in the other direction.'

Hot on the heels of the book launch, the party sent me on a seven-city visit – replete with rallies, rock music, cheerleaders and all the latest high-tech gadgetry and wizardry. The cross-country sweep was dubbed: 'The Leader of the Opposition Tour'. It cost nearly one million rands, but captured big headlines and large audiences. One breathless reporter in East London wrote: 'It was lights, camera and action at the Quigney Baptist Church here last night as DP leader Tony Leon hit town with all the glitz, glamour and razzmatazz of a charismatic preacher.'[113] It was somewhat audacious to proclaim me the 'leader of the opposition', and the DP as the biggest and fastest-growing opposition force, when objectively we were not. But the tour helped establish a fast-moving bandwagon.

Van Schalkwyk's NP tried to rain on this parade by announcing, at the tour's commencement, that the DP's deputy leader, William Mnisi, had left our ranks to join his. Mnisi – who, in a desperate bid to multiracialise our leadership, party members had appointed as my deputy in 1994 – was never up to the task. Although a member of parliament in the NCOP, his assigned duties were never properly fulfilled; his problems ranged from his finances, to health, family life and constituency duties. But of course his failures reflected badly on us and me as well. If we appointed 'on merit' then did this not raise questions about Mnisi? Unhappily I responded harshly and hastily to his departure, describing my defecting deputy as 'a confused and bedraggled rat who has clambered on to a sinking ship. He is in a poor state of health rather like the party he has chosen to join.' I was, appropriately, roasted by the media for these comments.

One happy outcome of this incident was the arrival of Wetshotsile Joe Seremane in our ranks as an MP, to replace Mnisi. Seremane's impeccable struggle credentials included a six-year prison sentence on Robben Island for his activities on behalf of the PAC. Joe and I met shortly before the 1994 election. To my surprise and delight he announced he would be voting DP. Thereafter, Mandela appointed him the National Land Claims Commissioner, but his tenure there was not happy. We had, however, remained in touch, and he agreed to enter parliament in our cause in late 1998. He is today the party's national chairman, and remains a personal friend.

During this time of fevered activity in the run-up to the 1999 poll, I received two quite separate, but in one sense related, approaches from two former leaders of my own party. The first was a note that Zach de Beer wrote me. He had been at all times warmly supportive. However, his missive was a jolt. Dated 29 September 1998, it read in part:

'As I told you at the time, I didn't really mind having Tertius Delport in the party. I was far more concerned about Hennie Bester joining the Western Cape cabinet. If recent opinion polls are even approximately accurate, we shall come to hold the balance of power in the Western Cape, and possibly in other provinces too. I don't know whether you have taken any decisions about what to do in this regard; but there are some indications – Hennie's position being one – that we might form coalitions with the Nats.

'As I think you know, this prospect horrifies me. It isn't just that the Nats are such a scruffy bunch, though in my view they are. Far more important – as I told FW de Klerk more than once – if the DP takes part in anything that looks like a white (or white/Coloured/Indian) ganging-up against blacks, this will tend strongly to undo all that we have aimed at over these many years. It is one thing – and a great thing – that there should be equal rights for all. It is a different, but also vitally important, thing that government should be widely representative of the different groups. That can only ever be achieved by our working … with the moderate section of what is today the ANC.

'I've thought carefully before writing this letter. If our party forms a coalition with the Nats, I really don't think I can live with it. If we were to do so with the ANC, I think the ride would be damn bumpy, and it might fail, but I would be happy that we should try, because it accords with what I think should be our strategy …

'I think it would be wrong of me not to warn you now that these are my feelings.'

On the racial polarity issue, I agreed with the potential danger to which he alerted me. But I felt South Africa's precarious democratic balance would tip in a hegemonic direction if we simply provided the ANC with the means and votes to take over the Western Cape. Sadly, but in a sense symbolically, Zach died in the very final week of the 1999 election campaign. His conflict between his party and personal loyalties and his consideration of principle and strategy were never put to the final test when we subsequently went on to form the coalition with the Nats in the Western Cape against which he had warned.

Then, in the middle of the 'Leader of the Opposition Tour' in November, Bill Johnson requested me to attend a dinner at the home of Van Zyl Slabbert in Parkview. My relationship with Slabbert, as distinct from Zach, was remote. Johnson advised me that I would find the purpose of the get-together 'intriguing and politically useful'. He did not elaborate much, except to indicate that 'Van is thinking of a political comeback in a leadership role in the Western Cape.' As it happened, Johnson could not attend the dinner and the only other guest was Professor Lawrence Schlemmer, the sociologist and pollster, who was a friend of Slabbert and an occasional adviser to me.

Slabbert served up a well-prepared tomato bredie (as I recall) of his own making, and plied our party with copious amounts of red wine. However, he was slightly more indirect about his intentions. Eventually, after some prodding from Schlemmer and me, he said he felt he might have 'one more campaign left in me' – and our attention turned to the Western Cape. I asked him whether he would consider standing as the premier candidate of the DP – although I had no idea how this would be squared with Hennie Bester, who legitimately had the expectation of the job. But I needed clarity about Slabbert's intentions. Schlemmer chipped in that he was polling political personalities in the province and would add Slabbert's name to the line-up.[114]

However, while Slabbert became ever more animated at the prospect of a political comeback, he emphasised that in the event of a hung parliament, the DP would have to align itself with the ANC, not the NP – for whom his loathing was still evident. I told him that this would be a deal-breaker;

our voters would never accept such a proposition. I then excused myself from the dinner and suggested to Slabbert that we keep the door open for further discussions. He faxed me the next day to advise that he would not be available: he had rethought overnight his putative re-entry to electoral politics, following our conversation.

As South Africa and my party headed into the festive season, my political activities yielded to matters far more personal and closer to my heart – literally and metaphorically. By December, for four months of intensive, frenetic activity, I had been criss-crossing South Africa with a ticking time-bomb between my ribs. A check-up in October – following persistent chest pains when running on a treadmill – led to my cardiologist Dr Graham Cassel pronouncing this verdict: I needed to undergo quadruple coronary bypass surgery, 'sooner, not later'. In view of my crammed schedule I managed to bargain with him for a postponement of the dread day until 3 December. But if my physical heart needed repair, this was to happen with the support of someone who had now taken occupation of my emotional heart.

Michal Even-Zahav was a striking, auburn-haired, intellectually smart and emotionally intelligent Israeli woman three years younger than me. I had first met her when the Israeli NGO she directed ('The Israeli Forum') invited me, together with a cross-section of Jewish legislators and ministers from across the world, to a conference in Jerusalem in 1991. These were biennial events of some interest to me, although falling in love with the conference organiser was not a probable outcome. At the time of our first few encounters she was married with two young children, and I simply noted her looks; was struck by our similarities in humour; and found that we had somewhat similar takes on certain of the more absurd and pompously self-regarding politicians who populated such gatherings. I left matters at that.

However, when at the suggestion of a friend I went on a short vacation to Israel to recharge my batteries after the municipal elections in June 1996, Michal's status had altered – and my life was about to change forever. She had recently separated from her husband, and we arranged a dinner date at a romantic restaurant which sat atop the old port of Jaffa, just outside Tel Aviv.

After dinner, we strolled along the beach promenade of Tel Aviv. The twinkling harbour lights, the warmth I felt from being with her, and the sentimental Celine Dion tune warbling over the loudspeakers ('Never underestimate the power of cheap music,' warned Noel Coward) conspired appropriately and agreeably. I had once asked a friend on the eve of his marriage how on earth he knew that his intended bride was 'the one'. He responded, I thought tautologously: 'You'll know it when you know it.'

That evening, as my feelings began to match the heat of the Tel Aviv summer, I knew that in Michal lay the end of my quest for a partner, and hopefully a wife with whom to share my life and whom I could love with the passion and contentment which so often seemed to elude my earlier relationships.

Our romance had, of necessity, to be of the long-distance variety. But it endured over both time and at other ends of the African continent while we snatched as many rendezvous, across Europe, the Middle East and South Africa, as our schedules permitted. The telephone and telefax – it was the pre-e-mail period – was a poor but sole substitute for the exchange of rhapsodic utterances between meetings. The moment she heard of my pending operation, she booked her ticket and arrived in Johannesburg on the eve of my admission to the cardiac care unit at the Milpark Hospital.

Buoyed by her and my mother's and family's support, the brilliance of the surgeons and tender care of dedicated nurses, I walked (or limped) out of the hospital just six days after undergoing a gruelling and fairly terrify-ing open heart operation (my chest was pinned open for over five hours – like a 'spatchcock chicken', I commented) and the heart stopped while the arteries were by-passed from grafts taken from my right leg and from inside my chest. I bore two enormous, although neatly constructed, scars, and felt huge discomfort – but not much else, physically.

After a few weeks at home, nursed by Michal and my mother and cos-seted by an army of friends and well-wishers, I flew off with Michal to Sharm el Sheikh, on Egypt's Red Sea coast. There the balmy waters and healing sun concluded, successfully, what the surgeons had started a few weeks before. I was now repaired, tanned and ready for the 1999 elections which, I felt sure, would mark a change in our political fortunes. But I did not underestimate the immense struggle that lay ahead. However, one of the epic battles, the finalisation of South Africa's constitution, had already been concluded.

CHAPTER 7

Constitutional Palimpsest

As one, you the representatives of the overwhelming majority of
South Africans have given voice to the yearnings of millions. And so it has
come to pass that today South Africa undergoes her rebirth, cleansed of a
horrible past, matured from a tentative beginning and reaching out to
the future with confidence.

PRESIDENT NELSON MANDELA

I

Woven into my early years in parliament – and of far more significance
to posterity – was the legislature's obligation to finalise the constitution.
The Interim Constitution, completed in November 1993, was, as its name
implied, not the last word, very far from the last word in fact. It provided
a framework of clauses to be incorporated into the final document – or
simply rewritten or discarded. The sole caveat imposed on the new draft
was that it had to comply with the 34 principles enshrined in the Interim
Constitution, which were immutable.

Sitting as a Constitutional Assembly, parliament was divided into a
number of 'theme committees'. In an early moment of ANC ecumeni-
calism, I was appointed co-chair of the theme committee on fundamental rights.[1] It was perfectly clear that the ANC's 62% dominance in the
Legislative Assembly meant that the new constitution would be written
in their image far more than the current document. However since, by a
small margin, they fell short of the two-thirds majority required for the
constitution's passage, there remained scope for the opposition to assert
itself in the drafting process.[2]

The final decision on whether the new constitution complied with the
enshrined constitutional principles was to be determined by the newly
enthroned Constitutional Court, the ultimate legal arbiter.

Although two years was set aside for the constitution-writing exercise,
the first 18 months were largely frittered away on 'reading scripts to each

other in the theme committees' – as I put it at the time. Even by the low standards of political theatre this left much to be desired. Every week our theme committee would convene and each party representative read out their preferred position on whichever clause was the subject of that week's 'theme'. The committees had no mandate to conclude agreements; and I quickly realised that they were little more than a form of political occupational therapy.

Coinciding with the theme committees, the Constitutional Assembly mounted a publicity drive to 'take the constitution to the people'. This was done at a cost of over R35-million. Whether a single clause or section was altered as a consequence of public input or pressure is doubtful. For example, the majority of representations and petitions by ordinary citizens and groups signalled the public's overwhelming support for capital punishment; but this made no difference whatsoever to the final outcome.

It was, however, illuminating to see how the truth of the old Watergate nostrum – 'Follow the money!' – began to impact on our proceedings. A Scandinavian government, I recall, bestowed over two million rands on a local NGO concerned with the promotion of 'children's rights'. Suddenly, from all corners, spokespeople, with speed, deliberation and earnestness, produced reams of position papers demanding the inclusion of all manner of clauses to promote the protection of young South Africans. For myself, instead of stuffing the charter with worthwhile desiderata, I felt a bill of rights should sketch a broad framework within which the legislature could develop detailed policies – the final adjudication and interpretation of which should then be left to the courts.

On a television debate with children's rights activists I couldn't help but observe that 'Japan's constitution devotes about three words to children's rights'; while Brazil (where, at the time, street-children were at times rounded up and shot by off-duty policemen) contained in its constitution a fulsome elaboration of over three pages on the subject. I asked: 'In which country are their rights better protected?' This led to name-calling about my insensitivity to such a 'pressing need'.

My ANC colleagues were completely convinced that one could and should legislate for every contingency and the betterment of the human condition. Indeed the ANC decided it was necessary to set forth a myriad of socio-economic rights, going so far as to guarantee every South African the 'right of reproductive health care'.[3] This led the *Financial Mail* to provide the acid rejoinder: 'Why not cardiac or dental health care as well?'[4]

While it was readily agreed that the right of access be afforded to everyone to housing, 'health, water, food and education', the dozen years that have elapsed since the Constitution's enactment have exposed the grim reality of daily life in South Africa. The gulf between the paper promises and the deplorable services shows conclusively how short we have fallen in translating words into deeds. A more modest document might have proven more realistic. But the majority party's determination to create, through the Constitution, a rod with which to beat itself was straight out of Lewis Carroll.

The ANC did not need a single provision from its laundry list of public goods to be placed in the Constitution; it could have used its legislative majority to enact any measure it wished. But ideological grandstanding and posturing took centre-stage by 'guaranteeing' certain (generally unaffordable) rights to which there could in principle be no objection, other than that the pestilential and abject conditions in which so many South Africans lived would mock the exercise as one of the greatest fatuity.

However, these socio-economic 'rights' became peripheral to the real crunch issues around which there was serious and fundamental disagreement. These were broadly: property rights, the proscription of hate speech, and whether the right to strike should be complemented, or cancelled, by the right of employers to lock-out their workers.

Each of these contentious issues – together with about sixty less headline-grabbing matters – was 'flagged for further consultation'. By February 1996 – with less than three months to the designated May deadline – there was no substantive agreement on any of them. Once again, the Ramaphosa-Meyer 'channel' – as their bilateral network was dubbed – took centre stage (or more accurately, offstage, since they tended to negotiate in secret).

However, Ramaphosa again held the whip hand, not simply – as at Kempton Park – because of his negotiation skills, but because of the prevailing realities of power. Although Meyer held the cabinet post of Constitutional Affairs, in reality Ramaphosa, as chairman of the Constitutional Assembly and backed by a big ANC majority, was the commanding presence. The ANC also dismissed minority dissent. Aiming particularly at the DP, its senior negotiator Pravin Gordhan airily advised the negotiations council: 'The minority parties are often concerned not with creating a democratic state, but rather with checking the power of the majority party in the interests of minority groups which are often racially based. The debate is often masked in democratic terms, but it is frequently used to protect the rights of the privileged.'[5]

While it is easy to deconstruct and intellectually demolish such rhetoric, it was nonetheless a revealing comment. Even Ramaphosa – usually a model of sang-froid – let the mask drop from time to time. In mid-April, he threatened to push ahead with a referendum if the ANC's demand for the formulation of the property clause was not agreed to. Now I experienced a sense of *déjà vu* when I learned (even as Ramaphosa spoke, so to speak) that preparations were well advanced for a R1,3-million party to 'celebrate the completion of the constitution' on 9 May. Yet the most contentious constitutional clauses remained seriously unresolved!

I happened to have lunch with Hugh Roberton, at the time political editor of the *Argus*. Over curry and rice I told him of my increasing disquiet at Ramaphosa's attempts to create a pressure-cooker atmosphere to force consensus and trample on minority concerns. Roberton, sensing a good story, immediately asked me to pen a statement along those lines, which I did. The next day's *Argus* proclaimed: 'ANC Slammed on Constitution'. The reaction of the ANC was swift, furious and disproportionate.

Notwithstanding the plethora of unresolved issues, the constitutional committee executive devoted its next meeting to venting its spleen against me and my umbrage at the million-rand bash. Ramaphosa announced that he had 'now lost all respect I could have had for the leader of the DP.' The Communist Party's Blade Nzimande demanded that I be 'summonsed to the council for displaying the worst kind of gutter politics', while his fellow-communist Gordhan said 'a motion would be placed before the council' for me to 'be interrogated'. Sustaining his contempt for minorities he declared it 'intolerable for a 1,7% party to use such publicity tactics'.[6]

It was left to Colin Eglin, our sole representative on an increasingly hostile body, to try and induce a sense of proportion and calm. I told the press that I declined to be treated as an errant schoolboy, and suggested the council address the substance of my critique. Eventually, the 'celebration' went ahead and despite my misgivings – in the spirit of reconciliation – I attended it, having that same day voted in favour of the constitution.

COSATU decided the temperature of negotiations needed to be raised by mass action. Smarting at opposition and business insistence that the right to lock-out appear in the final constitution, they announced a one-day national strike for 30 April, which happened to be the birthday of their secretary-general, my adversary from the labour law debates, Mbhazima Shilowa. Actually the strike was illegal, as I informed the Constitutional Assembly. It violated key provisions of the Labour Relations Act which mandated pre-strike ballots and various conciliation proceedings. Such legal niceties were swept aside, and on 30 April thousands of striking marchers gathered outside parliament. A COSATU leader, Ebrahim Patel, had apparently whipped up the crowd against me by informing them that I had 'mad cow disease'. Each party leader was invited by Shilowa to accept the strikers' petition. Accompanied by Douglas Gibson, EK Moorcroft and a former communist leader temporarily in our ranks, Joe Marks, I went to the sound truck to meet Shilowa and receive the document. He invited me to address his members; but I was booed and jeered when I attempted to speak.

After abandoning the futile effort, I made my way back through the crowd to the parliamentary gates. In those rather amateur-hour days, I had no bodyguards or security detail, although the towering Moorcroft probably resembled one. I suddenly felt a blow to my face, as a frenzied COSATU member hit me. I was startled, but not seriously hurt, though Marks was punched in the stomach. Unfortunately for COSATU, a sharp-eyed *Cape Times* photographer captured this magic moment. Unable to deny the incident, the COSATU leadership decided to brazen it out, accusing me of 'provoking' my own assault by leaving the rally.[7] The *Financial Mail* remarked that COSATU's defence of the indefensible reminded the editor of the old lag's protest: 'I didn't hit him, he walked into my fist.'[8]

Mathatha Tsedu – at the time writing for the *Sowetan* before briefly passing through a ruinous editorship of the *Sunday Times* en route to the ultra-Africanist *City Press* – was most revealing in his take on the incident. He proclaimed that Tony Leon had 'finally met his match'.[9] With a sniggering and contradictory disclaimer that 'violence can never be condoned, even when the person is Leon' he went on with Fanon-like logic to proclaim: 'But there was something of a kind of poetic justice in the reaction of the marchers – a rush of blood at seeing this man who at all times denigrated their efforts to uplift their lot, a man who at all times represents the moneyed classes.'

Tsedu also informed his readers of the 'suppressed glee' with which news of my assault was received in the newsroom of the *Sowetan* and ended with a dark warning: 'Watch it Tony, there is a limit to what the workers can take.'

A few days before the incident I had been beseeched via fax by Leslie Boyd – deputy chairman of Anglo American and a party supporter – to 'declare a dispute' in the negotiations, given the lopsided direction in which the labour relations clause was heading, favouring striking workers over employers. I accordingly decided to seek a meeting with Mandela, and we met on the evening of Sunday 28 April, at his Houghton home.

Boyd was not alone in his concern. A business delegation opposed to the ANC's support for COSATU had spent ten hours that very day with

Mandela. My impression was that there had been no breakthrough. When I met him he (somewhat bewilderingly) told me that business was as a whole 'quite satisfied' with the proposal to exclude the right to a lock-out from the constitution. I had taken the precaution of bringing Boyd's fax, and invited Mandela to read it. He airily dismissed its contents on the basis that 'Les Boyd is just a fire-eater' – a strange response to the concerns of one of the titans of South African industry. I was later informed by Marinus Daling, CEO of Sanlam, that the talks had proceeded extremely badly, but, 'What could we do? You have to go along to get along.'

I took the opportunity to express to the president some of our deep misgivings about certain as-yet-unresolved constitutional issues, such as the powers of the provinces; property rights; the limitations clause; and the right of independent schools to continue to receive a basic state subsidy. We didn't see the new constitution as a palimpsest which would simply write-over some of the critical areas of settlement in the Interim Constitution. Mandela urged me to write him a memorandum outlining our concerns, which I duly delivered to him the next day.

I tried to address our core concern at how the process had evolved in the immediate past and how I feared it might conclude: 'The DP has neither an inflexible nor hidebound approach to the new constitution or the negotiations surrounding it ... but [I added with reference to the increasingly secret bilateral ANC/NP negotiations conducted by Ramaphosa and Meyer] what we are seeing is contrary to the openness, transparency and inclusivity which the Constitutional Assembly promised ... We are deeply concerned that the new constitution should reflect a core of fundamental rights which will become the touchstone of value for the new South Africa. We are emphatically opposed to the constitution reflecting the worst common denominator of agreement between the two largest parties.'

As it happened, the second-largest party – the NP – was as per usual having an unhappy time. They continued, with ever-diminishing prospects, to pursue the power-sharing chimera. There were no takers, least of all from the ANC – who indicated that finally the sun was to set on this idea by the end of the current parliament in 1999.

The NP's other major concern was to entrench the right of mother tongue education (for them, Afrikaans) at school level. At various stages, they had declared this an 'absolute non-negotiable'. Their chief negotiator on the issue, Piet Marais, an estimably decent and mild-mannered MP from Stellenbosch, was locked in increasingly futile talks with the ANC/SACP's hardliner Blade Nzimande. Towards the end, he apparently suffered some form of health collapse. Whether this was because of the

ANC's hostility or the mixed signals he received from his increasingly yielding colleague Roelf Meyer, was never clear. But it was all to no avail. The ANC conceded the right in one breath of the relevant constitutional clause, but hedged it in with so many qualifications and caveats as to render it unenforceable. Within a decade the number of single-language Afrikaans schools had shrunk by a massive percentage.[10]

I had a little more success with the more modest suggestion that independent (or private) schools continue to receive state subsidies. Ramaphosa granted the concession, literally at the last moment of the final night of negotiation, in exchange for an implicit promise on our part that we would support the final passage of the constitution the next day – which we did. When this clause was discussed in the Constitutional Assembly, the voluble Nzimande felt obliged to add that the concession 'would not only be of benefit to Kearsney College in KwaZulu-Natal', a dig at my own alma mater certainly, but as it happened a reference to an institution to which, increasingly, members of the ANC elite were happy to entrust their children's schooling.

It was, inevitably, the property clause that excited some of the greatest passions and last-minute haggling before the constitution could be finalised. It was an issue, like the lock-out, which united the NP, the DP and the business community, although it did not result in the high dramatics of a national strike. An increasingly hawkish land lobby from within the ANC's 'broad church' was determined to rectify what it saw as the 'great sell-out at Kempton Park' three years previously. Their proposal, which held great sway inside the majority party, was essentially to nullify the payment of compensation in the event of an expropriation aimed at 'bringing about land reform'.

When I first saw the proposal, in December 1994, I immediately rang the alarm. As it stood, the clause would make 'millions of property owners uniquely susceptible to a land grab'; yet it would not 'advance meaningful land reform one jot'. By the final week the clause was still on the table – modified by the single proviso that any state appropriation of land 'to address the results of past racial discrimination had to be reasonable and justifiable in an open democratic society'. Dene Smuts, our bill of rights negotiator, described this as a 'Trojan Horse clause' which would, in effect, provide a very slim defence against state-sanctioned land seizures, sans proper compensation.

Despite our desire to accord reasonable protection to property owners, our options were limited. The right to property ownership was not one of the 34 principles with which the constitution had to comply. At Dene's suggestion, we arranged a meeting with Justice minister Dullah Omar and his colleague Kader Asmal. Eventually a slightly better formulation emerged, requiring any override of the protection of property to be in accord with the general limitations clause which required any derogation of rights to meet a number of specific tests and conditions.[11] I thought the clause marked a retreat from the carefully crafted compromise of Kempton Park. Still, it could have been worse.

Negotiations continued until the early hours of the morning of 8 May, the very day on which parliament was to convene and pronounce itself finally on the document. Colin Eglin, as our chief negotiator, had invested the best part of six years in helping to guide the constitution to its conclusion. Aside from his great personal and political investment, he saw the constitution, warts and all, as the justification of a life's work. He had tilled the stony soil of the opposition field when the very idea of such a document, securing equal rights for all, was dismissed by his Nat opponents as over-sophisticated rubbish.

I did not share all Eglin's unalloyed enchantment for the final product. I also faced at least one member of our caucus, Kobus Jordaan, who believed that we owed it to South Africa to vote against the document, mainly because of the property clause. As we convened around a coffee table, off the old assembly chamber of parliament, where the process was being wrapped up, I was persuaded by the remorselessness and elegance of Eglin's logic. We would support the constitution, although for the purposes of political theatre, would only indicate our assent towards the end of my speech the next day.

I had given very little attention to what form my speech would take. And since we only settled on our assent after midnight, I hurried back to our parliamentary offices across the road in the Marks Building to settle on some formula for what would be one of the more important speeches I would ever be called upon to make. To my great fortune I had recently acquired the services of a full-time speech-writer. Jennifer Cohen was a smart, tart-tongued, highly literate American who had stumbled into our employ via her husband, a political journalist, Tim Cohen. Her services were nothing short of heroic.

I dictated into a machine some rushed thoughts, a few pithy phrases, and a general outline of an approach. At 2 am I announced that I needed a few hours' sleep so that I could sound vaguely coherent the next morning. When our head of operations, Robert Desmarais, opened up the offices the next morning at 7 am there was Jennifer asleep at her desk — with a completed speech in her hands! After making some amendments,

I was satisfied. When after a procession of glittering speeches – including Mbeki's famously eloquent 'I am an African' oration – it was my turn to deliver the DP's view. I said:[12]

'I have been given this opportunity to tell my supporters and detractors alike whether the DP will endorse this constitution as it is written: my party asks, is it democratic? In many aspects, the answer is affirmative. It entrenches, most importantly, a true separation of powers. For the first time in our history the executive is to be checked by a democratically elected legislature and an independent judiciary, representivity, accountability, transparency and public participation – words never before attributed to South African governance are sprinkled through the document. Its bill of rights is one of the most liberal in the world.'

After noting our reservations, especially those relating to property, labour relations and the limitations clause, I reached my peroration: 'Finally, a constitution must be judged within the context of its capacity to protect and promote the interests of minorities. Let the words of Thomas Jefferson remind us:

> All too will bear in mind this sacred principle, that though the will of the majority is in all cases to prevail, that will to be rightful must be reasonable; that the minority possesses their equal rights, which law must protect, and to violate would be oppression.

'Our decision to support or oppose this constitution was fundamentally based on our deep-seated commitment to South Africa and its people. We want South Africans to walk the road ahead with a common purpose, a common road map, under our common flag. Despite our misgivings on individual clauses, we support this constitution and all it represents.'

Kader Asmal told me afterwards that he wept as he listened to me. The ANC, in a rare moment, broke into sustained applause at its completion.

Notwithstanding our support, we immediately instructed our attorneys, and in due course briefed expensive legal counsel to prepare papers for the Constitutional Court hearing where we attempted to obtain by legal process the redress we had unsuccessfully sought through negotiation. Some of our arguments found favour with the Court, although not our key concern on the non-inclusion of the lock-out provision. The Court, in its judgment on 6 September 1996, found that the Constitution in parts did not conform to the constitutional principles, although the text did 'comply with the overwhelming majority of the requirements'.[13]

Parliament then amended the text according to the precepts of the Court. On 10 December, Human Rights Day, I took my seat in the front row of a stadium in Sharpeville – scene of the terrible massacre that alerted the world to the true nature of apartheid – as Mandela assented to the final text and so symbolically turned the page of our bloody past into a more hopeful future. Five days later I celebrated my 40th birthday at my friend Clifford Garrun's house, which Mandela graced (with a warm and witty speech) along with 150 other guests. Among them were Tito Mboweni, Mangosuthu Buthelezi and Helen Suzman. Buthelezi's presence (and his present to me of a fine copper bust of his illustrious forbear, King Cetshwayo) added an amusing note to proceedings. On the day of my birthday, he had written me a gracious thoughtful open letter, which the *Sunday Times* splashed onto its front page with the somewhat trivialised and sensationalised headline: 'Leon urged to celebrate 40 as a Zulu'.[14]

At the party, Buthelezi, ever alive to being thought unmannered or impolite, quite unnecessarily apologised for 'embarrassing me with his remarks' – adding that he never meant to say that 'Mr Leon' (as he always persisted in calling me despite our growing friendship) 'should become a poor carbon copy of Mangosuthu Buthelezi.' He then went on in extravagant terms to praise me to the hilt (much to the delight of my mother and father, the latter in deep mourning for my stepmother Jacqueline who had died quite unexpectedly the month before):

'Those of us who accepted the invitation to be at this birthday party have done so as a tribute to a political leader of outstanding leadership qualities. A leader who has moral courage. A leader who refuses to be browbeaten. A leader who cannot be easily intimidated by any force on earth. A leader who achieved a position of leadership of an important political party so early in his life because of all these outstanding qualities … Happy birthday, a great son of South Africa. We salute you.'

It seemed a happy note on which to bring to an end one of the most tumultuous of years, the third of my leadership, which was then only really beginning.

Much of my leadership would be soon spent confronting some of the great challenges and one of the outsize personalities which now buffeted the 'Rainbow Nation', and which threatened to steer it sharply, and dangerously, off course – in the opposite direction of the hopeful future promised in the Constitution we had so recently inaugurated.

PART THREE

NEW ORDER CHALLENGES

CHAPTER 8

The Long AIDS Death March

It was not a fact. It was data from Stalin's parallel universe ...
the fact was that facts were losing their value. Stalin had broken the
opposition. He was also far advanced toward his much stranger objective
of breaking the truth.

MARTIN AMIS

I

The HIV/AIDS pandemic is the greatest tragedy of post-apartheid South Africa. In a history replete with wars, battles, famines and innumerable episodes of human suffering, none is so deadly as that which we are now enduring. Millions are dying early deaths; life expectancy has dropped precipitously in the past decade, from above sixty to below fifty.[1] One recent study estimated that in the absence of HIV/AIDS, South Africans would live twenty-six years longer, on average, than they do today.[2] An estimated 320 000 died of AIDS in 2005 – or roughly nine hundred per day,[3] about one in nine is infected with HIV, and the highest rates are among sexually active young adults. In 2005, 30,2% of women in antenatal surveys tested HIV-positive – a rate which continues to climb.

In human terms, the HIV/AIDS pandemic has devastated South Africa. What is even worse is that HIV/AIDS is a political tragedy[4] – one that could have been avoided or greatly mitigated if different decisions had been taken at the onset of ANC rule, and in the 14 years that followed.

Little was known of HIV/AIDS in South Africa at the dawning of democracy. Prevalence rates were still very low in the early 1990s; a national survey of pregnant women in 1990 found that only 0,8% were HIV-positive.[5] Scant attention was paid by political leaders: neither the National Party government nor the ANC had a sense of urgency.

Within a few years that changed. In 1992, a comprehensive national AIDS plan was drafted by a panel that included a variety of political figures as well as representatives from business, unions and civil society. Two of the drafters, Dr Nkosazana Zuma (later Dlamini-Zuma) and Dr Manto Tshabalala-Msimang, would go on to become national Health ministers in the governments of Nelson Mandela and Thabo Mbeki. The plan put education and prevention among its top priorities. Yet it was set aside, largely ignored for some years, apparently because of its association with the previous government.[6]

For much of Mandela's presidency, the pandemic was neglected: a fact later acknowledged by Mandela himself on several occasions, such as when he disclosed that his own son Makgatho had died of AIDS in January 2005. Official neglect reinforced the wall of silence surrounding the syndrome. There were issues of social and cultural taboo which made it difficult, apparently even for a head of state, to discuss a sexually transmitted disease openly and candidly. The main vector of transmission was heterosexual intercourse – a topic not often discussed in public. The Calvinist and Victorian sensibilities of the white population, combined with the traditional patriarchal values of many black communities, cast a shadow over public discourse, leaving the victims of HIV/AIDS in a shroud of shame and loneliness.

After stepping down from the presidency, Mandela made up for lost time, speaking out about the disease and even, implicitly, against some of the unhelpful policies of his successor in dealing with it. Nonetheless, Mandela's years in office were the period in which HIV/AIDS took root and expanded exponentially through the population.

I was in the audience in February 2002, at the Mount Nelson hotel in Cape Town, when at a Henry J Kaiser Medical Foundation function, Mandela gave an extraordinary explanation for the neglect of AIDS on his watch. In his frank manner he said that when he was first released from jail and started campaigning, he had preached the gospel of condom use and spoken of the perils of AIDS. At a school, a teacher admonished him; if he persisted, 'no one will vote for you.' This semi-apologia was coupled to a slightly veiled but stinging criticism of his successor's inaction. Later it became known that the issue led to an almost complete breakdown in their personal relationship.

If neglect marked Mandela's tenure, denial stamped Mbeki's. There was no initial attempt at prevention and treatment; and Mbeki actively questioned the link between HIV and AIDS – exaggerating the toxicity of antiretroviral drugs (ARVs). He and his Health minister embraced a spectrum of heterodox theories and outright quackery, resisting the findings of Western medicine, science, and the research of pharmaceutical companies, essentially on the basis of misconceived national and racial pride. Doctors who attempted to prescribe antiretrovirals – the only clinically effective treatment for HIV/AIDS – were occasionally punished, while non-governmental organisations that attempted to provide the drugs as prophylactics to rape victims were evicted from government hospitals.

The debates and confrontations erupting around these events and Mbeki's denialist stance caused severe damage to the president's personal reputation and the international standing of the country. South Africa's HIV/AIDS policy became a synonym for disaster.

Thus the African country best suited to fight HIV/AIDS – through its relative wealth and health care system – began lagging well behind poorer and less well-developed nations. Stephen Lewis, the UN special envoy to Africa on AIDS, wrote in 2005 that nearly every other country in sub-Saharan Africa 'is working harder at treatment than is South Africa, with relatively fewer resources, and in most cases nowhere near the infrastructure or human capacity of South Africa.'[7] South Africa led the world in the number of people infected with HIV until it was overtaken by India (with roughly twenty times the population) at the end of 2005.[8]

The consequences have been severe – not just in humanitarian terms, but in economic ones as well. The disease is most widespread within the age group comprising the most productive workers in the labour force. That means higher rates of absenteeism, and greater difficulty in retaining and transferring skills. There are many different models of the effects of HIV/AIDS on South Africa's GDP, but one of the most widely cited is a study by ING Barings in 2000 which estimated that our GDP would have been 17% higher by 2010 were it not for the impact of HIV/AIDS.[9]

In the initial period of democracy, South Africa was preoccupied with reconciliation and reconstruction, as described in chapters 6 and 7. HIV/AIDS was, at best, an afterthought – even though prevalence rates kept rising throughout the 1990s. Less than one per cent of the population was infected in 1990; but by the end of the decade, that percentage would approach ten per cent.

It was left to ordinary South Africans – in the main – to take up the challenge. Several NGOs began working on issues of prevention and treatment. One, the Treatment Action Campaign (TAC), was formed in December 1998 in Cape Town to protest the high prices charged by multinational drug companies for antiretrovirals. International HIV/AIDS conferences began choosing South Africa as a host destination – starting in the mid-1990s – seeing in the country both the danger of an unchecked pandemic and the potential for making a difference, not just in South Africa but across the continent.

Government, too, finally began to acknowledge the seriousness of the crisis. As deputy president, Mbeki told an audience in 1998: 'HIV/AIDS is not someone else's problem. It is my problem. It is your problem. By allowing it to spread, we face the danger that half of our youth will not reach adulthood. Their education will be wasted. The economy will shrink. There will be a large number of sick people whom the healthy will not be able to maintain. Our dreams as a people will be shattered … There is still no cure for HIV and AIDS. Nothing can prevent infection except our own behaviour.'[10]

But this rhetoric was undermined by government actions. There were missteps, mistakes and scandals as the ANC struggled to define the government's strategies and policies on HIV/AIDS. In 1995, then-minister of Health, Nkosazana Zuma, spent upwards of R14-million on producing a musical, *Sarafina 2*, which purported to be an educational drama about HIV/AIDS. Relatively few South Africans ever saw the play, which was apparently full of misinformation, and producer Mbongeni Ngema failed to justify the musical's lavish budget. (By comparison, the losing bidder in the government tender process offered to produce an HIV/AIDS play for R600 000.)[11] The minister struggled to defend her choice, one of the defining events of the new democratic dispensation.

Another serious scandal revolved around Virodene, a sham 'cure' for AIDS developed by three researchers in Pretoria who won the support of both Mbeki and Zuma. Just as the *Sarafina 2* scandal was blowing over, minister Zuma was approached in July 1996 by the developers of Virodene who touted their product as a potential cure for HIV/AIDS. The researchers proceeded to test the substance illegally on human subjects with the connivance of the minister (bypassing both the Medicines Control Council and the University of Pretoria Ethics Committee). Early the following year they returned to Zuma with the results, and on 22 January 1997 made a special presentation to the cabinet at her and Mbeki's personal behest. They claimed that Virodene could 'reverse' full-blown AIDS and 'destroy' the HI virus. Mbeki apparently stated that government would consider funding further trials and research. Subsequent analysis showed Virodene to be little more than an industrial solvent, and a potentially dangerous one at that.

By 2 March 1998, the DA Health spokesman, Mike Ellis, had accumulated enough *prima facie* evidence to lodge a complaint with the Public Protector concerning allegations that the ANC had a financial interest in Virodene. He stated that the Virodene developers had enjoyed high-level government support despite problems relating to the concoction.

These 'problems' were far from trivial. They included:

- the censure of the Virodene research team by a committee of the University of Pretoria for 'unethical behaviour' in conducting unauthorised human trials of the drug;
- the findings of a joint committee of University of Pretoria and the Gauteng Health Department that the active ingredient of Virodene was 'a toxic industrial solvent'; and
- multiple rejections by the Medicines Control Council (MCC) of the research protocols of the developers of Virodene.

Ellis also drew the Public Protector's attention to the 'highly irregular' presentation to the cabinet; and to suggestions that the Health minister might amend legislation to 'smooth Virodene's path by circumventing [current] requirements of the MCC.'[12]

The Public Protector eventually reported back nearly a year later.[13] It was Ellis's view that the dilatoriness was a stratagem to rob the issue of any currency. Predictably, the Public Protector accepted every assurance from Mbeki and Zuma and felt no need to probe further. He 'could find no evidence' that the Health minister or deputy president 'had any financial interest' in the development of Virodene; nor did he find 'any evidence' of any changes to legislation influenced by Virodene.

This delayed and superficial (five-page) response was predicated entirely on accepting every assurance or excuse offered by Mbeki and Zuma. The Public Protector accepted as 'perfectly normal' their personal attempts to resolve an internal, essentially commercial dispute between the Virodene researchers. The very idea of two of the most senior members of government meeting late at night and early in the morning with squabbling members of a private, profit-driven company was mind-boggling. But the lame suggestion was that Mbeki and Zuma were concerned that if the internal spat was not resolved 'it could have resulted in the sale of CPT [the company that manufactured Virodene] to persons who might sell Virodene at unaffordable prices.'

At the time the Virodene scandal surfaced, in early 1998, the Medicines Control Council (MCC) rejected Virodene's application for a licence. In a vengeful and entirely unjustified response to the MCC's seemingly sound and scientific rejection of Virodene, Mbeki and Zuma purged the MCC of its chairman, Professor Peter Folb, and its registrar and deputy registrar. Seized by the prospect of an African solution to HIV/AIDS, and of a drug that could rival those produced by Western pharmaceutical companies, Mbeki dismissed criticism of Virodene as motivated by racism, and complained that he and the Health minister were victims of a vicious public campaign.

He did so in these terms: 'The Virodene researchers themselves have had unbounded contumely heaped upon them. As expected, the minister of Health has not been spared the poisoned barbs ... In our strange world, those who seek the good for all humanity have become the villains of our time! ... I and many others will not rest until the efficacy or otherwise of Virodene is established scientifically. If nothing else, all those infected by HIV/AIDS need to know as a matter of urgency.'[14]

As for Ellis, he was attacked for 'consistently [pursuing] the interests of pharmaceutical monopolies and other forces opposed to the health policies and programmes of the government.'[15] In fact, Ellis's information had come from impeccable, deeply alarmed, members of the MCC astounded by Mbeki's involvement in a drug they considered 'dangerous to human life'. The DP was dismissed as holding 'the ANC and the masses it leads in contempt'. Zuma went even further: she claimed our party wanted 'all ANC supporters to die of AIDS'.

When Virodene was fully exposed as a fraud, Mbeki refused to apologise. The scandal seems to have hardened his resolve to stand by his eccentric views on HIV/AIDS.

There remain some very serious allegations – never proven – of how the ANC as an institution had the closest of links to the developers of Virodene, including owning some shares in their company and being involved in attempting to persuade Tanzanian authorities to carry out further testing in that country. This would suggest that Mbeki's advocacy of the substance – despite the scientific and ethical regimes it flouted – went beyond the mere eccentricity of philoafricanism.

Virodene brought to the fore a number of the least attractive features of the ANC and Mbeki's emerging leadership style: the playing of the race card when cornered; a diminution of science in favour of behind-doors charlatanism; and the potent power of ANC business interests. Mbeki and his handmaiden enjoyed personalising the issue as a means of obscuring its essential disgraceful elements.

2

I am not sure Mbeki ever gave up on Virodene. It is clear that the extraordinarily close collaboration between him and the manufacturers led – in part – to his ruinous opposition to mainstream antiretrovirals and his later policies of denialism. His resentment of the authority of medical experts and medical ethics presaged his approach to HIV/AIDS in years to come. After his ascent to the presidency in 1999, he might have been expected to lend new urgency to the fight against HIV/AIDS; instead, he threw the country's efforts into reverse by propounding a strange and dissident AIDS theory.

When I took my seat as leader of the opposition, I called on Mbeki to provide antiretroviral drugs to those who needed them to live. His response was to lead South Africa on a long, strange and destructive detour through the scientific wilderness. In late 1999, he publicly questioned the efficacy of antiretrovirals in a speech to the National Council of Provinces. He began his address by questioning the estimate that only one out of every 36 rapes in South Africa was reported to the police, and went on from there: 'Similarly, we are confronted with the scourge of HIV/AIDS against which we must leave no stone unturned to save ourselves from the catastrophe which this disease poses.

'Concerned to respond appropriately to this threat, many in our country have called on the government to make the drug AZT available in our public health system.

'Two matters in this regard have been brought to our attention. One of these is that there are legal cases pending in this country, the United Kingdom and the United States against AZT on the basis that this drug is harmful to health. There also exists a large volume of scientific literature alleging that, among other things, the toxicity of this drug is such that it is in fact a danger to health. These are matters of great concern to the government as it would be irresponsible for us not to heed the dire warnings which medical researchers have been making.

'I have therefore asked the minister of Health, as a matter of urgency, to go into all these matters so that, to the extent that is possible, we ourselves, including our country's medical authorities, are certain of where the truth lies ... I would urge the [NCOP] to access the huge volume of literature on this matter available on the Internet, so that all of us can approach this issue from the same base of information.'[16]

In questioning AZT – one of the most widely used antiretroviral drugs – and citing the Internet as his basic source, Mbeki opened a bizarre debate that confused and distracted South Africa's efforts to fight HIV/AIDS. He took his campaign further, openly questioning the link between HIV and AIDS. Encouraged by a small and largely discredited group of international AIDS dissenters, he portrayed HIV/AIDS as a form of conspiracy by pharmaceutical companies bent on testing and selling their products in

Africa, where the inhabitants could more easily be exploited.

In a seminal article in the *New Yorker*, Samantha Power observed:

'[The] fact was that antiretrovirals helped patients live longer – and HIV's role in causing AIDS had been confirmed by thousands of researchers. Yet Mbeki was starting to think like a conspiracy theorist. It was as if, having harboured dreams of African self-reliance, he couldn't quite bring himself to believe in a disease that could undermine all his grand plans. Mbeki denounced the notion that the disease had African origins as "wild and insulting". He insisted that his critics dismissed his arguments because they viewed Africans as "germ carriers, and human beings of a lower order that cannot subject its passions to reason".'

Mbeki was unmoved by those who urged him to buy the drug: 'I am taken aback by the determination of many people in our country to sacrifice all intellectual integrity to act as salespersons of the product of one pharmaceutical company,' he said. He linked his stand to larger moral principles, such as freedom of speech. Why was it that the mainstream was trying to muzzle dissent?

'Not long ago, in our own country, people were killed, tortured and imprisoned ... because the established authority believed that their views were dangerous,' Mbeki wrote in a letter sent in April 2000 to UN secretary-general Kofi Annan, British prime minister Tony Blair, and US president Bill Clinton. 'We are now being asked to do precisely the same thing that the racist apartheid tyranny we opposed did, because, it is said, there exists a scientific view that is supported by the majority against which dissent is prohibited.'

He charged that those who were supporting the use of antiretrovirals were actually trying to poison blacks. A statement from the president's office likened antiretroviral therapy to the 'biological warfare of the apartheid era'. It said: 'Our people are being used as guinea pigs and conned into using dangerous and toxic drugs.'[17]

Beyond contesting the efficacy of antiretroviral drugs, Mbeki began questioning the link between HIV and AIDS. Because AIDS was an immune deficiency 'syndrome' it could have a number of causes: HIV might be one, he suggested, but the real cause of immune deficiency was poverty. In September 2000, Chris Redman, International Editor of *Time* magazine, was in South Africa to interview Mbeki. He asked me what one question I would choose to ask the president; I said he should ask him 'whether you believe HIV leads to AIDS?'

When Redman asked him precisely that, Mbeki responded: 'No, I am saying that you cannot attribute immune deficiency solely and exclusively to a virus. There may very well be a virus. But TB, for example, destroys the immune system and at a certain point if you have TB you will test HIV-positive because the immune system is fighting the TB which is destroying it. Then you will go further to say TB is an opportunistic disease of AIDS whereas in fact TB is the thing that destroyed the immune system in the first place. But if you come to the conclusion that the only thing that destroys immune systems is HIV then your only response is to give them antiretroviral drugs. There's no point in attending to this TB business because that's just an opportunistic disease. If the scientists ... say this virus is part of the variety of things from which people acquire immune deficiency, I have no problem with that.'[18]

Earlier that year, Mbeki had announced he would be convening an international AIDS advisory panel to assist the government in responding to the pandemic. To the great dismay of AIDS activists, the opposition, and international observers, many of the world's most infamous AIDS dissidents were included on the panel, comprising roughly one-third of its members.[19]

The panel first met in May 2000; a year later, they issued a divided report. The mainstream scientists recommended HIV testing and antiretroviral treatment, including the specific use of the antiretroviral drug Nevirapine to prevent mother-to-child transmission (MTCT) of HIV. The dissidents, however, argued against both testing and ARV treatment.[20]

The effect of Mbeki's stance froze government policy precisely when international commitment to fighting the disease and the co-operation of pharmaceutical companies to assist with cheap or free drugs were beginning to coalesce. The president's spokesperson, Parks Mankahlana – who died later in the year, allegedly of AIDS – issued a number of highly controversial statements. He claimed, for example: 'There has hardly been a negative response to Mbeki's comments within the debate about AZT, from any personality of note from the Third World or any of the countries most affected by AIDS.'[21] The outrage over Mbeki's views was driven by profit-thirsty pharmaceutical companies, he claimed, adding: 'Like the marauders of the military industrial complex who propagated fear to increase their profits, the profit-takers who are benefiting from the scourge of HIV/AIDS will disappear to the affluent beaches of the world to enjoy wealth accumulated from a humankind ravaged by a dreaded disease.'[22]

Mankahlana also claimed that providing AZT to people with HIV would be unaffordable,[23] and that saving children from contracting HIV from their HIV-positive mothers would be too costly because the state would not be able to carry the burden of supporting AIDS orphans: 'A

country like ours has to deal with that ... that mother is going to die, and
that HIV-negative child will be an orphan. That child must be brought up.
Who's going to bring the child up? It's the state, the state. That's resources,
you see?'[24] Many felt this enjoyed official sanction, or closely reflected his
boss's view.

Mbeki did not refute or qualify these comments.

The reaction to Mbeki's stance within the HIV/AIDS activist community in South Africa was one of incredulity and frustration. My old friend
from Wits Law School days, now on the Supreme Court of Appeal, Justice
Edwin Cameron – who had himself come forward to declare he was HIV-
positive – gave an address in Durban in March 2000 at the gala dinner of
the Second Annual Conference for People Living With HIV/AIDS, in
which he took Mbeki and his administration to task:

'We know that governmental power can be powerfully used to change
the course of an epidemic. We also know that governmental power can be
misapplied to create confusion and to disempower people in the epidemic
... [It] simply does not seem that the government can begin to get it right
on AIDS. Amongst many people living with HIV/AIDS there is considerable grief and confusion about the government's policies ... There is too
much at stake for intellectual dilly-dallying.'[25]

Edwin also cited a speech by Dr Mamphela Ramphele, then-vice chancellor of the University of Cape Town, on 1 December 1999. Dr Ramphele
said that with respect to health care in South Africa, there was a 'subtle but
visible anti-intellectualism seeping into the body politic which discounts
the value that experts can, and do, add to human development.'[26] She
stated further that 'the bitter fruits of this anti-intellectualism' were to be
found in the government's HIV/AIDS policy, which was characterised by
'disregard' and neglect: it was 'nothing short of irresponsibility, for which
history will judge it severely.' Cameron commented:

'These are profound and scorching words. But as a person living with
AIDS, I cannot but endorse them.'[27] Cameron later told a group of lawyers
in London that 'AIDS denialism' was, at the end of the 20th century and
the commencement of the 21st, as great a crime and calumny as Holocaust
denialism.

Even personal appeals by Cameron to the president did not shift Mbeki's
position. In early 2000, as noted, the president sent a letter to various heads
of state, including Bill Clinton of the US, defending the dissident view of
AIDS championed by the likes of Dr Peter Duesberg, and accusing orthodox

scientists of conducting a 'campaign of intellectual intimidation and terror-ism'.[28] He wrote: 'The day may not be far off when we will once again see books burnt and their authors immolated by fire by those who believe that they may have a duty to conduct a holy campaign against infidels.'[29]

Reliable sources in Washington informed me that when the Clinton White House received Mbeki's missive, they assumed it was a hoax. When the South African embassy confirmed its authenticity the White House promptly leaked it to the press. Thus domestic criticism of Mbeki's AIDS policies was joined by growing international criticism.

By citing poverty as the root cause of AIDS, Mbeki was mixing fact and fiction. No doubt the poverty of the majority of South Africans was a huge contributing factor to the spread of HIV; but poverty was not the reason for HIV being passed from one individual to another. The virus itself passes from one person to another through certain body fluids, and HIV is the immediate and direct cause of AIDS. Poverty, then, is but an aggravating factor.

Mbeki's stand prompted South Africa's growing movement of HIV/AIDS activists, particularly the TAC, to shift focus. Protests against high prices had, to some degree at least, been successful, and more and more pharmaceutical companies began offering cheaper or free HIV/AIDS drugs to poor countries.

Initially, the government and the TAC had sided together against the pharmaceutical industry, but now the TAC found itself confronting the government over its refusal to provide AZT and other ARVs. The life-saving medicines were now being made available – and the only obstacle, other than the limited capacity of the public health system to distribute them, was Mbeki's denialist campaign. The political opposition, led by the DA but also joined by leaders from other parties, began demanding that government reject the denialist view and consider options for providing cheap or free HIV/AIDS drugs to those in desperate need of them.

The TAC tried to appeal to the ANC by pointing to the fact that many TAC leaders were members of the ruling party as well. But few ANC politicians were prepared to challenge Mbeki on HIV/AIDS. In later years, when the Health department insisted that the disease be referred to as 'HIV and AIDS' rather than the more conventional 'HIV/AIDS' – thus de-linking the virus and the syndrome – the ANC faithful complied obediently. Furthermore, there were a number of high-ranking ANC fig-ures who fully backed Mbeki's stance, and endorsed his refusal to provide ARVs. These were not only Mbeki's official spokespeople but political characters such as Peter Mokaba.

Mokaba was, in his time, a fairly powerful ANC luminary. His leadership of the ANC Youth had been mired in controversy. He rejoiced in his role as a hothead, mouthing slogans such as 'kill the boer, kill the farmer'. In contrast, his acquisitive penchant for luxury living and business ventures led to serious questions about his political and ethical probity. His attachment to Mbeki had been decisive in his ascent into a top ANC job: he was rewarded with a deputy ministry. Shortly before his death in 2002 (also reportedly from AIDS) Mokaba stated his position to Rachel Swarns of the *New York Times*:

'HIV? It doesn't exist. The kind of stories that they tell that people are dying in droves? It's not true. It's not borne out by any facts.

'Where the science has not proved anything, we cannot allow our people to be guinea pigs,' he said. 'Antiretrovirals – they're quite dangerous. They're poison actually. We cannot allow our people to take something so dangerous that it will actually exterminate them. However well-meaning, the hazards of misplaced compassion could lead to genocide.'[30]

Several other ANC officials who should have known better exhibited similar denialist attitudes. In a letter to the *Financial Times* in July 2000, the redoubtable Cheryl Carolus, high commissioner to the UK, disputed a description of AIDS in South Africa: 'I would have no hesitation in agreeing that many people in sub-Saharan Africa, including South Africa, suffer from the well-known sexually transmitted diseases as well as tuberculosis. The point is why these diseases in sub-Saharan Africa are described as AIDS, as your correspondent describes them. The question that arises is why the fundamentally unscientific claim is made that these are caused by HIV ...

'This constitutes a self-serving medicalisation of poverty. It is consistent with the argument that land shortage for the majority of rural Zimbabweans, who are concentrated in the communal areas, is a fiction invented by President Robert Mugabe to retain power.'[31]

Here Carolus managed to deny the HIV/AIDS pandemic and the political crisis in Zimbabwe simultaneously.

So while Mbeki's denialism was considered outrageous by many South Africans, it was endorsed by others, sowing confusion and misunderstanding.

His beliefs soon became a source of great embarrassment to the country. In July 2000, Helen Epstein, a medical writer for the *New York Review of Books*, wrote an extensive article, 'The Mystery of AIDS in South Africa', documenting and exposing the depths of Mbeki's denialism, from Virodene to the anti-AZT crusade. She recalled an interview Mbeki had done on television in the United States that May:

'On Tuesday, May 23, [Mbeki] was interviewed on *The NewsHour with Jim Lehrer*, and asked specifically about his AIDS policies. His replies were a series of evasions. He claimed that he had never said that HIV was not the cause of AIDS, but he did not deny that he had questioned the link between them. Nor did he explain why, if he did not question this link, he had invited [AIDS dissident Dr Peter] Duesberg and his followers to present their views to the presidential AIDS panel. When he was asked why he refused to make AZT available in public maternity wards for the prevention of HIV transmission from mother to newborn child, he answered that the state could not afford to make antiretroviral drugs available for life to all HIV-positive people in South Africa ...

'But he ... had not been asked why he didn't provide all HIV-positive South Africans with antiretroviral therapy for life. He had been asked why he didn't provide it only to HIV-positive women for a month, or perhaps only a week, around the time they give birth. This would cost about $50-million a year, which the Health ministry could well afford, especially in view of the fact that it will cost many times more to treat the children who might have been spared HIV infection when they eventually come down with AIDS.'[32]

In response, one of Mbeki's former colleagues in the South African Communist Party (SACP), Paul Trewhela, wrote a letter to the *Review of Books*, speculating on the motives behind Mbeki's stance. He cited Mbeki's leadership style – 'His instinct is to command support rather than to win it' – and wrote that Mbeki was still trying to compensate for 'the loss of his previous ideology' (i.e. Soviet communism). And there were other ideological roots: 'Mbeki's strange stance on the issue of the AIDS virus has two sources, one legitimate, the other not. It is fully appropriate that an African political leader should condemn the massive economic disparity between the rich, white West and AIDS-stricken Africa, where megadeaths are indeed the wages of poverty. The destruction of Africa's economically active population, aggravated by Third World debt and global terms of trade, is equivalent to the Great Hunger in Ireland in the 1840s. Hatred of the West will be the result for generations if this is not remedied quickly. In however strange a manner, Mbeki in part articulates this anger, as does Winnie Madikizela-Mandela.

'What confuses their case, however, is Africanist ideology relating to sexuality, most graphically expressed by Mugabe ... It is this implicitly racially governed as well as homophobic mindset that lies behind Mbeki's refusal of the judgment of the overwhelming majority in contemporary science on the nature of the AIDS virus. On the one hand such a view endorses an Africanist myth of a pure and primal Africa contaminated by a sinful West, a reversion to the race theory of the apartheid state. It reflects on the other hand the cloistered, driven mindset that produced the sham biology of Lysenko in the final years of Stalin.'[33]

The analogy to Lysenko seemed particularly apt. Trofim Denisovich Lysenko was a plant breeder who rejected genetics and the theory of natural selection. He believed in the discredited theory that organisms could acquire characteristics from their environment and pass them on to their offspring. Lysenko insisted that his views agreed with Marxism, and gained the support of Stalin's Communist Party. In 1938 he was made president of the Academy of Agricultural Sciences, and began persecuting scientists who did not agree with the official line on genetics and evolution. Many of his colleagues lost their jobs, were arrested, and were sent to die in the Gulag. Only in the early 1950s, after Stalin's death, did the Soviet Union admit that Lysenko had been wrong.

Mbeki persisted with his own fringe version of Lysenkoism.

3

By 2000 Mbeki's self-indulgence had been elevated into state policy. By now – on this issue – the parliamentary opposition could look abroad for support. American opinion had until this point been overwhelmingly on the side of the ANC. Broad international opinion saw little wrong with the party's centralism or race-driven agenda; however, the president's increasingly public AIDS denialism and his association with American AIDS denialists started to turn *bien pensant* opinion against him. What the Americans could not understand was why he had been so seduced – which was far more comprehensible to the DP and me, since we had long been exposed to the ANC's creeping racialism and hostility to dissent.

An opportunity to probe deeper arose during the president's budget vote debate in June 2000. I had little idea that my remarks would unleash Mbeki's full fury, notionally on drug-efficacy, but in reality about the subterranean factors which activated it.

I began, I thought, uncontroversially enough: 'I think the AIDS debate is an acute one. I quote the words uttered on 10 May this year by Charlene Smith, who herself survived a horrific rape ordeal. Let us listen to what she said about the government's and the president's stance: "If, instead of spending vast amounts of money on recreating the wheel, President Mbeki had taken up the Glaxo Wellcome offer – the lowest in the world at

R200 for twenty-eight days' supply of AZT – and made it available to rape survivors to prevent HIV, 10 000 rape survivors in South Africa would have got the drug. Eighty per cent of them would not have sero-converted and become HIV-positive if raped by an HIV-positive person.'"[34]

The president responded, fairly mildly: 'Tony Leon raises the matter of the use of AZT in the instances where women have been raped. It is illogical. I do not know if the manufacturing company here, that manufactures AZT, is in fact selling AZT for that particular indication or giving it out to patients who are in those circumstances, because if they are doing that, I am not sure it [would] be legal. The reason for that is that AZT is not licensed in this country for that particular purpose. Indeed, it is not licensed in any country in the world for that particular purpose. The reason for it is that the manufacturing company says that AZT is not a vaccine. Therefore, one cannot use it in this instance where somebody gets raped, possibly by somebody who is HIV-positive, and if one gives that person AZT, it will stop an infection. The manufacturing company … [has] never applied for the licensing of AZT for that purpose in any country.'[35]

In a narrow sense, he was correct. No countries had licensed AZT as a post-rape prophylaxis. This was partly due to the relatively low incidence of rape in many of the developed countries where AZT was widely available. The Hopkins HIV report of March 1998 noted that 'a national strategy to endorse PEP [post-exposure prophylaxis] for rape victims would be associated with the prevention of less than one HIV transmission per year.'[36]

However, doctors had studied and used AZT in cases of rape in the US and Canada, and PEP was already available to rape survivors in Britain from the National Health Service. A few South African hospitals, such as Chris Hani Baragwanath Hospital in Soweto, were already giving AZT as a post-rape prophylaxis from a supply of the drug given to it free by UNAIDS. Given the gravity of the HIV/AIDS crisis and the high incidence of rape in South Africa, it was understandable that many South Africans would have expected the government to consider the more widespread use of AZT as a post-exposure prophylaxis.

The following week I wrote to the president, assisted by James Myburgh's incisive research: '[With] respect to your response, I believe that my central contention is valid. You, of course, are correct to indicate that AZT is not a vaccine, which I did not suggest it was. It is, however, an antiretroviral medication which will prevent sero-conversion in rape victims who are raped by an HIV-positive person. I accept the accuracy of your statement that AZT is not registered with the relevant authority. But surely this is irrelevant? After all, Misoprostal, used in clinics by the government's own Department of Health to induce abortions, is also not registered by the MCC for that specific purpose.

'As I understand it, a 28-day course of AZT will boost the immunity of a woman raped by an HIV-positive person, thereby allowing her to fight the virus and increase her chances of not converting positive.'[37]

I had checked my facts with the local managing director of Glaxo Wellcome, John Kearney, who wrote to me that he could 'confirm that our reply to the president is essentially accurate on the scientific aspects of using AZT as post-exposure prophylaxis in individuals who have been raped.'[38] I enclosed his comments in my letter to Mbeki.

The president responded in writing at extraordinary length and fury. He attempted to refute my claims about AZT, saying they had 'no scientific basis whatsoever'.[39] Mbeki seized on a slight error I had made in my initial description of AZT. This was to be a fatal mistake – but for him, not me.

Mbeki cited a report by the Centers for Disease Control (CDC) in the US which noted that 'no data exist regarding the efficacy of [antiretroviral drugs] for persons with nonoccupational HIV exposure ...' The CDC, he noted, could not recommend for or against the use of antiretroviral drugs as post-rape prophylactic treatment.

It was clear to me that Mbeki had read and interpreted the CDC report selectively, taking note of only those sections that supported his claims, and misinterpreting important passages. For example, where the CDC reported that 'research is needed to establish if and under what circumstances antiretroviral therapy following nonoccupational HIV exposure is effective', the president seemed to believe this meant that ARVs were ineffective in such cases. Where the CDC had reported that the risk for HIV transmission in cases of 'receptive vaginal exposure' was only 0,1% to 0,2%, Mbeki incorrectly understood 'receptive vaginal exposure' to include rape. He continued to conflate prophylaxis with vaccine, and insisted I had argued that AZT be used as an HIV vaccine.

He scorned what he took to be my claims of superior scientific knowledge and claimed that manufacturers of ARVs, as well as outspoken AIDS activists such as Charlene Smith, were acting out of racist motives: 'I imagine that all manufacturers of antiretroviral drugs pay great attention to the very false figures about the incidence of rape in our country, that are regularly peddled by those who seem so determined to project a negative image of our country ... What makes this matter especially problematic is that there is a considerable number of people in our country who be-

lieve and are convinced that most black [African] men carry the HI virus
... I think that it is dangerous that any of our public representatives and
political parties should allow themselves to be used as marketing agents of
particular products and companies, including drugs, medicines and pharmaceutical companies.'

He also accused Glaxo Wellcome of 'disturbing behaviour' for encouraging the use of a drug for purposes for which it had not yet been approved
by the MCC. When the company's chief executive said Glaxo Wellcome
wanted 'to improve access to drugs for HIV-positive individuals' it had only
its own 'commercial objectives' in mind. He described support for the use
of AZT in post-rape prophylaxis as a violation of the law, and accused me
of a 'double standard' for opposing such claimed violations (involving state
violence) in Zimbabwe while encouraging the (supposedly illegal) use of
antiretrovirals in medical circumstances. A strange conjunction.

Among his conclusions: 'I trust that our discussion about AZT and rape
will convince you that despite the fervent reiteration of various assertions, supported by many scientists, medical people and NGOs, about the
existence of some unchangeable and immutable truths about HIV/AIDS,
as public representatives we have no right to be proponents and blind defenders of dogma ... I would like to suggest that you inform yourself as
extensively as possible about the AIDS epidemic. Again, for this purpose, I
would like to recommend that you access the Internet ...'

The president, perhaps confident that he had destroyed my arguments,
suggested that 'we make the correspondence between us available both to
the National Assembly and to the general public.' I thought this a good
idea, since I felt Mbeki had exposed the depths of his denialism, intolerance of criticism, and intellectual dishonesty in debate. I responded in
writing as follows: 'What is most disturbing about your letter is the way
you impute sinister motivations to the *bona fide* actions of others. You seem
to believe that the request by my party, Charlene Smith and others for
the government to provide AZT to rape victims, and the offer by Glaxo
Wellcome to provide it at greatly reduced prices, is all part of a giant conspiracy ...

'You imply that this conspiracy is the result of some unholy alliance
between a civil society motivated by racism and an international pharmaceutical industry driven by greed. It seems that underlying your letter is a
belief that civil society is once again being driven by an overriding desire
to reaffirm "its belief that its racist stereotype of Africans [is] correct"...
(For the record: neither I nor the Democratic Party have received any
financial assistance of any nature from Glaxo Wellcome.)

'Yet what is most worrying for South Africa is that it seems your party has actually started to believe its own propaganda. Instead of identifying, confronting, and then dealing with the immense problems facing our country, the ANC is perpetually chasing shadows. You seem more concerned with the possibility that high rape and AIDS figures might confirm the prejudices of some, than with the massive human tragedy in our country …

'You are entitled to your personal opinion on whether AZT is effective in reducing HIV transmission, and indeed, whether HIV even causes AIDS. However, it is wrong for you to use your current position (which was gained on the basis of political rather than medical talent) to block the provision by your government of such treatment. The point is that the physician and the patient must be left to make that decision. By denying rape victims AZT you are denying them the choice. With all due respect, you lack both the moral right and the medical expertise to make such a life and death decision.' I formally agreed with the president that we should make our correspondence public.

We sent the correspondence to Ray Hartley of the *Sunday Times*. The exchange created an immediate sensation, causing outrage at the president and placing his denialist views in the spotlight.[40] As for Mbeki's methods of argument, the *Mail&Guardian* editorialised the following week: 'An analysis of the president's letter by Leon … points to a distortion of fact by way of contextual manipulation which, if used by a second-hand car salesman, would verge on the fraudulent.'[41] Glaxo Wellcome, fearful of the damage the affair might cause, issued a statement clarifying that it had not recommended AZT for post-rape prophylaxis, and claiming I had misinterpreted their offer. However, the company also confirmed many of the other points I had made. These were conveniently ignored by Mbeki in his next letter, ten days later.[42] The drug company's attempt to buy itself some slack was to no avail.

Mbeki argued that the statements by Glaxo Wellcome contradicted each other, and reiterated his contention that I had spoken incorrectly in the National Assembly when I quoted Charlene Smith about the potential benefits of AZT. He also repeated his central thesis: 'I remain firmly of the view that had AZT been promoted and offered at reduced prices for rape cases, this would have constituted very disturbing behaviour on the part of Glaxo Wellcome, driven by nothing else except profit, with no regard for ethics and the health of our people. It would require that the government take the necessary action to stop what would have been illegal behaviour …

'I believe that STDs [sexually transmitted diseases] are very relevant to the collapse of immune systems among many Africans, including our own people, and therefore the acquired immune deficiency syndrome ... I hope that the international scientific panel on AIDS that we have convened will address the important issue of STDs. However, whatever the impact of STDs on the immune system, the correct medical response to infection with these is to treat them using established therapies. None of these include the use of AZT or any of the other antiretrovirals.'

Mbeki then returned to his argument about racist stereotypes of Africans, accusing Charlene Smith – a journalist, rape survivor and anti-apartheid activist, who went to jail for her beliefs – of racism. He accused me of failing to correct her perceptions of African men, and of supporting them by referring to high rape statistics in South Africa. 'To me as an African,' he wrote, 'it is both interesting and disturbing that the signatories of the so-called "Durban Declaration" return to the thesis about the alleged original transmission of HIV "from [African] animals to humans", given what science has said about AIDS during the last two decades. I accept that it may be that you do not understand the significance of this and the message it communicates to Africans, hence your queer observation that I seek to silence our critics, without responding to their arguments.'

Mbeki insisted that he had the right to interfere in medical matters: 'As a government, we will not abdicate our responsibility to work for the health of all our people, leaving this matter exclusively to "the physician and the patient" as you suggest. I may have no medical expertise, but I have grave doubts that the fact of being the largest opposition party means that you are best-placed to advise our government about the medical decisions it should take ...'

The president closed by complaining that I had already released our correspondence to the media. He now tried to claim that I had violated 'common courtesy' by not informing him that I intended to do so – which, in fact, I had. His final swipe: '[Possibly] we do originate from different planets with radically different value systems.'

When I showed Mbeki's letter to one of South Africa's most respected and learned AIDS activists (who himself was sick with the virus), he described its contents as 'stomach-churning' and 'nauseating'. In fact, the correspondence continued as I attempted to persuade the president – to little effect – by delving into the scientific arcana of HIV/AIDS through the assistance of a DA reseacher. Mbeki had evidently formulated his views on the disease from his tangled conspiracy theories, belief in rampant white racism, and refusal – isolated as he was increasingly becoming from the urgent medical deficits within society – to take stock of the actual needs of the masses whom he presumptively claimed to represent not just politically, but intellectually as well. And of course, his praise-singers simply echoed his inflection.

4

In my response to his letter, I had made an appeal to Mbeki to 'pull together' in the fight against HIV/AIDS, rather than reducing it to an issue of race. I also asked him to join me in following 'the conventions of reasonable, regular and frank discussion that were established during the constitutional negotiations and continued by your predecessor during the ANC's first term in office.' This, I argued, would not be an intrusion by the opposition on the government, but would send an important message to South Africans in a time of crisis.

In his response Mbeki questioned my patriotism and my understanding of democratic conventions. He spurned my suggestion that we campaign together on a joint platform to take an anti-AIDS message to the broad public. His words contained a barely suppressed anger:

'You state that the appearance of the president and the leader of the official opposition on the same stage, campaigning on the same health issue, would make "a very great public impact."

'You may very well be correct.

'But I can also imagine how many people there would be, at home and abroad, who would ask a particular question.

'That question would be – why does the elected president not have sufficient courage to discharge his responsibilities about the health challenge we face, without requiring that the leader of the official opposition should hold his hand!

'Surely, you must admit that the executive role you seek is somewhat strange in any normal democracy. It is also inconsistent with everything you say and do every day to convince all and sundry how rotten our government and its policies are.'

However, the basis of his approach appeared towards the end of his missive, when he chose to define and limit both the essentials of the problem and his meaning of patriotism.

'It would be obscene to reduce this to an HIV/AIDS issue, as you do. It would be a fundamental error to reduce the challenges we face to the incidence of disease in our country, as you do.'[43]

In my final response, I tried to address concisely many of the counter-arguments Mbeki had made. I pointed out that the legal opinions he had cited did not actually support his views. Once again, I noted, the president had been 'guilty of extremely selective quotation.'

I also drew Mbeki's attention to his gross double-standard: his championing of the scientifically repudiated Virodene and his claim that the scientifically tested AZT was 'toxic'.[44]

I received no response other than a presidential note on 1 September 2000 which merely asserted that the government was doing all it could 'to respond to the health challenges facing our people'; and that the correspondence was now closed.[45]

It may well have been on the level of written communication: but the debate around its implications continued. Excerpts were reprinted in national newspapers when the letters were published in full in the *Government Gazette*. Peter Bruce, editor of *Business Day*, later commented that Mbeki 'must regret allowing an exchange of letters with Democratic Party leader Tony Leon to be published ... Leon won, simply by finishing many of the quotes Mbeki had half-used to justify his position.'[46]

Despite the outcry against Mbeki's denialist views, he persisted. In October 2000, it emerged that during an ANC parliamentary caucus meeting, Mbeki insisted that there was no causal link between HIV and AIDS – and, furthermore, that the pharmaceutical companies were conspiring with the US Central Intelligence Agency to cover up the real truth about the disease.[47]

Many of the facts presented to me by our diligent researcher, James Myburgh, had been checked and researched by some of South Africa's leading medical virologists and immunologists. I was, therefore, fairly confident that the arguments I advanced – whatever the political fall-out – proceeded from a sound and verifiable basis. But who was advising Mbeki never became clear. It can be surmised that many of his opinions arose from a deep-seated ideological position. At a meeting in KwaZulu-Natal, even as the letters were passing to and fro, I remarked that he had a 'near obsession' with finding African solutions to every problem, even if this meant flouting science in favour of 'snake-oil cures and quackery'.[48] Mbeki responded viciously, as I recount in Chapter 15.

On 20 September 2000, in parliament, Mbeki announced to loud applause from the ANC that a 'virus cannot cause a syndrome'. That AIDS was caused by HIV was 'a thesis'. It was Dr Pieter Mulder of the Freedom Front who nailed Mbeki with a killer question: 'Madam Speaker, at the moment millions of people die in Africa and South Africa because of this pandemic. The president stated ... today that the Department [of Health] uses the thesis that HIV causes AIDS and that [their] whole campaign is based on that. Does the president agree that the debate at the moment as it is conducted here today and in the media out there, confuses the people?' Mbeki was completely at a loss and responded meekly: 'Yes, I would agree with the Hon. Mulder that perhaps all of us, myself included, because of the manner in which we handled this matter, might indeed have contributed to this confusion.'[49]

The accusations continued for several weeks, with the ANC describing DA proposals to provide antiretrovirals to the poor as an attempt to use Africans as 'guinea pigs'.[50] But the tide of public opinion was turning against the president, at home and abroad.

Drew Forrest, deputy editor of the *Mail&Guardian*, reflecting a year later on my correspondence with the president, and considering it alongside Mbeki's other utterances on HIV/AIDS, concluded:

'Whatever Mbeki's army of apologists may say, the hard fact is that our leader is an AIDS dissident. What clouds the picture is his awareness – sharpened by his rough treatment at the hands of foreign journalists – that dissidence is not an intellectually respectable position in the wider world. His views are, therefore, veiled by a smokescreen of "nondenial denial", academic quibbling and obfuscation ...

'Why does Mbeki unquestioningly accept the mainstream scientific view on other diseases caused by invisible pathogens – tuberculosis, polio, etc. – but not on AIDS? The answer seems to [have become] entangled with his hyper-defensiveness on race. A viral explanation of the rampant epidemic in central and southern Africa, in his mind, amounts to saying black people are polluted "germ carriers" who cannot control their sexual behaviour. His rejection of the African origins of AIDS as "insulting" has the same implications. It is absolutely unclear why an epidemic should reflect on the moral character of Africans. Who else but Mbeki, and perhaps the loony Right, has ever suggested this?'[51]

After so much controversy, which dogged him everywhere, Mbeki withdrew from the debate over HIV/AIDS. ANC spokesperson Smuts Ngonyama claimed: 'It is only a question of scaling down on the issue and not backing off. The president will still be involved in any public debate.'[52] However, at the same time that Mbeki's so-called 'withdrawal' was being executed, DA health researcher Julia Frielinghaus dug out the fact that the Health minister had been distributing, to all provincial health ministers, a bizarre conspiracy theory: 'Behold a Pale Horse'.

The innovative Julia had also worked out that the parliamentary medical aid was paying for antiretrovirals for 68 senior members of government and senior public servants, including a certain number – eleven, we were told by one source, although we were unable to confirm this – of ANC MPs, even as the government was denying the drugs to its own voters through the public health care system. She gave the information to the *Sunday Times* which emblazoned it on their front page under the headline: 'Hypocrites!'

Strangely, despite Mbeki's dissidence and the failure of his government to provide the drugs, some prominent commentators persisted in taking his side. Although tens of thousands of lives were at stake, much of the press comment was on the lines that while Mbeki might have erred, I should 'cool it'. Prominent ANC apologists like Nadine Gordimer and Anthony Sampson wrote to the *New York Review of Books* to, in effect, defend Mbeki against criticism of his AIDS policy. At home, the increasingly anti-DA newspaper the *Star* went further: its political correspondent, Robert Brand, actively took Mbeki's side in the dispute over ARVs, headlining his views (fatuously and inaccurately): 'How Mbeki won the great AZT and rape debate'.[53]

However, the government clearly realised that the president's views were a liability, and the duty of tackling the disease was handed off to the Health minister and to then-deputy president Jacob Zuma. The president's close aides, such as Essop Pahad, later tried to claim that the president never said HIV did not cause AIDS. The argument failed to convince anyone: Mbeki never recanted.

5

As the controversy over the president's beliefs about HIV continued, so, too, did the fight for antiretroviral treatment. ARVs were already available in private hospitals; most public hospitals, however, were not providing ARVs to their patients, and given government's attitude, were unlikely to do so any time soon.

The DA began considering a new HIV/AIDS policy: one that would provide ARVs to those who needed them, at a cost government could afford. We found there was some merit in the argument that providing antiretrovirals might prove too costly; the route to provision, therefore, was to negotiate the prices of drugs with pharmaceutical companies, or through political pressure. It was not unrealistic: Glaxo Wellcome, for example, had offered to make a 'cocktail' of ARV drugs called COMBIVIR available to the developing world at $2 a day.

Again, in 2001, 39 multinational drug companies who had sued government to protect their patent rights and prevent South Africa from using generic versions of their ARVs finally dropped their case. This led to the possibility that South Africa might purchase or produce generic antiretrovirals.

A major problem was then getting the drugs to the patients. One proposal was that the government should focus on treating other STDs, which increase the risk of contracting HIV, or on treating the opportunistic infections that affect those with AIDS. In my view, this did not go far enough: new infections had to be prevented through education, providing condoms, and the care of AIDS orphans, one tragic outcome of the pandemic.

It was possible for government to begin addressing all of these problems by focusing on mother-to-child transmission (MTCT). Drugs such as AZT and Nevirapine had proven very effective in preventing HIV-positive pregnant women from passing on the virus to their children. They needed to be taken by the mother and the infant only once, and therefore would be relatively cheap to administer. A report commissioned by the Department of Health in April 2000 found it would cost only a few rands per baby to save the lives of 14 000 babies every year.[54]

A nationwide treatment roll-out was actually in preparation. Government had appointed a National Steering Committee on mother-to-child transmission in September 2000, and planned to establish two research sites in each province. Here, initially, the groundwork would be laid for the wider roll-out. In April 2001, the MCC approved Nevirapine, and pilot studies began in July 2001. The manufacturer, Boehringer Ingelheim, had offered to provide Nevirapine free for five years.[55]

Probably because of the inertia at the top, government refused to extend MTCT programmes beyond the pilot studies, and refused to allow doctors in other public hospitals to provide Nevirapine. So tens of thousands of HIV-positive babies were still being born – each carrying an avoidable death sentence. Government claimed that providing the drug was too costly, given all the other health care services – testing, counselling, etc. – that needed concurrent provision. It claimed Nevirapine might lead to the emergence of drug-resistant forms of HIV; that the safety of the drug had not been assured; and that the health care system lacked the capacity to roll out Nevirapine.[56]

AIDS activists responded by taking the government to court. While this was pending, there was still much to be done. The opposition coalition – made up of the DP and the NNP – had governed the Western Cape since 1999. Under this regime, several public hospitals in the Western Cape had been providing MTCT interventions for almost two years, well ahead of the rest of the country. Favourable results allowed the programme to be extended. In August 2000 Health MEC Nick Koornhof announced that MTCT treatment would be available to some of the province's poorest communities: 'We started early, and this has made it possible for us to have this roll-out to six sites ... I understand that this announcement may cause controversy in certain circles, but we have taken this decision because it is the right thing to do, and not to play politics ... it would have been immoral for us not to proceed.'[57]

While Koornhof (who thrived on publicity but hated confrontation) tried to downplay the political dimension, it was clear enough: an opposition-controlled province was moving forward. In October 2000 I pledged to parliament: '[Wherever] the DA wins control of a local government in South Africa, there we will do everything in our power – subject to normal ethical and legal regimes – to make antiretroviral drugs available to HIV-positive pregnant women and rape survivors as a starting point.'[58]

Certainly, the pledge was made with the forthcoming local government elections in December 2000 in mind; but it was one the DA acted on immediately. Koornhof and I visited Europe in October 2000 to investigate the possibility of bringing the drugs into South Africa for use in Western Cape hospitals. Despite the refusal of any South African embassies to assist us, we were successful. We issued the following statement on our return:

- In the Western Cape, subject to provincial cabinet approval, ARV drug discounts will be negotiated directly.
- The cost-saving will enable more projects to be rolled out, particularly for unicity administrations.
- When parliament resumes ... the DA will call for the Portfolio Committee on Health to be convened urgently to take evidence on the true status and precise nature of the South African government's interaction with the expanded access initiative and the real reasons for [its] laconic or indifferent response.
- The DA, at all levels where it holds executive power, will seek to provide ARV drugs, as of right, in the cases of mother-to-child transmission and rape, where indicated and approved.[59]

Inevitably, exploiting a loophole allowing provincial and local governments not only to negotiate with drug companies, but to provide and dispense drugs, we pushed the fight against AIDS to the top of the political agenda. In his typical bare-knuckled way, our master strategist Ryan Coetzee flighted the following advertisement on various radio stations: 'If your daughter were raped, would you deny her access to drugs that could save her from AIDS? That is what the ANC does. The DA says make free anti-AIDS drugs available to rape survivors exposed to HIV infection. The DA government in the Western Cape already does. Isn't it time the rest of the country did the same!'

The furious ANC response was to accuse us of peddling 'poisons'. Caught in a device of the president's own making, they could not match our offer. Instead – in the words of journalist Mondli Makhanya – 'ANC spokesman Smuts Ngonyama accused the Democratic Alliance of something akin to apartheid-era biological warfare by providing toxic anti-retroviral drugs to black communities.'[60]

I have no doubt that the exceptionally soft underbelly of the ANC on AIDS, and Mbeki's disastrous mishandling of it, contributed – in part – to our very good showing at the polls on 5 December. The DA recorded the highest-ever percentage for the main opposition party since 1994, and swept to power in 25 municipalities, mostly in the Western and Northern Cape.

In 2001, I proposed that value-added tax (VAT) on AIDS drugs – and all the medicines on the Essential Drugs List – be removed. In November that year, the DA introduced a private member's bill in parliament to amend the Patents Act to allow government to permit the production of generic antiretroviral drugs and to declare a national AIDS emergency, which would, in accordance with international agreements, allow patent rights on life-saving drugs to be bypassed.

Towards the end of 2001, in October, speaking at Fort Hare University, Mbeki truly defined his stance on AIDS.[61] His well-known race consciousness and its impact on public health policy were now easier to understand:

'[Thus] does it happen that others who consider themselves to be our leaders take to the streets carrying their placards, to demand that because we are germ carriers, and human beings of a lower order that cannot subject its passions to reason, we must perforce adopt strange opinions, to save a depraved and diseased people from perishing from self-inflicted disease ... Convinced that we are but natural-born, promiscuous carriers of germs, unique in the world, they proclaim that our continent is doomed to an inevitable mortal end because of our unconquerable devotion to the sin of lust.'

Very few newspapers initially carried the speech with its strong, indeed extreme, denialist suggestions. However, after James Myburgh – an avid reader of the ANC's website – stumbled on it, he drew it to the attention of Drew Forrest at the *Mail&Guardian*. Forrest asked leading AIDS activist and lawyer Mark Heywood to deconstruct it. His analysis was damning: '[The speech] appears to describe those who believe AIDS is a virologically caused, mostly sexually transmitted disease that can be medically contained, as stigmatising and demeaning [of] black people ... [The] evidence tragically but inexorably suggests that the president is an unreconstructed AIDS dissident.'[62]

Nonetheless, other provinces began following the lead of the Western Cape. In January 2002, KwaZulu-Natal announced it would begin distributing Nevirapine to HIV-positive pregnant mothers.[63] It was no accident that the first two provinces to provide the drug were those where the opposition held power. Gauteng, where the opposition had a strong presence, became the third region to provide Nevirapine in February 2002.[64] But the other six provinces, where the ANC ruled by wider margins, laboured under denialism.

Meanwhile, in the courts, the government lost to the TAC at every level – right to the Constitutional Court in July 2002 where proponents of antiretroviral treatment won an historic victory. As court observer Carmel Rickard wrote in the *Sunday Times*:

'The court found the state had not met its constitutional obligations, and ordered that, to do so, it should remove the restrictions preventing Nevirapine from being made available at public hospitals and clinics that are not research and training sites.

'It found that there was no reason why the state could not continue to collect data and closely monitor the use of Nevirapine at its chosen pilot sites. But at the same time, it should provide the drug at its other birthing institutions where the facilities existed to do so. The state was also ordered to take reasonable measures to extend testing and counselling throughout the public health sector to facilitate the use of Nevirapine to reduce the risk of mother-to-child transmission of HIV.'[65]

Even before this landmark ruling, around March, the fight around Mbeki's stance was internalised within the ANC. The iconic Madiba was apparently shouted down when he attempted to persuade the ANC National Executive to change its position. At the same time, Peter Mokaba distributed a bizarre essay entitled 'Castro Hlongwane'. The document promoted the dissident view; and while authorship was unknown, suspicion fell on Mbeki. Our research department was sent an electronic copy, and I was told that when they checked its 'properties' it was discovered to have been written on Mbeki's computer. The *Mail&Guardian* did a similar check and came to the same conclusion.[66]

Despite huge celebrations at the Constitutional Court's decision, government continued to drag its feet. It again insisted that South Africa could not afford to provide ARVs directly to AIDS patients. This might have been true of the five million people living with HIV, but the DA argued that it was feasible to provide antiretrovirals to the most desperately ill patients – 500 000 of them. In 2003 we called for just such provision to be achieved within five years and funded through spending such as cancelling arms purchases.

New projects to provide ARVs were started in the Western Cape and elsewhere, often with the help of NGOs such as Medicins Sans Frontières. The TAC launched a civil disobedience campaign in March 2003 after government refused to honour an agreement reached at Nedlac in 2002 on implementation of a national HIV/AIDS treatment plan.

The ANC was extremely nervous about the TAC campaign, particularly the negative publicity it generated at home and abroad; the next general elections were only a year away. I also believed that our success in the 2000 elections had its political effect on the ANC, since the party ultimately adopted what was essentially the DA position ahead of the April 2004 poll. The roll-out, when it was announced, included providing ARVs as a post-exposure prophylactic for rape victims. This was far more than the judgment required, and placed government policy in line with DA practice in the Western Cape.

After receiving reassurances from the ANC, the TAC agreed to suspend its civil disobedience campaign following a meeting with Deputy President Zuma in early May. It hoped that a shift in government policy would be effected.[67] Indeed, in August, the cabinet announced a roll-out of antiretrovirals across the country; technical details would follow in subsequent months.

Did all this register an official Damascene conversion on the HIV/AIDS issue? No. International criticism and domestic protests made a significant impact, as did the upcoming elections. The Gauteng government, for example, announced a provincial roll-out of ARVs, ahead of the national initiative, just two weeks before election day. This opportunism was at least partial evidence that the ANC had not turned its back on the racial and ideological arguments it had used for years to defend the indefensible.

There was a distinct lack of political commitment to implementing the roll-out after the election. When the cabinet did announce its detailed plan for the roll-out in November, it set a target of 53 000 people to be treated with ARVs by March 2004. It missed this deadline, and missed its new deadline of March 2005 as well. However, the fact that the government had, notionally at least, performed a U-turn of spectacular proportions, suggested that certain aspects of democratic accountability were indeed active and alive in South Africa.

The ANC continued to insist, at home and abroad, that it had the largest HIV/AIDS programme in the world, in sheer size and expense. What it was not was the most effective or efficient. Prevalence rates continued to climb; hundreds of thousands continued to die in greater and greater numbers every year.

6

The main reason why the disease continued to spread was that South Africans failed to change their sexual behaviour. And one of the reasons for this was that government continued to send mixed messages about how the disease was spread and how it was to be treated. The ruling party now operated on the 'premise' that HIV caused AIDS: but the essential scientific basis of that 'premise' was never accepted by the president or his party. In September 2003 Mbeki told a reporter from the *Washington Post*: 'Personally, I don't know anybody who has died of AIDS ... I really, honestly don't.'

In a country where upwards of three hundred thousand people died of AIDS every year, and in which at least two of the president's close associates – Mankahlana and Mokaba – were thought to have died of AIDS, the statement seemed ludicrous and was widely interpreted as a sign of Mbeki's continued denialism and insensitivity.

The villain of the piece presented herself with astonishing effrontery. The minister of Health in succession to Dlamini-Zuma, Manto Tshabalala-Msimang – later to be described by the *Sunday Times* as 'a drunk and a thief' – continued to refer to ARVs as toxic. At the Fifteenth International AIDS Conference in Bangkok, Thailand, in July 2004, she announced that government was reviewing the use of Nevirapine because of potential risks.[68] In addition, she notoriously championed a 'nutritionist' theory of AIDS, a corollary of the fixation that poverty, not HIV, was the direct proximate cause of AIDS. Her quack belief held that better nutrition was the key to prevention and even cure of the disease. The minister recommended a concoction of olive oil, lemon juice, beetroot,

345

garlic and African potato. This diet, she maintained, was effective in boost-
ing immunity and fighting AIDS. Many mocked; but many – possibly
millions – believed her.

The minister's recipe was often presented as an indigenous alternative
to ARVs – the kind of 'African solution' that Mbeki had been looking for.
In reality, it was the invention of a Dutch woman, Tine van der Maas, a
one-time nurse who taught herself nutritional therapies.

Having gained the confidence of the Health minister, she proceeded
to provide her 'cure' to several AIDS patients. Some claimed her remedy
worked; for others, such as celebrity disk jockey Fana 'Khabzela' Khaba, it
did not. Khabzela was one of the rare celebrities to acknowledge his HIV
status; he publicly declared his intention to take ARVs and was regarded as
a hero. But he soon ended his course and tried alternative remedies. Van
der Maas was sent to help him, allegedly by Tshabalala–Msimang herself,
and administered her treatment for two months. Khabzela then died, his
immune system totally destroyed.[69]

Some studies indicated that the African potato could actually harm patients with HIV/AIDS, and could weaken the positive effects of antiretrovirals.[70] The Health minister was undeterred: in August 2006, she opened
the South African AIDS exhibition at the International AIDS Conference
in Toronto, Canada – her contribution featured brightly coloured displays
showcasing garlic, lemon and beetroot.

The minister announced 'with pride' that she enjoyed the nickname
'Dr Beetroot'.

Shortly after Toronto, 81 leading scientists wrote to the president urging
him to fire her. They declared: 'To have as Health minister someone who
now has no international respect is an embarrassment to the South African
government', and called for an end to the 'disastrous, pseudo-scientific
policies ... that have characterised government's response to the epidemic.'
At the conclusion of the pivotal conference in Toronto, UN AIDS envoy
Stephen Lewis charged: 'South Africa is the only country in Africa ...
whose government is still obtuse, dilatory and negligent about rolling out
treatment. It is the only country in Africa whose government continues to
propound theories more worthy of a lunatic fringe than of a concerned
or compassionate state.'[71]

This again led to a surge of local opinion for the minister's removal. But
as one cynic noted: 'The only way to lose your place in the Mbeki cabinet
is to die.'

It became increasingly obvious as the months passed, however, that she
was plagued by more than the demons of denialism. At a press briefing in

2007, she lost her place, asked for questions to be repeated, directed questions to the wrong people, and at one point broke into Russian.

All became – at least a little – clearer the next month, when a statement on 14 March from the Donald Gordon Medical Centre in Johannesburg made the astonishing anouncement that the minister had just undergone a liver transplant. Her doctors told the media that the cause was auto-immune hepatitis, but speculation was that the real cause was alcoholism. This allegation was initially made public when the *Sunday Times* reported that she had ordered nurses at a hospital in Cape Town to buy alcohol for her – and is an accusation that continues to hound her.

It was only when the Transport minister, Jeff Radebe, took over from the minister during her convalescence, and handed management of the department largely over to then deputy Health minister Nozizwe Madlala-Routledge, that a measure of direction emerged from the department. An updated antiretroviral roll-out took off, and a renewed sense of unity between government and civil society was restored.

Sadly, the détente was short-lived. Almost as soon as Tshabalala-Msimang was back to full health, the deputy minister was sent packing for not being a 'team player'. Although an ambitious new AIDS plan was made public in December 2006, just before the minister received her new liver, there is still a marked lack of detail about how the targets will be achieved; and it remains very much an open question as to whether government will truly put its money where its mouth is in committing the necessary resources to achieving these goals.

Tshabalala-Msimang clashed rep§eatedly with the TAC, as well as with the DA. We even started a website – www.firemanto.co.za – aimed at forcing the president to dismiss her. But she was retained after the 2004 elections, despite her abysmal performance in her first term. Following my long – and increasingly uneasy – correspondence with Mbeki, I was convinced that the president himself was the de facto minister of Health, Msimang his faithful messenger. Her political loyalty to Mbeki secured her tenure – and gave her the opportunity to retaliate.

The Health Department openly funded TAC opponents, and an association of traditional healers was encouraged by government to march against the Treatment Action Campaign on the pretext that it disparaged traditional medicine by supporting antiretroviral treatment. By far the most dangerous partnership was between government and the 'Dr Rath Health Foundation', led by Matthias Rath, an AIDS dissident who claimed that ARVs were toxic; and that they were being promoted by the TAC and DA as part of a global conspiracy involving pharmaceutical companies. He claimed his own vitamin treatments could reverse AIDS, and had established clinics in poor neighbourhoods in South Africa to distribute his products, none registered with the MCC or any other South African authority. Through slick marketing, publicity and staged confrontations with the TAC, Rath has caused even greater confusion about HIV/ AIDS, and enjoys the support of Tshabalala-Msimang. A few ANC figures, such as Ben Turok MP and former Education minister Kader Asmal, have spoken out against him, but Rath continues to operate in South Africa with impunity. He responds to criticism by filing defamation suits, many of which are later dropped.

In October 2004 the president appeared in the National Assembly to answer questions, and the DA seized the opportunity. Ryan Coetzee asked Mbeki whether he believed rape was widespread in South Africa; whether it could, in part, account for the spread of HIV; and whether the president would now play a more active role in leading the fight against HIV/AIDS. Mbeki proceeded to accuse Coetzee of seeking 'to engage in a televised debate that will help some people in our country to perpetuate the very dangerous pretence that racism in our country died with the holding of our first democratic elections ten years ago.'[72]

He went on: '[For] my part, I will not keep quiet while others whose minds have been corrupted by the disease of racism accuse us, the black people of South Africa, Africa and the world, as being, by virtue of our Africanness and skin colour – lazy, liars, foul-smelling, diseased, corrupt, violent, amoral, sexually depraved, animalistic, savage – and rapist.'

He cited an African-American professor who had written: 'We are portrayed as oversexed or lascivious, and yet the porn and adult entertainment industry is dominated by whites. It is African-Americans that get accused of being rampant sexual beasts, unable to control our urges, unable to keep our legs crossed, unable to keep it in our pants.'[73] For him, there was no debate about HIV/AIDS; there was only a never-ending, never-yielding debate on race.

The president had produced stereotypes of black people and Africans akin to the wildest rantings of the Ku Klux Klan, and claimed that this was what many white people – including his political opponents – really thought. Not only was this in itself racist, but it promoted such stereotypes by graphically imposing them on public debate and discourse. This irony is at the core of Mbeki's failed policy. His stance is based on a defence of black and African dignity. Yet it has condemned many of those suffering with HIV/AIDS, the vast majority of whom are black, to illness and death. The effects reach far beyond the victims themselves. HIV among teachers and nurses is having a profoundly negative effect on public education and health care in South Africa; HIV in the armed forces threatens their readiness and hence the security of the state.[74] As for the economy, it continues to grow, but at a far slower pace than it would if the government had acted quickly and decisively to fight HIV/AIDS.

I cannot but think that Mbeki's disastrous and wholly destructive AIDS policies in many ways destroyed – or at least deeply dented – his moral authority. It certainly smashed the aura of infallibility with which his presidency began. Beyond the tragedy of his views, there was great irony: Mbeki lambasted me for being 'a white politician', and preferred at all times to surround himself with – and indeed was often propped up by – a coterie of yes-men (and some significant women) who simply fortified his eccentric views and gave vent to his feelings of fury and displeasure at what he called 'my disdain and contempt for African solutions'. Yet, if Mbeki had in fact listened to the mainstream views I and so many others articulated (they were certainly not original) and had accepted that his opponents were not actuated by racial malice, his reputation would not have been so tarnished.

The impulses that drove South Africa's AIDS policy would also surface in confronting our greatest foreign policy challenge, across the Limpopo River, in Zimbabwe.

CHAPTER 9

Zimbabwe: The Fire Next Door

The fight against Zimbabwe is a fight against us all. Today it is Zimbabwe, tomorrow it will be South Africa, it will be Mozambique, it will be Angola, it will be any other African country. And any government that is perceived to be strong, and to be resistant to imperialists, would be made a target and would be undermined. So let us not allow any point of weakness in the solidarity of SADC, because that weakness will also be transferred to the rest of Africa.

ROBERT MUGABE, QUOTING THABO MBEKI

Sometimes, we must interfere. When human lives are endangered, when human dignity is in jeopardy, national borders and sensitivities become irrelevant. Wherever men or women are persecuted because of their race, religion or political views, that place must – at that moment – become the centre of the universe.

ELIE WIESEL

I

When I was nine years old, my brother and I were taken on a 'Flame Lily' holiday to Rhodesia. I had never left South Africa, and our northern neighbour seemed a different world – though the size of its economy was no greater then than that of the Durban-Pinetown area, and an hour-and-a-half's flight away in the sturdy and wide-windowed Vickers-Viscounts of Central African Airways. Almost all its white inhabitants spoke English; race relations – although strictly segregated – were said to be easier than in South Africa; and it seemed immensely more sophisticated because it had television!

Victoria Falls and the expanses of Lake Kariba were far less important than being allowed to watch TV for the ten nights of our stay. Of the politics of Rhodesia I knew and cared little. However, the year before, on 11 November 1965, Ian Smith, chafing at the colonial power, Britain, then shedding its Empire, had ushered in 15 years of conflict and diplomacy.

He made a Unilateral Declaration of Independence (UDI), an illegal and fateful step.

In Westville, where we lived with my newly re-wed mother and her husband (my first of two stepfathers), UDI was a cause for unmitigated celebration. Two neighbours, and the children with whom I played, were Rhodesian. Smith was a hero (in one living room, a copper relief bust of him stood proudly on the mantelpiece). His adversary, the pipe-smoking British prime minister, Harold Wilson, was disparaged and ridiculed in demonic terms.

My mother's liberal sentiments dictated a different response. But overwhelmingly, the white tide was in favour of Salisbury, the capital of the new white 'republic'.

Rhodesia was a constant – and increasingly dissonant – background noise in my childhood. I became reacquainted with its situation in my university years. It was 1978 and Smith was by then beleaguered by a widening bush war – essentially a civil conflict. He had decided that confrontation needed to be tempered by the politics of co-option. Accordingly, he turned his back on several failed or faltering international attempts to settle the question – which involved everyone from Wilson and his successor James Callaghan, to US secretary of state Henry Kissinger, South African prime minister John Vorster, and Zambian president Kenneth Kaunda.

Instead, he would embrace an 'internal agreement' excluding his main African nationalist rivals (Robert Mugabe's Zanu and Joshua Nkomo's ZAPU, which enjoyed mass support). His proposed deal brought in 'internal parties': a Zanu breakaway under its founding leader Ndabaningi Sithole (whom Mugabe had helped depose when both were imprisoned by Smith) and the United African National Congress, headed by the diminutive Bishop Abel Muzorewa. They cobbled together a new constitution, whose complexities could not hide the fact that while power-sharing was notionally the new order, Smith would continue in office and the Rhodesian security forces would retain their current command structures.

Donald Rallis and I, then on the Wits SRC, were curious to visit the war-torn territory when the new arrangement was to be tested in an all-race poll, which the exile forces boycotted. I sold some shares (a gift to me) to fund the visit, and Rallis arranged with the Rhodesian authorities for accreditation as observers. We hugely offended the Left.

It was rather different to a 'Flame Lily' excursion. The Air Rhodesia Viscount had its blue-and-white livery camouflaged by brown paint. We did not descend directly onto the runway, but performed a sort of spiralling, circular landing with the plane lights off – as the pilot informed his white-knuckled passengers, to avoid a strike from a surface-to-air missile similar to that which Nkomo's forces had used to blow up two planes a year before.

The skill of the pilot was in direct contrast to the political clumsiness of Rhodesia's leaders. We met personally only Sithole: a rather strange encounter in his suburban home where his garrulous son held court for an hour or so over tea, while his more famous father sat in gloomy silence, interrupting only to offer more refreshment. I don't suppose he understood what two unkempt students from Johannesburg could do for him.

The election proceeded peacefully enough; but the seemingly impressive turnout (augmented by white farmers who drove their workers to vote in trucks) did little to conceal the fact that the new arrangement offered little respite from the mounting war. There would be no legitimacy for the black participants in government, who were regarded as stooges and sell-outs.

Two years later, at the end of 1979, with the reluctant blessing of Margaret Thatcher, and the grudging acquiescence of Smith, a political gambler who had finally run out of cards, the British-sponsored Lancaster House talks ushered in a majority-rule settlement. This paved the way for all-party elections and Zimbabwean independence in 1980.

What seemed to be a successful and democratic conclusion to Rhodesia's travails would prove little more than a respite. For much of my political leadership period, there was no darker or more tragic shadow over Africa's hopes than Zimbabwe, the constitutional inheritor of Rhodesia.

When Zimbabwe – named for the great Zimbabwe ruins of the ancient Munhumutapa Empire – held its first democratic elections in 1980, it was the second-most-developed nation on the continent. By 2000, it was troubled by a host of political and economic problems – yet seemed poised to recover. But by 2008 it resembled a nation in ruins: her people denied basic civil and political rights, and surviving at the precarious edge of subsistence. Millions of Zimbabweans, facing poverty and starvation, had fled to South Africa; the country's scarce skilled workers have moved to Johannesburg, London and New York, perhaps never to return: a success story became an archetypal nightmare.

At the time of finally revising this book, in April 2008, it appeared that Zimbabwe might, against the odds, be poised to shake off the tyranny which had encased it for the preceding years: Zanu(PF) lost its parliamentary majority, and its president was entering into a final, perhaps fatal, endgame. But whatever the eventual outcome of its recent election, there were clear and grim lessons to be learned from its democratic implosion. Many of them centred around the man who brought about its collapse, who was also its liberator, Robert Gabriel Mugabe. For 28 years he held power uninterruptedly. In the words of Samantha Power, professor at Harvard University's Kennedy School of Government, he was, at the end, 'one of the last surviving members of the club of African big men' – having led bold opposition to colonial rule, such men became, in her words, 'addicted to power and its trappings ... Mugabe, acting less as a ruler than an owner of his land', followed a how-to manual of national destruction, as his support waned. Power thoughtfully entitled her piece: 'How to kill a country.'[1]

Mugabe was once a symbol of reconciliation. On taking office, the former guerrilla fighter pledged to put his country on the path of reconstruction: 'We will ensure there is a place for everyone in this country. We want to ensure a sense of security for both the winners and the losers ... I urge you, whether you are black or white, to join me in a new pledge to forget our grim past, forgive others and forget, join hands in a new amity and together, as Zimbabweans, trample upon racism.'[2]

At Wits, my hopes surged that this statesmanlike utterance would shed a guiding light on the darkness enveloping South Africa. Mugabe's betrayal tears the soul of every true African patriot who hopes that Africa's tomorrow can be better than its yesterday.

The ugly truth is that South Africa has played a largely ignoble supporting role in the Zimbabwean debacle. No country had been in a better position to influence events there; no party but the ANC had such intimate access to the inner circles of Mugabe's Zanu (Patriotic Front) party. Yet at most times President Thabo Mbeki refused to act – except to defend Mugabe's government and shield it from international criticism and diplomatic intervention.

A constant puzzle for our international allies was why a democratic South Africa did so little to staunch the erosion of Zimbabwe's democracy. What was less of a riddle was the psychology of Mugabe himself. In one of our many conversations, Nelson Mandela gave me some insight into part of the dictator's mindset. Shortly after his release Madiba visited an OAU heads of government meeting in Addis Ababa. Mugabe was holding court with the media and his fellow-presidents at a reception. But when Mandela entered, there was a stampede towards him and Mugabe was left standing practically alone. For someone so lionised at home and abroad as a frontline liberator, his eclipse by Mandela was deeply galling. It may well have been a factor which propelled him down the path he chose over the next few years.

I was subsequently to read that Mugabe's frail psyche and fragile ego impelled him to extreme reactions to slights and rebuffs, both major and trivial. It was suggested that his underdeveloped persona made it impossible for him to deal with rejection – whether from Ian Smith, recalcitrant white farmers or the perfidiousness of successive British governments. This was not initially apparent.[3]

Mandela introduced me to Mugabe during the latter's state visit to South Africa in 1994. He was charming and effusive, and inquired after the health of Helen Suzman of whom he spoke in glowing terms. We met again, indirectly, at Mbeki's second presidential inauguration in 2004. My on-occasion-fiery wife Michal described the rousing ovation Mugabe received from the serried ranks of ANC dignitaries as her most 'depressing moment in South Africa'. We stood directly behind him as we were lining up to leave the Union Buildings after the slap-up lunch which ended the festivities. Michal, not quietly, said: 'I wish he was dead.' Mugabe spun around and glared at her.

From the beginning of the crisis, the DA led the call for South Africa to take action in Zimbabwe. When I was there in February 2000, a brief window of opportunity opened when political change seemed possible. I suggested that potential aid and assistance – which South Africa had already extended to Mugabe's government – should be contingent on Zimbabwe allowing parliamentary elections to proceed 'without improper subversion or rigging by the authorities'. I added that aid should not be given unless Zimbabwe withdrew from the conflict in the Democratic Republic of the Congo (DRC) and returned to 'basic market principles' in its economic management.[4] While 'we should not overestimate the role and the influence we have in events rapidly unfolding to the north', these simple and straightforward steps could have sent a clear message at a crucial time.

But not only did South Africa do nothing; our government coddled Mugabe and frequently expressed admiration and support for his policies. When we protested, adding our voices to a growing international chorus, Mbeki complained that our motivation was racism: 'The reason Zimbabwe is such a preoccupation here, in the UK, in the US and in Sweden,' he told journalist Allister Sparks, 'is because white people died, and white people were deprived of their property … [All] they say is Zimbabwe, Zimbabwe, and Zimbabwe.'[5]

This was the first of many signals – coded and otherwise – that South Africa under Mbeki, with his lingering resentments to colonialism, white racism and the Cold War, would be an impediment to forthright action to restore democracy. I was to spend the next few years decoding the semiotics of this approach, and broadcasting my conclusions.

Mbeki and the ANC were so mesmerised by Mugabe's fulminations against whites and the West that they failed to notice that black Zimbabweans have suffered most from his misrule. Even if the world only noticed Mugabe's abuses because he targeted whites, that would not excuse his actions, nor justify South Africa's seven-year silence. This has revealed the ANC's deep ideological suspicion of democratic politics, as well as its enduring fixation on race.

2

There are many different opinions on the origins of the crisis. From the beginning, the ANC has argued that land is the root cause: and, indeed, prior to 2000, land ownership in Zimbabwe was highly skewed. Roughly four-and-a-half thousand white families owned the country's highly productive commercial farms, producing food and tobacco for export; 840 000 black farmers struggled on small plots in communal lands, producing staple crops.[6] Colonial policy and the Rhodesian government created and enforced this inequality. On the eve of independence in 1980, half the commercial farmland reserved for whites had belonged to blacks prior to the Second World War.[7] Land reform was, and is, an important issue.

There was general consensus that such reform was necessary, not just to redress inherited inequalities but to make the farming sector more productive. The expectation was that it would be carried out in a peaceful, orderly and economically sensible way.

The Lancaster House agreement of 21 December 1979 stipulated that land redistribution would happen on a willing-buyer, willing-seller basis, funded in part by the British and American governments.[8] In the 1980s, a significant amount of land was in fact redistributed, though the new owners struggled to make their farms succeed. And in a pattern that was to be repeated 20 years later, many farms went to inexperienced farmers, while many were gifted to political cronies. As Allister Sparks observed:

'Eighteen months after independence the Mugabe government had bought up 435 000 acres of white farmland, but resettled fewer than three thousand black peasants. In a pattern that was to become even more apparent in the years that followed, scores of government-owned farms were being handed out on leases to cabinet ministers, MPs, top civil servants and other senior members of the ruling party – few of which were put to productive use.

'The time bomb [of land hunger] exploded in the mid-1990s when a newspaper exposed the full extent of the land corruption scandal. Farms had gone to a former minister of Agriculture, to the head of Mugabe's office, to the commissioner of police and the former commander of the Fifth Brigade: in all 8% of commercial farmland had ended up in the hands of Mugabe's acolytes. Outraged, the British government, which at that point had spent £44-million to aid the land resettlement programme, stopped all further support.'[9]

In consequence, land reform virtually came to a standstill, and racial inequalities in land ownership persisted: the commercial farming sector continued to prosper and attract new investment, and by the turn of the century more than eighty per cent of white-owned commercial farmland had been purchased *during* Mugabe's rule.[10]

Though certainly an important challenge, land reform was by no means the most urgent political issue in Zimbabwe. In early 2000, a survey by the Helen Suzman Foundation found that only 9% of Zimbabweans thought the land question the most important obstacle ahead, against 76% who thought economic issues were most pressing.[11] A similar survey conducted by the Zimbabwe Election Support Network, focusing on rural conditions, found only slight disparities: 13% saw land reform as the major issue; while 60% cited the economy.[12]

Thus the 'land question' cannot by itself explain the crisis that exploded in 2000. What does need explanation is why Mugabe abruptly chose to carry out land redistribution then – and why in such a sudden and violent way. This points directly to Mugabe's short-term political motives. A somewhat different explanation is offered by the ANC: the so-called deficit spending theory, championed for a time by Mbeki. The idea is that during the 1980s Zimbabwe's investments in expanded social services and education, however noble, were financially unsustainable. The consequent fiscal crisis forced Zimbabwe to turn to lending institutions such as the International Monetary Fund (IMF), which imposed (the explanation goes) inappropriate structural adjustment programmes that pushed the country towards the abyss. As Mbeki put it:

'To meet the needs of the people and alleviate poverty, the independent state decided to adopt measures that would keep the cost of living relatively low, to ensure better mass access to essential goods and services.'

Mbeki listed the extraordinary budget-busting price-subsidisations of the Mugabe government, which forced it, cap in hand, to seek a bail-out from the International Monetary Fund (IMF). This, coupled with the 'counterproductive' structural adjustment programme it imposed on Mugabe's profligate regime, led Mbeki to reach a sympathetic conclusion.

'Contrary to what some in our country now claim, the economic crisis currently affecting Zimbabwe did not originate from the desperate actions of a reckless political leadership, or from corruption. It arose from a genuine concern to meet the needs of the black poor, without taking into account the harsh economic reality that, in the end, we must pay for what we consume.'[13]

Mbeki's argument contains a partial version of the truth. Zimbabwe did spend too much on a bloated state bureaucracy and social services; the debt was serviced through high taxes and a large, unsustainable budget deficit. But the government also pursued interventionist policies that choked investment and job creation. The structural adjustment programmes designed by international agencies were designed to address Zimbabwe's weaknesses by freeing the economy from political control.

These policies failed: partly because they were implemented too quickly, partly because the government refused to cut back on spending, including military spending.[14] But their failure was primarily the result of political choices. Over-spending on the civil service was a political ploy to provide sheltered employment and patronage for political supporters. In 1997 Mugabe gave – or was bullied into providing – a massive payout to 'war veterans' of the liberation struggle, which led the IMF to end financial support. The following year Mugabe sent troops to join the war in the Democratic Republic of Congo (DRC), exacerbating his financial problems but allowing senior political and military leaders to exploit Congolese resources for personal gain.[15] The financial crisis was not simply triggered by over-zealous public investment, or harsh structural adjustment programmes; but by choices made by Zanu(PF) to protect its own interests, not the least being its president's continuance in office. For over two decades, Mugabe and his inner circle centralised control, and made decisions based on short-term political considerations.

3

Mugabe had in fact salted many clues, from his earliest days in office, of the ruthless violence he would deploy when challenged. The crack-down, from 1982 onwards, on the opposition-stronghold of his wartime ally, and rival, Joshua Nkomo, resulted in the massacre of anywhere between eight thousand and twenty thousand Matabele. When Mugabe's Korean-trained forces ran amok during 'Operation Gukurahundi' the world averted its gaze, its focus being fixed far more firmly on apartheid South Africa. Again, as far back as 1990, the elections were reportedly rigged to prevent the success of another opponent and former ally, Edgar Tekere. These were simply bloody dress rehearsals for the political tragedy which followed after 2000.

In his treatise *The State of Africa*, Martin Meredith aptly describes Mugabe's style of administration in 'ordinary' times:

'He ruled through a vast system of patronage, controlling appointments to all senior posts in the civil service, the defence forces, the police and parastatal organisations, gaining a virtual stranglehold over government machinery ...

'Mugabe himself became an increasingly remote and authoritarian figure. His official residences in Harare were heavily fortified. He travelled only in large motorcades surrounded by retinues of armed bodyguards with screaming sirens heard for miles around. He spoke openly of his admiration for dictators such as Nicolae Ceausescu of Romania, praising him the day before he was overthrown by popular revolution. Party advertisements in newspapers paid homage to Mugabe as "our Consistent and Authentic Leader", emulating the style of communist personality cults. He lectured endlessly on the merits of communism, insisting that Zimbabwe's future was "better guaranteed under one single, monolithic and gigantic political party". Much of his time he spent on foreign travel, trading on his image as a revolutionary hero and cultivating a reputation as a key figure in the international campaign to defeat apartheid ... '[16]

When Mugabe finally turned his attention to land reform, the trigger was the failure of his campaign for constitutional changes to grant him greater power. A referendum was held in February 2000 to decide the issue, and Mugabe used a clever marketing campaign to build public support for his will.[17] The voters were not fooled. They rejected the changes by a margin of 53% against 44% in favour, handing Mugabe his first outright electoral loss in two decades.[18] The urban constituencies turned in the highest votes against the proposals, but even some rural areas opposed them, surprising many.[19]

Based on poll data, the Helen Suzman Foundation predicted that Mugabe would lose by a landslide. Reports of ballot stuffing and other forms of interference suggested that 'the Mugabe government had rigged the referendum – but still lost it.'[20] It was an historic victory for democracy, and a potential turning point in the country's post-colonial history. The June parliamentary elections were just months away, and a new opposition party, the Movement for Democratic Change (MDC), headed by trade unionist Morgan Tsvangirai, was now confident of its chances of victory.

I visited Zimbabwe with my counsellor, Nick Clelland-Stokes, in the immediate aftermath of the referendum to meet Tsvangirai and other opposition leaders. We found the mood in the country to be one of cautious exuberance. Tsvangirai struck me as engaged, courageous and level-headed. While expressing in private the need for opposition co-operation across the Limpopo, he later publicly changed his tune and started singing in the anti-DP/DA chorus – doubtless encouraged by the ANC. I dismissed this as part of the rent he felt obliged to pay for some kind of South African government support; which, incidentally, was never forthcoming.

What truly galled me, however, was Tsvangirai's soliciting (and receiving) funds from key DA donors in Johannesburg, whom he visited while claiming he had never done so. I thought such public disclaimers of known private realities revealed a troubling inconsistency. It confirmed that while courage is a non-negotiable of leadership, particularly of any opposition force in Africa, it must be coupled to strategic coherence.

After my visit, I issued a press statement: 'The referendum result has changed profoundly the political landscape in Zimbabwe. It has emboldened the opposition there, caused Mr Mugabe to pause, and requires South Africa to act deftly and appropriately in changed circumstance[s].'[21]

What had also struck me was the information that while the MDC was the first significant opposition force to emerge in Zimbabwe for a decade, it was only after the referendum that the South African high commissioner in Harare deigned to hold a meeting with Tsvangirai. This wilful disregard for an informed and inclusive diplomacy was the benchmark of the South African government's one-sided approach to events in Zimbabwe.

As the situation worsened in Zimbabwe – and following another visit I paid a few months later to inspect the farm seizures and worsening fuel situation – Colin Eglin urged me to seek a meeting with the Foreign minister, Dr Nkosazana Zuma. It would be fair to say that neither of us was a charter member of the other's fan club; but I heeded his advice. I detailed all I had seen and heard, offered some modest analysis, and suggested that perhaps our embassy in Harare should conduct a more thoroughgoing and inclusive approach to its information-gathering – and influence-seeking – operations. She listened in largely polite silence, took no notes, and the meeting was unwitnessed by any departmental official. I left the meeting dismayed, if not altogether surprised. It was clear that little would be done to deter Mugabe from proceeding down the road to tyranny.

Mugabe's response to the referendum result, after initially appearing to accept it, was an intensified campaign of land seizures, spearheaded by mobs of 'war veterans', some far too young to have fought in Zimbabwe's liberation struggles. These 'war veterans' terrorised white farmers, occupied land, beat farmers and their workers, and killed those who refused to leave their property. The police did nothing – even assisting in some cases. The army and the Central Intelligence Organisation (CIO) were thought to be involved in orchestrating the violence and the seizures.[22]

Mugabe was playing to his last remaining support base: the land-hungry poor of the rural areas, particularly in Shona-speaking regions. By whipping up old resentments and racial animosities, he hoped to rally the support he had lost in the cities and was fast losing elsewhere. The campaign was brutally effective; within a few months the exodus of white farmers had reached the point of no return. Many of the abandoned farms were not given to the poor, but – just as in previous 'reform' episodes – to Mugabe's political cronies. Few of the new farmers – whether Zanu(PF) loyalists or 'war veterans' – knew much about commercial farming, and many of the farms were soon defunct. The effect on the agricultural sector and the economy was to prove devastating.

The parliamentary elections of June 2000 were hugely anticipated. The opposition had the momentum of its referendum victory. Many outside observers felt an MDC victory was possible. RW Johnson, for example, wrote:

'An ageing liberation culture is being broken on the anvil of its own corruption and arrogance but in its death agony it is willing to pull down the whole country with it. It may succeed for a little while longer but its demise is now certain. Even if Zanu(PF) can somehow terrorise the electorate into giving it a fresh majority, there is no escape via that route.'[23]

Johnson proved to be too optimistic, if not premature. Mugabe was not prepared to risk another defeat. He used his presidential powers to modify Zimbabwe's Electoral Act in ways that favoured a Zanu(PF) victory. For example, postal ballots were sent to soldiers before they had actually applied for them.[24] Voters' rolls were not open to scrutiny until just a few weeks before the election.[25] These procedural irregularities, however, were minor compared to the political violence unleashed by Zanu(PF). As the Zimbabwe human rights NGO Forum later reported:

'In the two months before 24-25 June, political violence targeted especially white farmers and black farmworkers, teachers, civil servants and rural villagers believed to support opposition parties. Homes and businesses in both urban and rural areas were burned and looted. The *Daily News* Harare editorial offices were bombed and a subsequent bomb threat

traced to Zanu(PF) headquarters. Opposition organisers were killed, kidnapped and tortured ... Independent journalists experienced grave difficulty in covering violence in areas controlled by Zanu(PF), but when
they did, reported military planning and co-ordination of logistics for the
farm invasions ...

'All-night Zanu(PF) "political re-education" meetings ... brutalised
those forced to attend. It was widely feared that the executive was looking
for an excuse to declare a state of emergency and postpone the elections.'

There arose a climate of death threats; the actual death toll reached over
seventy; and the government used the Law and Order (Maintenance) Act
to prohibit the bussing of political supporters to all rallies except those
addressed by party presidents.

The Forum further reported: 'The EU observer mission reported 248
incidents of pre-election violence, only ten of which were directly witnessed. Eighty-five resulted in injury; 155 involved physical violence, including enforced attendance at rallies, and another 56 entailed psychological intimidation. By polling day, three opposition candidates had fled
their constituencies (one to a neighbouring country). Three others were
in hiding. One was in intensive care with critical head injuries ...

'There was little indication that the police would begin to uphold the
rule of law ... Then came the blanket presidential condonation of and
pardon for most acts of violence between January and the end of July
2000.'[26]

The violence was widely reported in the international media, and the
DA objected vehemently. In April 2000, after attacks against peaceful demonstrators in Harare, I urged President Mbeki to speak out against the land
invasions, and urge Zimbabwe 'to level the playing fields for all political
parties competing in the upcoming elections.'[27]

At one stage, I even wrote directly to Mugabe himself.[28] I reminded
him that the Southern African Development Community (SADC) Treaty
committed member states to uphold principles of human rights, democracy and the rule of law. He had also violated other international commitments, including (ironically) the Harare Declaration on human rights
and governance, approved in Harare in 1991. I called on him to uphold
the democratic outcome of the election, to stop the land invasions, and
develop a new macroeconomic policy to rescue his country from impoverishment. I noted: 'We respect, obviously, your sovereign independence
and we make this call with no desire to interfere in the political choices
of the people of Zimbabwe ... [But] the destiny of our people is linked
to that of your people. It is in this spirit of solidarity and support that we

look forward to the revival of democracy and the economic recovery of Zimbabwe.'[29]

I received no direct response. Indirectly, however, Mugabe found my interest politically useful. In the run-up to the election later in the year Zanu(PF) published a full-page colour newspaper ad with Tsvangirai portrayed as a puppet, his strings pulled by various masters – including Denmark, Canada, the World Bank, IMF, USA, the always-useful 'racist Rhodesians', and by two named individuals: Tony Blair and Tony Leon. The sign-off line was: 'If Tsvangirai wins, God forbid, who'll really be running Zimbabwe?'

My staff was fairly appalled. I was hugely amused and had it framed.

With more reports of new abuses every week, there were growing expectations that South Africa would, at least, condemn Mugabe's behaviour. But Mbeki did no such thing, preferring to consult privately with his Zimbabwean counterpart and ally, together with other African leaders. The meetings were trumpeted to the world as progress; but it was clear that 'quiet diplomacy' was at best ineffective and at worst a form of tacit support.

Ryan Coetzee was quick to realise the political advantage to our party. He arranged, and published, a series of newspaper ads with my picture (in 'fight-back' pose from the 1999 election) which led with the question: 'What is the difference between South Africa and Zimbabwe?' Answer: 'The DP's strong opposition.' The claim was that 'only strong opposition will ensure that South Africa never becomes another Zimbabwe.'

The campaign drew critics and caused Mbeki to refer to it, sneeringly, for many years. From a partisan perspective it was merited, and, in its way, effective. It highlighted a basic truth: that the co-option by Mugabe of his major rival, the ZAPU party of Nkomo, led to the collapse of effective opposition and paved the way for a one-party state.

While our domestic campaign around the Zimbabwe crisis resonated warmly with our support base (including, I noticed with some concern, the former white Rhodesians who in a previous era had backed Ian Smith to the hilt), I decided to internationalise it. In May I addressed the European Parliament in Brussels, and then took the case for strong action to London where I was warmly received by Peter Hain, Britain's Minister for Africa.

I remembered him as the *enfant terrible* whose demonstrations wrecked the 1970 Springbok tour to Britain. He had spent part of his youth in South Africa, and his parents were leading activists in the (South African) Liberal Party, before their harassment by the security police forced them to flee to Britain.

Hain by the time I met him was a coming force in Blair's Labour government (he was felled by a funding scandal in 2008). In his modest rooms set amid the period splendour and finery of the foreign office in Whitehall, Hain called the situation exactly right; he saw Mugabe's increasingly authoritarian behaviour as an issue of democracy, not of land. But he was also frank enough to express his dismay at South Africa's hand in the whole matter.

While I was in London, Mbeki appeared on SABC-TV and blamed the Zimbabwe meltdown almost entirely on what he called, euphemistically 'the Zimbabwe land issue'. Mbeki went further, in the same address (aiming his dart directly, no doubt, at our recent campaign), and accused his 'opponents' of making 'the noise of empty drums' on Zimbabwe and its problems. I had by now, however, come to the conclusion that Mbeki's strategy of so-called 'quiet diplomacy' translated in practice into silent support for Mugabe and his party.[30]

The EU later instituted a regime of 'smart sanctions' targeting Mugabe and Zimbabwe's ruling elite, but South Africa could not be persuaded to follow suit.

The consequences of this inaction became painfully apparent at home in the form of the rand's collapse against the American dollar, which was to continue through the end of 2001. A few ANC MPs began to realise the gravity of the situation: Dr Pallo Jordan openly admitted that the election in Zimbabwe would be neither free nor fair. But nothing was done to intervene to render a more equitable result.

The election was held as scheduled, amid reports of widespread problems and irregularities. The MDC had contested every single one of the 120 seats, for example, but was prevented from campaigning in three-quarters of them.[31] The implausible result, which few outside Zimbabwe credited, was a narrow victory for Zanu(PF), which claimed 47,2% of the vote to the MDC's 45,8%.[32] The MDC immediately launched a challenge, beginning a long and ultimately unsuccessful court process. The international community shrugged, hoping that the MDC would be satisfied with a strong showing, and that Mugabe would at least feel compelled to negotiate.

Mugabe had other ideas. As Martin Meredith recalls:

'Though the election was over, there was to be no respite from Mugabe's tyranny. Showing increasing signs of paranoia, he insisted that the strength of the opposition against him was due to a conspiracy by his old enemies – Britain, the West, the old Rhodesian network, white farming and business interests, even the churches – all trying to overthrow his "revolution" ...

[He] told members of Zanu(PF)'s central committee that it would be a serious miscalculation "to underestimate the forces ranged against us"...' The MDC was a manifestation of 'the resurgence of white power'. It was the task of Zanu(PF) to defeat them, 'using whatever methods were necessary'.[33]

Attacks on white farmers – as part of a 'fast-track' land reform programme that was actually a campaign of rural terror – increased, backed by the full force of the state. The leader of the 'war veterans', Dr 'Hitler' Hunzvi, began detaining and torturing members and leaders of the MDC. All this had, in retrospect, been predictable, given Mugabe's past behaviour in Matabeleland, and in the guerrilla war that preceded independence. He had come to power through force; now he was attempting to stay in power that way.

Scarce foreign currency evaporated as the value of the Zimbabwe dollar plummeted. Fuel shortages and queues became common. Foreign aid and investment withdrew, and the economy, which had recently enjoyed robust growth, began to implode faster than in any other peacetime country in the world.

Despite the obvious costs, Mugabe pushed ahead; indeed, he now began targeting the judiciary and the media, two of the last remaining independent institutions that could check his power. When the Supreme Court of Zimbabwe declared the 'fast-track' land programme unlawful, Mugabe instituted a campaign against impartial judges, and white judges in particular.[34] Chief Justice Anthony Gubbay, whom Mugabe himself appointed in 1990, was hounded off the Bench after mobs shouting 'Kill the judges!' had harangued the Supreme Court, and Justice minister Patrick Chinamasa said he could no longer guarantee Gubbay's safety.[35] Others who had blocked illegal land seizures were removed or threatened into retirement, and replaced with Zanu(PF) cronies. Information minister Jonathan Moyo crowed that Zimbabwe had eliminated 'Rhodesian' judges.[36]

The media was targeted by new laws and institutions, the most notorious of which was the Access to Information and Protection of Privacy Act (AIPPA).

Violence was also used: the presses of independent newspapers like the *Daily News* were repeatedly bombed by agents of the Mugabe regime, and journalists were routinely harassed, jailed and beaten. The economy was in free fall; democracy was on the run.

In response, there was no condemnation – indeed, plenty of outright endorsement – by the ANC. Mbeki was photographed holding hands with Mugabe, and defended him in the international media and forums. Mbeki presided, for example, over the Non-Aligned Movement (NAM) during this period, and supported its call (in 2003) for the lifting of sanctions against Zimbabwe, and condemned the withdrawal of financial assistance; and he strenuously opposed firm action against Mugabe. Mbeki's ministers fell into line. Finance minister Trevor Manuel continued to support 'co-operation, not criticism' of the Mugabe regime and to back economic aid for Zimbabwe.[37] Mbeki also ensured that Zimbabwe was provided with a steady supply of electricity and fuel, despite Mugabe's inability to pay his bills.

Some have suggested that Mbeki, hoping to extend South Africa's influence on the continent, has been reluctant to criticise a fellow African leader for fear of alienating potential African allies. There is, in fact, some degree of resentment towards South Africa in Africa, not only because of its dominant economy and international presence, but also because of the degree to which those assets are associated with the presence and history of white people in South Africa. Mbeki and the ANC were sensitive to this impression, and afraid of being labelled by fellow African leaders as servants of white interests; and the 'Leaders Club' of Africa was not to be found for action against one of its own.

Of course, Mugabe's real constituency was not the African 'masses' he claimed to represent, but the superannuated southern African post-colonial liberation elites. They were bound by common interests and a shared theology – a millenarian belief, according to RW Johnson, that the parties of independence are the final prophets of a messianic age, who can do no wrong. The possibility that any liberation party could be voted out is experienced by all such parties as an existential threat. That shared vulnerability is probably what bound Mbeki most closely to Mugabe.[38]

4

Mbeki also found Zimbabwe's plight politically useful in dealing with his most restive constituencies at home. The fate of Zimbabwe's white farmers and business owners was constantly dangled before South Africa's racial minorities as a warning of what could happen if they did not co-operate.

The internal economic consequences were severe: a drastic reduction in trade with a previously important regional partner; the influx of millions of illegal immigrants from Zimbabwe, exacerbating the country's unemployment crisis; the loss of foreign investment opportunities in Zimbabwe at a time when South African firms were expanding throughout the rest of the continent; and the direct loss of land and assets owned by South African citizens in Zimbabwe. In the first three years of the crisis alone, Zimbabwe's troubles were estimated to have cost South Africa 1,3% of our GDP.[39]

Politically, South Africa's international prestige suffered greatly as a result of Mbeki's silence: our hard-won reputation as a world leader in the field of human rights had been quickly and cheaply squandered. As I told parliament in February 2001: 'When the world sees President Mbeki smiling and holding hands with Mugabe, when it hears [then-ANC chief whip] Tony Yengeni praising Mugabe's handling of the election, when it reads Jacob Zuma approving of Mugabe's seizures of land and when it watches the heads of SADC giving their full support to him, it can only come to one conclusion: the South African government agrees with what Mugabe is doing in Zimbabwe.'[40]

Though he would continue to be welcomed as Africa's foremost spokesman, and an important voice in the developing world – President George W Bush described Mbeki as his 'point man' on Zimbabwe[41] – his stature declined. The damage was most visible in the stagnation and failure of several ambitious projects for African development championed by Mbeki. One was the 'African Renaissance' declared by then-Deputy President Mbeki in 1997. Mugabe has made a mockery of Mbeki's claim that a new age was dawning.

The newly formed African Union (AU), of which Mbeki was the first chair, also failed to deal decisively with Zimbabwe. In 2004, it adopted a report on human rights abuses in Zimbabwe prepared by the African Commission on Human and Peoples' Rights, but formal discussion of the report was delayed in deference to Zimbabwe, and no real action was ever taken.

Even Mbeki's proudest achievement, the New Partnership for Africa's Development (Nepad), was virtually strangled at birth. The implicit bargain of Nepad was that African states would commit to principles of democracy and good governance; and in exchange the developed world would provide investment for regional infrastructure and other projects. This was formally endorsed by the Group of Eight (G-8). Yet Africa fell at the first hurdle – Zimbabwe – and its failure was viewed more severely given that Mbeki was simultaneously Nepad's foremost advocate while also Mugabe's greatest ally. By 2006 Nepad's 20 flagship investment projects had failed to receive significant foreign funding.[42]

In February 2001, in a speech to parliament, I proposed that South Africa endorse international 'smart sanctions' by freezing foreign assets and funds owned by individuals in the Zanu(PF) hierarchy; restrict travel to South Africa by Zimbabwean ministers; and apply an arms embargo.[43] These were not drastic measures, nor unprecedented. As one newspaper noted, they were the same measures the ANC once demanded against the apartheid government: '[The] ANC is pursuing exactly the same policy on "constructive engagement" that it condemned when Margaret Thatcher applied it to South Africa in the 1980s. How odd that the sanctions against the ANC decried as insufficient then, should now be considered excessive.'[44]

As a backdrop to my speech I decided to pay a lightning 24-hour visit to Harare. I undertook the trip with some trepidation, since two months before Mugabe himself had denounced me, by name, as 'an enemy of the state'. But when Nick Clelland-Stokes and I arrived at the largely deserted Harare airport, we met the usual bureaucratic indifference of a bored immigration official. However, the changes that had overtaken Harare were palpable. Our taxi driver reeled off the daily miseries and privations which he and his family suffered from the fiscal profligacies and monetary mismanagement characteristic of Mugabe's regime.

We had arranged several meetings at Meikles hotel – where we were staying – with various interest groups, including the Commercial Farmers' Union, the opposition leadership, and several newspaper editors. On sitting down in the lounge we were surrounded by a half-dozen heavies in suits and dark glasses. The farmers told us that our uninvited observers were undoubtedly members of the CIO, the Rhodesian-named and inspired security police, whom Mugabe had turned into an instrument of fear and intimidation. I immediately adjourned the meeting and we met in a private lounge.

I was given a laundry list of the terror to which the farming community had been subjected: from the torture of workers to the plunder of crops and assaults on families by the 'war veterans'. As this litany of woe mounted, I noticed a tall, thin black man with a gold chain around his neck enter the room and take a seat at the table around which Nick and I were conferring with the farmers. He was instantly recognisable, even to me, as the appalling war veterans' leader Dr Chenjerai Hunzvi, who rejoiced in his nickname 'Hitler'. His name and photo flashed across the newspapers and TV screens of South Africa as the instigator of, and apparently active participant in, many of the acts of torture my interlocutors had just been describing.

We did manage to finish our meeting – and Hunzvi (shortly to die of

AIDS) left the room before we did. Then we set off to walk to the chambers housing Harare's advocates; on leaving the hotel were immediately and ostentatiously followed by the same group of CIO heavies. Once inside we realised that our foreign status and profile inoculated us from the sort of treatment then being meted out, on an almost daily basis, to all Mugabe's opponents, real and illusory. State-sponsored violence had now spread from the farms to the towns. Police and soldiers would enter taverns and smash people insensible. I was also played a tape of the ghastly Hunzvi announcing on state radio that certain members of the judiciary were 'devils and they must go and I will make sure they go.'

The worst atrocity to which my attention was drawn happened a month before in the rural area of Bikita, in a by-election. A staggering 41 people, aligned to the MDC, had been murdered, and not a single charge had been laid.

The denouement of this harrowing visit came in the evening. We had quietly arranged a dinner in my hotel suite with some senior opposition and press figures. While waiting for my guests, I stepped into the hotel bar and while enjoying a chilled local lager was alerted by the barman to the TV screen. There indeed was Mugabe's Goebbels-like Information minister Jonathan Moyo denouncing me as a 'fomenter of violence'.[45] He went on to say that 'anyone who wines and dines with Tony Leon is a traitor.' My dinner guests arrived despite the warning, and were unsurprised and – given the appalling climate under which they heroically operated – unfazed.

I left Harare the next day depressed but relieved to be going back to the relative normalcy of South Africa. The oppressive humidity of Harare, relieved by a burst of thunder, seemed an apt symbol of the change in the political weather over the past year.[46]

That afternoon in parliament I gave a vivid, but I believed accurate, rendition of what I had witnessed in the north. My call for limited and targeted 'smart' sanctions was dismissed by the ANC chief whip, Tony Yengeni, as 'irresponsible', and he warned me 'not to harp on the issue'. 'Let us leave the internal politics of our neighbours to the people of those countries,' he opined. This response was to become the wearying stock-in-trade mantra of the ANC government on the issue.[47]

The next day Yengeni's utterance gave Mugabe's mouthpiece the *Herald* an opening to defame the DA as part of 'an unknown alliance with forces that seek to derail the benefits of independence and revolution in southern Africa.'[48]

South Africa's distance from the rest of the world over Zimbabwe was most apparent during that country's presidential elections in March 2002. The MDC was struggling to overcome two years of repression – during which Tsvangirai had been arrested on trumped-up charges of treason – and international attention was once again in focus. Teams of observers arrived from around the world. Almost immediately, it became clear that the elections were to be rigged in Mugabe's favour – and that South Africa would approve.

It began to go wrong when the EU observers left the country, as journalist Andrew Meldrum (himself arrested, beaten and eventually deported) recalls:

'The large observer mission from the EU was determined to watch the presidential poll carefully, having judged the June 2000 parliamentary elections to be illegitimate. The Mugabe government refused to allow British observers to be part of the EU mission, charging that Britain was actively seeking to overthrow Mugabe and therefore could not objectively observe the polls. The EU did not accept this charge, but gave way in the interest of getting its observers deployed … [But when] the mission demanded to see the voters' roll, the Mugabe government balked. At a hastily called press conference, the head of the EU mission, former Swedish cabinet minister Pierre Schori, revealed that he had been ordered to leave Zimbabwe immediately, and the entire observer mission of nearly two hundred was to follow him out of the country.

'Since the presence of EU observers discouraged the most blatant violence, it was clear that the election would continue to be violent and the voting process opaque.'[49]

South Africa had its own observers, in various teams, including the SADC Parliamentary Forum Observer Mission. Several South African observers were actually attacked by Mugabe's 'war veterans' and Zanu(PF) youth militias when they attempted to visit MDC offices. The DA sent several members with a parliamentary delegation, including our chairman Joe Seremane, as well as Errol Moorcroft and Andries Botha. They faxed handwritten memoranda to our offices in parliament, making for chilling reading. A typical entry by Moorcroft, on 1 March 2002, was the following, after a meeting with farmers:

'I had asked them to restrict their reports to election matters only and to avoid speaking about land reform. This they did … They spoke of harassment of their workers, forced attendance of Zanu(PF) meetings, forced purchase of Zanu(PF) membership cards, restriction of maize handouts to party supporters only, etc., etc.; in fact more confirmation of everything we have heard about the violence and intimidation associated with this election thus far.'

Church leaders, trade unionists and opposition organisers produced similar stories and reports of widespread violence. Freedom of speech had been severely restricted; television coverage was almost entirely devoted to the ruling party; the Zimbabwe Electoral Commission was stacked with Zanu(PF) cronies; young people had been given paramilitary training and unleashed on the public; MDC rallies were blocked by authorities; venues occupied by Zanu(PF) supporters; and the police either stood aside or intervened on behalf of Zanu(PF).

The observers also visited Zanu(PF) strongholds. At one point, the state-controlled *Herald* printed a fabulist story accusing Moorcroft – 'a member of the South African Democratic Party led by well-known MDC sympathiser Tony Leon' – of chanting MDC slogans at a rally. On the eve of the elections, Joe Seremane – anticipating a whitewash by ANC parliamentarians – submitted his independent, personal observations: '[The] presidential election process cannot and should not be declared "free and fair" despite which way the results may go ...'

Among much else, he spoke of violence and intimidation; the removal of voters from the roll; the state monopoly and use of public media; and the use of food grants (limiting supply) as a campaigning tool. Without the recognition of these abuses, any vindication of the electoral process would sound like a 'fraternal and sentimental' closing of ranks, being totally oblivious to the 'deliberate distortion of the truth'.

Mugabe coasted to a fraudulent victory. MDC observers were abducted, and polling stations in cities slowed down to prevent a high Tsvangirai vote. In the end, the official results reported that the MDC had won the cities by small margins, while Mugabe had carried the rural areas in a landslide.[50] The Commonwealth observer mission declared that the election had been neither free nor fair;[51] so, too, did the SADC Parliamentary Forum, the Zimbabwe Election Support Network, a Norwegian observer team, and the excluded EU. Would South Africa do the right thing?

The ANC issued an official statement: 'The ANC congratulates the people of Zimbabwe for a successful 2002 Zimbabwe Presidential election ... [We] further offer our warm congratulations to Zanu(PF) and President Mugabe for a convincing majority win.'[52] This completely insupportable claim was repeated in parliament and became the government's official line. The DA observers could not, obviously, endorse this finding, and issued their own report of the elections, which presented an irreconcilable picture. It was clear to all but Mbeki and his acolytes that Mugabe was now a tyrant beyond control.

Mugabe's victory left Zimbabwe in a state of escalating hopelessness. In July 2002 *The Economist*, in 'From Breadbasket to Basket Case', chronicled its rapid collapse:

'Zimbabwe is facing its worst food shortage in sixty years, caused by drought and several years of violent harassment of the nation's most productive farmers. By the government's own estimates, nearly seven million of the country's thirteen million people will be without adequate food in a few months ...

'Mr Mugabe does not seem to care. After stealing a presidential election in March, his chief concern has been to punish those who dared to support his opponent, Morgan Tsvangirai. He suspects white farmers of having bankrolled Mr Tsvangirai's campaign ... [S]tarving peasants who are suspected of having voted for him are denied food aid in areas where the ruling party controls its distribution.'[53]

I had been persuaded by our party's Agriculture spokesman, the energetic and likeable Andries Botha, himself a successful and large-scale maize farmer in the Free State, that we needed to interact directly – and visibly – with the beleaguered Zimbabwean commercial farmers. He said (perhaps disingenuously) that the DA group would be unlikely to 'come to grief' if the leader was present.[54] I had actually reached an opposite conclusion, but swallowed my doubts. In early July 2002, I headed again by air to Harare.

We spent most of our time in the agricultural heartland of the country, especially the once-flourishing Mazoe Valley area some sixty kilometres north-west of Harare. There we saw some of the most ingeniously designed grain silos ever built in southern Africa standing empty, while in the neighbouring fields oranges rotted on the trees because it was now a criminal offence for the farmers to pick and process them. (Under the latest government decrees all farmers had been obliged to stop farming, preparatory to their forced exit from their farmlands scheduled for 10 August 2002.)

While inspecting this government-mandated devastation, we were introduced to a hitherto successful white farmer. In contrast with his neighbours, Mark Rain,[55] when served with a notice of 'compulsory seizure', had decided to collaborate; he would 'strike a deal' with the 'war veterans' as expedient as it was brutal. If allowed to remain on the farm and plant his crop, he would hand over 50% of the profits. He consented to this arrangement and paid up. The 'veterans' immediately told him it was not enough and announced, a week before our arrival, that they intended to move into his farmhouse and take over the farm. When he attempted to remove his tractors and equipment the occupiers took them from him by force. He pleaded with the local police for interdiction. They announced there was nothing to be done, since the matter was 'political'.

We also met the dispirited and nervous leadership of the commercial farmers. They showed us their own plan – a 'proposed Zimbabwe Joint Resettlement Initiative' – which offered the government over one million hectares of agricultural real estate in exchange for some form of normalcy on the remaining farms. This, needless to say, had been utterly ignored by the government, strengthening our view that resettling land-hungry people had never been the purpose or outcome of the land invasions.

After visiting the ground zero of African agriculture we returned to Harare. The activist German ambassador – in stark and pleasing contrast to South Africa's somnambulant high commissioner – had attempted with some success to intervene and save some of his countrymen's investments from government seizure. He hosted a dinner for us so that we could be briefed by him and some European colleagues on the situation. One diplomatic interlocutor pointed out that the caricature of Mugabe as either mad or demonic was exactly that – a caricature.

In fact, he said that while the head of state was extremely cruel, he was both cunning and essentially rational. He added that you needed to approach dictators with an actuarial calculation: Mugabe was by then approaching eighty: the way a dictator behaved, the diplomat suggested, depended on whether he was nearing the end of his career, or at the beginning. A young dictator will generally leaven doses of terror with doses of prosperity in order to stay in power. However, a ruthless tyrant, near the end of his regime, will be utterly unconcerned about the long-term implications of his actions and will simply hold onto power by all means possible. Tsvangirai was present, but said little other than to confirm the drastic deterioration.

However, the Mugabe government continued to display a fascination with my dining activities, and the next day in a huge five-column spread, the *Herald* newspaper provided its readers with a detailed – and largely fanciful – account of dinner and the most precise, and almost entirely inaccurate, rendition of the table conversation.[56]

In an allegedly hard news piece headlined 'State slams Leon over rumblings', my *bête noire*, the egregious Information minister Moyo, declared that my 'rumblings' in Zimbabwe (I had given an interview to the anti-government paper, the *Daily News*) were consequent to being 'a white man from south of the Limpopo trying to do politics in an African country undergoing economic emancipation from the shackles of colonialism, apartheid and neo-colonialism.'

Having dismissed me as the evil neighbour and representative of this triptych, the article went on to name all the guests at the previous evening's dinner (and threw in a few names who were not there at all, for good measure), and then proceeded to inform readers that the purpose of the dinner was for me to 'stir up trouble and encourage the MDC to revisit its plans for mass action.' A further claim made by the article was that this diplomatic confab was called to hatch 'plans on how the foreign missions would help the MDC in its [bid] to get into power.'

In my interview with the *Daily News* I had proffered another opinion as to why Mbeki remained quiescent in the face of Mugabe's tactics. Our president, I said, failed to act because he was 'overwhelmed by Mugabe's reputation': 'Mbeki fears his Zimbabwean counterpart, and Mugabe plays on the fact that he is the senior man and Mbeki the junior. Mbeki fears Mugabe because of his [Mugabe's] struggle credentials, which makes Mbeki very nervous about criticising him.'[57]

No doubt this remark further froze the already icy waters that separated Mbeki and me. But I believed the observation to be fundamentally accurate.

5

In fact, Mbeki was finally forced to act – though clearly against his own wishes. After the Commonwealth reported its observations of the Zimbabwean presidential elections, the troika it appointed decided, in March 2002, to suspend Zimbabwe from the Commonwealth, and reconsider the situation in a year's time. The impression was that the decision was taken against Mbeki's will. Certainly, it contradicted South Africa's positive remarks about the elections. Perhaps, having vented himself on the merits of majority rule, Mbeki was now out-voted and could do little else: he went along with the troika decision.

But Mbeki was far from happy with either the decision or the racial dynamics which he believed informed some Commonwealth members. In a petulant, and highly revealing, letter he penned in *ANC Today*, he pounced on an anonymous critic's description of the troika as 'two blacks and one white'. (The other members were Australian prime minister John Howard and Nigerian president Olusegun Obasanjo.) He also gave extraordinary insight into his real view of the crisis in Zimbabwe and Mugabe's critics:

'According to this view, the white world represents the best in human civilisation. The black world does not.'

Mbeki ended his tirade in a fashion which was to become emblematic of his worldview:

'The assertion is made that the view of the minority is both intrinsically and obviously correct and should prevail, simply because the minority is white. In the Commonwealth context, its defeat should never be ascribed to the vagaries of a rational debate. Rather, it should be attributed to a primitive black and African generic tendency towards dictatorship.'[58]

In March 2002, I had given Mbeki 'full credit' for his role in the suspension of Zimbabwe from the Commonwealth; however, he was evidently an unwilling participant and did his best to undo that suspension.

Mbeki later protested the way in which the troika had dealt with Zimbabwe, and accused Prime Minister John Howard – and the Commonwealth secretary-general – of all manner of uncollegial and unprocedural behaviour.

Mbeki's dislike for Howard, and Australia, was apparently not confined to his Internet columns and to the inner councils of the Commonwealth. In June 2004 the Australian high commissioner to South Africa abruptly quit his post in Pretoria, after just two years, to return to Australia. I learned that he, and other members of those branded by Pretoria as the 'white Commonwealth', were treated with open hostility by the South African Department of Foreign Affairs. For example, during his tenure he had failed to be granted, despite numerous requests, a single meeting with Foreign Minister Nkosazana Zuma. South Africa also apparently campaigned at the United Nations, post Abuja, to remove Australia from the chairmanship of the UN Commission on Human Rights.

Ultimately, Mugabe responded to the Commonwealth recommendations by leaving the organisation – just as apartheid South Africa had done decades before.[59]

Calls for a popular uprising against Mugabe did not succeed in the face of overwhelming shows of force by the government. However hated the regime was, the Zimbabwean people were not willing to risk their lives to replace it. They continued to vote with their feet by leaving the country as refugees. The focus shifted to the possibility of internal talks between Zanu(PF) and the MDC. In his State of the Nation address in 2002, Mbeki had declared: 'We will also continue to work with the people of Zimbabwe as they seek solutions to the problems afflicting their country. We hope that sooner rather than later these solutions will be found through dialogue among the leaders of this neighbouring country.'[60] Speaking alongside President Bush in July 2002, Mbeki claimed: 'We have urged the government and the opposition to get together. They are indeed discussing all issues. That process is going on.'[61] Pressed for details, Mbeki provided none.

Tsvangirai's response was one of dismissal: he accused Mbeki of making 'false and mischievous' statements aimed at 'buying time' for Mugabe: 'The Mugabe regime has remained intractable and sustained an arrogant and defiant program of violence, torture, murder, rape and all manner of crimes against humanity.'[62]

Tsvangirai was roundly rebuked in the press for having upbraided Mbeki so publicly; would it not have been better to give Mbeki credit in the hope of making real gains? But he was speaking out of sheer frustration – and he was probably speaking the truth.

Mbeki's promises were little more than a series of false dawns. In March 2003, for example, there were widespread reports that Mbeki had decided to get tough with Mugabe. 'Mbeki urges Mugabe to end land reforms' read one headline; 'Mbeki blasts land grabs' said another. But what the president actually said was: 'There is no dispute about it. We need land redistribution in Zimbabwe … It is now a matter of how to conclude the situation of land distribution in Zimbabwe; and we continue to discuss it with them. We must establish what remains to be done so we can come to a situation of normalcy in that country as soon as possible.'[63] So President Mbeki did not, in fact, urge Mugabe to stop his land grabbing; but gave him the green light to keep going and finish the job.

In any case, the ANC left no doubt about which side it backed. At its 51st National Congress in Stellenbosch in December 2002, Zanu heavyweight Emmerson Mnangagwa – head of the Central Intelligence Organisation during the Matabeleland massacres, and Mugabe's diamond baron in the DRC – was embraced on the podium and applauded by the ANC delegates. South Africa's Foreign minister, Dlamini-Zuma, said that the world would never hear one word of condemnation of Zimbabwe 'as long as this [ANC] government is in power.'[64]

So it has all been smoke and mirrors. In June 2003, Mbeki gave an explicit promise at the World Economic Forum meeting in Durban that the Zimbabwe crisis would be resolved within a year. In July, he went further, reportedly promising US president George W Bush that Mugabe would step down by December.[65]

Mbeki's promises were never fulfilled. His government had plenty to say about Israel's actions in the Palestinian territories; he himself became involved in mediation efforts in the Congo and the Ivory Coast, while sending deputies to conduct intense negotiations in Burundi. But in

Zimbabwe the *Daily News* was shut down and Mugabe was discovered to be building a R70-million mansion for himself, as the human rights abuses continued.

The ANC has continued to deflect criticism of its Zimbabwe policy as racist, and to echo some of Mugabe's anti-white rhetoric. One of his key apparatchiks, Dumisani Makhaye, spoke openly and honestly about the ANC's attitudes. Speaking at the ANC conference in Mpumalanga on 23 March 2002, he railed against international involvement in resolving the crisis in Zimbabwe: 'We are meeting here when the Western powers are geared towards rolling back the frontiers of liberation in southern Africa. They want to impose presidents of their choice in our region. *Zimbabwe is only a strategic hill, the objective is South Africa. The gross interference into the internal affairs of Zimbabwe by Western powers is a dress rehearsal for South Africa.*'[66] [author's emphasis]

6

The tyrant's heel remained firmly on the throat of Zimbabwe and its beleaguered people. Another gerrymandered parliamentary election in April 2005, replete with doses of intimidation and a host of irregularities, was again nodded through by South Africa. Soon-to-be deputy president Phumzile Mlambo-Ngcuka, heading the SADC delegation, congratulated Zimbabwe for holding a 'peaceful, credible and well-organised election'.[67]

My colleague, Dianne Kohler-Barnard, a fellow-observer, countered furiously, dismissing the poll as 'one of the most cynical frauds perpetrated in electoral history'. But even the stalled progress of the Zimbabwean opposition (which was soon to fracture) required retribution from Mugabe. Borrowing from the book of the Khmer Rouge, he launched 'Operation Murambatsvina' (or 'Drive out the Trash'). An estimated seven hundred thousand urban dwellers, in opposition strongholds, were forcibly removed from their shacks, which were subsequently razed to the ground.[68] Pretoria maintained its silence.

By the time I resigned as DA leader in 2007 I had concluded, dejectedly, that only Mugabe's death would resolve the situation. Thomas More's prescription *sola mors tyrannicida est* – 'death is the only way to be rid of tyrants' – seemed apt. Mugabe's longevity seemed to be matched, like Napoleon's generals, only by his luck: Zimbabwe's 15 minutes of world infamy (to transpose the famous phrase of Andy Warhol) was soon eclipsed post 9/11 by the more pressing and universalised Jihadist terror and the world reaction to it. He was also fortunate, as one cynical foreign observer put it to me, 'Because he grows tobacco – he doesn't have oil.' At critical stages he faced opponents he could either outwit or suppress, and most crucially of all, he mined the seam of residual resentments held by the regnant leadership elsewhere in Africa, especially in my own country.

A year later, however, another flawed set of elections appeared to herald a dramatic and regime-changing result. It appeared that faced with final economic collapse (inflation was set to reach a stratospheric 500 000% mid-2008) and complete immiseration, Mugabe's by-now-customised blend of vote-buying and rigging was unavailing, and the opposition had clearly outpolled the ageing dictator. Although the endgame remains unknown, the locust years which saw the destruction of one of Africa's greatest economic success stories and potent symbols of democratic reconciliation yields no end of lessons, most of them sombre.

In May 2008, the wave of xenophobic attacks across South Africa, largely targeting Zimbabwean refugees, pointed to the failure of Mbeki's approach and irresolution in dealing with Zimbabwe. It also drove home the dire local consequence of a misconceived foreign policy.

The real moral of the tale of our blighted neighbour was the relative ease and speed with which Mugabe could plunder his country and starve his people, pointing to the absence of a corrective, either internal or external. Zimbabwe demonstrated the severe limits of South Africa's willingness or ability to lead the African Renaissance to which Thabo Mbeki had committed his presidency. In the words of Samantha Power, faced with a real test he 'flunked it'.

But Power also identified the most significant lesson of Zimbabwe: the presence or absence of democratic accountability – an outspoken press, a healthy opposition, periodic elections and an independent judiciary. While rightly valued in themselves, she noted their greatest virtue to be practical: 'They deter and thwart top-down demolition.'[69]

Much of my time in politics was to be spent interrogating the health of these vital institutions at home.

CHAPTER 10

Parliament: Corrosion in the Corridors

The will to power came to take the place of the will to justice,
pretending at first to be identified with it, and then relegating it
to a place somewhere at the end of history.
ALBERT CAMUS

I

The parliament of South Africa represented the aspirations of the nation's new, non-racial, democratic order: the struggle against apartheid was, above all, a struggle for political rights and political power. Now the racial majority would finally be represented on the basis of 'one person, one vote', a prerequisite for all the struggle's other goals.

I had high hopes when sworn in as a member of South Africa's first democratic parliament in May 1994. Having been a 'tail-ender' in the Tri-cameral parliament, I knew its deficiencies. In the new era I had no doubt about the role the party should play. Inchoate thoughts were given voice by Archbishop Desmond Tutu. As the moral conscience in the old regime, he gave an early indication that he would be the ethical watchdog in the new order. I noted a warning he made at the time:

'There is nothing ... that in principle decrees that a democratically elected government, so hugely popular, should not give in to the allure-ments of power and privilege. Just because they have been democratically elected does not transform them magically into angels.' He concluded: 'We must hold our government and those in public office accountable. They are not God. We must expect standards of probity, integrity, honesty and public-mindedness, and be angry if they are absent.'

The new parliament – which also sat as the Constitutional Assembly until the passage of the final Constitution in 1996 – was everything the apartheid parliament was not: racially integrated, constrained by checks and balances, and representative of all the people. The early years (1994-1995) were filled with hope and promise; a spirit of innovation washed through

378

the stodgy halls, replacing old conventions with fresh perspectives and new aspirations. The legislators set about energetically dismantling what remained of apartheid's legal edifice; but it also introduced exciting new political and ideological debates whose depth was matched by their vigour. One example was the abortion debate of 1995, in which the full range of religious, medical and socio-economic issues was probed from a variety of perspectives in passionate but respectful exchanges.

The media had unprecedented access to parliamentary deliberations, and MPs were keen to carry out their duties, and to showcase their diverse array of traditional costumes and customs – never before given prominence in public. The aesthetic changes were more than the removal of old paintings and the hanging of the new South African flag; they reflected a seismic shift in the ethos of the whole institution.

We had the good fortune of being inaugurated in a time of great events, the election itself perhaps the greatest of all. Our challenge was to rise to that level.

The new parliament made use of many of the old one's best features. Ministers, for example, were summoned to 'question-time' in the National Assembly. MPs could thus scrutinise their decisions and debate them in short, intense interpellations. The president and the deputy president were not exempt from frequent grilling, and had to defend their positions against opposition challenges. The deputy president had to face questions every week. And added to all this, there were new reforms: an expanded system of parliamentary committees exercising direct oversight over each line-function ministry; and a Standing Committee on Public Accounts (Scopa) to monitor public spending. The new Speaker, Dr Frene Ginwala, was a high-ranking member of the ruling ANC, but set initially high standards for decorum and impartiality, winning respect.

My first run-in with government in parliament concerned an ugly incident in the dramatic and violent run-up to the 1994 April elections – the so-called 'Shell House massacre'. As I relate in Chapter 5, I had been caught in the middle of the Zulu protesters who marched on the building on 29 March only to be shot at – and killed and injured – by ANC operatives from within. The shootings were essentially unprovoked and disproportionate.

Far more disturbing were reports I received that the police, or elements in the hierarchy (scenting the impending change in power), had connived with the ANC leadership, including Nelson Mandela, to cover up the incident and protect the guilty. So my first questions in the new Assembly would not endear me to the new government.

Furthermore, I received an anonymous tip-off from deep within the police service that the answers being prepared to my questions (particularly relating to how the guards had obtained weapons) had, in essence, been doctored or falsified. This smacked of a cover-up. Forewarned, I waited for the hapless minister of Safety and Security to respond in parliament on 29 June; I particularly wanted to know whether the police had been given unrestricted access to Shell House to obtain evidence, particularly of a ballistic nature.

On this issue, the minister, Sydney Mufamadi, claimed: 'The police were not denied access to the building, but had themselves sought to rely on co-operation of the ANC in order to facilitate their investigation.'

This I knew to be false. So I leaped up and read from an internal police memorandum which had been leaked to me: '[Because] the police could not access Shell House ... no investigation was done inside and no one inside was asked any questions.'[1]

I also informed parliament that I understood no fewer than five different attempts had been made to obtain co-operation from the ANC – and that each had been rebuffed. I then read into the record a letter to the ANC from the police which stated in part: 'It is understood that you have since withdrawn the undertaking to allow the police access to Shell House...[We] call on you to honour your initial undertaking and arrange that the firearms used during the incident be handed over forthwith.'[2]

Without the arrogance and evasiveness that came to characterise this minister and many of his colleagues in later years, Mufamadi replied rather lamely: 'Until this morning I was trying to get further information relating to this question, and I was assured by both parties that the commitment to co-operate still stood.'

This was clearly contradicted by the facts in my possession. Douglas Gibson, our chief whip, put down a motion calling for an ad hoc select committee to be appointed 'to investigate whether Mufamadi had deliberately misled parliament with his answers.'

After some foot-dragging, a debate on the motion was held six weeks later and the committee was duly appointed and convened. Although (with its inbuilt ANC majority) it exonerated the minister, the exercise had interesting consequences.

The first concerned the sainted Madiba – President Mandela – who became so agitated about my probing of the shootings that he called a meeting with all ten members of our parliamentary caucus in his offices in Tuynhuys adjacent to parliament. There he berated me (unusually, since he was generally ebullient and affable) and said he had personally instructed the ANC guards to 'defend our headquarters' since the 'IFP was on its way to kill us all.' None of the ANC guards were ever charged, and the lack of co-operation between that organisation and the police continued.

Mandela's preoccupation with the matter troubled me. If he was correct that the ANC was 'under attack' and acted in self-defence, why had he and the hierarchy obstructed the police investigation at every turn. And why had the minister misled the House?

Later the following year, Mandela took another swipe at me in the Senate; he charged that as a consequence of our constant probing of Shell House, the DP had proven itself 'more right-wing than the National Party'.[3]

Irritated by the attention given to the 'Shell House massacre' he later reiterated that he personally had given the order to the guards to 'shoot to kill'.

Mandela's public put-downs were mirrored by his private remonstrations and explanations. At a discussion in May 1995, by far the most disagreeable between us, he concluded our meeting with the swipe, 'You're a young man and you want to make an impression, but your party is essentially all white.'

Time, in the form of the December 1997 judicial inquest into Shell House, would prove Mandela wrong on the issue: but his Teflon-coating was ultra-resilient. The incident pointed to a central paradox around Madiba. At one level he could be the most partisan of politicians. But on another plane, he was a global-celebrity-cum-secular-saint, beyond politics. The 'thunderbolt of error' bounced right off him.

History, I suspect, will largely ignore these events or consign them to a footnote in the chapter on the run-up to election day – and the dawn of freedom – on 27 April. But I had thought the parliamentary skirmishing was noteworthy since at the very commencement of democracy it was possible to believe that even if the government's huge majority insulated it from procedural or substantive defeats, there was a strong feeling that the nation's legislature was opening up. This proved to be, over time, both brief and illusory.

The ask-no-questions, brook-no-dissent exile liberationists began to find the scrutiny to which they were now subjected a little too uncomfortable.

The initial intake of MPs, particularly on the ANC side, represented a dizzying array of 'big name' activists, guerrillas, superannuated NGO types – and no small number of icons from South Africa's history. There was

Oliver Tambo's widow, Adelaide (whose stately progress around the House resembled a brightly coloured, well-upholstered couch in motion). Also in the widow's gallery of struggle heroes was Limpho Hani, spouse of the assassinated Chris Hani, whose death on Easter Friday 1993 accelerated the pace of the entire negotiation process and hastened the date of the freedom election. She sat right behind me – and we became very friendly for a while, even to the extent of having dinner together at my house away from parliament. She was, however, mercurial and ultra-conspiratorial; clearly she and Thabo Mbeki did not get on, and shortly after his accession as president she quit parliament and entirely disappeared from public life and view.

Paramount (at least in her own and much of the media's mind) was struggle queen and estranged presidential wife, Winnie Mandela, a home-grown hybrid of Imelda Marcos and Eva Peron. I have devoted a chapter to her (see Chapter 13).

This first batch included some very serious intellects, and activists who had burnished their credentials in the furnace of the struggle. There were Max Coleman (a businessman who turned radical when two of his sons were detained during PW Botha's state of emergency); ace trade unionists Johnny Copelyn and Marcel Golding; lawyer and human rights activist Willie Hofmeyr, tortured in detention; my former university colleague, Raymond Suttner, who had also been maltreated during his lengthy detention without trial; former political prisoner Barbara Hogan; church spokesman Saki Macozoma; and the formidable academic expert on the rise and fall of the Xhosa nation, Professor Jeff Peires. There were also no fewer than three Sisulus: Albertina, the famed Soweto matriarch and wife of Walter Sisulu, who along with Mandela and Tambo had formed the backbone of the liberation leadership, and two of her children, Max and Lindiwe; and Stalinist relic Brian Bunting, along with the more prominent Joe Slovo, whose deft pragmatism helped end many an impasse in the negotiation process.

Several mainstays of the grand apartheid era – blacks and Coloureds whose participation in the homelands or Tricameral parliament had provided the essential backbone of the collaborationist class – were also apparent; the Hendrickse family, for example, with patriarch Allan – once a member of PW Botha's cabinet, and leader of the Coloured Labour Party, along with his son Peter and son-in-law Desmond Lockey – together with Transkei's Bantu Holomisa and Stella Sigcau. They had all made the transition from Tricameral and bantustan co-option to ANC membership, the equivalent of immersion into the River Ganges to wash away all sins.

Oddest of the lot, in a sense, was the NP MP – who soon defected to the ANC – John Gogotya. His antics in Washington in the 1980s as a self-proclaimed leader of black South Africa were funded – it was later revealed – by the apartheid government, to denounce black majority rule in general, and the ANC in particular.

Then, alongside me and definitely and vehemently not in the ANC, was Freedom Front leader General Constand Viljoen. He had earned a fearsome reputation during his time as chief of the South African Defence Force, when PW Botha bestrode the presidency. Viljoen was seen as a 'soldier's soldier' whose attributes in battle included a propensity to parachute into the battle zone along with his troops. Retired from the military, he had become something of an icon of the hard Right. But, as related in Chapter 5, his decision to junk the rejectionist Conservative Party and set up an ethnic Afrikaans, pro-democracy Freedom Front was decisive.

Viljoen's charisma and message somewhat outweighed the DP's efforts in the 1994 election: his tiny parliamentary battalion was two seats larger than my own. Over the next five years I got to know him and his devoted wife, Risti, well. He was charming and humorous, personally secure in his own skin, if politically naïve, and he was listened to with respect by the ANC – though not a single suggestion he ever made was acted upon.

My other parliamentary neighbour, PAC president Clarence Makwetu, was an impressively tall figure of sartorial elegance. One of his disaffected members (and in the tiny PAC there seemed to be more leadership claimants than members) said the only reason he held the job was that 'he looked like Mandela' (which he did). The political gulf between us was as wide as it got in politics, and while he smiled and laughed easily, his small talk was limited. He was ousted after a year or two, and his place taken by the immensely affable – but politically ineffectual – former bishop Stanley Mogoba.

Less prominent and sitting further back – all members of the ANC caucus – were the Mahatma Gandhi's granddaughter Ela; and a quartet of Democratic Party crossovers, Pierre Cronje, Jan van Eck, Jannie Momberg and David Dalling. Dalling had told me before the election that as he imagined his absence of struggle history would prevent him becoming the new parliament's speaker, he would settle for chairmanship of the Justice Committee. In the event, he got neither post, and was made – more modestly – one of 25 ANC whips.

In all, the ANC's first parliamentary caucus comprised an eclectic fruit salad. The more talented and high-profile heavies were members of the cabinet; but the legislative ranks of the Congress were no less impressive.

Its strength was the intellectual depth and community credibility its members represented. This, alas, was not to last. With the completion of the Constitution in 1996, a steady trickle of the best and brightest, led by Cyril Ramaphosa, left legislative politics for the lure – and rewards – of the private sector, the parastatals, and the upper echelons of the public service.

By 1999 – with the second democratic election and the enthronement of Mbeki as president – the stream from parliament became a flood, led by talented cabinet members Jay Naidoo and Mac Maharaj (later ensnared in serious corruption allegations); and unfortunately, in most cases, their replacements were party activists of the third or fourth rank. A career in the National Assembly had little to offer the leading lights when it came to the stupendous salaries and perks for those whose 'know-who' was desperately needed by a private sector under immense pressure to 'blacken' its boardrooms.

The consequence for parliament of this brain-drain – and the scrutiny which real democratic accountability demands – has been fairly calamitous. It took time for the effects to be felt, but ten or twelve years on it had become apparent that much of parliament and its proceedings had become a pale shadow of the imperatives designated for it by the framers of the Constitution.

2

It was not simply the exodus that caused the vacuum. After an initial year of rushed legislation, broken quorums, and certain ministers' habitual absence from question time, I felt impelled to lead a DP delegation to meet President Mandela.

Despite not being a member of parliament, and having only indirect accountability to it, Mandela was keen on a lively legislature, and had a healthy – even reverential – regard for its importance. Over a lunch of lasagne at his Pretoria residence, he listened with some interest as the two veterans of our delegation (Eglin and Andrew) presented a laundry list of problems, and proposed solutions. Midway, Mandela interrupted and said the problem was that the ANC had gone 'straight from the bush into power'. He reminded us that the most significant previous regime change in 20th-century South Africa had been the ousting of the United Party government and its replacement in 1948 by the Nationalists' apartheid regime. Yet the NP had served a long spell in parliament as the opposition before assuming power: a long learning curve was inevitable and necessary.

No doubt, had Mandela served a second term as president, it is perfectly possible – even likely – that the legislature would have roused itself to fulfil its politically and constitutionally ordained function. However, his successor had none of Mandela's regard for the rigours, or niceties, of a robust legislature acting as both check and brake on an over-dominant cabinet. Whatever economic gains South Africa achieved, Mbeki had an impoverishing, indeed withering, effect on the politics of democratic accountability.

However, probably others must share the blame. At the dawn of the Mandela presidency, it became evident that tensions between party loyalty and parliamentary oversight would be settled in favour of the former. So, in 1994, party secretary-general Ramaphosa apparently compelled all ANC MPs to sign a code of conduct forbidding any 'attempt to make use of parliamentary structures to undermine organisational decisions and policies'.[4]

Ginwala's Speakership of the first parliament was, in the main, balanced. An interesting amalgam, she was high-born (an Indian Farsi) with impeccable struggle credentials (she had been extremely close to Oliver Tambo in exile in London); and a woman of formidable, even forbidding, intellect. Like all of us, she also had defects: that piercing intelligence was accompanied by a certain bossiness. Gibson quipped of her style: 'She can't decide whether she's Newt Gingrich or Betty Boothroyd' (a reference to the vastly differing styles of the then regnant speakers of the US Congress and the UK House of Commons).

Provided no vital ANC interest was threatened, Ginwala defended parliament as an institution and provided some protection to House minorities. She was often fairly candid – and not just in private – about deficiencies in her organisation, once memorably explaining why loyal struggle cadres make bad parliamentary democrats: 'The liberation movements have also brought a military style authoritarianism, combined with a tendency to close ranks defensively when attacked or criticised.'

Ginwala once chastised me for criticising some aspect of government, in these terms: 'The problem is, Tony, that some of us inside the organisation have been arguing exactly the same point. Now that you've identified with it in public, we're bound to lose.' I reminded her that good ideas do not become bad ideas because of their origins.

Whatever our complaints, the early democratic parliament now seems in retrospect like the 1968 'Prague spring' – a brief breath of freedom and openness soon smothered by a jealous government. It is clear that the danger to our democracy comes not from a rampant parliament, but from an all-powerful, centralised executive that acts with virtual impunity.

By 2007 it seemed fanciful to think any senior government members would openly challenge their own party's policies and behaviour. But in 1994 the minister of Housing, and South African Communist Party stalwart, Joe Slovo, was sharp on the proposed purchase of new naval corvettes: 'We have not been presented in this House or indeed at any other level of government with a thorough analysis of the potential threats to the security and integrity of South Africa which is capable of convincing me of the need for major capital spending on such items as submarines and ocean-going warships ... [A] couple of corvettes in the Navy can, in any case, never be much more than symbols... [We] need to be told clearly, before the next Budget is presented, what the purpose of all the high-tech, high-cost weapons systems the Defence Force is contemplating is; who it is they are going to protect us against; and why the current equipment is not sufficient.' A satisfied population would be South Africa's best defence.[5]

A decade later, parliament had become little more than an echo chamber, a platform for non-debates about non-issues. The ruling party controlled not only legislative agendas and outcomes, but parliamentary discourse itself, crushing alternative views. A few in the ANC shared this view. For example, then Finance Portfolio Committee chairperson Barbara Hogan said in 2002: 'Can we really say that debate emerges out of a really strong commitment to ensuring that we exercise our oversight role and are answerable to our constituencies? No, we can't say that. Without sounding outraged I simply say that it's a disgrace here in this parliament that we are not rising to the occasion as public representatives by assisting the executive ... [The] way we are dealing with the budget is perfunctory ... rubber-stamping.'[6]

Another definitive casualty of parliament's oversight role was the Standing Committee on Public Accounts (Scopa). For the first five years the DP's Ken Andrew – a person of painstaking punctiliousness and ethical rectitude – was given the chair. While I personally used to get quite frustrated by Ken's almost over-consensual style, he forged a powerful committee which cracked down hard and painstakingly on corruption. These good habits were carried on by his successor, drawn from the ranks of the IFP, Dr Gavin Woods, whose academic approach often belied a steely resolve. Woods, however, and the reputation of the Committee did not survive a collision with the cabinet over South Africa's corruption-ridden, scandal-plagued, multi-billion rand arms deal.

Not only was Woods elbowed out; the ANC's chief representative on

Scopa, the independent-minded Andrew Feinstein, was forced out of parliament entirely in 2001, after a falling-out with Essop Pahad and other
government heavies over its handling of the issue. He later told the *Sunday
Times*[7] that he was 'pressured by party leaders including chief whip, Tony
Yengeni [who later as I relate had to step down from parliament following an arms deal-related scandal], to stop investigating alleged corruption
relating to the deal.'

If relatively advanced modern democracies like Japan and the Netherlands
had their political foundations rocked by scandals relating to arms acquisitions, it was perhaps preordained that our new government's decision to
acquire a multi-billion rand defence equipment package would be controversial and crisis-ridden. More significant was how the ensuing trail of
corruption would lead to the highest offices in the land. The chief institutional casualties of the saga would be the very bodies entrusted by the
Constitution to root out maladministration and government malfeasance.

The arms deal began innocently enough with a comprehensive review
of South Africa's defence capabilities. This led to the Slovo salvo, cited
above, and a robust debate in civil society on whether, with its myriad
social needs and pressing claims, the modernising of the South African
Defence Force was the most pre-eminent and primary claim on the depleted Treasury. Whether it was the venality of certain top officials (such as
Defence minister Joe Modise, who died before the affair was investigated)
or a basic naïveté on the nullity of the much-promised, seldom-sighted
and essentially unenforceable industrial participation 'offsets' which every arms dealer promised the government, by 1996 a cabinet committee
agreed to 'the strategic defence acquisition'.

Parliament agreed in principle (but never in detail) to the package. The
cost – by then ballooning to over R33-billion – was never debated by the
legislature, although the detail, including the preferred bidders, was picked
over by the cabinet.

It subsequently emerged that the government official charged with the
procurement, Chippy Shaik (brother of the more infamous Schabir), met
in private – in flagrant contravention of the basic rules – with a number
of bidders before the final deal was concluded. Even worse, Shaik, despite
his official position, held a pecuniary interest in various entities that would
directly benefit from the deal he negotiated and finalised.

Mbeki himself appeared to play the role of both referee and player. In
2005 our indefatigable MP, Eddie Trent, received a copy of a so-called
'encrypted' fax suggesting Mbeki himself had held secret meetings with

executives from Thomson-CSF/Thales in Paris in 1997 when he was deputy president and chairman of the cabinet committee overseeing the arms package. (Thomson-CSF was later renamed Thales. Its South African subsidiary is named Thint.)

The implications were far-reaching. Firstly, it would have been in flagrant violation of the tender procedures governing the deal, since the company was bidding to supply a combat system contracted to the South African Navy. The second trapdoor was that the company, in the form of its South African subsidiary, Thint, was the same entity that ended up in the dock with Jacob Zuma (whom they were accused of bribing) on charges of corruption.

Information relating to these clandestine contacts was blocked by the Speaker, who went to extreme lengths personally to obstruct and obscure rigorous parliamentary and extra-parliamentary investigation of the package.

The initial allegations of corruption were first ventilated (without much substantiation) by PAC firebrand MP Patricia de Lille. But the first serious casualty was the slightly built and publicity-hungry old-order judge, Willem Heath. Since massive examples of corruption were emerging from the apartheid homeland of Ciskei, Heath, who hailed from East London, was appointed to head a special unit with wide-ranging powers of investigation and decision-making. Whatever his political inclinations, and however great his love of the spotlight, he developed a wide, justifiable reputation for tackling the proliferating frauds and forgeries prevalent in the dying days of the *ancien régime* and the early years of the new democracy. His powers were legislated, but the parliamentary statute which authorised his actions required that he obtain a presidential proclamation before he began poking into any specific matter. This proved fatal to his success.

The key to the Heath unit's power was his unique statutory authority to declare null and void any contract he thought the state had improperly concluded. Shortly before the new Defence minister, Mosiuoa Lekota, signed the final deal with international weapons suppliers, including Thomson-CSF, in December 1999, De Lille handed over to Heath whatever information she had, buttressed by material gleaned by one of the local bidders who was arbitrarily knocked out of the process. However, the judge could not get the minister of Justice to issue the necessary proclamation to allow him to start probing.

The parliamentary process dragged on for nearly a year before it hit paydirt. Acting on an initial report from the auditor-general, Scopa in September 2000 called for a multi-agency probe to interrogate major areas of concern relating to massive conflicts of interest, blatant lack of adherence to proper procurement procedures, and whether in fact the 'offsets' were 'feasible and sustainable'. Government claims that the package would inject R104-billion into the economy and create 65 000 new jobs were risible.

My role in the unfolding saga was marginal. However, as the party leader (at this time of a joint DP-NP caucus) I was determined that opposition representation on Scopa should be up to strength. I had privately been entreated by several journalists and the Scopa chair himself, Gavin Woods, to add more firepower to our team. I decided – after the obligatory consultation with my deputy, Marthinus van Schalkwyk – to dump the physically weighty but politically lightweight Dr Willem Odendaal (once a so-called high commissioner in a homeland). He was replaced by the politically junior but intellectual, savvy and media-friendly Raenette Taljaard. She had been plucked from academic obscurity by Gibson some years back and placed in our research department. She had become my speech-writer, and in 1999 I helped ensure her nomination to parliament as an MP from Gauteng. Although her role in parliament and the party would end abruptly in 2005 amidst some acrimony and grandstanding, her Scopa work was both brilliant and brave.

The displacement of Odendaal – entirely justified in view of our hitherto non-existent profile on the committee – together with a DP MP, the maverick KwaZulu-Natal farmer Graham McIntosh, whom I also side-lined, left pools of bitterness which Van Schalkwyk would scoop up when trying to break up the party a year or so later.

Another intervention by me occurred when the crisis around the corruption issue had reached its zenith in April 2001. The Swedish ambassador had invited me to address the EU ambassadors at one of their regular luncheons. I was bound by certain diplomatic restrictions, but thought this an excellent opportunity to point out that since allegations of bribery and corruption were swirling around South Africa and being investigated (or not), it would be no bad thing if the emissaries requested their own governments to look into the conduct of their own corporations alleged to have bribed our officials and politicians. The next day's *Citizen* carried a huge headline: 'Leon urges EU to probe arms deal'. These were my remarks, not anything disclosed to me by the ambassadors, and could have been made anywhere. But I had provoked diplomatic Nordic rage – though I believed it a disgrace that at the time the European contractors had not been charged or prosecuted with bribing the slew of South African officials implicated in the scandal. (This was to change, some years later, when the German authorities began to probe the matter.)

In parliament, meanwhile, Scopa's call for a multi-agency probe had been approved by November 2000. Practically every member of Scopa, including Woods and Feinstein, understood and intended 'multi-agency' to include Heath's unit, seen as effective and, most crucially, enjoying a healthy distance from the executive. Woods specifically requested the involvement of Heath and his unit in the probe.

Over Christmas the executive – clearly chagrined, if not frightened by where, and no doubt to whom, this investigation might lead – was galvanised into action. Early in the New Year, Mbeki used technical grounds to dismiss Heath as chief of his unit; the ANC fired Feinstein as its Scopa head; and the Speaker declaimed that parliament had not intended Heath to be in the probe (the text of the resolution was ambiguous). That she should do so was highly questionable, especially since parliamentary gossip was that the Speaker had personally attended a January 2001 ANC strategy meeting where the party heavies (led by the bullying Pahad) decided to stifle or close down Scopa.

Naturally the Justice minister was only too delighted to seize upon the Speaker's ruling (which he had apparently discussed with her beforehand) as a sort of fig leaf to partially clothe his nakedly partisan refusal to allow Heath a remit.

UDM leader, Bantu Holomisa, who on the occasions he could rouse himself to action was pretty effective in highlighting corruption, sent her a letter accusing her of a range of improprieties. Ginwala, he charged, had intervened in a 'grossly partisan manner'[8] in interpreting the Scopa report, and she had sought to defer its publication in order to deliberately slow down the investigation.

I again slammed the Speaker for converting parliament into 'an ethics-free zone'. The arms deal 'had not been her finest hour' and, I continued, 'where she should have stood up and defended parliament and its most powerful committee (Scopa) against executive-minded bullying and cajoling, she seems to have joined the other side.'

The 'bullying and cajoling' of which I complained became grimly apparent in late January when Mbeki made an extraordinary appearance on national TV. He waved around an organogram which he claimed Judge Heath had drawn up, and which he said contained a secret 'hit list' which the Judge had compiled naming Mbeki and his predecessor, Mandela, as the chief suspects in arms deal corruption. Mbeki used the diagram as part of his justification for dismissing Heath and his unit.[9]

On the heels of this surreal performance, the editor of the lively investigative journal *Noseweek*, Martin Welz, said he had personally drawn the diagram and believed Heath had never seen it before. Welz elaborated that 'the president was misinformed. The people who informed him did not understand what the documents meant. They [the documents] just sketched the power structure of who the most important people in government are – and whether their relatives and friends are involved in the arms industry [as indeed were both Mbeki's and Mandela's].' The documents did not prove anything, although sensational claims which surfaced six or seven years later suggested they might.

But back in 2001 Mbeki was clearly intent on smearing Heath. He was highly selective with the facts, cherry-picking those which agreed with his stratagem to insulate the executive from a real probe, and omitting or misstating those which contradicted his approach. I denounced his performance as 'arguments which would fail a basic ethics test.'

Amputated of an essential limb (Heath's unit), the 'multi-agency' investigation continued in attenuated form. It comprised the Public Protector (whose shyness when it came to holding ministers to account had already revealed itself in the *Sarafina* scandal); the National Director of Public Prosecutions (the former ANC chief whip in the Senate); and the auditor-general. None had either the hunger or the inclination to unpack the scandal and track its perpetrators, no matter what their office or status.

By November Scopa received the so-called 'Joint Investigation Task Group' report. It turned out to be at best a semi-dry squib. It held in essence that 'no evidence was found of any improper or unlawful conduct by the government.' Crucially, it absolved all the key political personalities of any responsibility or guilt or wrongdoing. 'The irregularities and improprieties referred to in our report point to the conduct of certain officials ... and cannot in our view be attributed to the president or the ministers involved.'[10]

The investigative troika (before parliament or Scopa could assess it) had handed over its work to the executive; and not simply to a ministerial committee but, apparently, to the president himself. Media reports and Woods's own sources indicated that the Presidency and others, including Pahad, had changed or severely sanitised the results to lessen their damaging conclusions and protect the cabinet. (Indeed, Mbeki, Alec Erwin, Mosiuoa Lekota and Trevor Manuel never denied that the original report was altered.) Scopa immediately called for the original report, which the auditor-general Shauket Fakie declined to do, stating that 'no material changes' were made to the original draft.

This was astonishingly disingenuous. Three years later, an unsuccessful arms deal bidder, through court action, obtained the original document. On it appeared hand-written notes (apparently in Pahad's writing) with the instruction that the report to parliament was to include the following:

'Add to overall conclusion ... the joint investigation team found no evidence of impropriety, fraud or corruption by cabinet or by government; and government co-operated with the investigation and assisted them with their endeavours.'[11]

Fakie's original draft made no such finding and drew no such conclusion. Yet the report when presented to parliament had been so altered.

Even more ominous than these self-exculpating additions were the omissions from the final report of key evidence given to the troika by the Defence secretary at the relevant time, General Pierre Steyn. The report neglected entirely to record the detailed and damning critique by Steyn of the entire package and the 'large-scale irregularities' which he stated had 'riddled' and 'flawed' the process. Steyn also stated in the draft (edited out of the final report) that the investigation was designed to give legitimacy to the 'political manipulation of the process' – exactly the conclusion the opposition had reached.[12]

When in March 2005 we demanded that Scopa recall Fakie and his report, we were ignored by the quiescent ANC majority. Woods had ceased to chair Scopa, and parliament had almost entirely abdicated its oversight role.

A bizarre footnote to this unedifying stain was an admission which Mbeki made to journalists on the eve of the 2006 municipal elections.[13] He acknowledged that an eviscerating and excoriating 12-page letter which Jacob Zuma had signed and sent off to the besieged Scopa head, Gavin Woods, had in fact been authored by the president himself. Having interacted with both men over a long period, I had always thought that the missive, with its peremptory, hectoring and highfalutin' tones and phrases, displayed entirely the voice of Thabo and the hand of Jacob.

Mbeki/Zuma defended the executive against Woods's and Scopa's request that the Heath unit be included in the arms deal investigation. The blistering conclusion: '[It] seems that the investigation you seek is tantamount to a fishing expedition to find the corruption and dishonesty you assume to have occurred.'

Yet, after all, if Scopa could not investigate allegations of corruption, who else could in parliament? There was also a distinct tone of menace in such phrases as: 'Special steps [will] be taken to correct this situation, to ensure that all of us, including Scopa and you, respect the rule of law

...'; and '[the] government will also act vigorously to defend itself and the country against any malicious misinformation campaign intended to discredit the government and destabilise the country.'

Within two months Woods resigned (probably before the ANC majority could push him out) as Scopa chair – and, effectively, parliament's probe of the deal ended.

The infamous letter received judicial attention in the subsequent trial of Schabir Shaik. Although the judge laboured under the misapprehension that Zuma, not Mbeki, was its author, Justice Squires noted: '[It is] almost as if the writer is taking a special delight in rubbing the collective nose of Scopa – and Woods in particular – in the rejection of the recommendations of Scopa.'[14]

The arms acquisition chief Chippy Shaik resigned following revelations that he may have improperly benefited his brother Schabir's companies during the bidding process. Schabir, in turn, in May 2005 was found guilty of corruption, and the target of his corrupt practices – for which the court jailed him for 15 years – was Jacob Zuma, whom Mbeki then fired from his post. He, too, was placed on trial for corruption. Yengeni also fell on his corrupt sword and got a jail sentence.

While it reflected a degree of health in the judicial and prosecution services that such notables were not untouchables, of the 24 individuals and 68 statutory bodies investigated in connection with the arms deal, nothing further was heard.

3

In any event, Zuma, Shaik and Yengeni were – in terms of the arms acquisitions – bit players whose convictions related to relatively tiny amounts of cash (or a luxury car discount) dwarfed by the billions spent on the armaments themselves. But there were to be no investigations, prosecutions or convictions of any of those higher up in the political decision-making chain. However, after Mbeki's defenestration in Polokwane in December 2007, Jacob Zuma's supporters pointed accusing fingers back at Mbeki, and demands surfaced for 'a TRC-process' on the arms deal: all bets were now off. When the first whiffs of bribery and backhanders emerged, a veteran businessman advised me that 'the corruption wasn't incidental to the arms deal, that was its central purpose.' Andrew Feinstein's[15] insider account of how its kickbacks funded the ANC's 1999 election campaign seemed confirmatory.

The glaring truth emerges: the people of South Africa are only represented in parliament in the most superficial and ineffectual ways – in art, but not in law; in word, but not in deed. Where once parliament was perhaps, briefly for a short period after 1994, the master of government, it soon became its servant, not of the people but of the executive. This was a damning comment on our incapacity to attain the proper understanding of democracy.

Another contributory factor in parliament's decline is the overwhelming electoral strength of the ANC. It has continued to grow in relative – though not in absolute – terms since 1994.

One-party dominance was achieved by a combination of the 'liberation dividend', opposition weakness and patterns of history. These accounted for the parliamentary weight of the ruling party. But the ANC chose to cement and extend its dominance through the Leninist practice of 'democratic centralisation'. Throughout this book I instance how this curtailed South Africa's democratic growth. But in parliament, the 'cadre deployment' policy proved withering at an early stage: MPs in the ruling party were subject to deployment or redeployment according to the diktats of leadership, stifling independence among members.

A second constitutional weakness, whose origins lay in my own party's 2001 split, was floor-crossing. Although the ANC has recently signalled its end, its effects on parliament for the six years it operated were calamitous: it extended ruling party dominance, further fragmented an already fissiparous opposition, and, most crucially, eroded public confidence in the legislature. My own experience was to prove the accuracy of the widely held perception that the national legislature was a political bargain basement – where trust is betrayed to the highest bidder.

The absence of directly electable MPs from a constituency to which they would have to account has been a third and reinforcing defect: it strengthened the hand of the party boss (including mine, I should add) and increased the remoteness, and perhaps irrelevance, of the average MP.

Parliament's behaviour – and the behaviour of the majority party in particular – greatly exacerbated these constitutional weaknesses. One of the most dominant features of post-1994 legislation, for example, was the frequency with which parliament delegated sweeping regulatory powers to the ministers, diminishing its own statutory role. A case in point was the Broad-Based Black Economic Empowerment Act (53 of 2003), which proposed dramatic changes to the structure of corporate South Africa. The legislation was only six pages long, though the original regulations ran to 36 pages, to be augmented several times over the next three years.

Ministers are not required to report their regulations back to parliament for amendment or approval – and even if they were, it is unlikely that the ANC-dominated Assembly would question them. There have been a few exceptions. A recent case – in 2006 – was the Icasa Amendment Bill, which establishes the mandate for South Africa's telecommunications regulatory body. The bill passed the National Assembly with all-party support, but was then amended by the National Council of Provinces (NCOP) in a manner that undermined the body's independence by ceding the minister of Communications the power to appoint its members. The DA protested, and Mbeki, acting on legal advice that the bill was unconstitutional, sent it back to parliament for amendment.

As early as the eve of the 1997 second session of parliament, I warned against the drift in our democracy by specifically citing and highlighting government's embrace of legislation giving ministers wide and loosely defined powers to draft regulations and promulgate rules that would never (at that stage, at least) have withstood the rigour of parliamentary scrutiny. In a speech at a DP gathering in Kenilworth, Cape Town, I asked rhetorically: 'Where is the "transparent and accountable government" to which the ANC committed itself in the 1994 RDP document?'[16]

Examples of the tendency included the two epic pieces of labour legislation: the Labour Relations Act, and the Basic Conditions of Employment Act, in whose passage through parliament I was intimately immersed, during this first phase of democracy.

An important consequence of my remark was the reaction of the then-president of the South African Institute of Race Relations, the historian Professor Hermann Giliomee, with an unsentimental – in my view realistic – view of the ANC in government. Giliomee stated that while my argument was 'important and timely' I had underestimated the situation and – in his view – not located, entirely accurately, the genesis of the problem.[17]

According to Giliomee, newly emergent governments make the 'shock discovery' that democracy is no cure-all: 'Cabinet ministers discover that the state's capacity falls short of the services, jobs and patronage their constituency expects of them. As their popularity recedes ministers panic and come to believe drastic action is needed. They demand increased powers; they become less and less inclined to face the scrutiny of parliament.'

If Giliomee believed I had understated the problem, one of my targets, the formidable minister of Health, Dr Nkosazana Zuma, believed I had unfairly castigated her. To my horror, the day after my comments were reported, Zuma strode across the aisle and, with some difficulty, squeezed in next to me in my bench. At menacingly close proximity to my eardrum she berated me on my views, which she took to mean that she was a dictator. I said my argument could be substantiated and offered to send her a detailed critique of how the law enforcing compulsory community service for newly qualified doctors gave the minister far too many discretionary powers. She offered to engage in earnest debate on receipt of my written argument. As soon as parliament adjourned I wrote her a detailed and I hoped balanced appraisal of the bill. I anticipated her response with eager relish. Seven years later, I am still waiting!

The pace of this tendency to rule by regulation quickened. It was fully in place by 1999. In the highly contested terrain of economic transformation one was most likely to find that scrutiny and transparency had been removed from the public gaze – and parliamentary participation – and placed in the hands of a minister. This gave him (or her) immense power over corporate South Africa, as events, and legislation, over the next eight years revealed.

After the 1999 general election, the Centre for Development and Enterprise, a Johannesburg-based NGO, published a critique of 'Policy-making in a New Democracy'.[18] Diplomatically couched, it nonetheless asked a series of pointed questions which led in a specific, negative direction: 'Will the ANC continue to allow and expand the role that opposition parties and outside interests can play in influencing government policy and legislation? Will the ANC government allow more scope and power to parliament in holding ministers and senior public servants accountable to parliament for their actions?'

Over the next six years the position worsened. Presciently and uncharacteristically Richard Calland, whose NGO, Idasa, was engaged to monitor parliament, started observing a trend which gathered momentum under the Mbeki presidency.[19] He noted: 'While the ANC ostensibly welcomes opposition politics and rigorous parliamentary debate, there appear to be disconcerting limits to its tolerance. Its MPs have on occasion resorted to labelling opposition politicians as racists if they disagree with ANC viewpoints.'

The howling down of opposition speakers also became a regrettable and monotonous feature of daily parliamentary life. The dismissive jeering and screaming which sometimes accompanied my speeches was dispiriting. However, since the ANC on parliamentary high days – such as the President's Budget or the State of the Nation address – felt that a modicum of decent behaviour was called for, I got away lightly compared to some of my colleagues who were screamed at and heckled in a manner which independent analyst Aubrey Matshiqi once described to me as (in the words of his father) 'bad manners dressed up as robust debate'.

Parliamentary committees possess broad powers to summon ministers to report to them, or compel individuals and institutions to supply evidence under oath. They also have the power to interrogate government budgets (although not to amend them), and are expected to report back on their activities to parliament itself every year. However, the committees rarely employ their full powers: many MPs do not even fully understand their role; under the direction of the ANC, in fact, committee chairpersons, until 2008, at least, behaved as if their responsibility was not to hold the executive accountable but to shield it from scrutiny.

The Ethics Committee allowed serious breaches of conduct by MPs and ministers to go virtually unpunished. How far parliament has fallen is the contrast in Scopa's treatment of former minister Winnie Madikizela-Mandela on the one hand, and Deputy President Phumzile Mlambo-Ngcuka on the other. In 1997, with the DA's Ken Andrew in the chair, Scopa investigated Madikizela-Mandela for unauthorised travel expenses, and ordered her to reimburse the government. In 2006, with a more quiescent Themba Godi of the PAC in the chair, Scopa declined to investigate the deputy president for her allegedly unauthorised use of an air force jet to fly family and friends to the United Arab Emirates over the Christmas holiday.

One of the more activist committees was the Portfolio Committee on Sport and Recreation. Rather than monitoring the dismal performance of the government in its interventions into South African sporting life, the committee – whose chairperson cheerfully admitted he knew nothing about sport at all – spent much of its energy criticising the racial balance of players in South African teams.

After the initial *glasnost*, changes in procedural rules were effected to protect the government and restrain the opposition. Within five years all debates, including the annual discussion of the president's State of the Nation address, saw the ANC reserve for itself the right of first response. This made South Africa one of the few legislatures in the world in which the government responds to the government before the opposition has a chance to speak.

4

During 2005, I felt it appropriate to inform readers of my weekly electronic newsletter, *SA Today*, that every advertisement calling for members of the public to give evidence to one or another parliamentary portfolio committee should be accompanied by a large health warning: 'Nothing which you say, no evidence which you adduce, no matter how compelling, will be of any effect or consequence should the majority (i.e. ANC) component of the portfolio committee receive a contrary instruction at any stage, from the executive.'

This was not simply hyperbole. At that time of writing, parliament enacted sweeping changes to legislation dealing with health care workers. The concerns of nurses who gave credible and laborious evidence to the appropriate committee were simply swept aside. Another example at the time was the Educational Laws Amendment Bill – which bolstered government's ability to interfere in school management. Painstaking compromises agreed to between the ANC and the opposition were disregarded after last-minute interference by the ANC minister.

Not every bill – or every committee – was railroaded in this manner. It all depended on the centrality or otherwise of the legislation to the ANC's grand project and political preoccupations of the day. Lesser matters in its hierarchy of political must-haves – ranging from bail-granting to national credit legislation – tended to enjoy a more inclusive and committee-orientated approach; and the legislation which flowed from such a process tended to be based on an all-party consensus.

The role played by the Speaker cannot be overlooked. Though Dr Ginwala was generally praised for her impartiality, her tenure was blemished, as I have noted, by her conduct in the arms deal controversy. Yet her independence – rickety though it proved at crucial moments – was too much for the Mbeki administration. She was suddenly replaced by Deputy Speaker Baleka Mbete shortly after the 2004 elections. Ginwala told me afterwards, somewhat ruefully, that she was not even consulted by Mbeki – or his parliamentary henchman, Tony Yengeni – about her axing. She told me she heard about it on the radio en route to a meeting of the ANC caucus. She later resigned from parliament.

Mbete was a staunch ANC loyalist and had been at the centre of controversy several years earlier when she was accused of receiving a driver's licence in improper circumstances – as a result of rank-pulling – when she was deputy Speaker. At least in America, when hotelier legend Leona Helmsley infamously said that 'only little people pay taxes', she did eventually go to jail for tax evasion. Mbete's contemptuous dismissal of an enquiry into her driving licence test was that she was 'too busy to stand in queues'.[20] This did nothing to halt her forward march in politics. I will return to her shortly.

Readers will have noticed that in this sorry tale of democratic decline, it was frequently the egregious Tony Yengeni who was the primary executioner, if not the author, of parliament's severe self-censorship of its constitutionally prescribed role of holding the executive to account. A brief diversion on this character is perhaps required.

Before his downfall, Yengeni's baleful influence was to be felt throughout parliament. He was appointed chief whip of the ANC, after the 1999 election, by President Mbeki; and his 'jackboot' approach to parliamentary democracy – so inimical to its functioning – became a feature of his operations. It was his greed in obtaining a massive discount on a swanky Mercedes 4x4 (which he fraudulently failed to declare in the Register of Members' Interests), from one of the arms deal bidders, that led to his disgrace, and ultimate, though brief, imprisonment.

His rise and fall in the space of two years was presaged by his antics as an ANC MP, a combination of the obnoxious and the oleaginous. Other than having the same first name, we had zero in common. Sitting just behind me in the first parliament he would generally chirp with disapproval whenever I spoke. His own speeches were laced with hate-filled, bilious, retributive sentiment – startlingly at variance with Mandela's inclusive Rainbow Nation vision. This made him popular with many in the ANC rank and file, and along with his struggle credentials (he was severely tortured during the final days when his guerrilla unit was interdicted in the Western Cape shortly before De Klerk inaugurated the negotiations era) made him a man to watch.

He was also unbearably smug; his bald and somewhat bloated Yul Brynner-like features were set off by the flashiest of clothes, apparently provided free (or perhaps at a hefty discount) by a *faux*-Italian outfitter from the Cape Town Waterfront. He harboured antipathy towards me, and it all exploded one afternoon during a humdrum parliamentary sitting in March 1998.

The DP's new star turn, a black female medical practitioner from the Eastern Cape, Dr Bukelwa Mbulawa, caused outrage in ANC ranks simply by being aligned with our party. To many it was inconceivable that she was not 'with the movement'. Accordingly, whenever she spoke in parliament – and she had a pretty shrill voice – a chorus of jeers, catcalls and insults would fly at her from the ANC ranks. Obviously, it got to her eventually. A year later she crossed the floor to her former tormentors, the ANC; but on that day she was in full battle mode, taking on the ANC for creating 'no-go areas' for opposition parties in the Eastern Cape.

To try and deflect her attention (and no doubt to goad me) Yengeni shouted out that Mbulawa was 'a token black'.[21] Such an epithet is 'un-parliamentary', since all racist references are deemed out of order. I put a demand to the Speaker that Yengeni withdraw the remark.

I had been witness to some far more vicious abuse in my time. A year or so earlier, for example, during his brief tenure as minister of Minerals and Energy in the Government of National Unity, the NP bruiser Pik Botha had called ANC trade unionist and MP Marcel Golding a 'golliwog'. Another memorable encounter was when ANC caucus chair, a certain Mrs Mentor, accused me of 'sabotage'. However, what was beyond the pale about Yengeni's utterance was that when called to order – as form required – and asked whether he had spoken the offending words, he dishonestly denied ever uttering them.

I called him a 'liar'. That was what he was, and I declined the Speaker's order to withdraw. Correctly, I was ejected. I thus earned the dubious distinction of being the first (and thus far, only) party leader to be kicked out of parliament since 1994.

Leaving aside the ensuing histrionics and headlines, I was amazed at Yengeni's barefaced effrontery in denying what he plainly had said (the recording devices did not pick up the exchange). It made me think then that the ANC member had a deep and fundamental flaw when it came to questions of integrity. His subsequent trial, conviction and four-year jail sentence for fraud (of which he served only a few months) came as no great surprise.

His negative impact on parliament would live on long after his personal shaming, since his first order of business after promotion as chief whip was the decimation of question time. In her political memoirs, Helen Suzman[22] records how skilful use of parliamentary questions permitted her to shine the harsh light of truth on the darkest recesses of the apartheid state. On average, she placed two hundred questions a year on the order paper. This so infuriated one cabinet minister that he shouted in parliament: 'You put these questions just to embarrass South Africa overseas.' She replied: 'It is not my questions that embarrass South Africa – it is your answers.'

For all the damage it wrought on the democratic fabric of South Africa, the National Party's respect for the vestiges of parliamentary procedure ensured that question time remained a primary, often lively, feature of MPs' life. When the new parliament assembled, it continued with the same question-and-answer format. This meant that MPs were given – through four 'interpellations' (15-minute mini-debates) as well as oral questions – the opportunity to grill ministers on a wide variety of topics.

This was a political godsend for a party as marginal as the DP then was;

through deft and fleet footwork we could get our questions in early – raising topical issues in a fairly tight framework. Initially we dominated the order paper, even though our MPs comprised less than two per cent of the total intake. Soon other opposition parties cottoned on, and the combined opposition posed something like 5 105 ministerial questions in the first parliament, compared to a limp 588 from ANC ranks.[23]

None of this appealed to Yengeni's controlling instincts. Shortly after he became chief whip, he used his party's majority on the Joint Rules Committee to scrap interpellations entirely, and introduced a quota system for questions. As Douglas Gibson explained in 2005: 'Instead of allocating questions on a first-come-first-served basis, questions were now apportioned according to how many seats a party held in the legislature. Question time is now dominated by ANC MPs who typically ask "sweetheart" questions that give the minister the platform to present his or her portfolio in glowing terms.'[24]

Yengeni even limited the number of follow-up questions which an MP could ask a minister. Now a minister could not be pressed or harried if the issue demanded it; the rules protected the executive from legislative probing.

Intended as a put-down – an insinuation of 'un-African' behaviour – the label 'Westminster' is affixed to politicians such as me to suggest that cut-and-thrust exchanges have little place in an emerging democracy. Yet it was precisely in Westminster when I sat in the Strangers' Gallery in the House of Commons that I saw the globe-trotting, world-acclaimed (before he invaded Iraq) Tony Blair bested and embarrassed by a humble opposition backbencher on the issue of long waiting lists in an NHS hospital. The obligation of a British prime minister to face a weekly grilling in the somewhat feared, sometimes theatrical Mother of Parliaments, seemed to me the modern equivalent of the Roman slave who stood behind Caesar as he received public accolades: 'Remember, Caesar, you are only human.'

There were few publicly critical cadres in President Mbeki's entourage. As a sop to the opposition, a rule was introduced formalising the president's obligation to answer questions at least four times per year. But this was often honoured in the breach, with Mbeki on occasion cancelling his appearances without sanction or disapproval.

And when he does appear in parliament to answer, the bulk of questions are of the 'how great thou art' variety, while the president has to answer only eight questions a year from all the opposition parties combined.

How did it happen? Part of the answer is that the peculiar personality and extreme prickliness of Mbeki not only came to dominate the ANC and government, but caused the very rules of parliament to be twisted and changed. It was said that President Richard Nixon had an extraordinary defect for a modern politician: he essentially disliked people. Mbeki, it seemed to me, had in addition another: he hated criticism and disdained any form of open scrutiny. His acolytes reinforced his shield by requiring that the Speaker 'vet' questions to the president to ensure that they were of 'national or international importance'. This extraordinary device was not, to my knowledge, activated during Ginwala's Speakership; but it was applied with alacrity by Mbete.

I have written of Eddie Trent's frustrated attempts to question Mbeki on the president's role in the arms deal. As time and the affair rolled on – and Mbete took the reins as Speaker – the spurious 'concessions' on question time rules engineered by Yengeni became entrenched (though not solely) on this particular issue.

While I was often critical of Mbeki's remoteness from parliament, when he did present himself in parliament on 22 October 2004 his performance was so startling – indeed frightening – that I rather wished he had stayed away and that Ryan Coetzee had never asked his question.[25] In essence, as I describe in Chapter 8, Coetzee sought a response from Mbeki on whether he believed rape was one of the prime reasons for the spread of AIDS.

The president refused to answer. He refused to state whether HIV causes AIDS; or to withdraw false accusations of racism which he had recently made against prominent local and international AIDS activists in his weekly newsletter *ANC Today*. Mbeki told parliament that he would not answer any questions about HIV or AIDS, even though the questions had been formally submitted to him and published by parliament in the question paper. Such questions, he said, were not his responsibility. Instead, the president said, he would talk about racism. And he did so, reciting a litany of racist caricatures that bordered on the pornographic, and implying that the DA believed them.

The DA interjected to remind Mbeki that parliament's rules prevent members from making racist statements, but the Speaker allowed the president to continue. And so he did – claiming, for example, that the DA and others believed that African women 'cannot keep their legs crossed' and African men 'cannot keep it in their pants'.

When the SABC television news carried a report on the debate that night, the exchanges between the president and the DA were edited to spare Mbeki embarrassment. The incident emphasised Mbeki's race obsession and underlined his AIDS-denialism. It also showed the essential disrespect he had for parliament, and contempt for the DA. The Speaker let him rave on uninterrupted.

5

However, within the ANC at least, Baleka Mbete played all sides. Wearing her customary '*doek*' (a sort of turban) the Speaker decided to attend the opening of the corruption trial of Jacob Zuma in Durban in late 2005 – as part of the ANC cheering gallery, ineradicably staining the formal independence of her office. In August 2006 she was on hand to wave Tony Yengeni into jail for his short and featherbedded stay there. Any expectation that the Speaker would cleave an independent path was misplaced. Clearly, however, she was adroit at playing ANC politics. She emerged, post Polokwane, as party chair. Unblushingly she then took over control of the powerful ANC political committee in parliament, the body which determines the ANC partisan tactics in the very legislature which had elected her to protect the interests of all parties, not just her own. Blemishing ineradicably the independence of her office was not, however, her only achievement.

She greatly enjoyed the high life – or perhaps the literal high-flying which government officials crave – which she came to regard as her due. In early 2006, it was revealed that she hired an entire aircraft to fly herself to Monrovia for the installation of the new president of Liberia. Apparently commercial airline schedules did not suit her; and the fact that South Africa was represented in the formidable form of both the president and the Foreign minister was of little concern – thus setting back parliament's budget by some R500 000!

The conduct of her deputy, Gwen Mahlangu, gave an even clearer indication of the ANC views of a Speaker's duties. While often incapable of making rulings from the chair or controlling parliament, the deputy was uncharacteristically effective during floor-crossing time. Mahlangu once notoriously abused her position by telephoning DA MPs during a floor-crossing 'window' and cajoling them to join the ANC – a particularly brazen gesture, given that only the Speaker's office knows at any given time which MPs have filled out forms indicating their desire to change parties.

During my period as leader of the opposition in parliament, I often accused the Speaker and her deputy of converting parliament into a branch office of Luthuli House (a reference to the ANC's head office). This seemed an accurate enough depiction of the real locus of parliamentary authority.

Ironically, the most blatant example of this tendency occurred after I had stood down in September 2007. The nation was then fixated on the state of, and circumstances surrounding, Health minister Manto Tshabalala-Msimang's new liver and claims of her apparent alcoholism and kleptomania. To the acute embarrassment of the ruling party, my intrepid colleague, Mike Waters, asked a written question enquiring whether the minister had been convicted of theft, in 1976, while employed at a hospital in Botswana, and whether she had disclosed her conviction to President Mbeki. At short notice (less than an hour before parliament was to meet for Wednesday questions) Waters was phoned and advised that the Speaker had ruled it out of order for containing 'offensive and unbecoming language', in transgression of parliament's rules. When Waters rose to protest his spurious muzzling that day in parliament, he was incandescent with fury, accusing Mbete of 'covering up for a thief'.[26] He was duly suspended for five days, but the minister was shielded from accounting for any ethical lapses or non-disclosures. Mbete subsequently never could explain how Waters's prosaically worded, but politically devastating, question transgressed the rule she invoked to suppress it.

The swiftness with which the Speaker acted to interdict and punish Waters stood in stark and unflattering contrast to her foot-dragging in the 'Travelgate scandal'. This episode placed the greatest stain on Mbete's tenure and also mocked the appellation 'honourable' affixed to MPs' names. It corroded, further, public confidence in parliament.

Initially, it was reported that more than two hundred MPs were being investigated by the Scorpions for allegedly defrauding parliament by falsely claiming reimbursement for travel vouchers they did not actually use, or abused for unauthorised purposes. Mbete, the deputy Speaker, and the cabinet ministers were cleared. The scam was uncovered by parliamentary officials in 2002, but only became public in 2004. It was disclosed in 2006 that the amount by which parliament had been defrauded could have been as much as R36 million.[27]

The ANC's response to this defining scandal was both instructive and contradictory: initially, in 2005, it orchestrated a volume of publicity when five implicated MPs were asked to resign. But soon enough, in 2006, two of them were 'redeployed' to local government, one of whom, Ruth Ntshulana-Bhengu, became a deputy mayor and subsequently was elected to the ANC National Executive.

Eventually, in February 2007, five years after the initial detection, 32 MPs accepted plea bargains, effectively admitting guilt and agreeing to pay fines. But the Speaker allowed them to hold on to their parliamentary seats. Six of these, senior ANC MPs, were demoted, but continued to hold their seats. (In terms of the Constitution MPs automatically lose their seats in the event of a minimum twelve-month prison sentence without the option of a fine.)

Parliament emerged from the saga deeply discredited; supposedly the heart of oversight and accountability, it has continued to protect the cheating MPs by avoiding, delaying and deflecting action against them.

In February 2007 the DA was forced to write to the Speaker to request the details of the names of the MPs who were repaying the money they stole and the amounts they were repaying. She had refused to make this information available, and we have yet to receive a response. By early 2008, my party – and the public – still could not access the forensic report which parliament obtained when the investigation commenced.

Not that the DA was spared embarrassment: one of our then serving MPs, Craig Morkel, and two formers MPs, were ensnared in 'Travelgate'. I suspended Morkel when he was charged, and advised him he would be expelled from the party if convicted. He crossed the floor to avoid this consequence, migrating ultimately to the ANC.

While there were, in terms of the Constitution and its own rules, limits to the action parliament could take against cheating MPs, the saga also cast an unforgiving light on Yengeni's successor as chief whip, Mbulelo Goniwe. Although he would within two years also exit parliament in disgrace (in his case for being a sex pest) we were subject to his full bullying vitriol during the height of the saga.

He was at his thuggish worst in 2005: 'One thing that you forget, is that you are here because of the magnanimity of the ANC. If we had chosen the path of the Nuremberg Trials, all of you would be languishing in jail for the crime of apartheid that you committed.'[28] Most DA MPs walked out in protest; it was not the first time in recent years that the ANC had accused the opposition of treason, or worse.

In early 2006, parliament's chief financial officer, Harry Charlton, whom many considered the whistle-blower in the Travelgate affair, was suddenly dismissed in what was widely regarded as an irregular and unfair fashion. The media and opposition felt that Charlton was being targeted, and parliament's stature continued to tumble.

Ironically, while parliament has been growing ever weaker, less independent of the ANC and increasingly tarnished by various scandals, the

ANC and parliament's own officials have grown ever more effusive in their self-congratulatory praise of parliament's role in our society. In one recent, repellent example, Secretary of Parliament Zingile Dingani – the man chiefly responsible for the dismissal of Charlton – issued a 'Special Vision Edition' of parliament's *Around the House* magazine (in late 2005) in which he appeared on the front cover with rays of light emanating from his head.

He identified himself as 'The People's Visionary' and included an interview with himself (conducted by an anonymous author) which yielded such insights as the following: 'The resonance between Mr Dingani's character and orientation and the strategic thrust of parliament is remarkable. He is a people's person in every sense of the word.' Beatification of the ANC continued in 2006, when MPs at the State of the Nation address were given a glossy copy of a praise poem to the president which read, in part:

> Hail Thabo Mbeki our hero
> Roar, Oh lion of South Africa
> You the famous and the revered
> In all the nations of the world
> You who knows the plight of the poor
>
> When you smile even the birds of South Africa
> Sing, rejoicing for the hero
> Your footsteps awaken
> History in the hearts of South Africans ...

Parliament also indulged in several costly junkets whereby the entire NCOP or National Assembly was relocated to a distant province for several days in the name of 'taking parliament to the people'.

A 'bread and circus' atmosphere was accentuated by lavish ministerial parties – including banquets at five-star hotels for MPs and their satraps. Following on budget votes, these became a virtually permanent feature after 2000. In 2006, the DA's research office analysed questions we had asked each department about the costs of the various budget parties. The total came to over two million rands between 26 departments for entirely pointless events. It was as though MPs were reduced to passive onlookers in front of an all-powerful executive that could buy off its members with slap-up dinners, lavish snacks and free drinks.

The more parliament sought to improve its image, the more striking its decay became. That was especially true in the case of the NCOP, theoretically the Upper House with the power to review National Assembly legislation, of which it seldom if ever availed itself. In 2004, following the controversial 'question time' session in the National Assembly in which Mbeki accused his critics of racism, DA whip in the NCOP Juanita Terblanche introduced a motion without notice condemning the president's insensitivity and inaction. To her own great surprise, the motion passed without objection – the assembled majority of ANC MPs being too sleepy or distracted to pay attention!

Only when the critical resolution was reported the next day did the ANC realise what had transpired. The president was reportedly furious, and demanded a retraction; rumour had it that he vowed never to address the NCOP again until the motion was corrected. This was achieved during a special NCOP session on a provincial visit to KZN, wherein the motion was duly overturned and replaced by one praising the president's leadership. The presiding officer invoked a rule that only allowed the heads of each provincial delegation – all nine of whom are ANC MPs – to speak, excluding the DA. The whole episode was ridiculed in the press, and highlighted the ineptitude of parliament.

The decline of South Africa's democratic parliament should have concerned all parliamentarians and voters, especially members and supporters of opposition parties. Tragically, however, many of these parties, at various stages, actually colluded with the ANC in weakening the legislature. Many, for instance, openly aligned themselves with the ANC – not, primarily, because this yielded better results for their voters, but usually because it bought more privileges, power and attention for their own party leaders. The NNP while it existed was the prime example; oftentimes Patricia de Lille's Independent Democrats (ID) followed suit.

The voting behaviour of these 'opposition' parties provided a useful X-ray of their backbone, or lack of it. Only the DA, the African Christian Democratic Party (ACDP) and the Freedom Front Plus (FF+) opposed a significant number of the ANC's budget votes in 2005, to take one recent example. Other opposition parties were either silent, acquiescent or absent. And only the DA was prepared to oppose a majority of the ANC's spending proposals, giving reasons and alternative spending suggestions. Furthermore, many opposition parties positioned themselves as 'friendly' alternatives to the DA, courting the favour of the ANC and contributing to attacks on the Democrats in parliament. Towards the end of my tenure as leader of the opposition, many parties, notably the FF+, involved themselves in the ANC's attempts to downgrade my office.

Although VI Lenin had a violent contempt for such bourgeois accoutrements as parliament, he did once famously ask, 'What is to be done?' In 2004, the DA introduced a discussion document: 'From Lapdog to Watchdog – giving Parliament back its Teeth'.[29] This gave a thorough analysis of parliament's malaise and over a dozen suggested solutions: the introduction of constituencies; changes to 'question time' allowing interpellations and appeals; greater power, resources and training for committees and their MPs; and numerous steps to reduce the power of the executive, including reforms to weaken the ANC's 'deployment' policy and the stranglehold it exerts over MPs.[30]

None of these suggestions has been implemented – and none is likely to be until there is greater political parity in parliament, either through an increase in the size of the DA or through a long-anticipated split in the ANC, or both. Only then will the need for a stronger, fairer legislature become a pressing priority. Too often, it seems, the DA has stood alone as the watchdog defending parliament and its role.

However, by 2006 help, or perhaps self-interest, had arrived in the unusual form of the South African Communist Party and COSATU. By then, emboldened by the succession debate in the ANC and the autocratic style of Mbeki, they joined our hitherto somewhat lonely stance on parliament's role. The SACP issued a discussion document charging Mbeki's 'management style' with 'undermining parliament's role in the country's young democracy'. They also held that 'presidential dominance' had reduced parliament to a 'rubber stamp'.[31]

Andrew Kenny – a friend, and an outspoken critic of the ANC – couldn't help but exclaim: 'All of this [SACP critique] is true, but look who's talking! The Communist Party complaining about centralisation of power! Every time communists have come to power, without exception, all power has been concentrated.'[32]

Despite the awkward embrace our ideas received from such strange quarters, COSATU – an even more traditional foe – was even more vivid in its denunciations of the denigration of parliamentary democracy. Its secretary-general, Zwelinzima Vavi, warned ominously that South Africa was 'drifting towards dictatorship' and cautioned that 'dictatorship never announces his arrival. It won't, like drum majorettes, beat drums and parade down the streets to announce that it has arrived.'[33]

I couldn't help but observe that on the issue of the withering of the institutions of democratic accountability – over Zimbabwe and AIDS – 'the Left was right'. However, their prescribed cure of having 'Dr' Jacob Zuma injecting doses of populist economics into our then healthy economy was perhaps even worse than the ailments they sought to cure.

In an almost mocking gesture, it was decided by the Speaker and ANC whips in 2005 that the constitutional definition and description of parliament's role needed to be buttressed by a new moniker. They embarked on a vastly expensive PR campaign, which saw the porticos of parliament's façade adorned with banners and placards proclaiming 'The People's Parliament'. No doubt the central committee of the South African Communist Party approved, as did all the ghosts of Moscow past. As Geoffrey Wheatcroft observed, in another context: 'It might seem odd that, at the end of the 20th century, anyone could be so tone-deaf to all the overtones of the adjectival "people's": people's courts, people's democracies, people's commissariat of internal affairs (NKVD), people's police …'[34]

If South Africa's economic posture contradicted the Soviet party line, there was much that was still admired by our comrades at home about the commandist politics of control that eastern Europe had today so determinedly shrugged off. Nevertheless, the burden of ensuring that our bold experiment with representative democracy did not wither on the vine was now shared by an eclectic group whose very diversity ensured that if not won, then, at least, the battle would be fought on several fronts – and for some time to come.

After Polokwane, parliament in 2008 showed some signs of revival, as ANC MPs keen to align themselves to the new political order began to press and harry the executive, still under the vanquished Mbeki's control. But only time will tell whether this will prove to be, once again, our home-grown version of the famous 'Prague spring'.

CHAPTER 11

Judging the Judges

Constitutionalism is about moral and political reasoning.
When judges go about the business of constitutional adjudication
they are involved in a form of politics.

JUDGE DENNIS DAVIS

The fact is that when judges are selected on any grounds
other than ability, judicial standards must fall.

SYDNEY KENTRIDGE SC

I

Politics and law have been inextricably conjoined throughout my life. While I studied and practised law more or less by default, from an early age the judiciary inevitably intruded into my childhood. My father's appointment to the Bench in Natal in 1967 brought this closed world into our family universe.

The deference by society, at that time, towards judges was remarkable. For their part, the judges took themselves even more seriously than the forelock-tugging, hat-doffing general public. Although extremely modestly remunerated, judicial office was a great honour; and membership of its small, cosseted, all-white and (with one exception) all-male universe was generally coveted by senior members of the Bar. Judges were exclusively drawn from that source.

I remember quite distinctly, on his appointment, my father acquiring a morning suit – replete with striped trousers, considered *de rigueur* for formal functions such as the opening of parliament. Much to the hilarity of my brother and me, we observed him preening himself around his Musgrave Road flat one Friday evening in a full bib-and-tucker, white-tie ensemble before the annual dinner for the Natal judiciary hosted by the state president at the castle in Morningside called King's House. Such were the formalities, on which little sunlight shone. The habit of deference, and obedience, was profoundly ingrained into white South Africans in the 1960s, especially to the Bench.

There was little direct, or even subtle, criticism of the judiciary. With the singular exception of LC Steyn's appointment as Chief Justice in 1959, there was no overt objection to judicial officers and their judgments.

However, John Dugard used his inaugural lecture as professor of law at Wits in 1971 to make a brave, pioneering call for judges to embrace a substantive vision of law rather than the narrow interpretative function to which the Bench generally reduced adjudication. Of course, the dominance of the apartheid state and large-scale judicial obsequiousness to its might made Dugard and others somewhat isolated, albeit splendid, iconoclasts.[1]

Under apartheid, judges were required – and largely chose – to enforce laws that were in many ways inconsistent with the basic principles of justice. While the judiciary was notionally independent, its humble powers of review were systematically undermined by the ruling National Party, which used its majority in parliament and control of appointments to ensure that no apartheid legislation would be rejected by the courts. While the courts were more effective in advancing principle by striking down subordinate legislation, such as ministerial regulations, even here the record was patchy and inconsistent.

There were certainly some outstanding, brave, independent-minded judges who stood by the fundamental principle that every person is equal before the law – even if every person was not equal before the government of the day. Indeed, from the onset of NP rule in 1948, the Appellate Division, the nation's highest court, was the seat of a quartet of judges of extraordinary character and intellect.

Of Chief Justice Albert van der Sandt Centlivres (and three other Appellate Division members, Justices Greenberg, Van den Heever and Schreiner) Sydney Kentridge SC, one of the greatest advocates produced by our system, observed: 'One would have had to have looked far to find in the English-speaking world a court superior in independence and ability.'[2]

Of Oliver Deneys Schreiner it was said that he was the greatest Chief Justice that South Africa had never had.[3]

The NP employed tactics to weaken the court – especially after it lost its first and second attempts to strike Coloured voters from the roll. It tried to give parliament a veto over any Appellate Division which struck down legislation. Then in a semi-fatal blow to the court's independence, it expanded the number of judges in the Division and appointed government sympathisers to the five new seats on the Bench. It increased the size of the Senate to attain the two-thirds majority necessary to push through constitutional changes and keep the courts at a safe distance.

Finally, in 1956, government secured the passage of the South Africa Act Amendment Act through a two-thirds majority vote in the Senate. This removed the constitutional protection of Coloured voting rights.

At primary school, great store was set on the boys arranging outings to visit the more interesting fathers at work – it was almost unheard of for the mothers of Clifton Preparatory to engage in employment. With a class full of the scions of sugar barons, department store owners, and even the editor of a local daily newspaper, there was no shortage of these coveted excursions. I soon arranged for my standard four class to attend one of the criminal trials my father was presiding over in the Supreme Court in Durban's Masonic Grove, just off the Esplanade.

The proceedings were, in fact, largely boring and to our young, untutored ears incomprehensible – with turgid altercations between the unfortunate (black) accused, and the (white) prosecutor via an interpreter. What struck me forcefully was the presence of a wooden bar in the middle of the witness box. When I asked my father about its purpose, he sadly explained to my shocked racial sensitivities that it was to separate white and non-white witnesses. Kentridge aptly summed up this physical intrusion of apartheid in the courts by noting: 'Historians looking back on this era will think this was a manifestation not merely of prejudice, but of actual insanity.'[4]

The physical segregation of the courts mirrored the relentless trampling of the rule of law and the suppression of civil liberties of the apartheid government. Earlier, more liberal manifestations of the courts gave way as one statute after another reduced the power of the courts and simply reversed, through legislative fiat, some of the more progressive judgments. As one learned observer noted, the Appellate Division 'never quite recovered' from the inflation of its numbers for political reasons. The NP was quite explicit in its desire to appoint 'more Afrikaners to the Bench in accordance with their preponderance in the white population'. Kentridge, for one, described this as the 'first application of affirmative action in [the judicial] field in South Africa long before that expression was coined'.[5] It was not to be the last, or even the most extreme, such application.

While the courts were generally mesmerised in the path of the apartheid juggernaut, they had to an extent recovered some of their spine by the 1980s and 1990s.

However, even by the time of my entry into politics in the mid-1980s, the NP – whose Justice minister Kobie Coetsee was perhaps the most reformist-minded in what, to be fair, was not an overcrowded room – was still playing jiggery-pokery with the judiciary. The most notorious manifestation was the decision of PW Botha's administration, in 1987, to appoint the outgoing Chief Justice (an executive-minded person), Pierre Rabie, to the constitutionally unprecedented position of Acting Chief Justice even though he had reached the compulsory retirement age of 70. The stratagem was designed to block the appointment of the next senior, more liberal possibility. (Five years before, as outlined in Chapter 2, my father was simply overlooked as Judge President of Natal, although he was the most senior judge at the time.)

2

When the old order crumbled, there were great expectations that a democratic state would reverse the erosion of the rule of law, and perfect – or radically improve – the system of judicial appointments. The inheritance was meagre. By April 1994, of the 166 judges in South Africa, 161, or 97%, were white males. Only two were white women, and only three were black men.[6] Both the new government and the appointing authorities had their work cut out. I had played, as I relate in Chapter 5, a large role in the dying hours of the constitutional negotiations in late 1993 in securing the creation of an independent body (the Judicial Service Commission) to appoint new members of the judiciary. Almost immediately after the 1994 election, as the newly appointed leader of a political party in parliament, I found myself observing my theoretical handiwork in action. The results were extremely uneven.

The introduction of a Constitutional Court, on an equal footing with the Appellate Division, was one of the most noteworthy elements of the Constitution. For the first time judges could strike down any parliamentary act or executive action found to be repugnant to the provisions of the new basic law.[7] However, another even more politically loaded and significant power was entrusted to the Constitutional Court: the right to certify whether the final Constitution drawn up by parliament, sitting as the Constitutional Assembly, conformed to the enshrined principles of the interim document.

Who would wield these powers in the Constitutional Court became, then, one of the most crucial tests of the fledgling new order. Under the relevant provisions of the Interim Constitution,[8] which reflected the uneasy compromises and last-minute horse-trading at Kempton Park, the president had to appoint four judges from the existing judiciary and a further six from a list of nine presented to him by the Judicial Service Commission (JSC). Intense lobbying in the run-up to the finalisation of the process was inevitable.

One evening during this period, at a state dinner at Tuynhuys at the invitation of President Mandela, in honour of one of the almost weekly stream of foreign heads of state then pouring into South Africa, I found myself seated next to Albie Sachs. I had frequently clashed with him at the Kempton Park negotiations where he served as an ANC delegate. Sachs had subsequently resigned from the ANC National Executive in order to prepare his 'campaign' for appointment to the Constitutional Court.

I found Albie an amusing, slightly whimsical figure. We had scant common ground on constitutional and legal matters. Some of my friends, in the upper echelons of legal practice and academe, were sceptical about his legal prowess, dismissing him as a romantic poet, not a serious lawyer.

Albie was, of course, perhaps best known as one of the most high-profile victims of the apartheid regime's brutal dirty tricks brigade. He had suffered grievous injuries when he was nearly killed in Maputo by a personalised car bomb despatched in 1988 from the apartheid security agent, Craig Williamson. He lost an arm – and wore his suits, quite unselfconsciously, with an empty sleeve. In fact, he usually quite openly introduced his 'stump' early into the conversation. This he duly did that night, regaling our section of the table with his encounter with Queen Elizabeth, in London, at some or other gathering of the Commonwealth. He told us that his disability somewhat nonplussed the normally imperturbable monarch.

I was determined not to raise the question of his looming candidacy to the court; but much to my surprise he raised it with me, asking in point-blank fashion: 'Why are you and your brother so opposed to my nomination to the court?' I was flummoxed by the question; not so much by my inability to answer it, but by what I thought was its extremely inappropriate nature, directed by an aspiring judge to an opposition political leader. I mumbled something about 'not being my brother's keeper' and indicated I personally had some problems with his previous writings on the 'dangers of Judocracy'. When the ANC was in exile, he warned of the dangers of a Constitutional Court with testing powers able to override the popular will – exactly the basis for the construction of the court on which Sachs now aspired to serve.

Albie then treated me to a lengthy jurisprudential discourse and we left matters at that. Needless to say, he was duly appointed by Mandela along with nine others according to the agreed formula. As Court President, Mandela chose Arthur Chaskalson, undoubtedly one of the most pre-eminent senior counsel then in practice, but also a formidable ANC partisan. Pius Langa, appointed Deputy President of Court, had only recently taken silk, and also had served on the ANC Constitutional Committee. Some of South Africa's finest judges – including John Didcott, Richard Goldstone and Johann Kriegler – were also selected. Analysing the background of the candidates, James Myburgh, in a text based on his Oxford doctoral thesis, concluded: 'While the court enjoyed some credibility in the legal fraternity because of the quality of a number of its judges, there was not a single person on the court who could be described as unsympathetic to the ANC.'[9] I had no idea whether every judge was ANC-inclined or not, but no doubt most were.

However, partisan preferences, of course, are never entirely accurate in assessing future behaviour and judgments. The one-time NP minister of Justice Oswald Pirow once famously observed: 'The problem with political appointees to the Bench, is that six months after their appointment, they assume they were appointed on merit!'

Indeed, during the first selection hearings, UCT academic Kate O'Regan was strenuously grilled on her acknowledged ANC membership. Yet in the course of her subsequent 12-year tenure she has not only, by rare common consent on such matters, come to be regarded as one of the finest jurists there, but has often, in minority dissenting judgments, ruled directly against the core political interests of her party.[10]

While under the 1993 constitution I had no role to play in judicial appointments, I fervently hoped that two former academic colleagues, June Sinclair and John Dugard, would make the cut. Neither was successful – despite outstanding claims based on their massive intellectual contribution to the very order whose judicial apex was the Court on which they were destined never to serve. The exclusion of Dugard was, I thought, shocking and ominous. I wrote him a letter of commiseration, and thought his reply rueful and revealing: 'Obviously I was very disappointed not to be included but I cannot say that I was surprised. I think/fear that it is easier for the proverbial camel to pass through the eye of a needle than it is for a liberal to enter the Kingdom of the New South Africa.'[11] (As I relate in Chapter 6, this was not Dugard's only knock back under the new order.)

I also, for the sake of form and courtesy, penned a congratulatory note to Chaskalson. I was amazed to receive from him a gracious response, over two pages, handwritten in the neatest of scripts, setting out his judicial wares, as it were, to an audience of one. Chaskalson explained his responsibilities, hopes and concerns to me thus:

'I am conscious of the responsibility given to the Court, to defend the Constitution and protect human rights. Time will tell whether the Court is able to live up to the expectations that the public has, and whether it is able to make a material contribution to the process of building a country in which rights are valued, and democracy exists in substance as well as form. I hope that it will be able to achieve its goals and that it will gain the respect of all sections of this community.'

I was impressed by his vision, and touched by his modesty and good manners. However, his tenure as head of both the Constitutional Court and the JSC was not without controversy or criticism, especially as racial transformation came, in my view, to overwhelm Chaskalson's more hopeful initial insights.

The JSC had the invidious task of seeking to rectify inherited imbalances on the overwhelmingly 'pale male' Benches in the various divisions of the Supreme Court. In terms of the compromise we reached at Kempton Park, the Constitution did not prescribe any minimum qualifications for judicial candidates, simply stating that judges had to be 'appropriately qualified'. For the 1994-1996 period the JSC consisted of 19 members with a fairly even balance between politicians and presidential appointees (six and four respectively) and nine members of the judiciary and legal profession, including, to my delight, Etienne Mureinik as the academic representative.

He summed up with his customary insight and clarity the essential change the new order imposed on both government and the judiciary. He termed it a 'culture of justification' requiring that 'every exercise of power is expected to be justified; in which the leadership exercised by government rests on the cogency of the case offered in defence of its decisions, not the fear inspired by the force at its command.'[12]

Initially the JSC struck a sane note on the imperative of transforming the judiciary. It emphasised the need for diversity, rather than blunt racial quotas, as the means towards the end of undoing exclusionary policies: 'Racial and gender representivity could not be understood to be the need to constitute a Court which represents race and gender in proportion to their share of the population … [If] the Constitution-makers had such a need in mind they would have enacted a system of proportional representivity.'[13]

The JSC was mindful of the supply-side issue: by 1999, for example, there were 1 550 white advocates practising at the Bar and only 300

African, Coloured and Indian practitioners.[14] I agreed entirely with the JSC's explicit approach. The old order was clearly unsustainable and needed a makeover. However, racial bean-counting was soon to both characterise and overwhelm the JSC and the judiciary.

Indeed, the sang-froid adhering to the JSC would soon be shattered. The first indication that race politics would trump rational debate occurred in September 1996. The Chief Justice, Mick Corbett, retired. Two candidates, the most senior judge in the Appellate Division (since renamed the Supreme Court of Appeal), Hennie van Heerden, and the deputy president of the Constitutional Court, Ismail Mahomed, squared off against each other. At that stage, the Appellate Division was the highest court in the land for all non-constitutional matters.

The waters were muddied early in the contest. Over a hundred (largely old-order) judges petitioned the JSC on behalf of Van Heerden, while with an almost Pavlovian predictability, black legal lobbies labelled Van Heerden and his backers – without any justification or evidence – as 'conservative elements opposing transformation'.[15]

I was actually extremely impressed with Mahomed: few could not be. We had served together on the Wits Council where his intellectual sharpness and impressive bearing were frequently on display. Although a person of mercurial temperament and personal awkwardness, his entire legal career was emblematic of the triumph of intellect and fortitude over an unjust racial order, which his advocacy did much to challenge.

Kentridge described vividly the personal humiliations heaped on Mahomed when he entered and rose in legal practice: 'When he first came to the Johannesburg Bar the law did not permit him to be a tenant of chambers in the centre of Johannesburg. When he first used to appear in the Appellate Division, it was illegal for him to stay in the Orange Free State without a permit.'[16]

Into this charged atmosphere rode Nelson Mandela, who pre-empted the consultative process he was constitutionally obliged to undertake with the JSC by publicly endorsing Mahomed.[17] Despite personally backing Mahomed, and despite my high personal regard for Mandela, I was strongly critical of the president's presumption. This led to his spokesman's absurd rejoinder that 'the president is just exercising his right, which any other citizen has.' Yet when the citizen happened to have the final say in the appointment, the response was risible. Mahomed was appointed.

Looking back now, it is clear that 1998 saw the commencement of a verbal and political assault on judicial appointments and the judiciary itself. Dressed in the rhetorical cant of redress and the garb of transformation, its purpose was radically to racialise the judiciary, and consolidate and extend the power of the ANC.

Part of the change was systemic. The final 1996 Constitution was far more tilted in the ANC's favour than the Interim Constitution had been. This was a consequence of the change in the balance of forces after the 1994 election. As the Constitutional Assembly, parliament drew up the final document. The final Constitution radically altered the composition of the JSC, notably by its massive inflation of politicians and presidential appointees – membership ballooning to 15 including the minister of Justice. It also did away with the Kempton Park compromise on appointments to the Constitutional Court. Henceforth, under the new regime, the president appointed all new members from a list prepared by the JSC 'with three names more than the number of appointments to be made'.[18]

The only essential restriction here was the requirement that, at all times, at least four members of the Court had to have been serving judges at the time of their appointment. The new Constitution also threw a bone, of sorts, to the opposition: the president was obliged to finalise his appointments only after consultation with 'the leaders of parties represented in the National Assembly'. In law, of course, 'after consultation' is something of a weasel phrase devoid if not of purpose, then of real meaning. It does not require the concurrence of the party consulted, simply consultation.

Under Mandela's presidency the forms and proprieties of the phrase were retained. I was to discover that when Mbeki ascended to the political throne, guided by his powerful legal adviser (whose influence and advice were not, apparently, confined to technical legalities), Ms Mojanku Gumbi, consultation descended into farce.

3

My first experience of things to come occurred after John Didcott's untimely death from cancer in 1997, creating a vacancy. The two most prominent claimants were Edwin Cameron and Zac Yacoob. Both were ANC-aligned, although Yacoob had been far more embedded in the hierarchy of the ANC-affiliated UDF and Natal Indian Congress. He had served as a 'technical adviser' (by ANC nomination) to Codesa, and helped draft the Bill of Rights. I regarded him as a staunch party man who never deviated from the ANC's positions on the Constitution.

Cameron was, legally at least, in a different class. Rex Welsh treated him like a son, and he was one of only perhaps three South Africans (along with Welsh) to be awarded the Vinerian Scholarship at Oxford University. However, he was neither black nor Indian, nor bore the devoted fealty to the ANC Yacoob displayed.[19] Mandela wrote to me advising that he was 'of a mind' to appoint Yacoob. However – and this was to be the distinctive difference between Mandela and Mbeki – he did at least proffer a courteous invitation to confer, stating: 'You may if you so wish advise me in writing whether or not you concur with the appointment, or should you wish to share your views with me in person, make an arrangement through my office to see me.'

I wrote back strongly motivating Cameron's appointment. A proper and respectful reply from the president followed, also expressing the highest admiration for Cameron, but confirming his intention to appoint Yacoob.

This decorous interaction did not permeate downward. In 1998 the JSC had to choose a deputy judge president for the Natal Division of the High Court. This appointment was of great significance since the incumbent judge president was due to retire, and precedent suggested that the deputy would shortly and automatically ascend to the top provincial judicial position.

Myburgh graphically detailed the showdown which split the JSC and whose conclusion indicated the triumph of racial solidarity which was to become the defining feature of most future appointments.[20] In fact, Farouk Chotia, a *Business Day* journalist at the time – broadly sympathetic to the ANC's goals of societal transformation – accurately pinpointed why playing the race card was not simply atavistic reflex. As he put it, the ANC's main priority 'is to see its political allies dominate institutions. In the judiciary it is more difficult to do so overtly. Race, therefore, becomes the main criterion, with the government secure in the knowledge that most blacks aspiring to be judges are party supporters.'[21]

That said, the Natal contest played out at the JSC and in the press pitted two deeply flawed characters against each other. Willem Booysen, a very senior Natal judge, had a massive and publicly known political skeleton in his cupboard. In 1992 he had been unmasked as a Broederbonder, at the time a semi-secret and influential lynchpin of the Afrikaner establishment. He resigned at the time of his exposure; but notwithstanding his politics, 16 of his brother judges endorsed his candidacy since he was regarded as an excellent and experienced judge.

His opponent, strongly backed by the ANC and its legal wing, the National Association of Democratic Lawyers (Nadel), was Vuka Tshabalala – whose judicial experience was scant (three years on the Bench in the Ciskei) and whose work as a Durban advocate did not mark him out as a future judicial leader. My father told me that Tshabalala was referred to as 'the late Mr T' because of his difficulty in arriving in court on time. But his real flaw was personal: he had a self-confessed drinking problem. He advised the JSC that he had sought and received professional help.

During the hearings the Natal judges wrote a further submission to the JSC advising that if Tshabalala was appointed 'he would not command the respect' of his fellows. The JSC resolved to be irresolute when each candidate received an equality of votes, and the two most senior judges on the body, Chaskalson and Mahomed, abstained from voting. This impasse and the judges' letter inflamed public discourse. Mandela's spokesman, Parks Mankahlana, entered the lists by accusing the Natal judges of 'attempting to preserve whatever remains of white domination of the judiciary'; adding for good measure that 'the Bench cannot remain as white as it is.'

This period was also marked by unprecedented ANC criticism of judgments which went against its interests. For example, the decision (by another Natal judge) to acquit a Richmond warlord (and ANC renegade) Sifiso Nkabinde on murder charges drew an extremist response from ANC KwaZulu-Natal cabinet minister (today premier) Sibusiso Ndebele that the presiding judge was 'an accomplished fascist'.[22]

This theme and line of attack was not confined to the provinces; it clearly enjoyed national approval. Justice minister Dullah Omar applied stern heat to the JSC by telling the National Assembly: 'It is imperative that both the JSC and Magistrate's Commission consciously and deliberately embark upon a programme which will transform our courts so as to make them representative in the shortest possible period of time.'

This statement was extraordinary, given Omar's own membership of the JSC which, as reported above, had four years previously rejected demographic bean-counting. But Omar's agenda was plain: he wanted more control over the judiciary, as Chotia had noted. A friend, who also held judicial office and was broadly sympathetic to the ANC, acidly remarked: '[Why] is it assumed that commitment to social justice, or even to the Freedom Charter, is the exclusive preserve of, or can only be carried out by, blacks?'

Omar's attack also created a following wind for his explicit attack later that year when Judge William de Villiers of the Transvaal Provincial Division made adverse findings against both Mandela and Sports minister Steve Tshwete, in the South African Rugby matter. Omar released a statement announcing that 'the apartheid judiciary ... was fortunate not to have been dismissed as the judiciary in the [East] German Democratic Republic had been after unification.'[23]

Omar's assault was not simply actuated by a political agenda; it was also helpful to his associates. Several partners of his one-time legal concern received judicial preferment, even though, in at least two cases, the candidates had no discernible qualities or qualifications which the legal profession could detect as suggesting advancement. By the time the JSC met again, in October, to resolve the stalled appointment of the Natal deputy judge president, it appointed Tshabalala, simultaneously choosing Bernard Ngoepe as judge president of the Transvaal. As Myburgh notes, Chaskalson led the surrender, advising the *Sunday Times*: 'I have wondered whether, when I evaluate people, I place too much weight on technical competence.'[24]

The real wonder was Chaskalson's wonderment.

The newly enthroned Ngoepe bluntly told the *Sowetan* that his prime objective in office would be to ensure 'that the judiciary reaches the stage when it is able to reflect the demographics of South Africa.'[25] He would soon be able to implement his vision, when subsequently appointed to full membership of the JSC.

My brother Peter was acutely aware – through his legal and political offices – of the machinations and governing motives of the JSC. He wrote to *Business Day* to signal in public what had largely been discussed less openly – namely 'that the ANC had a caucus in the JSC and an in-built majority there.'[26] This was buttressed by two legal scholars, Marius Olivier and John Bolard, who viewed the high number of politicians on the JSC with alarm: '[They] not only jeopardise the independence of the Commission, but also the perception of independence.'[27]

Peter had proclaimed this viewpoint – widely shared by many – in 1998. It was therefore with some sense of disbelief that in 2006 an extraordinarily disingenuous claim was made of the JSC and its workings. It was written by ANC apologist extraordinaire, Richard Calland, an arriviste member of our 'lumpen intelligentsia'. The occasion was the publication of a gossipy, faux-insider's account of the locus of power in South Africa, entitled *Anatomy of South Africa*. He 'made bold to say' that 'despite, and perhaps because of, the large number of politicians that now sit on the JSC, it is a body that is never criticised by either government or opposition parties; it enjoys a legitimately high position in the new institutional hierarchy.'[28]

I was deeply troubled: transformation had been reduced to a narrow racial zero-sum game. But as the Marxists would say, everything has to be seen in its historical context; and the 'motive force of history' at this point was the ANC's determination to impose its power throughout society, including the notionally (and constitutionally ordained) independent judiciary.

At the seminal 1997 Mafikeng conference, ANC spokesman Thabo Masebe stated that 'the time for self-deployment is over.'[29] He explicitly and ominously included the 'transformation of the judiciary' in the remit of the deployment grand design.

I experienced at first hand deployment under Mbeki. The ritual of consulting the opposition leadership on judicial appointments was much reduced. Yet even my diminished expectation was unsettled when Mojanku Gumbi despatched a peremptory letter to me in October 2002 advising that the president intended to appoint Judge Dikgang Moseneke to a vacant position in the Constitutional Court. She attached neither a motivation nor a suggested route for discussion, nor even bothered to inform me of the names of the other three candidates.

I called a very senior member of the Cape Bar and read him Gumbi's letter. He was appalled, and indicated that her approach was a total violation not simply of the Constitution, but of the settled meaning of the word 'consultation' under our common law. He suggested a suitable response; but while I was determined to draw some sort of line, I was equally keen not to personalise my response around the candidate.

I first met Moseneke (who then traded under his first name 'Ernest') at a World Council of Churches seminar on South Africa held in the splendid UN Palais de Nations in Geneva in early 1991. Although in a very different ideological zone from my own (the PAC), he struck me as an open-minded moderate. He was even game enough, on our return to South Africa, to address a meeting of party activists and donors in my constituency in Houghton. After his withdrawal from the chaotic world of PAC politics, he established an impressive practice at the Pretoria Bar, and later made a highly lucrative foray into business. At the time of his proposed appointment he was serving as a judge on the Supreme Court of Appeal, where the consensus appeared to be that he was a forthright and first-rate jurist. He was in my and my party's view a worthy candidate.

But the issue was what truly was meant by 'consultation'.

After a lengthy struggle to prise information from Gumbi, I said that 'with respect, from the beginning you have misconstrued the constitutional obligations and powers conferred on the president and you have dealt with me in a basically contemptuous manner ...' While I was certain Moseneke was 'an extremely meritorious choice' the so-called 'consultation' was 'basically a charade', undermining both the letter and the spirit of the Constitution.

Finally, like a stone disgorging water, she did provide a motivation and semi-plea: 'The president advises me that his choice of Mr Justice Moseneke is based on his outstanding legal, community-building and commercial credentials as set out in his curriculum vitae ... I am not aware of the length of time you need to consider such a matter. We will be guided by your good-self in this regard.'

The partial climb-down was in my view achieved because of the dangers faced by the Presidency, should any future litigant point to the flaws in the appointment process. In late November I received a rather plaintive letter from a decidedly less haughty Gumbi: 'Might we conclude that you are not opposed to Mr Justice Dikgang Moseneke assuming a seat on the Constitutional Court, but are unhappy with the consultation process?'[30]

I answered in the affirmative and the matter was settled. My dispute with Gumbi ensured that the quality of future 'consultations' would improve.

Whatever qualities may have been evinced by Moseneke could not necessarily be said, with candour, to apply to the next appointees to the nation's highest Court.

When Johann Kriegler and Richard Goldstone retired from the Constitutional Court, nine candidates were interviewed for the vacancies in November 2003. One, Jeremy Gauntlett SC, was one of the busiest and brightest advocates in South Africa; he had served as head of the General Council of the Bar; and was a member of the Appeal Court in Lesotho. He would, by common consent in legal circles, have made a significant contribution to the Court. But he was not one of the names forwarded by the JSC to Mbeki for consideration.

Of the four Mbeki did receive – judges Christopher Jafta, Barend 'Ben' du Plessis, TL Skweyiya, and JV van der Westhuizen – Gumbi advised that the president was 'considering appointing' Skweyiya and Van der Westhuizen. It was clear that the choices were flavoured by the nominees' close connection to the ANC. Senior members of the Bar and judiciary were dismayed at the exclusion of Du Plessis, who had already acted in the Constitutional Court, and was generally regarded as the top jurist in contention.

In response to Gumbi and Mbeki I decided to highlight what I perceived to be the real reason for Van der Westhuizen's preferment: 'It is ... inexplicable barring some other act which is not evident from the papers [you submitted to me] as to why Du Plessis has not been preferred, whereas, for example, Van der Westhuizen had no court experience preappointment [he had been an academic] and has not written any judgments of significance.'[31]

My coded letter was, by my standards, fairly diplomatic. I was close to a family in Johannesburg who were still waiting, at the time of my letter, for Van der Westhuizen to deliver a judgment on a relatively simple matter – a ruling on an exception two years after the argument in the case had been concluded!

Gumbi's response was instructive, because of what followed in respect of the next appointment to fill another vacancy. She stated:[32] 'The president has instructed me to inform you that he agrees that Judge du Plessis is a worthy candidate to be considered to appointment to the Constitutional Court. However, Judge van der Westhuizen has had much broader exposure to the constitution-making process in our country.'

When the next opening was occasioned by the retirement of Arthur Chaskalson, the Presidency overlooked a candidate with precisely the expertise which they had previously favoured. The choice was essentially between Professor Cora Hoexter and Ms Justice Bess Nkabinde. Sheila Camerer advised that Hoexter 'did an excellent interview and stood out as the obvious candidate.' Nkabinde was a relatively obscure judge from the remote reaches of North-West Province. Her record suggested no significant background in constitutional law. But Nkabinde was given the nod.

4

While race became the predominant issue in appointments, closeness or sympathy to the ruling party did not always trump the ethnic factor. Perhaps the most spectacular proof was the non-appointment – after three consecutive attempts at nomination – of Geoff Budlender SC to the Cape Provincial Division. Budlender was hardly sympathetic to the DA. On the contrary, he specifically endorsed the government's programme of 'transformation' and the ideology underpinning it. This was not merely lip-service. For the first period of democracy, under Mandela, he served as director-general of Land Affairs. His legal distinction and activities were even more impressive.

He was a co-founder of the Legal Resources Centre, which fought many of the most important court battles against apartheid. Furthermore, Budlender had also been involved in some of the most important hearings before the Constitutional Court, including the Grootboom case (2000) on housing rights;[33] the Treatment Action Campaign case (2002)[34] on the right to health care and antiretroviral medicines; and the landmark 1995 decision in which the Constitutional Court declared the death penalty unconstitutional.[35] Yet three times in a row, the JSC turned Budlender down; on the final occasion, he was passed over in favour of a black candidate regarded as competent but whose record was far less impressive than Budlender's.

Carmel Rickard, perhaps South Africa's most distinguished legal journalist, called on the JSC to 'be frank with the legal profession and say that white male lawyers should no longer apply for positions on the Bench.'[36] When I delivered a paper at the New York Law School in November 2004 I made the point after Budlender's exclusion that 'no white judge can possibly be good enough for appointment, no matter how sterling his legal career and political credentials.'[37]

It was no surprise then when Mbeki indicated to me that he wished to appoint Advocate Seth Nthai to fill a vacancy on the now highly controversial JSC.[38] A lawyer, Nthai was better known as an ANC politician, having served until 1999 as the MEC for Safety in the Northern (renamed Limpopo) Province. Even more alarming was that he had penned an article in a legal periodical applauding the fact that judges were coming under greater pressure from groups such as COSATU.[39] He was also in favour of JSC meetings taking place behind closed doors.

I advised Mbeki that the proposed appointment of Nthai would 'simply reinforce what appears to me to be the decline of the JSC from an independent and transparent institution to a partisan and closed body that functions as an arm of the ruling party.' While, as usual, Mbeki paid no heed to my warning, I was subsequently advised that Nthai, once on the JSC, appointed himself as the informal ANC ringleader and was vociferous on the body in advancing party choices for judicial preferment.

In the period following the Budlender exclusion and the Nthai appointment, it emerged that the minister of Justice and Constitutional Development, Brigitte Mabandla, had appointed a radical Africanist, Shadrack Gutto (my old adversary from Wits), as her special adviser on transformation. In 2006, despite being a foreigner, Gutto chaired the government panel recommending a ban on foreign land ownership. In early 2005 he told the *Mail&Guardian*:

'We still have a very archaic structure, an apartheid and colonial arrangement where you have judge presidents in charge of high courts, and the Supreme Court of Appeal, alongside the JSC. Judges and the legal profession currently regulate themselves, and these structures should be reviewed urgently so that we have a modernised system of justice where the judiciary is subject to review like any other branch of the state.'[40]

No less a personage than outgoing Chief Justice Chaskalson described

Gutto's recommendations as 'inconsistent with the principle of separation of powers and the independence of the judiciary'.[41] Gutto's criticisms were 'not warranted'.[42]

This presaged a form of 'fightback' from the judiciary. In October 2006, a high court judge with impeccable 'struggle' credentials, Azhar Cachalia, reportedly told the JSC that it would have to shift its priorities from transformation to experience. White lawyers, he asserted, believed there was a racial glass ceiling that blocked their attainment of judicial seniority. At the same time, inexperienced black judges were giving down judgments – especially in complex commercial cases – which were 'surprisingly shocking' and contain 'the kind of mistakes that should not be tolerated.' He added of the JSC's 'mistakes' in appointments over the last few years, '[Those] chickens are now coming home to roost.'[43]

The Supreme Court of Appeal heard a number of cases which showed that several of the new-order provincial judges were batting on wickets way out of their league of fitness or experience, or both. Decisions were reversed where judges could not grasp legal propositions which the Appeal Court held to be either 'trite' or 'so self-evident that nothing further needs to be said in this regard.'[44]

But whatever the qualitative problems occasioned by the transformation of the Bench, it had been quantitatively very effective. Within ten years, according to minister of Justice and Constitutional Development Mabandla, there were 214 judges in the superior courts, of whom only 128 were white males, representing 60% of the total. Sixty-one were black males, and 12 black females, 34% of the total. Thirteen, or 6%, were white females.

Fully 89% of the judges appointed since 1994 have been black ('black' in this context also refers to judges of Indian or Coloured origin). The change is even more far-reaching when one considers the magistrates of the lower courts, where black and female magistrates are being appointed quite rapidly. The magistracy is now 50% black and 30% female, according to the minister of Justice. Among the combined ranks of judges and magistrates, white males have ceased to be the majority.

The old legal saw 'hard cases make bad law' applied with a vengeance to a highly contested ruling of the Cape High Court in a pharmaceutical pricing case, which threw sharp relief on government's attempts at social engineering. It also opened a veritable Pandora's box on the inner turmoil of the Cape High Court and its controversial judge president, John Hlophe.[45]

The case threw a crisp issue into contention – the legal weighing of the right of access to health care against freedom of commerce. In terms of her powers, the minister of Health had created a system of pricing for retail pharmaceuticals. Dr Manto Tshabalala-Msimang had decreed – after a severely flawed and incomplete process of negotiation – that the maximum mark-up on any drug would be 26%, provided this could not exceed a maximum of R26 on items costing over one hundred rands.

When the case first came before the Cape High Court, it was heard by a full Bench of three judges, including Hlophe, Deputy Judge President Jeanette Traverso, and Judge James Yekiso. Yekiso and Hlophe found against the pharmacists and in favour of the government, with Yekiso writing the majority opinion; Traverso wrote a comprehensive dissent. Rumours then began to circulate that Hlophe, and not Yekiso himself, had actually been the author of the decision.

Hlophe accused white advocates of spreading the rumours, but an investigation by the General Council of the Bar suggested there was no evidence to support his accusation. The chairperson of the General Council, Norman Arendse, suggested that the rumours had not started among advocates, but among judges themselves. 'That one or two white judges are spreading the rumours is a cause for concern for all of us,' he said.[46] In response, Hlophe stated that racism against black judges and lawyers was widespread among members of the South African legal profession, and there was 'a calculated attempt to undermine the intellect and talent of African judges.'[47]

When the plaintiffs applied to the Cape High Court for leave to appeal, Hlophe refused. His ruling was described by legal experts as 'extraordinary'. To begin with, it was unusual – perhaps unprecedented – that leave to appeal was refused. It is almost always granted in cases when the Bench is divided. A split decision would suggest the possibility that the Supreme Court of Appeal (SCA) could arrive at a different ruling. Another strange feature was that Judge Hlophe took ten weeks to hand it down. Normally, leave to appeal is granted or refused almost immediately. As a result of the delay, the litigants, represented by Jeremy Gauntlett SC, made the unprecedented, but in legal circles understandable, decision to petition the SCA directly, before the Cape High Court had decided whether to grant leave to appeal.

After a tortuous process, the SCA – in a stern rebuke to Hlophe and the minister, who had intervened although deeply implicated in the case – ruled unanimously that it had jurisdiction to hear the case; that leave to appeal had to be granted; and that the ministerial regulations were invalid. The minister tried to stop the SCA's order from taking effect, but failed.

Before the matter reached the Constitutional Court, the ANC sprang into action. At its 93rd anniversary celebrations in Mthatha on 8 January 2005 it released a statement of enormous import: 'We are also confronted by the similarly important challenge to transform the collective mindset of the judiciary to bring it into consonance with the vision and aspiration of the millions who engaged in struggle to liberate our country from white minority domination.

'The reality can no longer be avoided that many within our judiciary do not see themselves as being part of these masses, accountable to them, and inspired by their hopes, dreams and value systems. If this persists for too long, it will inevitably result in popular antagonism towards the judiciary and our courts, with serious and negative consequences for our democratic system as a whole.'[48]

The timing of the ANC's attack was seen by many as a political attempt to soften up the Constitutional Court judges ahead of the pharmaceutical appeal. The inevitable furore generated caused a rapid backtrack on the part of the ruling party which insisted that the statement was 'an honest assessment of the state of transformation within the judiciary' and that it merely emphasised the need to reflect broadly the racial and gender composition of South Africa.

Hlophe came increasingly into prominence. In early 2005, he took the deeply uncollegial step of publishing a dossier on 'racism' in the Western Cape legal fraternity. Since he was the judicial leader of the Cape, his report (which he apparently leaked personally to a Sunday newspaper) was shocking. Cape advocates apparently 'despised' black judges. Yet if indeed racism was rampant in the Bar and the Bench, was this not a reflection of his leadership? I felt an anonymous, but on-the-record, comment by one of his judicial colleagues on Hlophe's motives to be close to the mark: 'It is clear to everyone in the legal profession that Hlophe acted out of spite because of the medicine price litigation and is now using racism as a smokescreen. The whole thing could explode in his face and could mean the end of his career.'[49]

The JSC took possession of the Hlophe report. They effectively buried it: but the damage done to the standing of the judiciary and public confidence in its workings and probity had been immense. Under Hlophe's benighted leadership the Cape Bench had been reduced to a sort of war zone.

A more ominous threat from a more significant quarter arose as 2005 drew to its close.

5

A British minister's spin-doctor once infamously suggested to her boss that the traumatic days following 9/11 were a good period 'to bury bad news'. The Department of Justice adopted a similar approach when it published for judicial comment, during the height of the 2005 Christmas holiday season, a proposed amendment to South Africa's Constitution.

The Fourteenth Constitution Amendment Bill proposed to vest 'the authority over the administration and budget of all courts' in the hands of the minister of Justice. Another bill released at the same time gave the government, not the judiciary, responsibility for the training of judges. A further amending bill proposed to give the president greater powers to appoint judge presidents, effectively cutting out the JSC. There was clearly some merit in certain of the proposals, but the bills rang the alarm bells for an array of jurists.

The legislation was condemned by senior jurists, black and white. Human rights lawyer George Bizos, who had defended Nelson Mandela during the Treason Trial, spoke out – warning that the bill could be 'the first step down that path' taken by the post-apartheid regime to subjugate the judiciary.[50] A senior judge of the Supreme Court of Appeal, my old colleague from the Wits Law School, Justice Carole Lewis, said at the time: 'The proposed bills ... undermine the independence of the judiciary in a way in which everyone in South Africa should be concerned ... The proposal of such radical change without a proper process of consultation is contrary to [our] democratic principles. The Justice Department's claim that there has been discussion of all the proposed changes is untrue.'[51]

Even former chief justice Corbett, whose own tenure had been remarkable for its lack of public (or even, apparently, private) contestation with government at certain crucial times, was moved to express his criticism in public: 'The world respects South Africa for what it has achieved ... [Its] continuance without attenuation is vital to our social order. I believe that the proposed amendments to the Constitution stand to do significant harm.'[52]

Stung by such widespread and vociferous criticism, from sources not usually given to publicly rebuking the state, Mbeki reiterated the government's commitment to the independence of the judiciary. Though he did not withdraw the bill, he promised to slow down its passage. Later in the year he was reported to have suspended the bills altogether until a 'buy-in' by the judiciary – which appeared unlikely.

The president knew the effect that the controversy over the bills was having on perceptions of his government. But he had also found that an independent judiciary could serve a useful purpose. For the courts played a major role in the unfolding legal battles around former deputy president Jacob Zuma, and succession battles within the ANC.

Zuma had been investigated for arms deal-related corruption by the national director of Public Prosecutions, Bulelani Ngcuka; but Ngcuka said publicly that the case was 'unwinnable' against the deputy president. Zuma and his allies retaliated by accusing Ngcuka of being an apartheid spy, and the president intervened. A commission of inquiry under retired Appeal Court judge Joos Hefer was appointed to test the allegations, and in late 2004 Hefer declared he had found nothing to substantiate them.

Then, as I record elsewhere, in June 2005 Zuma's financial adviser Schabir Shaik was convicted of fraud and corruption by Judge Hilary Squires in the Durban High Court, paving the way for Zuma himself to be charged with corruption. And in November, Zuma was charged with rape in the Johannesburg High Court, where he was acquitted by Judge Willem van der Merwe in May 2006. In October, the corruption case against Zuma was struck off the roll by Judge Herbert Msimang because of the state's exceptional dilatoriness in preparing its case. Zuma and his allies on the Left hailed this technical victory for the former deputy president as a vindication; but it was temporary. He was charged afresh in late December 2007, and is scheduled to appear in the criminal dock in August 2008. This potentially scuppers his ambition to succeed Mbeki as president.

Throughout this period, Mbeki said little about the judiciary as the courts held his main political rival up to scrutiny. Indeed, though the judges (and many of the lawyers) in these cases were white, there was scant comment from the public. In the eyes of South Africans, the Bench was already 'transformed' – and a 'white' judiciary was perhaps more useful to the president in the selective prosecution of opponents. Three black judges, after all, had recused themselves from the Zuma trials.

In this simmering atmosphere of conspiracy and tension, the unfortunate Hlophe lumbered into the frame again towards the end of 2005.

It was alleged that he had received a monthly retainer from the Oasis Management Group, a prominent investment consortium in Cape Town. He took leave from the Bench and was asked by the JSC to answer questions about the allegations. Hlophe claimed that he had received permission from the late minister of Justice, Dullah Omar, to receive expense payments from Oasis. The present minister, Bridget Mabandla, responded that she could find no record of this. However, the JSC, headed by Chief Justice Pius Langa, announced in December that 'there was no evidence to contradict Judge President Hlophe's assertion'; and that 'no useful purpose would be served in pursuing the matter any further at this stage.'[53] However, Langa's statement hid the fact that the JSC was, in fact, divided on the issue of Hlophe's credibility.

A year later, when further evidence emerged on the relationship with Oasis, the JSC split again, this time on the far more serious issue of whether impeachment proceedings against the judge should be considered. This time the split was explicit, and apparently racial, with the majority finding his conduct 'inappropriate', rather than career-ending.[54] I was amused to note that one of the 'victims' which this saga highlighted was my old nemesis, Judge Siraj Desai (whom readers will encounter in Chapter 17). Hlophe had given his beneficiary, Oasis, permission to sue his colleague Desai without initially disclosing his interest.

Like a bull who had run out of judicial china shops to smash, Hlophe again came into the sights of the Judicial Services Commission in late May 2008. This time the charge was even more serious: 'attempting to influence improperly' justices of the Constitutional Court. The fact, unprecedented in the annals of South African judicial history, that his accusers were the jurists from the country's highest court, suggested that early concerns about the judge president's inappropriate temperament for judicial office were well founded.

Hlophe's disgrace was matched, even exceeded, by another race warrior: Pretoria High Court judge Nkola Motata who, allegedly drunk at the time, gave new meaning to the maxim 'sober as a judge' when he crashed his car in early January 2007 into the wall of a private home in Johannesburg. Motata was also one of the key proponents – and beneficiaries – of judicial transformation. While his behaviour sullied his office, it was actually his sober remarks in a defamation case some years before which rang many alarm bells. The best traditions of our Roman Dutch law were simply not worth preserving, he said: it was time to scrap our 350-year-old heritage on the grounds that 'it had been thrown down our throats by the whites.'[55]

It is clear that the Constitution itself provides no fixed, permanent, self-evident set of meanings to those who read it; and even less so, perhaps, to those given the task of interpreting it. In the words of legal academic Pierre de Vos, 'the text of the 1996 Constitution is often vague, ambiguous and seemingly contradictory.'[56]

Under Chaskalson's leadership, the courts began to chart an independent course from the government for the first time in four decades. They also began to exercise their powers of review in striking down unconstitutional legislation. Early in its tenure, the Constitutional Court served notice that it was not to be found in favour of merely conceding to majority opinion when it came to controversial issues. The constitutional negotiators, for example, had ducked out of proscribing the death penalty in the Interim (and, indeed, the final) constitution. Its indecision was thrown to the Court, which duly outlawed the imposition of capital punishment in 1995. Ruling on behalf of a unanimous Court, Chaskalson held that 'if public opinion were to be decisive, there would be no need for constitutional adjudication. The protection of rights could then be left to parliament, which has a mandate from the public, and is answerable to the public for the way its mandate is exercised, but this would be a return to parliamentary sovereignty, and a retreat from the new legal order established by the 1993 constitution ...'[57]

A fine sentiment – though it struck me as odd that not a single other justice demurred – especially in the light of an opinion poll suggesting that 75% of South Africans wanted the death penalty reintroduced for serious violent crimes. Indeed, several legal academics were dismayed. One referred to it as 'a display of judicial amnesia in the face of a [crime] crisis';[58] while another suggested it 'compromised the credibility of the Court.'[59] However, I and South Africa were to discover that the Court's protection of and boundary-setting for minority rights and interests was to be a variable, if not fungible, barrier in future cases against a rampant, majoritarian government. The court had, at all times, to be sensitive to lingering anxieties about the 'counter-majoritarian' problem, the power of unelected judges to review laws passed by elected representatives on behalf of the majority of voters.

But the Court made several landmark findings against the state, often for its failure to protect or provide for citizens' rights. It found that the state had a duty to provide emergency housing to the homeless, even if the right to housing had to be 'progressively realised'. Perhaps even more important was the Treatment Action Campaign case of 2002, in which the Court found against the government and its refusal to provide antiretroviral drugs to pregnant women with HIV. The Court ordered the state to begin providing the medicines since the state had to uphold the constitutional right to health.

Government's setbacks in these cases incensed the ANC. Johnny de Lange, by now the literally pugilistic (he had once punched an NP adversary out cold on the floor of parliament) deputy minister of Justice, told the House that the judiciary 'must successfully prosecute the unfolding socio-economic and ideological transformation of our country.' Judges must not be found to be 'going out of their way to frustrate or undermine the legitimate and genuine choices and aspirations of the majority of South Africans.'[60]

I had my own concerns with how the courts treated the executive (or 'the majority' whom, on De Lange's interpretation, the former at all times represented). In three key cases involving the political interests of the majority party – versus my own – I found the court's approach both deferential to government's political interests and even contradictory.

In 1999 the DP took the minister of Home Affairs to court to secure a ruling that would declare sections of the Electoral Act unconstitutional. The New National Party, in a separate application, took the government to court on similar grounds.[61]

The Electoral Act included provisions requiring voters to present a bar-coded identity document to register and vote. These provisions effectively disenfranchised hundreds of thousands of voters who were still using old identity documents. The National Executive Committee of the ANC, openly eager to secure a two-thirds majority for the ruling party in the 1999 general election, overrode the views of some of its representatives on parliament's Portfolio Committee on Home Affairs, and made bar-coded IDs a requirement. The decision was taken on the same day that an independent study was released which showed that minority voters and opposition parties would tend to suffer most from such a requirement, while the ANC would suffer least.

It was estimated that roughly half-a-million voters could be disenfranchised in this way in the forthcoming elections – only the second such in South Africa's history.

The Constitutional Court was expected to rule against the government; only two weeks before it had ruled that prisoners could not be prevented from voting, and that voting laws had to be interpreted in favour of enfranchisement. However, in the bar-coded ID case, the Court backed the government. The majority ruled that parliament had acted 'rationally', concurring with Justice Zac Yacoob who argued that while 'the importance of the right to vote is self-evident', there was 'no point in belabouring its importance'.[62]

In a dissenting opinion, Justice Kate O'Regan ruled 'any alleged infringement of the right of citizens to vote had to be carefully and meticulously scrutinised.' She observed that a large number of voters stood to be disenfranchised and that there was no compelling reason to require bar-coded IDs for registration for the forthcoming election.[63] Yet her view did not prevail. The ANC was elated, declaring that 'the message of the ANC permeated through the Constitutional Court.'[64] A more sceptical observer wrote: 'The Court failed to stand up to the executive and the ANC on this key occasion – and its willingness to do so in the future is inevitably now more questionable than it was before.'[65]

I began to wonder whether the Court was prepared to be brave when it came to intense political (as opposed to socio-economic) questions of power. While hardly suggesting that the Court is a sort of glove puppet of the ANC, my unease was strengthened when my party received another knock-back shortly after the 2000 municipal elections. In the metropole of Johannesburg we obtained 59 seats, in contrast to the ANC's winning total of 131. The mayor then appointed ten ANC members (to the exclusion of all other parties) to his executive mayoral committee. Our lawyers insisted that the DA be allocated its proportionate share of the all-important committee. The Court, however, interpreted the section very narrowly and found against us. Again it was Justice O'Regan who dissented. She concluded that our contention was, indeed, correct.[66]

Far more controversial, and far-reaching, was the Court's finding on floor-crossing, brought before it by the UDM leader, Bantu Holomisa.[67] This completely flat-footed the DA, since we had argued in favour of floor-crossing before the Court when it certified the Constitution in 1996. On that occasion the ANC opposed our contention, and the Court found in its favour – upholding the anti-defection clause in the document. It pointed out that politicians 'would betray their voters' expectations' if the Court green-lighted floor-crossing. Then, owing to the tumult in the DA in 2001-2002, the ANC reversed its position in order to grab control of the city of Cape Town and the provincial government of the Western Cape.

Hoist by our own petard of principle, the DA went along with the ANC majority to allow floor-crossing, although I soon realised how much this decision would cost us. Holomisa, however, realising the avaricious ANC was eyeing some of his members as future recruits, rushed to court to stop it. He succeeded with an interdict in the Cape High Court and the matter was referred to the Constitutional Court for adjudication. Despite having voted for the legislation I privately hoped that the Court would uphold its previous position on the matter to save our position in the province and the city. But the Court essentially reversed itself and found that the government could legislate for in-term floor-crossing under the current system and that this was not a constitutional matter.

Van Zyl Slabbert's judgment was harsh but, I thought, essentially accurate. He accused the court of 'a disgraceful judicial flip-flop'.[68] Rob Amato, who before his death published a weekly column on constitutional matters, strongly inferred that the judgment was compensation by the Court to the governing ANC for its slap-down in the TAC case. He said if the Court was not exactly kowtowing to the ruling party, in those judgments 'on political structural issues the court has been against the opposition of the day.'[69]

As Judge Dennis Davis observed, in a general context, constitutionalism involves moral and political reasoning, and when the justices go about the business of constitutional adjudication 'they are involved in a form of politics.'[70] But whatever misgiving I felt about the court's approach on cases which went against my party's political interests, I was far more concerned at attempts to reduce the court's influence or weaken its independence. That was, at all times, the most important principle I tried to champion.

Voices of criticism from the opposition have lately been joined by increasing criticism from within the judiciary itself. Even Chaskalson remarked at a judicial colloquium: 'It's the early incursions into checks and balances which historically have been shown to open the way for later incursions to be made ... Once the erosion of fundamental principles of the Constitution is accepted, somebody else at some time can take it further. So any attempt to do so, no matter how small, is open to objection.'[71]

On balance, it appears that the judiciary remains well aware of its powers – and of the dangers of executive overreach. But there is hardly room for complacency. A skilled, robustly independent judiciary is a challenge to – and an uneasy fit for – a majority party whose 'national democratic revolution' wishes to control all levers of power. The winds which blew out of the ANC's Polokwane conference could signal even stormier weather ahead. Maintaining a court which owes its allegiance to the Constitution, not to the government, and to which every citizen can turn with assurance that his or her rights will be enforced competently and impartially, remains our great challenge.

CHAPTER 12

Trawling the Media

*It is a malaise born of a cynical political culture in which political leaders
brook no dissent, feed on public resources, and then tell the sick and
the poor to eat cake. Such political cultures never change until and
unless there is a political revolution that ushers in
a new leadership cadre.*

XOLELA MANGCU

I

On a visit to London in May 2000, I scheduled a meeting with the
Rt Hon. William Hague MP, then leader of the Conservative Party, and
thus leader of Her Majesty's Opposition in Westminster. Hague was remarkably young and very bright, and enjoyed, rather like me, a bad press
(with the exception of the *Daily Telegraph* and associated titles).

One of the great joys of visiting London is the daily luxury of reading a
range of quality broadsheets – and even the occasional tabloid. The London
papers are a feast, especially after the spare diet back home. On the morning of our meeting – shortly after Hague had made a controversial speech
– I glanced at that standard-bearer of liberal-Left *bien pensant* opinion, the
Guardian. It carried a full report of Hague's remarks – while on the op-ed
page there appeared a slashing editorial replete with a cruel caricature –
admittedly, Hague's bald head and baby face were easy pickings.

I was ushered into Hague's office on the first floor of the rather grand
Edwardian pile in Smith Square, down the road from the House of
Commons, which served as the Conservative headquarters. Hague was
genial and relaxed, and enquired in his Yorkshire accent: 'Well, Tony, what's
it like to be leader of the opposition in South Africa?'

'William,' I answered, 'one of the differences between your job and
mine is that with the newspapers in South Africa, after making a contentious speech, I can only be guaranteed an angry editorial or a vicious cartoon. It's entirely possible the actual speech will not be covered at all.' As if

to prove my point, on the day of the meeting SABC-TV outdid itself even by its own extreme standards of partisan bias. We had spoken of the crisis in Zimbabwe. However, while the South African television correspondent in London filmed the interview and transmitted it back to Auckland Park, I was axed from the evening news and replaced with an interview with the NP leader, Marthinus van Schalkwyk – who had followed me to London for the same purpose.

My remark to Hague was correct in its essence, certainly as far as the uneven, even hostile coverage and personal obloquy which the opposition and I received in much of the South African print and electronic media at the time. The standard response which I and the party received – in endless meetings and almost countless letters exchanged between us and local editors and proprietors – was that 'the ANC is equally unhappy' with its treatment. That didn't even address the point.

There would be a seismic shift on the print media's part when the excesses of Thabo Mbeki's administration were revealed (often, to their credit, by the newspapers themselves) and his authoritarian and remote leadership style began to be probed and criticised. His successor as party leader, Jacob Zuma, has had an even worse time of it, being held out in the media as a figure of loose morals, poor judgment and low intellect. But for the 13-year period of my political leadership, which of course coincided with the birth and after-birth pangs of the new order, I held a critical view of elements of the media, which they reciprocated with some enthusiasm, as I elaborate.

What I really objected to was the sort of *engagé* journalism which many in the English-speaking press used as forward cover to attack us, often on the slightest provocation and the slenderest of facts. To the best of my knowledge, I never launched public broadsides against the print media. I saw two fundamentals:

- As Enoch Powell had put it: 'For a politician to complain about the press is rather like a sailor complaining about the sea.' The media was part of your chosen environment, and helped to shape and form it in public consciousness.
- By the time I attained the party leadership in 1994, I had a conscious awareness of just how fragile – and hard-fought – free speech actually was. Our history was a constant companion as one faced the shock of the new. But freedom of the press was hardly a sturdy plant in our very stony soil.

One of the distinguishing features of apartheid was pervasive official censorship. Although we had preserved some of the external forms of democracy, a key missing element was media freedom. Pretences at membership of the 'free world' were mocked by the government's desperation to hide the truth and control its citizens' ideas.

Television only arrived in South Africa in 1976 – a full generation after it had been introduced in the rest of the world. Government had a profound fear that foreign programming would swamp local culture. Films, books and radio programmes were scrutinised for evidence of offensive or potentially subversive content. Journalists were subject to harassment, censorship and even imprisonment. Many whose ideas were deemed dangerous were subjected to banning orders.

The public broadcaster, the South African Broadcasting Corporation (SABC), endorsed the policies and worldview of the National Party government; it could not be trusted as a source of information. I remember as a child a particularly noxious five-minute slot served up nightly on SABC radio called 'Current Affairs'. It was delivered in rasping tones by one Alexander Steward, and its purpose was to force down our throats the essential justness of 'separate development' and denounce enemies of the state – internal and external – as godless communists or worse. (Alexander's son, Dave, now directs the FW de Klerk Foundation.) The Information scandal illustrated the regime's desperate attempts to dominate the media and crowd out opposing views.

The end of apartheid ushered in new freedoms for the media and expression in general. The new Constitution guaranteed the right to 'freedom of the press and other media', limiting expression only in cases of hate speech. It also provided for the right of ordinary citizens to access 'any information held by the state' and some private entities; and stipulated that the Independent Communications Authority of South Africa (Icasa) would be free of government control. Many media outlets, including the SABC, affirmed a new commitment to political independence and fair reporting. The arts community anticipated an era of fresh opportunities, including the use of long-overlooked indigenous tongues that were now included among South Africa's eleven official languages.

Not only did journalists relish the chance to reveal stories repressed for many years; they also (initially at least) turned their critical faculties on the new, democratically elected government – respectfully but doggedly holding its actions up to scrutiny.

In July 1990, shortly after the party was unbanned, ANC strategist and spokesman ('spokesperson' has now become *de rigueur*) Joel Netshitenzhe said: 'Government has no right to treat the SABC as though it owns the corporation exclusively. We demand that broadcasting should be jointly controlled ... It is no longer acceptable that it should merely represent the views and policies of one side.'[1]

Mbeki himself protested that the SABC leadership was appointed by the ruling party. In 1990, he reminded the Cape Town Press Club that the SABC was a public corporation and not the property of the National Party. The NP Home Affairs minister at the time, Gene Louw, declared, in defending the SABC: 'The fact that there is a government means that they make decisions and that they are at the centre of the debate.'[2]

On 14 February 1994, in the midst of the ANC's campaign for the first democratic elections, Nelson Mandela told the International Press Institute Congress: 'I have often said that the media are a mirror through which we can see ourselves as others perceive us, warts, blemishes and all. The African National Congress has nothing to fear from criticism. I can promise you, we will not wilt under close scrutiny. It is our considered view that such criticism can only help us to grow, by calling attention to those of our actions and omissions which do not measure up to our people's expectations and the democratic values to which we subscribe.'[3]

Soon after the ANC's ascent to power, I realised their fine polemics and philippics on press freedom were changing sharply. This inhibited my of-ten-felt desire to go after elements of the media in no-holds-barred fash-ion. For example, in May 1997, addressing journalists in Harare, Mandela complained that the South African media was run by whites: 'The press is still controlled by white conservative proprietors who don't really share our aspirations.'[4] The remarks caused an immediate stir: some wondered whether he had reversed his position on media freedom.

Even before 1994, there was ample evidence that the ANC was un-comfortable with the idea of a free and unfettered media. At a conference convened by the South African Institute of Race Relations in 1991 – the proceedings were subsequently published under the title *Mau-Mauing the Media* – several journalists reported harassment and intimidation by ANC 'comrades' in the townships. One, Thami Mazwai (of whom more), said: 'Little has been said about a new type of censorship that is around in the townships and poses the most powerful threat to press freedom in this country. We have a situation in which journalists are far less exposed to arrest, detention and incarceration by the government than they used to be, but are being threatened and manhandled by political activists in the townships, in the towns and everywhere, and are being told to toe the line "or else".'[5]

Ironically, Mazwai later became a figure of deep controversy when he denounced the idea of objectivity in journalism and justified the SABC's decision to cancel the airing of a documentary critical of Mbeki to 'protect the integrity of the president.'[5]

After a few years in power, the ANC began to chafe under media scrutiny. As deputy president, Mbeki spearheaded calls for 'common understanding' and 'broad consensus' which were not merely calls for reconciliation among different viewpoints, but carried the implication that opposition is disloyal and intolerable. His habit of imputing racist motives to critics became endemic.

At the ANC's defining 50th National Conference, in Mafikeng in December 1997, the Congress formally accused the media of using democracy 'as an instrument to protect the legacy of racism, graphically described by its own patterns of ownership, editorial control, value system and advertiser influence.'[6] It suggested that 'cadre deployment' should be used to ensure greater ANC control; and in its 1999 annual report, it claimed it was 'still faced with a primarily hostile press corps as media is still primarily owned and controlled by antagonistic forces with minority interests. The result has been a continuous onslaught of negative reporting on the ANC and the ANC-led government.'[7] There was no evidence to back up these claims.

The vendetta against the press escalated in Mbeki's first term as president of South Africa. In 1999, complaints about alleged racism in the media were filed with the South African Human Rights Commission (SAHRC) – ironically, by two racially exclusive organisations, the Black Lawyers' Association and the Association of Black Accountants.

The process was kicked off by Christine Qunta, a lawyer and radical ANC activist known for her anti-white views. When the *Mail&Guardian* published articles describing the torrid past of Emmanuel Shaw, a Liberian adviser to then-minister of Minerals and Energy Affairs, Penuell Maduna, Shaw sued and Qunta represented him. When they lost, Shaw left the country and Qunta blamed 'the racist white press'.[8] She laid complaints with the SAHRC against the *Mail&Guardian* and *Sunday Times*, accusing them of expressing racism through their coverage of corruption scandals in government.

Qunta went on to greater things, enjoying all manner of preferments and appointments from President Mbeki. It was hardly a surprise that by the time of the March 2006 municipal elections she was enthroned as a board member (in due course appointed its deputy chair) of the SABC and as a member of its news committee. While I was unsurprised when the DA received its usual dismal and slanted coverage in the run-up to the 2006 municipal polls, even I was taken aback when thereafter she attacked us in a prominent article describing the party as 'not a normal opposition party' and as 'the nemesis of progressive forces in South Africa'.[9]

In no democratic country in the world, I later protested to SABC CEO Dali Mpofu, could a board member of the public broadcaster make such comments about the country's official opposition and retain her board status. But in South Africa she did.

An interim report was commissioned by SAHRC chairman Barney Pityana – who had earlier called High Court judge Dennis Davis a 'racist' in a debate on national television – from the Media Monitoring Project (MMP), a Left-leaning group which had previously said little on the issue and found only a 2% incidence of racism in reporting about the 1999 elections.[10] The MMP suddenly found evidence of racism everywhere in the media.

Its report, compiled by researcher Claudia Braude, set out to show 'continuities between white supremacist narratives' of South Africa in the late years of the apartheid era and the early years of the democracy era. It was a highly selective reading of carefully chosen media stories across a mere six days in the South African news cycle. Braude's document – in her own words – 'aim[ed] to develop awareness among media professionals of the complex process of signification involved in their daily work, and the powerful way in which it can key into and thereby perpetuate racist and racialised perceptions.' The aim of this inquisition was to prove the lingering presence of incorrect and subjectively evil thought in the country's media, as well, perhaps, as to highlight the correct and good sensitivities of Braude herself.

The week she chose to analyse was late June 1999, immediately after President Mbeki had taken office. She gave examples of attempts – conscious or unconscious – to 'perpetuate racist and racialised perceptions'. She imputed malicious motives to coverage she disagreed with. Reports about an arrest warrant relating to a trust of which the new Gauteng premier, Mbhazima Shilowa, was a trustee, 'functioned implicitly and explicitly to associate his premiership with criminality.' Not coincidentally, this case of alleged bias involved the personal reputation of a senior member of the ruling party.

Throughout the report, Braude conflated media reports on government and the ANC with media opinion on black people generally. In the Shilowa case, for example, she wrote: 'The ease with which Shilowa was represented as criminal … occurs within an existing context in which black politicians (as blacks in general) are perceived as dishonest.' The media were identified with political opposition and with whites; Braude overlooked her own attempts to identify blacks with the government and the ANC. This highly racialised prism was then used to arrive at broad conclusions about the media.

Braude's report was released by the SAHRC as an interim report on 'racism in the media', and Pityana announced a formal inquiry for early 2000. Subpoenas were issued to editors demanding that they appear at the inquiry, which SAHRC chairperson Pityana appeared determined to conduct in the style of an inquisition. In fact, he had already stated his views in 1997, to the effect that the media 'continues to practise subliminal racism by creating a negative image of Africans. If we are to have any glimmer of hope of an African Renaissance, this type of reporting has to be seriously transformed.'[11]

The South African National Editors' Forum (Sanef) protested, referring to the subpoenas as 'a contravention of the fundamental freedom of the media clauses in the Constitution'.[12] Many other journalists and editors were firm in their criticisms of the SAHRC, lamenting its tone and direction. The editor of *Die Burger*, Ebbe Dommisse, said: 'It has less to do with racism and more to do with an attempt to get political control of the media.'[13] Mike Robertson, editor of the *Sunday Times*, added: 'The report reads like an undergraduate student's assignment.'[14] From overseas, the *Financial Times* wrote: 'This draconian approach [undermines] the very values the Commission itself is supposed to stand for – including freedom of speech – and which are entrenched in South Africa's Constitution.'[15]

The World Association of Newspapers (WAN) wrote a letter to President Mbeki in February 2000 complaining about the treatment of South African journalists. It noted that those subpoenaed faced a fine or a jail sentence of six months if they refused to appear. The Braude report contained 'numerous alarming examples of the arbitrary interpretation of what might or might not constitute racism.' The WAN concluded by calling on the president to reconsider the inquiry, its mandate and powers, and to have the subpoenas withdrawn.

The president's bizarre reply referred the WAN to 'the catastrophe imposed on our people by over three hundred years of racism, starting with the virtually genocidal annihilation of the Khoi and San people whom the European settlers found at the Cape of Good Hope in the 17th century.' The WAN was asking him to violate the Constitution by interfering in the inquiry; their appeal to him was 'dangerous and misplaced'.[16]

The widespread criticism of the racism hearings had some effect on their tone. At the opening on 1 March 2000, chairperson Pityana said: 'The hearings should not be turned into a court process.'[17] He added: 'It is not the purpose of the inquiry to find any individual journalist, publisher or title guilty of racism.'[18]

However, this signal of moderation also suggested that the inquiry would deal in generalisations. Braude, apparently chastened by public criticism of her role, reportedly distanced herself from the hearings when editors were subpoenaed to attend.[19]

For its part, the ANC reacted to the protests with disdain. It accused the media of seeking to place itself 'beyond reproach'.[20] Its contention was that the media should be held to account for its views and conduct; and journalists could not monopolise the role of watchdogs in society. This fallacious argument was the justification for the creation of a new 'current affairs' programme on SABC-TV whose stated purpose was to criticise other media outlets. In its posture the ANC imitated the attitude and methods of its National Party predecessor. Indeed, history seemed to be repeating itself – not only in the behaviour of the ruling party, but in the response of journalists who split along racial lines. When the SAHRC issued its subpoenas, white editors declared they would not obey, and would go to jail rather than submit. A group of black editors, however, agreed to co-operate. As Allister Sparks noted: 'Racial polarisation threatened to split the media community to a degree not experienced since the worst moments of the apartheid era.'[21]

The hearings themselves were a farce. There were bizarre imputations, such as whether a photograph of a marabou stork perched on a rubbish bin was implicitly racist. One lengthy submission by the ANC attacked JM Coetzee (later to win the Nobel Prize for Literature) and his Booker Prize-winning novel *Disgrace* for a chapter in which a white woman is raped on her farm by a group of black intruders. (Shortly afterwards, Coetzee emigrated to Australia.) In the end, Pityana concluded that the media had been guilty of a 'neo-colonialist conservative liberal agenda'; but the SAHRC made no findings against any journalist or publication. It had served its purpose: creating something of a climate of fear for journalists and editors that would not dissipate for many years to come.

Pityana, close to Mbeki's inner circle, was in time rewarded. He became vice chancellor of Unisa, South Africa's largest distance-learning university. However, three commissioners on the SAHRC (Helen Suzman, Rhoda Kadalie and Ann Routier) quit, in part because they were apparently appalled by his management style and ideological bias.

2

Another facet of the ANC's drive to dominate the media was the 'transformation' of South African newsrooms. This went beyond a push for greater racial integration, or equal opportunity for black journalists; it was aimed at achieving black ownership and editorial control, largely for ideological reasons.

One target was Howard Barrell, editor of the *Mail&Guardian*. The descendant of the anti-apartheid *Rand Daily Mail*, the *M&G* under Barrell continued, for a time, its fiercely independent stance. What irked the Presidency most was Barrell's scathing criticism of Mbeki's flirtation with AIDS denialism; his diplomatic failures in Zimbabwe; and his suppression of investigations into the government's corrupt multi-billion-rand arms deal. In one column he pointed out the hollowness of Mbeki's intellectual pretensions, not least his misquotations from Shakespeare. One headline asked: 'Is this man fit to rule?'[22]

Barrell was finally pushed out in 2002. He emigrated to the United Kingdom, and was replaced by Mondli Makhanya and then Ferial Haffajee.

In sum, there were three methods to ensure the 'transformation' of newsrooms. One was the direct attack – the ANC's broadsides against specific newspapers, or the president's singling-out of particular journalists. The second was to ensure that its own cadres were appointed to editorial jobs or in newsrooms. The third was to use the public purse to effectively buy the loyalty of private media outlets. Government spending on advertising ballooned during the Mbeki years; in fact government-sponsored adspend was the second highest in South Africa, beaten only by Unilever.

Black editors, journalists and publishers were, at this time, placed under as much pressure as their white colleagues. In a speech to a conference of editors in Midrand in 2003, Mbeki defined the media's task as being 'to report Africa to the South Africans, carrying out this responsibility as Africans'.[23] This meant that black journalists were expected to cover news in the manner government wanted it to be covered. Those who stepped outside the bounds of political correctness by portraying the government's weaknesses, or criticising it, would suffer – and suffer more, perhaps, than whites.

In 2003, national director of public prosecutions Bulelani Ngcuka gave an 'off-the-record briefing' to a group of black journalists concerning his investigations into allegations of corruption against then-deputy president Jacob Zuma. The exclusion of white journalists was a sign that they were not trusted, and that the expectation was that black journalists would adopt the line laid down by the ANC, readily and loyally.

Black journalists and writers who attacked the ANC – Xolela Mangcu, Vukani Mde, Rhoda Kadalie, Sipho Seepe and others – became the targets of unique and unrestrained opprobrium emanating from the Presidency. Often, they were made to feel socially isolated, the target of vicious rumour-mongering campaigns. William Mervin Gumede, who wrote a controversial biography of the president, published in 2005, found himself the target of harsh criticism from the ANC.

Eventually, even independent or mildly pro-ANC black journalists and commentators – including Tim Modise, Vuyo Mbuli and others who had put profession above party – exhausted the patience of government satraps. Sandile Memela, spokesperson for the Department of Arts and Culture, referred to them as 'coconuts'[24] – white on the inside, dark on the outside – and received no rebuke from his party or his employer for his blatant use of racist language to whip black journalists into line.

The response of the Presidency and the ANC was to concoct a series of 'indigenous' efforts aimed at counteracting 'neo-liberal' tendencies, rallying black intellectuals to their racial duty. These included the African Renaissance initiative, and each effort sought a unique African perspective and to recruit black intellectuals. Each failed, since ideas cannot be created by fiat, and intellectuals, whatever their hue, value freedom.

Frustrated by the critical debates it encountered in the mainstream media – even after the SAHRC hearings and its other attempts at control – the ANC decided in 2001 to launch its own online journal, *ANC Today*. In its first edition, Mbeki complained: '[T]he overwhelmingly dominant tendency in South African politics, represented by the African National Congress, has no representation whatsoever in the mass media.'[25] The president contended that throughout its existence, 'the national and political majority represented by the ANC has had very few and limited mass media' and that 'the white minority has dominated the field of the mass media.'[26] *ANC Today* aimed to set things straight.

Its first issue included an article proclaiming the President's decision to exclude the Heath Special Investigating Unit – which had the power to cancel contracts – from a probe into corruption in the arms deal as 'a victory for democracy'.[27] (In fact it was the opposite.) And soon *ANC Today* began including a regular 'Letter from the President' which presented Mbeki's reactions to current events, and surprising (perhaps unwise) and frank glimpses of the president's peculiar policy obsessions and ideological bugbears.

Mbeki began taking pot shots at those who had criticised the ANC, or who had merely said something which did not entirely jibe with his worldview. Victims of his harsh, sarcastic and cynical excoriation were journalist and AIDS activist Charlene Smith; Anglo American Corporation CEO Tony Trahar; Barloworld chief economist Dr Pieter Haasbroek; *Financial Mail* journalist Peter Honey; and many others – none of whom were given space to respond. The President also lashed out variously at the BBC, the *Sunday Times*, *The Economist* and *Business Day*, and at Internet sources.

The excuse was freedom of expression – but from the towering heights of the Presidency they had the opposite effect of severely damaging freedom of expression.

Criticism of the government – or even faint praise – continued to draw *ad hominem* attacks from the president and the ruling party. The hit man was Minister in the Presidency Essop Pahad, who brought a Stalinist bent to bear on freedom of the media in South Africa. Pahad became notorious for telephoning and berating journalists over what he considered unfavourable coverage of the ruling party. At an Independent Newspapers banquet in February 2001, to which the president declined an invitation, Pahad famously berated those present, accusing the media of 'rank hostility' to the government and president. 'What masquerades as "public opinion" ... is in fact minority opinion informed by the historic and social position occupied by the minority,' he claimed.

I was present in the splendid and historic surrounds of the Cape Town Castle. Independent Newspapers proprietor Tony (recently ennobled as Sir Anthony) O'Reilly was our host, and the evening looked promising. However, when Pahad took to the podium, he essentially destroyed, in one speech, not just the bonhomie and international goodwill prevailing, but gave the lie to the concept he claimed to uphold with a root-and-branch denunciation of the press and what he claimed was its singular assault on the person and integrity of the presidency.

Trevor Manuel, seated opposite me at the table, at first raised his eyebrows and then spent much of the time during Pahad's tirade with his face buried in his hands. It was up to host O'Reilly to save the evening. With Irish charm and lethal wit he duly did so by riposting to Pahad's denunciation: 'Oh, well, what can one say? A case of Essop's fables!' What was noteworthy as a hangover from the evening, however, was the Independent Group's willingness to publish Pahad's ravings prominently.

Pahad continued in this vein on many subsequent occasions. At the funeral of mining magnate and tax dodger (and according to post-mortem revelations, serial criminal) Brett Kebble in Cape Town in 2005, he accused journalists of overly zealous speculation about the causes and motives of Kebble's spectacularly gruesome death: '[Are] some of us so losing our humanity and sensitivity to pain that we do not think of the impact that what we say and write might have on the family?' It later came to light that Kebble had pumped millions into the ANC's cash-starved Western Cape Youth League operations. The rather paltry amount he donated to the DA was at the request of the liquidators of Kebble's bankrupt estate paid back by us without demur or delay.

I considered the Mbeki government to be not simply grossly over-sensitive to such criticism as the newspapers proffered of government's distinctly mixed record in power, but ungrateful for the generally defer-ential – and often cowardly – coverage they received. The opposition was given fairly short shrift by many newspaper groups. All this was to change radically in 2007, as the power shifts in the ANC achieved gale-force in-tensity and Mbeki's presidency of the party began to unravel.

When I entered parliament in 1989 an informal bonhomie existed between opposition backbenchers and the media in the gallery, usual-ly involving copious amounts of red plonk and the exchange of gossip. However, both government and opposition got a fair shake of the can. It was with the emergence of an unbanned ANC, and the shift of focus to the negotiations process in Kempton Park, that there came some loss of attention in parliament. This would altogether change with the advent of the new democratic order.

I never asked Harry Oppenheimer why Anglo American divested itself of its press interests, particularly the sale of the Argus newspaper group. Smart gossip suggested that Anglo did not want its mining and min-eral interests held hostage by its ownership of newspapers which, given the proclivities of the then stable of editors and writers, might well be in opposition to the ANC. They also said O'Reilly (whose media em-pire spanned the globe from Ireland and the UK, to America and the Antipodes) had his eyes on the Argus's cash-rich pension funds which he intended to repatriate to London and Dublin.

There was a meeting – in fact talks during a Caribbean holiday – be-tween Mandela and O'Reilly in which Madiba's blessing was sought and received for the acquisition of the Argus Group by Independent. It was widely understood that the newspapers would accelerate transformation and be broadly sympathetic to the ANC project.

One of my more controversial decisions as leader of the party in 1999, as I relate in Chapter 14, was to encourage Nigel Bruce, seasoned journalist and previously editor of both *Business Day* and the *Financial Mail*, to stand for nomination to parliament. He was duly elected amidst some controversy.

While I found Nigel witty and agreeable, to many he was an acquired taste: more high-Tory and less of a 'new South African' as preferred by the governing elite. Several editors – and ex-editors – actively ventilated their dislike, and no doubt his preferment also poisoned the well of our media relationships. But I enjoyed Nigel and liked his company. He was, in my view, particularly insightful on Anglo's fateful decision to sell its media interests, since in addition to his editorial tasks he had served as a board member of Times Media Ltd, which Anglo also owned, and which was also sold by them – not to O'Reilly but partly to foreign interests, Pearson, and a black empowerment consortium when Anglo divested itself of its stake in JCI.

I asked him to pen an account of this particular act of transformation, which he did: 'Anglo's sale of most of its newspapers to foreign interests in the 1990s and the gift of what was left to ANC-supporting interests was the most momentous event in the past fifty years in the media industry.' In his view and as far as democracy was concerned it was more significant than either the launch of the government-funded *Citizen* or the closure of the *Rand Daily Mail* (also at the behest of Anglo).

As for reasons, Bruce speculates that the Corporation hoped for a flourishing democracy which would mitigate the need for opposition-supporting papers. Anglo's stewardship of the liberal press dated back to the early years of apartheid. In effect, it controlled most of the English-language afternoon papers (in the Argus Group) and the morning papers within South African Associated Newspapers (later to become Times Media Ltd and then Johncom); as well as the *Sunday Times* and the *Financial Mail*, also in the latter group. This concentration, according to Nigel, aside from its commercial benefits, 'was to prevent acquisition by those who would stifle opposition.'

In Bruce's view: 'The Argus Group was a well-managed if editorially diffident company that saw itself, in the words of one manager, as the jewel in Anglo's crown. So it came as a shock when, with universal suffrage looming, it was sold on surprisingly beneficial terms to Irish newspaper owner Tony O'Reilly.

'O'Reilly's acquisition coincided with the slide in the value of the rand. This meant that to boost his returns on this investment he had to cut costs drastically, denuding newsrooms of experienced journalists and squeezing profits out of every nook and cranny. What saved him from the depredations of the weak rand was his decision to appoint editors who were sympathetic to the ANC.

'Their editorial output drove off white readers who were not replaced, as no doubt he thought would happen, by black ones. The outcome was a sharp fall in the circulations of all his newspapers. But that proved beneficial to the bottom line ... [since] when circulations fall, newspaper costs decline faster than advertising revenues. The margins of his newspapers widened, albeit temporarily, and with a little help from the group's substantial pension fund surplus, O'Reilly secured the return he desired. But, with such windfalls unlikely to be repeated, cost-cutting remains his key strategy.' I lacked Nigel's insider knowledge of the newspaper industry, but I found his account both interesting and iconoclastic, even if time and circumstance had moved on since he wrote it in 2006.

Nigel then takes up the strand of the second instalment of Anglo's disinvestment: 'Soon after the disposal of the Argus Company, Anglo was ready with another shock. The story was broken in the *Financial Mail* even before the chairman of Johannesburg Consolidated Investments (the mining house controlled by Anglo and which owned Times Media) was told of his fate. In its magnanimity Anglo had decided to give JCI, stripped of its platinum mines, to black political empowerment interests.

'JCI's remaining newspaper assets were part of the gift. However, Anglo decided that, while the demotic newspapers, such as the *Sunday Times*, would become entirely black-owned (which meant ANC-controlled), 50% of the financial journals, *Financial Mail* and *Business Day*, would be sold to Pearson, publisher of the London *Financial Times* (*FT*). A founding shareholder in the *Financial Mail* (*FM*), the *FT* had during the 1970s sold its original stake in the magazine for a paltry sum. By comparison, its re-entry as a partner in the new BDFM company was an extremely costly exercise.

'Pearson was intended as a sheet anchor to keep the *Financial Mail* and *Business Day* as independent editorial entities. But, with the *FT* having lurched to the Left in England, Pearson managers soon made common cause with South Africa's empowerment interests; editors were changed and the ANC became principal editorial beneficiary of the process.'

At the time of the second post-apartheid election, this sheet anchor was put to the test – and it held, but only just. All the Independent and Times Media (by this time Johncom) newspapers rooted for the ANC. The exception was the *Financial Mail*. In an extraordinary aberration its new editor (a former *FT* staffer) supported the party of former Transkei dictator Bantu Holomisa, who enjoyed just 3% of the vote.

'This caused a predictable outcry from empowerment interests and the ANC, but Pearson held firm and the editor survived. However, this was at best a holding operation. The editor of *Business Day* was prematurely retired and the *FM*'s man was switched to the editor's chair of that news-

449

paper. Ironically, *Business Day* is now more of a commercial and editorial success than the *FM*, to which the BDFM board appointed a succession of more tractable editors.'

In Bruce's view, the effect on opposition and public discourse has been profound: 'In these circumstances, if opposition parties – be they in parliament or provincial assemblies and councils – are denied access to a competitive and diverse press; they are also denied the means of being heard and doing their job properly. They are forced to resort to the depredations of spin.

'So after the turmoil of 12 years of transition, English-language newspapers have moved from the concentrated ownership of a benign corporation to an almost equally concentrated ownership of foreign interests, who have no regard for editorial standards and put hard-currency returns ahead of reinvestment.'

3

Initially, we did not see much change after the 1994 election. More or less the same group of hard-drinking, politically sceptical but broadly accurate and factually painstaking journalists remained in place. The tiny DP provided one of the few oppositional voices to the gargantuan Government of National Unity (comprising 94% of the seats in parliament). We received generous coverage, particularly of our various exposés which provided a diet of hard news and something of an antidote to the 'rainbow nation' chorus from the government benches.

However, within the first two or three years of the new democracy, not a single one of the experienced Argus journalists remained: John Maclennan, Anthony Johnson, Barry Streek, Peter Fabricius, Martin Challenor, Hugh Roberton and Donwald Pressly, each of them broadly of the liberal-Left, had disappeared from the parliamentary gallery. Either they cashed in their options, or were elbowed sideways, or were retrenched, or fled elsewhere. During 2004 I was interviewed by a newspaper expert from America's 'premier media monitor', the *Columbia Journalism Review*, Douglas Foster. He penned a penetrating analysis for the journal, 'The Trouble with Transformation'. In many ways he homed in on the phenomenon which Nigel Bruce identified above. Of the media skills-shedding situation he wrote:

'When Sir Anthony O'Reilly bought the *Star* [Johannesburg's flagship daily] many thought it would herald a new era of prosperity. The dilapidated facilities and overstretched editorial staff prove how illusory this prediction was ... When talented reporters get snatched up at double their salaries by government or corporations as spinmeisters; when someone gets promoted beyond his abilities, and even when a reporter gets a story wrong, "juniorisation" is the one-size-fits-all label used to shame newsroom denizens without mentioning explicitly that most of the "juniors" are black.'[28]

While I disagree with Foster's race-labelling – in my vexed experience with the political media, I often found that reporters who trumpet titbits of gossip as pristine fact are white – the point is valid. At the *Star*, he noted, the editorial staff had been slashed roughly in half over the past decade – and its much-lauded in-house cadet scheme had been scuppered at the very point that entry-level and advanced training were needed to 'ease the historic transition about to occur in the newsroom.'[29]

Extraordinarily, given the talent and experience available to them, the new bosses of Independent looked elsewhere for a group head of parliamentary and political reporting. Quite what journalistic ability the person assigned to this post, Zubeida Jaffer, had was not discernible to either her colleagues or the politicians she interacted with. I recall her using the occasional interview with me to deliver a prim message as to how 'the DP should position itself in the new South Africa' and other items of gratuitous advice, such as 'how you should encourage your supporters to do more to build the country.'

This didactic struggle activist became the apex of the parliamentary coverage of the most important press group. Her meteoric (and to her many detractors in her own company, unmerited) promotion was echoed elsewhere in the company. Titles were handed to new editors whose essential qualification was the colour of their skin.

In short order, the *Cape Times* and *Daily News* became the vanguards of this new approach, which proved disastrous commercially. Shortly after Ryland Fisher and Kaizer Nyatsumba became editors of the *Cape Times* and *Daily News* respectively, both papers began to haemorrhage readers and advertising; and the Independent group's overall profitability dropped. As it happened, the company's chief executive officer in South Africa, the close confidant (and hagiographer) of O'Reilly, Ivan Fallon, became involved in a public and ugly spat with me when he announced (with an atrocious lack of guts, I thought) that the newspaper industry (or his segment of it) would not get involved 'in a crossfire situation which could result in a situation we're trying to avoid.' This was in response to Mandela after one of his jeremiads against 'white conservative newspaper bosses'. In Durban, I called Fallon's response 'meek, rather than vehement or robust'.

Although he in turn accused me of 'making an idiot of myself', we opened a dialogue. I had heard Fallon was what the Americans call a kiss-up-kick-down person, disparaged by many in his newspaper stable as a ferocious cost-cutter and culler of journalists. I actually found him soft-spoken, socially gracious, quick-witted and not at all defensive when it came to discussing the shortcomings I identified in his group. It had to be said, though, that the easy dialogue we established was not matched by other Independent editors. I always said and genuinely believed that we asked for fairness, not favouritism. But with Kaizer Nyatsumba at the helm of the *Daily News* during and after the 1999 election, neither was to be observed.

Having been promoted from political editor of the *Star* to being the Independent's first black African editor, he seemed to decide that our previous reasonable – even friendly – relationship needed replacement with something far more rancorous and explicitly racist.

Nyatsumba's arrival at the *Daily News* led to a distinct change in the paper's profile, its positioning, and even its personality. It assumed an ardently Africanist, pro-Mbeki and anti-DA editorial line, with acres of op-ed space devoted to depicting me (and my party) as some sort of neo-Nazi, white-revanchist hybrid. Part of his newspaper's repackaging was to publish frequent large photographs of himself on the news pages, and the readers remained unimpressed. Sales and circulation plummeted, at one stage apparently shedding over twenty-five thousand readers. He did not last long and was sent to London.

However, while still at the helm in Durban he published a philippic declaring 'that all blacks hate the DP more than the NNP'.[30] I was not surprised at this denunciation. But my normally mild-mannered Durban-based parliamentary colleague, Nelson Raju, could not contain himself. He wrote a particularly pointed rejoinder to Nyatsumba, which read, in part: 'I must say that, in addition to his extraordinary gifts as one of the world's greatest editors and journalists and the self-appointed spokesman for black journalists anywhere, Mr Nyatsumba's gifts now extend into the realm of political prophecy.

'He states ... as a fact that all blacks "hate the DP more than the NNP". How does he know? Is this a poll? Is it an intuition? Is it based on the mutterings and musings of the new self-appointed elite of this country? The newly enriched chattering classes who use blackness as a passport to office and patronage? Or is it just a consequence of his own personal prejudice and bile?'[31]

Nyatsumba's 'transformation' efforts antagonised his own readers and he lost them. The same fate would later befall Mathatha Tsedu when he attempted an even more radical and costly exercise at the *Sunday Times*, owned by Johnnic; while Ryland Fisher's tenure in Cape Town also ended in tears and saw his editorial demise.

There was no doubt, however, that the DP (and later the DA) was having increasing difficulty in getting its message across. My earlier courting of the press, and their sometime reciprocal ardour, had not simply cooled – it had led (on their part) to basic hostility. One example was an exchange of correspondence during the 1999 election which I had with John Battersby (known for his hand-wringing posturing to his colleagues as 'John Batter-me'), then editor of the *Sunday Independent*. I drew his attention to a particularly offensive imputation about my then fiancée (later wife) Michal, which his newspaper had carried. For this he immediately and forthrightly apologised.

However, I thought the rest of his reflections summed up the general mood in his media stable. He wrote: 'I am not sure if my apologies will make any impression on you as you seem to have come to the conclusion that I have a personal axe to grind. That couldn't be further from the truth. Perhaps the reason I feel so strongly about the Democratic Party is that its principles most closely represent those which I hold dear. As I tried to convey to you at a dinner we had in February, I strongly disagree with both the direction of the party and its strategy under your leadership. I refer to the party's current obsession with white interests, its disturbing insensitivity to people of colour, its inability to retain any black leaders of note and the placing of some candidates – known for their jingoistic views and racist innuendos – high on your election list.

'Obviously, none of these personal views will divert me from my duty to cover fairly and proportionately the DP's election campaign and its performance thereafter ... I happen to like you as a person and enjoy your company. Since we met over dinner, I have actively tried to redress the grievances you expressed about our coverage. I have obviously failed but will keep trying.'

Battersby's view – that I had tugged the DP (and later the DA) away from its liberal democratic moorings – had salience elsewhere. Alan Fine, who for key periods in my leadership presided over politics at the influential *Business Day*, was a continuous critic. He often accused me of 'going for growth' at the expense of the party's principles (although in 1995, when I became leader, *Business Day* sneered that our then 1,7% support base meant we more 'resembled a desolate shack' than a real political force). Rhoda Kadalie, a friend, but a fiercely independent commentator (and later columnist for the same newspaper), was so incensed by one of *Business Day*'s attacks on me that she vented her spleen in typical and (I thought) splendid fashion in August, 2001:

'As a reader of your newspaper I strongly disapprove of your constant negative portrayal of the leader of the official opposition, Tony Leon ... [The editorials] are disrespectful, unfair and openly prejudiced ... Often your editorials read like ANC propaganda pamphlets, clear attempts to ingratiate your paper with the ruling elite. I hold no brief for the Democratic Party, but am extremely glad that we have some form of opposition in this country. If it were not for them we would not know about government corruption and there would be few to raise the crucial questions about delivery ...'[32]

Since I had a relationship – of sorts – with Fine, I asked him what he thought of Kadalie's attack. He responded by acknowledging: 'We have had some harsh things to say about you and your party over the years. Many, probably most of these have had to do with your handling of racial issues and related politics.' He then contextualised the series of attacks (which in 1999 led *Business Day* to endorse the ANC) by claiming 'the entire range of politicians seems to find gentle criticism of themselves vitriolic and a gentle criticism of their opponents fawning.'

I actually enjoyed my interactions with *Business Day*, including liquid lunches with its smart, if erratic, editor Peter Bruce, whose political affections and peregrinations were interesting to track. After the 2006 municipal election, he mused in a Monday morning column that I should make way as leader for Patricia de Lille (a bizarre choice, since at the time she was involved in machinations against us in Cape Town). Once more Rhoda leaped into the fray in typical combative and caustic style, noting how personalised much of the criticism had become:

'The only gripe people have about Tony Leon is that he is arrogant and combative – as though that has got anything to do with anything. Ninety-five per cent of the ANC is combative and arrogant. People never talk about DA policies or what Tony does, but comment on his personality, which is more a figment of the media and its white guilt than anything Tony is. I believed the media rubbish until I made an appointment to meet him. He is well-read, throws a good party, and is nice and irreverent.'[33]

Neither Battersby nor Fine saw out my period in politics from their editorial stools. Fine decamped to a public affairs position at AngloGoldAshanti. Battersby, who at one stage was sent to parliament by Independent (as group editor after the Jaffer appointment misfired), also in time left journalism entirely. He literally took the government's shilling and I last encountered him in London in November 2006, where he enjoyed the title 'country manager' for the South African government-sponsored 'International Marketing Council' (IMC). His remit was to lobby the UK media, write speeches for visiting South African government officials, and perform a basic propaganda function abroad. His new boss (on the government side) was Essop Pahad.

It was not surprising, therefore, to find him addressing various business and investment leaders on the bright prospects at home. He insisted that crime in South Africa was 'under control'; and while I have no doubt his new employer would have smiled with approval, I didn't think it edifying to see so seasoned and senior a journalist as Battersby transmogrified into a government stooge. To be fair, he was only following a well-trodden path: the crusading editor of the *Cape Times* under apartheid, Anthony Heard, was actually ensconced in the Presidency as Pahad's adviser, while several other editors had transmuted into government or parastatal spokesmen.

4

In March 2000, as a consequence of the continental drift in media control, we published a seminal document: 'All Power to the Party'. We drew attention to the ANC's key cadre redeployment strategy, a frankly Leninist stratagem at total variance with the best intentions and precepts of our Constitution. Under scrutiny was the wholesale takeover by the ruling party and its apparatchiks of all public service and non-party functions and structures. *Business Day* published a strong editorial, accusing us of 'McCarthyism' and arguing, strangely, that the approach of the ANC should not be taken at face value:

'Should we all be terrified of a tyrannical regime's pervasive tentacles, or should the DP be embarrassed at a McCarthyist effort to paint a false picture of the post-apartheid state? With the bulk of skilled blacks being ANC supporters, the trend the DP identifies was always going to be an aspect of South Africa's peaceful revolution.'[34]

The editor mischaracterised our motives and ignored the ANC's dismemberment of the Public Service Commission and its active takeover of the Judicial Services Commission. Yet five years later, *Business Day* had clearly thought again. Editor Peter Bruce wrote, in September 2005, of the ANC affiliations of all the investigative and political organs involved in the 'oilgate' scandal: 'The fact that [oilgate] involves funding the ANC, of which the head of police, the President, the minister of Justice, the head of the revenue service, the leadership at PetroSA [the parastatal involved in siphoning off funds to the ANC], the head of the Scorpions and the laughably termed "Public Protector" are all members, means it will never be investigated. It also means that anyone who comes too close to serious dirty tricks in the ruling party is going to find themselves being looked at hard by any one or more of the above.'[35]

Many of my detractors in the media genuinely believed that the DP/DA was 'offside' in the new South Africa – and didn't hesitate to say so. I also have no doubt that some of the negative vibrations stemmed from my own shortcomings. Rhoda Kadalie once advised me to spend more time 'drinking with the journalists'. We arranged agreeable and reasonably regular social encounters with the press gallery. However, Rhoda also advised that Patricia de Lille (whom she by then especially disliked) enjoyed disproportionate (until her Cape Town faux pas in 2006) coverage on the basis of her closeness with the media. Given De Lille's essential vacuity and almost serial inability to deliver or follow-up on various fatuous and sensation-seeking allegations, I felt it belittling and insulting to both parties that fair coverage could only be garnered in this fashion.

In addition, I have a congenital inability to hold my tongue or hide my feelings. I well remember attending the 2000 Alan Paton annual literary awards hosted by the *Sunday Times* and its editor Mike Robertson at the Hyatt in Johannesburg. Robertson, Edyth Bulbring (his wife and an excellent journalist) and I had been friends for many years. However, shortly before the awards I had been to Zimbabwe and witnessed first-hand the increasing tyranny of Mugabe and the fatuousness and failure, even back then, of Mbeki's quiet diplomacy.

The *Sunday Times* had recently endorsed the 'wisdom' of Mbeki's approach – which incensed me. I believed my relationship with Robertson was strong enough to withstand my forthright, perhaps vehement, disagreement with him on the issue. I was wrong. When I told Mike what I thought, he turned on me: '[The] difference between you and me is that your words have no influence on the government and mine do.' I riposted that 'Joel Mervis [the legendary *Sunday Times* editor in the 1960s and 1970s] must be spinning in his grave.' I was never invited back!

There was another reason why large sections of the English media strained, at least until 2005 or so, to justify the ANC and were so intensely critical of the DP/DA. It was not that basically intelligent and historically literate people were indifferent to government failings, hypocrisy and double standards. It was, in part, due precisely to their sense of history;

as Tony Judt described the liberal slideaway in the face of Soviet tyranny in Europe in the 1930s, there was 'a fear of being tarred with the brush of reaction'.[36] But as the famous communist apostate Arthur Koestler explained: 'This fear of finding oneself in bad company is not an expression of political purity: it is an expression of lack of confidence.'[37]

The idea of 'doing business with history' no doubt animated many journalists; but the lack of backbone on occasion meant that the first decade of democracy will not, I suspect, be judged as our press's finest hour. The maverick columnist Max du Preez, in mid-2006, pinpointed precisely this tendency: 'There is an old tradition among "progressives" of "the Left" in South Africa to be silent on certain problems or a trend if judged that speaking out would strengthen the arguments of the "reactionaries" or the "right wing". In this tradition, one would talk down crime and corruption, incompetence, and defend a sometimes indefensible foreign policy. I have also on occasion been guilty.'[38]

The headwinds in the media did start to shift.

Black journalists, in particular, led the charge – perhaps more emboldened because they are less susceptible to accusations of racism. In response to Pahad's rant at the Kebble funeral, for example, several newspaper editors hit back, including Jovial Rantao of the *Star*, who wrote: '[H]ere is a senior cabinet minister in the democratic Republic of South Africa saying things that skirt on the verge of stuff that dictators do best – violating press freedom ... It is the freedom of the press that we enjoy that makes it possible to write and disagree with a senior national cabinet minister – who has the ear of the president – without fear of intimidation or being thrown in jail.'[39]

In response to this backlash, presidential adviser Titus Mafolo helped organise a 'Native Club' of black intellectuals to promote government perspectives. This precipitated an outraged response, notably from several black commentators. John Matshikiza, in the *Mail&Guardian*, slammed the Club and described its open hostility to what it termed 'neo-liberal' intellectuals as 'a kind of neo-fascism that has no colour.'[40]

These reactions suggest that media independence not only has hope, but is reasserting itself in the second decade of democracy. However, the trouble remains that journalists, black and white, remain perturbed by an ambivalence about whether they should assist the government in its objectives, or hold its behaviour and policies to independent account. Some take their ambivalence further and project a false and unstable 'neutrality' making it mandatory that every criticism of government be 'balanced' by a criticism of the opposition; or every critical article 'balanced' by a positive one. This allows the ANC to constantly push the boundaries of what is acceptable in a non-racial democracy, and to continually hack away at the foundations of our new constitutional order.

Of course, not all media are alike. The curmudgeonly Johnny Johnson at the *Citizen*, who had so flayed me in the city council as a 'young Turk radical upstart', began warming to the DP – which my detractors would cite as proof of the party's 'lurch to the Right'. But when Johnson retired, his replacement, Martin Williams, an unabashed 'Old Prog', often alone in the English media, gave strong editorial support to the party.

On the other side of the linguistic divide, perspectives were shifting as well. Ton Vosloo, as chairman of Naspers (the multi-media and multi-national behemoth that controlled all Afrikaans newspapers in South Africa), gave an influential speech shortly after the onset of democracy in 1994. He pointed out that liberation was by no means a blacks-only affair. It had also, he said, freed Afrikaners to pursue political choices with no obligation to back the only political party which had hitherto guaranteed Afrikaans interests. His proclamation created a strong following wind in his group.

Shortly after assuming the leadership of the party in 1994, I visited all the country's editors. My warmest reception was from Izak de Villiers, editor of the immensely influential Sunday title *Rapport*. I was amazed to find that such a '*murg-en-been*' Afrikaner (a church minister before entering journalism) was an unabashed Anglophile. He expressed enthusiasm for my project of establishing a viable opposition, albeit with slender resources. He promised support, and in the years that followed was as good as his word. Given the Afrikaans press's historic role as the voice of the (former) establishment, De Villiers was, in his own way, deeply anti-establishment and even an iconoclast. He did not approve of De Klerk, or of his presumed successor, Roelf Meyer.

Die Burger in the Cape and *Beeld* in Johannesburg started to give the DP a far fairer look-in than previously. Ken Andrew told me that when in 1981 he took the scalp of Nat cabinet minister Dawie de Villiers in the Gardens constituency, he wrote off *Die Burger* because of its implacable opposition to the PFP. Afrikaans press support for the NP was so slavish that its organs were, with justification, dubbed '*Nat-pamflette*'.

This all began to change after 1994. The DP and I were direct beneficiaries of the alteration in the political weather; just as the increasingly faltering NP was blindsided by the fact that the Afrikaans press became intensely critical of it.

Nelson Mandela once told me that 'if you want to be really informed of what's going on in politics, you need to read *Die Burger* and *Beeld*.' Mandela had a fascination with newspapers – no doubt because of their scarcity during much of his imprisonment – and used to page through practically every South African title at the start of his day. For completely different reasons I did precisely the same; and I took his injunction to heart.

During the first phase of my leadership, I got to know Ebbe Dommisse, the humorous and intensely cynical editor of *Die Burger*. Before the advent of the popular tabloids *Die Son* and *The Sun*, it gave the best access to the bulk of Western Cape voters, brown and white. On Dommisse's watch, *Die Burger* began to question, with new-found frankness, the NP's ill-starred role in Mandela's Government of National Unity and (before that) the ineffectiveness of De Klerk's negotiation strategy at Kempton Park.

The Afrikaans press did not share the transformation imperatives and pressures of their English counterparts: relatively few black journalists used Afrikaans as their medium of expression, and the Naspers target market was (with the exception of *City Press*) largely white and Coloured. They had no new foreign owners with ferocious cost-cutting imperatives; 'juniorisation' was less prevalent; and while certain Afrikaans journalists retained an atavistic attachment to the NP, they could generally be relied on to report events accurately, and to separate news from comment.

I was fortified in my impression of Dommisse by the view of liberal UCT academic David Welsh (who edited my 1998 volume of speeches and essays), who told me that Ebbe was a close friend, with formidable acumen. Nor was spontaneous charm a substitute for analysis: he knew his readers and had a shrewd grasp of their political preferences. In consequence, he took an unprecedented decision in the 1999 general election and declined to endorse the NP editorially; an extraordinary decision given that his chair had been occupied by Dr DF Malan, the first apartheid PM after 1948.

This decision, coupled with *Die Burger*'s strong line on an NP-DP coalition after the election in the event of a hung parliament in the Western Cape (an accurate prediction), was most significant. The NP leader later told me that an NP-ANC deal in the province was impossible, given *Die Burger*'s implacable opposition to it. He would change his mind.

Before the media environment improved, matters actually grew worse. In 2000, to take one of hundreds of examples, the Democratic Party Federal Congress in Cape Town was barely covered at all by the *Cape Times*. The editor at the time, John Scott, acknowledged the error and blamed communication problems in the newsroom: 'Were you and your party colleagues to believe that this was all part of a *Cape Times* conspiracy to belittle the DP's importance, I could hardly blame you. I was shocked myself.'[41]

The following year, during the State of the Nation debate in February 2001, I was not entirely surprised to find my speech – the first opposition response to the president – barely visible in the next morning's *Cape Times*. Far more incredulous, since she had witnessed the event in parliament, was none other than Helen Suzman. She fired off a letter to the editor:[42] 'I was in the parliamentary gallery yesterday and listened to Tony Leon deliver his excellent even-handed speech in reply to President Mbeki's State of the Nation address on Tuesday. He gave due credit to the positive aspects of the government's policy, and attacked the government's neglect of what he called the "four dread horsemen of the Apocalypse" – crime, unemployment, the AIDS pandemic and corruption ... [He spoke] as the leader of the official opposition and I expected to find extensive coverage of his speech in this morning's *Cape Times* (Wednesday 14 February 2001). On the contrary, I had to search for the report and found it tucked away on page six in a couple of paragraphs.

'What has happened, I wonder, to the independent press that provided such a valuable service during my 36 years as an opposition MP?'

To its credit, the *Cape Times* carried her letter, and as a sort of ex post facto apologia later printed the speech as an op-ed article. Suzman's observations justified my remarks to William Hague in London the year before.

Other editors have not always been so forthcoming about their mistakes.

6

The problem was often one of emphasis. Allegations against the DA – for example, in the Harksen scandal of 2002 – were treated with banner headlines on front pages, while similar allegations against the ANC were at that time seldom pursued.

There are also certain columnists who could be counted on to adopt an anti-DA line, regardless of the facts. One such was Ashley Smith of the *Cape Argus*, who, during the 2004 election, expressed great admiration for Marthinus van Schalkwyk and, after the polls closed, promptly called for my resignation. He later left the newspaper in disgrace after being implicated in a scandal surrounding allegations that he and other journalists were in the pay of Western Cape premier Ebrahim Rasool.[43]

Another detractor was an oleaginous Independent Newspapers report-er, recruited from the SABC: Jeremy Michaels. He spent most of the 2004 campaign trailing Mbeki and me. Of the president, Michaels went into apoplexies of admiration for his touchy-feeliness (which, if it was visible during the election, was quickly suppressed thereafter). Michaels found nothing to approve in my campaign, and wrote me off as some form of semi-automated sound bite machine devoid of wit or warmth. This in-censed Michal, who was with me on the campaign trail and could scarcely believe how Michaels's reports twisted and slanted the real events which she too had witnessed.

Some time after the election Michaels disappeared on one or another scholarship abroad. I had forgotten him when in January 2007 I bumped into him at the annual eve-of-parliament cocktail function at the British high commissioner's sprawling Bishopscourt pile. With great pride he in-formed me that he left journalism to take up shop as the 'communications adviser' (or some such title) of the beleaguered ANC premier, Ebrahim Rasool. He was nonplussed at my tart response that he 'now got paid by an ANC government to promote it, something you previously used to do free of charge!'

In 2004 my communications and media director at the time, James Lorimer – himself a seasoned journalistic pro – had an encounter with an Independent Newspapers hack at our final KwaZulu-Natal joint rally with Buthelezi and the IFP, which, he said, literally staggered him. When Lorimer asked the *Mercury*'s Sipho Khumalo to share a copy of the speech I was about to deliver (until he could print off more copies) he was told to 'fuck off' since he was just 'another white boy'!

Lorimer did not have a racist bone in his body, and was generally un-flappable and unfailingly polite. But the slur outraged him – and he de-scribed it to Khumalo's editor, David Canning, as 'extremely offensive and naked racism'.[44] He suggested that aside from the reflection the re-mark cast on Khumalo and his professionalism, or lack of it, 'the more important issue' was how it reflected 'on the *Mercury* and on Independent Newspapers and the way they cover politics.' I was appalled and fascinated by this incident: no white journalist would survive for more than 24 hours if the roles and parties had been reversed. Yet without a shred of objective justification, Khumalo and his colleagues were quick to impute a racist subliminal motive to the DA and its campaign. I did not expect either a quick or an unequivocal response, and the editor did not disappoint me on either count.

It took Canning a full month to respond; the election was three weeks over before he put pen to paper. His explanation and half-baked apology was hedged in with qualifications and illogicalities. The responding letter was, of its kind and in its own way, a masterful fudge and an object lesson in timorousness and blame-shifting: it is worth reprinting in its original form:[45]

> Thank you for your letter dated April 5, 2004.
> My apologies for the delay in replying – our staff were out in the field during the elections and I have only been able to properly investigate the issue this week. This indeed appears to have been a most unfortunate incident.
>
> Sipho Khumalo is a seasoned journalist in whom I have great faith and confidence. He has given the DA plenty of fair and positive publicity in years gone by, including in this election. I have never before received such a complaint about his language or behaviour.
>
> He has a slightly different interpretation of the events that occurred on that day. In this case he had gone to some lengths to attend and cover a DA function but felt frustrated by a lack of facilitation and co-operation. He says what really angered him was his perception of racial bias in your personal attitude. He says that while you handed the white journalists present each a copy of the speech the black journalists were to share a single copy of the document in question. This presented difficulties for writers with competing deadlines.
>
> He concedes he did use intemperate language, although not quite as severe as you have stated, but for which he apologises. I have made it clear to him that such loss of temper and behaviour must not be repeated, no matter what the circumstances.
>
> I hope we can all learn some lessons from this unhappy incident and move forward positively from this point.

But there were constraints affecting editors, at the time, that were not simply political. As indicated above, the pressured atmosphere of rising costs and ownership demands for enhanced bottom lines placed pressure on editors, sometimes obliging them to act as ad salesmen. On one occasion, in the small corner of power which the DA occupied in 2000 (control of the Western Cape government), we involved ourselves in an arrangement which, when I heard about it, raised ethical questions all round.

Our chief executive, Ryan Coetzee, then advising (among a myriad of tasks) the marketing and advertising strategies for our premier, Gerald Morkel, had a visit from the new editor of an English-language Cape Town daily. His request was that the provincial government place (and pay for) a double-page advertisement in a forthcoming edition of the paper. As a 'sweetener' the editor promised in exchange a front-page lead on a subject of the government's choice. Ryan advised the premier and the cabinet against accepting the 'offer', but they greenlighted it anyway. So the newspaper received the revenue and the provincial government obtained a front-page lead some days later, to the premier's delight. But this was simply in one province.

The government of South Africa is one of the largest print advertisers in the country; and this alone suggests a great deal about the pressures which newspaper editors are placed under on a daily basis, betwixt shareholders and power-brokers.

Generally speaking, after the electoral dust had settled, post the 2004 election, a thaw began. I believe there was a recognition that an even mightier ANC required not merely robust parliamentary countering, but less fawning deference from the fourth estate. I also decided that the DA's ace-in-the-hole in terms of the media was Helen Zille, who had left the provincial arena and joined us in parliament. I appointed her national spokesperson for the party, with a direct brief that she interact with both editors and journalists. Her press background and general credibility helped, and while this assignment did her already considerable profile no harm at all, I looked forward to a more effective and productive relationship with the press.

I was also determined that if we did not always win affection, no one would beat us in terms of rapid response. I drummed into my team that while virtue and influence were important, ceaseless on-message, quality communication was a non-negotiable. Although some complained of our output, there was general consensus that the DA media operation was the most efficient and effective in parliament. While not every DA MP could rise to the rather modest demand for quick, informed comment, the lacunae were filled by the prodigious and relentless Gareth van Onselen, head of communications, and my own amiable communications head, Martin Slabbert – perhaps less gruff and abrupt than me.

There was also a corresponding changing – or reinforcement – of the guard among the parliamentary press. 'Juniorisation' started to give way to professionalism. A strong signal of this was the new parliamentary editor appointed by the Independent group, Angela Quintal. While considerably to the Left of the DA (and even of the ANC), she was a thoroughgoing professional: she understood, and sought out, news priorities; she played with a straight bat; and she sorted out errors and miscommunications.

The elevation of Peet Kruger, with whom I had a good professional relationship, to the editorship of *Beeld* opened up space in the parliamentary realm for two of the best-informed, toughest-minded political journalists of them all: Jan-Jan Joubert and Willem Jordaan. I often discovered more about events in my own party from them than from party insiders. Generally, they wrote pieces with accuracy and thoughtful intelligence. Other reporters such as Carol Paton, Wyndham Hartley, Linda Ensor, Brendan Boyle, Sue Segar and Mpumelelo Mkhabela could also be counted on to 'get the story right' – even if it contradicted, as it often did, my own partisan prejudices.

This goes to the heart of the issue. A free press in a democratic society should not treat political leaders with deference, but with defiance and even disdain if necessary. There is a story recounted by Jeremy Paxman of John Major's travails with the media, after Britain's ignominious, forced exit from the European exchange rate mechanism:

'On the night of black Wednesday, Kelvin Mackenzie, the editor of the *Sun*, rang [Major], Her Majesty's First Lord of the Treasury, the heir of Walpole, Peel, Gladstone, and Churchill, and told "John" breezily, "I'm holding a bucket of shit and tomorrow I'm going to throw it over your head."'[46]

Certainly, during the period I describe above, no South African editor dared to challenge the head of government, Thabo Mbeki, in these or in even slightly more decorous terms. Many were in thrall to a localised version of what the Albanian writer Ismail Kadare described as 'the obligatory optimism of socialist-society'. However, by 2007 I was pleased to note the emergence (particularly in the *Sunday Times* of Mondli Makhanya, and Barney Mthombothi's *Financial Mail*) of just such a no-holds-barred style. Our democracy deserves no less.

7

I have outlined my own, highly personalised account of the shifting relationship between the party and the print media. However, this privately owned sector was quite clearly entitled to its own prejudices and perspectives. A different set of considerations prevailed in respect of the public broadcaster, the SABC, especially the television service. Matters have changed radically since 1991 when the *Columbia Journalism Review* was moved to observe: 'Just as South African politics have opened up in the past two years, so has the SABC. Once-demonised politicians like African National Congress leader Nelson Mandela appear regularly on the air, and talk shows include representatives of South Africa's broad political spectrum, from communists to neo-Nazis.'[47]

By 2007 the status quo ante had been triumphantly restored, and the SABC had again become, in the felicitous words of one of its former staffers (with strong ANC convictions), Pippa Green, 'a political grazing ground for the ruling party faithful'.[48] The intersecting circles of ANC apparatchiks masquerading as broadcasting executives might have been helpful to the ANC's quest for hegemonic control, but it did considerable, perhaps lasting, damage to the state of our constitutional democracy.

I used to joke at party rallies (humour being a necessary antidote to my anger) that 'one of the differences between the presidencies of PW Botha and Thabo Mbeki is that when Botha felt enraged by something on TV news he used to phone the newsroom himself. In Mbeki's case that is quite unnecessary, since the TV news is designed with his total approval in mind.'[49]

In hundreds of campaign meetings and events designed by the party to commemorate public days of political significance (such as Freedom Day), the one constant on which I could generally depend was that SABC-TV would do its best to screw us into the ground. The attempts ranged from the comic to the outrageous. We often designed our events with a newsworthy angle or picture in mind, but the SABC paid little heed. Leading a DP delegation on a tour of the SADC countries, we met Botswana president Festus Mogae in Gaborone; and the event was filmed by the local SABC-TV crew. That night, despite a conspicuous lack of competition from other items, the meeting was neither shown nor referred to. On enquiry, we were advised that 'the tape got lost'.

On another occasion, when I met the king of Sekukuneland in Limpopo, 'technical difficulties' was the explanation proffered for our 'no show' on that evening's bulletin.

By the 2006 municipal elections, the ruling party's capture of the public broadcaster was complete and total. This was well illustrated by the SABC's decision to broadcast live the launch of the ANC election campaign yet totally to fail to provide the same coverage to any opposition party, including, naturally, the DA. As our media director Gareth van Onselen pointed out, this violated both the law and the spirit of the Constitution.

In a memorandum on the saga Van Onselen elaborated: 'Ahead of the local government elections, the Democratic Alliance wrote to the SABC's managing director of news, Dr Snuki Zikalala, to express its dismay at the public broadcaster's decision to broadcast live the ruling party's 8 January statement – effectively, the ANC's programme of action and the launch of its election campaign.'

The SABC did not simply exclude or severely limit opposition coverage on the news; it actively acted as cheerleaders to both the president and ANC cabinet members, no doubt boring viewers stiff with an endless parade of government announcements and opening ceremonies, converting the news into an echo machine of the ANC's worldview. Indeed, this enchantment of government and Mbeki was not confined to its newsrooms. After the 2004 election, it took out a full-page colour ad in all Sunday press titles wishing the president well after his election victory.[50]

Axing footage was one thing, direct news manipulation quite another. The most infamous example was when the SABC-TV censors declined to broadcast the booing of Mbeki's recently appointed deputy president Phumzile Mlambo-Ngcuka at a rally in northern KwaZulu-Natal by enraged Jacob Zuma supporters. My own experiences of such manipulation are legion. Towards the end of the 2006 campaign, it became clear that the DA had – owing to its demographics and good municipal leadership – a real chance of recapturing the Baviaans municipality in the Karoo vastness of the Eastern Cape.

Realistically, it was the only local government area in the province that was a toss-up between the DA and ANC. We planned a huge (by small-town standards) cavalcade culminating in a rally in a tent under the sweltering desert sun at lunch. When we flew in from Port Elizabeth I could scarcely believe my eyes. It seemed that the entire town (overwhelmingly Coloured) had turned out and lined the streets. I was driven through on the back of an open truck in the Karoo equivalent of a triumphal march. Thousands of hands (black and brown) reached out to me. And it was all filmed by SABC-TV.

Of course, that night they did not disappoint. There was a ten-second clip of me speaking and a tiny fragment of me on the back of the truck. They managed to edit out a single shot of the crowd and their supportive cheers. I might as well have been in the studio. (We won the municipality.)

I actually ran into the broadcaster's chief executive, Dali Mpofu, on the floor of the Independent Electoral Commission the day after the municipal elections. I knew him well from his days as a bright young law student whom I had taught at Wits. Clearly I had failed back then to transmit the important maxim *audi alteram partem* (hear the other side). For while we joked and exchanged greetings, I was still seething with anger at the way in which SABC-TV had, characteristically, editorialised and grossly misrepresented my views on minister Alec Erwin's extraordinary claim the day before polling that 'sabotage' at Koeberg power station was the cause of the power outage which had plunged Cape Town into darkness. (Erwin, five months later, incredibly, distanced himself from the remark, blaming 'linguistic difficulties' with the media.)[51] My full remarks relayed to both the wire service SAPA and SABC-TV were (as reported by SAPA):

'Leon expressed shock at what he described as the government's abuse of power in claiming sabotage was behind the recent problems at the Koeberg nuclear plant – which caused intermittent power failures in the Western Cape.

'"People know it is negligence," he said of Public Enterprise minister Alec Erwin's claims on Tuesday. Leon likened it to the apartheid government blaming "unknown elements" whenever anything went wrong.

'Authorities have known for ten years that capacity was going to run out, and blaming sabotage at the eleventh hour before an election was disingenuous, Leon said. "They must put the facts before the people."

'Asked if he thought government was lying, Leon said: "It is the last refuge of a scoundrel." He said there "might be" an element of sabotage involved, but incompetence was clearly to blame.'[52]

Yet the only words of mine which the SABC-TV broadcast were: 'There might be an element of sabotage involved.' (I was, obviously and uncharacteristically, covering my back; but at least indicated the essence of the problem which was soon to darken the whole country.) As I wrote later to Mpofu, SABC-TV 'deliberately distorts and decontextualises my views, usually using a voice-over to drown out my actual words.' It seemed to me a case of Pravda-TV. A follow-up meeting with him led to no change.

When I was interviewed in 2004 by the formidable Tim Sebastian for the BBC-TV current affairs programme 'Hardtalk', I was subjected to extreme third-degree trial-by-television techniques – his hallmark. He was pretty merciless, but I gave as good as I got and despite the gruelling encounter I enjoyed the experience. We both relaxed with a drink afterwards. Sebastian expressed amazement when I told him that our half-hour one-on-one interview (which the BBC broadcast to the world the following week) was more than I had ever been granted on SABC-TV despite, by then, having been South Africa's leader of the opposition for over five years.

The spirit of the takeover of the airwaves – in violation of the Constitution – rubbished the promise made by the ANC on the eve of its ascent to power. In a speech in November 1992 its then secretary-general Cyril Ramaphosa had stated: 'When the ANC wins the electoral support of the majority of South Africans, it will not seek to replace the National Party as the subject of the SABC's slavish loyalty. And we want to establish both the principle and practice of that independence now. The ANC is committed to public broadcasting which is independent of the government of the day, and which owes its loyalty not to any party, but to the population as a whole.'[53]

Famous last words in opposition were easy not to follow when in government.

As with much of the political and social space over which the ANC sought to assert its hegemony, its move on the SABC intensified. Broadly described ANC sympathisers such as Allister Sparks were replaced by outright party loyalists, such as Snuki Zikalala.

Of all those who helped snuff out the last vestiges of independent thought at Auckland Park, Zikalala is worthy of special mention and attention. He was one of the 37 senior ANC leaders who, in 1998, applied for amnesty from the Truth and Reconciliation Commission. He had left South Africa in 1974 to join MK, the ANC's armed wing; learned about bomb-making; and was based in Botswana before moving on to Lusaka and then Bulgaria, where he studied for a doctorate in journalism and worked for a Bulgarian newspaper. He wrote numerous political essays for *Sechaba* and the *African Communist*. He returned after 1990, working as an 'ANC journalist' before joining the SABC.[54]

In May 1998 Zikalala was catapulted from his job as a TV news labour reporter to the position of radio news deputy editor-in-chief. It was stated that his 'major area of focus in his new position will be to concentrate on establishing a single news department in the corporation in preparation for the 1999 election.'[55] In December 1998, once Sparks's contract was up, Zikalala was promoted to deputy editor-in-chief of both radio and television news; and by 1999 SABC news was being run by a triumvirate of ANC loyalists: Enoch Sithole, chief executive of news; Phil Molefe, head of TV news; and Zikalala, deputy editor-in-chief (then head of bi-media news).

An ANC assessment of the 'balance of forces' (published in 1999) noted that the media and public debate were 'critical' centres of power 'because even though we may have made progress in material terms, unless the forces for change are able to exercise hegemony, it will impact on our capacity to mobilise society.' It noted: 'The transformation of the SABC did take much longer than we thought and more needs to be done at middle management level.'

As Myburgh observed: 'There was something of a waning of party control of the broadcaster with the breaking up of the triumvirate in 2001. In that year Sithole resigned, and Zikalala and Molefe were pushed out of their positions following a boardroom reshuffle. Zikalala was then appointed spokesman for the minister of Labour. Although the SABC news could still hardly be described as non-partisan (its sympathies were firmly with the ruling party) there was some loosening up, and the opposition Democratic Alliance received relatively fair coverage during the 2004 national elections. However, in May 2004, after the SABC board was packed with Mbeki-loyalists, Zikalala returned as head of television news.'

In mid-2006, there was an uproar when it was revealed that a blacklist existed of certain public and political commentators who had been axed from appearing on the SABC because of their lack of political deference to the ANC and the party line. While Zikalala and his apparatchiks received most of the blame, a fair portion of the guilt vests with the SABC board itself. Take the metamorphosis of a key member, Thami Mazwai, from brave independent journalist in the 1980s to fully fledged party hack by the mid-2000s. His was a sad but illustrative journey of one whose once proclaimed and secure principles were steadily loosened to meet the requirements of government. He had also become a foremost member of the new class of race-holding rent-seekers, perhaps explaining the shift.

I noted at the time:[56] 'As a fairly prolific journalist in the 1980s and 1990s – mainly or *Business Day* and the *Sowetan* – Mazwai often wrote about the tenets of press freedom, warned against government interference, and highlighted the dangers of political bias in news reporting.

'His columns and articles are filled with such examples. In *Business Day* he wrote in 1990: "We believe that by being independent of any political bias we will best serve South Africa. From that position we will be able to criticise fairly and objectively. Our readers will be the ultimate judges. Freedom of the press is indivisible. It does not change from situation to situation, neither is suppression of the media by a black government less severe than that from a white government. Both abuse my rights as a human being."

'The following year, this time in *Finance Week*, he was even more explicit: "We should not, as professional journalists, proclaim membership or loyalty to political parties publicly. Nor should we be officials of these organisations. This affects our credibility and that of the publications we work for ..." And in 1992 he argued in the *Sowetan* that private media should never be state-funded, because "in no time the newspaper finds itself the mouthpiece of the government or any political organisation giving it funds."'

The bridge between the old Thami Mazwai and the new is perhaps best illustrated by a call he made in June 1995, as the national chairman of the Black Editors Forum, for the (ANC contingent of the) GNU to be given free airtime by the SABC. Why? Because: 'We cannot let the "media mafia" get away with consciously and unconsciously trying to compromise black political organisations which might allow FW de Klerk to spring back as a knight in shining armour because black governance has supposedly failed.'

From there on the slide rapidly increased pace. Objectivity, which he previously identified as a central tenet of an independent press, became 'an old cliché' that 'no longer addresses the challenges of the day.' The SABC's job was 'to interpret the bill of rights in African terms' and to 'inculcate national and continental pride.' As for political affiliations – this is what Mazwai told the *Mail&Guardian* about Zikalala:

'What I find disconcerting is that one of the allegations is that [Snuki] is ANC. What's that got to do with the price of mielie meal?' So much for professional journalists never proclaiming loyalty to political parties.

This dismal saga has no happy ending. At the time of writing, Auckland Park has more or less been surrendered to ANC control. Much of the narrative in my book focuses on how the governing party's desire for 'total control' makes it an uneasy, albeit dominant partner in a constitutional order premised on the foundation of an open society. Perhaps this ambition was too lofty and idealistic. But if our democracy is to take proper root and flourish, the fight for media freedom, and the unmuzzling of a multitude of viewpoints which have been silenced and sidelined, needs to be renewed and replenished.

CHAPTER 13

Tangling with 'The Lady'

Laws are like cobwebs, which may catch small flies,
but let wasps and hornets break through.
JONATHAN SWIFT

I

From my earliest political stirrings, Winnie Madikizela-Mandela emblazoned herself on my consciousness as an iconic figure in the liberation
struggle. The strikingly beautiful second wife of Nelson Mandela, she was
in earlier life a tragic and defiant heroine. Her husband sentenced to life
imprisonment on far-off (from Soweto) Robben Island, she epitomised
the incarnation and victimisation of black resistance. Unbowed by the
vicissitudes of her life, fiery in her response to the apartheid state and its
repressive apparatus, she struck me – and much of the world – as brave
and admirable; a profile in courage. With Mandela imprisoned she perforce became the single mother of two young daughters and was subject
to over twenty years of official harassment. In 1969 she served 17 months
in prison, and in the 1980s, in the wake of the Soweto uprising, she was
banned and forced into internal exile – banished to the tiny and isolated
Free State town of Brandfort.

If the intention of the state had been to decrease her visibility and
prominence, it had the reverse effect. Brandfort became a sort of political
Lourdes. Every visiting or local celebrity, from Senator Edward Kennedy
to Helen Suzman, stopped to visit and be photographed with the 'Mother
of the Nation'. Then came the turnaround.

By 1986, she simply disregarded her banning order and returned to
Soweto. Here she soon moved into palatial accommodation, built to her
specifications and apparently bankrolled by a black American businessman, who claimed he had been given, in exchange, the copyright to the
Mandela name.[1]

The first negative shock on the public's radar occurred two months after I became a Johannesburg city councillor. At a funeral in April 1986 she proclaimed, in a paragraph of incendiary infamy: 'Together, hand in hand, with our boxes of matches and our necklaces, we shall liberate this country.' As Tony Karon, then a local Left luminary, who at one stage edited the Marxist *New Era*, recounted, it was only four years later that she told talk show host Phil Donahue on US television that she had been quoted out of context. But as he put it, 'not even the most breathtaking rhetorical gymnastics could alter what she had said – a crisp, clear sound bite captured on tape for all time.'

Hardly novices in the dark arts of political propaganda, the National Party obliged in the 1987 election by using an image (they were prevented by copyright from publishing the original photo) of Helen Suzman embracing Winnie, with the infamous quote. This neatly paired the extremely non-violent PFP with Winnie's inflammatory words. Such was her allure, or spell, that even the Grande Dame of Houghton could not bring herself to repudiate her friend. The PFP was immolated at the polls that year.

The occasional press report surfaced on the activities of Winnie's personal phalanx of bodyguards, who rejoiced in the spectacular misnomer of the 'Mandela United Football Club'. They appeared to relish contact sports unrelated to soccer; and it was the murder of 14-year-old James Moeketsi Seipei, known as 'Stompie', which catapulted her and the thuggish 'footballers' into world headlines. On 15 February 1989, Stompie's decomposed body was positively identified. The next day, Murphy Morobe, a leading light in the Mass Democratic Movement (MDM), successor to the United Democratic Front and once more the ANC's doppelganger, voiced a stunning condemnation:

'In recent years, Mrs Mandela's actions have increasingly led her into conflict with various sections of the oppressed people and with the Mass Democratic Movement as a whole. The recent conflict in the community has centred largely on the conduct of her so-called Football Club, which has been widely condemned by the community. In particular, we are outraged by the reign of terror that the team has been associated with.'[2]

This was one of the very few occasions when the struggle code of no-questions-asked solidarity was decisively broken. There was a serious struggle within the struggle. It transpired that Stompie and four others had been kidnapped from the Methodist manse in Soweto and taken to Mandela's home where he was beaten senseless. Eight months after his body was found, Jerry Richardson – the coach of the club – was sentenced to death for the murder. However, in passing judgment, Mr Justice

O'Donovan held: 'Mrs Mandela punched and slapped each of them [the abductees, including Stompie] and called for a sjambok to be brought to her. Each of the four was beaten by Winnie Mandela.'[3]

A consequence was that the attorney-general of the Witwatersrand announced in September 1990 that Mandela herself would now face eight charges relating to the abduction and death of Stompie. However, the clear blue water which the MDM had attempted to place between it and the Lady was muddied by the ANC when it was unbanned earlier that year. Seemingly oblivious to the rotten foundation on which they were reincarnating their now legal movement, by August 1990 the Congress had awarded Winnie Mandela one of their plum positions: head of its social welfare department! Clearly her Eva Peron-like status with the masses precluded circumspection or caution.

At this time, in my first year as an MP, I met an extraordinary British journalist, John Carlin, who headed the London *Independent*'s bureau in Johannesburg. Hirsute and bespectacled, he was an arresting figure – with a string of beautiful girlfriends – who seemed better informed and more familiar with the tangled inner workings of the ANC and their external war with Inkatha than other writers; nor was it simply that Carlin had information, or the stock-in-trade of recycled gossip: his ground-breaking background research was of a calibre that set his reportage significantly apart from that of his competitors.

Carlin told me he was preparing a radio programme for 'File on Four' in Britain and a companion article for the *Independent* which, he assured me, 'would blow the lid on Winnie's nefarious activities.' When he subsequently gave me a copy of the tape of the programme – and the *Independent* piece entitled 'Terrorised by Winnie's Boys' – I realised his claim was an astonishing understatement. Here in gory and meticulous detail was the unmasking of Winnie Mandela as a sort of Madam Defarge on steroids, with a Sartre-Fanon-like penchant for gratuitous violence and terror. His chronicle revealed that Stompie's murder was merely the visible tip of a blood-soaked iceberg. Carlin's article was noteworthy not simply for its content, but also for the reaction, or more precisely the non-reaction, to it by Mrs Mandela and her lawyers. Generally – in the face of potentially defamatory and damaging publicity – the Lady either sued for defamation, or used the threat of legal proceedings to silence or intimidate her critics.

Now, however, the damning and detailed account in Carlin's piece and broadcast drew only silence – and no rebuttal – from Winnie or 'her boys'. In fact, about seven years later, the Truth and Reconciliation Commission's Special Investigation Unit confirmed most of the detail of the report (and drew attention to a number of other brutal incidents). Carlin had lifted the veil on the 'Football Club', and Winnie Mandela's role as lynchpin-patron. It was a chronicle of abuse, torture, kidnapping and murder. Most ominously, it also revealed a record of under-prosecution or calling to judicial account of Winnie Mandela by the state prosecuting authorities. As Carlin summarised his findings:

'We spoke to the relatives and the victims of attacks by a Football Club hit squad; to the mother whose daughter died in a revenge attack led by a prominent club member; and to a father who says he last saw his badly beaten son nearly two years ago being driven away by Mrs Mandela and members of the club. We learned that three former Football Club members are on Pretoria's death row, having committed 12 murders among them ... we heard about beatings allegedly handed out by club members at Mrs Mandela's home.'[4]

That home operated as a sort of informal court 'for all manner of social miscreants in the area, from car thieves to police informers'. During the heyday of the club, one of 'the boys' would enter details of an offence reported to her, and then Winnie – presumably operating as judge-prosecutor – would decide if the 'accused' should be summoned. In a detailed interview with one of the club's founders, Lerothodi Ikaneng: '[At] the house there was a kind of court in the yard. Winnie would come out of the house and listen to the case with other members of the "disciplinary committee" [also club members]. [She] might leave before the end of proceedings, but they would always tell her what they had decided. The punishment for anti-social behaviour was normally lashes, but for more serious crimes like car theft, it was lashes, kicks and punches. I lost count how many beatings there were.'

Ikaneng himself fell foul, in due course, of both the club and its patron. He was accused (and given the lethal appellation) of being a police spy. He was summarily hauled before Winnie, who 'lifted me up by the front of my shirt and hit me with punches and slaps, then she summonsed [two other club members] and told them to take me to her other home [the mansion] in Diepkloof Extension.'

He escaped and remained at large for 14 months. However, the week before Stompie's murder, the boy's killer, the heinous Jerry Richardson, accompanied by ten others, came across Ikaneng 'in a back street' and assaulted him with the blade of a garden shears which Richardson plunged into his neck. He was left for dead, but survived. Richardson was eventually convicted of attempted murder, but since Stompie was sucking all the oxygen out of the mediasphere, Ikaneng's saga got little attention.

Carlin exposed Mrs Mandela in the harshest and most savage light, and cast aspersions on the state's laconic, if not deliberately lax, approach to charging her, or at least calling her to testify in respect of serious crimes which she would have witnessed.

The first (February 1988) related to the murder by club member Oupa Seheri of two people in a Soweto shebeen. He was convicted and given the death sentence. The court record, read and reproduced by Carlin, revealed that the prosecution and defence had 'reached agreement' on a string of facts linking Winnie Mandela's home and car to the murders; and that her daughter Zinzi's bedroom had been used as a 'safe place' for the murder weapon. As Carlin put it: '[Curiously] neither Mrs Mandela nor her daughter was even called as witnesses at the trial. Not for the first time, as was to emerge later, Mrs Mandela was spared the indignity and the possible dangers of a court appearance after the defence and prosecution reached agreement on writing the admissions recording Winnie Mandela's home and car into the record.'

With perhaps one exception, scarcely a word of her involvement in this crime ever, to the best of my knowledge or memory, appeared in the local media at the time of the trial, presumably because the details were never aired in open court.[5]

The next bloody chapter came just three days before the MDM denounced Mrs Mandela (and might well, along with Stompie's murder, have triggered their decision). This time the victim was a leading 'Football Club' member, Maxwell Madondo. His killer, convicted of murder, was one Sibusiso Chili – who received the unbelievably light sentence of a year in jail. The judge's leniency was almost entirely based on what Carlin called 'the most incriminating piece of evidence against Mrs Mandela ever heard in court – evidence amazingly never reported in the South African press.'

When Chili and five others (among them Lerothodi Ikaneng) were charged with Madondo's murder, the defence announced that it intended to call two witnesses, one of whom, Katiza Cebekhulu, was to be writ large in the Stompie trial (and in my own later investigations). Cebekhulu, it was said, had made the statement that Mrs Mandela had chaired the meeting ordering the killing of Chili and Ikaneng. The state declined to call Cebekhulu, agreeing to a statement which the defence placed on record: 'The admission that the state will make is that the deceased Maxwell Madondo was a member of the Football Club and that a decision was made by Mrs Mandela and the Football Club to kill accused No. 1 [Chili] and accused No. 6 [Ikaneng].' While Chili received only a

12-month sentence, Ikaneng was acquitted, and another accused, Dudu Chili (mother of Sibusiso), had all charges against her withdrawn.

Mrs Chili, a senior ANC Women's League campaigner, was especially significant, as I would reveal to parliament six years later. The reason for her discharge was that a day after Madondo's murder, her home was petrol-bombed – according to her by 'Winnie's boys' – and her niece Finky Msoni killed in the blaze. (In due course, a Football Club activist, Charles Zwani, was sentenced to death for the child's death.)

By the time, then, of the article's appearance, Zwani, Seheri and Richardson were all on death row. Yet, incredibly, not one of them had implicated Mrs Mandela in their misdemeanours. (Mrs Chili had no such compunction.)

Carlin told me that the most outrageous act of violence concerned the case of Lolo Sono. Mary Tudor is reputed to have said, 'When I am dead and opened you shall find Calais lying in my heart.' In Carlin's view, for Winnie Mandela the words should be 'Lolo Sono', who disappeared on 12 October 1988. He was last seen, severely beaten, in the company of Mrs Mandela and members of the Football Club. Four days before his disappearance, two ANC-trained guerrillas were killed in a shootout with the police at the home of Jerry Richardson. Sono had been spending time at Mrs Mandela's home on many occasions. According to his father, Nicodemus, Winnie Mandela turned up outside the Sono home in Soweto in a Kombi on the last day (12 October) that he ever saw his son. He went out to talk to her, and she told him she did not trust Lolo; she thought 'he and a friend were police spies' – presumably implicated in the shootout.

Sono Snr told the *Independent*: 'I then saw Lolo in the back of the Kombi ... his eyes were swelling up. He was badly beaten. Now I tried to plead with her that, "OK, you can leave him with me." She said, "No, I'm not going to leave him, I'm taking him with me – the movement will see what to do." And when Lolo tried to talk, she kept telling him to "shut up". Then Winnie said they are taking him away. That's all she told me ...'

Sono told all this to the police. I accompanied him eight years later when he repeated the same harrowing story to the Truth and Reconciliation Commission, and personally interviewed the first post-1994 police commissioner, George Fivaz, on the matter. But to date, Lolo Sono has never been found, no body has been identified, and no one has been charged with either his abduction or his murder.

'Reign of Terror' seemed a lapidary metaphor for this chain of events. My parliamentary colleague, Lester Fuchs, and I were determined to use parliament to probe the minister of Justice, Kobie Coetsee, on the state's serial lapses in following up on the various cases in which Winnie escaped notice as either a witness or an accused. However, before we could do so, the cause célèbre in which she did indeed appear in the dock surfaced in public view: her trial, in relation to the abduction and murder of Stompie Seipei. Various youths had been accused – by Winnie – of engaging in sexual relations with Reverend Paul Verryn, the minister who ran the manse, and Seipei had been singled out as a police spy. All four were assaulted, Seipei fatally. The accusation against Verryn was never remotely proved, nor was any evidence offered to support the accusation.

Before the trial got under way in February 1991, two key witnesses, Gabriel Mekwe and Katiza Cebekhulu, disappeared. Cebekhulu – co-accused with Winnie – had apparently been whisked out of the country as early as December 1988. For inexplicable reasons, he landed in jail in Zambia, from where he was later rescued by British politician Baroness Emma Nicholson. Cebekhulu was also a key witness in the mysterious murder of the Soweto physician, Dr Abu Baker Asvat. Asvat was gunned down in his surgery in January 1987. Significantly, he had examined Stompie after his brutal assault.

Cebekhulu later claimed that Mrs Mandela was responsible for Asvat's murder. The prosecutor in the case that arose out of the killing – for which one TJ Dlamini was convicted – subsequently stated: 'My gut feeling all along was that there was something very strange about the Asvat killing. It was just too much of a coincidence. I just had the feeling that this was not an armed robbery or a murder, but an assassination. But we never had any hard information.'[6]

Cebekhulu's disappearance was a forerunner of things to come. The other key witness, Mekgwe, was kidnapped on the eve of trial, and two of the other kidnapped boys 'rescued' by Winnie from the manse along with Stompie (Thabiso Mono and Kenny Kgase) initially refused to testify. The generally ANC-leaning *Weekly Mail* declared: 'The prosecution did not know where its key witnesses were, and seemed unconcerned at its lack of knowledge.'

In an article I wrote about the trial, I said: 'Initially the ANC response to Mrs Mandela's prosecution was properly restrained. Its September 1990 statement simply noted that Mrs Mandela would remain as head of their social welfare department, but that "there would be no further comment". Yet comment the ANC certainly did. In a decisive intervention, on the eve of trial Secretary-General Alfred Nzo proclaimed, "It is the ANC which is on trial." He also accused the government of "violating the spirit of the agreements between ANC [and themselves]." In fact, had the state not prosecuted Mrs Mandela it would have been accused of overt political interference. But the ANC also threw hordes of demonstrators into the streets outside the Supreme Court in Johannesburg, and a legal friend said that what he witnessed "resembled elements of street theatre, a political rally, and a three-ring circus."'

Eventually, two of the recalcitrant witnesses testified (although Cebekhulu remained in Zambia) and notwithstanding the presence of ANC luminaries such as Nelson Mandela, Joe Slovo, Jay Naidoo and Chris Hani in the courtroom, Justice Stegmann duly convicted Mrs Mandela on four charges of kidnapping and being an accessory to assault.

In his inimitable fashion, Carlin wrote: 'She emerged with a broad smile of triumph, her fist raised in the air in response to the muted cheers of barely a hundred supporters. Nelson Mandela, who had taken a day off from attending to the nation's catastrophic affairs to be at his wife's side, looked as if his mother had just died.'[7]

Winnie was subsequently sentenced to four years in prison. Judge Stegmann called her 'an unblushing and unprincipled liar' – 'the moving force' behind the kidnappings. She immediately appealed.

Meanwhile, from sources deep within the Department of Justice, Lester Fuchs and I received fragments of information corroborating the *Weekly Mail's* and Carlin's thesis that the state (presumably on instructions from Kobie Coetsee) had prosecuted Mrs Mandela with great reluctance and had not investigated with any precision or zeal numerous other criminal matters. It was suggested that there was a deep concern in high government circles that if the law fell too heavily on her, the entire negotiations project – and its then-dim prospects of success – could unravel. A friend – both a lawyer and close to the ANC – made the cynical aside that 'the elite looks after its own, and don't doubt Mrs Mandela's membership of it.'

I also knew that Coetsee, who had brokered the government's first meetings with Nelson Mandela when he was still a prisoner, had arrived in this role through his relationship with her then-attorney in Brandfort, in Coetsee's home province. As Britain's Master of the Rolls, Lord Denning, once suggested, 'The arm of coincidence might be long, but it does not stretch unto infinity.'

When parliament convened the year after her initial conviction, Fuchs probed Coetsee on various matters relating to Winnie. Certain statements had appeared in the media, from various witnesses (post-conviction) that Mrs Mandela had concocted her alibi – which conveniently placed her in Brandfort at crucial times during the kidnapping of Stompie and the others. Fuchs asked whether the minister of Justice intended to reopen the criminal case against her. Coetsee obfuscated: 'The matter is *sub judice* [in view of Mandela's pending appeal against her conviction and sentence] and the requested information can therefore not be furnished.' He told parliament the police were examining 'certain allegations' which 'may affect the outcome of the investigation.'[8]

Needless to say, the 'investigation' led nowhere. After the appeal was disposed of by the Appellate Division over a year later, Coetsee did nothing to reopen the case.

A week later, at question time, Lester asked Coetsee whether investigations into the disappearance of the key witnesses – Cebekhulu and Mekwe – had been investigated, and whether any person or political party (i.e. elements of the ANC) was suspected of ensuring their 'non-attendance' at Mandela's trial, and whether any prosecutions would be instituted.

Coetsee confirmed that Cebekhulu was 'currently being detained in Zambia' and that Mekwe's whereabouts were unknown. The police 'were not able to gather any concrete, relevant and admissible evidence' linking anyone to Cebekhulu's disappearance.

A year or so later, the Appellate Division confirmed her conviction on the kidnapping charge, but substituted Mrs Mandela's jail sentence with a fine of R15 000. As the party spokesman on Justice at the time, I used a debate in parliament, a week after the Appellate decision, to describe the sentence as 'so lenient it induces a sense of shock.' Naturally, this led to a rebuke from one of the Appellate Division judges, who took it on himself to telephone me in my office and remonstrate with my views on the (correct) basis that I had not 'read the full judgment and had relied on media reports of it.'

I countered by saying that since kidnapping was a capital offence, a fine of R15 000 was 'paltry'. There was no doubt that Mrs Mandela's good fortune was hugely assisted by crucial witnesses 'disappearing', a sloppy and incomplete prosecution, and the clear, but covert, pressure brought to bear by the ruling establishment. What was noteworthy was that she never once dismissed her prosecution or sentence as 'political'. This was significant, given what was to follow.

In January 1994, the ANC placed Winnie high on their list of candidates for election to South Africa's first democratic parliament. The ANC decision violated one of its proclaimed principles: that common law criminals were barred from seeking public office. The movement dubbed her conviction for kidnapping as a 'political offence'.

As the DP's leader in the PWV (later named Gauteng) province I laid into the ANC: 'It is frankly startling that the ANC NEC has turned itself into a new high court … [It has] rubbished the Appellate Division which six months ago dismissed her appeal against her conviction on four counts of kidnapping.'

Yet when Winnie and I were sworn in as MPs after the April election, I was taken aback that despite my serial denouncements, she sought me out, threw her arms around me and burbled: 'We must get to know each other better!' I awkwardly hugged her back.

Mandela was on an upward trajectory. She was named as the deputy minister of Arts, Culture, Science and Technology, a benign enough portfolio; and her appointment was justified to me by an ANC heavy who invoked Lyndon Johnson's aphorism: 'It's better to have her on the inside of the tent pissing out, rather than the other way around.'

However, while she gadded around the world attending film festivals and the like, it did not take long for the old Winnie to re-emerge. In August 1994, she chose a Women's Day debate in parliament to issue (using parliamentary privilege) a ferocious attack on the 'apartheid courts' and their temerity in daring to judge her by 'white standards'. Her kidnapping conviction was scoffed: 'I was found guilty of kidnapping by those apartheid courts which were a disgrace to our judiciary.'[9] The head of the court which convicted her, Chief Justice Mick Corbett, had recently sworn in her husband as president, and had, together with his colleagues, retained his position in post-apartheid South Africa.

This was her response to my querying her fitness for office: 'There are men in this gathering who, in the calm of their Houghtons, literally fiddled and mounted the steps of power while our townships burnt and who today dare to question my membership of this august house.' As for the period of the Football Club, 'I lived in the terror of those times, and was repeatedly burnt by its fires. I did not flinch … though the press pursued me like a bloodhound.'

As she spoke, I was traipsing around the Northern Cape attempting to revive the party's depleted structures and political fortunes. However, I was determined to take her on at a speech in Kimberley. Not for the first time, though, my desire to get even with a detractor and get a headline led me to construct a trap for myself further down the line. I duly denounced her performance as constituting 'one of the most stupefying pieces of self-serving hypocrisy yet heard in the Chamber'; and announced my intention of raising 'serious questions' in the forthcoming budget debate on the Department of Justice. My tactical stupidity lay in giving the ANC notice of the counter-attack.

In the debate on Friday afternoon, 26 August 1994, the ANC front bench was better populated with ministers than such an obscure event would normally attract. The DP parliamentary team consisted of only six MPs in addition to me, and only one, Dene Smuts, would be with me for the debate. Early on the morning of the debate I set out to put the finishing touches to my speech – which by now included talks with some of the family members of victims of the Mandela Football Club, including the Sono and Chili families. My conversation with Dudu Chili that morning was even more revealing than Carlin's exposé four years previously.

My speech for parliament related to the events, cited above, around and about the murder of Maxwell Madondo. As Mrs Chili put it to me: 'Members of my family have systematically been hounded, harassed and ruined by Winnie Mandela ... my niece was firebombed and killed in my home on instructions of Mrs Mandela.' In a police raid on 20 February 1989 on Mrs Mandela's home (a fact disclosed and elaborated on at the trial of her son Sibusiso, one of the co-accused for the murder of Maxwell Madondo), a 'death list' containing eleven names – including three of her children – was unearthed. Yet no charges were ever brought against Winnie Mandela on this issue, but I never got that far in my speech. What I did read into the record was the following:

'Only this morning I had a conversation with long-time ANC activist Dudu Chili, who told me that her son was convicted on a charge of murder. She told me of the occasion in February 1989 when a member of the football team known as Dodo came to see her. He told her that Mrs Mandela had just finished chairing a meeting at which it had been decided that Dudu Chili's son, Sibusiso Chili, and Lerothodi Ikaneng should be eliminated. As a consequence of that and an assault on them by the football team, one of the members of the football team was murdered.'[10]

I managed to inform parliament of Winnie's role in the disappearance of Lolo Sono; the attempted murder of Lerothodi Ikaneng; and her serious conflict with the Mass Democratic Movement. But my address was interrupted on ten points of order from such luminaries as Thabo Mbeki's hatchet man, Essop Pahad, ANC whip Tony Yengeni, and the then-chairman of the Justice Committee, Johnny de Lange. In my one stroke of luck, that afternoon's presiding officer was not Frene Ginwala, the Speaker, who could be at times a fierce ANC partisan, but her deputy, Dr Bhadra Ranchod, a lawyer, and perhaps more importantly from my perspective, a member of the National Party. He was disinclined to allow any of the mostly spurious points of order to be entertained.

But the interruptions and heckling meant I could not quite finish and had to spend time answering the points raised. I was able to state that Mrs Mandela had on many occasions been protected by the apartheid regime: 'Mrs Mandela chose in her speech to address only the question of Stompie Seipei and his murder and kidnapping, dismissing her criminal convictions on the self-serving basis that she ... "was found guilty of kidnapping by those apartheid courts which were a disgrace to our judiciary."'

I went on to charge that court records, press reports and interviews suggested a 'string of unsolved crimes, unpunished offenders and a deliberate under-prosecution or laconic police work in all matters with which Mrs Mandela's name was associated since 1986.'[11]

My speech caused a sensation, as did the ANC's attempts to disrupt it. It was the first item on that night's TV news (this was before the ANC's takeover of the SABC board and editorial staff), while the next morning's *Weekend Argus* led with the headline: 'ANC Covers Winnie's Tracks As Leon speaks'. Journalist John Maclennan wrote: 'Members of the ANC launched a cover-up in parliament of Mrs Winnie Mandela's past by attempting to shout down DP leader Tony Leon ...

'Justice minister Dullah Omar said he would not dignify the "tirade" with a reply because Mr Leon was clearly seeking headlines. It is obvious, however, that Mrs Mandela's role is a very sore spot for ANC members who want to reflect an image of clean and respectable government. Questioned after the debate, one senior source said: "I just cannot bring myself to talk about her."'[12]

3

The ANC's laager around Winnie in public did not prevent several MPs from approaching me privately, or indeed via cupped hand, in parliament itself, and congratulating me on my 'exposé' of Winnie. Chief among the Lady's antagonists on the ANC benches was Limpho Hani, widow of the more famous Chris, with whom I was, for a while, quite friendly. Her dislike of Winnie was visceral, and she urged me to pursue matters.

By this time, I was in frequent contact with several of the families who had suffered the consequences, including the Asvats and the Sonos. However, one of the missing pieces in the puzzle, Katiza Cebekhulu, had resurfaced in Britain under the protection of Baroness Nicholson. A British journalist, Fred Bridgland, whom I knew, had written a harrowing account based on Cebekhulu's account of Stompie's murder and other elements in the chamber of horrors at the Mandela house in Soweto.

Among his more startling allegations, which were later published in a book – with independent corroboration – was that Winnie's alibi at her 1991 trial was fabricated by one of her lovers, whose affair with her precipitated divorce proceedings by President Nelson Mandela. The book also contained evidence from Albertina Sisulu showing that Mrs Mandela could not have been in Brandfort – as she asserted – at the time of the assaults on Stompie and others. So why had the police force not opened dockets against several people for perjury?[13]

Cebekhulu had been asserting since 1989 that he saw Mrs Mandela stab Stompie – in direct contrast to new evidence to the TRC of 'chief coach' Jerry Richardson, that Mrs Mandela ordered Stompie's murder and he, Richardson, had carried it out.

Bridgland told me Emma Nicholson was the key to Cebekhulu, but she was difficult and cagey, and had placed herself as a 'firewall' between Cebekhulu and the world. In March 1995 I visited London as a guest of the British Conservative Party. Our then head of parliamentary services, Robert Desmarais, secured an interview with Mrs Nicholson, as she then was (she later defected from the Conservatives to the Liberal Democrats and was seated in the House of Lords as Baroness Nicholson). I found her strange and odd; she was deaf, lip-read, and spoke in a booming voice. While she had indeed secured Cebekhulu's release from jail in Zambia and arranged his safe passage to Britain (where he was kept in a safe house), she adamantly refused to let me see him or speak to him. She insisted on 'assurances' from the South African authorities before she allowed either the police or the Truth Commission investigators to interview him.

On my return I contacted the national commissioner of police, General George Fivaz, who undertook to follow matters up. He sent a team to London later that year to interview Cebekhulu. The following year, I received a definitive response from him. Cebekhulu was an unreliable witness (to put it mildly) whose knowledge of Asvat's murder was based on hearsay; and he had given no fewer than 'four different versions' of the event. As far as all the other matters to which Winnie had been linked, he wrote: 'The attorney-general has been consulted concerning all the cases and is of the opinion that only in the event of new evidence coming to light, will he consider instituting criminal proceedings against Mrs Mandela, the only exception being the case concerning Mr Sono.'

The attorney-general had indicated that if the body was found, he would institute criminal proceedings. 'A possible site where Mr Sono was allegedly buried was pointed out to the South African Police Service. The site was thoroughly searched twice, aided by excavators and police dogs, but to no avail.'[14]

Cebekhulu's claims were clearly not sustainable. In July 1996 the Truth Commission initiated hearings in Soweto into the affairs of the Football Club and the conduct of Winnie Mandela. Forty-three witnesses gave evidence – including perpetrators; victims; former members of the Mandela United Football Club; other members of the Mandela household; her co-accused in the Stompie trial; religious and community members; and the South African Police Service and Security Branch. Mrs Mandela herself gave evidence – under subpoena – on the last day of the hearing. At his request, I accompanied Nicodemus Sono to the TRC. He gave his evidence in clear, sorrowful terms: evidence which went unchallenged by either Mandela's lawyers or members of the TRC.

The TRC transcript was a complete vindication of Carlin's article of six years before, of Nicodemus Sono's quiet but determined quest for justice; and a total damnation of Winnie Mandela and her cohorts in the Football Club. In all its gory detail, it read:

'Mr Sono testified that on Sunday 13 November, Mr Michael Siyakamela, Ms Madikizela-Mandela's temporary driver, came to his house. He was told that someone wanted to see him. When he went out, he saw Lolo sitting in the back of the minibus, with Madikizela-Mandela in the front seat. Lolo's face was swollen and bruised. Sono testified that Madikizela-Mandela informed him that Lolo was a police spy and that the MK cadres at Jerry Richardson's house had been killed because of him. Despite his pleas to Madikizela-Mandela to release his son, Lolo was taken away. Madikizela-Mandela allegedly told him: "I am taking this dog away. The movement will see what to do to him."

'This was the last time that Sono saw his son.'[15]

The commission heard and recorded further, intricate, devastating evidence of the terrible aura surrounding Mrs Mandela; and that, further, she had to 'accept responsibility for the disappearance of Lolo Sono' and one other. Members of the Soweto police were 'negligent in their duty': had they taken quick and decisive action the murders might have been averted. Most damning of all was the conclusion relating to her alibi during the

Stompie trial: 'The Commission finds further that Madikizela-Mandela was present at her home and not in Brandfort as submitted in her trial, and that she was present during the assaults, and initiated and participated in the assaults.'[16]

Of the subsequent killing of Stompie Seipei in January 1988, the TRC noted it had received three different versions of the events which led to his untimely death, of which a startling conclusion which could possibly be drawn was that Richardson killed Seipei because he (Seipei) had found out that Richardson was an informer.

The Commission concluded, in the light of what it termed 'corroborative testimony' placing Mandela on the scene and implicated in the assaults, that 'in all probability' she was aware of Stompie's grievous injuries, was responsible for his abduction, and had 'failed to act responsibly in taking the necessary action required to avert his death.'[17]

This single paragraph destroyed the alibi, the acceptance of which by the Appellate Division three years previously had kept her out of jail. Given that the TRC was headed by Archbishop Desmond Tutu and consisted, in the main, of persons of both eminence and strong allegiance to the ANC, its impression of Mrs Mandela's own evidence was less than complimentary:

'Ms Madikizela-Mandela's testimony before the Commission was characterised by a blanket denial of all allegations against her and of the attempts by the community leadership to defuse the situation arising from the abduction debacle. A detailed examination of some of these denials is contained in the investigation report. The picture that she sought to paint of herself was that she was right and everybody else was wrong. She called her former associates "ludicrous" and "ridiculous" and failed to recognise that these were the same individuals who had tried to support her in the face of criticism from community leaders.'

She refused to take responsibility for any wrongdoing. It was only at the end of her testimony, under great pressure from Archbishop Tutu, presiding over the proceedings, that she reluctantly conceded that 'things had gone horribly wrong.'[18]

On her culpability for the string of crimes which its investigations had unearthed, the TRC's conclusion was both unequivocal and condemnatory: Winnie Madikizela-Mandela was 'politically and morally accountable for the gross violations of human rights committed by the [Football Club]. The Commission finds that Ms Madikizela-Mandela failed to account to the community and political structures. The Commission finds that Madikizela-Mandela was responsible, by omission, for the commission of gross violations of human rights.'[19]

I was particularly interested in the TRC's corroboration of my premise about court and police laxity: 'The Commission was left with the distinct impression that the attorney-general was at pains not to prosecute her. Madikizela-Mandela's subsequent prosecution in the kidnapping trial, albeit over twenty-seven months after the abductions, suggests that the authorities had been left no other option in the light of the revelations of Richardson's trial the previous year. Strategic decisions with regard to the investigation and prosecution of Madikizela-Mandela appear to have been influenced strongly by the political circumstances and sensitivities of this period.'[20]

Towards the end of 1999 I was in Bloemfontein when I received a call from Kobie Coetsee, by then retired from politics and again living in the city. He wanted to discuss a matter with me. We arranged to meet in the VIP lounge at the airport, shortly before my departure to Cape Town. I had always found the former minister of Justice elliptical and impenetrable: this meeting was no exception. He expressed deep concern about the ANC's intention to 'damage the constitutional settlement'. 'We' should collaborate in its defence – but there were no specifics. I went on to ask him what he had made of the TRC's statement about the 'strategic decisions with regard to the prosecution of Madikizela-Mandela' being influenced strongly by 'the political sensitivities of this period'. He gave no direct response, simply fixing me with his sphinx-like smile. We were never to meet again – a few months later he died, on 29 July 2000.

A major point about the TRC hearings on Winnie Mandela and the Football Club was that at no stage had she sought indemnity for her acts and omissions. Indeed, her presence before it had only been secured on pain of subpoena. It therefore seemed entirely logical that she should be prosecuted in the criminal courts for the most clear-cut cases exposed by the Commission. Douglas Gibson and I – aided by our researcher Julia Frielinghaus – scoured the record and concluded that in three cases, at least, there was a compelling case for prosecution on charges of kidnapping, assault and possible murder. In the case of Stompie, the TRC had additionally found that her role had been far more intimate than the Appellate Division had determined.

Accordingly, in mid-December 1998, we met Advocate AP de Vries SC, attorney-general of the Witwatersrand Local Division of the high court, and presented him with a memorandum based on the TRC investigation report and other corroborating evidence. The three cases we had isolated were those where the evidence of the principal witnesses was 'unchallenged, corroborated, or not seriously contradicted or a combination of all three elements' – and *prima facie* indicated that prosecutions 'could and should' occur without further delay. De Vries listened with intent interest and promised to take matters 'under review'. In the spirit of his predecessors no further action was taken.

4

The timing of my meeting with the attorney-general coincided with the ANC's quinquennial National Conference at Mafikeng. There Winnie's star was in the sharpest of descents. She had already, more than two years before, been stripped of her deputy ministry for violating protocols relating to an overseas visit (an ANC insider told me this was simply an excuse to get rid of her). Nelson Mandela had divorced her in a blaze of humiliating and excruciating publicity which cast her in the most severe, philandering and money-grabbing light. Her attempts to be nominated from the floor of the conference for high office had been rebuked by the ascendant Mbeki, who was installed as party president.

Compounding her largely self-created misfortunes, the parliamentary standing committee on public accounts (Scopa) had fingered her for owing the state hundreds of thousands of rand for unauthorised expenditure while a member of government.

Although I did not see how I could take matters further in respect of criminal charges, her misdemeanours had been publicly exposed and her undeserved title of 'Mother of the Nation' seriously compromised. Yet her apparent disgrace did not prevent her nomination by the ANC for re-election to parliament – in the top ten names submitted on their national list for the 1999 general election.

There I left matters, until in March 1999, at home in Orange Grove, I received a telephone call. A breathless, agitated voice speaking in thickly Afrikaans-accented English announced himself as 'Alan van Zyl' [I have changed his name deliberately], an operative with the National Intelligence Service. He said he had information 'concerning your favourite Lady' which, he intoned, 'will blow you away' – or words to that effect. I arranged for him to visit me the next day.

At the appointed time my mystery visitor arrived. His breathlessness was explained by the fact that he was immensely fat and sweated profusely. Agitated and nervous, he sat at my desk. It transpired that Van Zyl was currently a member of the National Intelligence Agency, involved in 'secret

487

projects' for government. Amid his torrent of words, I gathered that he was under some kind of threat, and was owed considerable amounts of money for sundry services. I really didn't see how I could be of much assistance – except to suggest he seek relief under the generous provisions of the labour law. When pressed on information concerning 'the Lady' he took out a folded piece of paper on which a dozen or so lines of handwriting appeared.

I immediately recognised Winnie's handwriting. The note read: 'What infuriates me is the fact that I have confided in [Comrade] Thabo and some of the comrades present here about very sensitive information, which cannot be disclosed here. Some of the comrades about whom I hold certain information act the way they do because they fear I hold this knowledge ... The day I release that information would be the end of the ANC government!! [I] have kept quiet for the sake of the unity of the organisation.'

How had my visitor obtained the note? He told me it was part of a document prepared by Winnie Mandela and apparently read out at a recent meeting of the ANC's National Working Committee. He could not provide me with its context, and was extremely vague on how he had acquired it – deliberately so. Clearly he had an axe to grind against the government for which he currently worked, and felt hard done by. But I also had a strong feeling that his arrival with the note had been sanctioned by one or another element in the upper reaches of government. The timing was also fortuitous (or deliberate), since the following afternoon was scheduled as one of the last major debates of the session: Deputy President Thabo Mbeki's budget vote was up for debate and discussion. The intention of the delivery of the note had to be public dissemination of its contents.

On board the evening plane to Cape Town, I scrutinised my draft speech for the next day's debate and inserted into it the thermonuclear device my informant had handed me. (I also took the precaution in my office of checking the note against one Winnie Mandela had previously sent me. To even my unforensic eye, they seemed a perfect match.)

With more trepidation than customary, I was ready in parliament the next day, 23 March 1999, to drop what I presumed was a bombshell on Mbeki and an unsuspecting National Assembly. After a few preliminary remarks on aspects of ANC policy, I forged on: 'Yesterday, I received a copy of a document allegedly in Mrs Mandela's handwriting. It was apparently prepared for (or read out) at the NWC of the ANC.' I then read it out to parliament and asked: 'What is this information that could "be the end of the ANC government"? What dark secrets does Mrs Mandela hold? Is this why Mrs Mandela has been placed near the top of your election list?

'Is she holding you and South Africa to ransom? If so, for how long will we have to endure this? Is this why Mrs Mandela remains "the great untouchable of South African politics"? We deserve to be told.'

There was an immediate outcry from the ANC benches. I was far more intrigued to see how Mbeki would respond. *Hansard* records his reply: 'I indeed would not be surprised if, currently, there are some schemes going on in the country, precisely to cook up all manner of stories about the ANC. But we would not be surprised, it has been part of our history. I think it makes me feel sad to have the Hon. Tony Leon seeking to pursue and adopt methods that have been used by the old Special Branch in this country [applause]. He says he has a document written by the Hon. Winnie Madikizela-Mandela which says all sorts of things. I think it would probably be best and consistent ... that the Hon. Tony Leon focuses as much as he wants, as militantly as he wants, on the policies of the ANC, to criticise them. But to revert to what in this country was called dirty tricks, the resort to that kind of information, does not do him any honour.' [Applause][21]

Mbeki had either intuited – or had direct knowledge of – the provenance of my information. Mrs Mandela's office put out a blustering statement: 'Mrs Madikizela-Mandela wishes Mr Leon to note that her reconciliation with those elements who prosecuted her under the apartheid regime will rise above the Tony Leons of this world.'

Approached for my comment on Mbeki's response, I said that neither he nor Winnie had denied that the Lady held information of such a nature that publication would 'be the end of the ANC government'. Eight years on, no such information has surfaced.

Early the following month Winnie decided to smear me with the brush she had unavailingly used against Reverend Paul Verryn in the Stompie trial. She announced at an ANC election meeting that I 'disliked strong black women' – and wondered aloud about my 'marital status' (I was single at the time). The next day, addressing an election meeting at the University of Pretoria, a young female student stood up and asked me point-blank: 'Are you gay?' I was nonplussed, and retorted, 'No I am not. However, if Winnie Mandela was the last remaining woman in the world, I would seriously consider changing my sexual orientation.' The audience erupted in laughter.

I also decided, tongue-in-cheek, to pen Winnie a response to her attempted slur, dated 4 April 1999:

Dear Winnie,

I read your comment that I allegedly 'dislike strong black women'. You also wonder about my marital status – as indeed many do about yours.

The fact is I disapprove of your conduct in public life; I know the families of your alleged victims, and I do not think you should hold South Africa to ransom. This has nothing to do with my affection for women – black, strong or otherwise.

You should not ever draw general conclusions from the particular case – always a mistake, but usually the province of the racist and sexist! I'm surprised the ANC Women's League president is guilty of such a misjudgment.

I enclose a photo of my partner, Michal Even-Zahav. She's attractive and strong – but also pleasant. As and when we decide to get married, we'll be sure to invite you. You'd make a fetching, if somewhat superannuated, matron-of-honour.

Best wishes – Tony Leon

I made sure the *Sunday Times* received a copy of my letter, and it duly appeared in the 'Hogarth' satirical column the following weekend.

There my public tangling with this extraordinary woman more or less ended. Yet there was a private and more revealing side to her, which disclosed the fact that for all the monstrous acts she had committed, she was certainly not simply a latter-day political gorgon. Once after a furious exchange with Mbeki in early 2000, I was amazed to retrieve a voicemail message on my cellphone: 'It's Winnie here – you really got to the president. Good luck to you.'

However, like India rubber, Winnie Mandela would bounce back when Mbeki's leadership collapsed in December 2007, at the party conference: she stormed into top position for election to the ANC's National Executive committee.

More poignantly, and personally, a day or two after we had buried my mother Sheila in Johannesburg – in December 2001 – I was driving the car and Michal answered the phone, which she immediately passed to me, gasping, 'It's Winnie Mandela and she wants to talk to you.' There was the Lady, her unmistakable voice declaiming: 'I'm so sorry, Tony, to hear of your mother's death. I have only heard of it now, otherwise I would have attended the funeral. I gather your mother was a very strong woman and you must miss her terribly.'

I was completely amazed by both the fact and the warmth of her call, and thanked her as sincerely as I could. That had been a glimpse of the charming, comforting, beguiling 'Mother of the Nation'. History, if accurately and unsentimentally written, should record Winnie Madikizela-Mandela's role properly. How she stood up, with singular charisma and courage, to apartheid; but also how, in so many ways, like the legend of Perseus, she became the very embodiment of the political monster she attempted to slay.

PART FOUR

LEADER OF THE OPPOSITION

CHAPTER 14

Fighting Back

*With success comes criticism. More often than not, to be well liked
and respected is a sign that one is not seen as a threat.
The aim of Liberals should be to be less respected by their opponents
and better liked by their voters.*

FRITS BOLKESTEIN

*Mbeki's revival and updating of the African nationalist discourse
of the late 1940s and early 1950s ring loudly in a racist and unequal society.
Such a 'language' stands in the way of oppositional politics (as it does in
a wider democratic context) as well as in constructing an analysis for the
reconstruction of the dynamics of South African society.*

GERHARD MARÉ

I

South Africa's second democratic election on 2 June 1999 resulted in the
Democratic Party moving from fifth to second position in the political
line-up in parliament and the country. It elevated me from my peripheral place on the flanks of opposition to the formal position of Leader
of the Opposition. It saw the eclipse of the (New) National Party which
slumped from second to fourth place in the polls. And the African National
Congress's grip on power was further extended and entrenched when, on
the back of a declining national percentage poll, it gained 66,35% of the
votes.

These epic shifts and reversals coincided with the changing of the presidential guard from Mandela to Mbeki – marking the end of reconciliation
politics and the arrival of a full-throttle era of transformation. We fought
under the rallying cry of 'Fight Back'. On one level, this was stunningly
successful; yet on another made mephitic the already chilly waters separating the governing party from its new opposition. Then the electoral tidal
wave which all but drowned the NNP (as the NP had renamed itself in

495

one of the least successful rebranding exercises in history) led, a year later, to a fundamental reconfiguration of opposition forces.

Towards the end of 1998 I visited the Union Buildings in Pretoria late one summer afternoon to meet Mbeki, already the ANC president and the country's president-in-waiting. (Mandela had announced he was standing down the following year.) The purpose of the meeting was mundane: after Zach de Beer resigned his ambassadorship in 1996, I had success-fully arranged with Mandela for a DP provincial legislator, Western Cape educationist Professor Richard van der Ross, to receive a foreign posting (as ambassador to Spain). Now another political colleague had expressed an interest in an ambassadorship (I thought the job essentially routine and boring, a sort of glorified town mayor's role with little real power). My intention was to ask Mbeki whether the informal foreign posting arrange-ment reached with Mandela would continue. Van der Ross's term would expire on Mbeki's watch.

In marked contrast to our previous encounters, the occasion was dis-tinctly cold.

Mbeki suggested that if any DP MP wished to be considered they should 'join the Department of Foreign Affairs' and enter the public serv-ice. That disposed of my central concern. I then added conversationally that in respect of next year's election we should 'keep the channels of communication open' in case there was one or other matter requiring resolution. (I had in mind the chaotic events which had characterised the 1994 elections.) Mbeki responded curtly that the IEC (Independent Electoral Commission) would handle matters properly. The ease and af-fability of the past had vanished.

I was determined to use my immediate proximity to the nation's de facto most powerful politician to express again my concern about crime – then as now a matter of national concern. I suggested that if more con-crete measures and resolute actions were taken by government, this would arrest the considerable sense of demoralisation and fearfulness I felt had set in among many people. Mbeki looked at me bleakly and informed me that he had recently received a visit from the chairman of one of America's major auto manufacturers, who resided in Detroit – itself a crime hot-spot. His visitor, Mbeki told me, advised him that he felt 'perfectly safe in Johannesburg'.

I felt this missed the point, but realised there really was nothing left to discuss.

Driving back to Johannesburg, I pondered the change which Mbeki had undergone and which would mark his presidency. There was no easy explanation, but the warmth and contact which had characterised my relationship with Mandela would not continue with his successor. I would not seek further meetings with him. And if as I hoped the electorate conferred on me the leadership of the opposition, our relationship with the president would be determined by him – not by me as a supplicant, seeking crumbs of relevance from his table of power.

I never (contrary to various fabulists in the media who suggested otherwise) sought another meeting with Mbeki over the next eight years.[1] Given his attitude to me, on display that day, the lights were on but no one was at home.

Mbeki's transition from the clubbable smoothie of the mid-1990s to the distant, aloof figure of the decade's end was not confined to me. A very wealthy Johannesburg socialite-businesswoman with whom I was acquainted recounted a similar experience. She and her husband had frequently entertained Mbeki after his arrival back in South Africa in 1990 through the period of his deputy-presidency. She thought they were fast friends, the three of them often sharing late-evening nightcaps. In June 1999 she was invited to his presidential inauguration, and bounded up to him to say something along the lines of: 'Congratulations, Thabo.' He looked at her askance and said: 'I'm not your Thabo. I am the president.'

As Shakespeare chillingly related in *King Henry IV Part II*, on his assumption of the kingdom, Prince Hal turns on his old friend and mentor Falstaff and repudiates him: 'Presume not that I am the thing I was; For God doth know, so shall the world perceive, That I have turn'd away my former self ...'

Taking leave of President Mandela was altogether more pleasant. Parliament would with great frequency after 1997 be marked by ever-increasing ceremonials of state power and pageantry (in almost inverse proportion to its serious work as a legislature). But its farewell to Mandela on Friday 29 March 1999 was more than merited, as inclusive and joyous as the man's presidency (give or take Mafikeng in 1997). Aided by a speech, to which the articulate Andrew Kenny had added some sparkling prose, I was privileged to participate. My public tribute was a sincere attempt to express not only what the party and I thought of him, but what we genuinely believed he had done for our nation:

'There are three categories of great political leaders. The first is the great and the bad: this includes Hitler and Stalin. The second is the great and the good: this includes Winston Churchill and Franklin Roosevelt. And then there is a third category, also of good, but of a leader born with a special kind of grace, who seems to transcend the politics of his age. This is a very small category, and in fact I can think of only three such men in this century: Mahatma Gandhi, the Dalai Lama and Nelson Mandela.

'[He managed] to raise the sights of our politics ... We see how he was that rarest phenomenon – a committed politician and an unusually agreeable and generous man ...

'I am deeply honoured that I have been able to see from these benches the ending of apartheid and the beginning of full democracy under the presidency of Nelson Mandela. My respect and admiration for him is unconditional. He graces this House. He graces this country. He graces humanity.'²

I shed a tear at taking formal leave of this extraordinary phenomenon. At one level he was all too human, but at another he inhabited a plane out of reach of most mortal politicians. It had been a great gift that my political leadership had commenced under his presidency and had grown, not under his enormous shadow, but because of that special light which he shone on so many, including me.

2

The elements for our election campaign were cohering. Our poll numbers looked promising given our ambition of supplanting the NNP as the major opposition force. We rented campaign headquarters in Rosebank, Johannesburg. Our team had taken shape: Ryan Coetzee would manage communications; Greg Krumbock the organisation; Russel Crystal public events and my rallies; Douglas Gibson would chair the campaign committee and speak for it; and I would be its major salesman – its public voice and face.

We had an obvious selling point as an 'effective opposition'; yet in early 1999 still lacked a cohesive theme and overarching slogan. Into this vacuum stepped a leading Johannesburg businessman with a side-passion for politics and who – despite presiding over some major corporations – maintained an affiliation with international political consultants. In 1994 he and I became friends. He went on to play a hugely supportive role throughout my leadership.

In February, he told me he was bringing to South Africa, at his expense, 'two of the best political consultants in America'. Could they 'be of any use to you?' Indeed, yes. So I arranged a dinner in Cape Town to confer with his friends, Doug Schoen and Hank Scheinkopf, who were to play a significant, essentially unseen, role in our campaign.

Schoen, together with Mark Penn, headed a major New York polling and political consultancy. Their glittering client list included President Bill Clinton (Penn would go on to become Hillary Clinton's controversial chief strategist for her 2008 presidential campaign). He was neatly attired, smart and articulate, and had studied at Oxford under RW Johnson, which gave us another mutual acquaintance. Scheinkopf, intense, tousle-haired and frenetic, possessed a great reputation for campaign commercials, particularly on radio. Since Ryan had already decided the bulk of our advertising budget should be spent on radio, Hank appeared to be just the man to conceive our message.

Schoen and Scheinkopf told us what could be done and how our cause could be advanced through professional polling and the need for a disciplined, single-focus campaign which never strayed 'off message'. But what was that message? We were told that if we followed their strategy, it would emerge.

Marvellous stuff – until we broached the delicate subject of money. Their combined services would cost us about R2,5-million. By American standards this was, by comparison, an amount of great modesty; but by our standards it was huge. Not for the first time I uttered the words which often made my party colleagues sick with anxiety: 'We'll spend in faith.' (Eventually Gibson and I covered the Americans' bill with a spectacularly large once-off donation from a Stellenbosch businessman.)

We were drawing in more funds than ever before, but our campaign needs became, as their reach and grasp extended, ever more expensive. We often had to raise urgent short-term loans on an almost weekly basis simply to flight the many radio ads we had commissioned, and all of which had to be paid for in advance.

We had also engaged a local advertising/PR firm to conceive a communications strategy. It was apparently less than impressive. I did not attend the get-together between the Americans, the locals and our campaign team since I believed they needed to discuss how central (or otherwise) my role and projection should be.

I had a simple mandate: bring me the result and the theme and I will, if satisfied, sign off on it. The local advertising company apparently believed that a picture of a bull terrier should be used as the visual motif of the campaign, together with the slogan 'The guts to be the real opposition'. Schoen, Scheinkopf and Ryan Coetzee differed; they believed my face should be the visual, and that the slogan should be 'The guts to fight back', of which "Fight Back' would be the abbreviation.

I was waiting in my eyrie on the fifth floor of Marks Building in parliament, on a weekend afternoon in February, when Ryan Coetzee accompanied Schoen and Scheinkopf to deliver to me the verdict. Scheinkopf told me he had been doing a focus group in Durban, among potential Indian voters, and one of them said to him, 'I want a party to fight back for me against the crime, the corruption and the unemployment.' 'Well,' Hank then explained, 'we reckon it's your best shot: it's a fight back campaign.' He then suggested the slogan (which I heard now for the first time, although its echo would follow the party and me for the next decade): 'The guts to fight back'. I swallowed a little, immediately anticipating the uncomfortable frissons it would cause in some circles, including the more sensitive ones close to me. But I also thought it would be a stunning, simple, effective and fitting climax to our five hard years of tough-minded opposition.

I reasoned that, having hocked the party's finances for two such expensive experts, I would do well to follow their advice. I signed on, and the campaign went from conception to execution.

As opposed to our bit-player role and status in the 1994 poll, the DP campaign, with its provocative edge and professional delivery system, occupied centre stage in 1999 – not so much in our own estimation, as by the reaction and opprobrium of our opponents and the media. Within days of the 'Fight Back' posters – bearing a stern photograph of me – festooning lampposts and billboards, the ANC laid a complaint with the IEC that our slogan 'incited hatred'.

It was dismissed. However, the ruling party, clearly cut to the quick, launched its own short-lived retaliation. In colours and design mimicking our own blue and yellow livery, the ANC produced posters proclaiming: 'Don't Fight Blacks'. We succeeded in getting them removed by obtaining an IEC injunction that they misled voters into believing they were DP posters.

During a debate in parliament, in February, the ANC's Johnny de Lange, with whom I had frequently clashed, called me a 'Chihuahua – an arrogant little dog'. (I responded by referring to him as a 'bullfrog', to which he bore a more than passing resemblance.) While the chair ruled both expressions unparliamentary my tag stuck, notwithstanding my preference (in the small dog stakes) for the Dachshund breed!

On a slightly more cerebral level, in February, we published a policy document entitled: 'The Corruption of Transformation'. We accused government of crudely racialising its own affirmative action policy. We pointed out how it was simply advancing already largely well-off middle-class people with close connections to the ANC. We also asserted the view that demographic representation – a basically Verwoerdian assumption – was fundamentally flawed. It presumed that racial criteria should be the overwhelming, often the only, criterion in appointing and promoting individuals and filling key posts.

Its publication sparked the interest of *Financial Mail* editor, Peter Bruce, who decided to arrange, across the pages of his magazine, a debate, by way of a series of letters between the ANC's Saki Macozoma (who had left parliament to take over the reins as CEO of the government transport behemoth, Transnet) and me.

Macozoma dismissed our transformation document in peremptory terms:

'What is baptised as a systematic critique succumbs too early to the rhetoric of a marginal opposition which exercises the prerogative of the harlot – to be iconoclastic without the responsibility to put forward a credible alternative.

'The DP's befuddlement begins with the concepts of non-racialism, the rainbow nation and transformation itself. There seems to be an attempt by the DP to expropriate the concept of non-racialism and denude it of essential meanings.'[3]

I thought his critique misleading – especially since we had produced a forest's worth of policy documents on addressing poverty and South Africa's history of deprivation. It was also, in my view, evasive of our central criticism of the ANC's race-holding. I noted:

'The most important debate in South African politics is about how to achieve two goals: redressing the past, and ensuring sustainable growth in the future. The two steps must be taken together. It is immoral and impractical to redress imbalances by taking steps that will again entrench race as the central determinant of life chances in South Africa. Our alternative vision is the creation of the opportunity society in which the pursuit of happiness is made possible through ever expanding opportunities for all.'[4]

There might have been something of a personal edge to the debate. We had both been selected in 1995 by the US State Department to comprise part of a group of South African politicians to visit the United States. Macozoma and Bulelani Ngcuka (then ANC chief whip in the Senate, and later more famous as the National Director of Public Prosecutions and husband of the deputy president) and Janet Love MP were the ANC representatives on the trip. The visit proceeded reasonably amicably until we arrived at the congressional office of Congressman Ron Dellums – a well-known anti-apartheid US legislator in Oakland, California. The congressman was not on hand to meet us, and we had to make do with his office manager, an amiable African-American. After about an hour's worth of explanations on the intricacies and minutiae of servicing constituents, I thought it an appropriate moment for our departure, and our group headed back to our minivan. Once inside, Macozoma let rip at me with uncontained fury: 'It's only because our host was black that you so rudely terminated our discussion,' he snorted. I was completed nonplussed by his, I thought, utterly unprovoked and misguided assault. We passed the rest of the trip essentially not speaking. However, when we were in Washington DC a few days later, we had a 9 am appointment with the congressional black caucus. Macozoma and Ngcuka had the evening before left our hotel to stay elsewhere. The rest of our group arrived on time the next morning on Capitol Hill for the appointment, and our hosts, a large group of congressman, received us with warmth and effusion. They must, however, have been surprised at our largely white group and the glaring absence of the key ANC members. The meeting had been under way for over half-an-hour before Macozoma and Ngcuka arrived. I was unable to resist, and wrote Macozoma a note saying, 'Is it only because we are meeting with black congressmen that you arrived so late?' He was not amused.

But a happier relationship developed with another member of our delegation to America. Nicky Koornhof, a close confidant of Marthinus van Schalkwyk, and I became friendly. He was ambitious but irreverent, and we spent much time together. We remained in touch afterwards, and he signaled to me his increasing disillusionment with both his party and its new leader.

By 1999 Koornhof had become seriously exercised about his party's irresoluteness on committing itself to an opposition pact in the Western Cape in the event of no outright winner in the provincial poll. Van Schalkwyk, at that stage, was open-minded about cutting a post-election deal with the ANC. Koornhof was then the provincial minister of Health; but after some intensive persuasion by Hennie Bester and me he announced in late March that, despite his third placing on the NNP provincial election list, he was switching sides.

This was devastating to Van Schalkwyk, and a major boost for our campaign. Indeed, there was no shortage of serious candidates. Koornhof, who was rewarded with the No. 3 slot on our list, was joined by Cape Town education activist and former journalist, Helen Zille, who was given the fifth (and, it subsequently transpired, last electable) berth. In KwaZulu-Natal, the first Afrikaans-speaking head of the South African Chamber of

Business, Rudi Heine, was nominated alongside one of our youngest and most promising 'new look' candidates, Councillor Nick Clelland, formerly a DJ. In Gauteng, our one-time researcher (now my full-time speech-writer) Raenette Taljaard secured a winning nomination.

Not all our nominees received a rapturous reception.

I had long admired the intellectual pugnaciousness of Steve Mulholland, who after heading (and turning round) South African Associated Newspapers had moved on to Australia to run the large Fairfax newspaper group. Now he had recently returned to South Africa and I suggested he stand for election as a DP MP. After some discussion, he declined but indicated that his colleague and friend Nigel Bruce might well be available. Bruce, whom I admired for the strong editorial lines – and advocacy of the free market – he had pursued at the *Financial Mail* and more latterly at *F&T Weekly*, was amenable.

As I record in Chapter 12, a media feeding frenzy began. Bruce's previous editorials were exhumed, and a mother-lode struck with an infamous (if throwaway) line he had once penned singing the praises of a white waiter compared with the service of, as he chose to characterise it, 'some surly tribesman with his thumb in the soup and an eye on the clock'.[5]

I was pretty appalled when I read this, and told Bruce and the media that I thought it 'tasteless'. However, I declined the suggestion that Bruce step down though I did request him to apologise publicly – which he did. Nigel, however, added an explanation and a complaint: 'Sensitivities to race are nowadays so great that irony is neither understood nor accepted.'[6]

Bruce was not the only politically incorrect person we nominated. In KwaZulu-Natal, I had urged the party to nominate the former PFP MP Graham McIntosh. By 1999, on the back of his own considerable farming enterprises in northern Natal, he was head of the KwaZulu-Natal Agricultural Union. He was sensible on rural safety issues, and fluently tri-lingual in English, Afrikaans and isiZulu. However, I had discounted McIntosh's strong streak of religious fundamentalism and basic homophobia.

On our campaign 'battle bus' between Potchefstroom and Kroonstad in the Free State, I received an outraged call from Ian Davidson. In a newspaper McIntosh had launched a root-and-branch attack on Edwin Cameron, who had by then declared his HIV+ status in seeking nomination for judicial office. Apart from my regard for Cameron, I was appalled at McIntosh's social illiberalism. He, too, was required to apologise unreservedly and in public for his utterance; but I was to learn much later that in respect of this maverick, with McIntosh, at least, the old adage 'no good deed goes unpunished' was true.

When I was battling Van Schalkwyk for the soul of the DA in 2001, McIntosh proved to be one of the most disloyal and destructive of all my DP parliamentary colleagues at that extremely difficult time.

Our campaign went into high gear after a high-profile launch at Durban's newly opened International Convention Centre. Dressed in a black outfit fitted out for me by the owners of the über-fashionable Diesel franchise, I promised the party faithful that I would take the Fight Back campaign into 'every corner of South Africa, from Mmabatho to Muizenberg, from Manenberg to Mouille Point, from New Brighton to Nieu-Bethesda, and from Kraaifontein to KwaMashu'.

And so we did. By charter plane and 'battle bus' we crisscrossed the entirety of South Africa in search of voters, supporters and sound bites. Most of our campaign stops and events – orchestrated and choreographed with pinpoint precision by an increasingly ill-humoured but supremely effective Russel Crystal – were very successful. Sometimes I found myself way out of my comfort zone, as described by Suzanne Daley of the *New York Times*:[7]

'TZANEEN, South Africa – Tony Leon, the head of South Africa's liberal Democratic Party, a man with the slight lockjaw accent of those educated at this country's best English-style boarding schools, came here recently to pay homage to Chief Samuel Mpumulana Muhlava II and to make his pitch to the Tsonga people who live nearby.

'His campaign bus rattled up the dirt road and stopped before the run-down meeting house where a group of traditional dancers with drums and sheepskin anklets were ready to greet him here, 225 miles north-east of Johannesburg. Leon's speech was thick with deference to Muhlava, and skirted the rather thorny issue of how exactly you reconcile democracy with chieftainships, which are, after all, usually passed from father to son.

'South Africa, said Leon after he had removed his suit jacket and striped tie in the sweltering heat, needed to "carve a niche" for traditional leaders where they could continue to be "the voice of the people".'

We soon realised that our quest for black votes was more idealistic than realistic, given their unshakable attachment to the ANC. Nonetheless we spent a great deal of energy and time in predominantly black areas to advance the ideal of non-racial politics. One such foray took me to Ventersdorp in the North-West Province where the party had a strong pocket of black activists. Since this *mielie*-growing area was also the home of Eugene Terre'Blanche, leader of the neo-fascist Afrikaner Weerstands-beweging, I thought it appropriate to denounce the man and his politics to my overwhelmingly black audience. It made no difference – journalists, who did not accompany me to the event, simply wrote me down as 'courting the right-wing vote' by visiting Ventersdorp!

The press was engaged in its own flip-flop. Turned off by our message, which *Business Day* described as 'off key', most of the one-time DP-supporting media largely endorsed the ANC in 1999. Nevertheless, our support surged almost in inverse proportion to the media's switch of affection.

One journalist who was broadly sympathetic to our cause (notwithstanding, or perhaps because of, his one-time services in the ANC's armed wing, MK) was Howard Barrell of the *Mail&Guardian*. He accompanied me on a swing to the conservative southern Cape town of Oudtshoorn, until then a staunch Nationalist redoubt. In an article entitled 'Liberal Invasion of the Platteland'[8] he wrote:

'Leon may be forgiven for his inability to speak convincing Afrikaans. But in the latter case, the way he battled on, sounding almost camp at times, endeared him to many local folk … "I like him, man, he's *hardegat* (hard-arsed)," said a local farmer, a former member of the Conservative Party, who was among the sixty-odd people paying R100 each to attend a DP fundraiser at a beautiful Cape Dutch farm-turned-country-lodge outside Oudtshoorn last week. He was not the only former CP member there. So was Piet Retief (oh yes), whose motor business once straddled the Little Karoo. And the lodge-owner, Matilda de Bod, young wife and mother, and a former CP activist, who had organised the fundraising drinks. She had – bravely in a small town in which political loyalties can determine business opportunities – placed DP posters on the lodge's grand gates.

'Something extraordinary is happening. Opinion polls have shown that more Afrikaners now support the DP than they do any other party. Out of every ten Afrikaner voters, about three (30%) will vote for the DP, two (23%) support Marthinus van Schalkwyk's NNP, and one (11%) backs Constand Viljoen's Freedom Front.

'How can this be? How in 30 years can a party of *verdomde liberaliste* [damned liberals] become the party of biltong, *braaivleis* and *boeremusiek?*

'Why, I ask De Bod, this change in her politics? From CP to DP, for Chrissake? You, a Schoeman by birth, a member of the most prominent family farming in the valley? She laughs and walks off. I follow, repeating my question. She laughs and walks off again, as if there may be pain in her reason. "Because," she answers when I cut her off near a *hok* [cage] holding a pair of ostriches, "there's no place for the CP and its ideas in South Africa any more. Because we've got to find each other's hands and a way of holding them and of moving forward. And the DP gives us the best way of doing this."'

Meanwhile Van Schalkwyk campaigned in serene confidence that he would stave off the political assault we had launched in his political back yard. The young editor of a major Afrikaans newspaper later told me that six months before the election Van Schalkwyk had boasted to him that he would prevail over the DP. When the editor expressed his doubts, Van Schalkwyk responded: 'I know my people. They will never vote for a Jew.' Van Schalkwyk was to learn a series of hard and bitter lessons: and the first was that he didn't really know his people. If he did, he clearly underestimated them; or overestimated their capacity for prejudice.

But the winds of change were blowing through the Afrikaans establishment, and not in the direction Van Schalkwyk hoped. In September 1998 I was to bear witness to this weather change. After a lecture at the University of the Free State I was interviewed in Bloemfontein by an attractive young radio journalist, Martelize Kolver. After we had concluded the interview and she had switched off her tape recorder, she indicated that she was a fan of the party and myself. I was suitably impressed. She then told me that her grandfather had been involved in South African politics. I assumed he was some forgotten senator since the name 'Kolver' did not ring any bells in my political memory. So, more out of politeness perhaps than interest, I enquired who her grandfather was. Her reply completely blew me away when she told me he was John Vorster, the hardline National Party prime minister from 1966 to 1978.

She told me that not only did she intend voting for our party in the next election, but that her mother and father would also do so. She added that one of her brothers was voting for the Freedom Front and another intended to vote for the ANC. I then enquired of her, who, in her immediate family, was intending in 1999 to vote for the National Party which her grandfather had once led? 'Only my grandmother,' she replied.

I was single-minded in my determination to win every Afrikaans vote possible, precisely as Barrell had suggested. However, I was equally determined that in this quest I would not consciously betray a single party principle or personal conviction. Indeed, not all our Afrikaans supporters in any way accepted the controversial proceedings of the TRC. Many thought of it as an ill-disguised witchhunt against Afrikaners in particular and the old white order in general.

However, on the eve of the campaign when parliament debated 'the national response to the report of the Truth and Reconciliation Commission' I was absolutely straightforward in my response. Although I had misgivings about aspects of its operations and apparent bias, I had no doubt about its significance:

'The TRC report is over three thousand pages long. But we can sum up its conclusions in just three words: "abuse of power" ... The TRC has received many critical comments throughout its hearings. We are sympathetic to some of the criticisms. But there is one comment, heard quite often I regret to say, for which we have no sympathy. This is the comment, "Let's forget about the past." We must never forget the past. We must not forget one single horror that the TRC has exposed. Not one single killing, not one single bombing, not one single torture, not one single necklacing, not one single mutilation and not one single lie must ever be forgotten. Every outrage must be recorded and committed forever to the memory of our nation.'[9]

I knew that what I said would go against the grain of some in my new political fold. Yet the ANC's minister of Justice Dullah Omar used the same debate to reinforce, not reach beyond, the prejudices of his own constituency. In a particularly mean-spirited and myopic speech he declared that so-called 'white political parties' should be grateful that they were 'permitted to participate at the new democratic order without discrimination.'[10]

His remarks attracted little scorn and even less comment from the 'punditocracy'. Steven Friedman, for whom I was a particular *bête noire*, saw our campaign as an 'assault on post-apartheid South Africa'.[11] In fact, our 'assaults', such as they were, were aimed at the idiocy and unfairness which appeared to characterise much of the ANC's approach to redress, which had spread from the political centres to outposts where one perhaps least expected it to take root. One such place was the University of Natal in Durban.

3

During April I came across a report that an 18-year-old Indian girl in Durban, Privani Reddy, had been denied admission to the university's Medical School, although she had acquired a brilliant six As in her matriculation exam. Her enraged father launched court proceedings, citing the university's race quotas as the basis for her refusal. After meeting both Ms Reddy and her father and obtaining their permission, I led a group of DP picketers in a demonstration outside the Howard College campus. Our posters – 'Merit not Quotas' – drove the message home and proved that victims of the 'new racism' we were alleging were not confined to previously advantaged whites. On election day, the DP swept the boards in Chatsworth and Phoenix – the areas with the largest number of Indian voters. Our campaign around this issue was, in my view, decisive.

In the final week of the campaign, I decided to address our critics head-on. The hegemonic aspirations of the ANC seemed to me at the root of the loss of nerve among those from whom a more critical attitude towards government should be expected.

Most campaign speeches (including my own) are forgettable. However, the speech I delivered at Pretoria's Hoërskool Waterkloof on Monday 24 May was, I thought, of a slightly better vintage than most of my campaign rhetoric. Reading it over eight years later, I think it not only answered critics of our 'Fight Back' campaign, but raised larger questions about the future direction of South Africa under President Mbeki. Here is the relevant excerpt:

'We have always opposed racism. We have always stood for the principle of merit. We have always stood for individual rights irrespective of colour, religion or sex. We haven't changed – the real question is: why has the ANC changed? There are two reasons. The first is: why should the ANC see us as the most important target? One reason is that we represent the main real alternative. We are not, as is the National Party, just the remnant of something that used to be much more significant, a party of the past. We are, quite visibly, growing fast – we are a party of the future.

'We stand for a complete set of values – an entire political, economic and cultural vision ... merit, standards, hard work, and accountability. All these values run directly counter to the ANC's. What are the ANC's values? They seem to be encapsulated in the following statement: "The ANC must prevail and the ANC can do no wrong." But the ANC also feels challenged by us because they are not just an ordinary political party. It doesn't want to be just in government. It doesn't want to win just this election. This is a party which wants to dominate the whole of society – to dominate the economy, appoint its own people to the judiciary, the Reserve Bank and every other so-called independent institution. It wants to – indeed, it demands the right to – dominate all of civil society.

'It is this ambition for hegemony which also explains why the ANC wants to take not only a two-thirds majority but also why it wants to colonise every possible nook and cranny of our society. In addition, it even wants to tell the opposition how to behave and what posters we should have. It is affronted that there should even exist in this society a genuine, confident, unapologetic alternative. And yet this is the very essence of democracy – that there be such alternatives.'

I then decided to pivot the address to the rising chorus of anti-DP voices in the press.

'Why do quite a number of intellectuals, a significant number of journalists and some newspapers and, especially, the public broadcaster, the

SABC, subscribe to all this uncritically? Why do they endorse the ANC when they know what we all know – that it is a deeply illiberal, authoritarian and fundamentally power-hungry party? Why do they try to justify this by suggesting the DP is somehow guilty of *"swart gevaar"* tactics, when, in fact, we stand for the same liberal principles we always have?

'This is a question that goes right to the heart of our contemporary dilemmas, and the answer is very interesting. The Marxist theorist Antonio Gramsci, in part, provided the answer. He said that, for a movement or party to establish its complete cultural and political hegemony over a society, it needed to rely on what he called "organic intellectuals" to preach the new culture, enforce it in the universities, schools and newspapers, and teach children to see that hegemony as reality; people who [are] ... the carriers of the new dominant culture.'[12]

We rounded off our campaign with a mass weekend rally at the Johannesburg Standard Bank Arena with the largest crowd (over six thousand people) we had ever drawn to a single DP event. Helen Suzman was on stage to endorse us, and the auguries seemed propitious. However, the ANC drew seventy thousand to their Orlando rally on the same day (with Mandela as the drawcard) – and one saw reflected the different levels of the two parties' support.

Of course, while the target of our campaign was the ANC, our real opponents were the NNP. After voting early at Orange Grove Primary School, I visited a few other voting stations, did the rounds of party offices, and headed off with Michal (who had joined me for the last week of campaigning) to a hotel in Pretoria to await developments.

Although the calls from all our provincial and regional leaders sounded almost too good to believe, I was (as usual) exceedingly nervous. I paced the hotel room, watched the uninformative blather on SABC-TV, and confided to Michal that perhaps 'we gambled everything on a result we might not get.'

It had been arranged with our campaign leadership sequestered inside the IEC results centre that I should arrive (if I was to arrive at all) at the moment when the DP overtook the NNP on the electronic scoreboard. At about 2 am the following morning the call came from Greg Krumbock to Russel Crystal: 'Bring Tony, we've overtaken the Nats.' I was whisked at high speed to the counting centre and entered, not with the sometimes empty and exhausted feeling which can accompany a hard-fought victory, but with a sensation close to ecstasy: the tradition which the DP inherited and represented – 'so reviled, so battered, so trampled upon' in RW Johnson's words – had reasserted itself.

To be sure, the ANC was heading for a huge victory. But we had over one-and-a-half million votes, and had emerged from the near-death sentence imposed on us just five years earlier. South Africa had a new official opposition in parliament. And I was its leader.[13]

GENERAL ELECTION RESULTS
(Seats in National Assembly)

PARTY	1999 SEATS	1999 % OF VOTE	1994 SEATS	1994 % OF VOTE
African National Congress	266	66,36	252	62,65
Democratic Party	38	9,55	7	1,73
Inkatha Freedom Party	34	8,59	43	10,54
New National Party	28	6,87	82	20,39
United Democratic Movement	14	3,42	–	–
African Christian Democratic Party	6	1,43	2	0,45
Freedom Front	3	0,80	9	2,17
United Christian Democratic Party	3	0,78	–	–
Pan-Africanist Congress	3	0,71	5	1,25
Federal Alliance	2	0,54	–	–
Afrikaner Eenheidsbeweging	1	0,29	–	–
Azanian People's Organisation	1	0,17	–	–

CHAPTER 15

Blowback

*'Blowback' is believed to have been coined by the CIA,
in reference to the shrapnel that often flies back when shooting
an automatic firearm.*

WIKIPEDIA

*Most revolutions have two phases. First comes a struggle for freedom,
then a struggle for power. The first makes the human spirit soar and brings
out the best in people. The second unleashes the worst: envy, intrigue, greed,
suspicion, and the urge for revenge.*

ADAM MICHNIK

I

On 16 June 1999, a wintry Highveld morning at the Union Buildings, some forty million rand had been appropriated for Thabo Mbeki's inauguration as president of South Africa. I was there feeling rather pleased with myself: newly minted Leader of the Opposition, our parliamentary team five times larger than it had been before the election. My party was also installed as official opposition in two-thirds of the provincial legislatures. 'Not bad, not bad at all,' I thought.

However, as I stood in a marquee erected on the rolling lawns admiring Sir Herbert Baker's monument to British colonial rule, chewing a canapé and chatting to Douglas Gibson (now chief whip of the official opposition), I saw a tall, familiar figure striding towards me with purposeful intent. Julian Ogilvie Thompson was one of the most famous faces of South African business. As chairman of Anglo American, he bestrode a mining-industrial colossus which, at the time, was the most significant of the country's corporate behemoths. What did he want?

Although seemingly haughty and imperious, 'JOT' (as he was universally referred to) was possessed of a piercing intelligence and earthy wit. I had come to know him well since, in the tradition of his predecessor but one, HF Oppenheimer, he had continued to provide financial support to the party and had hitherto been warmly supportive of our new-found opposition role. Yet now there was anger and dismay in his countenance.

He was clutching a chicken kebab which he waved at me almost with menace. 'Tony,' he spluttered, 'you've gone to bed with people who have got political AIDS, and I've a good mind to switch off the taps.' I was taken aback, but not entirely surprised.

JOT was referring to the decision, just finalised amid great public controversy, to form a provincial coalition with the NNP in the Western Cape. This effectively shut out the ANC from governance, making it the only province in which they had no power. However, despite the Nats' vertiginous decline elsewhere – and the wholesale defection of most of their voting base to our ranks in June – the NNP had held on to 38,39% of the vote; the DP had finished with a disappointing 11,91%; while the ANC had edged into first place with 42,07%. So between them the DP and NNP had gained a combined 50,3% of the overall vote.

The DP agreed to honour our election pledge and seek an opposition-led coalition, although we did not exclude the possibility of a vestigial role for the ANC. NNP provincial leader Gerald Morkel and his DP opposite number, Hennie Bester, offered the ANC one cabinet post, which they spurned. Public speculation mounted, and I discovered that JOT's Union Building blast was not an isolated incident. Finance minister Trevor Manuel had obviously been working the phones: I soon received entreaties from various DP business backers urging me to take a more 'inclusive approach' to ensure that a 'significant portion of the Western Cape electorate was not shut out from governance'.

This was fair enough as far as it went – but it didn't go very far at all. Even while the ANC and their public praise-singers (which at that time included the *Cape Times* and SABC, naturally, and even the normally independent *Cape Talk Radio*) ratcheted up the volume, we were confronted with another coalition dilemma. This time it was from the ANC, which went some way in explaining the humbug and hypocrisy underlying true power considerations.

In KwaZulu-Natal, the previously dominant IFP had been cut back to 41,9% of the vote. The ANC was second (with 39,38%), leaving the DP and its 8,16% as the potential kingmaker in my home province. Almost immediately our provincial leader, Roger Burrows, was approached by the ANC to form a coalition shutting out the IFP. I vetoed this on the basis of our electoral promise of a 'coalition of the opposition' as a counterweight to the ANC. In KwaZulu-Natal the ANC had no consideration for the fact that a plurality had plumbed for the IFP, the very argument they were advancing for themselves in the Cape. On being rebuffed, the ANC in KwaZulu-Natal immediately went into talks with the IFP and formed a coalition as junior partner to Inkatha, thereby excluding the DP and thus the majority of whites and Indians who had in significant numbers supported us.

Despite the trade union federation COSATU launching rolling mass action in the Western Cape to bring succour to the ANC, and despite the sonorous intervention of Cape Town archbishop Njongonkulu Ndungane, I was determined we should stand our ground. I did, however, request Hennie to increase the offer to the ANC, which was upped to three seats. This too was rejected. So the opposition coalition went ahead.

On 24 June 1999 agreement was reached between the DP, the NNP and the ACDP (with one seat). We netted four cabinet posts including the crucial delivery areas of Education (Helen Zille) and Health (Nicky Koornhof). I received an irate message from former PFP grandee Ray Swart (who I had insisted to my mother should deliver the speech at my bar-mitzvah in 1970, in the forlorn hope that it might help his election campaign). Now he denounced me for 'selling out to the Nats'.

In my view, a well-administered, corruption-free, pro-poor provincial government would curb the ANC's hegemonic lust; it could also, by servicing all its voters irrespective of race, be a powerful template on which a future national political alternative could be modelled. Indeed, in the areas of Health and Education alternative policies to the nationally imposed denialism started to take root. A year later, when Mbeki had starved eight provinces of antiretrovirals, it was only in the Western Cape that such delivery first happened (although the IFP-led government in KwaZulu-Natal followed suit). When parliament convened for the post-election State of the Nation debate the ANC decided to blow back on our fight back.

We moved offices from our fifth floor eyrie to more spacious accommodation in the Marks Building which included, by the frugal standards I was accustomed to, a vast wood-panelled suite of offices allocated to the Leader of the Opposition.

We had 45 MPs including seven in the second chamber (NCOP). They came from seven provinces (in Limpopo and Northern Cape we failed to secure a national representative) and were, literally, in all shapes, sizes, age groups and races, and with distinct variabilities in terms of performance and competence. This was not surprising, and was perfectly captured by the story told to me by an NNP MP, Watty Watson (who would soon join the DP).[1]

He was assigned as counting agent for Komatipoort, in the southern tip of Mpumalanga near the Kruger National Park. The DP had no presence – yet the DP piled up far more votes than the NNP. So some of our MPs had arrived by design, others by default, but all on the back of the 'Fight Back' campaign: a stunning success, but one that resulted in a post-election hangover.

This was immediately evident from the rhetoric and dynamic in parliament. However, before the ANC launched its assault on us, Mpumalanga gave forth its first hostage of ill-fortune to Mbeki's new administration. As a consequence of a resolution taken at Mafikeng, all ANC premiers (and mayors, ministers and other lesser political beings) were to be appointed by the president. The provincial party structures were circumvented. It was a gift for the opposition which kept on giving.

Quite what qualities Mbeki discerned in his choice for Mpumalanga premier Ndaweni Mahlangu was one of his better-kept secrets. Even ANC insiders were aghast at the appointment of this former apartheid apparatchik to the top provincial job; he had served as 'Minister of Justice' as well as 'Minister of Education' in the KwaNdebele bantustan, and his 'struggle credentials' were slight to non-existent. Premier Mahlangu's first public utterance – from his corruption-ravaged provincial capital – became an instant classic. Defending a proven liar's appointment to his administration, he said it was 'permissible for politicians to lie in public'.[2] I suggested Mbeki fire Mahlangu as 'a golden opportunity to illustrate how he will handle corruption'. Mbeki did not: he rounded on me and the DP as pedlars of a 'soulless theology', 'home-grown Tories' who defined some races as 'sub-human and believed in the survival of the fittest.'[3]

In that speech Mbeki set all the markers for his presidency: mischaracterise his opponents; malign their motives; and stick by his appointments in public office, no matter how rotten, drunken or maladroit they turned out to be. He drew sycophantic and lusty cheers from the ANC benches, few realising that as his presidency evolved – and over time unravelled – he would use the same tactics against his internal party opponents.

Mbeki was, however, careful to pour honey on the head of the now much-diminished Van Schalkwyk, praising his 'constructive' approach to opposition. In the vanity, and ultimate venality, of the NNP leader, Mbeki had discerned the true character of his Nat opposite number far better than I could have known.

Speaker Frene Ginwala fawned over Mbeki, describing his attack as (presumably deliciously) 'murderous'.[4] However, the mission of demonising the new opposition in extreme and extravagant terms emerged clearly – but it was, on this occasion, a formality delegated to lesser forms of political life than the president. In particular, the poison in parliament flooded over a DP apostate: Dr Bukelwa Mbulawa who had become one of our MPs in November 1997. My former deputy leader, William Mnisi, had been left to his own – inadequate – devices, and I was determined to surround Mbulawa with care and attention. It was to no avail.

Perhaps frustrated by constant harassment from the ANC when she spoke from our benches, or from some inarticulate but deeply felt need to rejoin the majority, Mbulawa defected to the ANC on the eve of the election. Her reward was a seat in the new parliament, and the price of her return – as the first ANC speaker in the debate after I had spoken – was a savage take-no-prisoners assault on her former party and me.

It was easy to discern that she was reading from a prepared script. Under my leadership, the enlarged DP, she claimed, 'espoused a resurgence of neo-Nazism.'[5] *Die Burger* characterised her utterance as 'hate speech' and called on the ANC to 'repudiate her'.[6] That was objectively impossible. Mbulawa (who always claimed to be a staunch Christian) was no more than the paid messenger – the message itself was scripted by the ANC high command. A few days later ANC NEC member and KwaZulu-Natal spokesman Dumisani Makhaye again asserted that the DP was 'neo-Nazi' and compared the party to the 'Nazi perpetrators of the Reichstag fire'.[7]

This was a blood libel. Douglas dissuaded me from sending, via parliamentary messenger, thirty silver coins to Mbulawa. ('Rather buy yourself a drink, it will be less of a waste and more beneficial.') But this new and far more extreme obloquy had to be met and answered. I also noticed, one or two brave souls apart, how the ranks of the commentariat, always swift to label robustness or intemperance on my part as 'adversarial' or 'negative', were silent or averted their gaze. However, since my Jewish faith was to some extent part of the ANC's calculus of insult, I was unconstrained and unschooled in the injunction to 'turn the other cheek'. At the end of July I determined to provide some answering fire at a press breakfast in Pretoria.

I labelled the new tactics as the ANC's version of racial McCarthyism, which did, indeed, have a Nazi provenance. I told my audience:[8]

'"The masses have limited understanding, scant wisdom and a weak memory. Thus to have a major impact, political propaganda must focus on a small number of points and convey them through slogans. That will ensure that even the slowest member in the audience will understand the message."

'Those fateful words were penned by Adolf Hitler in *Mein Kampf* (as reproduced in *Haaretz*, Tel Aviv, 14 January 1999). They are the basis for the "Big Lie" theory of political propaganda. This technique was used with devastating effect by the NP government in the 1960s which smeared and labelled their opponents as "communists", even when such opponents were often staunch anti-communist liberals.

'The ANC – ably assisted by its satraps "redeployed" in critical positions of eminence and influence in the public and private media – are very different in both motivation and method from their NP predecessors. But in one respect their assault on the DP ... has the same authoritarian impulse: it is a desire to chill or still free speech and the democratic discourse. What the government – and others – really do and say when they label legitimate and democratic critics as everything from "racist" to "neo-Nazi" is to stop debate itself. The retort of "racist" effectively ends the debate since a racist's views are not worth considering, indeed, should be rejected at source, since he or she is a "moral criminal" whose motivation excludes him or her from a hearing.'

I concluded with the assertion that 'the Mbeki presidency must decide whether this is the sort of discontent it wishes to encourage.' Indeed, Mbeki was to walk this road with greater energy and determination than I ever imagined at its commencement. Race and race-labelling would over the next few years become his guiding star.

2

The assault on the DP coincided with attacks on a few liberal institutions unbowed by the gale-force nature of the new invective. The South African Institute of Race Relations, despite its impeccable role and painstaking research into the barbarities of apartheid, was not spared. Its outspoken criticism of the shortcomings and excesses of ANC governance led to rebukes and accusations of being 'right-wing' or 'pro-apartheid' by the ANC. Its robust director, John Kane-Berman, provided an explanation for the assault:

'The liberals in South Africa who are willing to be critical of the present government are in a very strong position in the sense that they have a track record of pretty consistent opposition to apartheid. That's part of the reason they are singled out.'[9]

One of the few black intellectuals who chose to embrace the liberal cause, Themba Sono, and who in due course served unhappily as a DA provincial legislator, gave what I considered an excellent elucidation:

'Political intolerance is a danger and has been growing very fast. The political left-wingers of this country, like the apartheid right-wingers, are incapable of surviving without an enemy. The new enemy is liberals and liberalism.'[10]

The ANC did not confine its attacks to parliament. It systematically stripped the DP of committee chairmanships and representation on outside oversight bodies (such as the Judicial Service Commission) in its quest for unbridled hegemony and its search for a more quiescent opposition.

A crucial question has often been posed: 'Did the DP's "Fight Back" campaign poison the wells of post-1999 South African politics?'

The answer is provided by an imaginary substitution: if we had fought the election under the slogan of, say, 'effective opposition' (as our under-inspired PR agency suggested) would the ANC's reaction and subsequent actions have been any different? That must be open to serious doubt. Our slogan might have offended, but the substance of our critique and insistence on stiff-spined opposition seemed to be the heart of their complaint against us.[11]

Leaving aside our incontestable electoral success, we certainly provided our opponents with a stick with which to beat us. But I am fairly certain that however anodyne or aggressive we chose to be, the result would have been much the same, unless we abandoned our style of opposition and drew back from the essence of our critique. Rooted in a liberal mould of promoting limited government, respectful of the rights of citizens and empowering them with access to opportunity – without predetermining either individual or group outcomes – we could do no other than vigorously contest the ANC's plans for socially re-engineering South Africa and fusing government and state.

My attention was drawn to the ANC document: 'Cadre Policy and Deployment Strategy: Facing the Challenges'.[12] Here, in infinite detail, was the end-point of the process commenced at Mafikeng two years earlier. In essence, the document stated that the accountability of all deployed ANC cadres lay to the party high command and not to the institutions in which they were serving. The party would place its officials in every key post in every institution, including those which the Constitution required to manifest independence. My initial critique of the approach was met with an asinine response. ANC spokesman Smuts Ngonyama described me as 'a childish but confused individual'.[13]

This jejune rejoinder hardly diminished our enthusiasm for unmasking the ANC's grand design. The DP research department set out to deconstruct the document and its intellectual forebears. The upshot was a tightly worded, closely reasoned analysis which we launched in March 2000 under the rubric: 'All Power to the Party: The ANC's programme to eliminate the distinction between party and state and extend its hegemony over civil society.'

The somewhat long subtitle summed up the essence of the 65-page tome, with hundreds of examples of how ANC cadres had been deployed faithfully across the whole of government, much of civil society, and throughout the public service, creating a dual authority – one the Constitution, the other the party. A close reading of both policy and practice left little doubt which centre would prevail. Much of our critique was already in the public realm although largely ignored or dismissed by the press and civil society's supposed watchdogs, such as Idasa, which throughout most of this critical period slept, or didn't bark. However, our study unveiled unique insights:

- The ANC's National Working Committee (NWC) was mandated to deploy cadres to all state institutions, including the public service, local government administration, statutory bodies, parastatals, the security forces, the Central Bank and the SABC.
- Control over deployments was centralised in the hands of the NWC.
- ANC cadres had been deployed to senior positions in almost all state institutions including those supposed to be independent of government.
- Hand-in-hand with deployment the ANC had established structures to ensure that the cadres remain *informed by and accountable to* the NWC.
- Under the official ANC policy of democratic centralism ANC cadres *in whatever sphere of state or society* are bound to defend and implement the will of the party leadership with 'maximum political discipline'.

In essence, the ANC was white-anting the Constitution and eroding the foundations of the liberal-democratic state.[14] One of Mbeki's later put-downs of me – that 'we live on different planets' – proved truer than he might have imagined.

3

At this time of fierce inter-party contestation, I was distracted by a squabble far closer to home than I might have wished. The 1999 regional election in Gauteng had more than doubled our provincial caucus there. It also elevated my brother Peter (who three years previously had elbowed

Ian Davidson out of the party's legislature leadership) to Leader of the Opposition in that chamber. His ascendancy was marred by a brutal falling out with his previous confidant and my one-time protégé, Jack Bloom, then provincial chief whip. Peter had apprised me of some of the background to the dispute, but I was utterly aghast when newspaper headlines proclaimed: 'Graveyard votes scandal rocks DP'.[15]

There were allusions to claims that so-called members of a 'liberal cabal' (an anti-Peter one) were using deceased members' names to fraudulently inflate party membership lists in the Gauteng South region. This brought to mind David Ben Gurion's quip that Israel would be a normal society only when it had its share of prostitutes and robbers. Our hitherto small and exclusivist party was now to be 'normalised' by the dark arts which characterised the larger political vehicle we had become.

I was dragged into the wrangle when an anonymous letter (emanating from the party office in the Gauteng legislature) referred to the 'megalomaniacal Leon brothers and their lackey Douglas Gibson'.[16] I was caught between the hammer of being Leader and the anvil of being a brother. 'When in doubt, appoint a committee' was a useful cliché. Errol Moorcroft MP – the party federal chairman – was appointed to head up the enquiry; but Peter became a pre-emptive casualty when he brought forward his intended resignation as provincial head 'in order to concentrate on his legal practice'. Bloom, a full-time politician, was allegedly concerned at my brother's division of time between his political role and his flourishing partnership at a top Johannesburg firm of attorneys. Party rules deemed that national and provincial MPs were to be essentially full-time legislators.

While the row created frissons of tension at my mother's Saturday lunch table, the strain between us disappeared after Peter left politics. But he remained resentful of what he regarded as the small-time, small-town prejudices and petty jealousies which he felt characteristic of the DP 'cabal' in South Africa's largest city and the party's most vote-rich province. Whatever the merits of the dispute and the resentments Peter's haughty style and sometimes remote-control leadership engendered among certain colleagues, it was on his watch and at his behest that the party in Gauteng had thrust open a series of corruption and conflict-of-interest scandals which had come to characterise ANC governance in Gauteng and elsewhere, and helped propel us to where we now stood.

Peter's political exit did not resolve the problem that the DP's rapid growth threw into sharp relief. Before 1999 the party organisation had in many cases been the political equivalent of a mom-'n-pop store. Many of the 'old guard' found it difficult to adjust to the realities of our new, larger political realm. They were mistrustful of outsiders, and the early tensions in Gauteng were a small dress-rehearsal for wider clashes and resentments.

Despite resistance in some party quarters to the imperatives of change, the party Federal Congress in March 2000 in Cape Town revealed to the world a very different animal, fast shedding the more pale, Anglicised and polite skins which some clearly happily inhabited. John Mattison – unusually as a South African political journalist at the millennium – combined some sympathy for our cause with trenchant powers of observation. He captured the scene well:

'The reaction of the thousand-odd delegates at the DP's [congress] to the unanimous re-election of Tony Leon as party leader illustrates the changing face of what was the party of rich, white, English-speaking suburbia. Someone shouted "*viva!*" Immediately after this, someone else shouted "*looi hulle*" (thrash them) ...

'The DP is not the party that it was in the days of Helen Suzman. Instead, last week in Cape Town it was the voice of the township and the former Afrikaner Nationalist. The DP won more Afrikaner support than any other party in 1999, making the liberal Leon the *Volksleier* of the year 2000.'[17]

The *Volksleier* was happy to bask in some of the party's new-found multilingual glory, but I was also seized with two imperatives. The first arose from a series of encounters and meetings under the banner of 'Sizakubona Tour' ('go and see for yourself'). This had taken me into some of the most forgotten, marginalised, overwhelmingly black and Coloured areas of continuing deprivation. The depressing pattern of life was bleakly uniform: communities in crisis because of stalled government delivery, non-existent employment prospects, faltering educational systems, and the deadly presence of a full panoply of poverty-related diseases from diarrhoea to HIV/AIDS. Whatever benefits Mbeki-Manuel economics was delivering, its reach fell short of this vast underclass.

With our Finance spokesman Ken Andrew in charge, we presented to congress a raft of explicitly pro-poor policies: vouchers for school leavers and, most controversially, a basic income grant for all South Africans (fully costed by a 1% increase in VAT). There should be accelerated privatisation, including the sale of state-owned property which we estimated would yield upward of R20-billion a year.

This message of pro-market, anti-poverty strategies, including achieving 6% annual GDP growth (which we announced six years before government swung behind it), was not aimed at rebutting our many critics on the Left, but also to address a much larger, more elusive voter market where the majority lived and suffered. We would dust off our fine-sounding principles and take them into the thick of the fight in black South Africa, which only the ANC appeared to be contesting. That long-term goal remains today central to the party.

More immediately within our reach was the consolidation of opposition. I conveyed my single-minded determination to achieve just that among our warring factions in the run-up to the year-end's municipal elections. It was to happen sooner and in far more dramatic fashion than anyone could ever have imagined. (See next chapter.)

Another message was that despite our improved fortunes, some souls were nervous at the barrage of criticism to which the party had been subjected. To be fair, some (including certain very senior MPs) were simply reflecting the anxiety of their constituents, especially the English-speakers who were the party's traditional backbone. I had always held deeply ambivalent views of this group, of which I, demographically at least, was a member. Although comprising almost two million South Africans (among its white membership) they were to an extent in a semi-permanent crisis of identity. They reciprocated my ambivalence.

The arrival of the NP in power in 1948 effectively saw them out of governance, and the arrival of the ANC in government seemed to place them further on the political periphery. They soon discovered that institutions previously their 'preserve' (such as the 'English service' of Radio South Africa) were now common property.

They feared the ANC and its power lust; and were deeply dismayed at the state's increasingly corrupt face and weak hand in tackling crime. On the other hand, they (and the big business panjandrums) were grateful that their properties had not been expropriated and, on the contrary, were being enriched by the appreciably steep rise in their market values. Most felt some guilt for the apartheid past in which many had been either complicit or unresisting. But they overwhelmingly voted for my party, although we were easy prey to those depicting it as 'anti-transformation' or 'out of tune with the new South Africa'. Many years later I read British journalist Jonathan Freedland's take on Israeli strongman Ariel Sharon and the unease he engendered in gentler members of the Jewish Diaspora: 'He was like a hulking, animated scarecrow … [You] might not boast of him in polite company, but you felt glad he was there.'[18] He could have been describing the response of many English-speakers to my brand of opposition and leadership.

At the congress, I affirmed there would be no let-up in my aggression: '[The ANC is] one of the last great nationalist dinosaurs, with a rhetoric replete with slogans from the ideological junkyards of the 1960s.' I added, taking direct aim at Mbeki's Manichean vision of South Africa, that 'you do not bind the wounds of our divided nation by ripping open the scar of racialism again and again when the government's petty political advantage-seeking and policy failures demand it.' Recourse to racial recrimination might fob off the black intelligentsia, but I pointed to what I thought its real purpose: '[It] is really forward cover to announce that if the ANC fails it will be the fault of whites, or anti-transformationists or some sinister third force.'

My seriousness was offset by the announcement that Mrs Carol Johnson of Manenberg on the Cape Flats had arrived to present her recently born baby to me; and so I was introduced to my namesake – young Tony Leon Johnson,[19] whom I inexpertly held in my arms as the cameras flashed. Since I was not to be destined to produce my own children, I had the consolation that long after me, Tony Leon would go on!

At the Rivonia trial, Mandela told the court: 'It is not true that the enfranchisement of all will result in racial domination – political division based on colour is entirely artificial and, when it disappears, so will the domination of one colour group by another. The ANC has spent half-a-century fighting against racialism. When it triumphs it will not change that policy.'[20] His successor gave notice in parliament in 1998 that ours was in reality a two-nation affair and the twain were unlikely to meet any time soon. He also gave early warning that on his imminent presidential watch race nationalism would be cranked up. Mbeki called a special debate to discuss the matter.[21]

'A major component of the issue of reconciliation and nation building,' he stated, 'is defined by and derives from material conditions in our society which have divided our country into two nations, the one black and the other white. We [Mbeki always used the royal plural] therefore make bold to say that South Africa is a country of two nations.

'One of these nations is white, relatively prosperous, regardless of gender or demographic dispersal. It has ready access to developed economic, physical, education, communication and other infrastructure ... The second and larger nation ... is black and poor, with the worst affected being women in the rural areas, the black population in general and the disabled.' This 'reality' was underwritten by the perpetuation 'of racial, gender and spatial disparities born of a very long period of colonial and apartheid white minority domination, [and] constitutes the material base which re-inforces the notion that, indeed, we are not one nation, but two nations.'

To make the point plainer, he also announced well in advance of his presidency that 'neither are we becoming one nation. Consequently, also, the objective of national reconciliation is not being realised.' Indeed, the nation was 'faced with the danger of a mounting rage to which we must respond seriously ... In a speech, again in this House, we quoted the African-American poet, Langston Hughes, when he wrote – *What happens to a dream deferred?* His conclusion was that it explodes.'

Nine years later, when Mbeki was heading towards the end of his presidency and was faced every day with riots and uprisings demanding service delivery, he expressed himself perplexed as to why the people were protesting. Clearly by then the two-nations reasoning which motivated his early remarks was wearing thin with a population weary of promises but no delivery. That came at the end of a very long and fraught race war which the Presidency decided to unleash on its opponents and the country.

Once established as president, Mbeki started to increasingly fine-tune his perspective. In parliament at the State of the Nation debate on 4 February 2000, he thought it necessary to draw the nation's attention to an e-mail sent by a racist engineer in KwaZulu-Natal (dismissed for his trouble). Mbeki was happy to provide the quotation in full:[22]

'I would like to summarise what the kaffirs have done to stuff up this country since they came into power ... If a white buys a house, he pays transfer duties. If a kaffir buys a house it is free of duties because he was "previously disadvantaged"... More than 20% of the GDP is embezzled by the kaffir politicians and corrupt civil servants ... The UIF and state pension funds have been embezzled ... Our girlfriends/wives are in constant threat of being brutally raped by some AIDS-infested kaffir (or gang of kaffirs) ... Every day someone you know is either robbed, assaulted, hijacked or murdered ... Half these black bastards have bought their drivers' licences from corrupt traffic cops ... and and and and and ... All I am saying is that AIDS isn't working fast enough!'

Quite why Mbeki saw fit to treat parliament to this vituperative filth was not clear. But he was prosecuting his race obsession – and his determination to place it back, front and centre on the political agenda. He indicated that government and the Human Rights Commission were to convene a National Conference against Racism which was held later in the year, and that also the country would be hosting the World Conference Against Racism in 2001 which he deduced was 'a great honour'.

He also caused outrage (apparently among friends of South Africa abroad) when he not only indicated that he was abandoning Mandela's emphasis on unity and reconciliation, but did so in the most emotive terms, quoting Brecht's *Arturo Ui*: 'The bitch is in heat again.' This was a reference to the resurgence of racism in the world.

Mbeki's generalised views on race and racists was about to home in on me.

I was in my parliamentary office late on a Friday afternoon in August 2000 when I received an urgent call from a radio station in Johannesburg. The president had launched a 'massive, personalised and racist' attack on me and 'would I care to respond?' I had not been named, but Mbeki had me in his sights. (See Chapter 8.)

Delivering the second Oliver Tambo Lecture – an 11-page ramble on race quoting all manner of authorities from Shakespeare to WF du Bois to Frantz Fanon to Malcolm X to Amilcar Cabral to Walter Rodney and even Ariel Dorfman of Chile – his opening paragraphs were – even by the standards of debate in South Africa – cognitively dissonant:

'Recently, a leading white politician spoke his mind either honestly or, alternatively, seemingly without inhibition. As with Prospero's brother [much of his lecture was based on a misreading of Shakespeare's *The Tempest*, either misquoted or misunderstood], circumstance had created the apparent necessity that he needs to be absolute Milan.

'Just over a fortnight ago, one of our newspapers reported that this white politician had said that the president of our Republic had damaged the reputation of the government. According to the newspaper, the white politician accused the president of suffering from a "near obsession" with finding African solutions to every problem, even if, for instance, this meant flouting scientific facts about AIDS in favour of "snake-oil cures and quackery".

'Our own absolute Milan, the white politician, makes bold to speak openly of his disdain and contempt for African solutions to the challenges that face the people of our continent. According to him – who is a politician who practises his craft on the African continent – these solutions, because they are African, could not but consist of the pagan, savage, superstitious and unscientific responses typical of the African people, described by the white politician as resort to snake-oil cures and quackery.'

The rest of the speech went on to preach against what he called 'the birth of a Caliban native petite bourgeoisie, with the native intelligentsia in its midst, that, in pursuit of wellbeing that has no object beyond itself, commits itself to be the footlickers of those that will secure the personal well-being of its members.'[23]

A few weeks earlier, at Stanger town hall on 25 July, I had specifically criticised what Mbeki had done by mishandling HIV/AIDS policy – and I had in mind his near-obsession with Virodene. My reference to 'snake-oil and quackery' did not refer to blacks but referred to white activities in the American South.

Howard Barrell in the following week's *Mail&Guardian* wrote: 'I am left with the conclusion that Mbeki has made this inflammatory charge without providing an iota of evidence. He has, instead, relied merely on a dubious grasp of the literary classics and assertion.' He pointed out that Mbeki had misconceived the role of Prospero and Caliban in *The Tempest* and co-opted them for his own purposes in 'a rather eccentric way'. For Mbeki, Prospero, the slave-owner, represents the oppressed. 'The coloniser is the usurper Antonio, who Mbeki tells us in his lecture, is personified by Leon and whites.'[24]

Barrell concluded: 'I spent several days this week trying to understand the basis on which Thabo Mbeki says Tony Leon is a racist. I have read, reread and read again the speech in which Mbeki did so and I am none the wiser.'

I responded: 'Mbeki must now explain to South Africa and the world why it was that he was as recently as two years ago championing the totally disreputable and medically, scientifically and legally discredited and now outlawed, so-called miracle AIDS cure, Virodene.' He had 'squandered his prestige on what might rightfully be called a form of quackery, and now takes issue with me because I dare to mention this blindingly self-evident fact.'

There was no let-up. The snake-oil and quackery jibe clearly cut deep inside the psyche of Mbeki and his circle. Smuts Ngonyama – head of the ANC Department of Communications in the Presidency – wrote to the *Citizen* on 18 August 2000: 'What more does a normal and serious-minded person need in order to know that this is a profoundly racist statement. Again, typical of his [Leon's] white supremacy stereotype, he does not accept that the ANC or the president should respond to this heap of garbage, precisely because his whole social consciousness does not make it easy for him to see that this is a racist statement.'[25]

Quite what I, or the general public, was to make of all this was not entirely clear. I pointed out in an article: 'I am not a Prospero, I am not even Prospero of a special type. I was born here, not shipwrecked and washed up on shores that are not my own. Our Constitution gives all South Africans full political rights and equal status. That means all here may write what they like, say what they must, and vote for whomever they want in power, black or white.'[26]

Mbeki's behaviour deeply disquieted me. I suspected there might be something in his background which compelled him towards his strange views. Some critics found the contrast between Mbeki and Mandela illuminating. In 1962, Mandela, then aged 44, went to prison until released in 1990, aged 71; in 1962, Mbeki, at 20, was sent to the ANC-in-exile for training (in England, the Soviet Union and Africa) and in 1990 returned to South Africa aged 47. James Myburgh and Stanley Uys pointed out: '[The man] who served 27 years in prison came out as a conciliator, while the man who served 27 years in exile came back racially driven.'[27]

That was reinforced by Professor Robert Schrire of UCT, who wrote in 1998 of 'the visceral dislike and contempt' Mbeki felt for the white minority, 'the former beneficiaries of apartheid'. Tom Lodge, a professor at Wits University and quite empathetic to the ANC's general perspective, believed 'Mbeki's weakness is the lack of a heroic liberation biography.'[28]

4

Mbeki continued to beat this drum throughout his presidency. His attack on me was given generalised form in a rare one-on-one interview with the media, in this case with Hugo Young in the *Guardian* on the occasion of a state visit to Britain. Mbeki opined: 'Many whites, I wouldn't say all, have a particular stereotype of black people. They would deny it, but it's true. They see black people as lazy, basically dishonest, thieving, corrupt. Most of all, they can't really govern any country. Look at what's happening in the rest of Africa – that would be the argument.'[29]

Having presented the entire white population in these terms it was relatively easy for Mbeki to claim his greatest concern was to create a non-racial society and that his failure to do so would be the greatest failure of his presidency. It was, however, to be a self-reinforcing process; over the next few years, the president didn't simply play the race card, he 'flamed' his opponents. I discovered that on the Internet 'flaming' refers to when someone uses a barrage of inflammatory, hostile or derogatory messages to provoke or intimidate another person. At an early stage, Mbeki had bought into this Internet phenomenon (he was a great surfer of the Net, for all its abundance of fake information); so he 'flamed' his critics to attack and silence dissent.

Mbeki was at least consistent. He outlined the most grotesque stereotypes of African people he could conjure in his fervid imagination and then he presented them as the 'ideals' his critics embraced. And yet, while putting the race 'debate' on steroids, Mbeki launched his New Partnership for Africa's Development (Nepad) which laudably made explicit an African pledge to 'promote peace and stability, democracy, sound management and people's sense of development and to hold each other accountable in terms of the agreements outlined in this programme.'[30]

It was exceptionally difficult to discern Mbeki's real motives as he increasingly withdrew from parliament and the South African media, which seemed to quite pusillanimously accept the fact they were going to be denied access to the president on a basis unknown during the Mandela era. Mbeki surrounded himself with a cocoon of loyalists and a wall of silence from which he would usually emerge with his weekly e-letter in the online ANC Today to take up his pet causes and put down his pet hates.

In this polluted atmosphere, few ventured above the parapet since they were likely to be shot down. Completely inured to this tactic, I decided to sally forth regardless. But the minuscule group of ANC-supporting whites had decided by the end of 2000 that it was time for a declaration of apology. Led by the ANC's Carl Niehaus and TRC commissioner Mary Burton, they prepared a petition for signatories to 'acknowledge the white community's responsibility for apartheid since many of us actively and passively supported the system.'

I described this hand-wringing as 'rubbish'. However, while the petition attracted no more than five hundred or six hundred signatures, it did in a sense create more moral distance between the black victims of apartheid and those who appeared to be white recalcitrants. I also felt the declaration contained an entirely self-negating clause that 'some people were deeply involved in the struggle against apartheid but they were very few in number.' The bulk of whites had to apologise for their existence.

I gave an official response: 'Either you did something to oppose apartheid or you did not. The fact that white anti-apartheid activists were a minority does not make them guilty by association with a majority of the same skin colour. Helen Suzman personifies the truth that the so-called white response to the apartheid years was varied, different and often honourable. One could say the same about black South Africans. Apartheid as a system could never have worked without the so-called collaborative class: many who made apartheid work in the homelands – the Public Works minister, Stella Sigcau, and the Mpumalanga premier, Ndaweni Mahlangu, for example – now find high office in the ANC. This should make the ANC pause before it tries rewriting our history.'[31]

It should have been possible to distinguish between Helen Suzman and Hendrik Verwoerd!

By the beginning of the following year the ANC was becoming irked by the fact that there were doubts about Mbeki's leadership mettle. But instead of tackling the question head-on – on AIDS and Zimbabwe, say – the party declared at the conclusion of a four-day NEC *lekgotla* in January 2001 that the real source of the country's problems lay with 'un-patriotic South Africans who besmirch the country at home and overseas.' The NEC member steering the statement, Sankie Mthembi-Mahanyele, added: 'We are talking about tendencies among some people to go over-seas and attack the government and the president [Thabo Mbeki] in bars, restaurants and meetings.'[32]

This proved to be a full dress-rehearsal for the year which followed, which in terms of race reconciliation was a true *annus horribilis*.

The first sign came on the eve of the opening of parliament in February 2001 when I received a copy of a letter that Steve Tshwete, the minis-ter of Safety and Security, had addressed in response to a petition from the Portuguese community, twelve thousand of whom had marched on the Union Buildings in an anti-crime initiative the previous November. I could scarcely believe its contents – not only in terms of the vitriol and vituperation with which a minister of state had attacked a significant por-tion of his own population, but because having known Tshwete reason-ably well over seven years, it seemed scarcely credible that he would have written such a letter himself.

In fact, when James Myburgh ran through his computer files he found many of Tshwete's phrases entirely redolent of the Thabo Mbeki play-book: 'It is perfectly clear to us [the government] that your initiative to march to the Union Buildings and deliver a memorandum addressed to our president was a conscious political act driven by your opposition to the government. I would even make bold to say [a vintage Mbeki phrase] that, in addition to your defining yourselves as our political opponents, you hold the government, our president and our continent in contempt.'[33]

Deep ministerial offence had been taken by the 'demand' that a public response be received by no later than the close of business on 20 November 2000. Tshwete railed that 'this was symptomatic of the contempt of which we speak.'

He went on denounce the entire Portuguese community in these terms: 'Our country has had a considerable Portuguese community for some time, including the apartheid years. We know of no occasion when this community marched to the Union Buildings to present a memorandum to the apartheid presidents demanding an end to the apartheid crime against humanity. You know very well that in its campaign of repression, the apartheid regime claimed the lives of tens of thousands of our people and those of others through southern Africa. In the face of countless massacres, you remained silent.'

Furthermore: 'Some among the Portuguese community you claim to represent, came to this country because they did not accept that the Mozambican and Angolan people should gain their freedom and independence from Portuguese colonialism. Accordingly, South Africa became a second home for these people, because our own people were not free.'

Then: 'These came here because they knew that the colour of their skin would entitle them to join the "master race", to participate in the oppression and exploitation of the black majority and to enjoy the benefits of white minority domination.'

It was a full-scale racist tirade. Tshwete – responsible for arresting the encroachment of crime – ended his missive by claiming that several members of the Portuguese group were actually themselves guilty of various criminal offences ranging from armed robbery to illegal trade in liquor and ivory.

I could not initially credit that this letter was genuine. I checked the minister's signature; and far from being a hoax published by some opponent of the ANC, it turned out to be the real thing.

In parliament deputy minister Aziz Pahad accused the media of 'creating a story'. He then put the blame again on the Portuguese, claiming that they had presented 'a bad memorandum'.[34] All this of course was grist to the mill of my own speech in response to Mbeki when I responded to his State of the Nation address (in which he did not mention the Portuguese). I pointed out that the people of South Africa wanted leadership in the struggle against crime: 'I am compelled to state that the minister of Safety and Security is failing to provide this leadership. On the contrary: instead of taking the fight to the criminals, he has declared war – in the most vile and racist terms – on the law-abiding Portuguese community. His contempt for his own citizens is palpable; his arrogance is despicable – his damage to our country is incalculable ...'[35]

At the time I was reading a masterful biography of Harry Truman by David McCullough;[36] and I quoted to parliament the tribute Mary McGrory had paid Truman when he died, and how she described his performance as president after the Second World War:

'He was not a hero, or a magician, or a chess player, or an obsession. He was a certifiable member of the human race, direct, fallible, and unexpectedly wise when it counted. He did not require to be loved. He did not expect to be followed blindly. Congressional opposition never struck him as subversive, nor did he regard his critics as traitors. He walked around Washington every morning – it was safe then. He met reporters frequently as a matter of course, and did not blame them for his failures. He did not use his office as a club or a shield, or a hiding place. He worked at it ... he said he lived by the Bible and by history. So armed, he proved that the ordinary American is capable of grandeur and that a president can be a human being.'

Truman's presidency, albeit in a very different time and place and under different circumstances, was a complete counterpoint to Mbeki's. He was open, accessible and 'a certifiable member of the human race'; Mbeki's behaviour had been in every respect different. Mbeki did not look up from his papers when I read out the quotation, but merely increased the pace of his furious scribbling.

Mbeki's racial obsessions and increasing dislike, if not contempt, for the parliamentary opposition was plain enough. But what I did not realise at the time was that his self-created national democratic revolution was about to start devouring its own members.

Warning had been given in a little-noticed article which appeared in a weekly column written by Dr Anthony Holiday of UWC. Holiday was a Marxist historian who had been imprisoned for his political activities during the heyday of apartheid. He wrote:

'There is the Leninist style of centralised leadership Mr Mbeki has insisted on adopting, whereby all the meaningful levers of power appear to be concentrated in his office. This arrangement was doubtless intended to increase his power and hence effectiveness ... sadly the system has had just the opposite of its desired effect.'[37]

Precisely how negative the centralised command presidency would become – and how ineffective it was in preventing Mbeki from being felled by his own opponents – emerged in May when again the voluble and ever-loyal Tshwete mumbled on a television programme that there was 'a plot' against the president. This was apparently based on the statement of an ANC operative in Mpumalanga, that Mbeki was somehow complicit in the assassination of Chris Hani in 1993.

The rumour had done the rounds on an almost continuous basis right through to 2007, but now Tshwete identified the three members who were behind this apparent plot: Cyril Ramaphosa, Tokyo Sexwale and Mathews Phosa, three ANC heavyweights, each of whom had in varying degrees fallen out with Mbeki.

Even the normally docile South African media sat up and took notice.

However, the local reaction (largely one of incredulity) was nothing compared to what it did to dent Mbeki's image overseas. *The Economist*, for example, headlined an editorial: 'Mbeki loses the plot ... and South Africa finds it has a paranoid president'. They did enquire whether, in fact, the outing of the plotters did not mean that Mbeki was going off the rails. They stated, '[But] Mr Mbeki is not barmy, merely paranoid. That, at least, seems the most likely explanation of the conspiracy episode. How comforting that should be to South Africans is another matter.'[38]

Mandela shortly thereafter rushed to the defence of the three, and the 'plot' was revealed to contain no substance. It indicated that the Presidency considered itself under siege, this time not from 'white politicians' like me, but from a fifth column within. This happened at the height of Mbeki's AIDS denialism, his maladroit handling of Zimbabwe, and discontent in his party about centralising, even dictatorial, tendencies.

By the time Mbeki headed off to London for his first state visit, he was seriously backtracking on both the plot and its presumed instigators. In an interview with John Snow on ITN he said that the matter of a plot claim arose only because of the suggestion that he was somehow complicit in the assassination of Hani. He stated, strangely, 'I think ... if the President was involved in a thing like that, the law will have to take its course, they have got to look at the question.'[39]

Snow riposted: 'But there is a suspicion too that you may have been trying to flush out your opponents. To smoke them out with these allegations?' To which Mbeki responded, 'They are not my opponents, there is no way. I do not know anyone who can demonstrate in one way or another that they are such opponents.'

The next chapter in the race wars was the decision by the ANC government to accept the invitation of the UN to hold the World Conference against Racism in Durban in September that year. I took advantage of a parliamentary visit to the Commonwealth conference in Australia and was happy to absent myself. However, before I left, I was invited to address the South African Institute of International Affairs, and I chose as my topic the racism conference: 'The Durban air will be thick with demand, complaint and compensation as many of the twelve thousand delegates to the UN World Conference against Racism seek the usual suspects in the form of Israel, colonialism and the wicked West. Arab states want Zionism equated with racism.'

Israel-bashing was more or less compulsory at such UN gab-fests. But it was noteworthy that a year before, during municipal elections in Cape

Town, the ANC had been responsible for a poster that stated: 'A vote for the DA is a vote for Israel' – with a Star of David with barbed wire and blood across it.

I then highlighted some of the choicer items from the conference – including a demand for an apology for slavery from the US and former colonial powers.

The ANC's own submission would slate globalisation, then starting to emerge as a force in the world economy, as 'the new apartheid'.[40] I pointed out, however, that Durban was a fitting locality for the conference since Africa suffered from some of the world's worst racist problems. There was the appalling genocide in Rwanda (at the dawn of South Africa's democracy). I also indicated that for sub-Saharan Africa, the Hutu-Tutsi madness was an elephant trampling on our gate. The Israel-Palestine conflict was a mouse scurrying far away – yet from the resolutions presented at the conference you would not have thought so. It was quite clear that the conference would be strong on Israel-bashing; and while one could be highly critical of the excesses of Israel in its occupation of the West Bank, there was no proportion or even-handed analysis of the situation in the Middle East.

I implored my audience 'to talk about racism in the widest terms and to proceed from A to Z. Start with Afghanistan's apartheid against women, and tackle Zionism at the end of the list, after Zimbabwe.' As for slavery – a trade ended by the major colonial powers over a hundred and thirty years ago – few at the conference were liable to single out fellow-attendee Sudan, whose government could give master classes on slavery, right then in 2001.

All this fitted very ill with President Mbeki's identification with the Nepad formulation. On the one hand he had a sophisticated grasp of economic reality; on the other, he had championed this Conference against Racism (on which the South African government spent R100-million) which appeared to be going in exactly the opposite and downscale direction.

By the time the twelve thousand conferees gathered in Durban, it was not surprising that one of the DA delegates to the conference, Jack Bloom, a passionate Zionist, noted that several pro-Hitler pamphlets appeared published by the Durban-based Islamic Propagation Centre International which itself had received at least three million dollars from Osama Bin Laden.

Naturally – given that tone – the conference was a complete fiasco. Its essential purpose was to draw attention to racial discrimination and xenophobia, but it soon descended into high farce. The American and Israeli delegations stormed out, citing anti-Semitic attacks outside the official meeting (such as the Hitler leaflets). They claimed the meeting had become a forum for racists.

In Canberra, Australia, I noticed the words of Elie Wiesel, the great Holocaust chronicler, who described the racism conference as a 'circus of hatred and a calumny of lies'.

The Economist painted an equally sorry picture of the conference organiser, Mary Robinson, UN Human Rights chief, who was meant to be running the show.[41] She tried to claim some success: eighteen thousand people had attended from over one hundred and sixty countries, including four thousand non-governmental activists and over a thousand journalists. However, the actual progress made on the 200 clauses of the final text was, in the words of the magazine, 'so tortuous that few expected a finished product by its close.' No one had benefited.

The World Conference in Durban (or 'hatefest' as its detractors labelled it) ended just four days before the Jihadist terrorists of Al Qaeda turned four commercial aeroplanes into missiles of mass destruction on 9/11. The immediate response in South Africa was instructive. I noted how Eastern Cape premier Makhenkesi Stofile suggested that the attackers should be regarded 'not as terrorists but as guerrillas' and that America 'should look into itself' for an explanation of what happened. In contrast, Mbeki's response was a powerful condemnation which placed South Africa on the right side of the international divide. But the ANC's forked tongue underlined an important policy ambiguity that was, in fact, grounded in a fundamental moral ambiguity towards the West, as the World Conference revealed, and which the invasion of Iraq would soon unleash again.[42]

Given the inanition within his own party to the juggernaut of Mbeki's triumphalism (and pained victimhood), one reflects on what Robert Conquest said in *Reflections on a Ravaged Century* when he spoke of the grip that Stalin held over the Communist Party. (Obviously Mbeki was in no way an equivalent to the murderous tyrant.) But the deference within his own party by many who knew things were becoming seriously unstuck yet who chose to keep their own counsel was striking:

'The astounding servility of the victors of 1934, who were as yet unterrorised, is usually explained as follows: if Stalin could not now be removed (they reasoned), he could at least be softened and mollified, flattered, humoured. What this amounted to was collusion in psychosis. They acted out Stalin's psychosis, and in so doing, predictably and disastrously, they fed and fattened it.'[43]

There was something in that as I contemplated the reality of the serried

– but largely silent – ranks of the ANC inside and outside parliament. What Mbeki was really doing in that relatively early period of his presidency was storing up a terrible rage which would all explode after he made the decision to fire Jacob Zuma as his deputy in 2005. That single event became a catalyst for a huge counter-reaction against Mbeki's excesses.

Meanwhile – with even Mbeki and his race warriors taken aback by the extraordinary events of the preceding 12 months – there seemed to be a cooling-off. However, it required a decisive intervention by Archbishop Desmond Tutu, later in November 2004, to allow real debate to resurface. In a seminal speech he criticised the tendency not to speak out against obvious wrongdoing within the governing party. I thought the speech was brave, principled, and a decisive break from the recent past:[44]

'I want our society to be characterised by vigorous debate and dissent where to disagree is part and parcel of a vibrant community, that we should play the ball, not the person and not think that those who disagree, who express dissent, are disloyal or unpatriotic. An unthinking, uncritical, kowtowing party is fatal to a vibrant democracy. I am concerned to see how many have so easily been seemingly cowed and apparently intimidated to comply.'

Framing his remarks around the president's long and disastrous dallying with AIDS dissidence, he made a much more powerful general point: 'Truth cannot suffer from being challenged and examined. There surely can't have been unanimity from the outset. I did not agree with the president but that did not make me his enemy. He knows that I hold him in high regard but none of us is infallible and that is why we are a democracy and not a dictatorship. The government is accountable, as are all public figures, to the people ...

'We should debate more openly, not using emotive language, issues such as affirmative action, transformation in sport, racism, xenophobia, security, crime, violence against women and children. What do we want our government to do in Zimbabwe? Are we satisfied with quiet diplomacy there?'

But for much of his presidency Mbeki appeared unfazed by or uncomprehending of how he had framed the level of public discourse. In June 2003, for example, he told parliament: 'I'd like to advise those who find it politically and strategically expedient to perpetuate the negative stereotype of the African which we inherited from our past, to take the greatest care that they do not start a fire they cannot put out.'[45]

In fact, the fire was one he had fuelled assiduously through much of his presidency.

CHAPTER 16

A Marriage Made in Hell

In politics the choice is never between good and evil,
but between the preferable and the detestable.
RAYMOND ARON

To think that a weak opponent is not dangerous misses
the point that a dog with rabies is in poor health, but it would
be a mistake to pat him.
ROBERT CONQUEST

I

Nothing divided the opposition so much as questions of unity. During the June 1999 election campaign various suggestions had been made in vague and general terms about the achievement of a consolidated opposition, devoutly desired by most non-ANC voters. UDM leader Bantu Holomisa had (I thought bizarrely) proposed that all opposition formations be 'de-commissioned' (appropriate from his militarist perspective) and attend a conference from which a new unified leadership would emerge.

While my call for closer co-operation, perhaps even a combination of parties, made good headlines, in truth I had little idea of what fruits it might yield. The campaign itself, especially our ruthless cannibalisation of the Nat electorate, had also poisoned the atmosphere somewhat. In the second democratic parliament, no fewer than 16 parties represented a highly fractured opposition spectrum ranging from the ultra-Africanist Azapo to the reincarnated Conservative Party – now the Afrikaner Eenheidsbeweging (AEB). Just over twenty-five thousand votes, spread across the entire country, out of nearly sixteen million cast, was sufficient to ensure the election of one MP. A plethora of parties represented the electorate, yet the brutal truth was that the total share of popular support for the non-ANC forces had declined by 3,8% since 1994.

The next electoral battle would be fought on very different terrain. In the nationwide local elections scheduled for the end of 2000, in addition to an allocation of seats via proportional representation, individual wards would be contested; and here the spectre of a split opposition would inadvertently favour the ANC.

Objectively, the party closest to the DP was the now much-reduced NNP. We largely drew votes from the same pool, representing similar minorities. But this proximity served only to sharpen differences and enmities, and relations between the parties were fraught.

Marthinus van Schalkwyk's much-criticised leadership had seen his party's reversal of fortune intensify. Initially, I quite enjoyed his company before his accession to the party leadership in 1997; but I had since developed a fairly healthy dislike of him. I found his puffed-up preening faintly ridiculous, and his oscillation between championing strong opposition while almost simultaneously swooning when Mbeki made siren calls irritating as well as revealing an essential lack of principle.

A friend had been a contemporary of Van Schalkwyk's at the Randse Afrikaanse Universiteit (RAU) in the 1980s. She told me his campus nickname was *Pofmuis* (which could be rendered as 'Puffmouse') – and that he enjoyed the promotion and preferment of the lecturing staff, not his student peers, as a consequence of which he had been propelled to the chairmanship of the Students' Council. He assiduously sought the approval and patronage of his seniors: a pattern which repeated itself under De Klerk who handpicked him as his successor. He was less successful in the court of public opinion.

Shortly after the 1999 election, we held, at his request, a desultory breakfast at the Radisson hotel at Cape Town's Waterfront. How should we approach the municipal elections? During October representatives of both parties met, although the DP side was divided. NP-turned-DP MP Tertius Delport told the meeting, baldly, there 'were no major philosophical differences between the two parties' – which mightily irritated James Selfe who thought, objectively, there were.[1] NP representatives Piet Matthee and Sheila Camerer expressed interest in a so-called 'umbrella option' under which both parties would retain their distinct identities but contest the election as a united front.

At that meeting, Selfe stated that before any common strategic objectives or tactical alliances could be considered, a basic trust needed to be established. However, for most of the DP rank-and-file, bleeding the Nat support base and pillaging their public representatives was far more agreeable and appetising. The alternative presented itself to them as creating a lifeline – or oxygen supply – for their seemingly dying corpus. However, asymmetrical considerations were at play in the Western Cape (thanks to the NNP's continued hold on the loyalty of the Coloured vote) and where we now exercised joint power in the only province in which the ANC was excluded from governance.

Matters nearly unravelled before they were resolved. Shortly after I moved into Van Schalkwyk's old office in the Marks Building, I was feeling quite hubristic – always a dangerous moment for a politician – but the intensity of the campaign, with its almost military-style discipline, had exhausted me.

In a wide-ranging interview with the skilled journalist Paul Bell of *Leadership* magazine, I had revealed my true feelings about Van Schalkwyk's party – I had described them as 'a bunch of losers': accurate but incautious given our alliance with them in the Western Cape.[2] When the interview was published some months later, one of those in the NNP most opposed to our alignment was the voluble and mercurial Peter Marais – of whom much more anon. He seized on my remarks to proclaim that the provincial relationship was 'in serious danger of being destroyed. Leon is kicking us in the teeth,' he told a Sunday newspaper.[3]

My words captured the essential ambivalence of the DP approach to the NNP (and the wider issue of opposition unity). We had fought so hard to emerge on top of the pile, and were deeply uneasy about the twin goals of entrenching our position while increasing the arc of the overall opposition's reach.

When the DP Federal Executive met in late November, I decided to spurn Van Schalkwyk's proposal of an alliance for the 2000 elections. I told the leadership we would fight the poll 'as a distinct party', but decided to increase pressure on Van Schalkwyk by inviting NNP councillors to join the DP 'by no later than March 2000' if they wished to contest the election under our banner.

This call chimed with the sentiments of the majority of our leadership; as did the knowledge that a July Markinor poll had shown the NNP's popularity rating to be in free fall.[4] It now stood at 4%, half what it had polled in June. Most NNP councillors would be out of work if they stayed loyal. I was confident we could decimate them from within, long before the following year's poll. DP leaders started actively canvassing NNP councillors to cross their own political Rubicon, a river which many of their electors had already forded.

I did not confine my efforts at enlarging the spectrum of opposition alliances to the NNP. Early in the New Year at the urging of the DP provincial leader in the North-West, Chris Hattingh, I met the old homeland hand and one-time president of Bophuthatswana, Chief Lucas Mangope. Mangope had reversed his 1994 rejectionist stance and had contested the 1999 elections, emerging in the province ahead of us as the official opposition (and with three times our votes, including an impressive 33% of the total in Mafikeng).

While I knew the purists in my party would be against the idea of breaking bread with this former prop of the bantustan system, I was fortified by the encouragement of Joe Seremane MP (soon to become party chairman), who had been one of Mangope's most staunch opponents. He not only thought it useful to meet Mangope, but attended the meeting. And since the ANC did not shrink from promoting all manner of dubious former apartheid compradors, it was time for the opposition to start playing catch-up.

I found Mangope quite charming in an olde-English way. Well-mannered, etiquette weighed heavily on him and he spoke in a modulated accent which made him sound somewhat like Prince Charles. Actually, we did not achieve much, other than a vaguely worded 'opposition co-operation pact' which never went much past the paper on which it was inked. But the symbolism both showed momentum and countered perceptions that our party could only fish in familiar waters.

In the New Year we extended our deadline for crossover public representatives from March to June. Russel Crystal proved adroit at the arm-twisting and coaxing; and by early June we went for a big bang announcement that 65 councillors from other parties (39 from the NNP, the remainder from five other political homes ranging from the ANC to the Freedom Front) had joined us. These defections from seven provinces were 'probably the largest single movement of public representatives to a new political home,' I said.[5]

The timing of the announcement was deliberate. At the DP Federal Council meeting in Durban in June, we wished to make our most audacious move yet.

In the run-up to Durban, Selfe produced a document (to give its full title): 'Entering Negotiations with the NNP. An Appreciation of the Strategic Landscape. An Assessment of the Balance of Forces.' While redolent of ANC-speak, the 54 single-spaced pages made interesting reading. Its key conclusions:

- Outside the Western and Northern Cape the NNP had no cards. They were bankrupt, organisationally weak, with little prospect of retaining existing support. Outside the Western Cape, our threat to kill them off one by one could be executed, as they knew.

- However, our threat had significance only until the elections were over. Thereafter we would have no stick with which to beat them for another three years.
- In the Western Cape the NNP could truthfully make the case that a significant section of their Coloured support would never vote for the DP; and in consequence the DP, even incorporating the NNP, would lose the city and the province to the ANC because some NNP Coloureds would vote ANC and some would stay away from the polls. This was the NNP's strongest card.

Given all this, it was probably accurate to say that the Western Cape NNP would never accept a merger on our terms – i.e. simply collapse itself under our banner and constitution.

The DP's aim should be to 'to incorporate the NNP into the DP without compromising our liberal ideology, brand integrity, organisational culture, and ensuring DP organisational dominance.' How, then, to achieve this?

2

When the party leaders met in the faded grandeur of Durban's beachfront Edward hotel, a cogent strategy had begun to crystallise. In the two-day discussion, it was appropriately Ryan Coetzee, our strategist *par excellence*, who defined the issue with clarity and crispness: '[Either] we continue the war of attrition against the NNP, "killing them off one by one", or we invite them on board our own ship and offer them the chance of contesting the election under the DP banner.'

The latter idea captured the imagination of the meeting, and I immediately faxed a letter to Van Schalkwyk advising him of the invitation. I issued a careful, diplomatically worded media statement, capturing the essence of the proposal:

'I have been mandated and authorised by a unanimous resolution of the Federal Council of the Democratic Party, the party's highest decision-making body, meeting in Durban on 11 June 2000, to invite the New National Party to contest the local government elections under the banner of the DP. This is a serious offer, sincerely made.

'Accordingly, I will discuss this offer with the NNP leader at a meeting with him as soon as possible. Making our democracy work, both politically and economically, is the basic responsibility and moral duty of every democrat in South Africa. The best way to ensure that democracy works is to build an opposition that can bring the ANC below 50% of the vote. One-party dominance ... has already resulted in growing corruption, cronyism, nepotism, authoritarianism, intolerance of the media and the opposition, and inefficient management of the state. These trends – if unchecked and unchallenged by democratic means – are going to become more pervasive over time.'[6]

I went on: 'It makes no sense for the DP and the NNP to continue fighting each other for the support of opposition voters ... The DP is a strong party with resources and a national organisation ... It would be senseless to give up this clear identity and our sharply defined message of strong, effective and principled opposition. It is thus the DP's duty to lead the consolidation of the opposition.

'And so I want to reach out to the NNP and to its leader Mr van Schalkwyk. The time has come to join forces for a greater purpose. To him I say, let us move forward together and take the fight directly to the ANC. You and I together can make a difference.'

As I headed for Durban airport, Van Schalkwyk called me. He was on the line, not as I half expected, with a rejection, but a proposal to meet as 'soon as possible' to discuss the proposal. We settled on breakfast the next morning at The Bay hotel, a stone's throw away from my Camps Bay residence.

Van Schalkwyk's dominance in the Western Cape had already been held over us when – in a furious response to the mass walkovers we had orchestrated the previous week – he had suggested that the NNP could consider terminating its regional coalition with us. This had made the quartet of DP ministers in the provincial legislature – Hennie Bester, Helen Zille, Nicky Koornhof and Glenn Adams – edgily nervous that they might be forcibly evicted from their offices. So while I held most of the advantages, I did not have them all.

I should have learned more from that breakfast. Disconcertingly, barely after we had shaken hands, came the appearance of a TV cameraman, replete with klieg light and reporter. The *maître d'* rushed to enquire whether we objected to being filmed.

I was completely taken aback. The last thing I wanted was a private discussion to be broadcast to the nation. So I objected and the cameras were banished. Since I certainly had not invited the media, I asked Van Schalkwyk how they had been tipped off. 'Oh,' he chortled, 'you know, word leaks out.'

That was an early warning (which I did not properly heed) of my pu-

tative partner's *modus operandi*: media leaks, protestations of feigned innocence, and always two agendas at play – the one on the table and another
hidden in a quintessentially self-serving mind.

Yet that morning he appeared brutally blunt: 'Look, Tony, I know the
situation. The NNP's essentially finished. We are prepared to go into business with you under your leadership. We are even prepared to drop the
name National Party. But we have to emerge with some dignity out of the
process, which would entail me becoming your deputy leader [with some
feeling he added, 'and not a deputy like William Mnisi'] ... We also cannot
simply join the DP; we would need to create some new vehicle.'

So here was the Nat leader surrendering; and we agreed to constitute talks on a more formal basis. I reported to my inner circle on Van
Schalkwyk's bottom lines, and I mandated Douglas Gibson to lead the DP
component. Van Schalkwyk selected Renier Schoeman, whom I would
soon enough learn had the morality of a puffadder. He would do Van
Schalkwyk's bidding, as their treachery unfolded.

As the formal talks commenced, it seemed a fortuitous moment to
reassure the liberal wing of the party that our roots were not about to be
ripped up. I had what I thought was an emblematic way of doing this. For
several months I had been engaged in a dispute with the Speaker's office
about reclaiming the portrait of Helen Suzman, which had in 1990 been
presented to parliament after party donors had commissioned it. For the
last period of the Tricameral parliament it had hung in a place of honour. But after 1994, her portrait, along with the entire rogue's gallery of
apartheid-era speakers and presidents, had been mothballed in the parliamentary basement. They made way for more politically appropriate works
such as 'artists against apartheid' (an aesthetically execrable display) and so
forth.

Eventually, after much wrangling, we exhumed the Suzman portrait
and hung it in our caucus room. At the ceremony, in mid-June, Suzman
announced herself satisfied that I and the DP parliamentary team were
'doing a fine job of carrying on the liberal tradition in parliament.'[7]

But on being asked whether Hernus Kriel's arrival in the ranks of her
party (he had recently defected from the Nats) and the current discussions
with the NNP derogated from the party's ideology or discomfited her in
any way, she responded: 'I admit that some odd characters have joined, but
this happens in politics. If you want your party to grow, people must join.
The important thing is to stick to your principles, and as long as our newcomers don't undermine our principles, I am prepared to stay on.'[8]

Actually, Suzman, over the next months and years, became steadily less enthusiastic about the 'odd bods' who joined us. She became an implacable opponent of the idea and of the soon-to-be reality of the Democratic Alliance. Once the overall deal with the NNP had been sealed, she phoned me on a Sunday night and, in one of her favourite phrases, told me 'in no uncertain terms' that it was a 'huge mistake' and you will 'come to rue doing business with those people.' She was even more incandescent at Colin Eglin's support for the new project.

It took about twelve days for the two sides – separated by aeons of mutual antipathy and an ocean of mistrust – to more or less reach accord. The NNP chanced their arm by reintroducing the retention of the word 'national' into the new name, and tried, on at least one occasion, to float the idea of a joint leadership. However, we were unanimous that our strength relative to the NNP would be an entrenched feature of the new set-up. I was determined that our negotiators should not fritter away through concessions the objective dominance which the DP held over the NNP. I remembered too well that precise outcome when the DP was formed to the disproportionate disadvantage of its largest component, the PFP.

Helen Zille, with her impeccable liberal credentials, accompanied by Ryan Coetzee, would negotiate over the new party's credo and principles. Instead of a long and disagreeable haggle, this aspect of the fusion was over in less than an hour. With minor modifications, the NNP accepted the entire ideological tenets of the DP, and Zille emerged from her meeting with the NNP's Shaun Vorster happily reporting that the principles could be stamped liberal-democratic.

There was intense pressure from outside, particularly from the Afrikaans media, to 'make a deal'. I knew that failure, after such heightened expectations, would be costly, if not ruinous. However, the negotiations did indeed often bog down when the NNP felt its dignity was being undermined. When, for example, Douglas Gibson put forward a proposal for two deputy leaders (one Van Schalkwyk, the other 'to ensure that the party's leadership is more broadly representative of South African society', possibly DP chairman, Joe Seremane) Renier Schoeman exploded with fury. He described the proposal as a '*berekende poging tot belediging*' ('a calculated insult').

Gibson responded on 23 June 2000, perhaps illustrating the lingering distrust: 'To suggest, as you have done, that the offer ... is a calculated insult, is to attempt to introduce an atmosphere into the negotiations which we have previously avoided.

'You know me well. If it is necessary to conduct these negotiations on an aggressive basis verging on warfare, I shall do so. If, on the other hand, you agree with me that the interests of South Africa and the opposition voter weigh far more heavily than the egos of the participants, let us agree that we will not start trading blows and insults.'

After this skirmish, there was progress and rapid agreement on the name – the Democratic Alliance, DA – and the leadership, myself as leader, Van Schalkwyk as deputy and Joe Seremane as chairman. The parties' federal councils would meet separately on Saturday 24 June 2000 in Cape Town to ratify or reject the outline.

In the days leading up to this self-imposed deadline, Hennie Bester for the DP and Piet Matthee of the NNP attempted to draw up a constitution for the DA. This proved to be a bridge too far; instead it was decided that, over time, the party's national management committee would tackle the task.

The focus switched to the all-important issue of how this body would be constituted. I had various entreaties from Van Schalkwyk that there should be an equality of representation – to which I was opposed. In the end the composition would be determined according to the 1999 election results which gave the DP a majority.

By the Saturday morning of the crunch meetings, there was no settlement of the issue of breaking deadlocks if the national management committee failed to reach agreement. In the end I told Bester that the DP would not proceed unless it had guaranteed management control of the entity: this was non-negotiable.

My domestic circumstances had changed. The year before, Michal and I had decided we would live together in South Africa despite the upheaval and disruption this would cause in her life and especially in the lives of her children. Her daughter Noa, then fourteen, and her son Etai, twelve, emigrated south and after an initial and unhappy stay in Johannesburg, Michal was adamant we would all live in Cape Town.

Although I preferred the familiarity and sociability of Johannesburg to the beauty of what I thought then was the smug insularity of Capetonians, I could not but agree to move to Cape Town. Michal had forsaken her friends, family and way of life for me; and I could hardly object to moving within my own country. Thus on the eve of the DA's formation, Michal, Etai and I (Noa had temporarily returned to Israel) were camped at my mother's holiday flat in Camps Bay, pending our move to a larger and more suitable family home in Newlands. As Michal recorded in her diary, I did not sleep well. She wrote:

'Truth be told, he agonised over the actual decision for a few nights, and then we had one long conversation starting at about five o'clock in the morning of a crucial negotiating Saturday. He then made up his mind: it was going to happen, but he would have to have a very good contract ensuring the power balance would be according to the voters' wishes, and that meant the DP was to have control and he would be in control of the party's political decision-making. The idea of a takeover – rather than a merger – was the only way he could have done it.'

3

The next day, at premier Gerald Morkel's office, I stated the position plainly: 'Gentlemen [there were no women present], the NNP component can have as many non-voting shares as you wish, but in the new line-up the DP will control the majority of the voting shares.' I said we needed management control and 'there will be no agreement unless we get it.' That cleared the air, and after a few ritual protests the point was settled. We signed and headed to our respective meetings.

After a few brief introductory comments I indicated to the DP meeting that I would sum up at the end of proceedings. Then Gibson outlined the proposal. He announced it as in essence a takeover of the NNP, though, constitutionally, a full-scale merger was impossible. Because of the anti-defection clause, the two parties would have to continue to exist separately in parliament and in the provinces – but would register the DA for the forthcoming municipal election. The new formation's municipal councillors would be representatives of the DA, but in the parliaments we would have to sit separately as DP and NNP until the 2004 general election – although we would caucus together.

This gap would give Van Schalkwyk room for endless manoeuvrings which would ultimately implode the party. I did not know that then.

The DP delegates dissected the deal; most, although not all, Afrikaans-speaking members favoured it, though Dene Smuts pronounced her scepticism: 'We're going to strap the rotting carcass of the Nats onto our backs.'

Helen Zille, in contrast, warmly endorsed the idea of the new party. Colin Eglin, who was rushing to the airport for an overseas plane, requested an early speaking turn. His intervention was to prove decisive. A person of unimpeachable credibility, Eglin said that if the formation of the DA would mean that we would be able to close down the debilitating opposition war, and take our party and principles into the terrain occupied by the majority of the electorate, then the risks were worth taking. As he left I could see in the body language of the delegates that he had, with his massive authority and crisp logic, swung many of the doubters. When the Federal Council voted, over eighty per cent of the DP delegates backed the formation of the DA.

Across town my former enemy and soon-to-be deputy, Van Schalkwyk, was having battles with his own party as he sought to convince them of the merits of the 'liberal English'. Some months later, in error, the DP (and later DA) executive director Greg Krumbock was given the tapes of the meeting. In essence, Van Schalkwyk apparently intimated that since the NNP had more party members than the DP (if not actual voters) then over time the NNP would be able to perform a reverse takeover. So he prevailed, at his meeting, at least.

We met the next day to sign the final deal, smile for the cameras, and set up our new political shop – one that now had 68 seats in parliament (the combined DP, NNP and Louis Luyt's Federal Alliance); control of one provincial government; and reasonable prospects in the forthcoming municipal polls.

The Afrikaans press was overwhelmingly affirmative. In an editorial, *Die Burger* welcomed the announcement of the deal. Under the headline '*Historiese Ooreenkoms*' ('Historical Union'), the newspaper declared:

'The merger agreement between the New National Party and the Democratic Party announced this weekend has the potential to irreversibly influence South Africa's history … Both the NNP and the DP have changed remarkably. The NNP has thrown off its apartheid past and accepted classical (in the European sense) liberal-democratic values. The DP has started to lose its English character and abandon its increasingly unsupportable – because of the repeal of apartheid policies – condescension towards Afrikaners.'[9]

The English media were more sceptical and cautious: their worldview was informed by the ANC. The governing party reacted with fury to the fact that the DA, initially at least, robbed them of their preferred tactics of playing favourites and divide-and-rule with the hitherto fragmented anti-ANC forces. The party's formation was a rebuke, as well, for Mbeki's attempt to woo Van Schalkwyk away from our embrace into his own. Smuts Ngonyama, head of the ANC Presidency, declared, 'The right-wingers have come together for a final onslaught. This is reminiscent of Verwoerd and his cohorts.'[10]

Kaizer Nyatsumba, an Independent Newspapers editor, as usual declared himself spokesman for the black majority. After conceding the correctness in principle of opposition unity, he intoned: 'Such a merger will without doubt, be read by the African majority to mean the ganging up against them of the country's minorities.'[11]

Following this theme, the *Financial Mail* declared the DP guilty of 'a gamble with political expediency'. It seemed to miss the point that the new party's purpose was to move on, in Eglin's words, to the arduous and essential task of winning recruits from the majority voting group. The *FM* editor thought this unlikely and gave me prescient, as it transpired, warning of the digestion problems I would soon enough experience:

'Having ingested the NNP to form the Democratic Alliance, Tony Leon's DP might pause for a moment to contemplate the old adage: "You are what you eat." By devouring the dwindling NNP instead of focusing on attracting black support, the DP has risked compromising its liberal principles.'[12]

Whatever the media's misgivings, our offices were flooded with congratulatory calls and financial pledges and I was festooned with invitations to speak and appear at everything from agricultural shows to cultural festivals. The DA was also surprisingly well received by our traditional business backers. The intensity of, for example, Julian Ogilvie Thompson's visceral disapproval of the DP-NNP coalition in the Western Cape a year before had given way to far more approving sounds. Ogilvie Thompson, Harry and Nicky Oppenheimer, and Bobby Godsell all signalled continued support. At this time I consulted South African Breweries chairman, Meyer Kahn.

Kahn, who knew more than most about branding and rebranding products, advised: 'Always give way on matters of dignity, but be unyielding on issues of principle,' he advised. I was soon to discover that, with the new leadership, it was impossible to disentangle the one from the other.

The indigestion of which the *Financial Mail* editor had warned arrived more swiftly than I imagined it would. In law school I had ingested the maxim *de minimis non curat lex* ('the law does not concern itself with trifles'). My new deputy leader, Van Schalkwyk, however, had attended a different law faculty. The weekend following our announcement, an expansive interview with me appeared in *Rapport*, the mass-circulating Afrikaans Sunday title. It had been conducted by Hanlie Retief, a smart and sassy interviewer ever alert to record and retell an incautious clanger. I certainly dropped a few. However, I was obviously not responsible for the headline: '*Die Joodse boytjie wat Kortbroek diep in sy agtersak gedruk het*' ('The Jewish boy who shoved Kortbroek into his back pocket').[13]

I blanched.[14]

Inevitably, Van Schalkwyk was in deep distress over the Retief interview. He told me the article had 'aroused fury in my ranks', adding with a disingenuousness which I would soon discover to be his norm, that while he was none too fussed, the remark I made buried deep in the text – 'Oh yes, the NNP wanted to retain the Christian national principle – "thing" – but it disappeared out of the window' – had set off a firestorm in his circle. I had truthfully answered Retief's question about whether liberal-democrat values were consonant with the NNP's Christian nationalism. I had pointed out that early on in the negotiations the Nats had dropped – at our insistence – any reference to this ethos, given its bad history in South Africa. Now Van Schalkwyk urged me to offer some assurance to 'my people'. I scribbled something for my secretary to send off to the editor, clarifying my meaning.

Was this to be my new fate? Every remark and utterance to be pored over, umbrage taken, and a cascade of calls from my deputy for rectification? I felt exhausted before we had even really begun. Part of me dreaded what was, inevitably, to follow.

And yet – I had shaken the liberal tree; the Nats were now in our midst, not at our throats; and we were applying the ANC politics of addition – this time to the opposition. Howard Barrell, the *Mail&Guardian* editor, was broadly sympathetic to the project and to me personally, and analysed my thinking well in a column:

'This line in recruits represents something of a break from tradition for the DP. Liberals of the old school have tended not to have the stomach for accomplices of this kind. Their delicate sensibilities have, more often than not, led them to conclude that it is better to belong to a small and (as they would see it) virtuously pure party than to suffer the moral blemishes that may come with growth and political relevance.

'But members of the disinfectant tendency no longer dictate the DP's rules of engagement. To the limited extent that they still raise objections to some of those now being drawn into their party's expanded embrace, their voices are surprisingly muted. Their doubts seldom rise above polite demurrals registered in the honeyed accents of our leafier suburbs.

'Tony Leon's leadership is a big factor in this change. Lachrymose liberalism is not the *volksleier's* cup of choice. For Leon, muscle and a little meanness are indispensable aids to morality. He is not in politics to be forever "right" yet forever irrelevant. Rather he is in opposition now in order to win power later – ten or fifteen years down the line.'[15]

Even my robustness was severely shaken when the DA went public with its first rally in the Eastern Cape town of Cradock. The night before, a fund-raiser was held in nearby Graaff-Reinet, where Seremane, Van Schalkwyk and I gathered to enthuse the local structures and haul in some cash. In truth, this somewhat conservative Karoo redoubt had little DP presence. Support the NNP retained in 1999 was largely concentrated here.

To my amazement and embarrassment the local NNP (now DA) leadership had seen fit to both invite and place at the main table – with Van Schalkwyk and me – General Johan Coetzee, the notorious head of the security police under John Vorster, and national police commissioner under PW Botha. That was the precise time when the securocrats unleashed their dirty tricks campaign against extra-parliamentary opponents. 'My God,' I thought, 'look who you have landed up with!' I wrote to Van Schalkwyk enclosing an adverse report on the sighting of Coetzee, and suggested 'caution' in such matters. He did not reply.

The new management committee quickly became a site of arm-twisting over all and everything: from the party's logo and livery to whether the national leader would feature alone in the iconography for local elections or with 'a more inclusive imaging' – which was Natspeak for including Van Schalkwyk on the posters and billboards. On some issues – the colours and emblem and the naming of a boardroom after FW de Klerk – consensus eventually prevailed. However, when the DP chiefs realised that the NNP's apparent plea for Van Schalkwyk's upfront inclusion in the promotional material was really an attempt to promote him as a co-leader, there was a staring-down.

These early dynamics gave the accurate assessment that at the top leadership level, at least, ours was to be a fairly loveless union, driven more by need and necessity than by affection. The 2000 municipal elections loomed.

4

In the run-up to the campaign it was suggested that I get to know NNP leadership figures outside the coterie surrounding Van Schalkwyk. The DP in the Western Cape was particularly keen that I make acquaintance with the two most powerful provincial Nats, Western Cape premier Gerald Morkel and the party's prospective Cape Town mayoral candidate, Peter Marais. Both had made their way up Coloured politics through the Tricameral system, but had little in common. Indeed there was a history of enmity and intense rivalry between the two, usually with Marais coming second.

I invited them to our home for dinner with Michal and me a few days after we found ourselves uneasily joined in the same party. In truth, I was unknown and somewhat suspect to two such significant figures in the new alignment. Morkel and Marais owed their allegiance and position to the NNP; yet now they found themselves in a newly minted party under a leader who until mere weeks before had loomed large in their demonology. Gossip held that I was aloof (perhaps), 'English-speaking' (guilty as charged) and 'not interested in Coloureds' (a lie).

The truth was that the DP had little traction among Coloured voters. And even here the NNP Coloured base was not the consequence of Morkel's or Marais's leadership – and even less so Van Schalkwyk's. It largely flowed from the community's reverence for FW de Klerk and its antagonism towards the ANC, in part attributable to an anxiety about marginalisation.

The dinner was an attempt to break down barriers, and I invited Douglas Gibson, in his words, 'to jolly things along' – one of his self-acknowledged social skills. I found Morkel, with his extraordinary resemblance to the movie star Charles Bronson, easy and affable. Marais and his wife Bonita were stiff and uncomfortable, although as the libations flowed, the evening eased up. Morkel, who had migrated to the Nats out of the collapsing Labour Party – whose organisational remnants the NP had largely captured, and which was the most established political machine on the Cape Flats – told us an interesting tale.

His family, while completely bilingual, were English-speaking. After the apartheid government started their manoeuvrings to remove the Coloureds from the voters' roll in the 1950s, his father declared: 'Henceforth, we will not use Afrikaans in this household.' Morkel was now the kingpin of an Afrikaans province and the provincial head of a Broederbond-directed party. Somehow conversation shifted towards music, and Gerald regaled us with his early career as an Elvis dancer, while Peter – a well-known crooner – told us of his prowess as a singer whose early career had been launched with ballads by the King of Memphis. I, too, was an Elvis Presley fan and had an impressive collection of his discs, which I played to our mutual enjoyment. Perhaps I would have done well to remember that one of Elvis's most famous ballads was entitled 'Suspicious Minds'.

We officially launched our campaign in mid-October with a big rally in Cape Town. Symbolically, a week later, we unveiled our manifesto in

Soweto; gone was the 'Fight Back' slogan of 1999 and in its place the pledge that the DA was 'for all the people'. With our pledges of free antiretroviral drugs in all municipalities which we controlled, and the promise of free basic water and electricity for all, I moved across the country, from township to shantytown, addressing large and enthusiastic crowds.

The *Financial Mail* ditched its initial cynicism about the DA and placed me on its front cover in early November. Its political correspondent (later to be editor of the *Mail&Guardian*) Ferial Haffajee wrote that 'Tony Leon is trying to break the political mould', and gave her readers a flavour of the efforts we were making to nudge South Africa politics in a more two-party, multiracial direction:[16]

'Tony Leon disputes the notion that his election poster has been touched up to give him a darker hue, but the Soweto launch of his party's election manifesto was an undeniably black *jol*. More than that, it borrowed liberally from ANC political tradition – the ubiquitous form of black politics. Bemused traditional white supporters who had made the trek from the northern suburbs of Johannesburg last month, in Panama hats and carrying picnic baskets, tapped their feet to the Retsi Jazz Band. "*Viva*" punctuated the speeches and, as Leon entered the Ubuntu Kraal in a casual navy blue shirt, the crowd rose to its feet singing a song that went, "Tony Leon-I, Tony Leon-I" – a struggle tune usually sung to the icon "Nelson Man-de-la, Nelson Man-de-la" …

'He's not doing the "Fight Back" of last year, a strategy that miffed black South Africans but brought a majority of Afrikaans and Indian supporters into the party's fold. The Sizakubona [see for ourselves] campaign was a political tactic to take Leon into black South Africa … "I put up with a lot of criticism about our campaign last year, which I never saw in the terms in which our critics or opponents saw it," Leon admits. "Sizakubona opened my own eyes. I went on my own voyage of discovery. Our party has to reconnect with its transformative roots."'

Polling day on 5 December saw the DA scale heights unmatched by any opposition movement since democracy's advent six years before. We received just on 23% of the national vote and swept the boards in the Western Cape, obtaining 53% in the all-important Cape Town metropole and control of nearly twenty municipalities elsewhere in the province, and a slew of district councils, as well as three other councils in Gauteng and the Eastern Cape.

The ANC's percentage of the vote had risen from 63% in 1994 to 66,4% in 1999; but now fell sharply to 59,4%. It was the worst performance of the ANC in the four elections since 1994. Our growth in the black electorate was modest – 4% nationally but much higher in specific areas such as vote-rich Johannesburg, where the party scaled to an electoral high of 33,7%. Our campaign strategists noted that many disillusioned blacks simply refused to go to the polls at all: they could, in future, be targeted by us.

The DA's strong showing attracted some international attention. Rachel L Swarns wrote for the *New York Times* that our Alliance was 'the strongest challenger to the governing ANC since apartheid ended four years ago [sic].'[17]

Quite how startled Mbeki's inner circle was by this development was made clear later that month in an article by the president's *alter ego*, Joel Netshitenzhe. He described his concern that our opposition was 'undermining the state':

'Add all these things up, and you start to wonder whether the official opposition considers itself, legitimately, as an alternative to the ruling party; or whether it is setting itself up as a state apart, a guardian of an alternative sovereignty! One might dismiss this as the effects of inexperience. But when it's consistent and calculated, and done to generate a similar attitude within the white community, then more than jingle bells start ringing. Search in other democracies for this kind of attitude, and you will realise that, even in politics, there are limits to indulgence!'[18]

I was appalled, describing his views as 'the single most disturbing sentiments expressed by a senior member of the ANC since 1994'. He was accusing the official opposition of 'engaging in treason'. Pertinently, I asked: 'If senior government and ANC officials are worrying that the official opposition is engaged in setting itself up as a guardian of an alternative sovereignty, then what is the government going to do about it? Where do thoughts like Mr Netshitenzhe's lead? What's the next step?'[19]

Over the next two years I was to learn the answer. The ANC would set about attempting to decimate the opposition – and would do so with the aid of a 'fifth column' within our newly created party. But before I was painfully to discover the perfidiousness of some of my new allies, I formalised a far happier, and more personal, union. On 10 December 2000 Michal and I were married at a rather splendid wedding at Cape Town's Mount Nelson hotel.[20]

5

At the time of writing this account,[21] six years after the initial implosion of the DA, I have more detachment than the deep emotions which the events back then triggered – although I still bear the scars on my back from the experience. There are no unambiguous answers to the welter of questions which arose from the DA's formation and subsequent split. In essence, we attempted to short-circuit history.

Those in the DP, led by me, who imagined that the conclusion of the Alliance agreement in 2000 would close down the war between us and the NNP leadership were naïve. We were to learn from bitter first-hand experience that the grafting of the NNP's support base on to our own was a 'gift constructed and delivered by Trojans'.

I was quickly to learn, after the municipal elections, that Van Schalkwyk did not consider himself to be a deputy leader in the ordinary or even political sense of the term. He saw – and over the next few months would seek to perpetuate – himself as essentially a co-leader. A foretaste of things to come occurred when I discovered that my statement on behalf of the party for Reconciliation Day, 16 December 2000, had been matched by one sent separately to the party and the nation by my deputy.

I wrote to him about it in a strongly worded letter on 15 December:

'Dear Marthinus – I think your view was adequately stated earlier this week. I do not think it is necessary, or desirable, for both of us to send out separate messages since this simply underlines the lack of cohesion within the party.

'Far more seriously in my view is that having requested you not to is-sue a statement, whatever the merits or demerits of doing so would be, you just promptly went ahead and did so ... If you felt so strongly about this matter why did you not discuss with my office, or with me directly, the proposed contents of the statement to ensure that it was absorbed into mine? This entire incident has left me with a somewhat unhappy feeling and I intend to ensure that, in decisive fashion, there is no repetition of instances of this kind.'

His response was both instructive and written in Afrikaans. It was dated 15 January 2001 and it read (my translation):

'I am concerned and disappointed by your letter. On a previous oc-casion I requested of you that we not behave in correspondence towards each other as if we were warring lawyers. I am available at any time of the day or night should you need to discuss or clarify anything with me. In my opinion, the collegial way for leaders to do business would be to co-operate and interact in a spirit of mutual trust and respect.

'You and I have an appointment on 24 January and I would rather discuss with you then a range of issues which I decided ... to leave until after the election ...'

The letter was typical of my deputy's *modus operandi*: assertion of moral indignation, avoidance of the issue at hand, and an attempt to recast the problem as one of trust and confidence. His insistence on face-to-face meetings was in fact indicative of his desire that there should be no paper trail on any matters of future contention. He would then have the ability to misrepresent agreements or assertions made in private meetings to paint me in an unreasonable and unflattering light.[22]

From the outset there were differences within the NNP – between Van Schalkwyk and his chief lieutenants (Renier Schoeman, Shaun Vorster and Daryl Swanepoel) whom I soon dubbed the 'gang of four'; and other mainstream leaders who quickly made the DA cause their own. Most of the latter were in the Western Cape government led by premier Gerald Morkel where DP-NNP relations were sound, perhaps because the DP component was the junior partner in the arrangement. MPs from other provinces, such as Sheila Camerer, were also committed to the DA programme.

At parliamentary and provincial level, the Constitution required us to maintain separate political identities. Douglas Gibson and I paid an early New Year visit to then deputy president Jacob Zuma, whom we asked to consider changing the law to allow both parties to close down legally and thus ensure that the DA – rather than the DP and NNP – became the sole remaining vehicle for the consolidated opposition. It was a proposal for a formal, national merger. Zuma promised to 'consider the matter'.

However, Van Schalkwyk insisted that the NNP retain its separate legal status until 2004. The continued co-existence of the NNP alongside the DA allowed the NNP to retain a separate identifiable leader, backed up by an office, staff, funding and visible perks. They retained a separate financial base for the maintenance of their structures, refusing to open their books to us on the basis of 'donor confidentiality'.

Although I instructed the DP rapidly to decommission itself and absorb all its attentions and energies into the new DA, many in my circle were nervous that Van Schalkwyk was attempting a reverse takeover of the party. I asked James Selfe (who by then was the chairman of the DA's national management committee), Ryan Coetzee and Greg Krumbock to prepare for me a confidential assessment of the situation. It made for disquieting reading. The section on the leaders' office and the Nat party's finances were instructive – and provided a summary of a marriage in obvious trouble:

- Leadership. Soon after the formation of the DA, it became apparent that Van Schalkwyk and his staff members Shaun Vorster, Daryl Swanepoel and Riaan Aucamp held a different view with respect to the role and function of the deputy leader to that of the DP component. Repeatedly the DP tried to integrate operations at national level, especially the office of the leadership, into one unit. At a meeting Van Schalkwyk refused point-blank to countenance this idea.

- Some people still report directly or indirectly to Van Schalkwyk, or will only carry out Leon's instructions if they are endorsed by Van Schalkwyk. This tendency may well be encouraged by Van Schalkwyk.
- The dispute about the maintenance of a separate office for the deputy leader with the disunity and the dysfunctional leadership relationship which that entailed continued intermittently for months. Leon finally instructed Van Schalkwyk to close down his office and integrate it with the leadership office two or three months ago. Van Schalkwyk refused to do so and instead used his separate office to headquarter his campaign to undermine Leon's position and advance his programme to take control of the DA.
- Finances. From the first days of the alliance, the NNP declined to disclose its assets and liabilities. DP requests for full disclosure at federal level met with stony refusals, with similar attitudes prevailing at many provincial and regional formations. In virtually every debate at the national management committee Van Schalkwyk has defiantly spearheaded the NNP's position.
- In February 2001 the DP became aware that the NNP had a massive undisclosed overdraft at federal level when ABSA bank turned down an overdraft request from the DA. This facility existed at the time of the formation of the DA and was probably written off in December 2000, although other sources indicate it may still be sitting in a non-interest-bearing account.
- Through the intervention of former president FW de Klerk, ABSA apparently wrote off an amount in the region of six million rands. This impacted extremely negatively on the DA in that ABSA and other banks refused overdraft facilities when these were absolutely necessary. It also destroyed what little trust remained with respect to the financial affairs of the NNP, with many party members left wondering what other NNP financial skeletons remained in the cupboard to be presented at a later date for payment by the DA.
- Van Schalkwyk's intransigence in integrating the finances and books of the DA facilitates an environment where dubious financial arrangements can flourish, as well as a conduit for funds flowing directly to the NNP which can then be used to finance a take-over of the DA.

The tensions inside the DA were not entirely of the NNP's making. Some in my team were not exactly choir-boys. Russel Crystal – for example – had great difficulty in hiding his visceral loathing of Van Schalkwyk, and seldom lost an opportunity to show his disrespect. He was also in charge of all our public events. When we held a rally on Human Rights Day on 21 March at Sharpeville, the sound system went on the blink the moment my deputy commenced speaking, but was miraculously restored to fine order when I took to the podium. The sudden change in volume was 'Crystal clear' in its source. Then I received complaints, particularly from Coloured councillors, of an impression of 'moral superiority' which some English-speaking DP members displayed towards them. I deprecated this, but it fuelled the fires for the forthcoming clash.

At a subsequent meeting to discuss the document, Ken Andrew summarised the cause of the party's turbulence: 'There is no problem about policy and principles. The disputes are about power.'

Colin Eglin, a veteran of previous party mergers and takeovers, pointed to the dangers of Van Schalkwyk's projection as an 'alternative leader and not as the deputy leader'. He also drew the meeting's attention to the role FW de Klerk was playing in 'keeping the NNP component alive'. Eglin, no doubt speaking on behalf of the vast bulk of DP supporters, warned: 'The decision to form the DA was entirely top-down. It was sold as a merger on our terms and anything less than that would lead to a different view of the DA.' His private warning did not remain hidden from public view. It soon appeared in print under the *Cape Times* headline: 'Concern at Van Schalkwyk's Profile'.[23]

By this time serious public leaks of party caucus meetings and other morsels had begun. As the NNP component fought unsuccessfully within the councils of the party for various concessions, and they were outvoted, information started leaking out on other matters, usually designed to portray me in the most negative and critical light. Invariably *Die Burger* and *Rapport* were the chosen vehicles. Two of their journalists, Peter Sidego and Eugene Gunning, became virtual stenographers for the NNP cause.

In February, addressing the parliamentary caucus, I said I expected a top performance from each member and that I had (with Van Schalkwyk's blessing) reassigned certain portfolios. I explained that my style of leadership was goal-directed and not inwardly focused; but no one was a prisoner and shouldn't feel bound to remain in the caucus unhappily or indefinitely. Such a comment was old news. However, within minutes, a distorted version of what I said was already in the media's hands. The weekend headline in *Rapport* screamed: '*Spanning tussen DP, NNP*' ('Tension between DP, NNP').[24]

Certain NNP 'sources' added a vicious spin – claiming DP MPs were displaying 'anti-Afrikaans feelings' and 'arrogance towards their former Nat colleagues'. It was clear that the culture wars and the ancient enmity between Boer and Brit were to be stirred up as Van Schalkwyk sought to improve his bargaining power.

Matters were ratcheted up much further and concentrated around the person – and personal computer – of my right-hand strategist, Ryan Coetzee. At one level, he was brusque and arrogant – but I trusted him completely and knew it was his imagination and intellect which had driven the formation of the DA in the first place. Nor was Ryan's passion for the turf wars and bureaucratic battles in which the NNP excelled, but to move the party on to connecting with the majority black electorate. That was the purpose behind the DA's creation, and he was impatient with those whom he saw as obstacles.

This was not at all to the liking of Van Schalkwyk and his lieutenants. They grew increasingly concerned as Ryan, with my encouragement, was appointed as communications adviser to the Western Cape government. His good relationship with Morkel and his key lieutenant, Finance MEC Leon Markovitz, was of obvious consternation to Van Schalkwyk, since it lessened the latter's hold on the premier. I was chiefly concerned, however, that we started communicating our vision as a political alternative, making a real difference to people's lives, especially in the poorer communities, from such sites of power as we commanded. I was confident that Ryan could perform and conceive such tasks with despatch and total commitment.

However, a short while after his arrival at the government offices in Wale Street, Cape Town, in February, his personal computer was stolen from his office. Some two months later, the thieves almost immediately hit pay-dirt, as I and the newspaper-reading public were to discover. By the time of the theft I had long forgotten a memorandum (he sent many) which Ryan e-mailed me the previous August, shortly after the DA was formed. In it he outlined, in depth and detail, how I, as party leader, needed to focus outwards towards the electorate and continue to engage in my activities in the black community.

In a single paragraph he addressed himself to concerns I and others had privately expressed to him about Van Schalkwyk's attempts to hog media attention and promote himself beyond his role as deputy. Ryan addressed the matter in his forthright way: 'Marthinus will pale into insignificance. The best way to deal with him is to forget about him … [He] can never compete with you when it comes to personifying a cause or articulating a message.'

That single, fateful remark was recorded eight months before it was fed in April to the media. The *Cape Times* breathlessly informed its readers of a 'DP plan to oust Van Schalkwyk'.[25] The fact that their 'exclusivity' was based on possession of a document sourced from a stolen computer was beside the point; and one paragraph suggesting I 'ignore' Van Schalkwyk hardly constituted a plan to oust him. However, publication was manna from heaven for the NNP leadership, allowing them to pump up the insecurity of their members by suggesting there was a plot 'to eliminate' Van Schalkwyk.

If elements within the NNP had not actually arranged for Ryan's computer to be stolen from a government building, they were the direct beneficiaries. Six years later, after the theft, the South African Police Service has yet to identify a culprit.

It was the end of our age of innocence. Hitherto, we had been recklessly naïve about such matters as securing documents, shredding memoranda, and locking offices. Change was now forced upon us. I also decided, henceforth, if possible not to have a single unwitnessed meeting with Van Schalkwyk. Our trust levels, never high to start with, were rapidly breaking down.

Inside the party a fight to the death had broken out over the issue of membership. This revealed most plainly that the NNP was indeed planning to reverse the terms of trade outlined when the party was created the previous year on the basis of the DP's relative electoral dominance. The final shape and composition of the party's structure had been left over; crucially, the DA constitution would determine who wielded the power at the Federal Congress at which the party's top leadership would be chosen.

The NNP favoured representation to be determined on the basis of party membership in branches and regions. The DP wanted delegates to be chosen largely on the basis of electoral support in areas across South Africa. There was a case to be made for both models, and some room for compromise.

The DP was the stronger vote-winner, but the NNP had swathes of paid-up members, particularly in the Western and Northern Cape. NNP structures started flooding the party's national head office with new members, and by June there were 55 000 of them – two-thirds from the Western Cape alone. It appeared, in the words of journalist Carol Paton, that the 'birth of the DA has given the NNP a new lease of life.'[26] True to my inclinations and Ryan's scripted advice, my focus was outwards; my NNP colleagues were clearly directing their energies towards the internal shape of the party.

The NNP had signed up more members in the sparsely populated Northern Cape than the DP had managed to enrol in Johannesburg. Johannesburg delivered more votes for the party than any other area in South Africa, and six times more than the Northern Cape. Yet on the basis of the NNP proposal, delegates from Kimberley would have greater representation than those from Johannesburg. It was unsustainable – and also a prospect underwritten by fraud. An internal audit discovered that at least twenty per cent of the new membership applications were tainted. In the case of the Northern Cape, 90% of the new 'members' had not personally paid their dues – as party rules required – or did not exist, or were dead. Unwisely, a senior DP figure (known to me) decided later in the year to leak our explosive internal audit to the *Financial Mail*.

It was an act of monumental self-indulgence. But when confronted he claimed in exasperated self-defence: 'I am sick of these Nats leaking fiction about us; it's time people learnt the truth about them.' By the time the article appeared, the party was all but over. However, it did give the essential reason for the Nats' behaviour:

'At the heart of the membership conflict is the NNP's drive for influence in the DA and the assertion of its political culture. The party cannot go it alone and struck the pact in the first place because it risked political oblivion. Its share of the national vote had plunged from 20% in 1994 to just under 7% in 1999. However, since the inception of the DA in June, 2000, the NNP has sought by stealth to take increasing control of the Alliance by signing up thousands of members to back up its demands in party constitutional negotiations, which continue.'[27]

At the height of this civil war I found the time and energy to go about the business of projecting the party to the public and urged our councillors to focus on the concerns of the voters, not on each other. I used my Youth Day address in Mamelodi on 16 June to try to reach out to the 'lost generation' and their successors:

'Twenty-five years ago the children of Soweto found the courage to fight back against an unjust order that denied them their dignity and disregarded their humanity. While the spark was a decision by the apartheid government forcing them to receive tuition in Afrikaans, the greater motivation for their heroic act of defiance lay at a deeper level: they rose up to assert their worth and dignity as human beings, to claim the equality they were denied, to declare to the country their determination to become full citizens in the land of their birth.

'But I look to the young people of today as inheritors of a very uncertain future ... Millions of young people have already become part of
a second lost generation. For the thousands who leave high school every
year, the prospects for meaningful, secure future employment are becoming ever more bleak ...

'What has today's lost generation got? What thoughts and feelings are
generated in the youth today, who face an AIDS pandemic, rampant crime,
poor education and the prospect of future unemployment, when they see
a picture of a fat cat like Tony Yengeni standing, proud as punch, in front
of his 4x4 Mercedes Benz? The ANC is in danger of generating in its own
supporters a deep sense of betrayal. They have switched from the power of
morality to the morality of power.'

I used the platform to acknowledge publicly glaring shortcomings (in
terms of black representation) in the DA's own internal structures and
public face, and that it would have to change.

Van Schalkwyk and his office – maintained despite my request that
he close it down – were strangely silent on what I regarded as a seminal
challenge to the party and its leadership.[28] He and I managed to maintain
the semblance of a relationship in public. But like a Potemkin village, the
outward appearance hid a bare inner reality. The party was set to explode,
and the agency was the mayor of Cape Town, Peter Marais.

6

I saw our newly won sites of government – particularly Cape Town – as
our 'shining cities on the hill'. Whatever my political colleagues thought of
my Mayflower metaphor, it was commonly agreed that DA-controlled municipalities had to be distinctive and exemplary, working examples of what
differentiated our style of government from the sleaze and self-enrichment
that became the depressing hallmarks of ANC local administration.

From the inception it was apparent that Peter Marais, who in terms
of the founding agreement of the party had been chosen by the NNP as
our mayoral candidate, would not fit easily into this high-minded mould.
Aside from dinner at my home, Marais and I spent time together on the
campaign trail in 2000. At this level, he was an astute worker, possessed
of the pithy phrase and strong populist instincts. However, he not only
hovered close to controversy, but actively courted it. The provincial ANC
leader, Ebrahim Rasool, called him 'a liar and a bigot'[29] – members of our
party became concerned when he denounced the Constitution since he

believed elements of it owed more to communism than to Christianity. He toned down his rhetoric afterwards, but there was little doubt, after our emphatic victory in December, that his tenure at the top would create ructions within the party.

Van Schalkwyk was acutely aware of the difficulties. In February 2000 he instructed Premier Morkel to fire Marais from his cabinet for a disciplinary infraction. He was reinstated after an apology, and Van Schalkwyk once confided to me: 'Peter is like my oldest child, but I know how to keep him under control.' If I felt that Marais's public gifts – his instinct for the underdog and championing of the Coloured majority – could be put to good use, I had severe doubts whether he could lead the city and our municipal caucus in an inclusive and goal-orientated manner.

From the outset he single-mindedly set about proving his doubters and detractors right. In a procedurally incorrect and politically ill-judged manner, he fired the city manager, Andrew Boraine. He then drew negative publicity for the party by splashing out on bodyguards, chauffeurs and cars for members of his executive. And almost from the outset, tensions surfaced in his caucus between DP and NNP members: on one occasion he dismissed the former on the basis that 'it did not know how to govern'.

I met him often and cautioned him that his prime responsibilities were to deliver on our municipal manifesto: the provision of antiretrovirals, the extension of free basic services, and the implementation of privatisation. Yet almost from the outset, any meeting on any issue of contention was leaked to the media. Marais was cast as the victim and I in the mould of a centralising dictator.

Marais made adverse comments about gays and lesbians; got into a race-tinged ruckus with the ANC over the banning of soccer from the Newlands stadium; and had an almost Mr Toad-like obsession for attention-grabbing schemes and stratagems. Then Van Schalkwyk and I – in early 2001 – received word that Marais was planning to splurge hundreds of thousands of rands on a lavish mayoral inauguration for himself, pillaging the ratepayers' purse. After being admonished by both of us, he pulled back and produced a scaled-down, but quite lavish, largely sponsored bash at the Cape Town Artscape. As an act of reconciliation I attended. Van Schalkwyk did not.

It was, however, Marais's determination to rename two of Cape Town's landmark streets, Adderley and Wale, after presidents Mandela and De Klerk, which unleashed a series of events that over three gruelling months shattered our new party's unity. While it would be untrue to conclude that Marais – or the minor issue of the street names – led to our demise, it was the final event that exposed our essential incompatibilities.

Peter Marais became a convenient instrument in the hands of my deputy to exit the party when his plans to take it over could not be realised.

The whiff of scandal that aborted Marais's renaming project arrived in my office in parliament on the afternoon of 24 July. The deputy mayor of Cape Town, the no-nonsense Belinda Walker, showed me an affidavit from a council employee that made for explosive and disturbing reading. There were serious instances of vote-rigging in the public participation exercise which the DA leadership instructed Marais to initiate before commencing with the name changes. The overwhelming majority of Capetonians were against it. Yet thanks to the energetic and illegal activities of two of Marais's officials, the result was manipulated – allowing the mayor to claim that most favoured it.

The DA's flagship city was about to sink in a sea of corruption. While my first instinct was to throw the affidavit into my desk and hope it went away, I quickly realised that far more proactive steps were required. I summoned the entire top leadership to my office that evening – including Morkel, Marais and Van Schalkwyk – and indicated that we needed to act decisively. Marais was saddened when we told him the scheme had to be abandoned and we appointed the corruption-busting former judge Willem Heath to head a commission to finger the culprits. We would make a clean breast of things. There was no disagreement, and the next day at a press conference we outed our own administration and outlined the steps we proposed taking to clean up the city's act. While the headlines almost wrote themselves ('Scandal rocks Mayor's office', proclaimed the next day's *Cape Times*) there was widespread public and editorial support.[30]

Marais's style of leadership and management dulled the sheen on our city and was beginning to seriously jeopardise our strategy of using our governance in the city to showcase our abilities. At about this time, Ryan Coetzee showed me the results of one of his voter surveys: Cape Town voters had a very low to indifferent opinion of their mayor, our helmsman: a 15% approval rating among Coloureds.

However, Marais proclaimed in a newspaper interview: 'I will survive scandal.' He claimed for the first time that there might be a conspiracy within the party ranks to oust him. 'The rumours are becoming more frequent ... maybe some people are not used to people of colour being assertive, having opinions and a character.'[31]

He was not only a loose cannon; he was crashing all over the deck. Having played the race card, he then proceeded a few days later to indicate that he was wrapping himself in the protective arms of the NNP, and would have no truck with the fact that he was a DA councillor answerable to the party's leadership. 'The DP cannot throw me out of my position as the NNP is the majority party in the council,' he claimed.[32] In fact, legally neither the DP nor NNP existed at council level, only the DA did; and Marais was notionally its municipal leader. In effect he was declaring war on his own party and one of its components.

Hennie Bester, provincial custodian of DP interests and Morkel's deputy, wrote to Gerald and demanded that steps be initiated against Marais, independently of any conducted by Judge Heath. In Bester's view, he found it 'incomprehensible how Mr Marais can hold these views, be allowed to conduct himself in this manner, and continue to hold [his] position in the DA.' He added that 'all of this damage is done not in aid or advancement of some matter of principle or critical programme of government, but to protect Mr Marais's personal position and power.'

Van Schalkwyk claimed that I was too pro-DP and promptly denied he had any hand in Marais's statements. He appeared blind – or deliberately deaf – to the damage.

We awaited the results of the Heath probe.

When it arrived on 30 August, the party leadership met at the premier's palatial Cape Dutch residence, *Leeuwenhof*. The report made damning findings against Marais and certain officials. Heath suggested that Marais be investigated by the city council for breaches of the municipal code of conduct, and that the provincial government probe affairs. Our meeting, which Marais attended, displayed rare resolve and placed a reluctant Marais on compulsory leave. But a short while later, the provincial government's appointment of Judge Edwin King to conduct the further probe was thwarted by a judicial decision which held that the regional legislature could not act on a breach by a councillor until the council itself had the opportunity to remedy the situation. Marais would be judged by a committee in his own council, dominated by his own allies.

We all knew the Marais saga and its spreading collateral damage had gone beyond a technical breach. The party agreed to appoint its own internal investigation into the continuing problems in the Cape Town unicity.

The next evening I was set to leave for Australia to attend a Commonwealth parliamentary conference. At 10.30 that morning Van Schalkwyk arrived in my office, having recently 'had coffee with FW de Klerk'. He said De Klerk had told him the problem was that 'Marais was out of control, but was an important vote-getter.' De Klerk had proposed a solution: Premier Morkel was in the wrong position and would be ideally suited to the mayoralty; and a position of prominence should be found for Marais. When I asked Van Schalkwyk who would replace Morkel as premier he offered himself.

I was intrigued, but indicated to Van Schalkwyk that merit aside and notwithstanding my positive views about Gerald, I foresaw immense problems with a white premier replacing a Coloured one. But I wanted to get the party back to its core business.

Van Schalkwyk advised me that the NNP provincial congress (allegedly convening to consolidate itself into the DA) was meeting on 24 September, and that before then 'Morkel will be pressured into resigning.' I was to learn later from Morkel that while I was away he, too, was invited to coffee by De Klerk who directly suggested to him that he stand down in Van Schalkwyk's favour. Morkel declined. It seemed odd that De Klerk – then enjoying a deserved international reputation for his role in South Africa's transition, and three years out of political leadership – was so involved in provincial machinations.

While I was in Canberra, tensions arose between Van Schalkwyk and Hennie Bester, which were relayed to me. I conveyed to my deputy the view that the matter required urgent resolution. The alternative would destroy the party and our public image. Marais could no longer continue as mayor, at the centre of divisions and mobilisation by the party's components. He should be relocated elsewhere, ideally in the provincial government, with perks and prestige sufficient for both his seniority and his ego. Van Schalkwyk assured me this proposed solution was 'on course' and, as premier, he would be able to 'keep Marais under control.'

By the time I returned on 14 September, Morkel's resistance had scuttled this plan. He was elected unopposed as NNP provincial leader (and DA premier) at the congress, at which Marais, although officially still on leave, made an incendiary speech and Van Schalkwyk, while pledging fealty to the DA, reminded his NNP members that they 'were a majority in the province and must act as one.'

We now headed full-speed towards collision. Van Schalkwyk made certain of that in public. He announced: 'Peter Marais is conducting himself in a manner that is satisfactory to me, and I will support him all the way to clear his name.'[33]

While not surprised by my deputy's perfidiousness, I also had to fend off pressures closer to home. Party formations elsewhere in South Africa could hardly contain their fury at what they saw as the Cape wing destroying their credibility. Ryan Coetzee was blunter; he burst into my office and said: 'You've got the power and you don't use it, it's pathetic.' His remark rankled, but matters could no longer be delayed. Bester, ever more exasperated, approached me in his typically earnest manner: 'If we don't act and fire Marais, the whole party will sink.' I told him we needed a sound legal basis to proceed, which he undertook to obtain.

On 1 October I convened a meeting in my office with Van Schalkwyk, Renier Schoeman and Douglas Gibson. The latter two had reached a stalemate on finalising the party constitution. However, on Marais, I told Van Schalkwyk that procrastination was no longer an option. I needed his assistance to find Marais a 'soft landing' and asked him to revert to me in 48 hours with a response, hopefully with Marais's concurrence. Van Schalkwyk hardened his position, saying he 'didn't need 48 hours' to consider a redeployment for Marais. Peter had indicated he would not willingly move. The management committee might have to address the matter.

The following evening, I, Van Schalkwyk and our wives were guests of FW de Klerk and his wife Elita in their beautiful Cape Dutch farmstead in the Klein Drakenstein area near Paarl. Elita and Michal had struck up a warm relationship. They were both foreigners, married to South African politicians, and had bonded. We had socialised with the De Klerks on several previous occasions, but this dinner was not merely social.

A few moments after the very delicious Coquille Saint Jacques shellfish starter had been cleared, De Klerk urged me to stand down from my hardline position on Marais. Any steps taken against him would create 'unnecessary tension between white and Coloured'. I assumed that Van Schalkwyk had briefed him closely on developments and my views. I replied by indicating that I had no problem with Marais having a high profile consonant with his dignity, but that he could not continue to 'lead and divide' the city.

When the DA exploded later that month, De Klerk was wheeled out to give his blessing to the new arrangement Van Schalkwyk was forging with the ANC. De Klerk showed, it seemed to me, his true colours, describing the DA – whose conception he had endorsed – as 'a pathetic failure'.[34] In a sharp exchange of letters I reminded him that he had taken the NNP out of the ANC-dominated GNU with the statement that 'continued participation would be equivalent to detention on a kind of political death row. The survival of multi-party democracy … depends on the existence of a strong and credible opposition.' However, I did think De Klerk redeemed himself in 2004 when Van Schalkwyk disbanded the NNP and placed what remained of it in the ANC; De Klerk resigned his membership of the party.

After the dinner party, while Michal and I were driving back to Cape Town, Van Schalkwyk phoned me and according to Michal's contemporaneous diary of events said he had felt 'exposed'. But why did Van Schalkwyk feel 'exposed'? He, after all, had invoked De Klerk's assistance. Had Marthinus omitted to tell De Klerk that I was not proposing to fire Marais, but seeking his relocation? This turned out to be an accurate assumption.

Three days later, predictably, the city council cleared Marais, and Van Schalkwyk immediately announced that he had 'been found innocent' and could return as mayor. Worse was to come.

By week's end I was attending DA functions in Limpopo. The local provincial leader Michael Holford was driving me to a remote outpost when I received a call from Freek Swart, political editor of *Rapport*. He told me his newspaper had information concerning my earlier meeting with Van Schalkwyk, Schoeman and Gibson. His newspaper would be publishing the fact that I had presented my deputy with 'an ultimatum' that Marais 'must leave active politics within 48 hours'.

I was shocked. *Rapport* was proposing to publish (the next day) an 'ultimatum' I had never made, ignoring my request that Van Schalkwyk assist in procuring a 'soft landing' for Marais. I knew well enough that the newspaper was being fed a particular line, the selfsame one Van Schalkwyk had duplicitously presented to De Klerk.

Rapport duly proclaimed: 'Leon's demand splits DA: Marais must go or else ...' There could only be a hard landing for Marais now; and the time for negotiations with Van Schalkwyk was at an end.[35]

7

On Monday 8 October I was convinced that I could not conduct a confidential meeting in my own office. I relocated to the nearby Townhouse hotel to confer with Bester, Selfe, Coetzee and Gibson. We would now move against Marais, supported by a legal opinion from Jeremy Gauntlett SC and Les Rose-Innes SC, which backed our junior advocate's position that Marais could be requested to relinquish the mayoralty on the basis that, as leader, I was entitled to make a political judgment on his position without recourse to a fully fledged labour relations-type disciplinary hearing. (The opinion turned out to be wrong, in law at least.)

Van Schalkwyk had presumably misread my previous concessions to party unity as weakness. Now I had to act. On Friday morning I requested

Marais to meet me; he made himself unavailable. A letter (drafted by our lawyers) setting out my terms was dispatched to his home. He was advised he would be eligible to attend the management committee meeting a week hence when the leadership would determine his fate. In my office I told Van Schalkwyk that I had now put Marais on terms – and to avoid the prospect of any misinformation or spinning of our meeting, I would convene a press conference in our caucus room at which I would explain exactly what I had done.

He was stunned. I left the meeting, briefed the media, fielded questions, and left. Van Schalkwyk then held his own impromptu briefing in which he denounced my decision: 'If you are leader in a party and you are not willing to stand up for one individual then nobody should ever trust you again to represent them ... [The] leader of a party must not and can never have the power to hire and fire people they dislike without justification. Never. Because if a party becomes that, it becomes a kangaroo court.'[36]

His self-serving hypocrisy nauseated me. After all, he had previously ordered the firing of Marais from the provincial government and was shortly to suspend Morkel from the party and jettison him as premier.

The next day was Michal's birthday. We had accepted an invitation from friends to spend the weekend in the luxurious environment of a newly opened spa resort and hotel in Kleinmond, near Hermanus. I owed it to Michal not to cancel – but my cellphone was never quiet and I spent much time peering into the precipice. As Michal's diary records, I was riddled with conflicts and far from happy, not the model of a romantic husband celebrating a joyous occasion with his wife:

'Tony took little notice of the extremely beautiful, pampering, impeccably serviced and incredibly well equipped hotel. It was a most unusual weekend. We were busy making a plan of how to tackle this huge obstacle that presented itself. Tony's political life, his whole career, his good reputation, his beliefs and his leadership were to face the biggest test he had ever had to take. Tony was really tortured. In some ways he had made the biggest mistake of his life in leading his small but very successful party into a very dangerous partnership. He felt like a failure. But he knew that it was too dangerous now for him to indulge in such thoughts: he had to get stronger and tougher, and banish these debilitating thoughts.'

Michal helped steel my resolve. The management committee would call Marais to account and if he failed to relinquish the mayoralty he would lose his party membership. Then we would move against Van Schalkwyk, and he would either accept the party's discipline and my leadership – or he too would be disciplined. I had the power within the DA to act decisively, but no control over the NNP. But, I reasoned, all their local councillors were DA members and the NNP, whatever else it chose to do, could not abandon them.

In my view – widely shared by the DP majority in the DA and many NNP representatives who could see through Van Schalkwyk's machinations – such considerations had to override the perks, patronage and status issues which so preoccupied my deputy and his followers.

Carol Paton, writing in the *Sunday Times* the next day, intuited my thoughts, in part, and the larger context: 'The truth is, that as important as Peter Marais likes to think he is, the fight in the DA is not really about him. For Van Schalkwyk, the fight for Marais is a last bid for power as the DA begins to take shape.

'The birth of the DA shortly before the local government elections last year was less of a merger between the Democratic Party and the National Party and more of a hostile takeover. Leon's idea of the merger was based on a vision of a bigger and better opposition. Within months of the merger being proposed, the two parties were jointly fighting an election campaign …

'The Alliance gave the DP what had never before been within its grasp – a foothold in government. The DA was soon in power in the Western Cape and controlling the Cape Town city council. According to the grand plan these were to be its flagships – its shining examples to the public that anything the ANC could do, it could do far better.

'To the NP, the alliance was a lifeline. From being a party in its death throes, it was now imbued with a new sense of purpose. But it brought many unsavoury habits and characters from the notorious past. Once elected, Marais did not intend to sit back and do Leon's bidding. His intention was to govern …

'The DA will survive. But Marais will not. Leon will use his majority in the Alliance to force him out.'[37]

The DA, with Van Schalkwyk still in it, lurched into its final phase. After returning to Cape Town from Kleinmond, I gathered my senior staff and close colleagues (James Selfe, Douglas Gibson, Ken Andrew, Helen Zille, Glenn Adams, Hennie Bester, Robin Carlisle and Colin Eglin) at my home and told them we would now meet here every night and operate like a war cabinet. Ryan Coetzee, who was seized with the metaphor, dubbed the operation 'Infinite Justice'.[38]

As a first step, Gibson sent Van Schalkwyk a letter – which he also released to the media – accusing him of lying about the so-called ultimatum.

He wrote: 'You have stated repeatedly that you were presented with an ultimatum to fire Peter Marais within 48 hours and that [Tony] required Marais to leave active politics by October. You know these statements are untrue and yet you continue to repeat "the ultimatum" in public and private.'

Our group was assured that our legal procedures were watertight, but that the biggest risk we faced was losing control of the Western Cape. This was underlined by information that Van Schalkwyk had commenced secret negotiations with the ANC, presumably to leverage the DP component out of the provincial government and align with the Congress. By then nothing about my deputy surprised me; but I knew many NNP representatives would be appalled. I held a press conference exposing his machinations and declaring both my own and the party's position in forthright terms, captured by the *Mail&Guardian*:

'Leon condemned secret talks between Van Schalkwyk's faction and the ruling ANC: "There is nothing more destructive of the opposition project in South Africa than a willingness to make an alliance with the ANC," he said. "The fact that an element in the NNP is prepared to do so proves beyond any shadow of doubt that the issue at stake here is not one of principle, but one of positions, privilege and perks."

'Leon said: "I wish to make it absolutely clear that the consequences of [Van Schalkwyk's] behaviour constitute a direct breach of faith with the people who gave their support to the DA in December last year, and could cause hundreds of DA councillors to lose their seats and hence their ability to represent the people who elected them …

'"I will not allow anything or anyone to place their personal interests above the cause of principled opposition in South Africa. I will do whatever it takes to ensure that the purpose and mission of the opposition in our country is protected and advances. That is my position, and it will not be altered. The DA must succeed," Leon added.'[39]

The party's national management committee met on Friday 19 October to deal with my request to Marais. It was the last occasion that the NNP leadership was to be present at such a gathering. The atmosphere was extremely tense, indeed, glacial, although restrained. Both Gauntlett and Rose-Innes were in attendance; Peter Marais arrived, also accompanied by his lawyers, and I motivated his relinquishing the mayoralty. It was neither a 'charge', nor was he to be 'convicted' of anything. I expressed a political judgment that he had 'failed to lead in a manner which unites, rather than divides, his executive and his caucus.'

In the afternoon, the committee accepted – on a split DP-NNP vote

– my resolution. Marais announced that he was leaving the meeting to seek relief in court. We then moved on to the second stage, which suspended Marais in view of his refusal to resign the mayoralty. Throughout, Van Schalkwyk and the NNP leadership remained rooted to their chairs. They did not follow Marais out of the room, but I guessed it was now only a matter of time before they did.

When the meeting ended Van Schalkwyk left in high dudgeon and described Marais's sacking as 'having the element of, let me put it bluntly, race. It has the element of an unfair process. It has the element of the individual not being treated properly or fairly.'[40]

The essential question was what would Van Schalkwyk actually do? I decided to play his own game and gave public notice of the conditions required if he was to remain in the party. Coetzee, with my blessing, briefed John Mattison of the *Sunday Independent*,[41] who reported on the thinking of our inner group:

'A rampant Tony Leon, leader of the embattled Democratic Alliance, has taken off the gloves in the fight with Marthinus van Schalkwyk, his deputy leader, and decided to go for broke, even if this means the expulsion of Van Schalkwyk and the dissolution of the Alliance.

'Demands on Van Schalkwyk could include a full public apology for his criticisms of Leon's handling of the affair; a commitment to implement the DA agreement in letter and spirit, including closing down his separate office; ordering the cessation of separate NNP meetings; and conducting himself as deputy leader and not a "co-leader", as some former DP members claim.'

Van Schalkwyk and I held a final desultory Tuesday meeting on neutral ground – the Vineyard hotel in Newlands. He was accompanied by Renier Schoeman and I by James Selfe. He suggested we try counselling, and proposed 'outside mediation by wise men and women'. But when he confirmed that he was personally fundraising for Marais's court challenge against our party (of which he was still, notionally, a member), I knew the game was up. I said the authority of the party was not divisible between him and me. Once the DA management had determined a position, the deputy leader could not move against it. In response to his remark that he 'supported my leadership' I advised him that 'deeds must follow words' and instead of supporting Marais he should be backing me.

We terminated the meeting. We never met again, and I have not spoken to him since.

8

The day before our meeting Van Schalkwyk had met secretly with the chairman of the ANC, Mosiuoa Lekota, to put the finishing touches to a deal between them which would be announced on Friday.

On Friday night, as Michal and I were attending a dinner at the splendid Grand Roche hotel in Paarl, a message on my cellphone ensured that I would spend the rest of the night away from the fine wines and food. Van Schalkwyk had announced that the NNP Federal Council had resolved to suspend its membership of the DA. I had been expecting this – but not the simultaneous statement by Lekota. The NNP and ANC had agreed to 'fast track' legislation which would allow the 1 400 DA councillors to leave the party and rejoin their original components. Both parties claimed they were 'moving towards an historic co-operative agreement'.

We could lose our position in the Western Cape government and Cape Town; many councillors could defect back to the NNP if the law was changed, and the DA could revert to a DP rump, shorn of credibility and fighting from a much-reduced position.

However, if the ANC emerged as the NNP's saviour, our salvation came in the somewhat unlikely form of premier Gerald Morkel's conscience (reawakened, he told me, by a call from his father). He turned on Van Schalkwyk and his proposed collusion with the ANC and denounced him as 'foolish and unprincipled'.[42]

By 1 November Morkel was unilaterally suspended by Van Schalkwyk, who, however, received a humiliating rebuff from his own rank and file. At a gathering of over a thousand largely NNP DA councillors at the Goudini Spa near Rawsonville, he was shouted down with cries of 'verraaier' (traitor), 'manteldraaier' (turncoat), and derided as ''n kortbroekleier' (a short-pants leader).[43] Morkel, not Van Schalkwyk, was the winner among the grassroots, and a unanimous motion was adopted rejecting Van Schalkwyk's move towards the ANC. I had some hope that the DA would survive Van Schalkwyk's exit, and that he would not take with him most of his own party structures.

I received the same impression a few days later when I addressed the DA Cape Town city councillors. Despite the preponderance of NNP members, and my move against Marais, they were also sticking with the DA. Morkel was also firm – but his position was unsustainable. Following his suspension (which Van Schalkwyk, in the face of a court challenge, was obliged to lift) his provincial ministers were bullied back into the Nat fold and it became clear that once the NNP and ANC coalesced at provincial level, he would lose his majority and his position as premier. He decided to jump first.

In a splendidly defiant speech a few days later in Mitchells Plain he announced he was not prepared to be a party to 'legislative larceny'. He quit the NNP, and shortly afterwards was elected provincial leader of the DA. (He already held this title and position as a consequence of the DA's formation, but at the party's Western Cape congress he was democratically elected to it later in November.)

In parliament I witnessed Van Schalkwyk's new dance routine. He was unfazed by the outpourings of bile in the media and apparently untroubled by a poll in *Die Burger* which recorded that 80% of historically NNP voters did not support his alignment with the ANC.[44] He poured honey on Mbeki's head and denounced me and the party of which, until a few days before, he had been deputy leader as 'representing old apartheid privileges'.[45]

Our media department had a field day publishing all Van Schalkwyk's recent denunciations and denigrations of the ANC. But it mattered little: he was on his way and unperturbed about anything so trivial as previous commitments and loyalties.

It was now all but over: by month-end the NNP and ANC announced a pact for the Western Cape government. Joining Morkel on the scrap heap were the DA ministers – Bester, Zille, Koornhof and Adams – each of whom had played a sterling role in creating centres of excellence in office. Morkel's former ministerial colleagues from the NNP – save one – found power preferable to principle. The exception was my friend and Morkel's confidant, Leon Markovitz, who resigned. He had a healthy contempt for Van Schalkwyk and was totally committed to the opposition project.

Marais was successful in his court challenge against his expulsion. But the ruling was academic. He resigned from the DA and was promptly installed, in Morkel's stead, as premier. In a further twist, no doubt bewildering even to the most avid follower of politics, Morkel was elected mayor by the DA Cape Town caucus.

On the day of Marais's inauguration as premier, he encountered Hennie Bester in the bathroom. He asked him to send me a message: 'Tell your leader that I will destroy him.' But as events unfolded, it was Marais who would be immolated and removed from office. In a final ironic turn, it was Van Schalkwyk – who had posed as his saviour – who would twist the knife in Marais to install himself as provincial premier in June 2002.

2001 had been the most awful of years. How stood the DA? The floor-crossing legislation proved far more complex to process than the Nats had imagined. So we retained (until September 2002) our grip on all DA councils and councillors. But we had lost power in the province, a severe blow to our attempt to provide a flagship of alternative government. It also meant the ANC now controlled – by arrangement in the Western Cape – all the provinces bar KwaZulu-Natal.

The fact that many former NNP members had stayed with the party was an encouraging sign. But I knew that I, too, had been damaged. Some of the mud flung around by the NNP had stuck: claims that I was too autocratic, too centralising and too insensitive – these clearly resonated, even in my own ranks. I was also aware that in the Western Cape the NNP-DA supporters and councillors who remained were hardly DP clones. They wanted the party to listen to them and not simply to press on as before.

I was to spend the next five years ensuring that, indeed, their voice was heard and they were not treated as '*bywoners*' (squatters) in their own home. I had high appreciation for the fact that by staying with the DA – and renouncing the Nats – they had turned their backs forever on the political party in which so many had been nurtured. I also knew that the DA in the Western Cape, post-Van Schalkwyk's departure, contained a strong Afrikaans, NNP-originating majority. This fact I was determined to respect. Indeed at the party's first congress in the province, at which Morkel was installed unopposed as provincial leader, the man who led the NNP rebellion against Van Schalkwyk, Theuns Botha, resoundingly defeated DP-DA rising star Helen Zille for the provincial chairmanship (214-109).[46] It was a sign that our party would not revert to its old form.

My own leadership would naturally be questioned. But while the circumstances had not been of my choosing, I could not see how matters could have been handled in a fundamentally different fashion. There was, however, in a year-end article by Willem Jordaan and Jan-Jan Joubert, a specific criticism I knew to be correct.[47] It quoted an anonymous MP who said that while he appreciated and had confidence in my leadership, I was 'too surrounded by a closed group of advisers and I needed to reach out to the party's broader base.' The same informant also observed that my style was akin to 'a Che Guevara guerrilla struggle … It worked very well in 1999 when he led his group out of the jungle, but it is time he demobilised and created a new style.' It was wise advice.

9

As the festive season began, I headed home to the comfort of family and friends. I assumed that I had been through the worst of all possible experiences: I was wrong. I would have done well to have remembered Shakespeare's injunction – 'the worst is death and death will have his day.'[48] That arrived on 19 December.

My mother had landed in Cape Town from her home in Johannesburg a few days before. She loved the city, and she certainly loved me and our family. She had been very unwell for most of the year. In May she had undergone a second, and essentially unsuccessful, coronary by-pass operation. By the time she arrived in Cape Town she was suffering from heart failure.

She was admitted to the Vincent Palotti Hospital on my 45th birthday (15 December). Neither she nor I realised quite how serious her condition was. She had an ability to downplay her illness, and used her wit and humour to deflect from the seriousness of her condition. But at 10 pm on 19 December, the hospital called and said my mother was in distress and asking for me. Earlier in the day I had noted the difficulty she had breathing, but had not realised quite how close she was to the end.

I sped to the hospital where Michal, who was at a meeting away from home, soon joined me. My own experiences of hospitals always invoked in me a feeling of discomfort. But here late at night – in the darkness and silence – it was especially grim.

My mother lay very pale and small in the last bed of the intensive care unit. Her difficulties in breathing had intensified, and she sounded awful. But she managed to say to me – more or less clear-voiced – 'That's it.' I couldn't believe it. But when she removed the oxygen mask from her face I could see the anxiety – perhaps fear – in her normally sceptical blue eyes.

Naturally, I responded dismissively and hopefully: 'Nonsense, Ma, you'll pull through, you always do.' Her cardiologist and friend Elwyn Lloyd then arrived. After examining her, he called Michal and me into the ICU lobby. He told us that Sheila's end was now very near. He took us back to her bedside and held her hand. Then he told me to take her hand as well and say goodbye. 'Soon she will be asleep forever,' he said. Then he left us alone.

I kissed my dying mother. I wept as her life – so eventfully lived – ebbed gently away. She, my greatest champion and protector, the fount of so much of what I became, was now gone.

The full ritual of death, and the essentially business-like logistics which ac-company it leading to the funeral – held in Johannesburg – distracted me from the intensity of grief which overcame me, often without warning, in the years ahead. After her funeral I returned home to Cape Town to read and answer the daily pile of cards and letters which flowed in as tributes to Sheila's life. Answering them provided its own form of occupational therapy. However, two notes of condolence stand out in memory. One was from my old university lecturer, Peter Vale, who eloquently expressed what I only then could vaguely discern:

'Mothers, alas, are a once in a lifetime offer. Mourn her well and very, very often. Because, although the rest of your life immediately beckons, it cannot be fully completed without her memory as a stable shadow.'

And with obvious empathy and sharing with me the place which the memory of his own mother held in his heart, Mangosuthu Buthelezi wrote to me from Mahlabathini:

'I have just learned of the tragic loss you and your family have suffered with the untimely death of your mother, Sheila. Throughout my life, I have been very close to my mother who has been for me a source of strength and inspiration. She died just a few years ago and I was devastated. I know well that at no age is anyone ready to endure such a terrible loss and that no matter when it happens, one's mother's death is perhaps the most devastating trial of life which one needs to survive.'

I found this profoundly moving.

CHAPTER 17

Darkest before Dawn

Here's how it all began on the night of Feb 25 1964, in Miami Beach, Flori-
da. At the end of the fourth, Cassius Clay retreated to his corner, almost blind,
and told his trainer, Angelo Dundee, that he wanted to throw in the towel.
Dundee was having none of it. 'This is the big one, Daddy!' he shouted in
Clay's ear. 'Cut the bullshit!
We're not quitting now.'
Clay went back out and finished off Sonny Liston in two more rounds, to
become heavyweight champion of the world.
MATHEW D'ANCONA

I

At the end of 2002 I was heavyweight champion of neither the world nor
South Africa, nor of anything else. I often doubted whether we could remain in the fight at all. But when the dust settled, our opposition project
was still intact – though only just.

In parliament, Van Schalkwyk, now freed of his ties to the DA, claimed
that under my leadership 'the DA had become the last colonial outpost.
Fear is their lifeline – to exploit, to fuel and to inflame.'[1] While self-respect
was never high on his list of personal attributes, even I thought his obsequiousness to government, and his rubbishing of the party he had helped
form 20 months before, reduced him further.

I took far more notice when my friend Mangosuthu Buthelezi mounted the podium and took aim at both Mbeki and me. His attack on the
president, on AIDS, was news-grabbing enough. As a minister in Mbeki's
government, Buthelezi had until then been extremely quiet on aspects of
policy with which he did not agree. Now he lifted the veil and declared:
'Our nation is dying of AIDS.'[2] But at the time government policy was to
deny the seriousness and the essential cause of AIDS and its treatment; so
this assault from a member of cabinet was regarded as outspokenly bold.

I took careful note of his remarks, in the same speech, on my own approach: 'I will say openly,' he declared, 'that at times I also have problems with the way the leader of the opposition expresses himself and the nature of his attack on government. At times he is not sufficiently sensitive to the collective psychology of the majority of South Africans who have been talked down to for centuries … [But] then we must realise that his abrasiveness is the product of a high intellect and the spirited position of a true patriot who means well.'

There might well have been substance in Buthelezi's view, even if offered to provide him with some covering fire for the 'line in the sand' that the media interpreted him as having drawn with Mbeki. However, I think what intensely irritated many of my critics was my refusal to carry the 'white guilt' which apartheid had engendered – and which the ANC was keen to reinforce. I had not supported the system; indeed, from earliest memory I had been cradled in recognising just how opprobrious it actually was. I was sensitive to Buthelezi's point about 'talking down' to blacks, but my style of opposition – as I conceived it – actually started from the opposite position. I did not believe that our democracy was served by a watered-down, half-hearted discourse and punch-pulling.

Indeed, there was something inherently patronising in the assumption that black people, and Africa in general, could only tolerate a sort of Potemkin-style democracy, resplendent in form but lacking the cut-and-thrust of robust debate and accountability. After all, vehement dissent had built the ship on which the opposition now sailed.

To my pleasant surprise, I found support for my approach (in the face of intense disagreement elsewhere) from an unlikely source. At a press conference launching the North Sea Jazz Festival in Cape Town in May, legendary musician Hugh Masekela put away his trumpet and sang my praises: 'What Tony Leon says is deemed unseemly … but if African people mouthed the same words we would honour them. When we were being shot at and imprisoned we were verbal and stood up for truth … [but now] we don't speak up at all. We have a population of 40-million, but only four are speaking out.'

His quartet was intriguingly ecumenical: Archbishop Desmond Tutu, Winnie Mandela, Patricia de Lille, and me. This endorsement would be of some comfort as events gathered pace and threatened to overwhelm both the party and my leadership.

Business Day took up the issue of our somewhat diminished situation in parliament: 'At the opening of parliament Tony Leon seemed to be carrying a weight on his shoulders and he did not look happy … [The] NNP is a party of serial turnovers [but] Leon and the DA are not, unlike the NNP, irrelevant ... [As] leader of a reduced entity on the political scene, Leon's aspect last week tells a new story. He is an awesome politician, but his job since the Nat defection has become equally awesome.'[3]

My face must have mirrored my inner concerns. I had to maintain the party's unity, although Van Schalkwyk and his ANC allies were eyeing the forthcoming floor-crossing episode with undisguised glee; there were some six hundred NNP councillors whom he had been forced to leave behind in the DA. The battle for their allegiance, when they had the opportunity to change parties, would be intense and unremitting.

On the one hand I would have to try to keep them in. On the other, the 'blue-rinse brigade' – as I mocked the more purist old-Prog types who constituted the DP's backbone – had been mightily disillusioned with the DA's implosion at the end of 2002. 'We told you so ... you can't trust those Nats. Good riddance', were fairly typical remarks. Yet there was no going back to the purist isolation of the past.

Our party was still, notwithstanding Van Schalkwyk's defection, bigger and more diverse than a political association of the upper-middle-class English suburbs. The party needed to be given a sense of common purpose. At the same time, the disillusionment in our support base was tangible and needed to be addressed. In addition, behind some of the attacks on 'my style' was an attempt to paint the DA as a political *cul-de-sac* – a shrill and impotent voice on the sidelines of some glorious renaissance where dissent was akin, at best, to recidivist racism or even 'counter-revolutionary' treason.

I had received various entreaties from a highly placed adviser to my critical friend Buthelezi. He was increasingly concerned at the instability of the IFP-ANC provincial government in KwaZulu-Natal, and wanted to show Mbeki that he had options outside the ANC. Burnt though I had been by my dealings with the NNP, I viewed a closer association with the IFP as meeting a number of my party's needs. It would negate perceptions that the DA was confined to minority racial politics. It would signal that our ill-starred marriage with the NNP had not foreclosed other options for opposition co-operation.

In fact, there was a long history of collaboration between the old PFP and Buthelezi's KwaZulu-Natal homeland administration; and he had warm personal ties to Helen Suzman and Colin Eglin. I also knew, however, that within my own current ranks, particularly in KwaZulu-Natal where the IFP wielded power, there was considerable unease about Inkatha. Some in the DA saw them as practising an antediluvian political and chauvinistic culture, replete with elements of cronyism tainted, on occasion, by corruption.

However, our provincial leader, Roger Burrows, was supportive of a closer association and I decided to proceed, but this time with caution – at least initially. In March the IFP and DA gathered over thirteen hundred of our Natal-based public representatives for a public show of strength and united resolve at Durban's beachfront exhibition centre. Both Buthelezi and I pledged to extend our existing co-operation, then confined to local government.

Buthelezi advised the media that our first public joint rally was 'just the start', a prophetic forecast.[4] I had no doubt then that circumstances could lead the DA into government in KwaZulu-Natal, but also knew that given the restiveness in my own ranks, I would have to 'hasten slowly'.

A significant ray of promise was emerging, suggesting that we could move beyond our traditional, narrow base. A Markinor poll commissioned by the SABC yielded significant information. Its results were a shock for both the ANC and ourselves: only 42% of all South Africans named Mbeki as the politician they most trusted (in sharp contrast to the 66% of seats in parliament he commanded), while 28% named me, putting Mbeki and me within closer range than we had ever been before – and suggesting that, despite the NNP defection, the DA still had considerable momentum.[5]

The SABC buried the poll in a single TV news report in the middle of the Easter holiday weekend. Still, I was even more heartened in mid-May when, in an all-black ward in the Albert Luthuli municipality in Mpumalanga, a DA by-election candidate polled 31,2% of the vote – up from 8% in 2000. Were we breaking new political ground?

The poll, rogue or real, put me in buoyant mood for the DA's first elective congress in April. It convened in the cavernous hall of Johannesburg's Nasrec centre, scene of the chaotic vote-counting in the 1994 election. The nearly two thousand delegates and observers – mostly black – indicated how far the party had travelled in six years. When I was led onto the stage to the pulsating rhythms of the Kwaito song 'Nkalakatha' I was emboldened to declare that the worst for the party was over.[6] I quoted Joseph Conrad's Typhoon: 'We have come through a storm of unparalleled velocity. At the end of Conrad's story he provided words of wisdom to those in the eye of the storm: "Always facing it, Captain McWhirr: that's the way to get through." And that's what we did. We faced it and I am proud to say that we got through.'

The delegates duly elected me unopposed as party leader, and left the conference feeling both purposeful and unified. My prediction proved to be hopelessly premature.

2

On the eve of the party congress, news broke that an insolvent German conman, Jurgen Harksen – resident in Cape Town and fighting off extradition attempts – had made donations to the DA in the Western Cape. The donations were allegedly procured by Gerald Morkel and Leon Markovitz when both were members of the provincial government. I happened to be reading the autobiography of British politician Michael Heseltine, who stormed out of Margaret Thatcher's cabinet because of the so-called 'Westland helicopter' crisis. He described the saga as follows: 'It grew from a cloud no bigger than a man's hand into what proved to be the most powerful storm of my political life.'[7]

This turned out to be a useful working description for the Harksen scandal, which came perilously close to severely tarnishing my own leadership and certainly the party's squeaky-clean anti-corruption image. However, it did not simply descend on an unsuspecting party in a vacuum. The NNP and ANC were determined to wrest control of our last governing outpost in Cape Town, and Morkel, our mayor, was our most important pivot in holding on to our power base. I also had been severely criticised for my so-called high-handed dismissal of Marais the year before; so from the start, I would have to proceed with maximum caution. To lose one mayor was perhaps incautious, but to lose two in one year could be politically calamitous.

The Harksen saga broke as parliament was putting the finishing touches to the floor-crossing legislation. Once enacted, the legislation would allow DA or any other councillors to switch parties. From the outset the pressure to move against Morkel (against whom nothing had been proven) was enormous; but I knew that if I did so I risked alienating the very councillors whose loyalty it was vital to retain.

Since lurid details of Morkel's close relationship with Harksen had been apparently leaked to the media by the trustees of Harksen's estate and by the Scorpions – the politically controlled national criminal investigation agency – it was clear that both our mayor and the party would be subject to severe scrutiny. The party Federal Council deemed Morkel and Markovitz's relationship with Harksen 'inappropriate'. We advised both that if either were to be arrested on any criminal charges flowing from such dealings, they would be suspended as members and expelled on conviction.

No charges were ever preferred against either. I felt there was breathtaking hypocrisy and double standards involved in the issue and the ANC's crowing. Firstly, Harksen had spread his bread fairly generously across the political waters of South Africa (which he denied in 2001, but admitted seven years later). The ANC had allegedly received a staggering $300-million from some of the most corrupt political leaders in the world, including Indonesia's Suharto and Gaddafi of Libya. Harksen was a tadpole, but a perfect one to delegitimise and destabilise the party.

Peter Marais had every intention of making good on his toilet threat to 'destroy Leon'. He proceeded rapidly. As premier he appointed a judicial commission of enquiry, urged on him by ANC provincial leader Ebrahim Rasool, to investigate the provenance and purpose of alleged security equipment (dubbed 'bugging devices') found in a basement in the provincial government building when the ANC-NNP administration took office in the DA's stead. Since Hennie Bester had been the provincial minister for Safety and Security and the provincial director-general was a former securocrat, Niël Barnard, it was easy to see where the investigation might lead. As for the choice of judge to head the probe, the premier did not approach the provincial judge president and request him to appoint a judicial officer. Instead he directly named Judge Siraj Desai to head the commission, and Desai accepted without seeking permission to do so.

Desai, a junior jurist, had an impressive track record, not so much in law as in the ANC. He had been a party branch chairman; was a house friend of Rasool; and had been a professional associate in the legal practice of Dullah Omar, until 1999 the ANC minister of Justice (and thereafter minister of Transport). Our collective brow furrowed when he immediately agreed to Marais's suggestion that his terms of reference be extended to investigate whether Morkel, while premier, had solicited or received donations from Harksen. So began, in Hennie Bester's words, 'a season of madness' in the Cape.

I was initially determined to stay out of the frame. I had already been burnt by the Marais saga, portrayed as 'judge, jury and executioner', and had been severely criticised for that by the Cape High Court. However, as the news broke I remembered well that in early December, Morkel had invited me to attend a lunch with 'business supporters and friends of mine'. An hour before the lunch, Gerald called me and said: 'I think it's only right to inform you that Jurgen Harksen will be one of the guests.' I knew vaguely of Harksen's reputation for being a 'legal wide boy', and his background, so I quickly phoned James Selfe to seek his counsel. He urged me to attend. I did not want to offend Morkel or the other business guests he had invited. No doubt unwisely, I split the difference by deciding to go to the Constantia Uitsig restaurant, make my customary presentation about the party's prospects, and then leave. The lunch was attended by about a dozen people, among them Harksen.

The occasion was neither clandestine nor did I solicit or receive Harksen's money. I left before the main course was served. The moment the Harksen story broke, *Die Burger* immediately contacted my office to ask about my involvement with Harksen. On 17 April my media officer released a statement detailing my one brief meeting and adding, quite accurately, 'there was nothing inappropriate and untoward about the occasion … Mr Leon has no relationship with Mr Harksen and has never met him on any occasion before or since.'

While the party, our opponents and the media braced themselves for Harksen's testimony before Desai, premier Marais was about to self-destruct. In May he was embroiled in a R5-million sexual harassment claim by a former ministerial colleague, DA MPL Audrey van Zyl. At a hastily convened media conference he burst into tears and claimed Van Zyl's suit was orchestrated by the 'DA gay lobby' which he claimed had 'taken control of the DA leadership in order to attack my image as a Christian.'[8]

I knew nothing of Van Zyl's claim and was quite unaware of this 'gay lobby' which had apparently seized the heights of my party. Marais rounded off his whine with another warning that 'any allegations of sexual sleaze might rub off on [the DA].' I was hugely amused: another of Marais's former female colleagues had made similar allegations.

Marais's bluster could not save him. Within weeks, his leader Van Schalkwyk said Marais faced a further probe, this time by the police into allegations of sexual harassment by an employee. The woman had worked in Niël Barnard's office; and now it was Van Schalkwyk who moved directly against Marais, whom he obliged to stand down as premier. On 1 June it was announced (by unanimous decision of the Western Cape NNP) that his replacement would be Van Schalkwyk himself. After a ten-month zigzag and multiple betrayals Van Schalkwyk's plan for the premiership was finally realised. Marais's alleged harassment became a forgotten footnote; and in October, provincial director of public prosecutions Frank Kahn announced that his office had found 'no reasonable prospect of a successful prosecution' in relation to the charge.[9]

On hearing the news of Van Schalkwyk's move to the premier's residence of 'Leeuwenhof' ('Court of the Lion') I noted that the place should be renamed 'Poedelpaleis' ('Poodle Palace'). It would be about my only stab at humour over the next two months, once Harksen took to the stand before Desai. In fact, two days before he did so, the judge informed Bester during his testimony (on the security issue) that '[it] is not in our terms of reference to determine whether any money was given to the DA.'[10]

Two days later Harksen happily started singing like a canary. He claimed he had given the DA some half-million rands in funding, and that he was the party's 'unofficial minister of fundraising'. He gave detail and colour, suggesting a close relationship with Morkel and Markovitz – but this was clearly not enough for Judge Desai, who, in my view in search of impaling the biggest DA beast of all, seized on Harksen's allegation that he had funded Morkel's court battles with the NNP the year before (in which Bester and Markovitz had been involved). Unprompted by any evidence, or the memory of his statement to Bester, Desai asked of Harksen: '[Who else] was aware of the fact that you were bankrolling this litigation, beside Mr Morkel, Mr Markovitz, Mr Bester, and who else?'

To which Harksen responded, equally without evidence: 'I would also think Mr Tony Leon.'[11] Later that day Desai stressed this point again: 'So is it correct to say then that the leadership of the DA at its highest level knew you were financing Mr Morkel's case?' To which Harksen, no doubt happy to be so led, replied: 'I have no doubt about this.'[12]

The next day's headlines were appalling for me: '*Tony Leon het geweet*' ('Tony Leon knew') screamed *Die Volksblad*,[13] while the *Star* front page was all of a piece: 'Harksen fingers Leon'.[14]

I could hardly blame the press for carrying his explosive testimony so sensationally. They would not wait for two months or so until our bulldog-like senior counsel, my good friend Peter Hodes SC, completely destroyed this tissue of fabrication in his devastating cross-examination. It was also of scant comfort to me in December when Desai eventually found, correctly, that Harksen's claims of my knowledge of his funding the Morkel litigation were 'false' and had been made to 'sensationalise his testimony' in May.[15]

The party and my reputation were thrown on the flames by the uncorroborated word of a serial liar, apparently encouraged by a judge who was running a commission that seemed far more concerned with politics than with law. We could not sit by and duck the blows, in the hope that at the end of this process we would emerge vindicated.

Our first attack dog of choice was Douglas Gibson, who took for the DA the unprecedented step of denouncing the entire Desai Commission as 'a kangaroo court'.[16] Apart from highlighting Desai's close connections to the ANC, we pointed out that under the relevant statute, Harksen could say whatever he wished before the commission without any of his evidence being used against him in any future criminal proceedings.

Gibson's robust attack drew howls of protest about the party descending into the dangerous arena of impugning the judiciary. But since it was our considered view that the entire set-up of the commission – and the judge's behaviour – was itself problematic, we felt we had no other choice. Indeed, buried within an editorial criticising Gibson's standpoint, *Business Day* wrote one line which went to the heart of how we conceived matters. It acknowledged that the Desai Commission was 'a weapon in the ANC's struggle for power in the [Western Cape] province and its capital city'.[17] In truth, of course, a commission chaired by a judge is a very different and far less protected judicial animal than a court of law.

In the interim we set up an internal party committee to investigate Harksen's sleazy pronouncements. But as leader I would have to respond in public. Scheduled to open the party's stand at the agricultural Royal Show in Pietermaritzburg, I chose my moment. The show – since we were being buried alive in agricultural manure of a vicious kind – was perhaps appropriate. On my way into the venue, a florid-faced, middle-aged white Natalian in an open-necked shirt (whom a DA canvasser would probably have marked down as a supporter) shouted at me: '[What] have you done with your German millions?'

In a carefully worded, closely referenced ten-page speech I set out the facts, as we knew them, and the background to the saga. I reaffirmed the party's commitment to take 'appropriate action against any DA member, no matter how junior or senior, who is found to be involved in corrupt or illegal practices.' I noted that there was in law or fact no basis to discipline Morkel, and moved on to Desai's role:

'The immediate political objective, quite clearly, is to damage the DA as much as possible on the eve of the promulgation of floor-crossing legislation, so that the ANC-NNP can maximise their chances of taking control of the city of Cape Town ... the last remaining major centre of opposition power in South Africa.'[18]

I drew attention to the fact that while the spotlight was on Harksen, President Mbeki had – according to the uncontradicted court testimony of former head of the Presidential Protection Unit, André Lincoln – held a series of private meetings in his office with the alleged mafia kingpin resident in the Cape winelands, Vito Pallazolo:

'Yet instead of Mr Mbeki dealing with such allegations in a forthright and considered manner he has not done so and the press has failed to report on it. Mr Mbeki has hidden behind the *sub judice* rule and simply declined to speak on this matter at all. This rule has also been available to my party in respect of the Harksen controversy, but we have never taken advantage of it.'

Beyond our legal battles, there was a direct, physical assault being meted out to the specifically black members of the opposition. I had recently accompanied Helen Zille to Cape Town's Crossroads township where one of our most prominent activists had been shot dead, while others had had their shacks and property destroyed and been forced to appear before 'people's courts' and generally harassed and intimidated.

The assault on us was four-pronged: the NNP-ANC deal to attempt to decimate the DA; the proposed floor-crossing; the misuse of state power in the form of the Desai Commission; and the harassment of DA black members. I warned that 'the ANC-NNP campaign to destroy opposition in South Africa will not stop here. It will go on. It will intensify. It needs to be resisted. But there are people in South Africa who engage in wishful thinking about the ANC. They don't want it to be true that the ANC of Mr Mbeki demonstrates certain dangerous anti-democratic tendencies. They prefer to think about the ANC as an organisation personified by other, kinder, gentler individuals. They avert their gaze from the worst aspects of the ANC's behaviour, or explain them away as aberrations ... Or they give up on the prospect of making South Africa the best it can be, and express a kind of limp gratitude that the ANC is not a great deal worse ...

'Let me be very clear about how the DA will respond to the assault on democracy: we will not be intimidated, manipulated or harassed into silence or submission. We will not stand back. We will not retreat into the minority *cul-de-sac* allotted us by the ANC. We will not respond with gentle, pleading words ... [We] will fight with the most potent weapon at our disposal: the truth. We will continue to tell the truth to the people of South Africa, and we will continue to win their support.'

I had not brought Mbeki into the mess for the purposes of sensationalism. Morkel had told me how the year before, when he was still premier, at a gathering of provincial premiers Mbeki had called him aside and said, in effect, 'You should get yourself out of your association with Tony Leon', leaving me in little doubt that the ANC's political assault on us enjoyed the highest sanction.

The immediate consequence of my speech came not from the ANC, but from its new-found ally, the NNP in the form of its executive director, Renier Schoeman, a man without much regard for morality or fact. He was a political operator, never over-fussed by his methodologies. However, his response was breathtaking: back in my Cape Town office a SAPA release carried his statement: 'Mr Leon's personal involvement in the Harksen scandal has unmasked the real Tony Leon: a political swindler who may well have been involved in serious corruption.'

The remarks were prefaced by the statement that the DA had been involved in 'questionable practices which potentially include actions that were criminal.' Schoeman suggested that parliament urgently consider 'appropriate sanctions' if I had compromised my constitutional integrity as Leader of the Opposition.[19]

'Those shits,' I thought, and no doubt told my staff. Aside from my integrity and good name, I had been placed in the middle of a web of criminal corruption. More than a mere verbal response was now required. I immediately consulted Hodes and Brian Doctor QC (in London). Both would normally have cautioned against one politician suing another for remarks in the public arena. However, when I read to them what Schoeman had said, they urged me to proceed with an action for damages based on clear and incontrovertible defamation. (Hodes immediately offered his services at no cost, if necessary.)

3

By 8 June, summons had been served on Schoeman, Daryl Swanepoel and the NNP. I stated: '[This] is the first occasion in my sixteen years in public office that I have taken such a step. The NNP leadership has crossed a line, the result of which has been to besmirch my good name and reputation with reckless disregard for the truth.' When the case (which was defended) arrived in the Cape High Court on 14 April 2003, Schoeman, Swanepoel and the NNP capitulated, paid our legal costs and published newspaper ads offering me an unqualified apology for the untruthful statements and allegations.

While I was now fighting back, our party was bleeding. Harksen's tales of 'whisky drinking in funky bars' with Morkel and Markovitz, and of having advanced personal moneys to both (which they strenuously denied), and of strong evidence of the laundering of Deutschmarks earmarked for the DA, had knocked us off our moral perch and we were in danger of drowning in a sea of sleaze. The origin of our misfortune was a German fraudster and liar whose untested utterances were amplified through a dubious commission and the media; but they were never questioned or scrutinised in the context of the wider assault on the DA.[20]

Two days after my Pietermaritzburg speech, on 28 May, I convened a meeting at my home of our core leadership group: Selfe, Seremane, Gibson, Coetzee, Bester and Theuns Botha. We agreed that Gerald, in particular, needed 'a ladder off the branch of the tree' which was in danger of breaking – with every indication that he could take the party down with him. We agreed on a forensic audit of the party's Western Cape books and the personal bank accounts of Morkel and Markovitz. We also knew that in addition to the vital role Gerald played in shoring up our councillors, there were no legal grounds for his suspension on the basis of untested allegations. We would simply have to tough it out.

Bester was helpful and constructive, and undertook to discuss our course of action with Morkel and Markovitz, who both readily agreed to our proposal. I detected nothing untoward or unusual in Bester's attitude or behaviour: as a lawyer and Morkel's deputy leader we knew how pivotal he was in the party's defence.

The next morning, my secretary Sandy Slack told me that Bester needed to see me on a matter of 'utmost urgency'. When a pale and distressed Bester arrived I assumed some complication had arisen with our proposed forensic audit.

I had guessed wrong. Bester, instead, told me that he had scheduled a press conference later that morning to announce his resignation from politics. I was dumbstruck. The party was in the middle of a war for its very survival – and here was one of our key generals deserting the field as it reached its most intense phase.

Bester said he 'couldn't take it any more'. On one level I empathised; on another I was furious: Bester, more than anyone else, had driven the DP to form its alliance with the NNP, and as a consequence had enjoyed ministerial office. The previous year, when the party was reeling from the Marais-Van Schalkwyk chicanery, again it was Bester who urged me to act against Marais, and established the (faulty) legal premise for so doing. Now he was walking away.

When I conveyed this unwelcome news to my senior colleagues there was immense anger. Some speculated he had been caught in the web of Desai's probe into the bugging saga. Others felt he had concluded that his ambition of becoming premier of the Western Cape was now beyond reach. Selfe, who had been a boarder at Bishops throughout his school life, laconically observed: 'He never went to boarding school; he was never forced to have cold showers or get thrashed. So now he quits.'

I put out a carefully worded statement noting that it was 'a tragedy that someone of [Bester's] enormous ability and great decency should feel it necessary to resign'.[21] However, my kind words hid the deep anger I really felt. At Bester's own press conference he indicated that his resignation was 'not unrelated to the Desai Commission', and in response to a question about Morkel he added, noncommittally, but slightly ominously: 'Morkel is the guardian of his own conscience and the master of his own fate.'[22]

Bester's resignation and the Desai commission meant that our attempts at damage control were severely diminished.[23] *Business Day*, for example, asked the by-now legitimate question, 'Will the DA survive the Harksen scandal?' while the *Mail&Guardian* plastered an anguished photograph of me on its front page, stating: 'Leon on the ropes: DA's frantic moves to limit the damage'.[24] Although I framed the page for my lobby, my outward show of *sangfroid* hid dread and anxiety.

One of my early-morning pleasures had always been to awake early, get the coffee on the boil, and head out to the front gate and retrieve the morning newspapers. Now, in June 2002, this agreeable morning ritual became an ordeal. It wasn't only the details of the so-called 'dirty money' we had received; it was, in my critics' view, the well-deserved reward for a series of misjudgments. For example, Drew Forrest wrote in the *Mail&Guardian*: 'The Harksen fiasco is further evidence of the morally corrosive effect on [Leon's] party of his grand plan: form an alliance with the NNP and then digest it quickly. Morkel, Markovitz, Marais and the rest were tainted cargo he should never have taken on board.'[25]

The *Star* wanted to know whether the hunter had become the hunted.[26]

In mid-June at a rally in Athlone, Morkel told the crowd that the DA would survive the 'dark times through which it was now passing'; and apologised for his 'foolish friendship with Harksen' which he publicly acknowledged as 'a grave error of judgment'. In turn I stuck the epithet of 'joiner' onto Van Schalkwyk, a term of opprobrium dating from the Boer War used to brand Afrikaner traitors who made common cause with the British. I knew it would hurt and thought it accurate. We also knew from our own internal polling that NNP support in the Western Cape had crashed to 6%, an all-time historical low, while ours was now four times greater.

Carol Paton of the *Sunday Times* attended the same rally and gave readers a more authentic account of how the party looked despite the scandals:

'There is a unique political culture in Cape Town's Coloured suburbs. When it comes to political meetings, people turn out in great numbers. They come for the entertainment, shout a lot and listen a little – but, nonetheless, they come.

'That's why petite Helen Zille, acting leader of the DA in the Western Cape, is on the stage of a "rocking" Cape Flats hall on Tuesday evening, stamping her foot and throwing her fist into the air: "*Viva DA, viva!*" she yells. "*Yayyyy!*" the crowd yells back ...

'Tuesday night in Athlone Civic Hall is typical of the style of politics on the Cape Flats. But it is also evidence of something quite profound: that since it split with the NNP in November, the DA hasn't gone back to being its good old liberal self. Instead, it has become a completely different party.

'On the negative side, it has lost its moral superiority.'[27]

The party Federal Council in June censured both Morkel and Markovitz, but declined to take any further action after both assured the leadership that neither had been involved in any unlawful act – a point eventually conceded by Desai when he reported in December. But there was a deep anxiety that any further humiliation heaped on Morkel would result in the loss of the unicity of Cape Town.

I had spent most of 2002 bolstering our Cape Town caucus, criss-crossing the country to try and staunch the expected exodus of NNP-DA councillors. It was a terrible time; many councillors were clearly weighing their options, but since we had no direct evidence of their intentions we could not act against them. There was also a significant swathe of Nats now in the DA who appeared totally committed to our party. However, recrimination, rumour and subterfuge now reigned and all but paralysed our councils.

The floor-crossing was due to commence at midnight on 21 June. Our position in Cape Town appeared dire. The NNP-ANC needed to attract 24 DA councillors to gain control, and applied enormous pressure – backed by huge financial incentives.[28]

In turn, we cajoled councillors to stay the course on the premise that in the long term the DA was the better option. In the case of most of the waverers, I did not doubt that the ringing of cash registers was more agreeable than moral suasion.

However, it was also clear that floor-crossing would not be a one-way street. I began meeting secretly with NNP MPs, bitterly unhappy with Van Schalkwyk's treachery and the prospect of living out the rest of their parliamentary and political lives under the heel of the ANC. Whatever our local losses would be, the DA at parliamentary level – the original floor-crossing legislation envisaged a simultaneous 'window of opportunity' at all three levels of government – would be bolstered by nine NNP MPs (out of a total of 28) joining the DA.

Then, before anyone could turn into a Cinderella at the midnight hour, Bantu Holomisa of the UDM obtained an urgent interdict to block the enactment of the law. After high drama and deep anxiety, the case was referred to the Constitutional Court. Since they would only deliver final judgment in October, all bets and looming defections were now temporarily off.

Meanwhile, in KwaZulu-Natal, the ANC was determined to lure floor-crossers and take control of the province from the IFP. Buthelezi was seriously alarmed when, with reckless precipitousness, the ANC prematurely announced that four provincial MPs (two IFP, two DA) were crossing over to it. This was in June. In view of the pending appeal, I knew that while the four putative defectors were the political equivalents of beached whales, the province could shift hands as soon as the Court made its pronouncement.

Until then the DA had been no more than an energetic bystander in KwaZulu-Natal. But when Buthelezi personally invited me to attend and address his party's National Conference in Ulundi, historic capital of the Zulu kingdom, it was an essential invitation. So I found myself in the midst of the IFP throngs patiently awaiting my turn to speak.

There was real anger among the delegates that their hard-won democratic gains in the province could be stripped away. To tap into this feeling and steer away from the hard reality that the DA had voted for the cross-over legislation (which I intensely regretted), I told the delegates that in the event of a change of government, then an immediate election should be called: 'The ANC claims to be a people's party. Well, let the people decide!'

The audience loved it. However, I hadn't gone all that way for an ovation. I spoke at length to Buthelezi and we agreed that our nascent co-operation needed to be taken a stage further. I told him – without at that time any mandate from the DA – that we would enter the government of KwaZulu-Natal if it appeared the ANC had any prospect of a takeover. We agreed to keep in close touch once we had clarity from the Court.

My closer moves to Buthelezi were instinctive and pragmatic. Roger Burrows supported my assessment – and would be a direct beneficiary of any move by the DA into the provincial government. I reasoned that if the DA balance sheet revealed a loss of local power, with no offsetting gains elsewhere, we would be in real trouble in the court of public opinion. Entering the provincial government of KwaZulu-Natal would improve the ledger.

I had long felt that while the ANC invoked the name of the poor at every turn, many of their policies – particularly on employment and public services – undermined their own rhetoric. What should be the opposition message? Certainly, we were associated with individual freedom and the market economy. In the waiting period I refined my thoughts, and at our April congress set out my stall in fairly radical language. Of course, fuzzy signals emanating from Harksen drowned out most of it, but the essence of what I had to say echoed my convictions:

'What we have to provide is not just a fundamental belief in individual freedom in a market economy, but also a social-democratic belief, a commitment to social justice, through action of the government. And that imposes on the rich minority in our country, which consists of all races, an obligation beyond simply obeying the law and paying taxes. We believe that the strong should help the weak. That the rich have a duty to the poor. That the able have a commitment to the disabled. These obligations – freely undertaken – will help make our country great. The powerful combination of a market economy and social justice is the key to the economic liberation we so desperately need.'

Ken Andrew, our researchers and I were struck by certain bleak and seemingly contradictory facts. The statistics suggested that half the country was living in conditions of deep poverty (about twenty million people); four million had no income at all; and nearly three million were without permanent shelter. Whatever else the ANC had achieved, their dent on poverty had been very slight.[29]

Starvation stalked the land – with one 1999 survey recording that over ten per cent of households with children under the age of seven went hungry most days of the year. While the state provided a patchwork of welfare grants – targeting the very young, the elderly and the disabled – there were huge numbers of South Africans who fell straight through the thinly spread welfare net. Grants were also conditional on means testing and often, at that stage, bogged down in problems of delivery and corruption.[30]

The minister of Finance, Trevor Manuel, resisted calls for an across-the-board basic income grant, deriding it as 'macropopulism'. But I knew that part of his reluctance stemmed from his persistent recoiling at raising, even modestly, the VAT rate, which was frozen at 14%. There was intense trade union pressure against any suggested rise.

But Andrew had arrived at the opposite conclusion. When he and our research team proposed that the DA support a modest basic income grant of R110 for every South African – and fund it with a 1% VAT increase plus a range of other fiscal measures to provide the necessary R15-billion required for its annual funding – I was immediately struck by this shift from our normal *laissez faire* approach, and its modesty: R110 was not a large handout.[31]

As a first step I arranged to buy a parcel of food worth R500 (for a family of five) and found that it could provide the bare basics for monthly nutrition, though not much more. This relatively small amount could make a big difference to many lives.

In November we publicly launched our basic income grant campaign in some of South Africa's poorest areas – in Atteridgeville in Pretoria and in a very poor section of the Umlazi township, south of Durban, where Statistics SA recorded a staggering 95% unemployment rate (over three times the national average).

The reaction of some of the party's business backers ranged from lukewarm to hostility. We also attracted the ire of COSATU which claimed, ludicrously, that our support would undermine its negotiations with government on the same issue.[32] I suspected that COSATU was embarrassed to find itself in the same company as its traditional 'class enemy'.

Human decency and social solidarity informed our approach. Our basic income grant campaign was to me an important marker in helping to connect the party to some of the poorest, often most wretched, enclaves in South Africa, and offer a practical proposal to those whom government appeared to have left behind, or forgotten, since assuming power.

4

During the same period I drove a campaign which unmasked the disdainful arrogance – and double standards – characteristic of the president's approach to crime and the unfinished business of the TRC. In May 2002 Mbeki pardoned 33 hardened criminals. Each had applied for, and been denied, TRC amnesty, which meant that the murders and violence for which they had been convicted failed to meet the tests of having been perpetrated with a political objective, or were 'proportional' to the cause involved.

Initially, Mbeki declined to name those pardoned. Then on 15 May, he and his Justice minister, Penuell Maduna, contradicted each other – the president claiming that their release was on the basis of their 'involvement in the struggle', while the minister told parliament the complete opposite: 'You will never find in our document a suggestion that they were pardoned because they were part of the struggle.'[33] I accused Mbeki of 'back-door amnesty' (he had always been ambivalent about the TRC). Then one of the freed killers – 27-year-old Dumisani Ncamazana (whose killing spree on the eve of the 1994 election took a gruesome toll of

various innocents), an 'APLA commander' – within two weeks of his release turned recidivist and together with his brother robbed a shop in East
London and murdered its owner, Martin Whittaker.

When Ncamazana was arrested in August, I was contacted by the
Whittaker family and flew to East London. They and the murdered victim's partner, Liesl de Villiers, were deeply angered that their lives had been
shattered by a deed committed by a man who, but for Mbeki's intervention, would still have been in jail.

More callous still was Mbeki's silence; he left it to his minister to proclaim that Whittaker's murder 'was neither here nor there'.[34] I denounced
Maduna and set about probing on what basis the 33 had been released.
Mbeki was constitutionally entitled to proclaim amnesty; but his judgment seemed impaired.

In September Mbeki revealed that in just three years in office he had
granted more than double the number of pardons (584) Mandela had
granted (274) in five years at the helm. Since Mandela's presidency had
spanned the period of reconciliation and transition, I pointed out that the
figures should have been reversed.[35] It seemed to me that pardons were
being used freely as a form of political point-settling, not to redress cases
of individual merit or hardship.

We soon learned that Mbeki's decision to pardon the 33 had been a consequence of a campaign by Eastern Cape premier Reverend Makhenkise
Stofile, of 9/11 fame (see Chapter 15), who had once shared a prison block
with five of them in the 1980s. But since neither apology nor explanation had been offered by the president or government for the reasons for
the release, I decided to invoke the provisions of the Promotion of Access
to Information Act and study for myself all the relevant and recorded
information.[36]

The documents made for startling and disturbing reading: none of the
33 applications appeared to have been processed on an individual basis; indeed, various key officials had recommended against granting presidential
pardons to some or all of the prisoners. What I found most alarming was
that Maduna – now the staunchest defender of the president's largesse –
had initially (in 2000) been against the decision. His about-turn was white-
washed on the unhelpful and uncorroborated ground that 'public opinion
inside as well as outside politics requires the 33 to be pardoned.'[37]

The documents also yielded the opinion of a key official in Maduna's
Justice department (Nic Grobler) who had sent Mbeki an 'explanatory
note' which stated in clear and unambiguous terms that 'the pardon should
not be granted to them.'[38]

That Mbeki chose to ride roughshod over the advice was all of a piece with his profoundly expressed view of – if not contempt for – the TRC processes, which at their best treated political offenders equally. For Mbeki there was in fact no equivalence: those who were even tangentially involved in the brutal struggle against apartheid were to be judged differently and benefit from pardons, notwithstanding the findings of the TRC.

At least a certain justice prevailed. On 12 December the High Court sentenced the two Ncamazana brothers to imprisonment for life for the murder of Martin Whittaker.

When the Constitutional Court finally delivered judgment on the floor-crossing legislation, it allowed crossovers at local level, but sent back to parliament the sections on national and provincial floor-crossing for rectification in line with the Constitution. This was the worst possible outcome from our perspective, and a matter of delight for our opponents. Our latest soundings had shown that we stood to haemorrhage councillors but gain MPs. I was in Israel – focused on the complexities and personalities of the Middle East – but hurried home to stick my finger in the dyke once more.

Shortly before 5 am on an October morning, James Selfe called me: 'Well,' he said mournfully, 'we've just lost Cape Town.' The bad news, so crisply delivered, propelled me towards my office to survey the wreckage. It was 8 October, the first day of a 14-day 'window of opportunity' (or 'opportunism' as I dubbed it) during which councillors could, finally, reveal their true colours.

How deep would the cut be? Objectively, the DA stood to lose the most; and we did not disappoint. Out of the 1 409 DA councillors across South Africa, 612 originated from the NNP. Since there were then no NNP councillors (each had been elected in 2000 under the DA banner), they had everything to gain and we faced a potential loss of over 40% of our municipal representatives. By the end of the 'window' some 340 NNPs left and 279 stayed. But in most municipalities under our control, the defection of a relative handful delivered power to the ANC-NNP coalition. We were pummelled: apart from the loss of Cape Town, we were to lose power in over a dozen councils in the Western Cape; five in the Northern Cape; and one in the Eastern Cape. We were left with a rump of ten councils in two provinces, and the consolation of sorts of retaining just over a thousand of our local representatives.

I called a press conference and was found by the media 'to be full of fighting talk'. Alluding to the cheque-book politics (courtesy of the ratepayers) which Van Schalkwyk had used to lure many defectors, I declared of the NNP leader and his born-again councillors: 'They would rather grab power through trickery, bribing and manipulation than win it fairly through the ballot box. These councillors are in breach of their contract with the people of Cape Town and they will pay the price.'

As for Van Schalkwyk, I dismissed him as the 'poor man's Joshua Nkomo of South Africa' (a reference to the quondam opposition leader in Zimbabwe who was co-opted into Mugabe's ruling party).

During this period, Gerald Morkel (who had lost his mayoralty to the ANC's Nomaindia Mfeketo) and I were on a series of walkabouts on the Cape Flats. We found many who had landed up being governed by default by an ANC administration they resolutely opposed. We rounded off with a giant rally in Cape Town city hall. On the advice of one of my staff, in tune with popular culture, I branded Van Schalkwyk 'mini-me', the midget in the Austin Powers movies, the clone of Dr Evil. At least I could enjoy the invective, while absorbing the losses.

Journalist Peter Wilhelm thought this all sounded an 'oddly triumphal note'.[39] But in fact, as I elaborated in an interview with him, the apparent triumph of the NNP was illusory, and their victory of 'the pyrrhic variety. By getting into bed with the ANC, the NNP have sacrificed their support base, and with it, their future. If they contest the next election [in 2004], it will come a distant third in the Western Cape and be wiped out in the rest of the country.'

This prediction, at least, turned out to be on the money. The NNP went on to lose every by-election they contested against us in the year that followed. In 2004 they were reduced to a parliamentary splinter of seven MPs, and Van Schalkwyk closed down the party a few months later, delivering his fragments into the ANC. Marais's fate was even worse. In February 2002 he, along with NNP provincial minister David Malatsi, was arrested for soliciting a bribe (of R400 000, in the form of donations to the NNP) from a dubious Italian businessman, Count Ricardo Augusta, in exchange for approving a golf estate development. (Marais was eventually acquitted, Malatsi convicted.)

While the NNP was, in the harsh but accurate description of Hermann Giliomee, given a well-deserved 'prostitute's funeral', its chief gravedigger, Van Schalkwyk, managed to parley his extraordinary act of political destruction – and the vandalism of his one-time opposition mandate – into a cabinet position under Mbeki.[40]

When he watched the ANC welcome the NNP apostates into their ranks during the floor-crossing, in what he said 'must rank as one of the most pitiful, the most crudely embarrassing images of "liberation politics",' satirist Robert Kirby concluded: 'As Groucho once said, some things give hypocrisy a bad name.'[41]

By December of 2002, Judge Desai delivered a damning report on Gerald Morkel and Leon Markovitz. Although he found no evidence of any personal enrichment, he disbelieved the origins of the Deutschmark donation. The day after Desai's pronouncement, Gerald resigned as Western Cape leader and I praised him for his 'admirable refusal to buckle under pressure', acknowledging both his brave stand and some errors of judgment – mindful that I had no shortage of those myself.

The concluding scene in the messy attempts to realign South African politics yielded for the DA script an apparently happier ending. The IFP premier in KwaZulu-Natal, Lionel Mtshali, was as a consequence of the ANC's moves against him (delayed temporarily since the provincial floor-crossing had been postponed until 2003) in a potentially imperilled position. He struck first, perhaps in the best traditions of his martial ancestors, and fired two ANC ministers from his cabinet. Buthelezi then invited me to consider joining the IFP government in the province.

In mid-November I addressed a distinctly lukewarm DA provincial council in Pinetown, many of whose members were opposed or edgy about full-blooded co-operation with the IFP. I had no doubt that if our by-now much battered 'alternative government' strategy was ever to proceed forward, the IFP invitation was a renewed opportunity. After much energetic persuasion, the doubters yielded. On 23 November in Durban North, the suburb where I was born, Buthelezi and I made our pact public, and the DA entered a new governing relationship.

The dark Cape storms had, I hoped, given way to a shaft of light from the East Coast.

CHAPTER 18

Against Goliath

When a movement turns into a clique,
The conqueror mused, as he stopped
By the sword his opponent had dropped:
Trophy or means of attack
On the rapturous crowds at his back?
He shrugged and left it, resigned
To a new battle, fought in the mind,
For faith that his quarrel was just,
That the right man lay in the dust.

KINGSLEY AMIS

I

In the run-up to the 2004 election there was a backwash of events and trends that had an impact on government, on the opposition and on wider society. They ranged from the epoch-defining to the mundane; and each shaped and pulled the contending forces of South Africa's democracy as the first decade of freedom drew to a close.

One should begin with whether poverty was conquered or was rampant.

The ANC held its 51st National Conference in Stellenbosch in December 2002, and declared its goal for the coming decade as the 'eradication of the legacy of colonialism and apartheid' which it hoped would culminate in 2012, which would see it win its final victory over poverty.[1]

The ANC was confident its ambitious goal was attainable; and served early notice in parliament the following year that South Africa was well on its way to that attainment – claiming the 'tide has turned in this government's fight for a better life for all South Africans.' Against the background of a decade of positive economic growth, Mbeki in his State of the Nation address reeled off a string of statistical pointers and ANC-initiated measures to bolster his assertion.

Certainly, the spread of social grants to the vulnerable and excluded, and 'social wages' paid by government to poor households – in the form of water and electricity connections, and the spread of new schools and health clinics – was an incontestable good. He and his administration deserved full credit – although the quality of these services was often far poorer than the statistics: for example, it was reported in 2006 that Telkom had disconnected nearly one million telephone lines of defaulting customers since 2000 – it had more than five-and-a-half million customers in 2000, which had shrunk to 4,7-million.[2]

In my rebuttal I pointed out that one in every three South Africans was unemployed; about seven million of the economically active were out of work; and black unemployment had actually worsened in the first decade of freedom from 46% in 1995 to 55% in 2001. I concluded that this was a direct consequence of government's policy choices, oxymoronically 'pro-Marxist but anti-growth, pro-labour but anti-poor'.

It seemed to me that despite the achievements of sound macro-economic management, there remained a real crisis which I termed 'the four horsemen of the Apocalypse: poverty, unemployment, HIV/AIDS and crime'. I thought Mbeki's 'tide has turned' line was distinctly Canute-like: not just in its misstatement of objective reality, but also for his stubborn refusal to even acknowledge the wave of AIDS deaths engulfing the country. He devoted fewer than forty words to the HIV/AIDS issue.[3] He had little to offer – and no comfort – for victims of crime, of whom by then 200 000 had been murdered, in the first decade of South Africa's 'freedom'.

I found an unlikely ally in the form of a maverick Stellenbosch academic – of a distinctly socialist stripe – Professor Sampie Terreblanche. He produced a fat tome: *A History of Inequality in South Africa*,[4] in which he spoke of the 'continued pauperisation' of half of the South Africa population since 1994, and a graph showing that this poorest half (23-million out of 45-million) possessed a mere 3,2% of the income in 2001. He described the post-1994 period in plain terms: 'From a socio-economic point of view, the poor have become marginalised, powerless and pauperised.'[5]

His assertion on inequality and its racial character went directly against Mbeki's thesis. Two other, more mainstream, academics, Nicoli Nattrass and Jeremy Seekings of UCT, challenged Mbeki's 'two nations' analogy for South Africa – asserting, 'In South Africa, black and white are no longer synonymous with rich and poor.'[6]

Then there was the tangled myth of the new elite.

While the poor and marginalised stayed stuck in the mud around their informal dwellings (literally, since so many were erected below urban floodlines) a new, multiracial middle class was powering ahead. Government's focus was intensifying on the issue of unequal wealth distribution on racial lines. From the outset, in 2003, when parliament enacted the legislative framework for Black Economic Empowerment (BEE),[7] I believed the ANC had the issue inverted: it was attempting to reframe the basic laws of the universe which placed creation first.

Just as with the economy, I thought, the emphasis should be first on wealth-creation – how to increase employment, ownership and entrepreneurship – and then deal with the demand side. Once again I found myself in interesting company, this time with Mbeki's own brother, Moeletsi, who became one of the most prominent critics of his brother's empowerment policies, stating in 2004:

'[Empowerment] takes the brightest among the black people who – instead of devoting their energies to creating new companies, to creating new products, to providing and creating employment – tend to spend most of their time, if not all of their time, looking for redistributing mechanisms to get shares in pre-existing companies. So what you are actually getting is that the brightest among the black people in this country, instead of creating wealth, building up their own companies, are becoming secondary fiddle players to the existing companies – and that in my view is not what is going to save our country.'[8]

He added: 'I think we should spend more and more and more money on skills ... I was reading a few weeks ago that we only have three thousand blacks who graduate with higher-grade mathematics at high school. Now, there should be a national campaign to change this kind of situation. Instead we're having campaigns about black economic empowerment.'[9]

A large part of government's empowerment policy then being enacted was through 'charters' to be applied throughout each industry in South Africa, described as 'one of the most rapid and sweeping transfers of wealth ever seen, and [one which] will put at risk both the solvency of the banking system and the strength of companies built up over many years.'[10]

The Economist took note and observed that the government's empowerment policy was hostile to investment and 'retards the economic growth that might make the poor less so.'[11]

The ANC's zeal to fit economic laws of supply, demand and investment into a racial straitjacket – based on pre-determined beneficiaries and pre-ordained outcomes – brought to my mind 17th-century Rome, when the church decreed that its religious views on planetary motion would prevail over the objective laws of astronomy. I was certainly no Galileo in

21st-century South Africa, though there were initially few voices raised in objection to the imposed economic order. The dissonant chorus would, however, grow as the process and its contradictions unfolded.

The irony was that instead of creating wealth for the majority of poor South Africans, empowerment proved little more than a costly way to shift wealth to well-connected members of the political elite.

Of the R42,2-billion in black economic empowerment deals in 2003, roughly 60%, or R25,3-billion, went to companies owned by only two men, both connected to the ruling party. The DA's approach would encourage empowerment through measures to stimulate economic growth, encourage small business development, boost savings, improve education, and expand employment. Without these broad-based measures aimed at uplifting the whole economy, real black economic empowerment would remain a dream.

But as South Africa headed down the road of dirigiste wealth transfers, the government increasingly and unjustifiably invoked the provisions of the somewhat antique Freedom Charter of 1955, instead of looking to its more recent and relevant GEAR macro-economics document (1996) which pinned the state's colours to international best practice. By 2003 the terms of trade were all defined by 'black economic empowerment', 'equity' and rectifying historic imbalances. Any challenge or dissent from this consensus was closed down before debate began.[12]

By 2003 practically all questions of economic principle and the non-racialism of the Constitution and Freedom Charter had been subordinated to questions of race and racial loyalty. Our researchers unearthed a document by Dr Hendrik Verwoerd in 1937: as editor of *Die Transvaler*, he proposed a 'solution' to perceived Jewish economic and professional dominance in South Africa, which he described as *''n botsing van belange'* ('a clash of interests') with under-represented Afrikaner interests. The state should intervene to ensure that each 'racial group' [among whites] would have its share according to its proportion of the [white] population.'[13]

Extraordinarily, while the NP government of 1948 never implemented such a radical plan, Verwoerd's notion of state intervention found direct approval – on a redirected basis – in the ANC's plan for comrade capitalism. Verwoerd's idea of 'balanced distribution' found its latter-day equivalent in the ANC's embrace of 'demographic representivity'. No society in the world had been made to use the power of the state to ensure equality of outcome without impoverishing the country. It seemed more sensible, if less politically sexy, to focus on the long-term, essential imperative of equality of opportunity and put it above racial or ethnic preferencing.

The ANC's near-dominance of the political terrain and its will to impose its writ across the whole of society seemed to me as leader of the opposition my greatest challenge. I had assumed that other, more powerful, actors in the business and civic realm would respond and fight their respective corners. I had made a wrong assumption.

2

The ANC's self-importance was global. Even before it concluded attempts to colonise boardrooms, the threat of conflict in Iraq consumed the energies of the governing party. In early 2003 the ANC invited me to join with it as part of a world peace movement 'to prevent the war in Iraq'. Mbeki declared that such activism – in the form of street protests and marches on the US embassy – was nothing less than 'an obligation'.

However, as I scanned Mbeki's *ANC Today* I found not a word of criticism of the tyrannous and murderous regime of Saddam Hussein. Nowhere was there a message on human rights, or a line about the rights of oppressed Kurds and the Shi'ite Muslim majority under Saddam's heel. I also thought the most absurd form of 'political tourism' was that Mbeki's deputy minister of Foreign Affairs kept shuttling off to Baghdad, as though his forays there could change the basics of the looming conflict. However, when the year before (July 2002) Saddam's deputy prime minister Tariq Aziz had paid an official visit to South Africa and been garlanded with praise and honour by deputy president Jacob Zuma, I found the spectacle revolting. What I did not know then was the proximity of profit for ANC front companies and individuals apparently benefiting from the UN 'oil for food' programme, easily manipulated and widely abused.

A report on the UN's oil-for-food programme, released in 2005, named Imvume Management among several other South African companies as having illegally benefited from kickbacks from the Iraqi government, and suggested that Imvume had an improper relationship with the ANC government. In February 2007 Mbeki announced a commission of inquiry into the allegations; the findings have never been produced.

However, President George W Bush's impatient determination to use unilateral action in Iraq gave South African anti-Americanism – mostly a noises-off phenomenon on the fringes of government and the ANC – a rare opportunity to shout defiance. I had no doubt the issue should be discussed on the merits and dangers of the emerging Bush doctrine of pre-emption; thus in my response to the invitation, which I declined, I noted that the 'UN is the primary safeguard of world peace and security, and unilateral action by any country undermines its authority. But our interests lie neither in kowtowing to the US nor in raising cheers for Third World tyrants and autocrats.'[14]

But, as ever in South Africa, race was close to the surface: it was in fact Nelson Mandela, not Thabo Mbeki, who attacked Bush, declaring the US president's contempt for the UN lay in the fact that its secretary-general, Kofi Annan, was black.[15] The stinging put-down to this bizarre remark came from the left-wing polemicist Christopher Hitchens. Writing in his blog *Slate*[16] he noted: 'It's a strong field in which to compete, but the contest for the most stupid remark about the impending confrontation with Iraq has apparently been won by Nelson Mandela.'

Taking its cue from the top, the ANC insisted that Iraq's (as it transpired, non-existent) weapons of mass destruction attracted the sort of scrutiny which Israel's did not – because 'Israel was white and Iraq black.'[17] This Manichean division of the world was absurdist and dangerous, but of a piece with Mbeki's railing against 'the white Commonwealth' which had demanded a stronger stand on Zimbabwe. I noted that 'our foreign policy has become so absurdly racialised that one half-expected the president to append a world map to copies of his speeches on which he helpfully indicates which parts of it are "black", "white", "mixed", or "other".' But in an atmosphere thick with political correctness and smug sanctimony, such invocations were frowned upon.

In foreign policy, as at home, ANC policy bore a striking resemblance to the 'doublethink' which George Orwell defined as 'the power of holding two contradictory beliefs in one's mind and simultaneously accepting both of them.' Mbeki was the progenitor of Africa's Nepad economic recovery programme – premised on obtaining millions of dollars of aid and investment from the G-8. Yet an uncritical 'Third World' solidarity appeared to explain other impulses behind South Africa's foreign posture, based more on reviving the Cold War than on facing the challenges and nuances of the unipolar global era.

But by then Mbeki had acquired a R650-million Boeing executive jet. By 2003 he had spent roughly two months abroad each year; and in that year alone, undertook four visits and 20 foreign odysseys, eclipsing his own previous record from 2000.[18]

The 'high flying' syndrome seemed to infect the entire cabinet. When Mbeki took off on a state visit to India in October 2003, 12 cabinet ministers accompanied him. This junketeering extravagance and the imposition of the 'big man' style of leadership had by then become ubiquitous. Shortly after the 1999 general election, walking in the parliamentary garage, I saw a gleaming line-up of brand new luxury German sedans and state-of-the-art 4x4s. We discovered that R20-million had been spent on getting the cabinet the best wheels – despite the shadow of poverty and privation.

Again, I frequently found myself driving to parliament along De Waal Drive from my home in Cape Town's southern suburbs, accompanied by blaring sirens and blazing blue lights. At first I assumed there was some desperate medical emergency; yet when I looked back it was to discover that the commotion was caused by the escort and entourage of some or other government minister, no doubt late for work.

Shortly after I first came to parliament in 1990 I encountered President FW de Klerk leaving the Union Buildings in Pretoria as I was entering them. South Africa was involved in a low-intensity but deadly civil war, and De Klerk was a marked man from Right and Left. Yet his entourage comprised two vehicles: his own Mercedes with a driver and bodyguard, followed by a police chase car. That was it.

Any encounter with Mbeki was very different. I noted in 2005, '[When] I saw President Mbeki's entourage, I managed to count 12 vehicles, including an ambulance, before I lost track altogether.'

Thus in the year before the ANC faced the electorate once more, it bestrode the national stage as a colossus – a super-majority organisation which elided the concept of party, state and society into itself. When, for example, DA party chairman Joe Seremane asked Mbeki in parliament to speak out on corruption allegations surrounding his deputy (twenty months before Mbeki acted) Mbeki snarled back: '[Mr Seremane] speaks on behalf of the people of South Africa ... we are in the fortunate position that the DA is not the people of South Africa.'[19]

Actually Seremane's point had been modest and self-evident. He had asked: 'How much longer must the people wait for you to lead in restoring the damage that has already been done?' But the reaction was clear: the right to speak on behalf of the people was reserved for the ruling party; the ANC was the majority party, and therefore the sole legitimate voice of the South African people. Opposition meant opposition to the people.

How was one to dent this behemoth? Mbeki had famously jibed that he and I lived 'on different planets'. It also appeared as though our views of politics and the place of opposition were based on two utterly contradictory theories: his universal view and mine being as dissimilar as the theories of general relativity and quantum mechanics.

Although I was a dud at physical science at school, I had seen a dramatic production in London which in an entirely non-scientific setting attempted to answer the question: 'Can it really be that the universe at its most fundamental level is divided – requiring one set of law when things are large and a different, incompatible set when things are small?'[20]

'Opposition' had been viewed as the polar opposite of loyalty in pre-democratic societies – where to oppose the king was to oppose the state. There seemed some danger that South Africa, on the eve of its celebrations of a decade of freedom, was in thrall to the same notion. I remained adamant that just as superstring theory reconciles the rules that govern the universe at macro and micro levels (subject to proof), the concepts of 'loyalty' and 'opposition' were not just reconciled in a modern constitutional democracy, but were a *sine qua non* for their attainment.

Academic-turned-businessman Dr Vincent Maphai gave voice to a different view; he singled out the DA as 'the only party that seldom, if ever, calls for national reconciliation. Instead the party defines its core identity in terms of opposing the ANC. It's like a rugby team that relies exclusively on spoiling tactics.'[21]

I considered Maphai's attack inaccurate in the extreme: yet he tapped into a widely held assumption that strong opposition was somehow 'un-African'. Sociology Professor Lawrence Schlemmer put him to rights, citing a 2001 South African Institute of Race Relations survey which found that two-thirds of African respondents did not concur that 'DA style opposition' was 'racist'. Sixty per cent of the same group believed that 'all this talk of racism' was uttered by politicians seeking excuses for their failures. He added that if Maphai 'wanted some kind of reconciliation pact' he should direct his attention 'as much to government as to the opposition, since the former continually exploits race in the scramble for political ammunition.'[22]

However, 2003 did foster a few positive signals. The much-delayed floor-crossing at parliamentary level in March gave the DA something to cheer about. Fed up with Van Schalkwyk's toadying towards the ANC and his breaking of faith with the opposition, nine NNP MPs,[23] including Sheila Camerer and Eastern Cape deputy leader Wilhelm le Roux, crossed the floor back to the DA. I described it as 'the first swell of a tidal wave that will destroy the NNP.' Actually, it was Van Schalkwyk who sank his own party, but I was happy to welcome back former colleagues who had never wanted to leave.

Before the floor-crossing I had been engaged in discussions with the

Pan-Africanist Congress's Patricia de Lille. She had established an impressive and flattering public profile as a corruption buster, and was given credit for exposing the scandal surrounding a South African arms package in November 1999. She had also once read out a list of apartheid 'spies' in parliament who were, she said, present in the ANC parliamentary caucus;[24] and had successfully enlisted the Cape High Court to set aside a parliamentary kangaroo-court-imposed gagging order.

I hoped to entice her into our ranks to add spice and credibility. Initially her backers included our mutual friend Rhoda Kadalie. While De Lille herself was reticent, those accompanying her made it clear that she deserved a 'leading role' in the party. During the Marais saga, a call from an intermediary informed me that 'Patricia was available to be mayor of Cape Town' – to which I responded that in the DA such positions were not baubles in the gift of the leader, but that the party determined and elected the top positions. By the time of the parliamentary floor-crossing, Kadalie had tired of De Lille, and her advisers were now flakier, such as Cape Town artist Beezy Bailey who described himself as her 'shadow minister of arts'. Our discussions went nowhere. De Lille crossed the floor to herself, as it were, and set up shop as the 'Independent Democrats'.

In our discussions I had concluded that despite her political attractiveness, she was essentially a vessel without much cargo – and her changing political views were driven by her vaunting ambition and the spin and flattery which encased her. On the formation of the ID, I noted: 'If De Lille gets votes from the ANC then that will be healthy, but if her purpose in life is to oppose the opposition then she will find it very difficult.'[25]

I had by then acquired in my office the crucial additional human resource of Joel Barry Pollak, a young South African-born American who joined as my speech-writer. He combined a brilliant and searching intellect with a rare understanding of the political environment. A polymath of note, he seemed to have an inexhaustible curiosity which he coupled with unusual gifts of eloquence and a phenomenal work rate. Then Nick Clelland-Stokes assumed a major role as our national spokesman. At his modernistic suggestion I initiated a weekly Internet blog to compete with Mbeki's *ANC Today*. Thus was born *South Africa Today* – a weekly platform to convey my views on any given topic, every Friday, to several thousand online subscribers and also to the media.[26]

If these developments pointed to cutting-edge debate, the actual to-and-fro was decidedly familiar. Mbeki continued to beat the race drum and close off any genuine discussion of policy. When I drew attention to this tactic and that he 'used race to deflect legitimate criticism' on key issues – from AIDS to corruption – he met my claim with the counter that I wanted 'to stop us from confronting the cancer of racism'. This was, of course, meretricious. *Business Day* responded: 'Mbeki's argument that the legacy of colonialism and apartheid will be with us for a long time is a valid one, but the president cunningly shifted the goalposts. Leon's original point was that Mbeki is inclined to use the race card to deflect criticism, and this was not addressed in the reply.'[27]

But by then I had concluded that the ANC and its leadership were the political equivalents of bulimics. They liked to feast from the table which had been laid by the settled presence and unfair advantages which had accrued to the white minority; yet this 'exceptionalism' inherited in 1994 also caused guilt and disquiet. They were not prepared to build on and extend the foundation: the entire edifice had to be rebuilt, root and branch.

This manifested itself far into politics and the economy: language became a site of conflict. Afrikaans and Afrikaans-medium educational institutions – indeed, all centres of independent educational instruction – were to be targeted. At its Stellenbosch conference the ANC had been quite explicit. It called for 'consciousness-raising and disciplining among teachers' as well as for 'reducing current protections of the middle class'.[28]

The Education Laws Amendment Bill which flowed directly out of the conference made race the most important criterion in the appointment of educators. It actually prevented schools from appointing the best candidates for vacant teaching posts by allowing a provincial department to override a school's choice for a teaching position – provided its selection was not based on 'equity, redress and representivity'. Factors such as competence, quality or ability did not enter into the issue.

This was a case of the education department saying that if not all schools could be excellent, none would be. The fact that the majority of black matriculants came from these 'model C schools' – formerly white schools whose catchment area had been increased, but were now again to be bureaucratically determined – was beside the point. The ANC conference was filled with scorn and revulsion for private schools as well, stating, 'We must either discount the private schools or ignore the cries of their lobby.' (Of course, practically all ANC MPs educated their children at private or at model C schools.)

Afrikaans posed its own set of challenges. It was viewed by many in the ANC as 'the language of the oppressor'; and had clearly been advantaged and developed by the apartheid government: at the onset of the transformation there were no fewer than five exclusively Afrikaans tertiary education institutions, and 2 700 schools. A decade later there were two universities, and Afrikaans single-language schools had shrunk by 90%.[29]

Since my party was now the repository of most Afrikaans votes, I used an address to the Afrikanerbond in Port Elizabeth to point out the dangers of 'pushing Afrikaners to the margins and destroying the language through educational policy'.[30] It seemed to me inconceivable that in the Western Cape, for example, where Afrikaans was the first language of most inhabitants, Stellenbosch University should not be maintained as an Afrikaans-speaking institution. (The province's two other universities were English.) However, the newly installed rector Professor Chris Brink did not share this view, and pressed ahead with a so-called 'T-policy' which was to erode the primacy of Afrikaans in its former citadel. Mbeki's own spokesman Bheki Khumalo (in 2003) referred to the remaining Afrikaans schools as a form of 'apartheid-style influx control', while in the same year the ANC Western Cape MEC for Education tried to force a school within his jurisdiction to drop its single-medium curriculum.[31]

The assault on language reached its absurd apogee when the police in the Western Cape were forced to conduct all formal communications in English, in defiance of the fact that most policemen, complainants (and probably criminals) were Afrikaans-speaking. This was not simply a case of rubbing some victor's salt in the wounds of the politically vanquished: it also went to the issue of control. More and more police station commanders who did not speak Afrikaans were transferred from the Eastern to the Western Cape, the better no doubt to ensure that policing did not – or could not – amount to some form of fifth-column challenge to the government.

3

The ease with which the ANC had moved from the spirit of non-racialism to the harsh ends of racial chauvinism was striking. It was also apparent that 'transformation' was fast becoming a 'weasel word' – a term emptied of all substantive meaning – or in our country, used to dress up the truth of racial transfers as something noble: never in truth mandated by the non-racial constitutional order.

It was one thing for Buthelezi and me to try and rearrange the opposition deck chairs, but the point was: could we alter the direction in which the ship was sailing, and how remote or real were our prospects of getting a turn at the wheel?

Before the 2004 election provided an answer, Harry Oppenheimer's son Nicky, by now chairman of De Beers, decided to influence the debate, or at least clarify its terms. He did so through accommodation and the use of what might be described as 'the politics of influence'. On 5 August 2003 I found myself at his residence 'Little Brenthurst' in Parktown. Of course, there was nothing 'little' about this grand residence. It was South Africa's premier residential accommodation in acres of pristine garden parklands.

I had previously been there as a guest at a small dinner party; but to-night's gathering was truly a collection of South Africa's political and eco-nomic 'good and great'. As I surveyed the ranks of the captains of industry and most of the cabinet, from Thabo Mbeki down, I speculated idly on the consequences were someone to drop a bomb.

We were there to be informed of the Mbeki-backed Oppenheimer-driven initiative to reconcile 'the conflicting challenges of transformation and growth': the 'Brenthurst Initiative'.

Nicky Oppenheimer had doubtless taken on the mantle of econom-ic statesmanship with which his family was associated. However, he had every reason to be personally a little nervous and self-interested. In 2002 as parliament adopted the Mineral and Petroleum Resources Development Act we witnessed the unpacking of the Freedom Charter. The state was to take possession, as custodian, of all existing mineral rights and future en-titlements. At best the existing mining houses could apply for conversion of their now 'old order rights' into 'new order' ones: but only on showing BEE credentials, and a substantial divestiture of ownership equity (in real-ity at least 26,1%) into black hands.

Oppenheimer had arranged for a team of management consultants to unveil the Brenthurst Initiative. In broad terms, it proposed that companies which achieved the government's black empowerment and associated tar-gets receive in return corporate tax relief. I thought it deserved credit for at least opening the debate; but was dismayed at its blinkered acceptance of government's racial approach to empowerment. There was no considera-tion for supply-side measures such as changes to labour policy and radical improvements in educational and skills advancement.

The proposal mooted a national transformation scorecard which was racially determined – and which would determine whether or not corpo-rate entities had complied with the government's determination of how much of their equity procurement had been placed in black hands. It all seemed a long way from the non-racialism which Harry Oppenheimer had preached, now as antique as some of the fine silver and rare objects on display in the cabinets surrounding us. But despite the president's blessing (or at least attendance), nothing more was heard. Not did it insulate De Beers or the mining houses from future attack.

For example, in September 2004, deputy minister of Minerals and Energy, Lulama Xingwana, attacked De Beers and Anglo American – accusing them of 'looting the country'.[32] And the demands of compliance with the new mining regime, on the back of South Africa's volatile currency situation, saw – as the minister of Minerals and Energy herself admitted in her budget speech in May 2005 – over eight thousand jobs lost in the gold sector alone over the previous 18 months.[33]

There was a studied contrast between the approach of South Africa's anxious business sector and the plain-spoken views of an expert outsider. I was part of the audience at Wits to listen to Robert Guest, the Africa editor of *The Economist*, who had just published a sad volume on Africa's failure to fulfil its promise: *The Shackled Continent*.[34]

Unconstrained by the forelock-tugging and scraping which so often arrested robust debate on BEE and empowerment in South Africa, Guest declared: 'South Africa has made legal a type of influence-peddling that would be described as corrupt in most other parts of the world ... I refer here to the frenzy of deals whereby white-owned firms are obliged to surrender large chunks of their equity to black investors, which they have to do at a discount ... [It] has not escaped the notice of foreign and indeed domestic investors that the beneficiaries of these deals are mostly senior members of the ruling party. Investors are generally too polite or nervous to say this publicly, but the way they see it is, if you want to do big business in South Africa you have to give a slice to the elite.'[35]

I was particularly struck by the phrase 'too polite or too nervous to say this publicly'. That to me was the essence of the problem – the cowering into silence of too many institutions. The audience at the Brenthurst Initiative had been a case in point. At least Oppenheimer attempted to start a sort of debate. But for the most part, he and the captains of commerce and industry nodded their heads glumly while the ANC went on to announce further BEE prescriptions.

In reality, South Africa's largest corporations simply moved the bulk of their investments offshore. On so many issues that the business community knew to be wrong or wrong-headed, such as the destructive labour laws or the policy of self-enrichment posing as transformation, there was a guilty silence. I called it 'a consensus of the embarrassed'.[36]

On certain rare occasions, business chiefs raised their heads above the parapet. Mbeki was waiting to snap them off. In 2003 when Sasol – South Africa's fuel corporation – in compliance with the statutory requirements for its listing on the New York Stock Exchange, rated BEE as 'a risk factor', the president accused it of 'bad-mouthing' South Africa.[37]

In September 2003, Anglo American's Tony Trahar suffered a similar response when he made the unremarkable observation that 'I think the South African risk issue is starting to diminish – although I am not saying it has gone.' Mbeki's response was furious: 'Was Anglo now saying that democratic South Africa presents the business world ... with a higher political risk than did apartheid South Africa?' There was no public defence from Trahar, though I termed Mbeki's tirade 'angry, intemperate and resentful'.[38]

Although Cyril Ramaphosa, Patrice Motsepe, Tokyo Sexwale and Mathews Phosa were fingered as the 'usual suspects' of BEE largesse, an entire army of ANC princes and princesses, politicians and businessmen were soon to benefit from the seeming bonanza of high reward and little risk – once again neatly inverting the normal laws of economics and entrepreneurship.

In September 2003 I proclaimed the DA's empowerment policy which we entitled 'Opportunity for All' – which I launched, appropriately I thought, outside a factory in a back alley of Crossroads, Cape Town; few – if any – of whose largely poor, and entirely black, residents were enjoying the benefits of the black empowerment billions. The essence of our approach rested on four pillars:

• Empowerment criteria should be 'plus' factors: but not the sole consideration when affirmative action appointments are made or contracts awarded.
• Compliance criteria for BEE legislation should be radically simplified by building in greater flexibility in how firms could make up their BEE score.
• Affirmative action legislation should incorporate sunset clauses to prevent legislative interventions from persisting long after they had served their purpose.
• Legislation should encourage companies to take bold action to empower their own employees rather than further empowering members of an already empowered elite.

The audience enjoyed it; the ANC ignored it – although the burden of our critique and the dangers to which it adverted were later echoed by many in the ANC's broad alliance, especially the trade unions. We were, not for the first time, being the canary-in-the-coalmine.

While it was self-evident that the concentration on redistribution and reracialising control and ownership would have little effect on narrowing

609

the vast gulf separating those astride the top of South Africa's wealth pyramids, this fact was also to become contested terrain.

The one argument which no amount of statistical manipulation or contestation could disguise was the increasing dread and horror which South Africans experienced, first hand, as victims of the criminals who marauded, unchecked, across the suburbs, townships and rural areas. Of all the failures of government this was the most glaring.

I frequently found myself visiting the bereaved families of victims of violent crime. I suppose any visit could give rise to claims of ambulance-chasing: but I wanted as often as possible to put names and faces to the statistical picture painted by the staggering, yearly average of twenty thousand murders. It was the least I could provide to the devastated.

Only a few days after my evening at the magnificence and safety of the Oppenheimer mansion in August, I found myself in Pretoria, only fifty kilometres away: essentially visiting a different world.

Clifford Rawstone, whom I went to visit, was perhaps typical of millions of suburban South Africans, living in an ordinary house in a nondescript neighbourhood. But he was almost the most extraordinary person I had ever met – and for all the wrong reasons. He had just lost his mother, Hester, his one-year-old daughter Kayla, and her mother (his fiancée Janine) in a triple murder committed by four hijackers in nearby Sunnyside, a few nights before.[39]

The fact that the three had been en route to celebrate Kayla's first birthday added an even greater note of pathos to the hideousness of the tragedy. As we chatted and I attempted, with difficulty, to find words equal to the violence that had destroyed his whole family, Clifford turned to me and said: 'Tony, you've got to do something to bring back the death penalty.'

As I left his house, I was doorstopped by a *Beeld* reporter and asked about my visit and the debate which this family slaying had again raised about the death penalty. I responded by saying 'it should be an option for sentencing'; but that I remained opposed to its reintroduction.[40] However, Clifford's plea – and the ease with which criminals with an apparently twisted perversity meted out violence, including raping babies and grandmothers – was beginning to shift my views. The moral certainty with which I had always approached the issue began to yield to a different consideration. Surely, society had the right in extreme cases, and subject to stringent safeguards of due process and appeal, to express itself and its terrible anger in judicial form? I had not yet decided the matter for myself with finality, but was certainly reconsidering my position.

There would be a firestorm of criticism when, during the 2004 election, outside a jail in Bloemfontein, I responded to a question, prompted, I was later to discover, by one of my pro-death-penalty colleagues. I declared, 'In extreme cases of violent crime, such as murder with aggravating circumstances, I believe the courts should consider the imposition of the death penalty.' This was immediately dubbed as 'Tony Leon backs the rope.' I knew the position to be controversial with some and popular with many. But I felt that the state and the judiciary should have the option – in specific and qualified circumstances – of meting out a 'terrible punishment' to the criminal army marauding, largely unchecked, across South Africa.

4

In January 2004, Nick Clelland-Stokes was supervising a photo-shoot in a back street of Cape Town. The purpose was my 'official mug shot', as he described the exercise of finding the right image to project in the campaign material. I pondered Groucho Marx's aphorism: 'I have inner beauty. The only problem is they haven't produced a camera which can show it.'

This sent me down a line of slightly dangerous thinking. How *do* politicians deal with 'fame' – and does it have any meaning? In many countries, politicians are well-known, but generally disliked. I recalled the Bledisloe Cup match (between Australia and New Zealand) at Sydney's impressively converted Olympic Stadium. It was the Wallaby captain John Eales's last match. He was massively cheered. For his part PM John Howard was roundly booed. That's Australian democracy and society: no deference.

Politicians in South Africa are often treated with a congruent sense of familiarity and awe – perhaps something to with the aura of television, but also a manifestation of the 'big man' syndrome, ingrained across many cultures.

Many whites had grown up under a severe, state-imposed custom of obedience to authority; many blacks found in the mythology of the freedom-fighter-liberator an image made flesh of future deliverance. I came from neither mould. But, as leader, I had become the image-custodian of the party. It worked well: 'leader worship' created instant crowds and enthusiasm, but downright scepticism in others. It was part of the showbiz element of politics, and having some attributes of the ham actor in my DNA, and being all-too-human, I quite enjoyed the sound of applause and the chanting of my name. However, I checked myself by recalling that the man who read the weather report on the nightly TV bulletin was far better known than me.

Churchill once observed that 'no man is a hero to his valet'. So those who really knew me were the keepers of a less-idealised reality than many of my public supporters, and certainly some DA voters were 'critical friends'. I distinctly remember campaigning in the high-income WASP enclave of Cape St Francis, where a flush-faced, well-attired, silver-haired gent – emboldened by his sojourn at the 19th hole – belligerently demanded of me: 'Why can't you be more positive? You're always attacking the government!' At least on that occasion I was amused when Donald Lee, one of our senior MPs, poked me in the ribs and said, 'You never hear that sort of remark in the Coloured community.'

Often the most irritating aspect of being in the public gaze was the unconstrained licence with which people felt they could freely unload their opinions. I once bumped into South Africa's queen of women's magazines outside a cinema. In response to some or other statement I had published that day, she delivered a mall-side lecture. The topic was Mbeki's nonresponse to another of Mugabe's excesses – not a matter much featured in her publications. But this did not inhibit her gratuitous advice as to how I should have couched my critique and what was wrong with what I had said. I thought, but did not say: 'I wouldn't presume to suggest how you edit a magazine; why do you presuppose you know my job and its constraints and our target market?'

On the other hand, it was often a snatched comment from someone in the crowd, or the words of a victim of crime, or the retelling of a horror story from the front line of some failed site of service delivery – like the woman in Hout Bay who claimed to have been waiting for 27 years for a house, as long as Mandela spent in jail – which informed my views and allowed me to express them in terms to which people could respond.

The imagery of the 2004 campaign, it had been agreed, would be positive and more reflective of upland sunlight than the fierce-faced 'Fight Back' of five years before. We borrowed and adapted our slogan from Tony Blair: 'South Africa deserves better – Vote DA for Real Change'. Nick selected a picture which had me smiling into some imaginary distant horizon, deliberately at variance with the normal scowling and hectoring poses which the press used to reinforce a particular image.

However, this was my sixth campaign as a candidate (and fourth as a national or provincial leader) and the early ego-injection of my face on a poster had passed. It all looked like wallpaper. Even so, the stakes were high: we had to motivate and mobilise our core base among the minorities, and also reach out to the majority. Van Schalkwyk's beleaguered NNP aimed what was left of their firepower on us in the Western Cape; while De Lille created excitement in the ladies' luncheon clubs and gay bars, and while moving around the Cape Flats.

The 'Coalition for Change' with the IFP created a vehicle with the prospect of some power. In order to prevent a minority switch-off (already evidenced in relatively low-level voter registration among whites, Coloureds and Indians), Ryan Coetzee decided we had to go for broke. Towards the end of the campaign we would announce that, combined, the Coalition could achieve a decisive and dramatic 30% of the vote. In a normal democracy, such a claim would invite derision. But measured against the 9,6% the DP achieved in 1999 (or even the 2000 municipal election high of 22%) it would sound like a real breakthrough.

On a very good day and in the best of all circumstances, it might have been notionally attainable. But 14 April 2004 was not to prove one of them.

In the words of one analyst, the election would see the DA 'scramble across the electoral landscape to scoop up old NNP supporters, pacify its existing liberal constituency, and make small inroads into the black voter market.'[41] I can attest that these 'multiple ventures' proved uneven and sometimes contradictory.

In designing our campaign to appeal to the broad black electorate, we wrapped our policies into a package of offers which research indicated met the most urgent and important needs of the majority. Our glossy, 33-page manifesto was an amalgam of ANC-bashing and 'a prospectus for the future based on real change'. In the introduction I wrote of the best and worst of our first democratic decade:

'South Africa has made significant and impressive progress as a nation over the past ten years ... But for millions of South Africans, these successes have been overshadowed by the ANC's broken contract ... its failure to deliver the better life it promised in 1994.'

I took to the campaign trail – in a fitted-out bus grandly christened 'Driving Change' – and to the air in a Pilatus turbo prop donated by a supporter. In the process I clocked up 45 000 km in a six-week campaign (twice round the world). But we were soon outgunned and massively outspent by the ANC. Nor was it merely the governing party's empowerment brigade paying their tithes. Heading into the election, lurid tales of the ANC's bankruptcy started appearing. (Telephones were cut off; rents and staff pay were outstanding.) I was told that the ANC was in hock to the banks to the tune of R100-million (twenty times our overdraft, which our bankers refused to extend). Yet their campaign belied their insolvency! Its forests of billboards, massive sound trucks and monster rallies indicated a R100-million effort!

The real source of much of their new-found wealth would emerge, sensationally, only a year after the election. In May 2005 the *Mail&Guardian* led with a story dubbed 'Oilgate'. The ruling party had pocketed R11-million when a front company, Imvume Management, paid this amount into its campaign coffers after receiving a 'facilitation fee' of R15-million for services (on which it defaulted) from the state-owned oil company, PetroSA. Imvume went insolvent as a direct consequence of its 'donation'.[42]

Subsequent testimony by PetroSA's board to parliament's Scopa revealed that Imvume had deliberately misled PetroSA on the true purpose behind its request, which it claimed was to pay its employees end-of-year cash bonuses.

Robert Guest's description of 'the vampiric African state' headed by a predatory ruling party was becoming a working description for the ANC. Reforming it becomes problematic, because the most necessary reforms reduce the wealth and power of the people in charge.

Another BEE-related funding controversy deserves mention. Set up as a front company by the ANC, Chancellor House quietly accumulated empowerment stakes in a host of industries and companies from mining to IT. Many of the tenders awarded by government went to its own company.

The late Brett Kebble was implicated posthumously in numerous dubious financial arrangements with ANC-associated bodies.

Before I could trade or receive any electoral punches, I had to attend to what Harold Macmillan once described as 'a few local difficulties'. Nothing more arrested the attention and provoked more backstabbing in the DA than the selection of election candidates. Under our devolved system, it is the one moment when party activists exercise real muscle and power, and literally make or break sitting MPs and their aspiring replacements.

To choose candidates, each province selected an 'electoral college' to pick the list (the fact that a few regional political influence pedlars tended to have disproportionate power in influencing selection did not pass unnoticed by me). As leader I had been accorded the right, if I chose to exercise it, of inserting a limited number of candidates into winnable positions on the list once the selection was concluded. I became increasingly dismayed with how – in some cases – the party went about its work.

Some candidates of exceptional merit moved down the list because they were unaligned to a faction, or deemed by some group to be antipathetic. (Mike Waters, quite one of our hardest-working Gauteng MPs, was almost bumped off the list as a consequence.) Other MPs (Raenette Taljaard and Nigel Bruce, for example) were deselected by the provincial party because their parliamentary prominence had been matched by a neglect of their constituency work – although Raenette's *prima donna* hauteur grated on many local political barons and baronesses who decided such matters.

As to my intervention, I had to have regard for the party's 'representativeness' – whether its public face would begin to look a bit more like South Africa, not a combination of the Rand Club and Broederbond (given a preponderance of white men in the initial line-up).

It was a vexed and unhappy exercise. I had the power of promotion which could save one parliamentary career at the expense of another. Many of my choices backfired: to retain talent I reinstated Raenette (who resigned within a year); and Richard Ntuli, an underperforming Gauteng MP, but our most senior black incumbent who crossed the floor two years later. In KwaZulu-Natal, the leadership gave me names who might 'improve' our reach into black and Indian areas (and all three, at various stages, later crossed the floor).

Nonetheless, my selections also yielded positive outcomes: Ryan Coetzee made his way to parliament, Donald Lee was restored to electability; as was Willem Doman in the Western Cape. They provided a collective refutation of the adage that 'no good deed goes unpunished'. And I knew many of the new crop would play a leading and lively role in the new parliament.

5

Of all people, Nelson Mandela provided me with the opening shot of the campaign. The previous July he had apparently raised – and promptly discounted – the spectre of Mbeki seeking a third term in office (the Constitution limited presidents to two five-year terms). He made the reservation, however, in the crab-like manner in which he always approached matters relating to Mbeki, declaring: 'Not the Mbeki I know. He could not do that. He will not change the Constitution in order to benefit himself.'[43]

I happened to meet Mandela shortly afterwards and asked him what led to his utterance. He told me he had met a group of British politicians who expressed precisely that concern – and that the matter be dealt with 'while I am still alive', he chuckled.

There was echo here. I remembered that Mandela, when handing over the ANC presidency to his successor at Mafikeng in 1997, had warned of the dangers of the presidency being used 'to settle scores with detractors, to marginalise, or get rid of them' and then immediately discounting the possibility that Mbeki 'would sideline anybody'.[44]

But lo! Key members of his own cabinet were indeed sidelined by Mbeki, and the 'plot' allegations levelled at three powerful potential rivals. I began to think these 'warnings' should be heeded, and that perhaps they underlay the deep sense of ambivalence that Mandela apparently felt about Mbeki.

So, shortly before the launch of our election campaign, I directly addressed the issue in Durban: 'Mandela has already seen fit to declare that Mbeki would never do such a thing [seek a third term] but our president himself has refused to answer. We need to clear the decks on this critical issue ...'

There was a fluttering in the dovecotes. I was accused by Mbeki's spokesman of 'electioneering' (actually, it *was* an election).[45] But since so much of the Presidency was shrouded in secrecy I could hardly expect anything unequivocal, least of all concerning Mbeki's political calculations. But once the issue achieved critical media mass, a denial eventually emerged.[46] One of Mbeki's chief admirers in the media, editor Mathatha Tsedu, denounced me as 'a racist'. Even raising the question 'is a great insult to many black citizens.'[47]

Tsedu's predictable – and thought-blocking – response did not prevent me from adding that even if Mbeki did not crassly move to amend the Constitution, he might seek the 'Lurleen option'. This referred to the name of the wife of one-time term-limited Alabama governor, George Wallace, who simply ran his cancer-stricken wife as governor and landed up back in power as a consequence. I suggested Mbeki might wish to continue as party president and have a surrogate elected to the official post. Events, as the ANC succession struggle unfolded three years later, pointed exactly in that direction.

The launch of our manifesto in February before 2 000 people at the Vista University campus in Soweto was orchestrated to show the party's new face. We served notice that we would campaign everywhere and go after every vote, especially those marginalised and forgotten by the ANC. When I read a generally sympathetic and balanced account of the event in the following week's *Sunday Times*, I was slightly irritated by the reported comment of one of our own members, Abel Ngwema, who declared that the main stumbling block to attracting black votes 'is the fact that Leon is white.'[48] In fact his indiscretion in public pointed to a larger truth, as the results would to an extent reveal.

To explain away or condone chronic delivery failures, corruption, and official indecision on HIV/AIDS, the ANC resorted to a local equivalent of *Animal Farm*, in which the pigs invariably react to criticism: 'You don't want Farmer Jones back!' And to deal with the inconvenient fact that I, and the bulk of the party, had in fact been in opposition during the apartheid years, the ANC panjandrums simply labelled us as more racist than Eugene Terre'Blanche. Shortly after the campaign ended, *Mail&Guardian* journalist Drew Forrest, normally a staunch critic and broadly sympathetic to the ANC, wrote:

'The April election witnessed an effusion of anti-DA venom, which went well beyond robust electioneering to suggest a co-ordinated campaign to demonise and delegitimise. The party was described as "a wolf in sheep's skin", savaged for "subtly" portraying Africans as inferior, and engaging in "lying propaganda" that was a "dangerous path South Africa should not be allowed to tread" – and for being "a virulent, unapologetic opponent of African liberation" ... One does not have to be a DA sympathiser to recognise the malicious caricature inherent in much of the rhetoric.'[49]

Actually Forrest missed some of the more extreme sound bites of the ANC propaganda machine. One of their chief race-baiters, KwaZulu-Natal's Dumisani Makhaye, labelled me 'the DA Führer'. He died shortly afterwards and was not mourned in my household.

As far as my caricature was concerned, Forrest noted that I had been portrayed as either 'a variant of Goebbels' (for my *Paratus* scribblings) or the 'son of a hanging judge' (based on the Zondo case). All this was in faithful mimicry of the 'big lie' technique.

We homed in on the wildfire spread of corruption under Mbeki. The arms deal scandal – by then ballooning to swallow up R53-billion from the exchequer, and mired in allegations of backhanders and bringing deputy president Jacob Zuma into the prosecution's sights – sat atop a growing mountain of sleaze. Mbeki failed to appoint a judicial investigation into the arms deal – and had, of course, closed down the initial probe launched by Judge Willem Heath. He maintained silence on a Nigerian oil scam in which it appeared he had lobbied the president of Nigeria for oil shipments that were never delivered, but appeared to have been paid over to a South African with strong ANC ties.

Whatever high-level misdemeanours were kicked into touch, it was far more difficult for the government to avert their – or the people's – gaze when it came to far less complex, more down-to-earth scandals at local level, where many officials and municipal councillors lived the high life. They often rapaciously misused their office for self-enrichment, while their constituents were deprived of basic amenities and services.

During the campaign I hit on an idea to highlight this issue and shine a light on Mpumalanga province, which, in a field of fierce competition, had emerged by then as the corruption capital of South Africa. My imaginative grasp – hiring a train we dubbed 'The Change Express' and stopping at various outposts of localised skulduggery – exceeded the reach of the railways: we arrived approximately three hours late at every stop. Nevertheless I was able to read out a laundry list to our patient supporters of multiple examples of tender-rigging, looted exchequers, and personal aggrandisement by local officials.

But these local boroughs of rottenness were all of a piece with the province itself. It had appropriated over R650m to build a palatial new legislature – shunting the province into bankruptcy. Yet in one municipality to which our much-delayed train travelled – Govan Mbeki – a quarter of the households had no annual income at all, while in another over forty per cent of the houses used candles to light their homes – despite a statutory provision obliging municipalities to electrify residences. 'It is no wonder,' I intoned, 'that South Africa has slipped in place on the ranking of percentage of corruption, issued by Transparency International, since President Mbeki took office, from 34th place to 48th.[50]

The campaign opened my eyes to many different and varied situations of suffering and hope. Easter Sunday fell just before polling day, and I was invited to join twenty thousand worshippers at the Suurbekom community outside Soweto. In view of the particular church's custom I had to remove my shoes. Feeling a little strange, barefoot in a suit, I nonetheless accepted an invitation to address the mass audience. I told my listeners that 'we might worship God in different ways, but the strands that unite us are so much stronger than the things that divide us.'

On another occasion, outside a rally in Colesberg in the Northern Cape, an old man approached me and looked at me curiously. In a flash of recognition he said in mixed languages: '*Hallo, meneer Tony Leon. Mister democratic man.*' I thought of it as a small moment with big meaning. But the campaign also deceived.

The week before the election in Empuluzi in Mpumalanga we held a huge meeting. There were over two thousand people there; it appeared as though much of the town had arrived for the event. They were hugely supportive, and roared with approval when I took to the stage. Yet on election day we received far fewer ballots than the number of people present in the audience that afternoon!

At our final campaign event in Midrand, Johannesburg, two days before polling, I tried to tie the strands together. It was, as had become our modern custom, an extravaganza of lights, dancing, fireworks and choreography, pleasing the thousands gathered and providing good visuals and pictures. After retelling our manifesto pledges I wrapped them up in the line: 'We believe that everyone in South Africa deserves a fair chance, and that no second-class citizen was ever born.' I then took some pot shots at other opposition parties (save the IFP) and the ANC, before declaring:

'There are a great many people in our land who have lost hope. They think there is nothing they can do to change anything, because they are so overwhelmed by poverty, by crime, by disease. Then let them hear this – the most important truth in South Africa today: many of our problems are historical, but the solutions are political. And if we want to get change, we need to vote for it.'

For the last 48 hours of the campaign I hurtled around the country in an attempt to shore up and bring out our vote in Cape Town, Durban, Johannesburg, finally ending in Pretoria on the eve of the poll. But as I moved from one locale – and photo-opportunity – to the next, I kept replaying in my mind a question which had been posed to me a few years before by then French prime minister Lionel Jospin when we met in Cape Town in June 2001. He conducted our entire discussion in French, through a translator; then towards the end of it all, he suddenly broke into perfect English to ask the essential question: 'Tell me,' he said; 'are you merely an opposition – or are you likely to become an alternative?'

After 14 April when the results piled in, I had the answer.

The DA was consolidated as the dominant opposition force in the country with over 1,9-million votes (12,37% of the total, an increase of some four hundred thousand votes over our 1999 performance). We now had 50 MPs in parliament, compared to the 28 of the third party in parliament, the IFP.[51]

While the results certainly confirmed our dominance on the opposition terrain, we were dwarfed by the ANC's haul of 69,69%, and the 266 MPs it netted. However, although their numbers had also risen since 1999, their overall increase had in fact been considerably less than ours in the election, and in terms of actual votes they had shed some two million supporters since 1994, although very few had migrated to the opposition.[52]

Most no doubt stayed home; but on a reduced overall percentage poll little of this size, detail and electoral arithmetic mattered. The ANC was overwhelmingly dominant. Our 'Coalition for Change' had not achieved its target; the IFP was rolled back in its KwaZulu-Natal heartland, losing our ministers, their premier, political control and patronage.

The NNP had managed to eke out 10% of the votes in the Western Cape, a vertiginous collapse from its previous dominance – but enough to provide the ANC with a bridge to take over the Western Cape. The ruling party was now master of all it surveyed: a super-majority in parliament, nudging towards 70%, and control of all nine provinces. Since democracy's separate centres of power are designed to check and balance each other, these results – plus the ANC's capture, through its cadre redeployment programme, of the constitutional citadels outside the legislatures – suggested that the majority party's power would be virtually untrammelled.

As the results sank in, part of me rejoiced that we had at least survived the messy divorce from the NNP in an enhanced position, capturing most of their supporters in the Northern and Western Cape, and improving our standing in eight of the nine provinces (KwaZulu-Natal was the exception). The result also proved, in part, that despite a vicious campaign of ANC invective, echoed by a largely supportive and, I thought, supine media, we had consolidated our opposition pre-eminence.

Racial cleavages endured. According to our analysis, 81,8% of the ANC's vote was from black people and 74,9% of the DA's from whites. Helen Zille had laboured mightily to advance our cause in the poor black Khayelitsha and Crossroads areas. Afterwards she related how, shortly before polling day, she telephoned the hundreds of individual constituents whom she had assisted directly in the preceding years. Would they vote for her? The generally uniform response was: 'We appreciate what you did, but we have to vote ANC.'

I did not think it was simply a case of intimidation – though there was a fair amount of that. But this was insufficient to explain the general phenomenon of the politics of identity trumping those of issue. Racial nationalism had triumphed again, and appeared to live on in the new nation as emphatically as it had held the old country in its thrall.

Why?

By 2004, South Africa had a relatively advanced economy and impressively sophisticated constitutional architecture. Democracy had arrived late – some forty years after the first Uhuru waves swept across more distant shores. Those – including me – who hoped that this confluence of

fact and time would create 'exceptionalism' to ethnic divisiveness, depress-
ingly evident elsewhere in Africa, were to have a rude awakening.

Martin Meredith, in *The State of Africa*, provided a rule-of-thumb formulation for electoral success: 'On a continent where class formation
had hardly begun to alter loyalties, ethnicity provided the strongest political base. Politicians and voters alike came to rely on ethnic solidarity.
For politicians it was the route to power. They became, in effect, ethnic
entrepreneurs.'[53]

Of course, while that might have been a good working description of
pastoral Uganda or the intensely ravaged state of Rwanda, it seemed to fit
South Africa – with a strong working-class industrial base, a vast rural reserve economy, and a First World service sector – less perfectly. But the net
electoral result seemed to point us in the direction identified by Meredith.

The ANC, in constructing and maintaining its 'big tent', ranging from
BEE billionaires to rural peasants, had found in racial solidarity and the
invocation of struggle a potent and durable tarpaulin to keep its increasingly disparate constituency under one roof.

6

My early pleasure at the thought of leading a parliamentary battalion of
50 MPs quickly gave way to depression. Had the racial fault line in our
politics, I reasoned, not reduced me to the political role of Sisyphus? Was
I destined to play a role of increasing futility or providing respectability to a system which was unchangeable and a government which was
unchallengeable?

Initially, the ANC confirmed my darkest (publicly unmentioned) forebodings. Thus, when parliament re-elected Mbeki president on 23 April
2004, I decided to reach out in reconciliation. After wishing him well and
reminding him that we were 'opponents, not enemies', I walked across to
his seat and to his, and everyone else's, surprise shook his hand. He seemed
warm and responsive. However, when parliament reconvened in late May
to debate the State of the Nation, the gesture was repudiated in specific
terms by one of Mbeki's closest lieutenants, Sydney Mufamadi, the minister of Provincial and Local Government. He repaid the compliment in a
swaggering currency:

'The contract between us and the masses cannot be supplanted by a
handshake. Thank you very much, Mr Leon, your hand must not cross the
floor. Keep it to yourself.'[54]

Mufamadi's approach – undoubtedly sanctioned by the ANC's collective leadership – was echoed by another minister, the shrill Geraldine Fraser-Moleketi: 'The voters have seen the wisdom of a single vision for South Africa.'[55] Even my old nemesis from Wits, Professor Malegapuru Makgoba (as William was now known), felt emboldened to proclaim: 'The electorate has declared loudly and clearly that it does not want a country characterised by opposition politics.'[56] I sighed at the prospect of the next five years.

Actually, it was the triumphalism of the ANC – their utter disregard for the choices of the 4,5-million South Africans who did not vote for them – and the dangerous Robespierrian representation of itself as 'the general will' that snapped me out of my post-election blues. The ANC now viewed itself as uniquely possessed of the right to rule both unchallenged and unchecked; yet I bore in mind Karl Popper's famous statement that the 'most fundamental problem of all politics' was the 'control of the controller, of the dangerous accumulation of power'.[57]

I thought a good place to start was to deconstruct the ANC's agenda.

Ryan Coetzee also recovered his equilibrium shortly after election day. 'Nothing,' he declared to me in late May, 'has essentially changed. But what needs to change is the narrative.' Indeed, it seemed to us that much of what passed for the other opposition parties, the media and business were desperately positioning themselves within the ANC's analysis – rather than challenging it or seeking an alternative vision. We decided, in two forthcoming back-to-back speeches, that we would attempt to present one.[58]

I would point to the dangers of the ANC's hegemonic impulses and the jeopardy it posed to our constitutional order. In 2004 government was engaged in a typical multi-million rand extravaganza around our founding document's tenth anniversary, I believed like Tolstoy's famous tree: 'The leaves enchant us more than the roots.' In the second address, we would articulate and unpack our contrasting vision – anchored in the philosophy of Karl Popper, suitably Africanised, of the 'open opportunity society'.[59]

In the first defined address, which I delivered to the Johannesburg Press Club on 10 June, I set out what I termed 'a sound analysis of the state of the transition to full democracy and a clear outline of why we rejected the ANC's revolutionary programme of "transformation" which informed its behaviour.' I pointed out that while the ANC had shelved its 'two-stage revolution to achieve socialism', it had replaced its communist objective with an Africanist goal.

I noted that the racial nationalism which the ANC had placed at the front and centre of its governance meant that the group, not the individual, would be both the beginning and end-point of state action – regardless of differences in outlook or interest or circumstance. Its insistence on 'demographic representivity' was not a temporary affirmative action remedy which – having achieved its aim – would fall away. Rather, I suggested: 'Demographic representivity specifically refuses to take into account the individual – and differences within the group. Under the ANC, demographics shapes destiny.'

I predicted that while this led to majoritarian democratic outcomes, the application of demographic representivity, and the conflation of the ANC with the state, moved the country towards what Fareed Zakaria had termed an 'illiberal democracy'.[60] It would close intellectual borders and loosen crucial restraints on the abuse of office. The party was also reversing its 1996 GEAR commitment to redistribution through growth. In its place was the idea that the state was the essential agent of 'economic emancipation'.

My critique would inevitably provoke a reaction; so I proceeded in my second speech, delivered on Youth Day, 16 June, to set out a liberal answer and alternative. For us, I said, 'society is comprised at its most basic level of individuals, and not of racially defined groups, or classes, or ethnic associations ... This does not mean we believe people are simply individuals. Identity is a complex thing, and is shaped by many forces – psychological, economic, genetic, cultural and historic – and each of us is at least in part the product of these forces.

'But as liberals we believe people are more than the sum of forces that shape them; because the combination of these forces produces an individual with a unique outlook, who can construct his own meaning and is best placed to fashion his own truth. This basic construct – the individual versus the racial group as the building block of society – is the root difference between the two [ANC and DA] worldviews.'

An opportunity society had to be built on the back of a socially and environmentally responsible enterprise economy. It needed a responsive public sector targeting effective education, safety and health care. And we had to build ladders out of poverty and degradation, crime and grime.[61]

I wanted to show that we were neither indifferent to the great challenges posed by the legacy of apartheid, nor purveyors of a negative or narrow vision of South Africa and its future. I did not know whom the speeches would reach. We mailed thousands of copies to key South African stakeholders, and embarked on an active selling and spin-job with the media. However, one person not on our mailing list was the president.

When Mbeki addressed parliament a few days later – in his budget vote – he had clearly read my texts closely; and used them as a springboard to attack both my critique and propositions. However, he did at least conclude, 'there was room for debate', suggesting, I thought disingenuously, that 'this had never been a problem.'[62]

The president asserted that 'an insistence that people should be treated as individuals and not as part of a group that was being oppressed is to deny the very history of South Africa ... To get there he [Leon] believes, among other things, he must convince us that the African majority in our country was not oppressed and exploited as Africans but as individuals, and that the legacy of the past impacts on this majority not as African, but as individuals ... I do not know what will happen to Hon. Leon when he wakes up one day and discovers that there are individual Africans who belong to the African national group, that there are individual workers who belong to the working class, and that each of these has been combining to act together exactly because they shared common interests.'

We were debating the state of the nation!

I reminded him I had never suggested reducing the role of the state to the libertarian desire for 'a night watchman' concerned only with defence, law and order and the administration of justice. 'But,' I countered, 'there is a world of difference between a smart and compassionate state on the one hand and a large and inefficient one on the other.' That was a more accurate delineation of the 'ideological gulf' which he had correctly identified as separating us.[63]

I drew parliament's attention to what Mbeki's state had, in fact, created: 'The past ten years have seen a proliferation, a veritable alphabet soup of state agencies and structures – the Sector Education and Training Authorities, ministers and members of the Executive Council, South African local government associations, and the like – which have coincided with (or caused) an increase, not a reduction, in the very problems they were set up to resolve and manage.

'And so we have a schools crisis in this country, alongside a government-structured and taxpayer-funded education and training authority. We have a crisis in local government, accompanied by a mushrooming of local government structures and taxpayer-funded bodies. And we have dysfunctional provinces and their delivery systems, running parallel to an increase in the provincial and national bureaucracies.'

At much the same time that Mbeki and I engaged in debate on the role and reach of the state, the South African Institute of Race Relations's John Kane-Berman pointed to the practical realities: 'A picture emerges of a government which has extended its reach beyond its capacity to act effectively in carrying out its core functions. Whatever ideological arguments may be mustered in the liberal versus socialist debate, the practical application in South Africa is that the state does not have the capacity to carry out all the development work it aspires to. There is a tragic dimension to this, because most victims of state failure are the illiterate, people with AIDS, social pensioners, the homeless, people without their own cars, petty offenders too poor to pay bail, the jobless and the destitute – each and every one of them an individual.'[64]

The *Sunday Times* thought that the debate 'cuts to the heart of the state' and discerned a *glasnost* in our relationship, intellectually at least. Parliamentary correspondent Brendan Boyle wrote: '[The civility of the debate] was a light moment in a stormy relationship that has seen the president largely ignore the opposition leader's ideas and arguments. And it does underline a change happening in South Africa's political debate. Leon has rinsed off the stained liberal banner his party has stored in a basement of little-used political ideas, and paraded it back into parliament after a disappointing election result.'

He concluded: 'Perhaps, for the first time, Mbeki and Leon are talking to each other and not past each other. That would be a good omen for political debate in South Africa.'[65]

I was not as sanguine. While my text had pricked Mbeki's interest, I never imagined that he would alter course or concede flaws in his own approach. Indeed, 'rule by charter' became ever more evident as the ANC sought to impose on the business sector its transformation agenda. The DA continued to produce and publish policy alternatives – not simply to stimulate debate, but to encourage investment and scarce capital resources.

There appeared to be a shift of sorts – and a concession – towards some of these imperatives when ANC deputy Finance minister Jabu Moleketi presented a discussion paper in July 2004 to the ANC's National Executive. Many of his suggestions for sweeping economic reform closely mirrored our policies – including rapid liberalisation of excessive controls; the exclusion of small firms from collective bargaining agreements between large employers and big unions; extending exemption for firms from certain regulations by raising the size threshold from 50 to 250 employees; and creating a two-tier labour market with flexible wages at entry level.[66]

However, this package was strangled in committee, and nothing more was heard of it.

When, in March 2005, our finance spokesman, Ian Davidson, highlighted in parliament our idea that tax breaks be used to stimulate employment both in the domestic worker sectors and among small businesses, the minister of Finance, Trevor Manuel, was scathing. He dismissed the idea and accused our spokesman of 'wanting to be waited on hand and foot by black people who will carry and fetch.'[67] Actually, while the budget debate was going on Manuel's short-fuse temper was also directed to Donald Lee MP, our sports spokesman, who had criticised the ANC's use of race in sport – and in particular drew attention to the then recent selection of Kevin Pietersen for the England cricket team. Pietersen left South Africa because of what he perceived as the operation of a racial quota compromising his prospects of selection for the South African Proteas. Manuel was outraged when Lee compared Pietersen's departure to England to that of the other and more famous exile, Basil D'Oliviera. He wrote Lee a note in parliament, declaring, 'I cannot express my outrage sufficiently.' Of course, the point was that Manuel, Lee and D'Oliviera were Coloured.

I speculated at the time that Manuel's dyspepsia was perhaps due to the succession debate then emerging in the ANC. Alone apparently in the pantheon of successful finance ministers in the modern world – of whom he was undoubtedly one of the select – Manuel's name never entered the speculative lists as a future president. And he was certainly the best performer in a cabinet of, admittedly, lesser talents. It was undoubtedly his colour, or insufficiency of it, which counted against him. In my view his a priori exclusion was first-hand confirmation of the hollowness of the ANC's commitment to non-racialism and the further assertion of what it tortuously described as its 'continuing battle to assert African hegemony in the context of a multicultural and non-racial society'. This indeed was a battle Manuel could never win – he had been excluded at birth.

But whatever limits 'the national question' (as the ANC, borrowing from Stalin's lexicon, described racial and ethnic minorities) placed on Manuel's future ambition, he was a fully paid-up member to Mbeki's views that the 'developmental state' was the answer to South Africa's myriad socio-economic challenges.

Nothing perhaps more starkly contrasted Mbeki's grand theorising and the grim reality than yet another of parliament's grand displays of pageantry, this time on 6 May 2004, to commemorate the tenth anniversary of democracy in South Africa.

As Mbeki pontificated in parliament on the virtues of 'the developmental state', our research department unearthed a recent case concerning the Eastern Cape Department of Welfare. It had taken them three years to decide whether a certain Mrs Nontembiso Kate, an ageing victim of chronic arthritis, was entitled to a disability grant. Her story was brought to light through court proceedings that culminated in a judgment by the Supreme Court of Appeal earlier that year.[68]

It was a moving account of the suffering and struggles experienced by an ordinary South African in her fight for economic survival. She was eventually given a grant in April 1999 – thirty-six months after her initial application. What should have taken three months took an agonising three years, during which time Mrs Kate's condition worsened and her financial situation became increasingly desperate. Mrs Kate was devastated to find that the provincial department was prepared to give her only R6 000 in back pay, instead of the R18 315 to which she was entitled.

In his heads of argument, the senior counsel acting for Mrs Kate in her Supreme Court of Appeal hearing, Advocate Wim Trengove SC, stated: 'Mrs Kate's fate is one shared by tens of thousands of the poorest and most vulnerable people of the Eastern Cape. Their provincial government acts with utter disregard for them and indeed as if "it were at war" with them. … It persists in conduct in flagrant breach of its duties under the Constitution and the most fundamental rights of its weakest and most vulnerable citizens.'

The Court ordered the provincial government to pay damages to Mrs Kate for having caused her that loss. And while I welcomed the fact that individuals were able to seek, and gain, relief from the courts in our new constitutional dispensation, the fact remained that for many of the other ten million South Africans who were meant to receive state grants, there was no relief in sight. They continued to deal with an incompetent, un-compassionate and uncompromising bureaucracy, day in and day out.

Clearly, despite the president's fine words, government's track record on socio-economic rights had been patchy at best. Housing delivery had slowed to a trickle, public health facilities were in an advanced state of decay, and the number of dysfunctional schools in the public education system had increased dramatically. It seemed that the only unwavering priority was to affect the policy and practice of racial transfers – coupled with party loyalty.

However, whatever grand and interventionist roles the government envisaged for the state and its agencies, evidence from the ground pointed in another direction entirely. At the very moment at which the ANC ambitiously expected the state's role to increase, its machinery was seizing up, or had been allowed to grind down to a point of collapse.

7

These existential conditions on the ground were made worse by a form of parasitic capitalism, which soon enough collapsed the distinction between the bureaucracy and business. A revolving door had begun to operate with displaced ministers and top officials straying into the fields of business over which previously, often just months before, they had held regulatory sway. It was also brought to my attention that senior officials, including ministers, were directly 'advising' companies as to whom their 'empowerment partners' should be. Such BEE credentials were necessary for compliance on which state-sanctioned licences – from mining rights to cellphone networks – depended.

Corruption reached gale-force intensity. I had 12 years before drawn attention to a single building in Polokwane, Limpopo, where back-handers paid to the 'right official' in the 'right department' had seen one of the poorest provincial administrations massively overpay for an essentially obsolescent office block. By 2007 it appeared that an ANC provincial MEC – and junior officials – were involved in a R 500-million tender scandal relating to no fewer than five buildings acquired for provincial purposes.[69]

Housing projects, children's feeding schemes, even parliament's own security systems – all fell victim to rapaciousness and greed and the get-rich-quick mantra with which public office (and proximity to it) had in short order become the rule of thumb.

In addition to resembling elements of Guest's 'vampire state', South Africa had also become an 'enclave state', where key government departments, from Home Affairs to the critical Department of Trade and Industry, had ceased in key areas to function effectively or professionally. Out of the 167 annual audits conducted by the auditor-general on the 34 government departments and public entities from 2001-2002 to 2005-2006, there were only ten clean reports. Four of those ten departments had received qualified or worse audit opinions three times in a row – or more.[70]

Characterised by audits of improper expenditure, underspent budgets and unauthorised costs, the government passed it all off as 'capacity problems'. Yet Mbeki vigorously demurred when the exposition suggested a step-change in approach, or that a replacement of the minister might improve the capacity of the state. It was, in my view, the direct consequence of too many policy contradictions, too much over-regulation, and a singular ideological rigidity – pinned on race – which made the 'better life for all' a vote-winning slogan, but for too many simply empty rhetoric. The exceptions were the Department of the National Treasury, the

South African Revenue Service, and the Transnet turnaround; perhaps the brightest ray of light was the award by FIFA in May 2004 to South Africa of the hosting rights of the soccer World Cup in 2010.

In his weekly online newsletter in August 2006, Mbeki focused on the lack of positive coverage of the continent, declaring that the vast majority of stories out of Africa fell into three categories, 'AIDS, development and conflict ... In time these stories begin to define who and what we are.'[71]

It was an irony, perhaps the crowning paradox of the Mbeki presidency, that he had presided over a state which in key areas, both by design and through neglect, helped fuel the stereotyping he so correctly identified and condemned.

8

And yet there had been had been one 'brief shining' Camelot moment when it appeared that Mbeki had the will to staunch the flow of corruption and uphold the now tattered banner of good governance. It happened in parliament on Tuesday 14 June 2005, which I rated as second only to De Klerk's 2 February speech, over fifteen years before. Ten days before, Deputy President Jacob Zuma had been severely implicated in a Durban High Court judgment against his financial adviser Schabir Shaik, who was found guilty on multiple charges of corruption and fraud.

Although the National Director of Public Prosecutions, Bulelani Ngcuka, had found 'a prima facie case' against Zuma he had, at this point, declined to prosecute him (his successor, Vusi Pikoli, would eventually change his position and charge Zuma, initially unsuccessfully, with corruption and fraud – see Chapter 19).

In fact eight days before Mbeki detonated his big bang announcement on Zuma (which would, two-and-a-half years later, immolate his own leadership), the DA had moved a motion of no confidence in Zuma. The Speaker, predictably, ruled it out of order. What I noted that day, however, was while the ANC back-benchers howled in outrage, the grim faces of Zuma's ministerial colleagues were a study in contrast. Many years after the event (in August 2007) minister Ronnie Kasrils told Douglas Gibson, 'The DA should be remembered for one thing at least: making Jacob Zuma's continuance in office impossible. It is your greatest service to democracy.' The flattery was, no doubt, overblown, and the prediction, at the time of this writing, seemed vastly over-optimistic.

Mbeki's action against Zuma created a tidal wave of resentment and recrimination, still washing over his party and the country more than two years later. Zuma had yet to be indicted (this was to occur in December 2007), but he revelled in his victim-status and became a lightning rod for the ever-growing circle of party cadres and formations who regarded his sins – real or imagined – as the lesser in comparison with Mbeki's conduct and *modus operandi*. Indeed, from within ANC circles phrases such as 'vindictive', 'dictatorial' and 'anti-democratic' were being applied to Mbeki.

Mbeki's later refusal to take action against erring and ethically compromised cabinet members such as Health minister Manto Tshabalala-Msimang added fuel to the perception that Zuma's axing was motivated by internal political considerations. However, in contrast to Zuma, Tshabalala-Msimang (described by the *Sunday Times* as 'a drunk and a thief') was a fierce and dependent Mbeki loyalist, and her husband, Mendi Msimang, was a key figure – as treasurer-general – in the ANC.

An even more glaring instance of the dual standards at the heart of the Mbeki government – in addition to the contest over the state of the Health minister's liver – was Mbeki's decision to retain his personally hand-picked National Police Commissioner, Jackie Selebi. In November 2006 this man had acknowledged a friendship with a mafiosi kingpin, Glenn Agliotti, one of the accused in the sensational Brett Kebble murder.

I immediately called on Mbeki to appoint a judicial commission of enquiry into the Selebi saga. The cabinet refused, and claimed that 'there was no indication of wrongdoing or involvement in illegal activities by the National Police Commissioner.' Aside from begging the question and offering the hollow promise to act 'on production of such evidence' (only obtainable by the commission Mbeki refused to appoint), I was struck by the president's complaint (not public) of 'a trial by media' aimed at Selebi.[72]

But, of course, in September 2003, precisely to put to rest 'a trial by media', Mbeki had appointed a full-blown commission of enquiry to expunge the stain against one of his other court favourites, then National Director of Public Prosecutions, Bulelani Ngcuka. Presumably in this case Mbeki was fairly confident that the commission, headed by retired Justice Joos Hefer, would exonerate Ngcuka of the claim (made by two of Zuma's chief backers, Mo Shaik and Mac Maharaj) that Ngcuka was an 'apartheid spy'. In due course, the Hefer Commission exonerated Ngcuka of any involvement with the apartheid regime.

The Hefer probe indicated how selectively the Presidency used judicial commissions. Mbeki also wrote an exceptionally revealing letter on 19

January 2004 to Judge Hefer on receipt of his report.[73] Thanking Justice Hefer for his main report, Mbeki wrote:

'I also fully agree with you that "anything which may discredit either the institution or the office of the National Director, or the person holding the office, is manifestly of constitutional significance and indubitably of public importance."

'Given the public controversy that had broken out around the spy allegations, I thought it absolutely critical that this matter be dealt with as speedily as possible to enable us to act on the matter without undue delay. It was clear that to delay action on the matter would cause a lot of damage. This required that the truth about the allegations should be determined without delay.

'I thought that the best way to address this requirement would be to appoint a Judicial Commission of Inquiry. I remain convinced that this was the correct way to proceed. Like you, I therefore did not, and do not, accept the observations made by some that the inquiry was irrelevant, was of interest only to the ANC, and so on.'

When the president correctly said of the Ngcuka allegation that 'this required that the truth about the allegations should be determined without delay' he did not apply the same test and standards to the Selebi allegations. In law and fact, and in terms of the national interest, the Selebi accusations were far more serious than those made against Ngcuka. (Mbeki was forced, finally, to act against Selebi in January 2008, but by then the damage to both his reputation and the country's institutions was far gone. See Chapter 21.)

A year after the Zuma firing, I found myself in parliament again facing Mbeki. This time I placed myself in the unusual position of defending the president against the charge of 'being a dictator'.[74] But I also took the occasion to repay his infamous 2001 attack on me when he misquoted *The Tempest*. I used the Bard's words in *King Lear* (I hoped in accurate context) to point to the source of his own malaise:

'Honourable President –

'Like Shakespeare's King Lear, you are trying to solve a succession problem. But as Lear's Fool says: "Thou has prepared thy wit o' both sides, and left nothing i' the middle." The truth is that, like King Lear, you have frustrated your own intentions.'

Professor Njabulo Ndebele, vice chancellor of UCT, had written in the *Sunday Times*:

'Could it be that part of the problem is that we are unable to deal with the notion of opposition? We are horrified that any of us could be seen to have become "the opposition". The word has been demonised.'

I continued: 'Honourable President, it is intolerance towards opposition, both internal and external, that has divided your government against itself. You claim: "Our movement is neither 'rudderless' nor 'at sea' about anything of importance."[75] Yet your own governing allies, COSATU and the South African Communist Party, say that South Africa is "drifting towards dictatorship" and that we have an "overly powerful Presidency".'[76]

But for the next two years much of the critical business of the nation became absorbed and suborned by the increasingly bitter battle – between Mbeki and Zuma – for the ANC succession. Mbeki chose to deny the crisis entirely. When in September 2005 I questioned him about it in parliament, he claimed that 'this particular controversy has no impact on government whatever.'[77]

Within months his reassurance was obsolete, and within a year it appeared absurd.

CHAPTER 19

Cape Hope?

For democratic structures to endure – and to be worthy of endurance –
they must listen to their citizens' voices, engage their participation,
tolerate their protests, protect their freedoms
and respond to their needs.
LARRY DIAMOND

I

It would be wrong to read from this account that my exertions were ex-clusively spent on days and nights of high political drama. My efforts in the post-2004 period were more engaged in the practicalities of running an opposition. Typically, I began my day with an early-morning scan at home of the newspapers, followed by calls to Douglas Gibson (chief whip) and Gareth van Onselen (head of Media) and a discussion with my chief of staff (variously David Maynier, Gareth van Onselen, Tim Harris and Paul Boughey). We sketched out responses, reactions and anticipations of the next 24-hour parliamentary and news cycles.

In short, we spent as much time launching pot shots at various failing government departments and ministers – and engaging with the ever-spreading corruption fronts – as in responding to the increasing number of attacks on ourselves and on me. I was never a paid-up subscriber to the school of thought which proclaimed: 'It doesn't matter what they say about you, provided they spell your name properly!' My parents had, in any event, blessed me with idiot-proofing against any prospect of my name being misspelt. I was, however, a paid-up subscriber to the view which proclaimed, 'Leave no charge unanswered.' And answer we did, hoping to puncture the caricature which presented the party and me as variants of an anti-transformation Beelzebub.

After initial discussions Douglas would convene a 9 am meeting with key staff and MPs and mull over various statements, motions and parlia-mentary questions. I would go to my office, engage my secretary in tasks of correspondence, then attend to the business of the party. This often involved dealing – not pleasantly – with recusant provincial or municipal leaders (of whom there was no shortage), complimenting and encouraging good performers, or suggesting an initiative for a portfolio holder. The daily routine almost always included a fundraising call or attendance at a party event.

I had been sensitised to the criticism that the party leadership was too 'top-down'. But after the 2004 election I went on a listening tour across the country to hear, first-hand, how the party and its formations felt at having to confront an environment where one party – not their own – seemed to hold a permanent lock on power, and on many, if not most, of the levers of control outside government and parliament as well.

I think the process helped many to unburden themselves of their angst and dissatisfactions. They were probably too polite (or intimidated) to direct much criticism towards me personally, but I had no doubt that the warm affection and regard with which I was held by many in the party was matched by others who waged proxy wars against our national head office – or demanded greater power and control by the provinces or regions.

I accepted some of these views as genuine, discounting others when I sensed a personal agenda. At all events I certainly took note, particularly at how the party was collectively responding to the rigours of continued opposition; and whether its heart and soul were still engaged in our project of building a bigger party.

There were those who maintained a zealous determination and understood precisely how important a role we had to play. Others – including some in the upper echelons of parliament and the provincial assemblies – appeared to be on what I termed 'pension watch' – far preferring what might be the 'civilised management of steady decline' rather than the bare-knuckled pushback which I believed to be our appropriate posture. Yet others – and here the circles overlapped – were masters and mistresses of the petty intrigues of office politics, far more chary of the grindingly hard daily work of holding government to account and identifying and driving issues of concern to voters and public.

It hardly surprised (but slightly disappointed) me that some in my own ranks were succumbing to the political ennui which had begun to afflict the minority community in the country. Demoralised by a constant demonisation from the ANC, a few even longed for what could be defined as 'remission by baptism'. When bantustan president Kaizer Matanzima died in June 2003, Thabo Mbeki delivered a bizarre graveside eulogy, suggesting that you could be co-opted into the elect, even posthumously, and your previous sins of omission and commission were of no relevance. On another occasion, a group of '107 Afrikaans businessmen'[1] felt obliged to pen a statement of fulsome praise for the president, after meeting with government. When the DA leader in the Western Cape legislature was goaded on this declaration, he responded frankly: 'But I know what they say about the ANC and its president around the braai.' Mbeki knew too, but that wasn't the point. The purpose of such exercises was to square away any form of political dissent and make the constitutional opposition, led by me, an outpost of isolation, suggesting to both its members and supporters that life would be more congenial if they kowtowed to the reality of single-party dominance. The chilling effect this had on civil society, a vital prop of our constitutional order, was brought home to me during the 2006 municipal elections, described below, when I made an appearance at my old school, King David High School, in Linksfield, Johannesburg.

Afterwards I learned of an e-mail sent by the outgoing executive director of the South African Board of Deputies, the umbrella body of the Jewish community, to the ANC. It purported to describe my address to the students. The grossly inaccurate description – the executive director of the Board was not even present during my visit – was accompanied by several disparaging remarks such as '… if you are bored and need some toilet reading material ill [sic] send you more details of the Tony rhetoric, let me know.' The e-mail was subsequently forwarded to others by its intended ANC recipient, who commented smugly: 'Look what the Jewz [sic] think of leon [sic].' After the e-mail surfaced, the Board commendably fired the author of the e-mail and distanced itself from its contents. There was a welter of evidence, however, that many across the broad spectrum of civil society sought favour, absolution and accommodation from the ANC. To me this was a form of surrender and a negation of citizenship.

While physical emigration (see Chapter 21) was the preferred option of many, the reduction of political engagement in my own ranks by previous stalwarts was another constant and depressing feature of my time in leadership. This was, I suspect, consequent to arriving at the same conclusion which I had jotted down when a leading Kenyan white 'settler' living in that country's highlands – Michael Cunningham-Reid, a member of the famous Delamare clan – said: 'We stayed out of politics. That's the big taboo. We must be no challenge to the black man's political power.' Happiness in Happy Valley apparently came with this price tag.

I could never have led the party or the opposition if I had deferred to this imperative, but I didn't doubt its local salience. My colleague Dr Kraai van Niekerk had pointed out how perilous such an internal 'immigration' had been for Zimbabwe's white farming community. At independence in 1980 they largely opted out of political involvement, concentrating their efforts and energies on their successful agricultural enterprises.

But after ten years of 'keeping their heads down', politics came back to haunt them and destroy their livelihoods. The absence of organised and effective opposition in Zimbabwe – and its resurrection far too late in the process – meant that Mugabe's forward march on their lands and liveli-hood could not be resisted.

The party had by now massively increased the number of black activists in its ranks – a pleasing and positive feature. But if the backbone of the party's current white base was opting out, lying low, then the non-racial, colour-blind principle of the party was not succeeding in binding the minorities into continued political engagement. I did note, however, that English-speaking South Africans – including some in the DA – were more susceptible to the Cunningham-Reid 'big taboo' injunction than other minorities. Perhaps it had always been like that.

It became integral to my mission to address the twin notions of the fear of isolation and the perils of minority withdrawal.

An opportunity presented itself in March 2005 when a series of lec-tures honouring Helen Suzman was arranged in Cape Town, following the opening of an exhibition in honour of her life and work. With great accuracy and without malice, Colin Eglin described the crowd at the im-pressive ceremonial inauguration as 'a cross between a bar-mitzvah and a Prog old boys' gathering'.[2]

Both the age and the demographic profile of the audience comprised many of the best elements of a bygone era and the 86-year-old matriarch being honoured. But I was determined – after due and generous acknowl-edgment to Helen – to assess whether the liberal cause had any further relevance in the new South Africa. It could hardly be done in one speech, and I certainly claimed no exclusivity or special insight: but a careful read-ing of the growing anti-DA and anti-liberal discontents (liberal critics of the party were quick to claim they were not the same) revealed that part of the malaise in my own fold arose from an internalisation of the critique (indeed, calumnies) offered by our intellectual and political opponents.

Again, Mbeki had recently provided presidential respectability for the assault. In January 2005 he had bracketed Helen Suzman politically with John Vorster and other 'lesser agents of colonialism'. Mbeki approving-ly described Suzman's liberalism (sung by 'a sweet bird') as monumen-tally hypocritical in the fight against apartheid. He caricatured her and her stance as, 'I am in favour of change ... but determined to prevent change.'[3]

There was protest and outrage from the liberal camp at Mbeki's ignobility in attacking Suzman. But I had realised that invoking good deeds done under apartheid was an insufficient answer to those who now regarded liberalism and its exponents as the prime ideological enemy.

In my lecture[4] I linked South Africa's seemingly beleaguered liberal enclave to a rich and durable international hinterland. From it had emerged some significant and principled common threads: the inviolability of the individual and his rights, and the rejection of the notion that the collective will must in all circumstances trump the claims of the sovereign citizen. This, in the South African context, made it difficult to reconcile our ideology with the proponents of a 'national democratic revolution'. In fact, it was Arthur Koestler – the erstwhile European Communist – who turned his back on his earlier faith and proclaimed in his greatest novel, *Darkness at Noon*:[5]

'I don't approve of mixing ideologies ... there are only two concepts of human ethics and they are at opposite poles. One of them is Christian and humane, it declares the individual to be sacrosanct and asserts that the rules of arithmetic are not to be applied to human units. The other starts from the basic principle that a collective aim justifies all means and not only allows but demands that the individual should in every way be subordinated and sacrificed to the community. Humbugs and dilettantes have always tried to mix the two conceptions; in practice it is impossible.'[6]

It was the pre-eminent 20th century liberal philosopher Isaiah Berlin who provided in his 1938 essay 'Two Concepts of Liberty', in his influential delineation between 'positive and negative' liberty, the reason why liberalism was treated with such scepticism in the developing world, including South Africa. As I put it:

'Whereas "negative liberty" was merely the freedom not to be coerced by the state, "positive liberty" was the freedom to realise some greater good – such as basic material needs for all, or some overarching Utopian vision of a new society.

'The great fallacy of the Left in the 20th century was that "positive liberty" was the superior and more urgent kind – that the state had to provide "positive liberty" to the poor, even at the cost of sacrificing the "negative liberty" of the rich. It was an illusory bargain, as Berlin demonstrated, because when the state is allowed to interfere with the "negative liberty" of the rich, it eventually interferes with the freedom – both "positive" and "negative" – of the poor as well.'

I went on to caution the audience that 'countless examples have confirmed Berlin's conclusions. Indeed, the political and economic crisis in Zimbabwe today can be described as a direct consequence of the state denying its citizens the "negative liberties" of property and political freedom under the guise of providing the "positive liberty" of land reform.

'Yet having said that, we must also note that liberalism cannot and must not neglect "positive liberty". Particularly in a society like South Africa, where social and economic inequality are just as much a threat to "negative liberty" as they are to "positive liberty", liberalism must strive to maintain a balance or a creative tension between the two.'

While the DA in 2005 was by no means exclusively liberal – our base was now at least eight times larger than South Africa's liberal hard core of about 250 000 voters (roughly the number who voted DP in 1994), I felt that our broad approach and policies were liberal democratic, even if there was no fetish about ideology.

Our critics tended, when it suited their purposes, to lump the party and the ideology together – or to claim we had abandoned our belief system and were now 'illiberal'. The essence of the assault lay in the Mbeki line that liberals 'were in favour of change, but determined to resist it.' ANC stalwart Pallo Jordan had taken the argument further: he entirely discounted the liberal contribution to South Africa's 'liberal democratic constitution'. Unisa vice chancellor Barney Pityana was even more extreme, declaring in 2002: 'Liberals are the ones who would have perpetuated apartheid by their opposition to economic sanctions and the isolation of the apartheid regime.'

I responded to this airbrushing of history with an acknowledgement: 'The reality is that while the contribution of liberals to bringing down apartheid was modest, it was essential and, at times, decisive. The presence of a small but vocal liberal opposition came at the moral cost of participating in a whites–only parliament, but always kept alive the idea and the hope of a democratic alternative to apartheid.

'And the information yielded by the government in reply to the parliamentary questions put forth by Mrs Suzman and other MPs was of great use to the anti-apartheid movements, both at home and abroad.'

The issue of whether liberalism did or did not bring liberation seemed little more than question-begging, although I did attempt my answer. The more immediate question was whether our principles and polices could provide South Africa today with answers to fight the ills of unemployment, crime and disease. The old Nationalists had sneered at 'wealthy

English-speaking liberals' in the heyday of apartheid. So the target had not changed, simply the source of the attack.

The goal, then and now, was to discredit liberalism among the ethnic, racial and economic majority of voters by identifying it with ethnic, racial and economic minorities – who are, in today's South Africa, by implication, associated with the evil of apartheid.

I quoted approvingly from John Kane-Berman's elegant summation of how, at its best, the liberal state was pro-poor:

'The liberal state ... removes barriers to market entry that stifle individual opportunity and enterprise. It is frugal with taxes, recognising that they are the fruits of human labour, not the property of the state. It is prudent with expenditure. Where it collects taxes to redistribute, it does so in a way as to help the poor start climbing the staircase of self-reliance and success. It avoids doing things – such as generate electricity or run harbours and airlines – that profit-driven entrepreneurs can do more effectively. Where it has to make trade-offs, it favours liberty above restriction, the poor above the rich, and consumers above producers.'

I moved towards a conclusion: 'There is no greater investment a government can make than in the freedom of its people. And if we, as liberals and as democrats, place the liberty of the individual as the highest priority, then our course is clear and determined. We cannot rest easy at a time when millions of South Africans are still denied the most basic freedoms to express themselves in their own language; the freedom to live beyond poverty.

'The evil of poverty is that, among other things, it removes people's choices. They have no opportunity to be independent, and so poverty affects not only their way of life but also their spirit and their humanity. It robs them of their dignity. Yet when poverty is our nation's main focus, liberals must remind South Africa that freedom and democracy are often the worst enemies of want and the best guarantors of prosperity.'

I was determined that our cause could not allow its most vehement detractors to define it. We could not allow a negative, fatally flawed stereotype to undermine our resolve and legitimacy.

2

But such philosophising had to yield, yet again, to the relentless ticking of the electoral clock. The 2006 municipal elections across South Africa would be my fifth appointment at the polls since assuming leadership, and in its own way as decisive as the other electoral contests fought. If the party was to have any chance of improving its fortunes in the 2006 election, then two separate – equally vital and grisly – tasks needed to be concluded in the run-up to the polls. The first was to raise sufficient funds; and the second, restore a semblance, if not the substance, of unity to the deeply divided Western Cape, in which our most realistic hopes of victory lay.

Money is the mother's milk of politics; but fundraising is the 'chemotherapy of elections' (to paraphrase a failed candidate for the US Senate). But like the painful treatment for cancer, it was an absolute requirement for success.

The DA, despite its tag as 'the party of the rich', lived much of its life on the financial edge. Only smart month-end juggling prevented us from 'going under'. There were, as I have recorded elsewhere, well-substantiated rumours that the ANC owed the banks over R100-million – but as the governing party (which in the heavily regulated financial services sector counted for a great deal) they hardly lived in fear of imminent foreclosure. For the opposition there were no such certainties.

We were generally able to secure enough money to run a reasonably competent, professional and well-funded campaign. Between elections, however, the situation was much tighter. Despite receiving constituency allowances from the (probably unsuspecting) taxpayer, our debt by the beginning of 2005 was dire. Part was historical: aside from defaulting on their own bankers, the NNP had effectively swindled the DA out of some R5-million by simply walking away from their financial obligations for the 2000 municipal election. (Of course, chronic indebtedness never prevented their leader, executive director and two secretaries-general from acquiring the latest Mercedes and being met at every stop by a liveried chauffeur. Van Schalkwyk once – in all seriousness – informed me: 'My people expect it.')

Debts from 2004, although we had been well funded, had left us owing several million rands.

The obverse of the funding crisis was an accurate reflection of South Africa's current politics. One of the unarticulated premises of BEE was to combine rapacious rent-seeking with the fetish of control – and get as many ANC-aligned directors as possible onto the boards of all public (and most private) companies. This created an atmosphere in most (although, crucially, not all) boardrooms in which donations made to the DA could become radioactive. While many prospective corporate donors were sympathetic, they simply switched off the taps or gave vast amounts to buy off the ANC. Some did dole out a small percentage to us to rebut accusations

of the very thing they were in fact doing, buying favour. Some contributed to the party to balance the moral or ethical books; but there were some
standout examples of those who were quite explicit about their financial
backing – the late Harry Oppenheimer and Cape Town businessman Ben
Rabinowitz were two such examples – but the general rule remained that
big business now favoured the ANC.

We had met these funding crises quite well over time. After the 1999
election Greg Krumbock had pioneered a telesales marketing campaign
which, over a six-year period, grossed the party some R50-million. We
thus had some fourteen thousand small donors – at its peak – who typically gave us between three hundred and five thousand rands apiece. The
modus operandi was quite robust: for example, a 'getaway' car was despatched
from the call centre to collect the donation before the donor changed his
mind. The great advantage of this funding system was that it lessened our
dependence on 'big money' and the private-sector corporations whose
traditional support and ideological preference for the DA was not worth
their alienation from the all-knowing and potentially vengeful ANC.

Notwithstanding Greg's heroic efforts and my endless fundraising sor-
ties to Johannesburg, by 2005 the party balance sheet had too little black
ink and enough red to make a communist blush. In one of his first acts
as newly appointed CEO, Ryan Coetzee gave us focus with his normal
intensity. He yanked the estimable and meticulous David Maynier from
running my office to re-jigging the party finances and fundraising. The
essence of the new approach was to use me even more extensively in visits
to business.

My frequent-flyer account soared into serious realms as I set about,
with the dogged assistance of Doug Gibson, Helen Zille, Sheila Camerer,
Sherry Chen, Brenda Bedborough and Brian Goodall, to visit literally
every enterprise that would receive us.

Post-Harksen, we also had to be ultra-careful to screen potential donors
and wipe from our slate any dodgy entrepreneurs. (The ANC, it was to
become apparent, laboured under no such constraint.) With exhausting
effort we clocked up about two hundred appointments in the year, and
raised just under twenty million rands. There was a bizarre, even surreal
flip side of the fundraising grind. One titan of South African industry
informed me, 'They bug my office and even my home', before making a
substantial donation in the seclusion of his garden.

Later when the widespread nature of mutual paranoia and surveillance
began to leak from various agencies such as the National Intelligence
Agency (NIA) – not least of the ambitions of businessmen deemed to be

'off side' in the ANC succession battle – my bizarre little garden visit took on a sinister perspective.

On another occasion, I went with Douglas to see a major business-woman – of huge wealth – who had been a modest donor to our cause, giving about twenty thousand rands a year – rather grudgingly surrendered, mostly for reasons of historic identification with the old Progressive Party. We were immediately treated by her to a laundry list of the party's shortcomings and an exasperated sign-off line: 'Well, I suppose I'll keep giving you something, because hopeless as the opposition cause is around here, I guess we need one.'

Something in me snapped. With rising passion I told her that we were the thin blue line separating South Africa from one-party status. Perhaps she should more profitably examine what South Africa – and the business climate – would be like without any opposition at all. The truth at the moment was either to make us – through funding – more viable, or dispense with an opposition. 'That,' I concluded, 'is the brutal reality and you must accept this.'

I suspected I had blown the situation, when the quiet millionairess behind the desk said to us: 'Yes … well, I'm rearranging certain assets so I will now be sending you one million rands before year-end.'

Having made enough progress on the fundraising front to put enough petrol in the electoral tank for 2006, I turned my attention to the vexed issue of unifying the party in the Western Cape. Despite the migration of many of the Nat leaders to the ANC, most of their local public representatives, members and voters had remained in the DA.

By far the majority of party members and activists and representatives in the Western Cape were much less interested in the battles – and parties-of-the-past – and were completely committed to taking on the opposition's major opponent, the ANC, rather than each other. But there was a fringe group of outriders in both camps who tended to inflame passions or invoke – legitimately or otherwise – a key principle which they believed the 'other side' was violating. The issues varied, but the intermittent flare-ups often reverted to old Prog-Nat fault lines.

Theuns Botha – the former mayor of the southern Cape town of Riversdale – was our provincial leader. He came from a 'strong Nat' background and his father had been mayor of Kimberley. As I have related, he had played a pivotal role twice in the short, turbulent history of the DA: Botha had given voice to and become the public face of the NNP's rejection of Van Schalkwyk's chicanery within the DA.

He had also stepped into the breach and assumed the provincial leadership when Gerald Morkel resigned in 2002. In my view, to the extent that any politician is 'owed' anything, Botha was 'owed'. He was also a binding force for the party in the *platteland* (rural areas) and represented a core element of our constituency. I personally got on very well with him, and I admired his fluency as a platform speaker and – on a personal level – his good relationship with his wife Sarie and pop-star son, Willem. But he was also susceptible to the suasions of advisers whose self-interests did not, in my view, always coincide with the party's needs or principles.

However, most of the provincial voters – and our supporters – resided not in the small towns dotted around the Western Cape hinterland and coastline, but in the metropolitan area of Cape Town. And here the undoubted leader was the redoubtable Helen Zille, whose role in the provincial government – as Education minister – had been stellar. She was not simply from the 'DP wing' of the party, but embodied the liberal heritage itself, having been – for many years – far closer to left-leaning NGOs such as the Black Sash and the End Conscription Campaign than to the DP, which she joined formally only in 1999.

She had also spent many years as a well-respected political journalist at the liberal flagship *Rand Daily Mail*. This not only gave her 'street cred' with the usual suspects who berated the DA for being 'against history' by opposing the ANC, but also – almost uniquely – gave her a firewall which insulated her from press criticism. Both the press and the ANC enjoyed parading Helen as either my successor or an inhouse coup-leader, ready to topple me from office. I never experienced an iota of disloyalty from her, and came to admire her political courage and completely unromanticised view of the ANC's power lust and how to oppose it.

After the fall of the DA from power in the Western Cape, Helen had led the opposition in the province; and after the 2004 election had been elected to parliament. I had appointed her party national spokesperson (see Chapter 12).

However, in human terms, Helen was very complex. She had an often obdurate single-mindedness, and, I thought, seemed ultra-sensitive to plots and stratagems she thought were being unleashed against her. She and Botha were not natural allies: but both needed the other if our ambition of regaining power in Cape Town and beyond was ever to be realised.

I had little doubt that an agreeable *modus operandi* would have evolved between them. However, in the run-up to the elections there was much at stake, and internal ructions and rumblings in the party did not make for pleasant viewing.

To her supporters, Helen was something of a latter-day female Savonarola, the 15th-century Dominican preacher who, in the words of a biographer, 'fearlessly hammered corruption among the princes and prelates.'[7] Quite who needed to be cleansed of wickedness was not always clear; but to some former NNPs in the party, they were the targets. To others it was almost a revival of the Anglo-Boer War of over a century ago, played out in the narrow confines of the DA.

Much of 2005 was spent trying to mediate between the factions. James Selfe, chairman of our Executive, laboured for months – with seemingly limitless patience – to create peace. He had little to show. I had meanwhile concluded that our best prospect of victory in Cape Town – and the best available mayor – was Helen Zille. Any fear I felt about potential divisiveness was, in my view, outweighed by her considerable intellect, media image and utter incorruptibility. This would make her both electable and, crucially, a safe pair of hands in which the reins of governance could be gripped.

I faced three obstacles: to persuade her to take the job; to persuade one party component to accept her candidature without civil war breaking out; and, finally, to put in place a nominating mechanism for the mayoral and all other municipal candidates in Cape Town. After ever-escalating internal machinations, an internal audit had revealed severe irregularities in the recruitment tactics of certain branches, ranging from 'sponsorship' (each member should pay his own dues, not be 'sponsored') to more serious allegations of fraud.

Membership determined the branch's role and strength in nomination contests – so we clearly had a major problem, if not crisis, on our hands. I resolved this matter by getting the Federal Executive to ram through a set of regulations which allowed for an expanded local executive to choose all Cape Town candidates, including the mayor. We bypassed the branches and the problem of inflated or improper membership rolls. Neither side was happy, but by the time the decision was taken the electoral cycle was so advanced that this makepiece – and broadly democratic – solution was the only alternative.

Helen kept oscillating between a desire to stand and 'do good in the city', and a reluctance to give up her national role. She was also extremely – and understandably – anxious not to fall between a failed mayoral bid and giving up her parliamentary seat.

After many meals, meetings and disclaimers, Helen eventually threw her hat into the ring. Somewhat like the eunuch in the harem, I had the desire but not the power to see her nominated. Unwisely in my view Theuns

Botha backed Zille's opponent for the nomination, Lennit Max, previously Western Cape police commissioner before entering politics in 2004 as Patricia de Lille's standard-bearer in the Western Cape. He had seen through De Lille sooner than most, and crossed the floor to the DA.

While I felt Lennit had many fine qualities and attributes (and the advantage of being Coloured), his recent arrival meant he should bide his time. I was also by now absolutely convinced that Helen's nomination would galvanise reluctant or even disaffected supporters to get behind the DA and add a few crucial points to our base.

While I didn't have the formal power to choose Zille, I had influence with the makeshift selection committee, which met in Cape Town on 7 December 2005. The selectors were fairly evenly split along the old, familiar lines of division – except that Helen and I had persuaded at least five of the former Nats to back her candidacy. She also gave an exemplary speech, and remained utterly unruffled in the face of hostile, even vicious, questions from her opponents. She emerged triumphant, winning by 22-16. Now, I felt, the campaign was reasonably on course towards success.

After the election, described below, a school of conspiracy (there was no shortage of eager students in my party) put it about that I had 'located' Helen in the mayoralty to keep my leadership out of harm's way and her grasp. Since, as I recount in Chapter 20, I was already setting the sun on my own position, this assertion had no credence. I simply wanted to secure the most electable and credible person for the position, and believed then, as now, that Helen provided that in spades.

3

In most democracies, the opposition could have been expected to win by a landslide.

Indeed, opposition parties, led by the DA, secured significant gains in the nationwide local government elections on 1 March. The DA increased its share of the vote from 12,3% in the national government elections of 2004 to 16,3% in 2006 – by far the largest increase of any opposition party. That 4% gain matched a 4% loss for the ANC, which won nearly 70% in 2004 but fell to 65,7% in 2006.

The ANC retained control of the overwhelming majority of municipalities: but the DA dealt it a critical defeat in Cape Town, cracking the dominant party's monopoly over South Africa's major metropolitan councils and shutting it out of government in most Western Cape municipalities.

But we should have won!

Or, if not won – done far better. Consider the rot which had set in. Nearly half of the nation's 284 municipalities were officially classified as 'dysfunctional' and in need of urgent intervention by central government. Protests erupted onto township and city streets as residents – frustrated by failing public services – vented their anger. Corruption in ANC-controlled local structures had reached such proportions that even President Mbeki himself warned that his party was 'degenerat[ing] into an ignoble, blood-sucking and corrupt parasite, an enemy of an immensely heroic people.'[8]

The DA responded with a stark campaign slogan: 'Stop corruption, start delivery.' And 1,6-million South Africans gave us their support.

And yet millions more chose to stick with the ANC – even increasing its majority in several of the places it had governed worst, such as Delmas which had been ravaged by a typhoid epidemic. ANC support there increased to 72% from 65%.[9] Why was South Africa's political opposition failing to gain from the ANC's mistakes?

The short answer was that the ANC's soaring percentages masked the reality of plummeting voter turnout. Nearly sixteen million South Africans voted in 2004, but fewer than ten million did so in 2006. The 6,5-million who voted for the ANC in these elections represent slightly more than half the number who voted for the ANC in the historic 1994 elections. The percentage turnout of 48,4% was, in fact, among the lowest ever in the post-apartheid era (second only to the turnout of 48,1% in the 2000 local elections). Furthermore, pre-election surveys suggested that less than half the electorate was planning to vote ANC, as opposed to more than two-thirds before the 2000 local government elections.[10] Those who came to the polls for the ANC this year were its core supporters; most of its previous voters stayed home. But the six million ANC votes lost since 1994 did not migrate to the opposition column.

It was apparent at the campaign's commencement that fewer people than ever were buying ANC propaganda. More and more journalists found the courage to expose its failures. Carol Paton observed in the *Financial Mail*: 'For the crisis is that local politicians are pushing out competent officials and replacing them with ANC lackeys who allow councillors to do as they wish.'[11]

Many municipal councils under ANC control had become little more than thieves' banquets, with local mayors and councillors feasting off ratepayers' munificence and skimming a percentage off public tenders and contracts. South Africa's coastal cities and hinterland had become places where officials and councillors positioned themselves to take advantage of their office on the basis, as the old adage went, of 'get your snout in the trough or you'll freeze in the cold.'

Take the 'gravy plane' debacle.

In mid-January the intrepid *Beeld* revealed a secret trip which the deputy president, Phumzile Mlambo-Ngcuka, embarked on – for a private vacation – using an air force Falcon 900 jet. It cost the taxpayers upwards of half-a-million rands. She was accompanied by her husband Bulelani – the former National Director of Public Prosecutions – and the nemesis of Jacob Zuma, whose job Phumzile had taken!

The 'gravy plane' saga was manna to our propaganda, since it underlined the widely held perception of 'high-flying adored', and the use of public resources for private purpose. We were also mightily assisted by the government and the deputy president's welter of contradictory explanations for the trip, and suggestions that securing her husband's BEE interests was the real motive for a visit which was varyingly described as 'a private visit' or 'part work, part vacation'.[12]

The election was also foreshadowed by the open warfare which had emerged in the ANC between the camp followers of Mbeki and Zuma. Following Zuma's ejection from the deputy presidency, Mbeki had been stunningly and surprisingly rebuffed when, in July 2005, his party's national general council refused to countenance Zuma's resignation as party deputy president. Instead, he was triumphantly reinstated, a package of pro-market reforms favoured by Mbeki were defeated, and effigies of the president were burnt outside the meeting. The die was now well and truly cast, although a cease-fire temporarily endured during the election campaign.

One way in which the president sought to rebuild public support was by launching a broader battle against corruption: hence his railing against 'blood-sucking parasites' in October 2005. The ANC made all its councillors sign an oath promising not to be corrupt, and to work for the public interest 'without motives of material advantage or personal gain'. But Mbeki's critics, inside and outside the ANC, noted that corruption scandals close to the Presidency were conspicuously overlooked.

The top-down presidency had its effect on the primary vehicles of information on the election itself: the Independent Electoral Commission (IEC) and the SABC, the latter doing its best to harm the DA. As per usual, the SABC frequently failed to turn up at DA events and rallies; and when it did cover the DA, the television news almost always lumped us together with smaller, regional opposition parties in a 'package' story. The SABC refused to inform the public that the DA existed as a national alternative to the ANC.

The apogee of the SABC's performance and prejudice was revealed on the Sunday following the 2006 poll. The SABC took out giant ads in national newspapers hailing President Mbeki as one of South Africa's 'two phenomenal presidents' (the other being Mandela). How SABC reporters were meant to cover the president responsibly while their editors and bosses – loyal ANC cadres, almost to a one – praised him to the heavens was, of course, moot.

Roughly five weeks before the election, the Zille campaign drew attention to the failing state of the city's firefighting services, a result of staff and equipment shortages, budget cuts and low morale. Coincidentally, within the next 24 hours a massive wildfire – allegedly started by a British tourist who threw a cigarette butt out of a car window – engulfed Table Mountain. The blaze lasted for days, destroyed several homes and killed a hiker on the mountain. It also drove home the point that the ANC-run council was woefully unprepared for such a disaster, and had slowed down a plan to upgrade the fire department which the DA had introduced when it controlled the city several years earlier.

At the same time, power failures hit the city and the province, starting in December and running right through election day. The immediate cause was a generator failure at the nearby Koeberg nuclear power plant, ostensibly due to a loose bolt. However, it soon became clear that the ANC government, at a national level, had failed to plan for the country's growing energy needs, and there was no contingency plan to deal with the electricity cuts. Hospitals lost power and could not perform surgery; sewerage systems backed up and filled streets and rivers with the stench of human waste. This was a full dress rehearsal to the national crisis which was to grip South Africa from January 2008 when suburbs, townships and even the mines were plunged into darkness.

The ANC's response to these crises was instructive. On the eve of the election, the minister of Public Enterprises, Alec Erwin, called a press conference at which he claimed that the damage at Koeberg had been a deliberate act of sabotage. Of course he was forced to backtrack after the election; but the accusations were repeated by other ANC officials, who implied that the DA itself was responsible. The real cause – bad planning, poor management and racial prescriptions – would be revealed in due course.

For the 48 hours preceding polling day, 1 March, Russel Crystal had determined there were over a dozen municipalities across the Western Cape which were so marginal – or poised on such a knife-edge between victory and defeat – that I should visit them to maintain momentum through to polling day.

To criss-cross the province effectively, a donor had lent us a Beechcraft Baron turboprop aircraft. With some trepidation, in view of its unpressurised and unheated cabin, Theuns Botha and Martin Slabbert – my media officer – and I took off from Cape Town airport early on the Monday morning. Previously, when in need of an aircraft we had borrowed or hired the faster and smoother Pilatus or Kingair, but given our ever-dwindling cash supply (we had borrowed – with the help of one of our donors – R8-million from the bank two weeks prior to election day) we could hardly reject this lesser, but free, craft. When we landed at Theewaterskloof, close to the apple orchards of Grabouw and Elgin, I thought it extremely unlikely that we would win the Bergsig/Uitsig ward which we visited that day, but two days later it was won by exactly one vote, and the momentum was enough to allow us to construct a governing coalition there and oust the ANC.

Who knows what counts as momentum? Reflecting afterwards on that slim margin of victory (and on that in a very poor Coloured area in Port Elizabeth where we tramped for three hours in bad weather, door to door, despite me feeling increasingly feverish; and discovered afterwards that we won by just nine votes against a floor-crossing councillor) I recalled the time when I won my own seat for the first time by fewer than forty votes. In a close race, no effort is wasted and every bit of campaigning helps. The aircraft, however, developed a malfunction and we were forced on our last leg to make an emergency landing in George, which nearly caused me to miss a final visit to the Cape Flats. Fortunately I hopped on an about-to-depart commercial flight.

4

Our journeying across the province finally brought me home, exhausted and fairly rumpled from such a lengthy and varied day on the trail. I was greeted by Michal and Etai with the great news that there had been another power outage in Cape Town; our house was again in darkness, with no prospects of either a hot dinner, or, even more crucial, a warm bath which, together with a large whisky, had been my fantasy since freezing my innards off in a benighted plane earlier that day.

We hastily decamped to the local pizzeria which had its own generator. It was packed with fellow-residents of Newlands, also in search of hot food. Several came up to me and indicated that the recurrent – to use an apt adjective – crisis in electricity in Cape Town was a consequence of both bad government and shoddy planning. They indicated that this latest outage had increased their determination to go and vote the next day.

Having recently transferred my vote from Johannesburg to Cape Town, I awoke on polling day knowing that my own vote had a fair chance of being cast for a party and person who could actually achieve power and not simply be marooned on the opposition benches for the next five years.

So with hopeful expectation Michal and I left with my security detail for the local polling station. The other advantage of casting my first vote in Cape Town was that the stone cottages opposite the majestic Kirstenbosch Gardens, nestling in the shadow of Table Mountain, must rate aesthetically and environmentally as one of the most beautiful voting stations in the world.

The somewhat anxious mayoral candidate, Helen Zille, and a gaggle of media met us. We visited a few party offices and voting stations in our strongholds (in the southern and northern suburbs); then went on to the airport via a stop at the crucial Mitchells Plain headquarters. This area – with the bedrock and bulk of the Cape Town Coloured vote – was a 'must-win'. The enthusiasm of our workers there, under the leadership of Robin Carlisle, my friend and grizzled veteran of more campaigns than most, seemed greater than the tempo of our voters who were dribbling, rather than streaming, to the polls.

We transferred to the IEC centre in Pretoria, to audit early results and computer projections of our showing. By now I had been involved directly as a candidate, or as party leader, in some dozen elections, and the expectations and anticipation never diminish with time. This day was no exception.

We camped at the IEC centre for the next 24 hours. The tedium of 'hanging around' the counting centre was interspersed with media interviews and some light-hearted joshing with our opponents. There was an amusing moment when President Mbeki's wife, Zanele, who struck me as altogether more relaxed and warm than her husband, related to us an amusing incident that occurred the previous day when she went to cast her vote.

Apparently, she arrived at her local polling station in Killarney, Johannesburg. I thought it odd that she voted in Johannesburg, while her husband was registered at the official residence in Pretoria – but odder still was the fact that no one recognised her and she could not find her name on the electoral register. However, she told us how the gimlet-eyed DA polling agent (a local councillor, Nico de Jager) did recognise her and sorted the matter out. She had been unilaterally and against her instruction, apparently, registered under her married rather than her maiden name. She concluded: 'I was tempted to vote for my rescuer.'

Later in the afternoon, at the airport, we encountered an anxious-looking Patricia de Lille in a business lounge where, at 4 pm, she sequestered herself in the smoking booth to relieve her *angst* with cigarettes and a couple of glasses of wine. This was probably indicated, since while the Cape Town results had not been finalised it was a close-run thing, with the DA edging towards ninety seats, the ANC on just over eighty and the ID on twenty. Seven smaller parties had, between them, about a dozen seats. The council – the key and unpredictable prize of the whole election – would remain 'hung' and unresolved until its first meeting ten days hence.

The sensationalist eve-of-election claims of opposition 'sabotage' of the electrical system were accompanied by the ANC's attempts to manipulate the voting process. At several voting stations in black townships across Cape Town, DA observers witnessed – and photographed – ANC activists handing out identity documents to would-be voters at ANC offices and ANC information tables. Zille herself was physically pushed out of the ANC's office in the township of Crossroads when she used her cellphone to take pictures of identity books on a table, awaiting distribution. There was no way to ascertain whether the documents were real or fake – and no credible explanation as to how they ended up in the hands of the ANC on election day.

The police were asked to intervene, but refused, saying that it was an IEC matter. The IEC, in turn, refused to take any action. IEC provincial electoral officer Courtney Sampson told the *Cape Argus*: 'I spoke to an official at Home Affairs who assured me that it was part of its normal distribution of identity books ... There was nothing sinister about the process.'[13] In the end, this apparent attempt at vote-rigging failed to deliver Cape Town to the ANC. But it may certainly have affected the final margin of its loss.

The final results of the 2006 elections were mildly encouraging for the DA. Not only had we increased our national percentage since 2004 by more than any other party, we also increased our vote in eight out of nine provinces and consolidated our position as the only national alternative to the ANC. We came in second to the ruling party everywhere except

KwaZulu-Natal, where we as usual finished third behind the ANC and the Inkatha Freedom Party. An analysis by the Council for Scientific and Industrial Research (CSIR) suggested that the DA enjoyed greater loyalty among its voters than any other party. Roughly 98% of those who chose the DA in 2004 chose it again in 2006; the percentage was 95% for the ANC, and only 70% for the Independent Democrats (ID).[14]

In Cape Town, the final tally showed that the DA won with 42% to the ANC's 38%; our chief opposition rival, the ID, achieved only 11%.

Though De Lille still claimed to be the 'kingmaker', her share of the vote was not enough to put the ANC in power without drawing in other parties. In the complex negotiations which followed, the DA was in the strongest position to form a governing coalition, which indeed we did, installing Zille as mayor by the hairbreadth margin of just two votes. The council meeting at which the new mayor was elected finally gave our supporters and members something to cheer about; but there was an ominous, darker underside well described by veteran journalist Wyndham Hartley in *Business Day* on 25 April:

'The alarming part [of the council meeting] was that those who voted with the DA had to face the wrath of the ANC. Some ANC members of the council looked at the opposition members from whom they had expected support and drew imaginary knives across their throats. This in open council ...

'[The] most disturbing thing was the visceral nature of the ANC's response to failure in an election and its patent failure to accept the result with any dignity.'

The ANC certainly did not take defeat well – or even, perhaps, believe that they had lost. Two days after Zille's installation as mayor, the media[15] reported that several Cape Town councillors had been 'attacked, intimidated and threatened for aligning themselves with the DA's multi-party governing caucus. A Khayelitsha ACDP [a party in the DA governing fold] councillor Sipho Xazana told the paper, for example, that a senior ANC member had attempted to run him over twice with his Mercedes Benz.'

Zille's attempts to address communities in Crossroads and Khayelitsha were thwarted by ANC hoodlums who violently disrupted her meetings, even on one occasion threatening her with a knife. Despite the menacing atmosphere, and the undemocratic behaviour, Zille seemed to thrive on it all, and indicated to me that it was not without its usefulness. It showed South Africa how profoundly contemptuous the ANC was about democratic outcomes that, in rare cases, went against it.

Many, not just in my circle, began to speculate on how the ANC would behave when its national, not simply metropolitan – Cape Town – grip was loosened: would they 'do a Mugabe' was a question which admitted of no reassuring answer. On a lesser note, Patricia de Lille was to execute a dizzying series of flip-flops: contrary to the expectations of her voters who were opposition-minded, she initially refused to join the multi-party coalition which we assembled to install Zille as mayor. To the intense anger of many (including her hitherto-adoring press) and against her own pledge, she sided with the ANC's maladroit incumbent Nomaindia Mfeketo. After this stratagem misfired, De Lille faced plunging polls in two subsequent by-elections which the DA won. Ultimately she threw in her lot with Zille's coalition which then stabilised, but De Lille was exposed, in the process, as essentially unstrategic and shallow. I suggested at the time that her dalliance with the ANC made her an 'unsuccessful Kortbroek'. She had a similar penchant for avoiding scruple and principle, but lacked Van Schalkwyk's guile and shrewd intellect to deliver on her betrayals.

I felt broadly satisfied with the DA's overall performance, an improvement on its 2004 showing but not as spectacular as our 2000 local government haul. This time we netted 1 107 councillors nationwide, had grown significantly in the Coloured community, and had advanced, slightly, our very modest toehold in the African electorate. After four gruesome years of party splitting, losing control of the provincial and local governments, and the wearying effects of floor-crossing, we had claimed back our political relevance. I was also pleased with the tier of leadership in place in certain key municipalities: Mayor Anton Bredell in the Swartland and the young John Steenhuizen in Durban were two stand-out examples.

But we had also failed to convince the electoral majority that, notwithstanding their obvious and visceral disenchantment with their government, our party was an alternative home. I knew that winning Cape Town was our 'get out of jail' card from perceived impotence and marginalisation, but realised, yet again, how heavily the issue of race determined electoral outcomes. I was determined to address it within the party afresh.

5

Shortly after the results were known – and after Michal and I had spent a splendid weekend at a wine estate in Franschhoek, as guests of its owner – I returned to my office for a potentially difficult media interview.

The *Financial Mail* whose editor, Barney Mthombothi, had previously opined how ill-starred Mbeki and I were for our respective roles, sent journalist Peter Wilhelm to conduct the interrogation.

Wilhelm told me the *Financial Mail* was thinking of doing a cover story on the DA and on me. I immediately intuited, given some of the background press chatter, that it would not be a friendly one. Indeed, I even told him it would be entitled: 'Leon must go'.

Peter looked somewhat taken aback[16] – and said that whatever his editor had planned, this was not the article he was writing, since the facts on the ground contradicted such a thesis. In the event, the article was pretty positive, and summed up my mood and feelings – and the party's objective state – fairly accurately:

'Far from having emerged from the election chastened, the DA, and certainly its terrier-like boss, are facing the coming years, at least until the general election of 2009, with optimism and enthusiasm. This does not mean that the DA – contrary to the dreams of most opposition parties worldwide – has realistic hopes of becoming the government any time soon. Indeed, there is a sense in which Leon, who sets the entire tone for his party, enjoys his combative, adversarial role. Of the electoral outcome, he told the *Financial Mail*: "Obviously we would be more happy if we got more votes; but we got a lot more than we got in 2004."'

The article was revealing for the fact that the magazine had made extensive background enquiries of my parliamentary colleagues in an effort to detect dissent – or the murmurings of a backbench revolt against my leadership. Wilhelm reported, in the same piece:

'The *Financial Mail* has been entirely unable to find anyone in the DA caucus who – whether they "like" Leon or not – can name anyone who could, at this point, take his place. One said, "He is the most honest fellow I have ever met. I have never heard him tell a lie." (When told of this anonymous tribute, Leon smiles: "I probably have told a lie. But I try not to."). The caucus member went further: "Look at his executive, the skilful people he has assembled around him ... [Without] him, [the DA] would have collapsed and died from 1994 on. His place in history – which someone will write in 100 years – is that he created a viable opposition. I just don't see anyone else to replace him."'

The article hazarded a guess that I would lead the party until 2009, because as it put it, 'for the medium term, the sole credible opposition is the DA, and Tony Leon is irreplaceable, love him or leave him.'

Not every journal, or journalist, was either as kind or as fair. Indeed, 18 months later, the *Financial Mail*'s chief rival, *Finweek*, would announce it was time for me to 'move over'; but that is another story, told later.

6

The weekend after our successful outcome in Cape Town the party Federal Council met in fairly jubilant mood. I had decided that we now needed to use the space afforded by the relatively successful election to confront and act on the two fundamental and irrefutable facts of political life in South Africa: first, that seven out of every ten voters were black; and second, that without the white community's active buy-in and participation the country had no future based on real prosperity and long-term growth.

The ANC had dealt very well with the first fact and very poorly with the second. For us the situation was almost exactly reversed.

I told the meeting that we faced a most important strategic and political choice – not an easy one, but imperative. It was whether to fight for pole position as the political representatives of racially defined minority groups, or to create and serve 'new categories of voter interest'. I recommended that we move boldly into the second option – but not to abandon the interests and concerns of the broad majority of our current base.

The meeting was enthusiastically in agreement. Of course, such sentiments were easier to express than to achieve. But I was fortified in my views when I received a report from a formidable intellectual resource and long-standing party member whom the party had asked to investigate the causes and consequences of the 2005 parliamentary floor-crossing debacle which saw four of our black MPs exit the party for the embrace of the ANC – against whom, only days before, each of the defectors had expressed deep disdain, if not revulsion. Her response was noteworthy. She indicated that the mood music should change: 'Having a party which looks, sounds and feels multiracial is a key step to making defections unimportant.

'Potential new voters need a bridge into the party. Some people will jump a chasm if the city behind them is burning, but more of them will cross a bridge.'

From these elegant insights flowed the consequences:

Saturation attacks on an opposing party will not in themselves ensure anything like a mass defection. There needs to be sufficient difference between the parties to make the move worthwhile, and enough similarity to make it possible and plausible.

In this process, symbols, language, policies, and visibility and purpose of action play a significant role in making a switch of allegiance thinkable or unthinkable. A black voter who has seen only white faces on DA posters from Auckland Park to Witkoppen may hesitate to transfer his loyalty. What symbolic message is conveyed when DA posters look like those of the FF+ and the Christian Front? Ordinary voters must be given words, hopeful words, to explain why they are moving to a good party alignment, not why they are leaving a bad one.

Only a majority black party can hold power in South Africa. So a change of government requires a breaking of the nostalgia vote – and a substantial movement of voters from old party loyalties and sympathies. And for new votes to be gained, at least some traditional ones will have to be lost.

The DA – currently the most viable opposition party – needs to provide a language which voters can believe in and which also explains any move towards either active or passive DA support. This must be a positive, not a negative, language, and will entail a vision for the future, as well as a critical analysis of the present.

In the light of this memo – and notwithstanding the party having burned its fingers by promoting black talent only to see the prodigies of yesterday become the defectors of tomorrow – I felt we had to press on with an even stronger emphasis on genuine affirmative action within our ranks. That, at least, would allow us to address the first and fundamental fact of political life in South Africa.

I did not underestimate the difficulty of the task. Black skills in South Africa then, as today, were at a premium, and the life of a black opposition MP was not necessarily one of ease and repose. The DA had also become both gun-shy in terms of potential defectors, and often despairing about the reluctance of independent-minded people of colour to identify openly with the party after 12 years of race-labelling.

I had an anecdote for the meeting which a former US ambassador had told me. US president Jimmy Carter advised his secretary for the army that the time had come for the appointment of the first black (one-star) general, and he was to find an appropriate nominee. The Joint Chiefs of Staff reported back that they were unable to find a suitably qualified person. Carter responded: 'Then go and look again.' They duly found, and promoted, General Colin Powell who, of course, shot straight up the ranks to become chairman of the Joint Chiefs and then the hugely admired and widely respected secretary of state under George W Bush.

What this search could yield before the 2009 election remains to be seen. But, self-evidently, the party needed to fill its ranks with black South Africans.

I also felt the party needed to change its stance on floor-crossing.

Our position on the issue was vexed – if not downright contradictory. Shortly after the 1994 elections, Colin Eglin had championed the abolition of what was called the 'Anti-Defection Clause' of the Interim Constitution. This provision (which was retained in the final Constitution) disallowed members of parliament from retaining their seats if they joined rival political organisations.

Eglin's position was – on the face of it – sensible and principled. If the icepack which froze South African politics every five years was to melt, parliament and other legislative bodies should reflect that change. Since South Africa had a closed-list proportional representation system, inordinate power vested in the hands of party bosses, as I relate in Chapter 10. MPs could not exhibit or vent maverick views based on principle for fear of incurring the wrath, if not the axe, of the leadership. Indeed, the only overt act of defiance of party orthodoxy which I ever saw on the ANC side was when singer-turned-politician (she wished to sing her maiden speech) Jennifer Ferguson deliberately abstained when parliament voted to liberalise the hitherto stringent abortion laws. She left (or perhaps was pushed out) shortly thereafter.

Eglin's views were ignored. Indeed, when the DP discussed the idea in parliament in 1998 it was vehemently opposed by the ANC. Shortly after the DA was formed, James Selfe drew up draft legislation which would have allowed parties, subject to fairly stringent conditions to prevent opportunistic party-hopping, to merge and MPs to cross the floor. We needed this legislation to cement the Alliance at parliamentary level.

Our explanatory memorandum provided one significant caveat: '[It] needs to be recognised that members of legislatures elected on lists do not have an original mandate from the voters, unlike those representing geographic constituencies. Therefore, the merger, splitting or resignation of members from political parties must occur in an ordered and regulated manner to ensure that the wishes of the voters are not frustrated.'

One safeguard in the bill was the stipulation that the Independent Electoral Commission would need to be satisfied that 'the party that nominated him or her [i.e. a public representative] has deviated significantly and materially from the policy and principles on which that member was elected.' That requirement was removed by the ANC when parliament was presented with floor-crossing legislation two years later.

In the form in which the floor-crossing legislation was rammed through, it was – as I have indicated elsewhere – to salvage Van Schalkwyk's immoral union with the ANC. Political expediency had gutted whatever principle lay behind our original proposal.

The worst – or most politically pernicious – aspect of floor-crossing, which we had blithely ignored when first promoting the principle, was the manner in which it was manipulated to fragment the opposition and strengthen, artificially, the ruling party, through a combination of inflated threshold criteria and all manner of taxpayer-funded inducements.

The Federal Council rectified the error of our previous support for floor-crossing and endorsed a decision now to call for its scrapping (duly adopted by the ANC in December 2007). The meeting also endorsed, enthusiastically, my renewed views on the genuine affirmative action steps needed to help the party's makeover (but at the time of writing this process remains incomplete).

Shortly before the election, the ANC civil war erupted afresh as Jacob Zuma lumbered into the frame of the criminal courts as the accused in a rape trial.

Zuma's trial gave us the spectacle of a man who showered after sex with the complainant because 'this minimised the risk of contracting the [HIV/AIDS] disease.' It also spotlighted another persistent issue which had been buried — albeit in a fairly shallow grave — in the aftermath of the ANC's emphatic 1994 victory and their energetic rewriting of history. This revision of history included the suppression of inconvenient human rights lapses during the struggle against apartheid: violence and rape in particular. There were many accounts of sexual abuse against women at various ANC camps around southern Africa. Indeed, Zuma's insouciant manner (in 2007 he became more popular than Mbeki), his disregard for women and his sexual proclivities were apparently the merest reflection of the real situation in ANC-run units during military operations against the South African government.[17]

The media naturally devoted forests of pages to the Zuma trial, especially the prurient and lascivious details which spewed out of the courtroom, consequent to the explicit testimony of the witnesses — not least those of both the complainant and the accused. I thought the correspondent of the London *Financial Times*, John Reed, was utterly correct when he wrote:[18]

'The Zuma trial has laid bare the rainbow nation's shadowy underside. It has highlighted South Africa's problems with violence against women and continuing struggle with HIV/AIDS which affects some six million people. It has rekindled tribalism, a borderline-taboo topic in politics. It has exposed deep divisions over policy and leadership style within the ANC … [The] discord casts a shadow over South Africa's otherwise brightening prospects.'

While Zuma's supporters outside the court were screaming 'burn the bitch' at his accuser, inside parliament yet another debate was held on women's rights.[19] The great, tragic irony was, of course, that Zuma, when deputy president, had led both the government's HIV/AIDS council and its moral regeneration campaign – perhaps explaining, in part, the conspicuous lack of progress on both fronts. But when Zuma was triumphally acquitted, in May 2006, among his supporters and conspiratorialists generally a visible relief gave way to vented anger. The corridors inside and outside parliament buzzed with talk that it was a set-up: he had been 'honey-trapped'. The trial was intended to be the denouement – to seal his presidential ambitions. Not for the first or last time in this saga did this prove to be a gross miscalculation.

But while Zuma's ongoing legal battles both sensationalised and sectionalised the ANC, crime generally preoccupied everyone else.

In the 1980s, during the intense and most violent phase in the struggle against apartheid in the townships of South Africa, I had on occasion attended funerals in Soweto and Alexandra. At these gatherings, priests substituted for political leaders then exiled or imprisoned. The mourners often unfurled the forbidden flags of liberation movements, and fists of defiance were raised as thousands sang for a freedom whose imminence and peaceful arrival appeared exceedingly improbable.

In April 2006, a dozen years after that unlikely freedom had indeed arrived, and with it the hopes of a civil peace underpinned by legitimate order, I attended another funeral. The manicured lawns of Johannesburg's West Park cemetery were a study in contrast to the dustbowl conditions of most township grave sites, and on this day there were no flags or clenched fists or political priests. But there were thousands of mourners present, and there was a terrible anger. It was a funeral service for Brett Goldin, a talented 28-year-old actor whom I had seen perform on the stage, and whose mother, Denise, was a political supporter from Sandton, Johannesburg. The weekend before, Brett and his friend, 27-year-old fashion designer Richard Bloom, had been hijacked at gunpoint on a Saturday night after leaving a dinner party in Cape Town's highend Bakoven suburb. Drug-fuelled gang members from a Cape Flats outfit, as part of a grotesque rites of passage initiation ceremony, had then thrown them into the boot of the car, stripped them naked, and later executed both Brett and Richard. They were then tossed onto the side of the highway where their bodies were subsequently found. This terrible crime, and Brett's theatrical eminence, sent a shudder through the country.

At Brett's funeral, which followed immediately after Richard's, his grief-stricken mother gripped my hand and implored me to ensure that 'Richard and Brett will not have died in vain.' As Douglas Gibson and I left the cemetery I mulled over this despairing plea. In truth there were few public platforms and occasions on which I did not address crime. There were no shortages of policy prescriptions and calls for actions which had been made to government, most of which had been brushed aside.

As we drove towards Douglas's townhouse in Craighall Park, in northern Johannesburg, police yellow tape blocked off access to Hamilton Avenue near his home and we were obliged to detour. We soon discovered this was occasioned by another murder of another person with whom I happened to be acquainted: while the Bloom-Goldin funerals were under way, a widow, Mrs Tessa Goldworthy, who had once run a bookshop which I used to frequent in Sandton, was being murdered in her driveway.

And these terrifying and terrible instances happening simultaneously in the same locale were simply those that touched me personally.

The month before, the four-year-old granddaughter of Transvaal Judge President Bernard Ngoepe, Makgabo Matlala, was murdered in Lenasia, south of Johannesburg. Her 57-year-old nanny was gang-raped by the murderers. It was a robbery, and it took the police, who contrived to make the Keystone Cops appear competent, an entire day to find Makgabo's body, in her family home.

In the same month, April, in KwaZulu-Natal, an elderly couple was at-tacked on their farm by a group of armed thugs who burned the 82-year-old farmer's feet so badly with scalding water that his soles came off. (In fact, violent psychopathy, including the gratuitous use of torture, appeared to be a special and gruesome feature of the increasing severity of attacks on farmers.) And the frequency of farm murders in democratic South Africa exceeded by a wide margin the combined death rate at the height of the Mau Mau insurrection in Kenya and the civil war in Rhodesia respectively.

One of the practical steps that I did take following the brutal Goldin-Bloom murders was to read out in parliament an open letter to President Mbeki written by Brett's impassioned and articulate sister Samantha. She pleaded with the president to use her brother's murder as a spur for de-cisive action against the crime wave. Mbeki never responded to the letter in parliament, nor did he contact the family. Since parliamentary debates were one of the few forums where the president and government minis-ters can be directly challenged, I thought I would use my last State of the Nation debate as Leader, in February 2007, to press the government again on crime. I had received, in late December 2006, another heartfelt letter from a person I had never met.

Her name was Vi Rathbone, and she hailed from Warner Beach on Kwa-Zulu-Natal's South Coast. In perfect handwriting, and at some length, she poured out her anguish about, at the age of 80, having decided to emigrate to Australia. With thousands following the same route, hers was not an exceptional tale. But I sat up and took note when she informed me that she was the grandmother of the well-known rugby player Clyde Rathbone. He had, amidst much local disparagement and patriot-questioning, emigrated a few years before, to Australia, where he had been selected to play rugby for the national team. With her permission, I later read out in parliament a portion of the letter: 'The full story of my grandson Clyde Rathbone's decision to relocate to Australia and play rugby there is not known. His mother is lucky to be alive, as when their home in Warner Beach was broken into the robbers dragged her by the hair to the upstairs balcony and pulled her over the balustrade. She sustained some injuries, but fortunately did not become bedridden for life.'

I wanted parliament, and South Africa, to know that while Vi Rathbone felt obliged to leave South Africa for Australia to be near her family which had fled the country as a consequence of crime, it was also important to hear the heart-wrenching remark which she wrote at the end of her encomium: 'I will miss South Africa, which I love, and I will never run it down.'

I also drew parliament's attention – and that of the government – to the brutal dismemberment, rape and murder of a 14-year-old girl, Thato Radebe, which had occurred that week in Johannesburg. I wanted to underline the message that the criminals drew no distinctions in age, class, colour or geographic location when it came to victim-selection. (In fact, the overwhelming majority of crime victims are black and poor, rather than white and middle-class.) On this occasion in parliament, the government did not ignore the letter, although it did not bother to acknowledge the horror story of 14-year-old Thato.

The normally sensible and balanced minister of Defence, Mosiuoa 'Terror' Lekota,[20] unleashed his guns on the 80-year-old emigrating grandmother. In responding to her patriotic plea and my remarks on crime, Lekota said in parliament: 'Let them go to Australia.' Outside the House, at a press conference, he took the insult much further. It was all of a piece with the infamous call made the year before by the minister notionally entrusted with Safety and Security, Charles Nqakula, that those who complained about crime and demanded government perform its basic duty could either 'whinge or emigrate'. He said that Mrs Rathbone was leaving South Africa because in Australia 'white people are still the law.'[21]

The antipathy between the South African and Australian governments over such issues as Zimbabwe was, by then, well known. I thought, however, that the minister of Defence would have done well to have pondered the reality that many of the emigrants fleeing South Africa were in fact its backbone: boilermakers from Bellville, fitters and turners from Mitchells Plain, and nurses from Soweto.

The ethic of governmental excuse and blame-shifting was a poor substitute for the resolute action required to root out the weeds of crime and corruption – the two objective conditions which continue to militate against the flowering of the new constitutional order.

CHAPTER 20

Exit

Though politicians dream of fame
And hope to win a deathless name,
Time strews upon them when they've gone
The Poppy of oblivion.
TONY BENN

Too much of a good thing can be wonderful.
MAE WEST

I

There were many congratulatory calls after the DA's relatively stunning electoral success in the December 2000 municipal election. With our newly formed party grabbing 23% of the national total, the arrival of two-party politics in South Africa was heralded.

One curve-ball bounced back at me – from my old friend Laurence 'Lacky' Kaplan. Lacky and I had been friends in the army, and had gone through university and articles of clerkship together. He went on to make a fortune as a commodities trader, always retaining his frankness and humour. 'Well, Tone,' he said, 'now's a good time to quit!'

Somewhat taken aback, I asked him to elaborate. 'It will never get any better than this. Go while you are at the top of your game, while they all still want you to stay.'

Lacky's concern with my place in posterity was touching, but impractical. There remained the substantial task of getting the DA to cohere as a party and moving it forward to the next terrain of battle, the majority electorate. Had I known at the end of 2000 what an *annus horribilis* loomed, I would probably have done well to take his advice, but my own stay at the top had to be subordinated – in part – to the needs of the party. It was essentially at my behest and vigorous insistence that the DP had folded its tent into the DA – I could hardly have deserted an entity so recently conceived and comprising such fissiparous elements.

There were many moments over the next six long years when I yearned to let go, to find out who Tony Leon was when not leading a political party, free of the tasks of arbitrating disputes or, as Douglas Gibson put it so piquantly, 'cleaning out the lavatories'.

Increasingly the waters of my own party and South African politics became generally muddy; indeed, at times, downright mephitic.

In 2001 the fight for the soul and allegiances of those NNP councillors being courted to abandon the DA and rejoin the unscrupulous Van Schalkwyk was at its height. Ken Andrew passed on to me a sports slogan: 'Winners don't quit, and quitters don't win.' It was very Nixonian, but I used it to good effect at rallies – and more importantly applied it to myself. I was determined to guide the DA out of the floor-crossing and Harksen morass; that there was some light at the end of the tunnel, not greater darkness.

Certainly, in the run-up to the 2004 elections, we began to win back ground apparently lost through floor-crossing, as proved by successive by-elections. But, as recorded in Chapter 18, 2004 was a disappointment, even though we gained 400 000 new voters – more, as our propaganda ceaselessly pointed out, than any other party. But our quest and hope for even a modest share of the black vote continued to be the political equivalent of the search for the Holy Grail.

On the evening of Thursday 15 April 2004 when, as the results came in, the party gathered for a celebratory function at the Johannesburg Country Club in Auckland Park, I turned to Russel Crystal, who had painstakingly plotted every step I took in the gruelling campaign, and said: 'That's it, Russel, this is my last election.' He did not disagree.

The campaign was planned in a manner that provided me with some rest and always with comfortable accommodation. At one level it was backbreaking, yet at another deeply boring. Ten weeks of public rallies, visiting old-age homes, chatting to children, exhorting the volunteers, and putting up with an ever more hostile media environment had taken its toll. I felt I had gone one round too many.

After the election, however, with a new parliamentary caucus to lead I settled back into leadership. Of course, increasing restlessness was ever-present. I had been leader for a decade – and for most of the earlier nine years, faced terrifying challenges. With time, those challenges had become fairly routine and humdrum. Like a poor man's Alexander the Great, were there any more kingdoms to conquer? The ANC with its increased majority was more arrogant and unresponsive than ever – and while I set about deconstructing its agenda and some of its more ludicrous pretensions, I was clearly not as passionate about the enterprise as I once had been.

The November 2004 party congress in Durban re-elected me unopposed as leader, but my irresolution must have been apparent to those who knew me. Douglas Gibson snapped: 'For God's sake, Tony, if you're going to be the leader, then lead!' That – and a rumoured challenge for the leadership by Helen Zille, which she strongly denied – put the fire back into my belly.

The electoral timetable gave us focus after Durban. The party faced the 2006 municipal elections and needed to be put on the right footing – organisationally, financially and politically.

I could not afford to become too self-absorbed. There were thousands of supporters and activists who looked to me for inspiration and resolve. I was determined not to let them down. Many had made sacrifices for our cause which in their own way were as large as, even greater than, mine – yet received no kudos, no publicity, and no public affirmation.

2

My increasing ambivalence and detachment from politics gave way to the routines of parliament and the demands of the party. Once again I entered the closed universe that had been the habitat of much of my adult working life. But my moth-to-the-flame ambition for party, country and self was clearly reaching some form of burn-out. I was also playing on a wider stage: my overseas odysseys took me to places and encounters that were enough to sharpen and reinvigorate even the most jaded palate.

Attending the Democratic Party National Convention in Boston – in August 2004 – where Senator John Kerry was nominated to take on President George W Bush was an eye-opener to the kind of political extravaganza on a scale that made our domestic politics seem very provincial by comparison (which, I suppose, they objectively were).

On a spiritual level, I had long admired and quoted the words of His Holiness the XIVth Dalai Lama – and read every book and seen the movies made of his life and struggles for Tibet. Then I met him. In March 2006 (after a 350-km road journey from Kashmir to Dharamsala which took a bone-crunching six hours) I finally met and conferred with arguably the world's most extraordinary monk. He combined, in almost perfect measure, deep wisdom and earthy humour. He described his faith as 'simple, my religion is kindness'; and we also met nuns and young children who had escaped the continued persecution of the Chinese overlords in Tibet. This was exposure to a vast universe of discourse and dispute.

A year earlier I had travelled to the heartlands of Tibet's nemesis, the People's Republic of China, where our delegation had been wined and dined. An epic banquet in Beijing put me off Peking duck forever, since we ate the poor bird from beak to webbed foot as the communist mandarins explained their views, with exquisite politeness, but quite plainly, on everything from Taiwan to Tibet. Like good tourists (I was accompanied on the visit by Douglas Gibson, our wives and my head of office, Tim Harris) we clambered up a portion of the Great Wall of China. It is well over six thousand kilometres long, and was built in 400 BC. It is one of the greatest and most enduring architectural wonders of the world.

Yet in sharp contrast – and as an appropriate metaphor for the two Chinas, ancient and modern – we flew a thousand-plus kilometres south-west to the Three Gorges Dam. This extraordinary and environmentally controversial project will be, when completed in 2009, the most powerful dam ever built in the world, and will tame the waters of the Yangtze River, third in size only to the Nile and the Amazon. It will contain the largest hydro-power plant in the world to help meet China's huge energy needs – but the project has involved the relocation of nearly two million people.

Much as one might find such a project inhuman – the consequence of gerontocratic central planning – realpolitik intrudes. China's links to Africa, including our own country, are ever-increasing: its rapacious demand for our natural resources is a key factor helping to fuel Africa's growth cycle.

The contradictions which permeate this impenetrable society are not easily resolved. Early on I found myself in a heated debate with a communist over free markets. As a committed free-marketer, I was used to arguing in favour of dismantling trade barriers, and do not often find myself arguing against them. Yet there I sat, trying to convey to this hardened veteran of the People's Revolution the damaging effect on local production of overly rapid trade liberalisation. This encounter was typical: a country that was once ideologically crippled and poverty-stricken has now turned, through a quarter-century of market-driven reform, ruthlessness and sheer hard work, into a potential superpower.

Such contradictions are inherent in the tension between the economic management of the state and its system of government. Widespread reforms and economic liberalisation have boosted growth to over nine per cent per annum, yet China remains a centralising and, in many ways, an autocratic state which radically limits the freedom of its people.

The current ideology in China – namely 'socialism with Chinese characteristics' – has a kind of genius. It allows China the freedom to relax oppressive state control of domestic economic affairs to fire up economic growth and investment, all the while justifying this (as one high-ranking official did) as the first step in a long journey towards perfect socialism in which private ownership is abolished. This vision is so flexible as to render it meaningless: capitalism winks at socialism and moves right on.

These journeys – and countless others which I will spare the reader – were the agreeable flip side to the routine, sometimes humdrum nature of domestic politics. I took care to remind myself that it was my office, not my sparkling personality, that led to the blizzard of foreign invitations.

The 2005 parliamentary floor-crossing window saw five DA MPs join the ANC. One of them, Dan Maluleke, had chosen to sit next to me at lunch in parliament, having already signed on with the ANC, which he announced that afternoon. This brought me crashing back to earth. If this also was the chemotherapy of politics – as I have described fundraising – I was not sure that I could endure much more of it. The treachery, the view of politics and party choices as a form of job-hopping, was not to me what politics was about nor why I had become a politician. It wasn't that I claimed any moral superiority. But to me, however badly or well I would be treated by my party, I didn't join it because of career enhancement. I belonged because I believed. But it sickened and revolted me (and I am no boy scout) at what a bargain basement business parliament and politics, at many levels, had become.

I kept my eye, however, steadfastly focused on the 2006 municipal poll, and was pleased when we emerged with a strongish hand (not nearly as good as 2000, but better than 2004) (see Chapter 19).

Now I could, with more equanimity and without too many petty urgencies to distract me, contemplate the future – the party's and my own, and the potential severance of these hitherto joined-at-the-hip concepts.

British-American scribe Tina Brown once described the House of Windsor's attempts to lessen the role of Princess Diana as 'a thousand cuts of quotidian smallness'. Her observation was a useful working description for the personalised nature of the ANC's constant attempts to diminish my office, which, over time, cast a pall on my mood. For example, after the 2006 election, at a meeting of parliament's Constitutional Review Committee, ANC members (with the enthusiastic support of the Freedom Front) indicated they were of a mind to amend the section of the Constitution which gave recognition to the leader of the largest opposition party in the National Assembly as 'The Leader of the Opposition'.

In practice – apart from increased office space, staff and a salary incre-
ment – the title meant little. Part of me hoped the ANC would proceed,
since it would reveal – plainly and precisely – their arrogant disdain for
their constitutional opponents. My colleague, Sheila Camerer, who sat on
the committee, described the move as 'spiteful'.

She went on to say: 'The DA believes this spiteful move specifically
targets DA leader, Tony Leon, as the issue was never raised when FW de
Klerk and Marthinus van Schalkwyk were the incumbents.' She pointed out that if the ANC succeeded it would create a negative impression
around the world that the government had become increasingly intolerant
of opposition.

The mean-spiritedness of the plan depressed me. South African politics
had not yet sunk to the level of Uganda, where the opposition leader was
acquitted of trumped-up charges of rape, so flimsy that he did not even
bother to mount a serious defence. He was arrested, his lawyers claimed,
simply to prevent him campaigning in that country's February 2006 presidential election.

But the ANC's proposed jiggery-pokery with the Constitution simply
to diminish my status was nonetheless debilitating. I couldn't help but
think that it had its origins close to the Presidency, if not with the great
man himself. A leading KwaZulu-Natal businessman who had profited
mightily from the ANC's ascent to power – but who liked to keep in with
the opposition, as well, by doling out cash donations at election time –
had recounted to my colleague Mike Ellis how, when he had told Thabo
Mbeki, a few years before, that he had 'greatly enjoyed' a lunch with Tony
Leon, Mbeki had snapped: 'Why do you lunch with that traitor?'

Needless to say, the plan was not proceeded with after I announced my
intention to resign.

One of the real pleasures of my life, for the past twenty years or so, has
been to subscribe to the British magazine, the *Spectator*. High Tory in its
politics, irreverent in its put-downs, and rumbustious in its forthright and
well-written opinions, its arrival in my home invariably lightened my
mood and was my weekly intellectual fix. (The late Tertius Myburgh once
recounted that he viewed its appearance in his post box with the same
pleasure he got as a child on seeing a copy of the *Beano*.)

During various visits to London I had met members of its editorial staff
and become quite friendly with the extraordinary Boris Johnson, the tousle-haired editor and Tory MP for Henley (and, latterly, mayor of London),
whose somewhat deliberate bumbling lightly hid a piercing intelligence

and massive intellect. Boris was always warmly supportive of my opposition efforts down south, and even invited me to sit in on his editorial conferences, which, at face value, appeared so rambling and discursive that I often wondered how such an excellent and crisp magazine was produced each week. But aside from Boris's personality and humour, he was – and remains – a brilliant and incisive writer.

It was winter in Cape Town (mid-July 2006) when, sitting in my study, and lazily glancing through a copy of the *Weekly Telegraph*, I encountered a piece by Boris ruminating on the reasons why Tony Blair was so reluctant to exit Downing Street, which I read with close interest. He wrote:

'It is a necessary fact of political biology that we never know when our time is up. Long after it is obvious that we are goners, we continue to believe it is "our duty" to hang on, with cuticle-wrenching tenacity, to the privileges of our post. We kid ourselves that we must stay because we would be "letting people down" or that there is a "job to be finished". In reality we are just terrified of the come-down … [All] politicians are masters of procrastination, but there is no day they find easier to postpone than the day of their own resignation.'[1]

I saw in Boris's piece my own political epiphany. Surely, now, I should go? I totted up the sums and realised I had been leader of the Prog-orientated opposition longer than anyone else. By the time of the next congress I would have served in the post for just on 13 years. Steytler, mostly out of parliament, did 12; Eglin, in two stretches, a combined ten years; Slabbert, seven; and De Beer six. Only in the United Party had Sir de Villiers Graaff stayed on for 21 years, and with each election he led an ever-diminishing party.

I had been fortunate to preside over growth, but if I stayed on too long it could all start going in reverse. In any event, the party was now far more stable and in reasonable fighting trim. I was not, in truth, certain that there was much more I could do to take it further than it now stood.

Aside from revisiting the gallery of past leaders, I was determined to give my successor enough time and space to establish himself (or herself, as I reckoned with some foresight) to stamp authority on the party before the next national election over two years hence. Having lived through the trauma of Slabbert's precipitous exit, I had no wish for the party to be shattered by another sudden departure.

If Boris Johnson's piece rang a warning bell, it was the arrival of a far plainer but more immediately relevant memorandum by Ryan Coetzee which convinced me to set in process my own resignation. Marked 'strictly confidential',[2] it was entitled 'The DA and Black Voters'. It was, in typical Ryan style, closely reasoned and coldly logical. It outlined why the party had failed to attract significant numbers of blacks; elaborated on serial obstacles in the party's quest; and went on to outline how the DA needed to change its identity in order to rediscover its 'heart' – one which would beat in sympathy with the country's majority.

The paper warned, correctly, that should the party simply give up on the objective of winning black votes, this would be 'a disaster' for it and South Africa. Over time, demographics would whittle down the party's current base, and the failure of the DA would mean the country would have to forego the prospect of a non-racial alternative to the ANC – which was, after all, the *raison d'être* for founding the party in the first place.

Ryan concluded: 'It is unclear whether or not it is possible to change the DA's identity. In this regard, the key thing to understand is that the DA's identity is simply a reflection of the identity of the people in it, in particular of its leadership and, most especially, of its national leader. The identity of the party's leader and the identity of the party are impossible to separate.

'In order for the DA's leadership to have an identity with which black South Africans can identify, one of two things must happen: either those leaders must develop that identity if they don't already have it, or they must make way for others that do …

'At this point the fact is that the DA doesn't have enough existing leaders with the right identity, and there don't seem to be others in the party with the requisite leadership skills.

'It may be possible to change the DA's identity by importing new leaders into the party from the outside. The question then is, are there people on the outside who have the right identities and are willing to take up leadership positions in the DA?'

He cautioned: 'If the DA's identity is to change, its leaders need to change, or be replaced by people with the right identity.'

I knew Ryan well enough to know that he actually regarded my continuance as leader as indispensable to our project going forward. He didn't cite, or know of, an acceptable or credible alternative. However, approaching fifty, I felt I was unlikely to undergo a substantial makeover or re-invention. If the leader was standing on a plateau, it could in time become a precipice – in which case it was certainly time to depart.

More to the point, I had had enough of the job. I didn't think I could do much more with it; and leading an opposition without immediate prospects of power was akin to making bricks without straw.

The following month I convened a carefully selected group of people ostensibly to discuss Ryan's document, but actually to tell them something few could have discerned: I was going to quit.

The people I chose to inform were those in high party positions whom I believed I could absolutely trust. I had no desire to unsettle the party and preside over a panicky and disorderly succession by announcing my intention too long in advance. But I needed to level with my inner circle. Thus in mid-August at a hotel in Dunkley Square, near parliament, I told Ryan, Douglas, Russel Crystal, James Selfe, Greg Krumbock and Mike Ellis of my decision. They had been with me the longest, literally from the beginning when we turned around the DP and created the DA.[3]

I did not wish them to dissuade me. I was completely and utterly resolved after stating my intention. There was silence, but soon enough, as the shock dissipated, led by James, the participants each requested reconsideration, having been completely taken aback. In the back-and-forth which followed, Ryan sent me a note:

'I knew you would say this today and yet I still feel very emotional about it. I suspect that even you don't know how much you have achieved.'

While I agreed – out of friendship – with James's suggestion that I 'reconsider', there was no turning back: I felt an immense lightening of that invisible but heavy load which leadership places on one's back. I had no clear idea what I would do after exiting, but like Mr Micawber trusted that 'something will turn up'.

We agreed to keep the tightest lid on the decision, since we estimated that the party should be informed only six to eight weeks before its congress. When, for logistical reasons, the congress was postponed to May 2007, I judged I should make the announcement immediately after the conclusion of the State of the Nation debate in parliament in mid-February. Aside from consideration for the party's internal stability – which a leadership vacuum was likely to cause – I didn't fancy a long recessional for myself either. It was not in my nature to operate as a lame-duck leader.

The party was engaged in a long-overdue but internally difficult reengineering exercise to overhaul its structures and cut down the jealously guarded fortresses of its myriad local barons. Instability at the top would be an impediment to this process. The news remained confined within the circle of confidence.

3

In November I set off for the UK to address the South African Business Club in London and to speak in a debate at the Oxford Union on climate change – a topic of great universal relevance, but of which, until I started preparing, I knew disgracefully little. Fortunately Gareth Morgan, our international relations liaison, was both expert and passionate on the topic. Gareth and I then flew to Morocco to attend the Liberal International Congress, of which I was a vice president.

Coups generally happen when the president is abroad. As Gareth (to whom I had not confided my leadership intentions) and I were driving through the rugged splendours of the Atlas mountains, matters were being driven in a particular direction at home.

Shortly after my return I was told – in agitation and consternation – that Dr Tertius Delport had been trawling the corridors of parliament and whispering there, and at a regular Acacia Park braaivleis for DA MPs, that *'Tony moet loop en Helen [Zille] moet sy plek neem'* (Tony must go and Helen must replace him). Other colleagues confirmed the essence of this. I was now in a dilemma: Delport did not know that he was pushing against a door I had already unlocked.

I requested him to attend a meeting, but he advised my secretary he was 'busy with the Magistrate's Commission' of which he was a member, and could meet only in early December. When we did eventually speak he denied all knowledge of the rumours, swearing: 'I was only the messenger.' This was at considerable variance with the retelling of others, but there I left the issue for the moment.

Matters came to a premature head when I was advised that *Finweek* (a financial journal), an unlikely vehicle for a political putsch, was probing the relative merits of Zille's leadership mettle and the apparent demerits of my own brand.

On the morning of Friday 24 November I was travelling to Cape Town airport to fly to Johannesburg to attend a series of functions which were to culminate in a large fundraising dinner in Krugersdorp. Ironically the two guest speakers were Helen Zille – then enjoying an enormous public bounce from her besieged Cape Town mayoralty – and me. En route to the airport I heard the SAFM announcer doing a regular review of the weekly media. He turned to *Finweek*, scheduled to be published on Monday, and said: 'Here's something of interest. *Finweek's* cover article is about why Helen Zille would make a better leader of the opposition than Tony Leon.'

My options seemed to boil down to two. I could ignore the brouhaha which the article would create – but how to answer the obvious enquiry 'Are you standing again as leader?' without dissembling? Or I could fast-forward my announcement from the following year to Sunday or Monday. I was determined, however, not to allow the magazine to explode a mushroom cloud over what had been – in my own mind until now, at least – a carefully considered and planned exit strategy.

By the time I arrived in Johannesburg later that morning, the intrepid public relations operative (and Russel Crystal's wife) Lauren Winchester assured me she would obtain a copy of *Finweek*, even though it was due to hit the streets only on Monday. Midway through a lunch with a foreign diplomat, she burst into the hotel dining room waving the offending item. The cover showed an attractively posed shot of Helen Zille and the headline 'Move over Tony'. Inside was a hatchet job of note, with Richard Calland and Patricia de Lille commenting negatively on my leadership attributes and extolling Zille. Only Ryan Coetzee's affirming comments and those of an anonymous MP (Dene Smuts, I later discovered) provided any semblance of balance.[4]

I knew I would have to move quickly and tear up my carefully conceived timetable. Nonetheless I still got through three party events. In the far West Rand town of Randfontein, where the enthusiastic party organisation of the old political trouper Roy Harris had converted this one-time CP/FF fortress into strong DA territory, my leadership was held in deeply felt regard. The occasion was used to shower me with various gifts for my looming 50th birthday – of which a bottle of Johnnie Walker Blue Label whisky would prove most medicinal for the fraught 36 hours that followed.

I then arrived in Krugersdorp for my double act with Zille. I knew she had been made aware of both the article and my anger at its content and timing – although, in fairness, she had no idea of my intentions. She looked as if she had seen a ghost – which of course, I would soon become, politically. In a serious and sombre speech she interspersed lashings of praise for my leadership. I managed to give an enthusiastic and witty performance, leaving my audience with no hint that this was, in Krugersdorp at least, my last hurrah.

At about midnight I was deposited in my suite at the Rosebank Hotel. It had been a day of high emotions, but I was not done yet. Informal soundings from my inner group and family members fortified my decision to go public with an announcement on Sunday. Michal, who was scheduled to depart for Israel the next day, managed to postpone her trip by 24 hours. Ryan and Gareth van Onselen would also arrive in Johannesburg the next day to set up the logistics for the press conference. I advised James Selfe to arrange for a teleconference of the Federal Executive for Sunday morning. All was moving into place, except what was I going to say and how was I to couch my announcement? I knew this was one draft no one else could write.

673

In a pair of shorts and T-shirt, I took a generous swig of the gift from Randfontein, and wrote out a draft in longhand. When I passed it around my small circle the next day, no one thought it necessary to change a word. This is what I wrote:

RELEASE: EMBARGO AGAINST DELIVERY: 'MISSION ACCOMPLISHED'
STATEMENT BY TONY LEON MP,
   LEADER OF THE DEMOCRATIC ALLIANCE,
SUNDAY 26 NOVEMBER 2006 AT 11H00.

I wish to announce today that I will not seek, nor will I accept, nomination for the leadership of the Democratic Alliance when the party Federal Congress convenes in May 2007.

I am deeply conscious of the enormous responsibility that the Democratic Alliance – and its predecessors – has placed in my hands since 1994, when I was first elected leader of the Democratic Party. It is my wish to discharge the inevitably difficult issue of succession in the most responsible and least divisive manner possible.

After very careful consideration and intense personal introspection, I first made this decision, entirely of my own accord, in August of this year. I communicated my views at a meeting – which I convened in that same month – to the senior line function officials of the party, including the chairman of our Federal Executive, the chief executive officer and the parliamentary chief whip.

They were unanimously of the view that I should not relinquish the leadership at the congress and should lead the party into the 2009 election. However, for the reasons which follow, I could not, with regret, accede to their request.

In the light of my commitment to the party and its internal stability it was my intention to announce my decision closer to the congress in May 2007. However, speculation has already arisen – prematurely and publicly – in a different quarter. I have no wish, nor do our party and its millions of supporters deserve, to be involved in debate and a contestation on either my merits or an argument regarding continuance in office, which is entirely moot and academic in view of the conclusion which I had myself reached four months ago.

The reasons for my decision are as follows:

- First, by May 2007, when I intend to relinquish the party leadership and the office of Leader of the Opposition, I would have been party leader for almost 13 years. I regard this as the absolute upper limit of effective leadership. There is a danger, over time, no matter how healthy or vigorous the internal workings of an organisation and no matter how effective its public representatives, that the identity and branding of the party will be almost completely absorbed into the identity and personality of its leader. This is not good for the health of the party – or the nation – and, come to think of it, not particularly good for my health either! In other words, it is time for the party to move on, and for me to move on as well.
- Secondly, in view of the fact that the next general election is scheduled for the first quarter of 2009, I believe that it is only fair and proper that my successor should have a reasonable time to establish his or her leadership and to engage the public and the party with their vision, both for the opposition and for the country.

There is, of course, never an ideal time to depart. There are always reasons which can be advanced, quite legitimately, as to why an extension in office is preferable. However, in reaching this decision, I was always determined that my successor should commence their term of office with every possible advantage.

I do believe that I bequeath to my successor – and to the party and the country – an organisation which is stable, united, in good shape and size and, most importantly, which is going forward.

It is certainly almost unrecognisable from the shattered organisation I was bequeathed after the 1994 election. Today we have two million supporters, 57 members in both houses of parliament, 47 provincial MPs across all nine provinces, 1 100 municipal councillors, and control of over twenty municipalities in three provinces.

While I intend to continue to discharge my role as leader energetically until the last hour of my last day in office, permit me to make an observation about the immediate future. The DA needs to engage in an intelligent and constructive debate about its future leadership and direction. I have seen too many political leaders and politicians leave the scene and their post trying to dictate and determine their own succession. Such efforts are always, in my view, a mistake. As we have seen in our own country and elsewhere in the world, inevitably they fail and end in rancour and recrimination.

I wish to make it clear that I do not belong to this dismal school of political leadership. Our party must freely and democratically choose its leadership, without let or hindrance.

I do, however, give my successor one categorical assurance: when the party has chosen its new leader I will give that person my loyal support, just as my predecessor, while he was alive, gave me his – something which I have also been humbled to enjoy from the overwhelming majority of DA public representatives and supporters in all my years in office.

I have been enormously privileged – and am deeply grateful to my party and to the people of South Africa – to have been given the opportunity to lead this party for so long. I have enjoyed the great victories our party has achieved, and have been fortified in the defeats, which are inevitable in such a business, by the sustained support of my colleagues and our many foot-soldiers on the ground.

I have tried my level best to advance our interests and the national interest as well. I have always believed and tried to advance the principles and grand vision for South Africa embedded in our noble Constitution, which document I was also privileged to have had a hand in crafting.

In 1994 I set out – with a handful of colleagues – with a mission and a purpose: to establish and entrench the concept of opposition as a legitimate and absolutely essential cornerstone of our new democracy. This was, and remains, no easy task in either our country or continent. However, as our battalions have grown and advanced, and as our cause has taken root – often on hitherto stony ground – I believe that the mission has been accomplished.

It will be up to my successor and the party – which I have served in its various incarnations for nearly forty years – to take it forward and to lead it to the next level.

I intend to remain as a member of parliament until its term of office expires in 2009, by which time I will have been an MP for 20 years, which is also, I believe, the outer limits for effective national service in the country's highest legislative body.

On a personal note, I would like to acknowledge the support, which I never asked for but always received, from my family and friends, particularly my wife Michal, my late mother Sheila, my father Ray and my brother Peter. They and the countless men and women of the Democratic Alliance have ensured that no matter how difficult and arduous the task, there was always love and loyalty to sustain me. For this and for so many other blessings which I have received I will always be intensely grateful.

4

I felt, as a courtesy, that I should advise Thabo Mbeki of my decision. I was conscious now that one of my unhappy bequests to my successor was a dysfunctional relationship with the president. It was too easy for me to think it was entirely at his behest that this was so. At about 9 pm on that Saturday evening, by arrangement, his office phoned (he was at an Imbizo in the Eastern Cape) and we had a slightly stilted conversation, he no doubt surprised either at my decision or that I should be advising him of it in advance. After a brief chat, he wished me well – but when he paid tribute to me in parliament two months later he noted his appreciation of the 'courtesy I had done him' of informing him in advance of the announcement. Like my late grandmother, Ray, he set a high premium on good manners.

The following morning I began calling select MPs and party elders who would not be on the teleconference. Colin Eglin provided as ever a sage word: 'You won't feel so good now, but in a few days you will start to feel a great sense of relief.' Theuns Botha and Kraai van Niekerk expressed dismay, and our young MP and national spokesman, Motlatjo Thetjeng, urged reconsideration. But the die was cast and my entourage moved on to the Hyatt hotel for the press conference.

The room was packed with journalists, editors, numerous local MPs and councillors, and a sprinkling of personal friends I had invited. Michal sat with me and the party top structure up front, and James Selfe introduced me. I managed to get through it until the end when I read out the last paragraph. The memory of my mother, gone to her rest five years before, choked me. She had so ardently made my causes her own, and had taken such immense pride in whatever I had accomplished – and at the end of it all, it was only her memory I could invoke. I saw that some of my colleagues and friends, Ian Davidson, Janet Semple and Lesley Goodall, were openly weeping.

Public reactions varied. The ANC Youth League compared me to Adolf Hitler. In contrast the chief rabbi of South Africa phoned to tell me my place in eternity had been assured. IFP president Mangosuthu Buthelezi – apparently deeply shocked – was as ever graceful and generous: 'I am proud to call Mr Leon a friend as well as a political colleague. Whatever we thought of Mr Leon's acerbic and robust style of opposition … there is no doubt that he is a staunch patriot to the tips of his fingers.'[5]

Writing in the *Citizen*, Andrew Kenny expressed fulsome praise:[6] 'South Africa owes a debt of gratitude to FW de Klerk and Nelson Mandela for delivering our democracy. But it also owes a great gratitude to Tony Leon for defending our democracy with the utmost clarity and vigour.

'More than anyone else in the past 12 years, Leon has shown the world we pass the test of true democracy: we have a genuine opposition, loyal to South Africa but unafraid to criticise the faults of the ruling party, and to criticise it loudly for all the honest world to hear.

'In 1994 the DP won 1,7% of the votes and was a small opposition party. It now has more than 12% (the greatest increase of any party in South Africa) and is the official opposition. This is mainly because of Leon. Tony Leon, who will step down next year, has done wonderful service for South Africa. He is a great liberal and a great patriot.'

Allister Sparks, whom I had met face-to-face precisely once, weighed in with the gratuitous remark that I 'lacked warmth and charm';[7] while in oxymoronic tribute-rebuke, commentator Xolela Mangcu described me as 'a brilliant strategist but poor leader'.[8]

I actually thought, on balance, it was *Business Day* – often a frequent critic – which provided the most balanced assessment.[9] Under the head-line 'The New Opposition' it commented: 'The leaders of political parties, even those in opposition, very rarely go willingly. They usually have to be prised out of office. This makes Democratic Alliance (DA) leader Tony Leon's [decision] to step down next year unusual and, upon reflection, admirable.

'Between now and the DA's Federal Congress in May many people, particularly those who both worked with him and voted for him, will be trying to decide exactly what Leon's legacy is. A successor will also have to be chosen. Neither will be easy. From the moment he upstaged Helen Suzman's hand-picked successor in the Houghton constituency in 1989 to this weekend's announcement of his planned resignation, as leader Leon has seldom been far from controversy.

'He is by most accounts difficult to work for and to work alongside. Indeed, the relentless pace at which he works is legendary within the party. No one worked harder for the electoral successes which the party achieved after its profound drubbing in the first democratic election in 1994. Also legendary is his impatience with those who work for him if things are not going well …

'That may change in the hands of someone who can reposition the party in an attempt to succeed where Leon failed – to attract significant numbers of black voters. And that will certainly require authentic black leadership. Unless a powerful new vision can be created and implemented by strong and capable leaders, the Tony Leon legacy – the idea of opposition – will wither and die as voters increasingly lose interest.'

It was quite clear from the acres of comment and correspondence that my departure from political leadership would be every bit as contested as my arrival. On the Thursday following my announcement I was busy in my parliamentary office dealing with media interviews and answering a mountain of letters ('I should resign more often,' I quipped to my staff), when Nelson Mandela rang from his home in Maputo, Mozambique. It was vintage Madiba. He bantered about 'giving me such a shock at my vast age with your decision', but then intoned, more seriously (and I hoped accurately), 'You know, Tony, you will be missed much more than you might realise, because you have played such a very important role in our country.' I was deeply touched.

The one issue on which I was resolved not to interfere with – or influence – was my succession. In the new year the party was to embark on a series of open forums to give the membership an opportunity to weigh up and assess any would-be successor. There was plenty of precedent, both locally and internationally, as to why leaders should not try to rule from the political grave, as it were. I well remembered the mutual bitterness created between Helen Suzman and me when she supported, unsuccessfully, my opponent for the Houghton nomination, and how it cast a pall over her own retirement and my entry into parliament. And, of course, South Africa was paralysed by the crisis caused by the subterranean desire of Thabo Mbeki not to be succeeded by Jacob Zuma.

The person whom the press immediately dubbed as my likely successor came calling just days after my announcement. Helen Zille was deeply discomfited by the suggestion that she had been complicit in either the Delport manoeuvrings or the *Finweek* article. She pointed out that she had agreed to the interview and photo-shoot on the basis that it was a profile of her mayoralty, not an attempt to grab my position. My decision had startled her, since she had thought I would not consider going before the

2009 general election. I had no reason – or evidence – to doubt her word, and we then went on, in a more relaxed manner, to discuss whether she would indeed be a candidate.

She told me she was under 'immense pressure' to declare her candidacy, but that she would only decide 'after very careful consideration'. In the event, she only finally declared her hand in March 2007, by which time the popular momentum which had gathered in support of her candidacy placed her in an unbeatable position.

Objectively, the biggest obstacle to her leadership was her mayoralty of Cape Town. I expressed some doubt as to whether two such disparate and time-consuming roles – mayor and party leader – were capable of successful combination. She listened carefully, and went away. Zille ultimately decided that she could in fact do justice to the two positions. At the time of writing, this arrangement appears to work tolerably well. I remain today, however, of the same opinion I expressed to Helen then: the national opposition needs to be led and motivated from a national platform which only parliament – notwithstanding its flaws – provides.

In the interregnum I had various discussions with the two candidates who had declared themselves earlier than Zille. I had walked a relatively long road together with the party chairman, Joe Seremane. I had sat next to him in parliament for several years and he had shown me the anonymous notes he received from various ANC MPs after he had made a speech, accusing him of being 'the white boss's boy' and various other juvenile insults.

He was a man of iron character and steely resolve. His years on Robben Island prevented him from being swayed by either the blandishments of flattery or the cold calculation of insult. He had been, at all times, most loyal and cheerful. However, at 69 I doubted whether he would relish all the tasks of leadership – from fundraising to strategising, which had never particularly excited him. I also told him that in my frank assessment he would not beat Helen Zille, should she stand. He did not, at this stage of his career, need the potential humiliation of a resounding defeat.

Joe listened carefully, but offered no comment. He duly declared his candidacy, but his campaign never went into high gear, as the ultimate result reflected.

Athol Trollip was a horse of a very different colour. Completely trilingual in English, Xhosa and Afrikaans, he had impressed me with his performance as Eastern Cape leader, welding together a very fractious party and growing its base in a no-nonsense fashion. He also had youth on his side, being five years younger than me (Zille was seven years, and

Seremane nearly two decades, older than me). However, Trollip's light had been hidden from much of the party, and certainly from the public, as he ploughed his political furrow in the remote provincial capital of Bhisho. Certain key members of my inner circle were actually backing his candidacy – but I declined to make any public endorsement.

I did, however, tell Trollip that he had little to lose by losing, as he eventually and predictably did. Zille, through her own efforts and merits, created a wind of excitement and approbation in the party and the public. Her considerable attributes were amplified by a hugely supportive media: not an advantage my leadership had enjoyed. Her accession, in the locution of former CIA director, George Tennant, was a 'slam dunk'.

My family, close friends and I celebrated my 50th birthday in high style in South America, en route from Buenos Aires to Rio de Janeiro. I would be returning to a political stage on which I would soon not be starring.

The 2007 State of the Nation debate in February was my last as Leader of the Opposition. I set out what I believe to have been the successes and failures of 13 years of democratic rule. It was, I reminded an unusually attentive audience, the equivalent of South Africa's bar-mitzvah, which heralded the onset of maturity in a young person's – or nation's – life.

The ever-escalating crime wave and the response to it by business threw into sharp and uncomfortable relief the shortcomings and deficits of our brand of democracy. Spurred by the murder of famed Zulu historian David Rattray early in the new year, a leading bank – FNB – had been emboldened to commence a R20-million campaign to obtain a positive and sympathetic response from the seemingly disengaged Mbeki by inviting the public to petition him, via postcards, with their own crime stories.

Disgracefully, I thought, the supine leadership of Business South Africa muscled in and after a visit from the minister of Safety and Security, FNB capitulated and abandoned the campaign. Such pathetic knee-bending in the face of government pressure pointed out the fragility of our democracy. I drew on the words of the former Soviet prisoner of conscience, Natan Sharansky, whom I had met in Israel, to which he had immigrated, and where he achieved ministerial office. Sharansky had drawn an important and influential distinction between a 'free society' and a 'fear society' (which he tested by positing the consequences for a person who walked into a town square and denounced the government).[10] Drawing on the unhappy FNB campaign abortion, I told parliament:

'In 1994, we made the choice to become a free society, constitutionalising our choice two years later. Yet sometimes we display the characteristics of a fear society. A major characteristic of the latter is limited space for criticism. That is why the effective muzzling of the FNB campaign was disturbing and disappointing.

'As a leader it is finally always better to ensure that the space for criticism is protected. Tolerance of criticism wins respect; suppression of it breeds resentment.'

I also had in mind the all-out war raging in the ANC about Mbeki's own succession, which, unlike the DA's now open contest, was being ferociously waged behind closed doors and via media leaks. Much of the criticism was being directed against the president himself, widely regarded as being utterly intolerant of dissenting views and opposing opinions. The SACP deputy secretary-general had, a few years before, been upbraided for suggesting that the smothering of internal opposition within the ANC had amounted to a 'Zanufication' of the party.

However, in his reply, Mbeki was unusually generous in his response to me, as recorded in *Hansard*:

'I am certain that all of us will miss his lively engagement as a party leader in the public debate. That must and will continue, whatever our views about the arguments he advanced and the manner in which he advanced those arguments.'

As a parting shot, he also decided to elevate me up the canine chain, declaring: 'From where I sit in the government benches, I never had the courage to argue that he served merely as a chihuahua, because indeed he had the bark of a bull-terrier.'[11]

The fight for my succession appeared to be orderly and reasonably conducted, although it had all the hallmarks of a one-horse race. As the party prepared to gather for its congress in early May, I arranged a farewell meeting with Mbeki. I sought no publicity for the visit, but hoped by this gesture that we could end our relationship on better terms than before. The Presidency, however, had other ideas, and when we met in the Union Buildings there were present a battery of cameramen, TV operatives and a roomful of bantering journalists. It was our first formal meeting in the eight years of his presidency. Mbeki had clearly decided that nothing became my office so much as my leaving it!

With the media battalion escorted out, Mbeki and I had an animated chat about old times: the state of our respective parties, my likely successor (although I politely refrained from enquiring about his), and the challenges facing the country. He was warm, engaging and very frank: exactly the opposite of how he had been (to me, at least) throughout his presidency and reminiscent of the person I had found so animated and forthright as Mandela's deputy. The enigma and the contradictions around his personality remained unanswered, and the fissionable nature of our latter-day relationship went unaddressed, although it appeared – at that moment – to have largely dissipated.

He escorted me to my car; we shook hands again; and I departed wondering how differently matters might have turned out but for the vagaries of our political and personal dealings.

I was now literally in the last lap – and days – of my leadership. On the Friday night before the congress, the party held an awesome function for me at the former Hyde Park residence of one-time apartheid oil trader Mario Chiavelli, now a sumptuous public facility – 'Summer Place'. It was a warm occasion, with splendid tributes from Bobby Godsell, Mangosuthu Buthelezi and Mosiuoa Lekota, the ANC chairman, which gave an ecumenical touch to what was largely a gathering of the party faithful.

Helen Suzman was present in a wheelchair, and received, appropriately, many tributes as well. She had previously indicated that, in view of her frail health, she would only stay for 15 minutes. But the atmosphere that night was clearly agreeable, and she stayed on beyond 10 pm. Most touchingly for me, aside from the presence of so many people who had been with me on what I described as my long, incredible and exciting journey, was the company that night of two of my best friends and political allies, Brian Doctor, who arrived from London, and Cecil Bass, from Australia. They had been with me at the very start, and were here now at the end.

The family was also present: my then 82-year-old father from Durban; Noa from Rhodes University, looking more than ever like Angelina Jolie as she had shed her customary jeans and jersey for an altogether more glamorous black ensemble. Etai – more a friend than a stepson – accompanied Michal and me. I decided to speak unscripted, and made light-hearted references to everyone present. For my own family I dredged up the remark I had made at our wedding six years before: 'I have great sympathy for the Palestinians because I know what it is like to live under Israeli occupation.'

If lightness and informality of touch was appropriate for the occasion, a degree of heavy lifting had gone into my final leader's speech which I was to deliver the next day. Joel Pollak, from Harvard, had volunteered an excellent draft. But I needed to conjoin the personal with the political: to talk a little of my own background and the impulses which drove me into politics and sustained me for so many years.

I wanted to convey to the delegates and the country that although we had won some electoral battles, our greater net losses at the ballot box had been offset by victories elsewhere. As it happened, the previous November, one of the most significant economists of the 20th century, Milton Friedman, had died at 94. In its editorialised tribute to him, *The Economist* reprinted a paragraph from his memoirs, co-written with his wife Rose. 'Judged by practice,' they declared, 'we have been, despite some successes, mostly on the losing side. Judged by ideas, we have been on the winning side.'[12]

Would that be my own political epitaph? What I truly wanted to convey to the party was just how important, ground-breaking and deeply relevant our ideas remained; and how we needed to continue to 'take them into the thick of the fight for a better South Africa'. After a lot of last-minute fiddling, and rephrasing, early on Saturday morning I was ready for the congress – which would turn out to be a one-day love-fest for me, on the Saturday, and on Sunday would be focused on electing my successor and handing the reins over to her.

I could feel the love and support – and no doubt relief from some – as I entered the congress hall in Gallagher Estate. Russel, Greg and the team had prepared what I called a 'five-tissue special', with a video casting my leadership in extravagantly heroic terms, followed by various leadership figures delivering from the stage paeans of fulsome praise. It was all heady stuff, and I particularly relished Robin Carlisle's put-down of my many critics within the liberal circle: 'If it weren't for Tony,' he declared, 'liberalism over the past ten years would have died of malnutrition.'

Into this semi-North Korean arena of adulation I delivered my final speech. I suppose, objectively, I could have read out a grocery list, and they might well have cheered me off anyway. But in my message to the faithful inside (and those beyond the party walls)[13] I wanted to give an affirmation of courage and hope in carrying the cause onward. I had shed tears in its preparation, but was dry-eyed and clear-voiced in presentation.

I concluded my 40-minute address by reminding the audience of the indispensability of courage in the years ahead. 'All is not lost if courage remains. ... We can make South Africa great. We can fulfil the dream of freedom. We can do it if, together, we have the faith to trust, the courage to endure, and the resolution to build. Good luck. God bless you. And goodbye.'

One person in the audience who was considerably more lachrymose than me that morning was the black academic Sipho Seepe, who wrote about the congress a few days later in his column in *Business Day*.[14] He declared:

'At the risk of losing my friends, I admit that I was moved to tears when Tony Leon gave his farewell speech ... [He] was in his element – almost evangelical. I was moved by his tenacity; his courage to stand up for what he believes in, whatever the consequences. I was moved by his achievements in a difficult terrain. I appreciated the emotional toll it must have taken on Leon in the past ten years as Leader of the Opposition. He had to contend with many insults, character assassination and labelling.

'Imploring the tear-filled and racially diverse crowd, he observed: "Sometimes sustaining your belief and your value system is hard, when the tide is against you, when the majority is of another opinion, or when the task seems futile."'

The next day I performed my final remaining task. Like a Hollywood presenter at the Oscars, I was handed the envelope in which the delegates' votes had been tabulated. I read out the result: 'The next leader of the Democratic Alliance is Helen Zille.'

She made her way, at the head of a triumphal march of her many supporters who snaked across the hall, to the stage. It was now her moment, and her party to lead. We embraced and waved. Helen was now the gravitational pull around which the party would revolve.

I stepped back and then walked down, one final time, off the platform and into Michal's arms – into the future which now beckoned. My political mission was complete. It was time for renewal.

PART FIVE

THE FUTURE

CHAPTER 21

Future Imperfect

You had all the advantages ... but you chose to act as if you had never
been moulded into civil society and had to begin everything anew.
You began ill, because you began by despising everything that belonged to you.
You set up your trade without capital.

EDMUND BURKE

I have also worked under minority and majority forms of nationalism.
The former, in my experience, has nothing whatsoever to recommend it,
and the latter a good deal less than its protagonists would have one believe.
Nationalism, exclusivist by nature and guarded by zealots,
tends to marginalise not only outsiders
but sections of its own citizenry.

CHARLES VAN ONSELEN

Among all forms of mistake, prophecy is the most gratuitous.

GEORGE ELIOT

I

One afternoon in about 1992 I found myself in a Sea Point restaurant engaged in discussion with Dennis Davis – the impish and amusing legal academic and later High Court judge. South Africa was at the height of its tumultuous political transition. Although a man of the Left, Davis's social – if not ideological – flexibility allowed us to maintain a friendship.

Dennis was more excited than usual. He described how film-maker Roberta Durrant had been commissioned by SABC-TV to produce a series which he, Davis, was to present. Its ambitious mandate was to inform viewers of the range of contentious political and economic issues then dominating the constitutional negotiations; allowing some of the leading politicians ('you among them', Dennis advised temptingly) to debate them.

It is, perhaps, an interesting commentary that the state broadcaster, then in the process of freeing itself from the shackles of obedience to the National Party worldview, should have initiated such a project. Initiation and realisation are always separate, but the programme was indeed broadcast over the next year or two. Yet like much else from that exhilarating period, the 'Prague spring' at Auckland Park – where the voice of the state immures itself – was not long for South Africa. The SABC is today, once again, neo-Soviet in its obeisance to state power: the only difference is that today it genuflects before African, rather than Afrikaner, national authority (as I relate in Chapter 12).

Dennis told me that the series was provisionally entitled 'Hypotheticals'. I told him that while I thought the idea excellent, the title was exceedingly dull. 'Well, what would you suggest, Tone?' he enquired. Reaching back to my barely remembered school Latin grammar, I suggested 'Future Imperfect'. And so the series was named.

'Future Imperfect' remains a useful, appropriately ambiguous, working description for what might become – hypothetically, one might say – the next phase in South Africa. However, I am reminded of the perils of prediction, whether expert or amateur. A few years ago, *The Economist* confidently predicted that the price of crude oil would plunge to US$10 a barrel. At the time of writing, it is touching the US$150/barrel mark. Locally, former editor and newspaper boss Steve Mulholland once archly told me, 'Ever since I was five years old, I had been told that South Africa has only five years left before it explodes. Well, I'm now seventy.'

I often thought about the future as I listened to Thabo Mbeki's presidential speeches in parliament. I have recounted how within the brief span of a dozen years of democracy, that body became little more than a ceremonial relic, more engaged in all manner of pageants and celebrations of state power than in a serious-minded or substantive checking and balancing of governmental authority.

While on occasion during his presidency Mbeki used his appearances to demonise phantom enemies in the opposition and elsewhere, more often than not his State of the Nation speeches trumpeted forth a raft of his government's achievements and successes. It must be a bitter irony for him to now contemplate the fact that his real enemies were sitting right behind him in the ranks of his own party. His perorations could, without the flourish, have been penned by Harold Macmillan, at least in terms of that famous slogan: 'You've never had it so good.'

The year 2006 was no exception. The president once again informed parliament that it had been a year of remarkable progress; Professor Roger Southall has usefully summarised the address as a 'highlight of triumphs, more than tears'.[1] In Mbeki's view, government was performing splendidly in meeting the nation's challenges.

Among other things, on the basis of sustained positive economic growth since 1994, government claimed to have provided access to potable water to some ten million South Africans; allocated two million housing subsidies to the poor; spent particularly heavily on education, with nearly 100% enrolment of all eligible learners – with primary and secondary school enrolment touching 85%; and had raised the gross annual value of what Mbeki referred to as the 'social wage' (essentially welfare payments) to around R88-billion by 2003, with the poor being the principal beneficiaries.

Overall, Mbeki argued, under the ANC government, a significant number of people have been leveraged out of poverty: in 2001, 4,1-million out of 11,2-million households in South Africa lived on an income of R9 600 or less each year, whereas this had decreased to 3,6-million households by 2004, even after accounting for differences in prices.

Although the president always had a penchant for selective quotation and neatly eliding promising facts to disguise more pressing and inconvenient ones, I thought my response to this State of the Nation paean of self-praise would be both churlish and dumb if it did not acknowledge the achievements on Mbeki's watch. Yet there was a far darker side to the glowing picture painted in the National Assembly. This included another slate of facts and figures which government generally avoided addressing, but blamed on 'the legacy of apartheid' – or simply contested their existence. But some of these inelegant truths stubbornly persisted.

For example, South Africa's sharp slide down the global rankings of the UN Human Development Index (HDI) had been vertiginous.[2] Indeed, according to the HDI, average life expectancy in South Africa was no more than 49 years between 2000 and 2005 – a figure not sighted in the developed world since the time of the Industrial Revolution. This reality can largely be attributed to the AIDS pandemic, arguably Mbeki's and his government's greatest failing. To put the scale of the problem in context, consider this: South Africa – which houses just 0,7% of the world's population – accounts for 14% of the global population of people living with HIV/AIDS, and provides the world's highest number of AIDS deaths, over a tenth of the global total.

Again, while the economy was – in headline terms – in robust shape, more than eight million people within the expanded definition of unemployment (which includes those who have given up even the search for work) were without jobs. Most were young and black, under-educated and unskilled, and they accounted for an alarming 40% of the potential workforce.[3]

According to Professor Ricardo Hausmann of Harvard's Center for International Development, if job-creation in South Africa simply achieved the levels attained by Brazil, Thailand and Mexico, for example, employment would be 50% higher. This would mean that an additional 6,5-million South Africans would be working.[4]

While in and of itself our GDP growth rate is impressive, it flatters to deceive – since its rewards are so grossly uneven. The richest 10% of households in South Africa account for nearly half (45%) of the national income. South Africa is at the top of the range of countries with the severest inequalities on the planet. Our measurement on the (admittedly contested) GINI Co-efficient measures 0,6 (0 being the perfectly equal society, and 1 being the most unequal).[5]

In any event, by the end of the first quarter of 2008 South Africa's GDP growth rate had spiralled downward to 2,1%, while inflation breached the 11% barrier. A perfect storm now darkened a hitherto bright economic skyline.

The country is wracked by soaring levels of violent crime. Our murder or homicide rate (as at March 2005) is possibly the second highest in the world after Colombia.[6] In my view, and based on a welter of anecdotal evidence which has acquired critical weight, this crime wave has fuelled a mass exodus from the country. More than any morbid attachment to the vanquished apartheid glory days, nearly one million, mostly white, skilled and largely young South Africans have used their mobility to emigrate since 1994. And while corporate South Africa largely acquiesced before the ANC hegemony – and for the most part uncritically applied its policy prescriptions – the major companies moved their listings and most of their assets offshore.

Crime's evil twin, corruption, had – after less than a decade in office – metastasised the ANC, a one-time revolutionary movement, into what RW Johnson described as 'a conglomerate of factionalised commercial interests – most of them highly parasitic on state power … determined to enrich themselves by raiding public money.'[7] ANC secretary-general Kgalema Motlanthe was even more brutal when he admitted that 'this rot is across the board … almost every project is conceived because it offers certain people a chance to make money.'[8]

In 1994 the new government inherited an impressive, if unevenly distributed, infrastructure. But by the mid to late years of the first decade of the new millennium, South Africa was, literally, creaking at the seams. Skill-shedding at the state's electrical supply parastatal, Eskom – necessitated by the rigid application of racial quotas – was an aggravating factor. But the 'load-shedding' which plunged suburbs and industries into darkness (and which continues even now) almost mocked the fact that South Africa had abundant coal supplies and, at one time, boasted the cheapest electricity in the world.

The expansion of industry was crippled; foreign investment looked increasingly at hazard. On a more practical level, ordinary commuters are constantly faced with traffic lights out of order, and our clogged highways have become a daily irritation. At the time of final editing of this book (May 2008), a new survey revealed that South Africa has the world's highest brain drain and the worst skills shortages of 55 countries surveyed, coupled with plummeting productivity: a lethal cocktail likely to produce a severe economic hangover going forward.[9]

2

How does one explain such contrasts, and how can one country synthesise such ambivalent demands from various interest groups – including the voters? How does one nation remain intact, keeping faith with past commitments, all the while attempting to make its way in an intensely competitive, increasingly flat or globalised world?

Thomas L Friedman, globalisation's most-read pundit, noted in *The Lexus and the Olive Tree*: 'Every government lives under the fear of a no-confidence vote from the herd of investors, every day of the year.' And while bond and equity flows surged into South Africa in 2006 (reaching a record high of R131-billion), long-term Foreign Direct Investment (FDI) into plant, factories and mines all but collapsed from R40-billion in 2005 to a negative R6-billion in 2006.[10] Tellingly, the largest outflow was occasioned by the sale of foreign gold mining interests in the local industry.

Mining had long been the flagship of South Africa's economy. Yet in the face of an almost unprecedented worldwide commodity boom, mining production actually contracted by 6% between 2004 and 2006, while the number of people employed on the mines dropped an alarming 20 000 in the same period.[11] The dirigistic prescriptions, replete with racial ownership requirements and ministerial discretions,[12] was clearly affecting investor sentiment: between 2003 and 2006, South Africa had slipped from

693

25th to 53rd place in the survey of nations identified as a desirable destination for investment in minerals.[13] Indeed, government contrived to lace its 'business-friendly' policies with even more state regulation and control. Mining was perhaps the most noteworthy recipient of our homegrown version of 'market Leninism'. (This account was written before the severe, and ongoing, electricity 'load-shedding' forced the mines to cut production, and on one grim January 2008 day to halt mining entirely.)

Also, without having South Africa specifically in mind, Friedman pointed to the most exposed flank of our economy: our huge current account deficit – currently measuring 6% of Gross Domestic Product. This is financed largely through short-term portfolio flows which are highly susceptible (and easily reversible) to any change in global economic conditions and levels of demand. The crisis in the US sub-prime credit market has yet to play itself out fully, or at all, and its impact on developing economies such as South Africa could barely be glimpsed at the time of writing. The consequences could be devastating.

South Africa's reliance on foreign capital has been a constant, and depressing, feature of its history.[14] As of 2007-2008, the rise once more into the ascendancy of ANC leadership of the men and women of the Left (bearing their demands for what Trevor Manuel once derisively termed 'macropopulism') could easily turn mildly positive sentiments towards South Africa in world financial markets in the opposite direction in very short order.

Even before it started to unravel, Mbeki encased his presidency in (apparently self-delusional) spin. He blindly promoted its achievements while downplaying or ignoring its failings.

On the other hand, there are a great many foreign observers (and, no doubt, a few at home) who view South Africa through the lens of the 'Africa as a basket case' paradigm: doomed in perpetuity to a marginal and pitiable existence at the ebb of human affairs and on the periphery of a fast globalising world.

In contrast to both these perspectives, I consider the broad facts outlined above – the good and the bad – to be a far more realistic appraisal of the state of the nation.

But will the South African story end happily and reasonably peacefully? Can South Africans dare hope that they can build, or at least aspire to achieve, a one-nation model; a country in which aspirations and opportunities are more widely shared; where life chances increase instead of shrink; and where hope replaces fear as the common currency of people currently traumatised by staggering levels of violent crime and blighted by corruption and delivery failures? Can it overcome its dysfunctional education system and a constitutional democracy which today more resembles 'a bonsai tree than the mighty oak' we thought we had planted in 1994?

Will the very recent xenophobic violence that engulfed South Africa metastasise into attacks on other groups, or will we finally address both the causes and the symptoms of our national malaise?

On these large and compelling questions, Thabo Mbeki's government has not provided sufficient or reassuring answers. The extent to which the president could not see far enough was evident when in late 2007 his own rank and file expressed its dissatisfaction and challenged his presidency and his power from within. It appeared to be more a *cri de coeur* than a *coup d'état*. But apparently his closest allies were unaware of it – and deaf to the howling cries for change.

A case in point: the business class section of South African Airways sometimes throws up some interesting seating combinations. Thus, in late August 2007, I found myself on a Cape Town-bound flight seated next to a very senior ANC minister, a close confidant of Thabo Mbeki. He and I had clashed on several occasions, publicly and quite acrimoniously; I considered him an interesting and by no means isolated example of someone who had suppressed a powerful intellect and ideology to serve power and retain office. He was, accordingly, a firm favourite in the court of King Thabo.

My departure from frontline leadership some three months earlier had clearly softened attitudes and improved the atmosphere between us; indeed, he expressed considerable surprise at my decision to step down voluntarily.

After some agreeable banter on the topic of my past and my immediate plans (this was on the eve of my departure from South Africa for Harvard), I turned the conversation to the more vexed – and intensely contested – issue of the succession struggle, and the crisis gripping his own party. Mbeki's decision to stand again as party president in December against Jacob Zuma had already led to open warfare in the ruling party. The frequently servile media no longer regarded the president as untouchable.

So now press commentators and Zuma-backers in the ruling Alliance were presenting Mbeki as a figure of preening rectitude and intellectual arrogance – remote from the people, dismissive of his critics, and a dangerous manipulator of power who needed to be stopped.

Nor was Zuma having an easy time. His ethically challenged and morally hobbled persona – from the stain of corruption, to his inappropriate sexual conduct and backward-looking social views – were trumpeted as proof of his unfitness for leadership. Yet at the time he appeared to be involved in a gravity-defying political resurrection. Houdini-like, it appeared he might yet escape the chains of the looming criminal charges he faced. He and his supporters had alchemised the corruption allegations into a conspiracy against a brave victim: and there was evidence enough for both the charges and this perspective.

I thought the momentum was with Zuma, but my airborne companion was having none of it. As we munched on the canapés in pressurised comfort, the cabinet minister put me to rights. He was utterly confident in his assessment:

'Look, you people outside the ANC, particularly the press, don't understand how the ANC works.' He outlined a visit he had just made to his own constituency. 'Of course, the youth leaders there have been swayed by the hotheads in the Zuma camp. But after I spoke to them and explained what is at stake, they were smart and disciplined enough to accept the imperatives which necessitate Thabo's continuance in office. Over the next few weeks, the broad collective leadership of the party will spread out across the formations. By the time of the [leadership] conference there will be a unified position which will be dramatically different from the sort of stuff you're reading about today.'

Certainly, although under severe challenge, Mbeki did appear to be political master of all he surveyed. The road to Polokwane – where the leadership would gather in December – was to be littered with the political corpses of those who dared to cross him. The ferocity of the battle would also be measured by the number of public institutions and constitutional instruments damaged or manipulated by both sides in this struggle.[15]

Mbeki continued to voice full confidence in his failing ministers and rotten officials. On policy, he saw no need to change course despite his failures – especially with regard to crime and public health. As Henry Kissinger once observed: 'When enough prestige has been invested in a project it is easier to see it fail than to abandon it.'

Yet in mid-December, in the northern conclave at Polokwane, Mbeki's presidency went south. His overwhelming defeat by Zuma – he received just four out of every ten votes cast – was more than a decisive rejection. It was a full-scale democratic palace revolution within the ANC. After Mbeki's defenestration, the party proceeded to vote off its National Executive no fewer than eight of the nine provincial premiers, the country's deputy president and eight other cabinet ministers.

At the time, I was, literally, at the other end of the world – enjoying my new-found freedom visiting a wine estate in Sonoma in northern California. When I later read the full results on the Internet, I was amused to see that my cabinet informant – to the last apparently adamant, with the other Mbeki courtiers, that their side would prevail – was among the casualties. More alarmingly, my old nemesis Winnie Mandela had made a storming comeback: she had been voted into top place on the National Executive.

She was not the sole convicted criminal to benefit from the dénouement. High places were awarded to the likes of Tony Yengeni (attending the conference as a parolee) and Ruth Bhengu, a 'Travelgate' fraudster who had been removed from parliament for misusing official air tickets. They were not alone: a survey by the *Mail&Guardian* revealed that 29% of the newly elected ANC executive were either convicted criminals, or were currently being investigated by the criminal justice authorities, or had resigned from public office owing to 'ethical lapses'.[16]

A study in contrast was the fate of Trevor Manuel, the fiscally conservative and personally incorruptible Finance minister. He tumbled 50 places down the list, compared to his top showing at the previous conference five years earlier when the Mbeki forces held sway. The drop in just over a decade from the moral supremacy of Nelson Mandela to the morally compromised Jacob Zuma had been very steep and relatively swift.

By then Zuma was far from an unknown figure: yet he remained an enigma. One ought to recall that at the time of Mbeki's accession, very little of personal relevance was known about Mbeki himself. He was a blank – from his religious beliefs (if any) to whether he could drive a car. By contrast, almost every element of Zuma's personal life had been intensely scrutinised. The court processes which had engulfed him – and in which he would soon again be embroiled – had cast a blight on him, and it was not flattering. He was a polygamist, a traditionalist with more than a dozen children and a penchant for casual unprotected sex. He enjoyed a lavish lifestyle he clearly could not afford.

He had also been correctly condemned for outrageous remarks about gays and for the infamous shower which he claimed washed away the dangers of HIV/AIDS after the sexual encounter which resulted in his rape charge. But he did at least – in welcome contrast to the incumbent president – promptly apologise for his verbal transgressions.

His funding had come in large measure from a (now convicted) criminal, whose guilt in part was determined on the basis of his corrupt relationship with Zuma. And there were others in a circle that provided him with money and support – hardly reassuring figures, possessed of neither moral probity nor a personal or financial disinterest in Zuma's march to power. His five-year spell as a KwaZulu-Natal provincial minister and his six years as deputy national president had left scarcely a mark.

Nonetheless, there were those who felt that Zuma might be the antidote to the imperial presidency of Mbeki. And yet, at crucial stages, he had headed the 'cadre redeployment' desk of the ANC. Mbeki was, indeed, the central architect and guiding spirit of the ANC project to capture, within the tentacles of the ruling party, the army, the police, the bureaucracy, intelligence structures, the public broadcaster, parastatals and agencies such as various state regulatory bodies.[17] But Zuma was the chief of personnel in the quest to 'extend the power of the National Liberation Movement over all levers of power.'[18]

In more personal, less political terms there were obvious and stark differences between the two leaders. While I had occasionally been exposed to flashes of Mbeki's warmth and at times thoughtful intellect, more frequently I, with his other opponents, had felt the lash of an at times baleful, brooding anger and withering resentment. Zuma, by contrast, oozed emotional intelligence. My few personal meetings and many parliamentary encounters with him suggested someone perfectly comfortable in his own skin.

In 2003 Zuma and I were jointly hosted by my friend, the ebullient Bill Lambert,[19] as guests of honour at the annual Durban July Handicap at Greyville racecourse. We spent most of the afternoon in the air-conditioned luxury of the stewards' pavilion, interspersed with visits to the parade ring and winners' circle. We hugged on meeting and departing; he joked and laughed easily, and told Michal at length of the pleasure and joy he derived from his many children. To this social encounter he brought none of the rancour and distance which – at that stage – characterised the political and parliamentary relationship between our parties. Yet such easy charm was, apparently, deceptive.

A senior American official, intimately involved with Zuma in his peace-broking efforts in Burundi, told me how he had witnessed first-hand the brutal (and in his view entirely necessary) manner in which Zuma threatened recalcitrant parties in the drawn-out negotiations. 'There's nothing sweet and cuddly about him when the chips are down,' I was told.

On another occasion, discussing with Nelson Mandela my poor relationship with Mbeki, he advised me to seek the counsel of 'JZ': 'He's a key man,' Madiba informed me. Although I did not take up this suggestion, I took careful note of Mandela's high regard for the often – at least at that stage – underestimated Zuma.

The man's parliamentary performances, while neither remarkable nor memorable, were also characterised by spontaneous ease and affability – which appeared as genuine as it was effective. An American political eminence I met at Harvard noted somewhat grimly (vis-à-vis George W Bush's re-election in 2004) that 'likeability' was a potent factor in presidential politics. South Africa was not entirely different, it seemed.

3

It is clear to me that Polokwane represents an extraordinary, even exceptional, moment in the modern history of South Africa. Strangely, given the essentially negative vibrations that characterised our relationship, I felt more sympathy than *Schadenfreude* at Mbeki's public humiliation; but as I absorbed the importance of the event, I was almost overwhelmed by several rich ironies. For one thing, its impact on the future remained unclear – except that the Zuma forces had been right in predicting that a tsunami-like force would carry their man to victory.

There were now two centres of power in South Africa: one in the party and the other in the state, both clearly set to use and doubtless abuse their separate bases to thwart and outsmart the other. I also strongly suspect that the wave will be far from spent by the next election in 2009, and that South Africa will live with its consequences for years.

Another reaction to Polokwane was to celebrate the reanimation of democratic vigour within the ruling party. South Africa's history militated, in the short term, against the country going for the democratic gold of changing governments as a consequence of Mbeki's serial failures. I dubbed the Mbeki–Zuma contest 'the evil of two lessers' – a borrowed, but apt, description. Second prize – the silver medal – would have been a compromise candidate who could bring renewal and the necessary ethical leadership without the populist fervour powering the Zuma insurgency.

But the ousting of the *entire* top leadership of an all-powerful party not facing any immediate electoral threat was rare in the democratic world. Margaret Thatcher's decapitation as PM by her Conservative Party in 1990 was one modern exception – yet, at the time, her party sensed electoral peril. In the younger democracies, and certainly in Africa's nationalist formations, it was unprecedented to remove, democratically, an all-powerful president. So South Africa qualified for a bronze medal; perhaps better than none.

There appeared, in the immediate aftermath of Polokwane, to be three other, less noted, but positive outcomes: the revival of a spirit of criticism and dissent; the apparent submergence of tribal politics; and some respect for constitutional limits.

A little elaboration:

Firstly, I had often been amazed that those who obviously knew better willingly suspended their disbelief as Mbeki visited upon South Africa a range of sometimes cranky policies and undemocratic practices. A party which prided itself so much on the richness of its democratic traditions (often, in reality, the stuff of liberation mythology) had apparently happily permitted one man to centralise vast powers in his office and person. Now, clearly, every policy and state action would be contested – and that included fingering the central culprits in the arms deal scandal, to the beneficiaries of government-mandated empowerment deals. The 'noises off' could be heard across the political board – not confined to the 'usual suspects' in the anti-Mbeki camp such as COSATU and Communist Party blowhards. The genie was out: it was unlikely to be bottled again soon.[20]

I had been one of many who bought into the myth that Mbeki was an Africanised version of Machiavelli – a master of the dark arts of political survival, and a ruthless but successful backroom manipulator. The endgame at Polokwane proved that I (and the bulk of the media and the political classes generally) had believed in a false analogy. Mbeki, in the end, resembled the Wizard of Oz: he had intimidated people with the giant shadow he cast from behind the screen of power. When this was ripped away he proved in some ways the local equivalent of the old man from Topeka, Kansas, who when revealed in his weakness responded to the charge 'You are a bad man' with the meek rejoinder: 'No, I am just a bad wizard.'

Secondly, under Mbeki's presidency, the drive for racial unity that characterised Mandela's acclaimed rainbow nation leadership gave way to a more monochromatic, less expansive, and essentially Africanist project. Most political disputes and policy challenges were met or resisted by silencing opponents with references to the racist past or by dangling our shameful history – justified or not – in front of leaders of minority groups and parties such as myself. While this was effective in seeing off external opponents, it provided forward cover for a range of disastrous policies, failing ministries and blatant corruption. It could not be used at Polokwane. Perhaps as a consequence the debate had been advanced, or at least shifted slightly, from the race-holding and name-calling which had atrophied recent political discourse.

For much of the post-apartheid phase of South Africa's political life, I was the recipient of confident assertions, primarily from Africans, and particularly in my own party ranks, that, stripped to its essence, the ANC represented a sort of closed ethnic supremacy. The 'Xhosa nostra' was a camp phrase much in vogue. On the grounds of his Venda origins, for example, Cyril Ramaphosa's candidacy was ruled out by some, whatever his private intentions. Yet not only is Zuma – as the T-shirts of his supporters proclaim – '100% Zuluboy', but his broad trans-ethnic support, including deep political pockets within the Eastern Cape, appear to shatter this shibboleth.

Yet one cannot discount the dragon of tribalism arising again in the future. Events in Kenya furnish a potent recent example of how close to the surface ethnicity lurks in apparently even long-settled and broadly democratic African societies. Indeed, claims of tribalism remain a handy alibi for some in the Zuma camp to bat away the corruption charges against their hero. Nonetheless, the efficacy of full-blown tribal politics ripping South Africa apart appears (for the present) to be at bay.

The intra-African xenophobia that rocked South Africa and shocked the world in May 2008, and left 50 foreign residents dead and saw 50 000 persons displaced, suggests, however, that ethnic warriors plough a very fertile, if not bloody, field in the once-admired 'rainbow nation'.

Thirdly, and on balance another positive outcome of the ANC succession struggle, was perhaps unintended: a limit on the scope of the Presidency. Mbeki and his cadres were shamelessly explicit as they 'extended the power of the National Liberation Movement' and blunted the very instruments which the Constitution had fashioned to guard precisely against such encroachment. When I pointed this out or warned against the threat of a third term presidency,[21] I was either dismissed as a scare-monger or warned off as 'unpatriotic' or going against the grain of the 'national consensus'. Such stereotyping became a useful, and dangerous, catch-all intended to asphyxiate any pesky critic.[22]

Even worse was to draw attention to the impact the Soviet Union had had on the thinking and character of some ANC leaders, including Mbeki. The National Party's 'Reds under every bed' scare tactics had made disreputable any parallels, however valid, between Moscow and the ANC. However, it wasn't simply past attachments but the present incumbent in the Kremlin, Vladimir Putin, who eerily resembled Mbeki at the height of his power. David Remnick's taxonomy on Russia's new Czar appeared in the *New Yorker*. He wrote:

'In recent years, Putin has ensured that nearly all power in Russia is presidential. The legislature, the state Duma, is only marginally more independent than the Supreme Soviet was under Leonid Brezhnev. The governors of Russia's more than eighty regions are no longer elected ... they are now all appointed by the Kremlin ... [The] business community must also obey the commands and signals of Putin's circle.'

With the necessary substitutions, this could have accurately described Mbeki's massive top-down enforcement of power and manipulation of constitutional institutions, although it must be said that this analogy has its limits: Mbeki has never been as ruthless as Putin towards his opponents. Where an opposition-supporting businessman in Moscow received an eight-year jail term in eastern Siberia, in South Africa his local equivalent was more likely to be the recipient of a vicious and public e-mail from the president. Nor was he as effective as Putin – who overcame constitutional limits on the Presidency by becoming prime minister, a post he attained through total political dominance.

South Africa's Constitution made no provision for a prime minister. Hence Mbeki's decision to extend his power and retain his influence by seeking re-election as party president misfired.

That was not his only miscalculation. He and his satraps had spent a decade stripping South Africa's constitutional instruments of real authority and locating effective power in the hands of the party, particularly its National Executive Committee (NEC).[23]

Whatever the effects of the extension of the powers of the Liberation Movement – and it has done great damage to our fledgling democratic order – it was always premised on the ANC as a unified organisation, controlling both party and government. So long as Mbeki held both positions this was no problem in terms of enforcing his control. After Polokwane, he – and the country – faced the prospect of all decisions of government and cabinet being held hostage to the edicts of the party executive, a body controlled by his implacable foes.

Here lies the supreme irony: Mbeki's deliberate collapse of the divide between party and state rendered the residue of his presidency a study in impotence.

On the other hand, Mbeki is quite unused to defeat. At the time of writing, he still held the formal reins of power, although like Achilles in his tent he shrunk from contact with the country, no less than with his party, the very organisation that has defined his life's work and which had so decisively now rejected him. This did not prevent him, however, from denying the self-evident political crisis in Zimbabwe after that country's 2008 presidential poll, and in this respect his political autism was as depressing as it was consistent.

Crucially, he also effectively controlled many of the country's national institutions – especially the public broadcaster, the National Prosecuting Authority and the National Police Commissioner (whose own arrest Mbeki effectively headed off in 2007, until he was obliged to act against him in January 2008).

With that fact as backdrop, the state moved swiftly to serve fresh corruption charges on Zuma in late December 2007. He was no doubt still savouring his victory when he was summonsed to appear in court in August 2008 to defend himself on 18 counts of corruption, fraud, money-laundering, racketeering and tax evasion.[24]

The indictment had scarcely been served (as if Zuma's Christmas present had been wrapped and delivered by Pandora) when Mbeki's swelling ranks of enemies within his party denounced him. A leading Zumaite, and a kingpin in his campaign, ANC Youth League president Fikile Mbalula, spat out: 'The decision to charge Jacob Zuma is not a decision of the judiciary; it is a decision of the state, and the state is led by Thabo Mbeki. This is a blatant and desperate attempt to block Zuma's ascendancy to the highest office in the land.'[25]

Many – not just Zuma's allies – are deeply suspicious that Mbeki will use the remnants of his considerable state power to prevent Zuma from adding the state presidency to the ANC's top offices. And some do not confine their rage, or their threats, to the person or office of Mbeki. Signalling that Zuma will not go quietly to court, for example, COSATU's KwaZulu-Natal provincial secretary let rip with a threat of mayhem: 'People are now angry. This time there will be blood spilt in the courtroom. People are ready to put themselves in the front line, we will not be held responsible for their anger.'[26]

Here lurks the greatest and most obvious danger – the negative which could cancel out any of the positives. The Polokwane decision to dismantle the Directorate of Special Operations (the 'Scorpions') was perhaps the most ominous indicator. Its sting had been felt by some of the very leaders, including Zuma, who now bestrode the party.

4

As a country, we have now been placed on notice that the ANC's civil war could spill over into society as a whole, jeopardising judicial institutions and compromising even further their independence. This is a real prospect. The NEC's decision of 8 January 2008 (eight months ahead of Zuma's designated trial) that Zuma will be the party's presidential candidate in 2009 is essentially a declaration of war against the state and its judicial authority.

In the event of Zuma being prosecuted successfully, even his political death-defying skills may well not be sufficient to ensure his presidential candidacy in 2009. In that event, the country's next president could be his newly elected deputy in the party, Kgalema Motlanthe, a former trade unionist with an almost invisible public profile and of largely unknown views. Under either candidate, the trade union barons of COSATU win: Motlanthe is from their ranks, and Zuma owes his victory in large measure to them.

Should Zuma prevail, most South Africans have no clear idea where he will lead the country. For some, the words 'President Zuma' are an unnerving prospect. But he rushed around investment centres in South Africa, London and the US, assuring nervous financiers that he will not change our reasonably successful, if job-crushing, economic policies. However, his union and communist allies chafe at restraints imposed by the current economic orthodoxies implemented by Mbeki. They want looser monetary and fiscal policies with less inflation targeting – and are deeply opposed to any further trade liberalisation.[27]

To an extent, all this is merely gazing at the tea-leaves. Where Zuma claims to be a servant of the party 'collective', Mbeki's personal style was often solitary and iconoclastic. Yet on the rare occasions when he justified his actions, he too defended himself by invoking 'the collective'. In August 2007, for example, he defended his dismissal of the popular deputy minister of Health, Nozizwe Madlala-Routledge, by deprecating her 'inability to work as part of a collective'.[28]

Zuma appears far more genuine in his commitment to such a 'duty'. 'I go with the overwhelming feeling of this country; if the majority says, Zuma do this, I will do it,' he told *Time* magazine.[29] This might have reassured the restive party rank and file, but was far less reassuring to a national and international community which looks to the top of South Africa's ruling party for strong, moral leadership. It seemed a negation of that personal responsibility which is, as much as national unity, a key ingredient of successful modern leadership. Majorities, in any event, are changeable, and are influenced by political direction. What signals, if any, Zuma would send, and who – if not the top man – would be setting the tone should he ascend to the presidency, was, on this reading, bewilderingly unclear.

However, on such crucial issues as AIDS and Zimbabwe, Zuma and his allies in COSATU and the South African Communist Party ranks are more democratically mainstream than Mbeki's essentially denialist, narrowly Africanist and politically tone-deaf approach. On crime, for example, Zuma has been far more frank than Mbeki, who routinely rounded on critics, and even victims, of the country's crime wave as being actuated by either racial malice or ignorance. Zuma, by contrast, correctly identified violent crime as 'a threat to our democratic order'.

Well he might. Even as he received his own charges, on the weekend before the 2008 New Year, in a Pretoria suburb four armed robbers viciously attacked the departing Tanzanian high commissioner and his guests at a farewell party. The unfortunate diplomat, Emanuel Mwambulukutu, reportedly told the robbers, 'Gentlemen, God bless you.' They replied: 'We don't care for God, let's stab the dogs.' This they proceeded to do, leaving the high commissioner seriously injured and unconscious, while his wife was stabbed in the head. The only solace for the couple might have been that they did not join the more than nineteen thousand South Africans murdered over the past year.

In such matters Zuma appears plugged into the real concerns of his country's people. This would be a welcome departure from Mbeki.

The fear remains that because of his dubious personal associates and past moral choices, under a Zuma presidency South Africa could revert to a stereotype of 'Big Man', African-style kleptocracy replete with redistributive and populist economics with lashings of demagoguery.

Of course, as Roger Southall indicated, corruption and crony capitalism billowed under Mbeki. But that is no inoculation against its deepening.[30]

Accordingly, the crucial shift required at home and abroad – not least for a world that requires South Africa's democracy to succeed – is to place less reliance on the country's leaders – singular or collective – and less faith in Dostoyevsky's all-powerful Czar leading the country into an illusory golden age. We need to invest more effort in building and defending our democratic institutions. These can outlive the best and the worst of presidents. That is where the opposition, alongside a reinvigorated media and civil society, has a continued and crucial role to play.

Whatever shape South Africa's new leadership takes, immense challenges have to be met. Do we want to be nostalgically remembered as a fading footnote in world history, commemorated for the one big thing we got right in 1994 – but with a sense of aching possibility about opportunities lost, dreams deferred and goals missed since then? Or will we become – perhaps against expectation – a success story of renewal, taking our place in the front row of winning nations, applying thoughtful policies and best practices, with equal measures of good governance and self-restraint, transcending the divisions and iniquities of our history?

In 1986 I started my journey in politics and in the public life of South Africa. I was a callow young city councillor representing an unfashionable suburb in Johannesburg; the candidate of a party whose leader had just given up. The dark night of apartheid seemed without end. But it was, in the sweep of history, simply the darkest hour before dawn. In truth I did not then imagine – or dare to dream – that it would happen: that a privileged and protected minority would relinquish its hold on power. I never dared believe that a brutalised majority would accept the constraints imposed by a settlement negotiated with its former oppressors, basically without vengeance. That the process would be far less bloody than feared, as well as occur in a relatively short time frame, seemed improbable.

The conventional wisdom of two decades ago certainly bet against the prospect of my country enacting a democratic constitution, replete with one of the most progressive bills of rights in the world. Or that its new, apparently revolutionary government would practise sound financial and fiscal management over its economy. Or that the same country would catapult itself – in a few short years – from international pariah into a respected and valued member of the comity of nations.

But, perhaps more darkly, no futurologist could have foreseen the ways in which some, although crucially not all, the clothes discarded by the departing regime would be picked up and worn so eagerly by the government which supplanted it: arrogance of power, corruption of institutions, the triumph of ideology, the fetish with race, and the cosying-up to repressive international regimes. These, too, seemed to pass, almost without pause, from the white nationalists to the black nationalists: in power, the noun proving more permanent than the adjective. And viewed through the lens of the 1980s, perhaps the most surreal event of all was never in view: the decision in 2004 – albeit forced by electoral humiliation – of the New National Party to abandon ship and clamber aboard the vessel steered by its one-time nemesis, the African National Congress. Or maybe it simply mirrored the seamless transition on the economic front: former black socialists and white, one-time backers of the apartheid regime acquiring staggering and conspicuous wealth under the new order while the bulk of the people stayed poor, or became even poorer.

George Orwell, as he did on most of the important events of the 20th century, had decades before preordained it. It was in his conclusion to *Animal Farm*, the powerful allegory which I first studied in my far-off high school days. He recounts the arrival back of Farmer Jones – the former oppressor who returns to the farm. He sits down to drink and play cards with the pigs, the liberators, who had driven him out in the first place: the shivering creatures, the masses, stood outside this charmed circle and

> looked from pig to man, and from man to pig, and from pig to man again, but already it was impossible to say which was which.

As I battled to conclude this book, an icy dark December winter encased the Harvard Yard in Cambridge, Massachusetts, and I realised I had still not answered the question: would hope or fear win the day in South Africa? On the second Sunday of Advent I found myself in the packed Memorial Church. In a galaxy of academic and intellectual luminaries the star of Reverend Peter J Gomes, Plummer Professor of Christian Morals and minister in the church, was one of the brightest. Reflecting on my country's – and my own – uncertain future, I found the mesmerising words of his sermon compelling, and scratched them down on the back of the Order of Service. We did not share the same faith, but he appeared to answer, persuasively, my own ambiguity and doubts:

> Lighting a candle does not remove the darkness.
> But it does light the path in front of you.
> Hope is an act of defiance in a cynical world against the
>   conventional wisdom and the mendacity of mediocrity.
> Hope is better than the alternatives.
> When in doubt, believe.

The future is imperfect, but it is ours to make.

Appendix

CAUCUS COLLEAGUES: MEMBERS OF PARLIAMENT

Democratic Party: Elected 6 September 1989 General Election

House of Assembly

Andrew, Kenneth Michael

Burrows, Roger Marshall

Carlisle, Robin Vincent

Charlewood, Carole Heeley

Cronjé, Pierre Carel

Dalling, David John

De Beer, Zacharias Johannes (Co-Leader)

De Waal, Louis Arnold

De Wet, André Eloff

Eglin, Colin Wells

Ellis, Michael James

Engel, Geoffrey Craig

Fuchs, Lester

Gastrow, Peter Hans Paul

Goodall, Brian Bradford

Haswell, Robert Frederick

Hulley, Roger Rex

Jordaan, Jacobus Adriaan

Leon, Anthony James

Lorimer, Rupert John

Malan, Wynand Charl (Co-Leader)

Momberg, Jan Hendrik

Moorcroft, Errol Knott

Nel, Wessel Uys

Rogers, Robert Harry Doherty

Schwarz, Harry Heinz

Smuts, Dene

Soal, Peter George

Tarr, Michael Ashton

Van Eck, Jan

Walsh, John Jasper

Worrall, Denis John (Co-Leader)

House of Delegates

Abraham, Michael
Rajab, Mahmoud
Singh, Amunsingh

President's Council

Gant, David Walter
Rennie, James
Selfe, James

Democratic Party: Elected 27 April 1994 General Election

National Assembly

Andrew, Kenneth Michael
Eglin, Colin Wells
Ellis, Michael James
Gibson, Douglas Harvey Monro
Jordaan, Jacobus Adriaan
Leon, Anthony James (Leader)
Smuts, Dene

Senate

Mnisi, William Fettie
Moorcroft, Errol Knott
Selfe, James

Democratic Party: Elected 2 June 1999 General Election

National Assembly

Andrew, Kenneth Michael
Bell, Brian Gordon
Borman, Gloria Mary
Botha, Andries Johannes
Bruce, Nigel Strathearn
Clelland, Nicholas John
Cupido, Paulina Wilhelmina
Da Camara, Manuel Lima
Davidson, Ian Ormiston
Delport, Jacobus Tertius
De Vos, Pierre Jacobus
Eglin, Colin Wells
Ellis, Michael James
Farrow, Stuart Brian

Gibson, Douglas Harvey Monro
Gore, Vincent Charles
Grobler, Godfried August Josephes
Heine, Rudolph Jacobus
Kalyan, Santos Vinita
Lee, Trevor Donald
Leon, Anthony James (Leader)
Maluleke, Daniel Kapeni
McIntosh, Graham Brian Douglas
Moorcroft, Errol Knott
Ntuli, Richard Sibusiso
Opperman, Sydney Edward
Pillay, Sigomoney
Schalkwyk, Philippus Johannes

Schmidt, Hendrik Cornelius
Selfe, James
Semple, Janet Audrey
Seremane, Wetshotsile Joseph
Sigabi, Nomareledwane Bernice
Singh, Amunsingh
Smuts, Dene
Swart, Paul Stephanus
Taljaard, Raenette
Waters, Michael

National Council of Provinces

Botha, Celia-Sandra
Gouws, Embrensia Claassens
Krumbock, Gregory Rudy
Lever, Lawrence Gerald
Raju, Nelson Moonsamy
Theron, Jacobus Lodewikus
Versfeld, Antoinette Maria

Democratic Alliance: Elected 14 April 2004 General Election

National Assembly

Blanché, Johannes Petrus Izak
Boinamo, George Gaolatlhe
Botha, Celia-Sandra
Camerer, Sheila Margaret
Coetzee, Ryan
Davidson, Ian Ormiston
Delport, Jacobus Tertius
Doman, Willem Phillips
Ellis, Michael James
Farrow, Stuart Brian
Gibson, Douglas Harvey Monro
Haasbroek, Sarel Francois
Henderson, Ross Kirby
Jankielsohn, Roy
Kalyan, Santosh Vinita
King, Ryno Johannes
Kohler-Barnard, Dianne
Labuschagne, Leslie Bernardus
Lee, Trevor Donald
Leon, Anthony James (Leader)
Lowe, Christopher Mark
Maluleke, Daniel Kapeni
Masango, Suhla James

Minnie, Karel Johannes
Mnyandu, Bhekinhlahla Jeremia
Morgan, Gareth Richard
Morkel, Craig Mervyn
Nel, Adriaan Hermanus
Nkem-Abonta, Enyinna
Ntuli, Richard Sibusiso
Opperman, Sydney Edward
Rabie, Pierre Jacques
Sayedali-Shah, Moulana Mohammed Rafeek
Schmidt, Hendrik Cornelius
Selfe, James
Semple, Janet Audrey
Seremane. Wetshotsile Joseph
Smuts, Dene
Steyn, Arron Cecil
Swart, Marius
Swart, Paul Stephanus
Swathe, Mpowele Mexan
Taljaard, Raenette
Trent, Edward William
Van der Walt, Desirée

Van Dyk, Salomon Maritz
Van Niekerk, André Isak
Waters, Michael
Weber, Hilda
Zille, Helen

National Council of Provinces

Chen, Sherry Su-Huei
Krumbock, Gregory Rudy
Lamoela, Helen
Le Roux, Jacobus Wilhelm
Loe, Shelley
Robinson, Denise
Terblanche, Juanita Frederika
Thetjeng, Odysseus Motlatjo
Watson, Armiston
Worth, Darryl Arthur

Notes

INTRODUCTION

1 *New York Times*, 12 October 2007.
2 Thomas Nagel: 'What is Liberalism? An Assessment', *New York Review of Books*, 25 May 2006.
3 Arthur M Schlesinger, Jr: 'Journals 1952-2000', The Penguin Press.
4 Andrew Sullivan: 'Why Obama Matters', *Atlantic*, December 2007.

PART ONE: PATH TO LEADERSHIP

1. IN MY BEGINNINGS

1 Debates of the Constitutional Assembly, Vol. 3, 8 May 1996, at column 436.
2 Mendel Kaplan: *Jewish Roots in the South African Economy*, Struik, 1986, passim.
3 Kaplan, op. cit., at p. 52.
4 The editorial is quoted, undated, in my father's unpublished memoir: 'Truth in Action: Justice observed in South Africa', 1988.
5 *Spectator*, 19 August 2006.
6 Statement to the Senate, June 1954; see ANC.org.za/books/reich//.html.
7 *Natal Mercury*, 3 August 1960.
8 Christopher Hitchens: *Why Orwell Matters*, Basic Books, New York, 2007.
9 *De Minimis*, Law Students' Newspapers, August 1981.
10 AK Heard: *General Elections in South Africa, 1943-1970*, Oxford, 1974, at p. 113.
11 Heard, op. cit.

12 *Sunday Times*, 19 December 2004.

13 My mother Sheila married three times. Her first marriage was to my father, Ramon, from 1954 to 1965; her second, to Richard Arthur (Dick) Prior, lasted from 1965 to 1971. In 1980 she married Paul Ferdinand Wilhelm Schulz, a German industrialist. It also proved in time to be an unhappy union, but survived until my mother's death in December 2001.

14 On 11 November 1965 Ian Smith, prime minister of Rhodesia, a British colony, made a Unilateral Declaration of Independence from Britain in order to maintain white control.

15 Quoted by PS Thompson: *The British Civic Culture of Natal South Africa 1902-1961*, Brevitas, 1999, at p. 105.

16 Robin Lamplough: 'Opportunities seized – a History of Kearsney College', 1999, at p. 279.

17 Republican Publications (Pty) Ltd v Publications Control Board 1972(3) SA562(D).

18 The details of Hofmeyr's career are contained in the memoir of his biographer, Alan Paton: *Towards the Mountain*, David Philip, 1980, at p. 134.

19 Op. cit., at p. 136.

20 Voortrekkerhoogte, literally 'Voortrekker Heights', was the name assigned by the incoming NP regime to the military complex, outside Pretoria, which the British had named 'Roberts Heights' after the British commanding general who led his troops into Pretoria during the Anglo-Boer War. On ascending to power in 1994, the ANC rebranded it as 'Thaba Tshwane' after a local legendary African warrior. All these renamings – one per epoch, as it were – proved the validity of Nehru's observation that 'history is almost always written by the victors and the conquerors.'

21 Bob's brother, Pat Rogers, had also served with me as a Johannesburg city councillor.

22 Speech of Essop Pahad, National Assembly, Parliament, 13 February 2002.

23 Statement by Khulekani Ntshangase, ANC Youth League, 1 July 2003.

24 Speech of Essop Pahad, National Assembly, Parliament, 13 February 2002.

25 *Hansard* of Gauteng Provincial Legislature, No. 36, 1998: Fifth Session, First Legislature, 9 November 1998, Brig.-Gen. Bosman, p. 7774.

26 Udo W Froese and Ronald Roberts, *Sowetan*, 28 November 2000.

27 Quoted in Tony Judt: *Postwar: A history of Europe since 1945*, The Penguin Press, 2005, at p. 100.

28 Statement, 26 March 2004.

29 She was following a well-trodden path of black elite co-operation with apartheid structures. Nelson Mandela's own father-in-law, Columbus Madikizela – Winnie was his sixth child – had taken the apartheid shilling when Matanzima co-opted him into his cabinet at the onset of limited self-rule in the 1960s.

30 Speech of TS Setona MP, National Council of Provinces, *Hansard*, 18 May 2005.

31 A 'rating' is naval parlance for someone who holds neither commissioned nor warrant rank; in other words, an ordinary seaman, the equivalent of an army private, my rank.

32 James Sanders: *Apartheid's Friends – The Rise and Fall of South Africa's Secret Service*, John Murray, 2006, at p. 2.

33 The death toll in the uprisings is officially given as 174 blacks and two whites; the number of wounded as 1 222 blacks and six whites; the number of persons arrested as 1 298. Property damaged or destroyed is officially listed as 67 state-owned beerhalls and bottle stores, 53 administration buildings, 13 schools, eight state hostels, 154 vehicles,

as well as banks, clinics, bus sheds, hostels and factories, public buildings and amenities built up over the previous 25 years.

2: DANCING WITH DIALECTICS

1 Belinda Bozzoli is today the distinguished deputy vice chancellor of Wits; Gareth is the DA's head of Special Projects. Their husband/father is Charles van Onselen, arguably South Africa's finest living social historian.

2 Hermann Giliomee: 'Manipulating the Past' in *Political Correctness in South Africa*, SAIRR, at p. 103.

3 John Kane-Berman: *South Africa's Silent Revolution*, SAIRR, 1990.

4 Frantz Fanon: *The Wretched of the Earth*, circa 1962, Penguin, London, 1967, at p. 147.

5 Tony Judt: *New York Review of Books*, 21 September 2006.

6 Isaiah Berlin: *Two Concepts of Liberty*, 1958, at p. 10.

7 Mark Lilla: *New York Review of Books*, 25 April 2001.

8 Paul Johnson: *The Enemies of Society*, Weidenfeld & Nicolson, 1977.

9 Paul Johnson: *A History of the Modern World*, Weidenfeld & Nicolson, 1983.

10 *Wits Student*, 20 February 1979.

11 Letter to Anthony J Leon from Edward M Kennedy, United States Senate, Washington DC, 15 March 1979.

12 David Owen: *Time to Declare*, Michael Joseph, London, 1991, at p. 423.

13 Vorster had been 'kicked upstairs' into the presidency in September 1978, just as the Info scandal was breaking. The final report of the Erasmus Commission into the Information Department, published in March 1979, revised its initial exculpation of Vorster and stated that he (together with Connie Mulder) had to bear 'joint responsibility' for irregularities in the department during his tenure as prime minister. Vorster resigned as president on 4 June 1979.

14 I hasten to add that our stroll through the Reeperbahn was out of curiosity, not to partake of any of the merchandise – animate and inanimate – on offer.

15 Tager, who was avowedly non-political and status quo-minded during the turbulence of the 1980s, magically transformed herself, after 1994, into a queen of transformation and a pillar of the new order's political correctness. She was rewarded with the plum appointment of chairman of Transnet, the state-owned transport behemoth. However, her tenure there was neither long nor particularly distinguished.

16 It is an interesting commentary on South Africa in 2006 compared to the country 24 years before, that the study of labour law was then confined to a three-week course slapped onto the tail-end of public law. Today it is a major academic specialisation, entailing several years of full-time study.

17 See, for example, Lijphart, A: *The Politics of Accommodation: Pluralism in the Netherlands*, University of California Press, Berkeley, 1980; Lijphart, A: 'Federal, Confederal and Consociational Options for the South African Plural Society' in Rothberg and Barratt (eds), 1980.

18 Quoted by Professor Hermann Giliomee in *Opposing Voices*, Jonathan Ball, 2006, at p. 69.

19 The sophisticated voting system required students to fill out a computer form which allocated points to each candidate in accordance with the preference of each elector:

e.g. ten points for the voter's first-choice candidate, down to one point for his tenth, or last-preference choice.

20 *Star*, 4 December 1980.

21 *De Minimis* – 'about very little'.

22 This ministry, which dealt with black affairs, had started life under the first apartheid government as the Ministry of Native Affairs. It was euphemistically rechristened every few years thereafter and transmogrified into 'Bantu Affairs', then 'Plural Affairs', and finally 'Co-operation and Development', although there was little sign of either.

23 They had designed the legal architecture, or firewalling, as the case might be, which allowed some of the city's and South Africa's major enterprises to take off.

24 From my first days as a ward councillor through to leader of the opposition in parliament, I have always published my home telephone number in the local phone book. Residents and constituents, aside from the occasional crank, have seldom abused my public accessibility. I believe that every paid public official must be accessible to the constituency that elected him or her.

25 Michael Savage: 'The Imposition of Pass Laws on the African Population in South Africa 1916-1984', *African Affairs*, Vol. 1, No. 339, April 1986, at p. 181.

26 In May 1983 the Appellate Division made a decisive intervention which improved the lot of employed migrant contract workers in the urban areas. Their landmark judgment, Rikhoto v East Rand Administration Board, granted the applicant the right to permanent urban status, allowing 150 000 blacks the right to apply to have their families unite with them.

27 The advertisement was published on 23 October 1983 and included the names of Clive Corder, Dr Frans Cronje, Eric Ellerine, Robert Enthoven, Dick Goss, Dirk Hertzog, Leslie Frankel, Sol Kerzner, Louis Luyt, Ted Pavitt, Sydney Press, Bennie Slome, Eugene van As and Bill Venter. They, and the other signatories, constituted some of the most powerful business voices in the land. Some among their number are still active in commerce and industry today.

28 Amos Elon: *The Pity of it All: A portrait of Jews in Germany 1743-1933*, Penguin, 2002, at pp. 193-194.

29 Ibid.

30 See maiden speech of ME Mbili MP, 17 October 2006, Unrevised *Hansard*.

31 *Hansard*, Joint Sittings of both Houses of Parliament, 25 February 1999, at column 81.

32 1985(4) SA 709(D): For comment on the case 806 *South African Law Journal*, Vol. 103, 1986, at p. 344 and, especially, Professor LJ Boulle in *South African Journal on Human Rights*, Vol. 1, 1985, pp. 251-260, and John Hlophe in *South African Law Journal*, Vol. 104, 1987, at p. 183.

33 *Sunday Tribune*, 21 June 1987.

34 *Sunday Times*, 21 June 1987.

35 A full-blown national state of emergency was proclaimed the following year, in 1986.

36 Derrick Mercer: *Chronicles of the 20th Century*, at p. 144.

37 Henry Kenney: *Power, pride and prejudice*, Jonathan Ball, 1997, at p. 356.

38 Max du Preez: 'Explaining the Miracle' in *Turning Points Book 6 : Negotiation, Transition and Freedom*, joint publication of the Department of Education and Institute of Justice and Reconciliation, and STE Publishers.

39 Botha's speech not only failed to live up to the over-hyped expectations of it; he delivered a merciless slap-down to the reforms which Heunis and others suggested. He

stated, for example: 'I know for a fact that most [black] leaders in their own right in South Africa and reasonable South Africans will not accept the principle of one-man-one-vote in a unitary system. That would lead to domination of one over the other and it would lead to chaos. Consequently, I reject it as a solution.'

40 Indeed, one of the emigrants to New Zealand is a former colleague of Chris de Jager's from the CP, the immensely likeable and bright Cehill Pienaar, who arrived with me as a member of the 1989 intake to parliament, as MP for Heilbron in the Free State.

41 *ANC Today*, Vol. 6, No. 43, 3–9 November 2006.

42 http://www.anc.org.za/ancdocs/pr/1980s/pr850816.html.

43 See next chapter: 'Into Politics'.

44 A full analysis of the Mdlalose case, and the background facts and controversy it spawned on the campus, appeared in an article by the editor of the *Natal Witness*, David Willers, published in the newspaper on 16 April 1992.

45 *Sunday Tribune*, 12 April 1992.

46 Quoted by me in a speech to parliament on the University of Witwatersrand, Johannesburg (Private) Amendment Bill Debate, 20 May 1997.

47 *Sunday Times*, 12 November 1995.

48 *Financial Mail*, Johannesburg, 17 February 1995.

49 On 2 November 1995, Makgoba's attorney Ismail Ayob caused the hitherto confidential letter to Charlton to be published.

50 Interview with Mark Gevisser in the *Mail&Guardian*, 13 July 1995.

51 Etienne Mureinik: article in *Mail&Guardian*, 22 December 1995 to 4 January 1996, entitled 'Do we want quality or ethnic cleansing?'

52 Ibid.

53 *Business Day*, 10 November 1995.

54 *Star*, 8 November 1995.

55 *Sowetan*, 3 November 1995.

56 Letter from the minister of Education to the university vice chancellor, dated 15 November 1995.

57 Letter from Ismail Ayob attorneys to the university vice chancellor, dated 30 November 1995.

58 Ibid.

59 SAPA media report, 7 December 1995.

60 SAPA media report: 'Government will not allow Wits University to implode'.

61 See Chapter 4: 'The battle for Houghton'.

62 Interview with Helen Suzman, *Business Day*, 3 November 1997.

63 I ceased to be a member of the university Council in May 1997 when, in terms of a new statute, direct election of Council members by Convocation was scrapped.

64 *Mail&Guardian*, 22 December 1995 to 4 January 1996. (My two decades of intense involvement with Wits, starting as a lowly student and ending as a governor, ended. Aside from addressing one of its graduation ceremonies, I have had no further contact with the university since then.)

3: INTO POLITICS

1 I was very soon to discover that the PFP majority I was defending was, in fact, an illu-sory comfort blanket.The ward had rapidly changed its population since the preceding election. The 'Jewish' advantage my candidacy was meant to bring was considerably offset by the fact that much of the (voting) population in the area were Portuguese immigrants, largely refugees who had been arriving steadily since the collapse of the colonial empire in Angola.

2 A singular exception to this trend in the white Left in Yeoville/Bellevue was my friend David Ferreira. David was one of the brightest and most left-wing student politicians, a few years behind me at Wits. We disliked each other, fairly intensely, on campus, but became fast friends when he arrived to do his articles at Edward Nathan. His stellar academic track record and personal qualities ensured a Rhodes scholarship. Despite our political differences he voted for me and persuaded others to do the same when, as the result revealed, every ballot counted.

3 Unfortunately no doubt for some residents, old-age institutions are ideal and necessary stops on a candidate's and leader's political schedule. Aside from the concentration of a significant number of voters registered at one place which makes the visit politically necessary, the candidate is also, generally, guaranteed a full hall if he visits during tea time. This makes for good pictures and is immeasurably more reassuring for the can-didate and his team than an empty-looking venue which relies on people to come in off the street.

4 House of Assembly debates, 7 February 1986, column 428.

5 It is probably fair to say that the PFP never recovered from the rupture caused by its departed leader and the manner of his going.The party was comprehensively clobbered the following year in a general election. It limped on for two more years.

6 *Sunday Times*, 9 February 1986.

7 *Citizen*, 13 February 1986.

8 *Star*, 13 February 1986.

9 *Sunday Star*, 23 February 1986.

10 *Sunday Times*, 23 February 1986.

11 It was fantastically creepy (but no means unique in the hypocrisy of our politics) that about ten years later Bloomberg actually joined the ANC, while I – the so-called ANC appeaser – became the ANC's public enemy No. 1.

12 Even today, in ward contests where the DA and its opponents have registration tables at polling places, the head count of voters at a table is usually a highly accurate predictor of the final result.

13 Harry Truman once archly – and largely accurately – observed that 'if you want a friend in politics get a dog.' Bass and fellow councillors Claire Quail and Paul Asherson were the exceptions that proved the rule, starting a friendship at council level and remaining (at least until Paul's death) friends for life. In parliament I was also blessed with lasting friendships that transcended the petty jealousies and intrigues which are the staple of so much of political life.

14 *Star*, 27 February 1986.

15 *Weekly Mail*, 28 March to 6 April 1986.

16 'Past imperfect, future Tense' by Paul Bell in 'The Watershed Years', *Leadership*, 1991.

17 Davidson, Asherson, Bass, Quail, Walton and I constituted the core of the Young Turks,

a collective political label rather than an age-accurate description.

18 Ian McEwan: *Saturday*, Jonathan Cape, London, 2005.

19 See, for example, Jabu Kuzwayo: 'Developing mechanisms for civilian oversight over the armed forces' in *African Security Review*, Vol. 7, No. 5, 1998; Max Coleman: 'State violence: A study in repression', Centre for the Study of Violence and Reconciliation, Seminar No. 6, 1996.

20 *Saturday Star*, 21 April 1990.

21 Ibid.

22 *Sunday Star*, 22 April 1990.

23 Report of the Hiemstra Commission, September 1990, at p. 31.

24 Ibid., at p. 35.

25 *Business Day*, 25 March 1988.

26 *Star*, 25 March 1988.

27 MJ Cohen and John Major: *History in Quotations*, 2004.

28 *Saturday Star*, 14 August 1988.

29 *Saturday Star*, 24 September 1988.

30 *Sunday Times* Magazine, 16 October 1988.

31 *Star*, 21 September 1988.

32 *Beeld*, 22 September 1988.

33 *Business Day*, 28 October 1988.

4: THE BATTLE FOR HOUGHTON

1 *Business Day*, 23 October 1989.

2 *Saturday Star*, 8 April 1989.

3 *Star*, 11 April 1989.

4 *Business Day*, 23 May 1989.

5 *Sunday Star*, 21 May 1989.

6 *Business Day*, 26 June 1989.

7 *Star*, 25 May 1989.

8 *Citizen*, 29 May 1989.

9 Ibid.

10 *Sunday Star*, 2 April 1987.

11 *Citizen*, 23 June 1989.

12 *Sunday Star*, 25 June 1989.

13 The phrase was used to describe so-called 'verligte' Afrikaners who rejected the NP policy, but were disaffected by PFP-style opposition – presumably, 'third force' Afrikaans-speakers were in the ultra-Right forces.

14 *Sunday Times*, 6 August 1989: the article spoke of me as 'the leader of the young ones. His reputation as the tough, no-compromise leader of the DP in the Johannesburg city council precedes him, but everything points to the fact that he will live up to his billing.'

15 *Star*, 27 April 1989.

16 *Star*, 13 April 1988.

17 *Sunday Star*, 30 July 1989.

18 *Star*, 8 October 1989.

5: PRESENT AT THE CREATION

1 Tony Judt: *Post War*, op. cit., at pp. 524-525.
2 See F van Zyl Slabbert, Heribert Adam and Koglia Moodley: *Comrades in Business*, Tafelberg, 1997, at p. 53.
3 Willem de Klerk: *FW de Klerk: The Man in his Time*, Jonathan Ball, 1995.
4 *Sunday Times*, 26 April 1992.
5 *Hansard*, 13 February 1990, column 806.
6 *Hansard*, 7 May 1990, column 8150.
7 See for example Slabbert et al, op. cit., at p. 61.
8 M Albeldas and A Fischer: *A Question of Survival: Conversations with Key South Africans*, Jonathan Ball, 1987, at p. 483.
9 Patti Waldmeir: *Anatomy of a Miracle*, Viking, 1997, at pp. 160-161.
10 Slabbert et al, op. cit., at p. 61.
11 Waldmeir, op. cit., at p. 166.
12 Reported in the *Star*, 5 July 1990.
13 *Star*, 5 July 1990.
14 *Star*, 10 August 1990.
15 *Daily Mail*, 13 August 1990.
16 *Sunday Star*, 12 August 1990.
17 'Never mind the coffee, just pray they don't shoot', *Star*, 7 September 1990.
18 Waldmeir, op. cit., at p. 183.
19 Waldmeir, op. cit., at p. 186.
20 *Die Burger*, 22 June 1991.
21 Margaret Thatcher: *The Downing Street Years*, Harper Collins, 1993, at p. 167.
22 Waldmeir, op. cit., at p. 193.
23 Waldmeir, op. cit., at p. 198.
24 In truth, while the party's incompetence and feuding were factors, there was no doubt that the DP's administration of Johannesburg was also alienating the party's core supporters.
25 *Star*, 21 November 1991.
26 *Star*, 20 November 1991.
27 *Star*, 22 November 1991.
28 Waldmeir, op. cit., at p. 191.
29 Waldmeir, op. cit., at p. 241.
30 The CP won with a big majority of 2 140 votes, reversing the 1989 NP 1989 majority of 1 583. The percentage poll was 75,4%.
31 *New York Review of Books*, 21 December 2006, at p. 38; writing of leader Ariel Sharon.
32 The winning 'yes' campaign received a 68,7% affirmative vote in an 86% poll.
33 *Sunday Times*, 5 April 1992. There was a great, indeed amazing – and at that stage unknown – irony at play here. The DP and the NP did eventually join together in 2000 in the Democratic Alliance, of which I became leader. The NP, however, broke away a year later and ultimately disappeared into the bowels of the ANC. Thus Dalling found himself in the same party eventually, together with remnants of the Nationalist leadership he so despised!
34 David Dalling MP, Jan van Eck MP, Jan Momberg MP, Robert Haswell MP, Pierre Cronje MP.

35 *Sunday Times*, 26 April 1993.

36 Waldmeir, op. cit., at p. 201.

37 Waldmeir, op. cit., at pp. 202-203.

38 The ANC and NP top negotiators met apparently on over forty occasions between the breakdown of talks after Boipatong in July and official resumption of ANC/government talks in September. De Klerk, in a response to the national and international outrage consequent to Boipatong, arranged for an international independent inquiry to examine the massacre and allegations of security force complicity with it. They found no evidence of this, but excoriated the SAP for its poor investigative procedures afterwards.

39 *Sunday Times*, 8 October 1992.

40 Waldmeir, op. cit., at p. 216.

41 South African Institute of Race Relations 1992/93 Survey, p. 440.

42 *Business Day*, 23 October 1992.

43 See speech of Tony Leon MP in parliament, 21 October 1992.

44 *Hansard*, 21 April 1993, column 5524.

45 Waldmeir, op. cit., at p. 226.

46 Adam, Moodley and Slabbert, op. cit., at p. 55.

47 *Financial Mail*, 5 March 1993.

48 *Financial Mail*, 24 September 1993.

49 Billy Paddock in *Business Day*, 19 November 1993.

50 Statement by Tony Leon MP and DHM Gibson MP, 12 November 1993.

51 *Citizen*, 31 November 1993.

52 *Sunday Times*, 31 November 1993.

53 *Business Day*, 16 November 1993.

54 Ibid.

55 *Sunday Times*, 21 November 1993.

56 *Sunday Telegraph*, London, 21 November 1993. (Elsewhere I recount how the independence of the Judicial Service Commission was essentially whittled away over the first decade of democracy.)

57 *Hansard*, 22 November 1993, at column 13850.

58 Treurnicht died in April 1993, leading Douglas Gibson to observe in his inimitable way that since he could not decide whether his rejectionist party should participate in the all-race election, he solved the problem by 'choosing a third way and going to heaven' – a vintage Gibson remark.

59 In exchange for his participation in the election, Viljoen obtained a constitutional agreement to inaugurate a 'Volkstaat Council' which sat for several years after 1994, produced lengthy plans and was then phased out, yielding nothing at all for his supporters.

60 Waldmeir, op. cit., at p. 245.

61 Interestingly enough both Botha and Meyer had become either ANC members or supporters; perhaps proving their detractors – who bitterly accused them of 'selling out' – profoundly correct.

PART TWO: LEADER OF THE PARTY

6: NEW SOUTH AFRICA, NEW LEADER

1 The latter – in the form of the IFP – finally entered the electoral contest a week before polling day; while the former continued with a fitful, violent campaign of carnage and bombings right through to 27 April 1994.

2 *The Democratic Party Vision for the New South Africa*, South Africa Foundation Review, October / November / December 1993,Vol. 119, Nos. 10, 11 and 12.

3 *Sunday Times*, 15 May 1994.

4 *Sunday Times*, 17 April 1994.

5 *EP Post*, 20 April 1994.

6 *Cape Argus*, 14 April 1994.

7 *Mail&Guardian*, 21 April 1994.

8 *Sunday Times*, 8 May 1994. (Former president Richard M Nixon had recently died, in April 1994.)

9 *Sunday Times*, 22 May 1994.

10 *Argus*, 21 May 1994.

11 Only the party Congress, scheduled for November 1994 in Durban, could formally appoint the leader. But it was widely understood and accepted that whoever prevailed in the contest in May would be confirmed at the Congress – as I was later that year, unopposed. This remained so in every successive Congress until I voluntarily resigned 13 years later at the party's 2007 Congress.

12 The seven National Assembly MPs – Colin Eglin, Douglas Gibson, Mike Ellis, Kobus Jordaan, Dene Smuts, Ken Andrew and I – were augmented by three senators: James Selfe, EK Moorcroft and William Mnisi.

13 *Financial Mail*, 27 May 1994.

14 *Star*, 15 June 1994.

15 Ibid.

16 *Star*, 22 June 1994.

17 *Sunday Times*, 19 June 1994.

18 He was suffering from advanced cancer and was to die two years later.

19 Allister Sparks in *Beyond the Miracle* (pp. 182-193) gives a lucid, though highly romanticised, account of the evolution of ANC economic policy from the heavy strategic interventions envisaged for the state in the economy under the aegis of the 'Ready to Govern' policy document of July 1991 right through to the 'Growth, Employment and Redistribution' (GEAR) model, replete with its growth-orientated market orthodoxies, unveiled by Manuel in parliament on 14 June 1996.

20 Fortunately, Colin Eglin, whom I retained as the party's chief negotiator for the purposes of finalising the new Constitution, and Dene Smuts, our human rights spokesperson, were (although without formal legal training) among the best and most intelligent interpreters of constitutional and rights-related issues I ever encountered, inside or outside of parliament or legal practice.

21 The Labour Relations Act 66 of 1995; Basic Conditions of Employment Act 75 of 1997;

Employment Equity Act 55 of 1998; Skills Development Act 97 of 1998.

22 See next chapter.

23 The economic and employment figures and GEAR targets appear in Sparks, op. cit., at p. 198.

24 Nedlac was established by statute of the new parliament (Act 35 of 1994). Section 5(1) (c) of the Act states: 'Nedlac shall consider all proposed labour legislation relating to labour market policy before it is introduced in Parliament.'

25 At the time of the bill's passage (1995) the Small Business Development Corporation estimated that 49% of the economically active population was involved (as employer or employee) in some form of small enterprise, while only 24% were employed by big business.

26 *Hansard*, 12 September 1995, columns 3889-3993.

27 *The Economist*'s description of Sir Menzies Campbell's lot as leader of Britain's Liberal Democrats: *The Economist*, 3 March 2007.

28 Frielinghaus, over thirteen years later, is still a centre of excellence in our parliamentary research office.

29 Desmarais stayed three years and today remains one of my closest friends.

30 'Leon's DP Fast Proving that Dynamite Comes in Small Packages', *Sunday Tribune*, 28 August 1994.

31 In a rare media interview in 1997, Oppenheimer was quite open in his support for the party and me. He told the *Mail&Guardian* (7-13 March 1997): 'I think the DP talks a lot of sense and I think Tony Leon talks a lot of sense. The DP is really the only party I could support.'

32 As I explained my rationale for the merger, Oppenheimer quietly broke in: 'I might not understand this deal entirely, but it seems to me you are saying that we have created and are now part of something larger … and I think that's a jolly good thing.' It was to be our last meeting. He passed away three weeks later. I described him as 'a prince among men' and noted that without his continued support and financial generosity there would have been no liberal political party in South Africa – neither the Progressives nor the DP. I miss him to this day.

33 *Daily News*, 24 October 1994.

34 Gertrude Himmelfarb: *The Moral Imagination: From Edmund Burke to Lionel Trilling*, Oxford University Press, December 2004.

35 The DP was then emphatically pro-choice.

36 *Sunday Times*, 3 August 1995.

37 *Beeld*, 7 February 1995.

38 Quoted by the author in an article in the *Sunday Times*, 10 December 1995.

39 Statistics quoted by author, *Sunday Times*, 10 December 1995.

40 *Sunday Times*, 22 October 1995.

41 Overall in the Western Cape (when the metro result was added to the rural areas which had voted the previous year) the party barely gained 5% of the total vote, down on the provincial total obtained in 1994 and just ahead of the nugatory 4,2% which we received on the national ballot from the province in the same election.

42 President Mandela's remarks were quoted to parliament by IFP president and minister of Home Affairs, Dr MG Buthelezi MP, in the debate on the budget of the Presidency, on 2 May 1995, in columns 716-722 of *Hansard*.

43 *Hansard*, op. cit., at column 719.

44 *Hansard*, op. cit., at columns 819-820.

45 *Citizen*, 24 February 1995.

46 *Sunday Tribune*, 13 February 1995.

47 Quoted by *Business Day*, 24 April 1995.

48 *Sunday Tribune*, ibid.

49 Ibid.

50 *Sunday Times*, 30 April 1995.

51 *Business Day*, 24 April 1995.

52 *Star*, 24 April 1995.

53 *Mail&Guardian*, 8-14 December 1995.

54 See for example *Hansard*, 4 June 1997, columns 1331-1334; and *Hansard*, 5 November 1997, columns 3483-3484.

55 SAPA, 6 June 1999.

56 On 22 September 1998 a 600-strong South African military task force entered Lesotho on the instruction of acting president Mangosuthu Buthelezi, who claimed that this was part of a combined SANDF/ Botswana Defence Force initiative to help the government restore law and order after election-related unrest.

   Amid the chaos, unruly civilians took to the streets of Maseru in an orgy of looting and arson, which the intervening troops could do little to stop. With downtown Maseru in ruins, the South African government insisted that the military intervention was not an invasion, but rather a response to a written invitation by Lesotho's prime minister and head of government. But further controversy resulted from the revelation that the prime minister had left it until South African troops were already in the country before informing King Letsie III.

   Shortly afterwards I made the point that the SANDF was willing to spend millions of rands on an invasion with an unclear purpose, but when I had asked why the army could not be used to protect vulnerable South Africans in rural areas, it pleaded poverty.

57 Mandela's remarks were quoted by Jack Bloom MPL in a speech, 'The case for George W Bush', to the South African Institute of International Affairs, Johannesburg, 5 September 2006.

58 Jack Bloom MPL, South African Institute of International Affairs, 5 September 2006.

59 SAPA, 1 March 1996.

60 *Cape Times*, 4 March 1996.

61 *Saturday Star*, 9 March 1996.

62 *Star*, 16 March 1996.

63 Quoted by James Myburgh: 'The last Jacobins of Africa: Thabo Mbeki and the making of the New South Africa', unpublished manuscript, 2007, at p. 82.

64 *Hansard*, 10 June 1997, columns 3246-3261.

65 Myburgh, op. cit., at p. 82.

66 *Hansard*, 10 June 1997, columns 3671-3676.

67 James Myburgh, op. cit., at p. 95, quoting an unnamed ANC official reported in the *Chicago Tribune*.

68 http://www.anc.org.za/show.php?doc=ancdocs/history/conf/presaddress.html.

69 James Myburgh, op. cit., at p. 97.

70 The document is contained in *Umrabulo* No. 5, Third Quarter 1998, as quoted by Myburgh at p. 117.

71 *Hansard*, 10 February 1998, columns 39-57.
72 'Death of the Rainbow Nation: Unmasking the ANC's Programme of Reracialisation', DP discussion document, February 1998.
73 Quoted in 'Who is Thabo Mbeki?', *The Economist*, 1 November 1997.
74 *Business Day*, 5 March 1998.
75 *Business Day*, 8 March 1998.
76 The arms deal was eventually called off, apparently consequent to America's heavy arm-twisting on the matter.
77 *Sowetan*, 31 January 1997.
78 *Cape Times*, 24 January 1997.
79 *Mercury*, 24 January 1997.
80 *Volksblad*, 10 January 1997.
81 *Citizen*, 30 January 1997.
82 *Weekend Argus*, 15-16 February 1997.
83 *Cape Times*, 27 February 1997.
84 This was a reference to President Robert Mugabe of Zimbabwe, who after ruthlessly and violently crushing his political opponent (and quondam ally) Joshua Nkomo – and his ZAPU party – had co-opted him into his government. It was, I thought, an unfortunate and revealing analogy.
85 *Die Burger*, 4 March 1997.
86 *Pretoria News*, 7 March 1997.
87 *Star*, 10 May 1997.
88 *Sunday Tribune*, 10 March 1996.
89 SAPA, 22 May 1997.
90 A good and reasonably dispassionate summary of the TRC's *modus operandi* and reactions to it appears in Martin Meredith's work *The State of Africa*, Jonathan Ball Publishers, published in the US as *The Fate of Africa*, New York, Public Affairs, 2005, at pp. 654 onward.
91 Meredith, op. cit., at p. 657.
92 Ibid.
93 Meredith, op. cit., at p. 659.
94 As quoted by Sparks, op. cit., at p. 161.
95 Immediately prior to its public release, De Klerk sought a court order to have findings relating to him excised from the publication, particularly relating to the Commission's findings that De Klerk had been an accessory after the fact to the bombing of Khotso House and Cosatu House. The court ruled that the sections should be blacked out until it had had an opportunity to consider the case properly. After lengthy discussion, the report was published – but with the removal of some of the references to which De Klerk objected.
96 I was to have later confirmation of the ANC's approach when, years later, I challenged Mbeki about the naming of a national intelligence agency (NIA) academy after Mzwandile Piliso, who was the head of the ANC's security department in exile from 1981 to 1987 and had subsequently died. I wrote a letter to Mbeki on 30 May 2005, in response to a speech he made to parliament in which he disparaged the naming of the town of Grahamstown after Colonel Graham, whom he described as one of the most 'brutal and most vicious of the British commanders on that frontier [of the eastern Cape]'. Defending the ANC's proclivity to change a host of town and street names,

Mbeki moaned, 'Yet we have a town – Grahamstown – named after him. The question must arise: Why do we celebrate a butcher? This place has got a name; it's called iRhini. But we celebrate a butcher!'

Having remembered Piliso's own, more recent, butchery and acts of torture, highlighted by both the TRC and the ANC's own internal commissions of enquiry into gross violations of human rights at the ANC's notorious Quatro camp (or 'Morris Seabelo Rehabilitation Centre', to give it its full Orwellian title) in Angola, I thought the opportunity too good to miss, and in my letter to Mbeki sent a reminder of the acts of torture which Piliso directly oversaw and which the TRC and the ANC's 1992 Skweyiya Commission reported on. As I detailed it to the president, they included the following:

- lengthy isolation in solitary confinement;
- regular beatings under the feet or elsewhere with guava tree sticks or with coffee tree sticks;
- 'Napalm': being rubbed with (or rolling naked on) hairy beans or leaves of a plant which caused itching;
- 'Pompa': blowing out one's cheeks or pumping them up so that a guard could slap the cheeks causing excruciating pain to the ears;
- 'Pawpaw': being covered on the face with the skin of a scooped out pawpaw fruit, then beaten;
- 'Beirut': flogging while naked and lying in a face-down position;
- 'Helicopter': being tied hand and foot and suspended on a pole or log like a pig on a spit;
- being tied to a tree and remaining there in public view for a long time;
- having red ants introduced into clothing and being bitten by them;
- 'Slaughter': being placed in a shoulder-deep hole and then beaten on the head and shoulders for obeying an instruction to climb out;
- 'Starvation': being denied food as a form of punishment;
- chopping wood for hours on end;
- drawing water and pulling a 1 000-litre tank uphill with others, while being beaten in the process; and
- third-degree interrogation – non-stop interrogation for two days or more.

When he eventually responded, Mbeki replied: 'The naming of a South African Intelligence Academy and of a city such as Grahamstown are obviously different questions. In the cases you raise, there is no equivalence. This is the more so when one takes account of the intentions of the two persons involved – indeed, their lives stand in direct opposition to each other. In the one case, the person was involved in the subjugation of the people of South Africa and, in the other, the person fought in a struggle for democracy on behalf of the people of South Africa.'

Clearly, in the ANC president's worldview, even the worst and most malignant foot-soldier was a hero – worthy of the highest honour. It is doubtful whether the so-called 'prime evil' of the apartheid state, Colonel Eugene de Kock, who was sentenced to two life sentences plus 212 years imprisonment in 1994 after being found guilty of 89 charges from his activities as head of the apartheid state's Vlakplaas unit, was necessarily aware of Mbeki's embrace of the ANC's chief torturer. But he had been, already, long abandoned by his own political masters – correctly in my view – but probably not in the minds of many NP supporters.

97 Gant had served as the chairman of the DP Federal Council and Executive until November 1994. The farm was later sold to the business mogul, Christo Wiese.

98 A leading businessman later dispelled my illusion, advising me many years later that he had placed Meyer on his corporate payroll from the moment he left parliament in 1997 until his return there after the 1999 election.

99 Bantu Holomisa joined the Transkei Defence Force in 1976 and quickly rose through the ranks to major-general. In December 1987 he led a successful revolt against the then prime minister, Stella Sigcau. Tutor Ndamase was made prime minister, and Holomisa remained in power as commander of the Transkei Defence Force until Transkei's re-integration into South Africa.

Holomisa then began to build his career in the ANC. He styled himself a populist, and used information obtained from his close ties to the apartheid intelligence services in his former life to help his career. He set about exposing some of the work of the SADF's Department of Military Intelligence, including the Goniwe 'death signal' sent by General Joffel van der Westhuizen. In 1996 he obtained the highest number of votes in the ANC National Executive Committee. http://www.anc.org.za/ancdocs/misc/holomisa.html.

100 SAPA, 1 August 1996.

101 *Argus*, 26 August 1996.

102 *Business Day*, 3 February 1995.

103 *Sunday Times*, 14 September 1997.

104 *Citizen*, 4 June 1997.

105 The same sound bite was conveyed in print in several newspapers, e.g. *Rapport*, Sunday 18 January 1998.

106 Two prominent Eastern Cape NP politicians, Donald Lee MP, its most senior Coloured leader there, and Embré Gouws, a former rural mayor and current PE councillor, who were personally close to Delport, followed his lead into the party. Both were returned, along with Delport, as DP MPs in 1999.

107 Speech to Democratic Party Regional Council, Rosebank Hotel, 2 March 1998 (published in various media).

108 JP Landman was a noted local political commentator, Afrikaans-speaking and progressive in outlook.

109 *Sunday Times*, 17 May 1998. '*Gatvol*' is an Afrikaans term which can politely be rendered as 'fed up'. It adumbrates unease at the TRC, eviction from power, affirmative action, and denigration of their language, culture and history.

110 Ibid.

111 Helen Suzman: Foreword in Tony Leon: *Hope and Fear: Reflections of a Democrat*, Jonathan Ball, Johannesburg, 1998, at p. ix.

112 As a tribute on my 50th birthday in December 2006.

113 *Daily Dispatch*, East London, 13 November 1998.

114 When the poll was produced, Slabbert – contrary to the expectations of that evening – scored a low 5%, or thereabouts, in terms of popularity among Western Cape voters.

7: CONSTITUTIONAL PALIMPSEST

1 The ANC largesse to the opposition at this stage included the appointment of Ken Andrew as chairman of parliament's Standing Committee on Public Accounts (Scopa), by far a more significant appointment than the title conferred on me by the Constitutional Assembly.

2 However, the opposition's veto – and it was far from certain that the various oppositional factions would or could agree – was not as potent a weapon as it appeared. A key section of the Interim Constitution stated that in the event of parliament not assenting to the final constitution, it would be 'referred by the president for a decision by the electorate by way of a national referendum' – and the constitution could then be ratified by a simple majority of voters.

3 Such a right was indeed enshrined in S.7(1)(a) of The Constitution of the Republic of South Africa 1996 ('The Constitution').

4 *Financial Mail*, 1 December 1995.

5 Quoted by Paul Bell in 'The Making of the Constitution', published by the Constitutional Assembly, March 1997, at p. 42.

6 *Citizen*, 18 April 1996.

7 *Citizen*, 1 May 1996.

8 *Financial Mail*, 17 May 1996.

9 *Sowetan*, 3 May 1996.

10 See section 29(1) and (2) of the Constitution, as originally enacted in 1996.

11 See sections 25 and 36(1) of the Constitution, as originally enacted in 1996.

12 Debates of the Constitutional Assembly, Vol. 3, 8 May 1996, columns 436-441.

13 Certification of the Constitution of the Republic of South Africa – CCT 24/1996.

14 *Sunday Times*, 15 December 1996.

PART THREE: NEW ORDER CHALLENGES

8: THE LONG AIDS DEATH MARCH

1 UNAIDS: *2006 Report on the Global AIDS epidemic* (May 2006) [online publication] http://data.unaids.org/pub/GlobalReport/2006/2006_GR_CH04_en.pdf.

2 Chuks Jonathan Mba: 'The Effect of HIV/AIDS Mortality on South Africa's Life Expectancy and Implications for the Elderly Population' [online abstract] http://agingaidsnet.psc.isr.umich.edu/projects/detail.html?id=102.

3 South African Department of Health: *National HIV and Syphilis prevalence survey* (2005) [online report] http://www.doh.gov.za/docs/reports/2005/hiv.pdf.

4 South African Department of Health: *National HIV and Syphilis prevalence survey.*

5 Alan Whiteside: 'Painting the picture – Impact of AIDS on Development in Africa', *Science in Africa*, May 2003 [online article] http://www.scienceinafrica.co.za/2003/june/aids.htm.

6 Jani Meyer: 'The AIDS plan that never saw the light of day', *Tribune*, 10 October 2004, p. 8.

7 Sharon LaFraniere: 'UN Envoy Sharply Criticizes South Africa's AIDS Program', *New York Times*, 25 October 2005 [online article] http://query.nytimes.com/gst/fullpage. html?sec=health&res=9C01E4D8103FF936A15753C1A9639C8B63. See also Stephen Lewis: *Race Against Time*, Toronto, House of Anansi, 2005.

8 'India "has most people with HIV"', BBC News, 30 May 2006 [online article] http:// news.bbc.co.uk/2/hi/health/5030184.stm.

9 'Economic Impact of AIDS in South Africa', ING Barings, Johannesburg, 2000.

10 Thabo Mbeki: Declaration of Partnership Against AIDS, address, 9 October 1998 [online text] http://www.anc.org.za/ancdocs/history/mbeki/1998/tm1009.htm.

11 'The Sarafina II Controversy', *Phila Legislative Update*, June 1996 [online article] http:// www.hst.org.za/pphc/Phila/sarafina.htm

12 Letter by Mike Ellis MP to the Public Protector, 2 March 1998.

13 Response of the Public Protector, 24 January 1999.

14 Thabo Mbeki: 'ANC has no financial stake in Virodene', March 1998 [online article] http://www.anc.org.za/ancdocs/history/mbeki/1998/virodene.html.

15 ANC statement of 3 March 1998. http//www.anc.org. 30/anadocs/pn/1998/pn0303b. htm/.

16 Thabo Mbeki: Address to the National Council of Provinces, 28 October 1999 [online text] http://www.dfa.gov.za/docs/speeches/1999/mbek1028.htm.

17 Samantha Power: 'The AIDS Rebel', *New Yorker*, May 2003.

18 Tony Karon: 'Mbeki – Africa's Challenges', *Time*, 11 September 2000 [online text] http://www.time.com/time/europe/magazine/2000/0911/mbeki.html.

19 David Rasnick: letter to Dr Aluko, 27 December 2004 [online text] http://www.utexas.edu/conferences/africa/ads/204.html.

20 Mike Cohen: 'President's Controversial Advisory Panel Releases AIDS Report', *AP*, 4 April 2001 [online text] http://www.aegis.com/news/ads/2001/AD010515.html.

21 Parks Mankahlana, 20 March 2000.

22 Ibid.

23 Parks Mankahlana, *Citizen*, 28 March 2000.

24 Parks Mankahlana, quoted in Jon Cohen: 'South Africa's New Enemy', *Science* 288 (5474) [online article] http://aidscience.com/Science/Cohen288(5474)2168.html.

25 Edwin Cameron: 'Involvement of People Living with HIV/AIDS – How to Make It More Meaningful', address to gala dinner of the Second National Conference for People Living with HIV/AIDS, Durban, 8 March 2000.

26 Ibid.

27 Ibid.

28 Thabo Mbeki, quoted in Suzanne Daley: 'A President Misapprehends a Killer', *New York Times*, 14 May 2000.

29 Thabo Mbeki, quoted by Robin McKie and David Beresford: 'Africa's fate hangs in balance', *Observer*, 7 May 2000, p. 18.

30 Rachel L Swarns: 'An AIDS Skeptic in South Africa Feeds Simmering Doubts', *New York Times*, 31 March 2002 [online article] http://query.nytimes.com/gst/fullpage.html?sec=health&res=9C01EEDA173AF932A05750C0A9649C8B63.

31 Cheryl Carolus: 'This absurd myth of African AIDS epidemic', *Financial Times*, 6 July 2000.

32 Helen Epstein: 'The Mystery of AIDS in South Africa', *New York Review of Books*, 20 July 2000 [online article] http://www.nybooks.com/articles/9.

33 Paul Trewhela: 'Mbeki and AIDS in Africa: A Comment', *New York Review of Books*, 19 October 2000.

34 Charlene Smith, quoted by Tony Leon: speech on the occasion of the president's Budget Vote debate, 13 July 2000, National Assembly, Cape Town.

35 Thabo Mbeki: response to the president's Budget Vote debate, 14 July 2000, National Assembly, Cape Town.

36 John G Bartlett: 'Post-Exposure Therapy for Prevention of Non-Occupational Transmission of HIV', *The Hopkins HIV Report*, March 1998 [online article] http://www.hopkins-aids.edu/publications/report/march98_4.html.

37 Letter to President Mbeki, 19 June 2000.

38 Letter from John Kearney to Tony Leon, 4 October 2000.

39 Letter from President Mbeki to Tony Leon, 1 July 2000.

40 *Sunday Times*, 9 July 2000.

41 *Mail&Guardian*, 14 July 2000.

42 Letter from President Mbeki to Tony Leon, 17 July 2000.

43 Letter from President Mbeki to Tony Leon, 5 August 2000.

44 Letter from Tony Leon to President Mbeki, 24 August 2000.

45 Letter from President Mbeki to Tony Leon, 1 September 2000.

46 *Business Day*, 16 April 2007.

47 David Beresford: 'ANC backs down on AIDS,' *Guardian*, 25 October 2000.

48 SAPA, 11 August 2000.

49 National Assembly Interpellations, Questions and Replies, Vol. 36C at 3408, September 2000, p. 20.

50 Smuts Ngonyama, quoted in David Beresford: 'ANC backs down on AIDS', *Guardian*, 25 October 2000.

51 Drew Forrest: 'Behind the smokescreen', *Mail&Guardian*, 26 October 2001 [online article] http://www.mg.co.za/articledirect.aspx?articleid=217658&area=%2farchives__print_edition%2f.

52 Smuts Ngonyama, quoted in Tim Butcher: 'Mbeki accepts defeat after protests over AIDS policy', *Daily Telegraph*, 18 October 2000.

53 *Star*, 18 October 2000.

54 Minister of Health: reply to DA question in parliament, 13 September 2000 (internal question paper number 44).

55 George J Annas: 'The Right to Health and the Nevirapine Case in South Africa', *New England Journal of Medicine*, 20 February 2003.

56 Ibid.

57 Nick Koornhof: Statement on Prevention of Mother-To-Child Transmission of HIV/AIDS: Roll-out of Programme in Western Cape, 29 August 2000.

58 Tony Leon: speech in the National Assembly, Cape Town, 10 October 2000.

59 Tony Leon: statement at media conference, 27 October 2000.

60 *Sunday Times*, 29 October 2000.

61 Address by President Thabo Mbeki, University of Fort Hare, 12 October 2001 http//www.anc.org.za/ancdocs/history/mbeki/2001/XM11012.btm/.

62 *Mail&Guardian*, 26 October 2001.

63 Agence France-Presse: 'S Africa-AIDS: ANC Stalls on Issue of Anti-AIDS Drug in

Second S African Province', 23 January 2002 [online article] http://www.aegis.com/NEWS/AFP/2002/AF020138.html.

64 Afrol News: 'South Africa: ANC Might Bow to Pressure on Antiretroviral Drugs', 21 February 2002 [online article] http://ww2.aegis.com/news/afrol/2002/AO020203.html.

65 Carmel Rickard: 'State routed in Constitutional Court's Nevirapine Judgment', *Sunday Times*, 7 July 2002 [online article] http://www.aegis.com/news/suntimes/2002/ST020709.html.

66 *Mail&Guardian*, 19 April 2002.

67 UN Integrated Regional Information Networks: 'Johannesburg: Chronology of HIV/AIDS Treatment Access Debate', 19 August 2003 [online article] http://www.aegis.com/news/irin/2003/IR030817.html.

68 *Mail&Guardian*, 15 July 2004.

69 Liz McGregor: 'Hungry for Life, the Hip Deejay Clutched at Futile Straws', *Sunday Times*, 7 March 2004 [online article] http://www.sundaytimes.co.za/2004/03/07/insight/in01.asp.

70 Caroline Hooper-Box: 'Study casts doubt on African potato remedy', *Sunday Independent*, 30 January 2005, p. 30. See also Jillian Green: 'Manto's Concoction "Could be Harmful"', *Star*, 9 June 2004, p. 3; and Edward Mills: 'Impact of African Herbal Medicines on Antiretroviral Metabolism', *AIDS* Vol. 19, No. 1, 3 January 2005, pp. 95-7.

71 *Sunday Independent*, 20 August 2006.

72 Thabo Mbeki: response to questions by Ryan Coetzee MP, National Assembly, Cape Town, 21 October 2004 [online text] http://www.anc.org.za/ancdocs/anctoday/2004/at42.htm.

73 Edward Rhymes, quoted by Thabo Mbeki, 21 October 2004.

74 JA du Plessis: 'South Africa: Arguing the Unthinkable – The Emerging HIV/AIDS Pandemic', Management Briefing, May 2004.

9: ZIMBABWE: THE FIRE NEXT DOOR

1 Samantha Power, *Atlantic Monthly*, December 2003.

2 Robert Mugabe, quoted in David Blair: *Degrees in Violence: Robert Mugabe and the Struggle for Power in Zimbabwe*, Continuum, New York, 2002, p. 14.

3 Heidi Holland: *Dinner with Mugabe*, Penguin Books, 2008.

4 Tony Leon: 'South Africa Must Engage in Zimbabwe to Advance Democracy and Secure Economic Change', press statement, 20 February 2000.

5 Thabo Mbeki, quoted in Allister Sparks: *Beyond the Miracle*, Jonathan Ball, Johannesburg, 2003, at p. 327.

6 Craig J Richardson: *Learning from Failure: Property Rights, Land Reforms, and the Hidden Architecture of Capitalism*, American Enterprise Institute for Public Policy Research, No. 2, April 1996 [online paper] http://www.aei.org/publications/pubID.24196/pub_detail.asp.

7 Andrew Meldrum: *Where We Have Hope: A Memoir of Zimbabwe*, John Murray, London, 2004, p. 128.

8 Ibid.

9 Sparks, op. cit., pp. 319-20.

10 Richardson, op. cit., p. 3.

11 RW Johnson: 'If the people could choose', *Focus*, No. 24, December 2001.

12 Zimbabwe Human Rights NGO Forum: 'Human Rights and Zimbabwe's 2000 Election', January 2001 [online document] http://www.hrforumzim.com/special_hrru/Special_Report1_2000_elections.rtf.

13 Thabo Mbeki: 'The people of Zimbabwe must decide their own future', *ANC Today*, 9 May 2003 [online newsletter] http://www.anc.org.za/ancdocs/anctoday/2003/at18.htm#preslet.

14 Teddy Brett and Simon Winter: 'Origins of the Zimbabwe crisis', *Focus*, 30 June 2003 [online article] http://www.hsf.org.za/%23articledatabase/article_view.asp?id=49.

15 Mahmoud Kassem et al: *Final Report of the Panel of Experts on the Illegal Exploitation of Natural Resources and Other Forms of Wealth of the Democratic Republic of Congo*, United Nations Security Council, 16 October 2002 [online report] http://www.grandslacs.net/doc/2477.pdf. 8.

16 Martin Meredith: *The State of Africa*, Public Affairs, New York, 2005, pp. 628-629.

17 Meldrum, op. cit., p. 120.

18 Zimbabwe Human Rights NGO Forum, ibid.

19 Ibid.

20 Johnson, op. cit.

21 Tony Leon: statement, 20 February 2000.

22 Meldrum, op. cit., p. 126.

23 Johnson, op. cit.

24 Zimbabwe Human Rights NGO Forum, ibid.

25 Ibid.

26 Ibid.

27 Tony Leon: 'South Africa must speak out against Mugabe's misrule', press statement, 2 April 2000.

28 My parliamentary colleagues and I decided we would highlight the contents of the letter by marching from parliament up Roeland Street (where the Zimbabwe mission in Cape Town was housed) to deliver the letter personally. However, on hearing of our impending arrival the Zimbabweans hastily exited the building and bolted the door. So I read the letter out to the waiting media and, without trying to emulate Martin Luther, but through necessity, pinned it on the door.

29 Tony Leon: letter to Robert Gabriel Mugabe, 13 April 2000.

30 SAPA, 4 May 2000.

31 Zimbabwe Human Rights NGO Forum, ibid.

32 Ibid.

33 Meredith, op. cit., at p. 640.

34 Ibid.

35 Meredith, op. cit., at p. 641.

36 Reuters: 'We'll weed out Rhodesians – Govt', *Citizen*, 23 February 2001.

37 Trevor Manuel, quoted in Nicol Degli Innocenti: 'S Africa firm on aid for Zimbabwe', *Financial Times*, 20 March 2001.

38 RW Johnson, *Focus*, No. 25, 1st Quarter 2002, pp. 8-10.

39 Mike Schussler: 'The Cost of Zimbabwe to the South African Economy', Zimbabwe Research Initiative, 2003.

40 Tony Leon: speech on Zimbabwe, Parliament of South Africa, 26 February 2001.

41 George W Bush: press conference, Union Buildings, Pretoria, 9 July 2003 [online transcript]. http://www.whitehouse.gov/news/releases/2003/07/20030709.html.

42 *Business Day*, 7 June 2006.

43 Tony Leon: speech during special debate on Zimbabwe, Parliament, South Africa, 27 February 2001.

44 'Standing up to Mugabe', *Daily Telegraph*, 19 February 2001.

45 Moyo and Mugabe were later to suffer a spectacular fall-out which led to the former renouncing his master and winning a seat as an independent MP in the 2003 parliamentary elections.

46 I wrote about my visit in an essay for *Time* magazine entitled 'South Africa's defining moment', *Time*, 23 April 2001.

47 *Business Day*, 28 February 2001.

48 *Herald*, Harare, 27 February 2001.

49 Meldrum, op. cit., p. 195.

50 Meldrum, op. cit., pp. 197-200.

51 Meldrum, op. cit., p. 201.

52 ANC: 'Outcome of the Zimbabwe Presidential Elections', press statement, 13 March 2002 [online document] http://www.anc.org.za/ancdocs/pr/2002/pro313a.html.

53 'From breadbasket to basket case', *The Economist*, 29 June 2002, pp. 41-2.

54 The delegation consisted of MPs Clelland-Stokes, Botha and Dan Maluleke.

55 Not his real name.

56 *Herald*, Harare, 4 July 2002.

57 *Daily News*, Harare, 3 July 2002.

58 *ANC Today*, 8 March 2002.

59 Thabo Mbeki: 'We will resist the upside-down view of Africa', *ANC Today*, 12 December 2003 [online newsletter] http://anc.org.za/ancdocs/anctoday/2003/at49.htm.

60 Thabo Mbeki: State of the Nation address, Parliament, South Africa, 8 February 2002.

61 SAPA, 10 July 2002.

62 Ibid.

63 Mmegi: 'South Africa criticises Commonwealth suspension of Zimbabwe, but also criticises land reform there', *Reporter*; also SAPA, 21 March 2003 [online article] http://www.sadocc.at/news/2003-080.shtml.

64 http://www.zimbabwesituation.com/may25_2003.html.

65 Basildon Peta: 'Secret deal paves way for Mugabe exit this year', *Independent*, 15 July 2003.

66 Speech by Dumisani Makhaye, ANC NEC member, opening the ANC's Mpumalanga provincial congress, 23 March 2002.

67 http://www.allafrica.com/stories/200504041132.html.

68 http://www.news.bbc.co.uk/1/hi/world/africa/4715635.stm.

69 Samantha Power, op. cit.

10: PARLIAMENT: CORROSION IN THE CORRIDORS

1 *Hansard*, National Assembly, Interpellations, Vol. 3, 1994, at p. 11.

2 Ibid., questions and replies.

3 *Cape Times*, 2 June 1995.

4 Cited by Douglas Gibson in *Focus*, published by the Helen Suzman Foundation, *Focus*, No. 38, 2005, quoted from A Bernstein, CDE: 'Policy making, etc.', 1999, at p. 28.

5 Joe Slovo, quoted in Pregs Govender: 'Farewell and Thank You', farewell speech in the National Assembly, 30 May 2002 [online text] http://www.anc.org.za/ancdocs/speeches/2002/sp0530.html.

6 'Hogan slams Parliament for budget oversight', *Mail&Guardian*, 14 June 2002.

7 *Sunday Times*, 8 February 2004.

8 *Sunday Times*, 27 May 2001.

9 SAPA, 22 January 2001.

10 Joint statement by the Auditor-General, National Director of Public Prosecutions, and the Public Protector on the Joint Investigation Report into the Strategic Defence Procurement Packages, 15 November 2001.

11 http://www/da.org.za/da/Site/Eng/campaigns/arms.asp.

12 *Pretoria News*, 3 March 2005; *Natal Witness*, 31 March 2005.

13 'Zuma letter was mine – Mbeki', interview, *Sunday Independent*, 26 February 2006.

14 *Business Day*, 3 June 2005.

15 Andrew Feinstein: *After the party*, Jonathan Ball, 2008.

16 'RDP': 'Reconstruction and Development Programme' produced by the ANC before the 1994 election.

17 Hermann Giliomee: 'Shortcuts betray Democracy', *Cape Times*, 21 August 1997.

18 'Policy-making in a New Democracy', Centre for Development and Enterprise, August 1999, at p. 21.

19 Richard Calland in 'Report Commission' ed by CDE, 1998, at p. 11.

20 *Natal Witness*, 16 April 1997.

21 *Herald*, 11 March 1998.

22 Helen Suzman: *In No Uncertain Terms*, Jonathan Ball, 1993, at p. 114.

23 L Nijzink: 'Opposition in the new South Africa', paper presented at Konrad Adenauer Foundation Conference, 2001; cited by Gibson, op. cit.

24 Gibson, ibid.

25 *Hansard*, House of Assembly Debates, Question No. 2, 21 October 2004.

26 *Independent Online*, iol.co.za, 6 September 2007.

27 *Mail&Guardian*, 27 January 2006.

28 Mbulelo Goniwe: speech in the National Assembly, Parliament of South Africa, Cape Town, 25 May 2005, Final *Hansard*.

29 'From Lapdog to Watchdog', DA Discussion Document, 28 October 2004.

30 The DA developed 17 proposals that we believed would in some way bolster parliament's ability to oversee the executive. Some of the most important are:

   Legislation that prohibits MPs and ministers from being employed by parastatals or government agencies for two years after leaving parliament.

   Questions to be allocated on a first-come-first-served basis, instead of in proportion to party strength, thereby giving proactive MPs, irrespective of party allegiances, more opportunities to call ministers to account.

   An appeal mechanism that gives the Speaker the power to ask the minister or president to respond to a question adequately.

   The re-introduction of four 15-minute interpellations per question day.

   The removal of the limit on follow-ups to stimulate debate and put pressure on ministers to respond to questions satisfactorily.

The current convention of ten days for a minister to respond to written questions to become a hard and fast rule of parliament.

MPs to be required to undergo rigorous training, specifically on oversight.

Every MP to be assigned their own researcher, as in many other legislatures around the world. If the cost is prohibitive, then specialist researchers should be employed to assist groups of members of committees.

Committees should be compelled to submit a report specifically on their oversight activities.

Committees should be given the power to amend a budget.

The Speaker should not participate in caucus meetings and activities of the majority party in parliament.

Regulations should be submitted to the relevant portfolio committee for approval. In Australia, for example, regulations are submitted to the relevant portfolio committee to consider their constitutionality as well as whether the regulations are in line with policy.

31 *Star*, 29 May 2006.
32 *Citizen*, 30 May 2006.
33 *Mail&Guardian*, 26 May to 1 June 2006.
34 Geoffrey Wheatcroft: *The Strange Death of Tory England*, Allen Lane, 2005, at p. 241.

11: JUDGING THE JUDGES

1 See 'Rainbow Jurisprudence' by Professor A Cockrell, *South African Journal on Human Rights*, Vol. 12, No. 1, 1996.
2 Sydney Kentridge: 'Law and Lawyers in a Changing Society', University of the Witwatersrand, 22 September 1987.
3 Ellison Kahn: 'Oliver Deneys Schreiner: A South African' in *Fiat Justitia: Essays in Memory of Oliver Deneys Schreiner*, ed Ellison Kahn, Juta, Johannesburg, 1983.
4 Kentridge, op. cit., at p. 4.
    Some fifteen or so years later I was to witness the apogee of the 'insanity' to which Kentridge referred in its modernist and most bizarre manifestation. When in legal practice I had to attend a matter in the Kempton Park magistrate's court, near Johannesburg airport. This hideous edifice, erected a few years before, was not simply an egregious example of monumentalist architecture. It provided for the most extreme form of public segregation I had ever witnessed. There were racially segregated entrance and exit points, and the interior of the building was so divided that blacks and whites entering the East Rand portal of segregated – and no doubt unequal – justice would never meet, or God forbid, brush past each other, since inside there was a duplication of facilities and rooms and courts, each reserved for the different races. I can't recall exactly where Coloureds and Indians fitted in, but even after a young lifetime of growing up under apartheid the Kempton Park experience induced a sense of shock.
5 Kentridge, op. cit., pp. 4-5.
6 Brigitte Mabandla: speech of the minister of Justice and Constitutional Development, National Assembly, Parliament, Cape Town, 22 June 2004.

7 Section 98(2) of the Constitution of the Republic of South Africa Act 200 of 1993 (the Interim Constitution).
8 Chapter VII of the Interim Constitution.
9 James Myburgh: 'The last Jacobins of Africa: Thabo Mbeki and the making of the New South Africa', unpublished manuscript, 2007, at pp. 69-70.
10 Naturally, or at least formally, at any rate, all judicial appointees in South Africa are expected to withdraw from party membership on assuming office.
11 Letter from John Dugard to Tony Leon, 6 November 1994.
12 Etienne Mureinik, in *South African Journal of Human Rights*, 1994.
13 Judicial Service Commission: 'Guidelines for questioning candidates for nomination to the Constitutional Court', 26 September 1994.
14 *Business Day*, 12 January 1999, quoted by Myburgh, op. cit., at p. 112.
15 *Citizen*, 17 September 1996.
16 Kentridge, op. cit., at p. 9.
17 S.174(3) of the Constitution of the Republic of South Africa Act 108 of 1996 (The Constitution) empowers the president to appoint the Chief Justice after consultation with the JSC.
18 S.174(4) of the Constitution.
19 Letter from President Nelson Mandela to Tony Leon, 28 October 1997.
20 Myburgh, op. cit., at p. 113.
21 *Business Day*, 12 November 1998.
22 *Sunday Tribune*, 3 May 1998, quoted by Myburgh, op. cit.
23 SAPA, 14 August 1998 (Myburgh, op. cit.). However offensive, Omar's statement was mild compared to his party's position on the judgment. In a media statement of 18 June 1998 Judge de Villiers was accused by the ruling party of 'belonging to a class of dinosaurs that internalised the workings of white domination.'
24 *Sunday Times*, 22 October 1998.
25 *Sowetan*, 19 October 1998.
26 *Business Day*, 21 October 1998.
27 M Olivier and J Bolard: 'Towards a legitimate South African Judiciary', *Journal for Juridical Sciences*, 26(1), pp. 31-50, at p. 36.
28 Richard Calland: *Anatomy of South Africa*, Zebra Press, 2006, at p. 221.
29 *Die Burger*, 10 December 1998, quoted by Myburgh at p. 118.
30 Letter from Ms M Gumbi to Tony Leon dated 25 November 2002.
31 Letter from Tony Leon to Ms M Gumbi, November 2003.
32 Letter from Ms M Gumbi to Tony Leon dated 15 December 2003.
33 Grootboom and others v Government of the Republic of South Africa and others, Constitutional Court – CCT 38/00, 21 September 2000.
34 Minister of Health and others v Treatment Action Campaign and others: Constitutional Court – CCT8/02, 5 July 2002.
35 S v Makwanyane and another: Constitutional Court – CCT3/94, 6 June 1995.
36 Carmel Rickard: 'The bench is closed to pale males, struggle credentials or not', *Sunday Times*, 18 July 2004.
37 Speech to New York Law School, New York City, 1 November 2004, at p. 12.
38 Mbeki's right to appoint four members of the JSC is contained in section 178(1)(15) of the Constitution. This provision obliges him also to 'consult' leaders of political parties in the National Assembly on his choices – hence the correspondence.

39 *De Rebus*, August 1998.

40 Shadrack Gutto, quoted in Nic Dawes and Rapule Tabane: 'Government plans new clamps on judges', *Mail&Guardian*, 18 February 2005.

41 Arthur Chaskalson: 'Unjustified criticism of judiciary', *Mail&Guardian*, 27 February 2005.

42 Ibid.

43 *Cape Times*, 16 October 2006.

44 See, for example, analysis of Carmel Rickard in the *Weekender*, 28-29 October 2006.

45 Case No. 4128/2004 in the High Court of South Africa (Cape of Good Hope) in the Matter Between New Clicks South Africa (Pty) Ltd and Dr Manto Tshabalala-Msimang and Professor D McIntyre NO and Case No. 4329/2004 in the Matter Between Pharmaceutical Society of South Africa and Six Others and the Minister of Health and the Chairperson of the Pricing Committee; judgment delivered on 27 August 2004.

46 South African Broadcasting Corporation: 'Report clears white advocates of "racism"', 5 October 2004. http://www.sabnews.com/south_africa/crime1justice/0,2172, 89196,00.html.

47 *Cape Times*, 6 October 2004.

48 http://www.anc.org.za/show.php?doc=ancdocs/history/jan8-05.html.

49 *The Witness*, 28 February 2005, quoted in 'DA Judicial Review', 20 April 2005, at p. 10.

50 George Bizos, quoted in 'Judiciary under Threat – Bizos', News24.com, 21 February 2006 [online article] http://www/news24.com/News24/South_Africa/Politics/0,2-7-12_1885236,00.html.

51 Carole Lewis, *Business Day*, 23 January 2006.

52 Michael Corbett: 'Ambiguous Legislative Proposals Threaten South Africa's Young Democracy', *Business Day*, 16 May 2006.

53 *Cape Times*, 9 December 2006.

54 *Legal Brief Today*, Issue No. 1935, 29 October 2007.

55 *Sunday Times*, January 2007.

56 Pierre de Vos: 'A Bridge Too Far?' *South African Journal on Human Rights*, 2001, at p. 3.

57 http://www.constitutionalcourt.org.za/uhtbin/cgisirsi/20080408061152/SIRSI/0/520/J-CCT3-94.

58 Max du Plessis (University of Natal) in *South African Journal on Human Rights*, 2006, p. 5.

59 Lourens du Plessis (University of Stellenbosch) quoted by Max du Plessis, op. cit.

60 *Hansard*, Vol. 57, columns 130-140.

61 Democratic Party v Minister of Home Affairs and another: Constitutional Court – CCT11/99. The ruling was joined to a separate application on the same issue by the NNP in New National Party v Government of the Republic of South Africa and others: Constitutional Court – CCT9/99. The rulings in these cases were conjoined.

62 New National Party v Government of the Republic of South Africa and others: Constitutional Court – CCT9/99, 13 April 1999.

63 New National Party v Government of the Republic of South Africa and others: Constitutional Court – CCT9/99, 13 April 1999.

64 Smuts Ngonyama: 'Ruling of the Constitutional Court on the Issue of Bar-Coded IDs', press statement, 13 April 1999. http://www.anc.org.za/ancdocs/pr/1999/pr0413.html.

65 Anthea Jeffery: 'Every vote counts' in *Focus*, No. 20, 2000, pp. 17-21.

66 SAPA: 'Concourt dismiss DA's appeal on mayoral committee', 12 December 2002.
67 United Democratic Movement v President of the Republic of South Africa and Others (2003): SA 495 (CC).
68 *Sunday Independent*, 24 September 2005.
69 *Sunday Independent*, 27 July 2003.
70 Quoted by Max du Plessis in 2002 (18) *South African Journal on Human Rights*.
71 Arthur Chaskalson, quoted in John Kane-Berman: 'A looming constitutional crisis', *Fast Facts*, No. 4, April 2006.

12: TRAWLING THE MEDIA

1 Inter Press Service: *South Africa: Debating the Future Role of the SABC*, 25 July 1990.
2 *Weekend Argus*, 26 May 1990.
3 Nelson Mandela: address to the International Press Institute Congress, Cape Town, 14 February 1994 [online text] http://www.anc.org.za/ancdocs/history/mandela/1994/sp940214.html.
4 Mandela, quoted by Ivan Fallon: address to Johannesburg Press Club, 9 July 1997.
5 Mazwai, quoted in Raymond Louw: 'SABC is flirting with "insult laws"', *Business Day*, 30 June 2006.
6 http://www.anc.org.za/ancdocs/history/conf/conference50/presaddress.html.
7 http://www.anc.org.za/ancdocs/annualreports/1999/Section%20c.html.
8 *Mail&Guardian*, 10-16 March 1999.
9 *Star*, 4 March 2006.
10 *Mail&Guardian*, 10-16 March 1999.
11 *Sowetan*, 25 August 1997.
12 Lakela Kaunda, quoted by Stephen Mulholland: 'Eyes Right!', *Moneyweb*, 17 February 2000 [online article] http://moneyweb.iac.iafrica.com/shares/sangoma/356918.htm.
13 *Die Burger*, 10 April 2000.
14 *Sunday Times*, 27 August 2000.
15 Editorial comment: 'South Africa overreacts', *Financial Times*, 22 February 2000.
16 SAPA, 1 March 2000.
17 Barney Pityana, quoted in SAPA: 'Newspaper editors welcome SAHRC's approach for media racism hearings', 1 March 2000.
18 Barney Pityana, quoted in SAPA: 'Media racism hearings no court process: Pityana', 1 March 2000.
19 SAPA: 'Editors pitch up for opening of media racism hearings', 1 March 2000.
20 African National Congress: press release, 14 February 2000.
21 Allister Sparks: *Beyond the Miracle*, Jonathan Ball, 2003.
22 *Mail&Guardian*, 26 April 2001.
23 Thabo Mbeki: address at the Sanef conference on the media, the African Union, Nepad and democracy, 12 April 2003.
24 *Business Day*, 16 May 2006.
25 Thabo Mbeki: 'Welcome to *ANC Today*', *ANC Today*, 26 January 2001 [online article] http://www.anc.org.za/ancdocs/anctoday/2001/ato1.htm#welcome.
26 Ibid.
27 'Heath decision a victory for democracy', *ANC Today*, 26 January 2001 [online article]

http://www.anc.org.za/ancdocs/anctoday/2001/ato1.htm#welcome.

28 Douglas Foster: 'Letter from JHB: The Trouble with Transformation', Columbia Journalism Review, September/October 2004, at p. 8.

29 Ibid.

30 Daily News, 21 June 2000.

31 Letter of Nelson Raju MP to the Daily News, 21 June 2000.

32 E-mail of Rhoda Kadalie to the editor of Business Day, 15 August 2001.

33 Business Day, 13 March 2006.

34 Business Day, 20 March 2000.

35 Business Day, 27 September 2005.

36 Tony Judt: Postwar, 2005, at p. 219.

37 Ibid.

38 Max du Preez, Star, 3 August 2006.

39 Jovial Rantao, quoted in Kevin Bloom: 'The point of journalism', Mail&Guardian, 1 November 2005.

40 John Matshikiza: Natives are Regrouping, Mail&Guardian, 22 May 2006.

41 John Scott: letter to Tony Leon, 6 March 2000.

42 Letter from Helen Suzman to the Cape Times, 15 February 2001.

43 SAPA, 6 December 2005.

44 Letter from James Lorimer, Director of Media and Communications in the Office of the Leader of the Opposition, to David Canning, editor, Mercury, Durban, dated 5 April 2004.

45 Letter from David Canning, editor of the Mercury, to James Lorimer, dated 5 May 2004.

46 Jeremy Paxman: The Political Animal: An Anatomy, Penguin, 2003.

47 Quoted by James Myburgh: 'Ever Faster News', 23 July 2006.

48 Mail&Guardian, 4 July 2006.

49 The reference to Botha related to an infamous moment in the 1980s, when he was so enraged by the TV portrayal of Coloured leader Allan Hendrickse's defiance of him that he personally phoned the news producer in mid-broadcast to demand a rectification, which duly happened at the end of the broadcast.

50 In addition, a member of the SABC Board, Christine Qunta, in her personal capacity helped fund a series of full-page newspaper advertisements – one wishing Mbeki a happy birthday, and another defending his controversial views. Qunta sat on both the board and the news committee of the SABC at the time of the birthday advertisement.

51 www.polity.org.za, 17 August 2006.

52 SAPA, 1 March 2006.

53 Myburgh, op. cit., p. 1.

54 Beeld, 14 May 1998.

55 Finance Week, 4 June 1998, quoted by Myburgh, op. cit.

56 South Africa Today: 'SABC Board needs to start putting journalistic ethics at top of its Agenda', 11 August 2006.

13: TANGLING WITH 'THE LADY'

1 Tony Karon, Die Suid-Afrikaan, April/May 1991, at p. 26.

2 Quoted by John Carlin, *Independent*, London, 21 September 1990.
3 Karon, op. cit.
4 Carlin, op. cit.
5 Nomavenda Mathiane, *Frontline*, March 1989.
6 *Christian Science Monitor*, 6 April 1992.
7 *Independent*, London, 14 May 1991.
8 *Hansard*, Questions and Replies, 6 May 1992, at column 936.
9 *Hansard*, 9 August 1994, columns 1010-1017.
10 *Hansard*, 26 August 1994, columns 2099-2105.
11 Ibid.
12 *Weekend Argus*, 28 August 1994.
13 Emma Nicholson and Fred Bridgland: *Katiza's Journey: Beneath the surface of South Africa's Shame*, Macmillan, 1997.
14 Letter to Tony Leon from General George Fivaz, National Commissioner, South African Police Service, 6 May 1996.
15 Truth and Reconciliation Commission of South Africa Report: Special Investigation: Mandela United Football Club 1998, Vol. 2, Chapter 6, pp. 565-567 ('TRC Report').
16 TRC Report, op. cit., para. 57, at p. 568.
17 TRC Report, op. cit., para. 60, at p. 570.
18 TRC Report, op. cit., para. 98-99, at p. 578.
19 TRC Report, op. cit., para. 110, at p. 581.
20 TRC Report, op. cit., para. 104, at p. 579.
21 *Hansard*, 23 March 1999, at column 3075.

PART FOUR: LEADER OF THE OPPOSITION

14: FIGHTING BACK

1 More agreeably, my final encounter with Mbeki occurred in May 2007, on the eve of my standing down as party leader.
2 Tribute to Nelson Mandela, *Hansard*, Parliament, 26 March 1999, columns 194-196.
3 *Financial Mail*, 26 February 1999.
4 Ibid.
5 Requoted in *Guardian*, London, 21 May 1999.
6 Ibid.
7 *New York Times*, 27 April 1999.
8 *Mail&Guardian*, 30 April to 6 May 1999.
9 Speech in Parliament, *Hansard*, 25 February 1999, columns 100-105.
10 Parliament, *Hansard*, 25 February 1999, columns 62-68.
11 Quoted by Giliomee, Myburgh and Schlemmer in *Opposition and Democracy in South Africa*, edited by Roger Southall, Frank Cass, 2001, at p. 177.
12 I continued: 'We live in a country of falling incomes, collapsing services and a currency that has halved in value, a nation with the world's worst crime rate. When we question

that – and when we stand up and fight back against it – we are accused of being unpatriotic, racist or somehow against transformation. But the worst aspects of this election have been those who would deny reality itself.

'There is another neurosis and anxiety in South Africa – the factor of guilt over the past. Now there is much to regret about our past and there are many individuals who have good reason to feel guilty for their past behaviour – indeed, some who should be severely punished for it. But it is not a healthy thing for whole classes of people to feel guilty. It doesn't do them any good and others invariably exploit it in a way that leads to long-term anger and cynicism.

'It is certainly an actively bad thing when it leads to kowtowing to a grasping new elite which is also often greedy and unscrupulous. But I am afraid that some people in our society have also adopted a deference, a bowing and scraping to a new form of *baasskap*.

'We want the DP to do well in this election and not only because a stronger opposition can speak up more loudly and effectively. We want to do really well because the very sight of such an opposition will give people more courage. We want our victory to be felt by all our voters. We want them to feel, as our posters say: "You have the power". Because that is the best way to build the society we want. A society composed of free, equal, confident citizens. Show some courage – don't accept the *baasskap* of the ANC.'

13 The election results are tabulated in *Opposition and Democracy in South Africa*, edited by Roger Southall, 2001.

15: BLOWBACK

1 He is today the DA leader in the National Council of Provinces.
2 *Cape Times*, 29 June 1999.
3 *Star*, 1 July 1999.
4 Ibid.
5 *Star*, 29 June 1999.
6 *Die Burger*, 30 June 1999.
7 *Natal Mercury*, 26 July 1999.
8 Address to *Pretoria News* executive breakfast, Wednesday 28 July 1999.
9 *Financial Times*, London, 24 August 1999.
10 Ibid.
11 In a careful analysis of the DP 1999 Fight Back election campaign, DA sympathiser but credible academic analyst Professor David Welsh found no evidence to support the branding of the campaign as either racist or right-wing. In a study called *Election 1999: South Africa from Mandela to Mbeki* (David Philip, 1999, at pp. 88-100) Welsh states:

'Errol Moorcroft MP is quoted as saying that: "There is nothing like a spell-out of power to help someone appreciate liberal values – such as tolerance of dissent and minority rights. Having railed against liberalism for decades as a threat to their survival, many Afrikaners now identify liberalism as the guarantor of their future as a language group whose members, unsurprisingly, most enjoy each other's company."'

No credible case could be made for regarding Moorcroft's comment as 'proof' of a rightward shift: minority rights are not only entirely consistent with democratic principles, their protection in a multicultural state is a likely condition of that state's stability. The past five years have given Afrikaners some grounds for supposing that their constitutionally guaranteed language rights were under threat of dilution, as the trend towards English as the de facto official language inexorably continues.

It was perhaps the DP's campaign slogan 'Fight Back' that provided most grist to the critics' mill. It was, opined Idasa, 'an inherently conservative message' since the most realistic analysis was that its 'subliminal message' is 'Fight Change'. How this interpretation was reached is unclear. An even more remarkable interpretation was advanced by Eve Bertelsen:

'Tony Leon offers the voters "The guts to fight back" sometimes glossed with "for a better future". Since these slogans clearly contest the ANC's claims to be "Fighting for change" and "A better life for all", an inescapable inference must be that the DP fight is somehow poised against change, with the hope of a better life for some.'

'Change' is a neutral word since change can be for good or ill; or it may embody well-intentioned policy that is likely to fail or have disastrous consequences. The inescapable inference to be drawn from both the above comments is their assumption that the ANC has a monopoly on virtue and insight when it comes to 'change'. To challenge this monopoly then becomes little short of *lèse majesté*. Both criticisms are absurd. (It should also be pointed out that the DP had decided upon its slogans and posters before the ANC's slogans were known.)

Likewise, the assumption that 'Fight Back' was aimed against blacks (as the ANC alleged in a poster that they were ordered to remove) ignores its connotations, clearly spelled out in DP literature and by DP speakers – 'We fight back against crime, corruption, unemployment, unfairness, racism and power-abuse.' In response to those who detected a subliminal racist message in the slogan, I responded: 'Only those blinded by a bizarre racial bigotry could assume it was directed at any group.'

12 *Umrabulo*, No. 6, First Quarter 1999.
13 *Daily News*, 2 August 1999.
14 'All Power to the Party: The ANC's programme to eliminate the distinction between Party and State and extend its hegemony over civil society', March 2000, at iv.
15 *Sunday Times*, 5 December 1999.
16 *Mail&Guardian*, 10-16 December 1999.
17 *Sunday Independent*, 12 March 2000.
18 *New York Review of Books*, 21 December 2006.
19 The parents were strong DP supporters and decided during the 1999 election that their new baby should have my name. I felt very honoured.
20 Quoted by Joel Joffe: *The State vs. Nelson Mandela: The trial that changed South Africa*, One World, 2007.
21 Thabo Mbeki: debate, Parliament, 29 May 1998.
22 www.anc.org.za/ancdocs/history/mbeki/2000/tm0204.html.
23 Thabo Mbeki: Second Oliver Tambo Lecture, 11 August 2000.
24 *Mail&Guardian*, 18 August 2000.
25 *Citizen*, 18 August 2000.
26 *Sunday Times*, 20 August 2000.
27 Stanley Uys and James Myburgh: 'Thabo Mbeki's Presidency and Policy: A Psychological Profile', *Internationales Afrikaforum*, 3rd Quarter 2002.
28 *Financial Times*, 28-29 April 2001.

29 *Guardian*, 29 May 2001.
30 'The New Partnership for Africa's Development Founding Document', October 2001,
    p. 204.
31 *Sunday Times*, 17 December 2000.
32 *Business Day*, 15 January 2001.
33 *Citizen*, 13 February 2001.
34 *Citizen*, 13 February 2001.
35 Speech in Parliament: Leader of the Opposition, 13 February 2001.
36 David McCullough: *Truman*, Simon & Shuster, 1992, p. 989.
37 *Saturday Argus*, 1 October 2000.
38 *The Economist*, 5 May 2001.
39 Interview with ITN – John Snow, London, 4 May 2001.
40 'Non-Racialism in Action: Acknowledging the Past, Changing the Present, Building
    the Future', submission of the African National Congress to the World Conference on
    Racism NGO Forum, August 2001.
41 *The Economist*, 8 September 2001.
42 Tony Leon: speech, Cape Town, 19 September 2001.
43 Robert Conquest: *Reflections on a ravaged century*, Norton, 2000.
44 *Star*, 24 November 2004.
45 *Hansard*, columns 5347-5358.

16: A MARRIAGE MADE IN HELL

1   James Selfe: letter to Tony Leon dated 19 October 1999.
2   *Leadership*,Vol. 16, No. 4, 1997, pp. 53-62.
3   *Sunday Times*, 28 November 1999.
4   Ibid.
5   *Star*, 8 June 2000. A few days later, with even greater public attention and press com-
    ment, former NNP Western Cape premier, Hernus Kriel, deserted the NNP and
    joined us. To offset the negative comment I expected from the announcement, I had
    arranged on the same occasion for the hitherto unaligned academic, Professor Themba
    Sono, also to announce his defection to the party (in exchange for a vacant seat in the
    Gauteng legislature). Sono's arrival was practically ignored by the controversy sur-
    rounding Kriel's. The fact that neither was to enjoy a long shelf-life in the party perhaps
    spoke eloquently of the haste with which I was determined to create the appearance of
    momentum based on growth without being overly fussed by the consequences.
6   Tony Leon: media statement as leader of the Democratic Party, 21 June 2000.
7   *Cape Times*, 20 June 2000.
8   Ibid.
9   *Die Burger*, 26 June 2000.
10 *Business Day*, 27 June 2000.
11 *Cape Argus*, 21 June 2000.
12 *Financial Mail*, 30 June 2000.
13 *Rapport*, 2 July 2000.
14 I was about to leave on an overseas trip. I was in London and Michal in Israel when she
    phoned to tell me that the Israeli Ecclesiastical Court – the Beth Din – through which

all marriages and divorces in Israel have to be processed, even for those as minimally religious as Michal and her former husband, had finally granted her a divorce. In the middle of Covent Garden I proposed marriage over the telephone. Unromantic? I always believe in acting immediately: she accepted, and we were wed by year's end.

15 *Mail&Guardian*, 23-29 June 2000.
16 *Financial Mail*, 10 November 2000.
17 *New York Times*, 7 December 2000.
18 *Star*, 29 December 2000.
19 *Star*, 9 January 2000.
20 Five days after the 5 December election Michal and I were married at a warm and, we thought, stylish ceremony at Cape Town's Mount Nelson hotel. Most of the 175 guests were family and friends – Michal's from Israel and mine from across the Diaspora of émigré South Africans, from Boston to Perth, and those who like me had remained at home. But the full spectrum of politics was also on hand to celebrate with us: Helen Suzman, Tito Mboweni, FW de Klerk and Bridget Oppenheimer. Of course, we also invited my deputy, Marthinus van Schalkwyk, to signal our new-found unity. However, as events would soon confirm, my marital relationship would prove far more affectionate and enduring than the political partnership I had entered into just six months before, which would unravel sooner than either of us thought.
21 August 2007.
22 He was no newcomer to subterfuge. At university he was in charge of an apparently independent youth movement, '*Jeugkrag*', which was later revealed to have received, at his request, but without his disclosure, secret state funding channelled via the covert account of the South African Defence Force (see, for example, 'FW's heir was MI agent', *Mail&Guardian* online, 29 August 1997).
23 *Cape Times*, 25 June 2001.
24 *Rapport*, 18 February 2001.
25 *Cape Times*, 2 April 2001.
26 *Sunday Times*, 5 August 2001.
27 *Financial Mail*, 12 October 2001.
28 I followed up the speech by conducting personal visits in August to South Africa's heartland and the ordinary people who made the country work. My so-called 'Day in the Life' campaign saw me spending a day as a nurse in Cape Town; a night with the police patrolling the mean streets of Hillbrow; a session as a shift worker driving (or more accurately sitting alongside the person engaged in the task); a morning with a street vendor in Chatsworth; and an afternoon accompanying a taxi driver in Cape Town. This series of on-the-ground experiences left me better informed about the conditions and hardships confronted by people who really were the country's backbone, and far more positive about the country's future than I felt about even the short-term prospects for my own political organisation.
29 ANC press release, 9 November 2000.
30 *Cape Times*, 26 July 2001.
31 *Cape Times*, 27 July 2001.
32 *Sunday Times*, 29 July 2001.
33 *Business Day*, 27 September 2001.
34 *Daily Dispatch*, 1 November 2001.
35 *Rapport*, 7 October 2001.

36 Verbatim transcript of M van Schalkwyk media conference, 12 October 2001.

37 *Sunday Times*, 14 October 2001.

38 The group met on a nightly basis at my home for the next two weeks. The proceedings were both businesslike and sombre in view of the gravity of the party's situation. About the only moment of levity was provided when, one Sunday evening, Jeremy Gauntlett SC arrived to brief us on the latest state of play on the legal front. One of the participants commented on the fact that he was wearing a pair of shorts. Gauntlett instantly responded, 'Oh, I thought the party dress code was still the *kortbroek*' – a reference to Van Schalkwyk's nickname. In fact the Cape High Court did not concur with Gauntlett's stratagem that Marais's resignation could be achieved as a consequence of a leadership judgment. The reversal was a blow to our credibility, but it was thought fruitless to take it to appeal. Events were to overtake its significance.

39 *Mail&Guardian*, 19-25 October 2001.

40 Ibid.

41 *Sunday Independent*, 21 October 2001.

42 *Die Burger*, 1 November 2001.

43 *Die Burger*, 5 November 2001.

44 *Die Burger*, 10 November 2001.

45 *Cape Times*, 7 November 2001.

46 *Volksblad*, 28 November 2001.

47 Ibid.

48 Richard II, Act 3, Scene 2.

17: DARKEST BEFORE DAWN

1 SAPA, 13 February 2002.

2 *Star*, 13 February 2002.

3 *Business Day*, 14 February 2002.

4 *Sunday Independent*, 17 March 2002.

5 Poll result: Mbeki 42%; Leon 28%; Buthelezi 19%; Van Schalkwyk 12%; analysed by Professor Hermann Giliomee in *Die Burger*, 2 April 2002.

6 Kwaito is a music genre that emerged in Johannesburg in the early 1990s. It is based on house music beats, but typically at a slower tempo and containing melodic and percussive African samples which are looped; deep baselines; and often vocals, shouted or chanted. The name is derived from the Afrikaans word *kwaai*, meaning 'angry'.

7 Michael Heseltine: *Life in the jungle: My autobiography*, Hodder and Stoughton, 2000, at p. 293.

8 *Saturday Argus*, 9 May 2002.

9 *Herald*, 10 October 2002.

10 Transcript of Desai Commission of Enquiry 2002, at p. 199.

11 Transcript at p. 272.

12 Transcript at p. 272.

13 *Volksblad*, 25 May 2002.

14 *Star*, 25 May 2002.

15 *Daily News*, 3 December 2002.

16 Statement of Douglas Gibson MP, DA Chief Whip, 23 May 2002.

17 *Business Day*, 28 May 2002.
18 Speech by Tony Leon, Pietermaritzburg, 26 May 2002.
19 SAPA, 26 May 2002.
20 The media virtually ignored the harassment of our black activists or mentioned that the wilder claims that the Scorpions were about to arrest Morkel and Markovitz were being leaked to them by the Scorpions themselves; and that the Scorpions' chief was one Bulelani Ngcuka, former ANC chief whip in the Senate and the husband of an ANC cabinet minister.
21 *Citizen*, 30 May 2002.
22 Ibid.
23 The cherry on the top was an admission by ABSA bank official Erik Marais, a DA branch chairman, that he had, at Morkel's request, 'laundered' DM 90 000 which he received in cash from an unnamed donor, whom Markovitz identified only as 'Hans'.
24 *Mail&Guardian*, 31 May to 6 June 2002.
25 Ibid.
26 *Star*, 10 June 2002.
27 *Sunday Times*, 16 June 2002.
28 For example, Van Schalkwyk as premier suddenly announced an expansion – at a cost of R10-million in additional salaries – in the number of municipal sub-councils, allowing the ANC/NNP to provide higher-paying positions to would-be defectors to whom he offered the chairmanships.
29 Statistics SA recorded in 2002 that the poorest 50% of South African households had, in fact, become poorer between 1995 and 2002, the exact period in which the ANC had been in power.
30 See the DA's social welfare policy: 'Freedom from Want'. http://www.da.org.za/da/Site/Eng/Policies/Downloads/Poverty.asp.
31 The 1% VAT increase would deliver one-third of the total (R4,7-billion). We proposed taking back one-third of the tax returned to taxpayers in the current budget (R5-billion) while we targeted a budget deficit of 2,6% (providing R5,4-billion). While the grant would notionally be available to anyone who applied, it would carry a tax value twenty times larger for income tax purposes, which would mean those earning more than R7 500 a year would pay more in tax than the value of the grant. This would eliminate applications from those who did not need it.
32 *Mercury*, 25 December 2002. (Some five years later, in 2007, these 'negotiations' have yielded nothing.)
33 *Business Day*, 20 May 2002.
34 *Argus*, 1 August 2002.
35 *Argus*, 18 September 2002.
36 Received by author's office in October 2001.
37 *Daily Dispatch*, 21 October 2002.
38 *Sunday Times*, 20 October 2002.
39 *Financial Mail*, 9 November 2002.
40 When in August 2004 Van Schalkwyk finally and formally took his remaining band of cronies into the ANC, having secured his seat at the cabinet table and sunk his own party, Colin Eglin, by then retired from politics, spoke to me about this final, sorry chapter in the NNP's existence. As I recorded it in *SA Today* (13 August 2004), Eglin described it as a strange reversal. 'When the ship goes down, the captain usually goes

down with it,' he said. 'Or, at least, he must evacuate the women and children first. Van Schalkwyk has done the opposite. He jumped on a R750 000 life boat [his annual cabinet salary sans perks] and let his passengers drown as he was towed to the safety of the shore.' Exactly.

41 *Mail&Guardian*, 15-21 November 2002.

18: AGAINST GOLIATH

1 Patrick Laurence in *Focus*, No. 30, 2003, Helen Suzman Foundation.

2 http://www.lawlibrary.co.za/notice/updates/2006.

3 AIDS is fully explored in Chapter 8. By 2003-2004 it had moved from a fairly marginal disease in 1994 to a full-blown pandemic. By then an estimated one in ten South Africans was infected, striking hard at the core of South Africa's labour force, where a far higher prevalence of infection was estimated. (CIA World Fact Book 2004)

4 S Terreblanche: *A History of Inequality in South Africa 1652-2002*, University of Natal Press, Pietermaritzburg, 2002.

5 Quoted by Laurence, op. cit.

6 *SA Today*, 28 March 2003. Harsh realities.

7 The legislative framework for BEE is contained in the Broad-Based Black Economic Empowerment Act No. 53 of 2003, which enables the application of 'codes of good practice' and transformation charters to business sectors. The legislation requires that companies be rated according to seven criteria, including employment equity, skills development, preferential procurement, enterprise development, socio-economic development, ownership and management control. Charters for different sectors give slightly different weightings to these criteria.

Companies' scores affect their ability to access state tenders and contracts. Their scores also indirectly affect their business dealings in other respects as empowerment ratings are increasingly included in evaluation of businesses.

In August 2007 the Department of Trade and Industry announced it wanted a host of laws that apply to business to be reviewed to make firmer empowerment demands on employers, and in particular calling for more legislative clarity to deal with fronting of companies by black people – the inevitable consequence of a scramble for a limited number of potential BEE partners in order to fulfil the requirements of the legislation.

A plethora of funds have also been set up to give budding black entrepreneurs access to support. The biggest, the National Empowerment Fund, was intended to provide start-up capital to new ventures and originally was to be financed by the allocation of shares from the privatisation of state assets including 5% of Telkom, 10% of Acsa and 5% of Eskom. But privatisation was derailed and it was left grossly undercapitalised.

It was relaunched in 2004 when it was reported that there were seven different agencies and organisations aimed at facilitation: including the NEF, the IDC, Khula, Umsobomvu, Ntsika and the Apex Fund. The DA reported at the time that almost all had failed to deliver on their overlapping mandates. In 2002 the (then) minister of Trade and Industry Alec Erwin expressed an intention to form an integrated financing agency, but the idea has fallen away.

BEE deals have been shrouded in controversy, with many involving generous handouts to the same persons over and over again. A few more encouraging private-sector BEE approaches have been seen lately involving low-cost share sales to many investors, rather than high-value sales to a few. These include Multichoice's sale in 2006 of 45-million shares worth R2,25-billion which has seen their investment value increase sixfold. Naspers's Welkom Aandeleskema sold 5% to small investors which on an outlay of R1 000 was in mid-2007 worth R31 000.

8 Alec Hogg: 'Moeletsi Mbeki: Deputy Chairman, South African Institute of International Affairs', interview posted 10 September 2004. http://www.mineweb.net/radio/classic-mining/346622.htm.

9 Ibid.

10 RW Johnson: *South Africa: The First Man, the Last Nation*, Jonathan Ball, Johannesburg, 2004, p. 224.

11 'A decade of freedom', *The Economist*, 7 April 2004.

12 Taken to its logical conclusion, government's ambitious black ownership targets – which it set at 25,1% in ten years across most industries – would need huge advances of funding: in excess of R700-billion according to Azar Jammine, a leading economist (source: RW Johnson: *South Africa – A short history*). Raising this kind of money from capital markets could undercut cornerstone elements of government economic policy. According to *The Economist* (15 January 2004) it could drive up inflation by as much as ten per cent, which in turn could halve the growth rate.

13 *Transvaler*, 1 October 1937.

14 *Business Day*, 1 February 2003.

15 www.iol.co.za, 30 January 2003.

16 Christopher Hitchens, 1 February 2003.

17 *Saturday Star*, 25 January 2007.

18 *SA Today*, 16 October 2003.

19 *Hansard*, 18 September 2003, column 3716.

20 Brian Greene: *The Elegant Universe*, Jonathan Cape, 1999.

21 *Sunday Independent*, 9 November 2003.

22 *This Day*, 19 November 2003.

23 The MPs who joined us were Sheila Camerer, Willem Doman, Wilhelm le Roux, Sakkie Pretorius, Frik van Deventer, Craig Morkel, Maans Nel, Pierre Rabie and Charles Redcliffe; and the Western Cape MPLs were Gerrit van Rensburg, Ryno King and Alta Rossouw.

24 In October 1997.

25 *Business Day*, 27 March 2003.

26 I would go on to publish 201 weekly newsletters during the remainder of my leadership (51 months). It was a weighty but rewarding challenge, augmented by Pollak's pen and in its last stages by Dr Guy Willoughby who replaced him. I often wrote the pieces on the fly, prompted by something I had read or breaking events. The overwhelming bulk concerned the state of South Africa's democracy, including criticisms of ANC governance. One was written from the unlikely locale of the Great Wall of China; another from the Dalai Lama's home in exile, in Dharamsala, in the foothills of the Himalayas.

27 *Business Day*, 23 June 2003.

28 ANC: *Umrabulo*, No. 16, August 2002, 51st National Conference edition.

29 Speech by Pieter Mulder MP during the Education debate, Parliament, on 20 May 2003.

30 *This Day*, 2 November 2003.
31 *SA Today*, 25 February 2003.
32 *Star*, 15 September 2004.
33 Budget speech by the minister of Minerals and Energy, Phumzile Mlambo-Ngcuka, 19 May 2005.
34 Robert Guest: *The Shackled Continent – Africa's Past, Present and Future*, Macmillan, 2004.
35 Quoted by Professor Laurence Schlemmer, *This Day*, 26 May 2004.
36 Tony Leon: speech to Western Cape DA structures, Somerset West, 12 June 2004.
37 *Financial Times*, 13 September 2004.
38 Tony Leon: speech to Safmarine Breakfast Club, 11 November 2003.
39 In fact there was a fourth victim of this gruesome triple slaying. En route to executing Janine and Kayla (Hester had been murdered first, in the vehicle), the killers stopped to pick up a young teenage girl in Stinkwater, near Hammanskraal. She, together with Janine, was raped and shot, but in her case not fatally. The DA in Pretoria started a fund to assist her recovery.
40 *Beeld*, 6 August 2003.
41 Susan Booysen in 'Electoral Politics in South Africa', edited by Jessica Piombo and Lia Nijzink, at p. 129.
42 *Mail&Guardian*, 20-26 May 2005.
43 *Citizen*, 29 July 2003.
44 Speaking at the ANC's 50th National Conference in December 1997, when Mbeki was elected unopposed as leader of the ANC.
45 *SA Today*, 30 January 2004.
46 http://www.iafrica.com, 7 March 2004.
47 *City Press*, 15 February 2004.
48 *Sunday Times*, 14 March 2004.
49 *Mail&Guardian*, 3 June 2004.
50 'The ANC has made Mpumalanga South Africa's corruption capital', www.DA.org.za, 14 March 2004.
51 On this side of the ledger the result was even more impressive when viewed against the DP's dismal performance in 1994 (338 426), but it was well down on the 23% achieved by the DA (with the NNP) in the 2000 municipal elections. However, the NNP decision to break away from the DA and move into alignment with the ANC was resoundingly rejected by the voters in 2004. Van Schalkwyk's party received a derisory 1,65% of the vote, meaning that on his watch he had reduced the inheritance of 82 MPs he was bequeathed by FW de Klerk in 1997 to just seven MPs in the National Assembly. The IFP also suffered a further reversal in the election, polling 6,97% of the overall total, a net loss of nearly one million votes compared to its 1994 position. (In KwaZulu-Natal, their drop-off was most marked: from 50,1% in 1994 down to 36,8% in 2004.) 2004 saw eleven opposition parties represented in parliament.
52 ANC results: 1994 12 337 655
              1999 10 601 330
              2004 10 880 915
53 Martin Meredith: *The State of Africa: A History of Fifty Years of Independence*, Jonathan Ball, 2005, at p. 56.
54 *Daily Dispatch*, 27 May 2004.

55 *Sunday Times*, 2 May 2004.

56 Quoted by Max du Preez, *Star*, 15 May 2004.

57 Karl Popper: *The Open Society and its Enemies*, 1945.

58 Both speeches were published by the Democratic Alliance in a pamphlet entitled 'Two visions for South Africa: The open opportunity society versus the National Democratic Revolution: Two defining speeches by the Leader of the Opposition', June 2004.

59 Sir Karl Popper, the Viennese-born (1902) British philosopher; in *The Logic of Scientific Discovery* (1934) he proposed that knowledge cannot be absolutely confirmed, but rather that science progresses by the experimental refutation of the current theory and its consequent replacement by a new theory, equally provisional, itself open to subsequent refutation, when more data is available. *The Open Society and its Enemies* (1945) is a critique of dogmatic philosophies such as Marxism. He, no doubt, would have provided a trenchant political critique of the ANC's National Democratic Revolution.

60 Fareed Zakaria: *The Rise of Illiberal Democracy*, 1997. http://www.fareedzakaria.com/ARTICLES/other/democracy.html.

61 The speech contained a codification of our economic, safety, health care, education, affirmative action and welfare policies.

62 *Sowetan*, SAPA, *Star*, 25 June 2004.

63 Speech, op. cit.

64 John Kane-Berman, Chief Executive, South African Institute of Race Relations: 74th Annual Report, 1 April 2003 to 31 March 2004.

65 *Sunday Times*, June 2004.

66 http://www.mg.co.za, 23 May 2005.

67 *Business Day*, 16 March 2005.

68 Member of the Executive Council: Welfare v Kate – 2006 SCA 46 (SA). The judgment can be viewed at http://www.law.wits.ac.za/sca/summary.

69 Statement: Mpowele Swathe, DA spokesperson on Water Affairs and Forestry, *City Press*, 26 August 2007.

70 Democratic Alliance; National Audit Outcomes; Auditor-General's reports for the 34 budget votes 2001/2 to 2005/6, http://da/fishworx.co.za/da/Site/Eng/campaigns/DOCS2001-2006.pdf.

71 *ANC Today*, 11 August 2006.

72 *SA Today*, 24 November 2006.

73 Ibid.

74 Speech in Parliament: President's Budget Vote debate, 7 June 2006; *King Lear* I iv.

75 Thabo Mbeki: 'Committed to build a new nation!' *ANC Today*, 2 June 2006 [online letter] http://www.anc.org.za/ancdocs/anctoday/2006.

76 South African Communist Party and Congress of South African Trade Unions, quoted in Mde, Vukani and Karima Brown: 'Mbeki faces open revolt from angry ANC allies', *Business Day*, 26 May 2006.

77 National Assembly, 8 September 2005.

19: CAPE HOPE?

1 SAPA, 30 November 2004.

2 Milton Shain (ed): *Opposing Voices*, Jonathan Ball, 2006, at p. 7.

3 *ANC Today*, 7-13 January 2005.
4 Tony Leon: speech, 'South African Liberalism Today and its Discontents', Cape Town, 6 April 2005.
5 Arthur Koestler: *Darkness at Noon*, Penguin Books, 1964, p. 128.
6 Koestler, op. cit.
7 *Spectator*, 15 April 2006.
8 Thabo Mbeki: 'A titan that serves the people of South Africa!' *ANC Today*, 14 October 2005 [online newsletter] http://www.anc.org.za/ancdocs/anctoday/2005/at41.htm#preslet.
9 Vicky Robinson and Rapule Tabane: 'It's the ANC or no vote at all', *Mail&Guardian*, 3-9 March 2006.
10 Mike Cohen: 'South Africa's Ruling ANC Leads in Local Elections (Update 3)', *Bloomberg.com*, 2 March 2006 [online article] http://www.bloomberg.com/apps/news?pid=10000085&sid=afd5ZnayZazo&refer=europe.
11 Carol Paton: 'Rusting Republics', *Financial Mail*, 9 September 2005 [online version] http://www.eprop.co.za/news/article.aspx?idArticle=6209.
12 *SA Today*, 13 January 2006.
13 Norman Joseph: 'Home Affairs accused of ID irregularity', *Cape Argus*, 2 March 2006.
14 SABC News: 'Party loyalty highest with DA voters', *SABCNews.com*, 3 March 2006 [online article] http://www.sabcnews.com/politics/the_parties/0,2172,123138,00.html.
15 *Cape Argus*, 27 March 2006.
16 *Financial Mail*, 10 March 2006.
17 During Zuma's rape trial some of this evidence emerged. His accuser gave detailed descriptions of three earlier rapes while she was a child in exile. Other women subsequently came forward with similar allegations of sexual abuse. While claims were investigated by the ANC internally at the time, it would appear that the perpetrators were only lightly reprimanded.
18 *Financial Times*, 20 March 2006.
19 See the 'call to action' in which top South African women, including Gill Marcus, Mavivi Myakayaka, Wendy Appelbaum and Cheryl Carolus, denounced the signal sent out by Jacob Zuma's rape trial, published at http://www.mg.co.za/Contentimages/266888/zumacallaction.pdf.
20 *SA Today*, 16 February 2007.
21 http://www.eyeoncrime.co.za/?q=node/42.

20: EXIT

1 *Weekly Telegraph*, 5-11 July 2006.
2 It was leaked to the media immediately after my own resignation was made public on 27 November 2006, apparently to advantage a putative contender for the leadership.
3 I also naturally confided my decision to my wife, my father and my long-standing secretary, Sandy Slack.
4 *Finweek*, 30 November 2006.
5 *Beeld*, 27 November 2006.
6 *Citizen*, 5 December 2006.

7 *Cape Times*, 30 November 2006.
8 *Business Day*, 4 December 2006.
9 *Business Day*, 28 November 2006.
10 Natan Sharansky: *The Case for Democracy*, Public Affairs.
11 http://www.anc.org.za/ancdocs/history/mbeki/2007/tmo215.html.
12 *The Economist*, 23 November 2006.
13 In an extraordinary and unprecedented moment, nudged on by the president apparently, the SABC carried the speech live on both television and radio.
14 *Business Day*, 16 May 2007.

PART FIVE: THE FUTURE

21: FUTURE IMPERFECT

1 Roger Southall: 'State of the Nation', HSRC, 2001, p. 1.
2 Here, any comparison with FW de Klerk did Mbeki no favours. In the first year that De Klerk assumed the presidency (1990) South Africa ranked 85th out of 174 countries then surveyed by the UN. By the fourth year of Mbeki's presidency (2006) we were down to 120 out of 177 listed nations.
3 This is a stark and sombre total in its own terms, and is even more extraordinary when compared with, for example, the Great Depression in the 1930s – when even at its height no more than a quarter of the potentially employable workforce in the US was without jobs. And the employment situation is just as bleak in comparison with the typical levels achieved by 'comparator' countries – nations in the developing world whose stage of economic development roughly resembles our own.
4 Presentation and workings of the international panel on ASGISA; posted at http://www.CID.Harvard.edu/southafrica/index.html.
5 Jeffrey Herbst: 'Mbeki's South Africa' in *Foreign Affairs*, November/December 2005.
6 In contrast, the USA, dubbed by Professor Christopher Stone as 'the most violent rich country in the world', has a murder rate only one-seventh that of South Africa, which in turn is 28 times that of the United Kingdom (South African Institute of Race Relations, quoted in *South African Strategy*, 16 November 2007).
7 *Business Day*, 24 January 2007.
8 *Financial Mail*, 19 January 2007.
9 Survey of 55 countries by Productivity SA and the 2007 IMD World Competitiveness Yearbook: SAPA, 14 April 2008.
10 'Country Report on South Africa', Economist Intelligence Unit, June 2007.
11 PSG Leon: 'Resource Nationalisation'; address to Harvard Law Students, 1 October 2007.
12 Elaborated in the Mineral and Petroleum Resources Development Act of 2004, which legislated state custodianship of mineral rights and provided the minister with vast discretionary powers.
13 Fraser Institute: 'Annual Survey of Mining Companies 2006/2007'. In 2003-2004 the

Survey recorded that South Africa ranked 25th in the 53-country survey.

14 Among other economic realities, this reliance on foreign capital pointed repeatedly to the absence of domestic savings and the large-scale collapse of the country's manufacturing sector. In consequence, demand for imports vastly outstripped and outperformed the struggling export sector of the local economy. It also underlines the essential unsustainability of the current, apparently rosy, growth figures: the diagnosis should have been the prediction of a credit-led boom at a time that the country was borrowing heavily to make up the difference between exports and imports. While South Africa can hardly control the world economy, its own domestic circumstances can profoundly affect international investor sentiment.

15 In August 2007 Mbeki fired the popular and hard-working deputy minister of Health, Nosizwe Madlala-Routledge, allegedly for indiscipline but in reality for questioning the official line on hospital conditions and HIV/AIDS. He retained Health minister Manto Tshabalala-Msimang despite revelations of her kleptomania and drunkenness. Tshabalala-Msimang was known to abet the president's AIDS-denialism, and was the spouse of the powerful party treasurer-general, Mendi Msimang. More significantly, in October 2007, the president suspended Vusi Pikoli, the National Director of Public Prosecutions, reportedly for moving to arrest, on allegations of corruption, the National Police Commissioner and Mbeki loyalist, Jackie Selebi. Selebi enjoyed a close relationship with organised crime boss, Glenn Agliotti, who in turn was an accused in the murder of Brett Kebble, a gangster-businessman closely tied to the ANC leadership, though on the Zuma, not the Mbeki, side. Selebi was, after much wrangling, placed on 'extended leave' in mid-January 2008, following the final decision of the prosecuting authority to press ahead with charges of corruption and defeating the ends of justice.

16 *Mail&Guardian*, 18-24 January 2008.

17 Joel Netshitenzhe: 'Explaining transformation' in the ANC journal *Umrabulo*, 4th Quarter 1996.

18 Ibid.

19 Chairman of Gold Circle Racing and leader of the DA in the Umsunduzi (Pietermaritzburg) city council.

20 The former Education minister, Kader Asmal, proved to be an ever-reliable weathervane in determining the shift in the political weather and presidential fortunes. For seven years (and for the entire length of his cabinet service) he remained utterly silent on the tyranny in Zimbabwe, despite his noted volubility on most topics. In the run-up to Polokwane he found his voice once more and spoke out against Robert Mugabe. He even felt emboldened to (vainly) muster support for the presidency for the ANC's Hamlet, Cyril Ramaphosa. ANC MP Ben Turok was another, equally revealing, example of how the power paradigm had shifted. In the early years of Mbeki's presidency, my colleague Ken Andrew made a scathing remark about the president, entirely within the bounds of parliamentary protocol. Turok would have none of it. Outraged (and mistaking proceedings in parliament for an episode of *Law and Order*) he leaped to his feet and demanded that Ken's utterance 'be struck from the record'. After Polokwane, in January 2008, Turok was busily writing letters to the newspapers criticising Thabo Mbeki.

There was something distinctly familiar about all this. It was rather reminiscent of the National Party at the height of its power when '*Die Hoofleier*' was revered and held to be above criticism and beyond reproach. The moment the mask of power slipped the fawning servility which once encased him went with it. Paeans of praise gave way to scorn and derision. That was, on balance, considerably better than the fate of deposed leaders in full-blown authoritarian societies.

21 Mbeki also decided to accept the formal constraint of the Constitution which limited the country's presidency to two five-year terms. But his decision to seek a third term as party president suggested an intention to influence, decisively, both the formal succession process and informally hold decisive sway over the next state president.

22 One acclaimed local cartoonist lampooned me as a sort of town nutcase, foaming at the mouth and ringing a bell proclaiming 'the end is nigh'.

23 A fascinating insight into what this relocation of power meant, in terms of accountability, was provided by Tito Mboweni in an interview with Padraig O'Malley in December 1996: '[Those] of us in government are answerable to the NEC. I can't just proceed because I'm minister of Labour and do whatever I want because I'm governing. I didn't fall from heaven. I became minister of Labour because I went into government on an ANC platform, was deployed by the president in that position, [and] so I am answerable to the president, yes, of the Republic but fundamentally in terms of policy and politics I'm answerable to the NEC of the ANC.' Of course Mboweni is no longer the minister of Labour, but the governor of the Reserve Bank – an institution which by definition *must* be independent from the state. If Mboweni is to be believed, however, he takes his cue from the NEC.

24 These relate to some four million rands he allegedly received from his 'financial adviser' Schabir Shaik, currently serving a 15-year stretch in jail for corruption and fraud, including soliciting a bribe, on behalf of Zuma, from an arms supplier and manufacturer.

25 SAPA, 29 December 2007.

26 *Sunday Times*, 13 January 2008.

27 On my reading, there was support for a range of economic initiatives and recommendations outside the Manuel/Mbeki box. The National Treasury-commissioned international study on the growth potential of the South African economy, for example, advocated a far more competitive exchange rate based on a real depreciation of the currency, a build-up of foreign reserves and a recalculation of the consumer price index (see Harvard Center for International Development Working Papers, op. cit.). They also suggested a review of black economic empowerment, trade and industrial policies. Clearly, current orthodoxies need reconsideration. But on fiscal policies Zuma's allies stand alone in suggesting a more expansive approach.

28 *Sunday Independent*, 12 August 2007.

29 *Time*, 8 August 2007.

30 Southall, op. cit., pp. 18-19.

Index